Encyclopedia of
Children and Childhood
In History and Society

Editorial Board

Encyclopedia of
Children and Childhood
In History and Society

Paula S. Fass, Editor in Chief

Volume 1
A-E

MACMILLAN
REFERENCE
USA™

THOMSON
GALE

New York • Detroit • San Diego • San Francisco • Cleveland • New Haven, Conn. • Waterville, Maine • London • Munich

THOMSON
———★———™
GALE

Encyclopedia of Children and Childhood: In History and Society
Paula S. Fass, Editor in Chief

©2004 by Macmillan Reference USA.
Macmillan Reference USA is an imprint of
The Gale Group, Inc., a division of
Thomson Learning, Inc.

Macmillan Reference USA™ and Thomson
Learning™ are trademarks used
herein under license.

For more information, contact
Macmillan Reference USA
300 Park Avenue South, 9th Floor
New York, NY 10010
Or you can visit our Internet site at
http://www.gale.com

For permission to use material from this
product, submit your request via Web at
http://www.gale-edit.com/permissions, or you
may download our Permissions Request form
and submit your request by fax or mail to:

Permissions Department
The Gale Group, Inc.
27500 Drake Road
Farmington Hills, MI 48331-3535
Permissions Hotline:
248-699-8006 or 800-877-4253, ext. 8006
Fax: 248-699-8074 or 800-762-4058

While every effort has been made to
ensure the reliability of the information presented in this publication, The Gale Group,
Inc. does not guarantee the accuracy of the
data contained herein. The Gale Group, Inc.
accepts no payment for listing; and inclusion
in the publication of any organization,
agency, institution, publication, service, or
individual does not imply endorsement of the
editors or publisher.

Errors brought to the attention of the
publisher and verified to the satisfaction of
the publisher will be corrected in future editions.

LIBRARY OF CONGRESS CATALOGING-IN-PUBLICATION DATA

Encyclopedia of children and childhood : in history and society / edited
by Paula S. Fass.
    p. cm.
    Includes bibliographical references and index.
    ISBN 0-02-865714-4 (set hardcover : alk. paper) — ISBN 0-02-865715-2
(Volume 1) — ISBN 0-02-865716-0 (Volume 2) — ISBN 0-02-865717-9
(Volume 3)
    1. Children—Encyclopedias. I. Fass, Paula S.

HQ767.84.E53 2003
305.23'03—dc21   2003006666

This title is also available as an e-book.
ISBN 0-02-865915-5

Contact your Gale sales representative for ordering information.

Printed in the United States of America
10 9 8 7 6 5 4 3

Contents

Editorial and Production Staff

Editorial and Production Staff

Linda S. Hubbard
Editorial Director

Jeffrey Galas, Jennifer Wisinski
Project Editors

Guy Cunningham, Ellen Hawley, Peter Jaskowiak, Anna Nesbitt, Kathleen Roy, Mary Russell, David E. Salamie, Linda Sanders
Copyeditors

Beth Fhaner
Proofreader

Wendy Allex
Indexer

Jennifer Wahi
Art Director

Dean Dauphinais, Robert Duncan, Lezlie Light
Imaging

Margaret A. Chamberlain
Permissions

Datapage Technologies International, Inc.
Typesetter

Mary Beth Trimper
Manager, Composition

Evi Seoud
Assistant Manager, Composition

Rita Wimberley
Buyer

MACMILLAN REFERENCE USA

Frank Menchaca
Vice President and Publisher

Jill Lectka
Director, Publishing Operations

List of Selected Illustrations

VOLUME 2

VOLUME 3

Preface

Preface

The history of children and childhood is a new and energetic field of inquiry that provides critical insights into the human past and contemporary social experience. By gathering articles by the best investigators and by approaching the subject both with a global focus and from an interdisciplinary perspective, the *Encyclopedia of Children and Childhood: In History and Society* provides the interested reader with a necessary introduction to the wide range of issues that define the field. In devising its selections and choosing contributors, the editors aimed to offer general readers as well as researchers a significant means to embark on an exploration of the very latest scholarship in an exciting and burgeoning area of social research.

Starting in the early 1960s, historians began to probe the past for insights into lived experience and became newly attuned to the many social and community institutions involved. Family relations, religious experience, and various forms of education including schooling, work life, peer and voluntary organizations, sports, and recreations all became areas for disciplined historical study. Together investigations into these areas began to yield significant knowledge about the texture, meaning, and complexity of human experience in the past. In turning their attention to a fuller people-centered history, historians also turned to the tools and questions of allied disciplines, especially sociology, anthropology, and psychology, to better understand human behavior and the nature of social organization. This explosion of historical scholarship into previously underexplored or unexplored arenas was one of the signal achievements of social science in the second half of the twentieth century. Social history broke down the tight walls of earlier historical scholarship that was largely confined to an exploration of the people at the top and the politics of power.

In breaching those walls, scholars allowed children to come into view. Largely excluded from active politics (with a very few exceptions such as infant rulers or as participants in youth politics), children and adolescents became everywhere visible as the family, the school, and work in factories and fields were opened to investigation. Discovering the presence of children in history was exciting to many of us who began to work in the new field of social history in the later 1960s and early 1970s. The *Encyclopedia of Children and Childhood* brings the full range of that new work together for the first time.

Just as exciting was the growing understanding of the crucial role that childhood played in how cultures defined themselves, fashioned their instruments of socialization, and sought to control their futures. In 1960 Philippe Ariès's seminal book, *L'Enfant et la vie familiale sous l'Ancien Régime* (published in English in 1962 as *Centuries of Childhood*), encouraged historians to think about childhood itself as an invention, a historically driven phenomenon, not a transcendent category. Linked to a complex and subtle argument about how European society isolated childhood as part of a wider process of social differentiation, Ariès's provocative thesis about the absence of childhood before the seventeenth century stimulated a wide range of inquiries. Most questioned his conclusions but were firmly indebted to his most profound insight: childhood is a historically embedded definition that opens up deep layers of culture by exposing how societies code the earliest period of life and organize it in consequential ways. The definition of childhood is connected to fundamental institutions, technologies, and a range of social relationships. Gender was an especially important aspect of that definition, and as the fields of women's history and then gender studies evolved in the 1970s and 1980s, children's history developed alongside its many insights.

By the late 1970s, children and childhood were firmly part of a refashioned vision of the past. That past was made new by the work of scholars seeking out materials hitherto hidden in birth registers and wills, tomes of philosophy and psychology, slender volumes of poetry and novels, private diaries and letters, paintings and photographs, toys and the built environment. In other words, as the full panoply of human experience came into view as a setting for real children in the past as well as for how our ancestors thought about and imagined children, a whole range of sources could be refreshingly brought to bear on these matters.

The three volumes of the *Encyclopedia of Children and Childhood* draw upon that extraordinary range of historical sources. In examining its pages the reader will immediately encounter the wealth of pictorial means through which children and youth have been represented at various times and in various settings. They can be found at play and at work, in school and in war, as the embodiment of innocence and the absence of experience, as well as knowing and sexually seductive. The illustrations, provided through the skills and special knowledge of one of our editors, Anne Higonnet, are only the first taste of the wide array of issues awaiting the reader's plain curiosity or more scholarly needs. These volumes include short biographical introductions to the important thinkers through the ages who have understood the centrality of childhood—from Plato and Aristotle through Erasmus, John Locke and Jean-Jacques Rousseau, to Sigmund Freud, John Dewey, and Jean Piaget. In seeking to understand children globally, the editors have invited scholars who specialize in most of the regions of the world, such as Africa, Latin America, China, India, and Australia, among others, to add to the knowledge that American and European historians have been accumulating over the past thirty years. Similarly, we have tried to include the great religious traditions, Judaism, Islam, as well as the early Catholic Church fathers and the innovations of the Protestant Revolution, in our understanding of global childhood. And we have urged the authors to try to adopt a cross-cultural perspective in many of the general essays, such as those on naming, infant mortality, games, sexuality, and adolescence. This wide-ranging comparative perspective adds to the historical depth we have tried to create with articles on childhood over time in the West from ancient Greece and Rome through the Middle Ages, early modern Europe, and European colonialism, down to the modern world.

Modernity (Europe and the United States since the mid-eighteenth century) has offered scholars the richest range of sources as well as the most complex focus for investigation. This is largely because childhood as we now understand it, with its elaborate emphasis on the early years of life and its drive to protect the young and to prepare them for adulthood, is largely an expression of the European Enlightenment and the institutions of the nation-state. Modern schooling and developmental psychology, which are its products, have provided a set of questions and an institutional focus that now largely take this perspective as a categorical given as they have refined our modern Western understanding of childhood and children. The *Encyclopedia of Children and Childhood* explores these issues in great detail, including notions of proper child rearing and parenting, schooling and other forms of instruction, the role of various emotions, the nature of child development, and the importance of age. In a technological culture where child survival has become an expectation, issues of birth and conception have come prominently into view and the editors of the *Encyclopedia of Children and Childhood* have given special attention to its many expressions in contemporary reproductive issues.

The encyclopedia also includes adolescence and youth in its definitions of the child and childhood because modern schooling, modern psychology, and the modern state with its laws and labor regulations have made the period from twelve to eighteen (and increasingly even beyond this) a feature of youthful dependency and development. We have many articles that focus on this period of life—from its definition and bodily transformations in puberty, to rituals of dating and sexuality, to youth's commercial entertainments, political engagements, and socially problematic behaviors (drinking, smoking, delinquency, pregnancy). We pay considerable attention to the schooling of adolescents, as well as to younger children, especially in Europe and the United States, and include articles on a variety of public and private school contexts and related contemporary issues. Schooling is often also addressed in the entries on other countries and parts of the world in the globally framed articles.

While work has, in the twentieth century, become a marginal experience for most children in the industrialized world as school has replaced it as focal feature of daily and weekly activity, children have been important economically in the past and remain very important workers in many parts of the world to this day. Many entries address this experience, from the lives of slave children in North America and in colonial Brazil, to industrial workers in Europe and part-time workers in the modern American consumer economy.

In the modern world, play became almost synonymous with our views of a proper childhood. The *Encyclopedia of Children and Childhood* contains many entries on theories of play and the experience of play from the sports field to the computer screen, with many steps via the long history of toys (dolls, trains, teddy bears). Eager to provide readers with a sampling of the books that, since the eighteenth century, have been an important ingredient in the lives of Western children, we include articles on Bible stories, ABC hornbooks, and fairy tales, as well as the tales of Christopher Robin, Peter Pan, Nancy Drew, and Harry Potter (among many others) as well as the comic books that defined the reading experiences of twentieth-century children. Indeed, we chose to emphasize literature written for and read by children, rather than the great varieties of literature that portrayed children (which began to proliferate in the nineteenth century), because children's literature is written by adults with very particular views in mind of who and what their readers are like. Even in a compendium as wide-ranging as this one, choices have to be made because the field has grown so vast and so bountiful that we simply could not hope to include all aspects and elements of the latest scholarship.

In choosing representations of childhood we leaned heavily in the direction of the visual rather than the literary. And we have chosen not just to illustrate our entries but to include major landmarks in the history of art as they pertain to children. Thus the reader will be given an introduction to many of the most important and iconic images of children, representations that have helped to organize how we see and think about children over the past several centuries. These images are therefore in themselves primary sources in the history of childhood. In so doing, we expected both to engage the reader pursuing the subject and to entice the casual reader who flips through to proceed from these to the equally enticing array of articles on almost every facet of the life of children and the concept of childhood in the past and present, from conception and birth through passages to adulthood. The *Encyclopedia of Children and Childhood* thus hopes to make the study of childhood and children, first nurtured in the university library, laboratory, and classroom, a compelling subject for a wide array of professionals who work on children's issues and want to know more about its past, including doctors, lawyers, teachers, and social workers, as well as students of all kinds eager to learn about their own childhood, that of their parents, and of the many diverse people of our shrinking world.

There are 445 articles in the *Encyclopedia of Children and Childhood*, arranged in alphabetical order for easy reference. The articles range from five hundred to five thousand words in length and are written by over three hundred scholars from many parts of the world who are active researchers in history, social science, literature, education, medicine, law, and art history. Each signed article features several carefully chosen cross-references to related entries, indicated within the text with small capital letters or listed at the end of the article, as well as an up-to-date bibliography of print and Internet sources. In Volume 3, readers will find an annotated collection of fifty primary sources, reproduced in whole or in part, identified by the editors as essential documents in the field. A topical outline appears in Volume 1. It groups articles by broad categories, thereby offering teachers and readers alike an informed map of the field. A comprehensive index in Volume 3 provides yet another entry point to the set, encouraging readers to explore the information contained in these three volumes.

In selecting a group of editors and creating a board of consultants, I have sought to include experts with different backgrounds and specialties. Peter Stearns, himself the editor of Scribner's *Encyclopedia of European Social History* and an early creator of the field as the pioneering editor of the *Journal of Social History*, is the author of dozens of books in both European and American history and a founder of the new field of the history of emotions. He has recently become an important presence in matters of world history and global history. He brings all these varied experiences to this project. Ning de Coninck-Smith, a Danish scholar familiar with the field of childhood history as it is currently practiced and developing in Europe, also brings a deep knowledge of the history of education and the material culture of childhood to her work as an editor. Anne Higonnet's writings brought the study of the representations of children powerfully into the history of art, and her knowledge of the history of photography and illustrations has grounded that enterprise in the everyday experience of people as well as the more refined precincts of the museum and exhibition hall. Stephen Lassonde's work on American schooling, immigration, children's work, and definitions of age makes his knowledge of the institutions of childhood and the varied contexts of child life an invaluable one in an enterprise oriented to exploring the many differences as well as the similarities in the lives of modern children.

Our consultants are an eminent group of scholars whose unparalleled knowledge about both childhood and the wider contexts within which childhood functions and their broad-ranging acquaintance with practitioners of this history have been critical to the success of the project. They include Natalie Zemon Davis, the leading cultural historian of early modern Europe and an intellectual with a truly international stature; historical sociologist Viviana Zelizer, whose book *Pricing the Priceless Child* was, together with the work of Philippe Ariès, seminal in how we have come to define the field of childhood history; Michael Grossberg, editor-in-chief of the *American Historical Review* and the most prominent historian of the law as it pertains to children and family matters in the United States; and David Kertzer, whose deep research on a range of family-related subjects and several edited volumes make his contributions to our understanding of children and their families in the modern European past preeminent. In addition, Susan Schweik has generously shared her knowledge of children's literature with me, and Tobias Hecht provided an invaluable introduction to scholars and issues in Latin American history.

I am indebted to all these individuals for their advice and assistance. I also want to thank the staff of Macmillan Reference USA, whose patience, devotion to the project, and hard work have been essential to its successful completion. From Anne Davidson's initial commitment to the idea, this has been a subject that Macmillan has supported warmly. Especially critical throughout has been Jill Lectka's friendship, support, and constant assistance and good sense. It has been a pleasure to work with her as well as with Jeffrey Galas and Jennifer Wisinski, whom I have known only as e-mail correspondents and on the telephone, but for whom I have developed great regard and affection. The staff at the History Department at the University of California at Berkeley, especially Sherrill Young, Chris Egan, and Jennifer Sixt provided important assistance at various stages of my work. Several of my wonderful graduate student assistants have also made critical contributions to this project. They include Andrea Kwon, Laura Mihailoff, and especially Rachel Hope Cleves whose good cheer and energetic work made the excellent collection of primary sources in Volume 3 possible. Finally, Jack Lesch has been through my excitements at the very possibility of such a project coming about, the long labors to sustain it, and the exhilaration at its completion. He allowed me the time, sustained my energy, and provided the emotional resources that helped to make it happen. My thanks go to all of these people and to the several hundred contributors who are making the field of children's history in its many varieties and different cultural settings flourish as we go to press.

PAULA S. FASS

List of Articles

List of Contributors

List of Contributors

Inge Aaen
  LEGO Company, Denmark
  Construction Toys

Laura S. Abrams
  University of Minnesota, Twin Cities
  Addams, Jane (1860–1935)
  Social Settlements

Kimberley Stratemeyer Adams
  Guilford, Connecticut
  Keene, Carolyn

Annmarie Adams
  McGill University
  Children's Spaces

A. Cassandra Albinson
  Getty Research Institute
  Cassatt, Mary (1844–1926)
  Geddes, Anne
  Gutmann, Bessie Pease (1876–1960)
  Mann, Sally (b. 1951)
  Smith, Jessie Willcox (1863–1935)

Ronny Ambjörnsson
  Umeå University, Sweden
  Century of the Child
  Key, Ellen (1849–1926)

Astri Andresen
  University of Bergen
  Bastardy

P. Gayle Andrews
  University of Georgia
  Junior High School

Lori Askeland
  Wittenberg University
  Brace, Charles Loring (1826–1890)

Joe Austin
  Bowling Green State University
  Youth Culture

Arianne Baggerman
  Erasmus Universiteit, Netherlands
  Autobiographies
  Enlightenment, The

Beth Bailey
  University of New Mexico
  Sexuality

Leonard L. Baird
  Ohio State University
  Private and Independent Schools

Samantha Barbas
  Chapman University
  Child Stars
  Temple, Shirley (b. 1928)

Lynn A. Barnett
  University of Illinois at Urbana-
  Champaign

*Organized Recreation and Youth
  Groups*

Sara Beam
  University of Victoria, British
  Columbia
  Charivari

Sandra L. Beckett
  Brock University, Ontario, Canada
  Dumas, Alexandre (1802–1870)

Ellen L. Berg
  University of California, Berkeley
  Gulick, Luther (1865–1918)
  Kindergarten
  Teen Drinking

Jay R. Berkovitz
  University of Massachusetts at
  Amherst
  Judaism

Gai Ingham Berlage
  Iona College
  Baseball

Marie-Jeanne Liengme Bessire
  Department of Education, Canton of
  Jura, Switzerland
  Piaget, Jean (1896–1980)

Amy L. Best
  San Jose State University
  Proms

Carlos Kevin Blanton
Texas A & M University
Bilingual Education

April Bleske-Rechek
University of Wisconsin—Eau Claire
Intelligence Testing

Nils Eric Boesgaard
Independent Scholar, Denmark
Toy Soldiers (Tin Soldiers)

Ruth B. Bottigheimer
State University of New York at
Stony Brook
Bible, The
Fairy Tales and Fables

Kevin J. Brehony
University of Surrey, Roehampton,
UK
*Froebel, Friedrich Wilhelm August
(1782–1852)*
Montessori, Maria (1870–1952)
Nursery Schools
Theories of Play

Ulrich Breuning
National Film School of Denmark
Movies

Barbara Brookes
University of Otago, New Zealand
Menarche

Jeffrey P. Brosco
University of Miami
Pediatrics

Stig Broström
The Danish University of Education
Vygotsky, L. S. (1896–1934)

Marilyn R. Brown
Tulane University
Images of Childhood

Alyson Brown
Edge Hill, United Kingdom
Child Prostitution

Guy Brunet
Université Lyon 2, France
Orphans

Elizabeth Bryan
Multiple Births Foundation, United
Kingdom
Multiple Births

Vern L. Bullough
State University of New York
Age of Consent
Homosexuality and Sexual Orientation

Catherine Burke
University of Leeds
Theories of Childhood

Emily D. Cahan
Wheelock College
*Child Development, History of the
Concept of*

Nancy Campbell
Rensselaer Polytechnic Institute
Drugs

E. Wayne Carp
Pacific Lutheran University
Adoption in the United States

Benedict Carton
George Mason University
Africa

Susan P. Casteras
University of Washingtom
Victorian Art

J. J. Chambliss
Rutgers University
Aristotle (384–322 B.C.E.)

Anne-Marie Châtelet
Ecole de l'architecture de Versailles,
France
Open Air School Movement
*School Buildings and Architecture:
Europe*

Nupur Chaudhuri
Texas Southern University
British Colonialism in India

Howard P. Chudacoff
Brown University
Adolescence and Youth
Birthday

Beverly Lyon Clark
Wheaton College
Disney

C. Antoinette Clarke
Ohio Northern University College of
Law
Juvenile Justice: United States

Rachel Hope Cleves
University of California, Berkeley
Alcott, Bronson (1799–1888)
Dr. Seuss (1904–1991)
Guns
Little Women and Louisa May Alcott
*Societies for the Prevention of Cruelty
to Children*
Wayland, Francis (1796–1865)
Wright, Henry Clarke (1797–1870)

Lisa Forman Cody
Claremont McKenna College
Conception and Birth

Robert Cohen
New York University
Great Depression and New Deal

Lorinda B. Cohoon
University of Texas at El Paso
Boyhood

Barry M. Coldrey
Thornbury, Australia
Placing Out

Michael C. Coleman
University of Jyväskylä, Finland
American Indian Schools

Peter W. Cookson Jr.
Teachers College, Columbia
University
School Choice
School Vouchers

Catherine Coquery-Vidrovitch
Paris, France
Female Genital Mutilation

Rotraud Coriand
Friedrich-Schiller-University Jena,
Germany
Herbart, J. F. (1776–1841)

William A. Corsaro
Indiana University
Play

Andrew M. Courtwright
University of North Carolina
Smoking

David T. Courtwright
University of North Florida
Smoking

Gordon Cox
University of Reading, United
Kingdom
Music Education

Hamilton Cravens
Iowa State University
Aid to Dependent Children (AFDC)
Children's Defense Fund
IQ
Laura Spelman Rockefeller Memorial
Social Welfare: History
Sheppard-Towner Maternity and
  Infancy Act
Welfare Reform Act (1996)

Hans van Crombrugge
University of Ghent, Belgium
Rousseau, Jean-Jacques (1712–1778)

Gary Cross
The Pennsylvania State University
Consumer Culture
Economics and Children in Western
  Societies: The Consumer Economy
Toys
Vacations

Hugh Cunningham
University of Kent, United Kingdom
Work and Poverty

Laura Curran
Rutgers University
Foster Care
Orphan Trains

William W. Cutler III
Temple University
Parent-Teacher Associations

Ann Dally
University College London
Birth Defects
Sudden Infant Death Syndrome

Ning de Coninck-Smith
The Danish University of Education
Pedophilia
Social Welfare: Comparative
  Twentieth-Century Developments

Martin J. Dedman
Middlesex University
Baden-Powell, Robert (1857–1941)

Rudolf M. Dekker
Erasmus Universiteit, Netherlands
Autobiographies
Enlightenment, The
Fear
Frank, Anne (1929–1945)

Crista DeLuzio
Southern Methodist University
Puberty

Richard L. DeMolen
Our Lady of Tahoe Parish, Nevada
Baptism
Communion, First
Confirmation

Rachel Devlin
Tulane University
Girlhood

Jerry G. Dickason
Montclair State University
Playground Movement

George Dimock
University of North Carolina at
Greensboro

Hine, Lewis (1874–1940)
Photographs of Children

Dwayne Emil Dixon
Center for Documentary Studies,
Durham, North Carolina
Ewald, Wendy (b. 1951)

Gail Donaldson
Union College
Freud, Anna (1895–1982)
Klein, Melanie (1882–1960)

Brendan Dooley
Florence, Italy
Campus Revolts in the 1960s

Charles Dorn
Bowdoin College
Grammar School

Ana Cristina Dubeux Dourado
Federal University of Pernambuco,
Brazil
Brazil: History

Kirsten Drotner
University of Southern Denmark
Media, Childhood and the

John M. Efron
University of California, Berkeley
Mortara Abduction

Nika Elder
Wellesley College
Church, Charlotte (b. 1986)
Spears, Britney (b. 1981)

Susanna Elm
University of California, Berkeley
Ancient Greece and Rome: Self-
  Formation
Perpetua, Saint

Amy L. Elson
Belloti v. Baird
Ex Parte Crouse
In re Gault
Twenty-Sixth Amendment

Nicole Eustace
New York University
Emotional Life

Hughes Evans
University of Alabama at Birmingham
Children's Hospitals
Incest

Paula S. Fass
University of California, Berkeley
Abduction
Dating
Lindbergh Kidnapping

Antoinette Fauve-Chamoux
Ècole des Hautes Études en Sciences
Sociales, Paris
Inheritance and Property

Elizabeth Warnock Fernea
University of Texas at Austin
Middle East

Joanne M. Ferraro
San Diego State University
Early Modern Europe
Family Patterns

Sarah K. Fields
University of Georgia
Sports

Agnès Fine
Université de Toulouse, France
Godparents

Barbara Finkelstein
University of Maryland at College
Park
Violence Against Children

Yochi Fisher-Yinon
The Hebrew University of Jerusalem
Bundling

Lene Floris
Holbaek Museum, Denmark
Pram

Miriam Forman-Brunell
University of Missouri, Kansas City
Baby-Sitters
Barbie

Michael J. Foster
Rector, Chase Benefice Dorset,
United Kingdom
Boy Scouts

Lara Freidenfelds
Harvard University
Artificial Insemination
Egg Donation
Sonography
Surrogacy

Willem Frijhoff
Vrije Universiteit, Netherlands
Gymnasium Schooling
Latin School

Elise P. Garrison
Texas A & M University
Ancient Greece and Rome: Overview

Eileen A. Gavin
College of Saint Catherine, St. Paul,
Minnesota
Bühler, Charlotte (1893–1974)

Philip Gavitt
Saint Louis University
Medieval and Renaissance Europe

Gerald R. Gems
North Central College
Basketball
Boxing

Victoria L. Getis
Ohio State University
Delinquency

Brian Gill
RAND
Homework

Jonathan Gillis
The Children's Hospital at
Westmead, Australia
Pacifier

John R. Gillis
Rutgers University
*Life Course and Transitions to
Adulthood*
Rites of Passage

Clay Gish
ESI Design, New York
Street Arabs and Street Urchins

Jeffrey Glanz
Wagner College
*Holocaust, Jewish Ghetto Education
and the*

Mona Gleason
University of British Columbia
Canada

Howard R. D. Gordon
Marshall University
*Vocational Education, Industrial
Education, and Trade Schools*

Lynn D. Gordon
University of Rochester
Women's Colleges in the United States

Deborah Gorham
Carlton University, Canada
Gendering

Jeanine Graham
University of Waikato, New Zealand
New Zealand

Julia Grant
Michigan State University
Scientific Child Rearing

Jan Price Greenough
University of California, Berkeley
School Shootings and School Violence

Michael Grossberg
Indiana University
Law, Children and the

Marta Gutman
University of California, Berkeley
*School Buildings and Architecture:
United States*

Elizabeth Haiken
El Cerrito, California
Cosmetics

Lesley A. Hall
Wellcome Library and University
College, London
Masturbation

Robert L. Hampel
University of Delaware
Progressive Education

Peter E. Hanff
The Bancroft Library, University of
California, Berkeley
Wizard of Oz and L. Frank Baum

Hal Hansen
Suffolk University
Apprenticeship
Urban School Systems, The Rise of

Jørn Hansen
University of Southern Denmark
GutsMuths, J. C. F. (1759–1839)

Michael Hardin
Bloomsburg University of
Pennsylvania
Tattoos and Piercing

Lisa H. Harris
University of Michigan
Fertility Drugs
In Vitro Fertilization

Amy Harris-Solomon
Easter Seals of Tennessee
Child Care: In-Home Child Care

Roger A. Hart
City University of New York
Sandbox

Harry Haue
University of Southern Denmark
Education, Europe

Joseph M. Hawes
University of Memphis
History of Childhood: United States

Dinah Hazell
Independent Scholar
Lord of the Rings and J. R. R. Tolkien

Tobias Hecht
Independent Scholar
Brazil: Contemporary

Kirsten Hegner
University of Copenhagen, Denmark
Furniture

Steffen Heiberg
Fredriksborg Museum, Denmark
Infant Rulers

Kenneth J. Heineman
Ohio University—Lancaster
Youth Activism

C. Dallett Hemphill
Ursinus College
Manners

Colin Heywood
University of Nottingham, United
Kingdom
European Industrialization

Anne Higonnet
Barnard College
Child Pornography
Japanese Art, Contemporary
Lolita

Diane E. Hill
University of California, Berkeley
Juvenile Justice: International
UN Convention on the Rights of the
Child
UNICEF

Hugh D. Hindman
Appalachian State University
Industrial Homework
Working Papers

N. Ray Hiner
University of Kansas
History of Childhood: United States

Kerstin Holmlund
Umea University, Sweden
Child Care: Institutional Forms

Margo Horn
Stanford University
Child Guidance

Elliot Horowitz
Bar Ilan University, Israel
Circumcision

Mark Hunter
University of California, Berkeley
Globalization

Patrick H. Hutton
University of Vermont
Ariès, Philippe (1914–1984)

Paula E. Hyman
Yale University
Bar Mitzvah, Bat Mitzvah

Joseph E. Illick
San Francisco State University
Native American Children

Rael Jean Isaac
Independent Scholar, New York, NY
Recovered Memory

J. Thomas Jable
William Paterson University
Interscholastic Athletics

Juliane Jacobi
University of Potsdam, Germany
Francke, Aug. Hermann (1663–1727)

Anette Faye Jacobsen
Danish Institute for Human Rights
Child Labor in Developing Countries

Lisa Jacobson
University of California, Santa Barbara
Advertising
Allowances

Monika Janfelt
Southern Denmark University
War in the Twentieth Century

Hans-Christian Jensen
University of Southern Denmark
Bicycles and Tricycles

Knud Jensen
The Danish University of Education
Kerschensteiner, Georg (1854–1932)

Kristina Tegler Jerselius
University of Uppsala, Sweden
Child Witch

John W. Johnson
University of Northern Iowa
Tinker v. Des Moines

Niels Jonassen
Humlebaek, Denmark
Cars as Toys

Kathleen W. Jones
Virginia Polytechnic Institute and State University
Healy, William (1869–1963)

Marshall B. Jones
Pennsylvania State University
White House Conferences on Children

Jerome Kagan
Harvard University
Child Psychology

Josh Kagan
New York University, School of Law
Head Start

Gene Kannenberg Jr.
University of Houston—Downtown
Comic Books
Tintin and Hergé

Tabitha Kanogo
University of California, Berkeley
Abduction in Modern Africa

Harvey Kantor
University of Utah
School Desegregation

Melissa R. Katz
Brown University

Madonna, Religious
Madonna, Secular

Timothy Kelly
Saint Vincent College
Catholicism

Gavin Kendall
Queensland University of Technology—Carseldine, Australia
Literacy

Kathleen Kete
Trinity College, Hartford, Connecticut
Pets

Bjarne Kildegaard
Rudkøbing, Denmark
Collections and Hobbies

Wilma King
University of Missouri, Columbia
Slavery, United States

Jan Kociumbas
University of Sydney, Australia
Australia

Nita Kumar
Center for Postcolonial Studies, Varanasi, India
India and South Asia

Elizabeth Anne Kuznesof
University of Kansas
Latin America: Overview

Andrea Kwon
University of California, Berkeley
Title IX and Girls' Sports

Margareth Lanzinger
University of Vienna, Austria
Naming

Thomas Laqueur
University of California, Berkeley
Sendak, Maurice (b. 1928)

Stephen Lassonde
Yale University

Age and Development
High School

John M. Last
University of Ottawa, Canada
Contagious Diseases
Polio
Vaccination

John T. Lauridsen
The Royal Library, Copenhagen, Denmark
Hitler Youth

David Levine
University of Toronto
Economics and Children in Western Societies: From Agriculture to Industry
Fertility Rates

Kirsten Linde
Akershus Fylkesmuseum, Norway
Swaddling

Kriste Lindenmeyer
University of Maryland, Baltimore County
National Child Labor Committee
Teen Pregnancy
U.S. Children's Bureau

Anne-Li Lindgren
Linköping University, Sweden
Radio

Alison Klarmont Lingo
University of California, Berkeley
Obstetrics and Midwifery

Amanda H. Littauer
University of California, Berkeley
Same-Sex Parenting
Victory Girls

Bogna Lorence-Kot
California College of Arts and Crafts
Eastern Europe: Poland

Zvi Lothane
Mount Sinai School of Medicine
Freud, Sigmund (1856–1939)

Thomas Lyngby
University of Aarhus, Denmark
Aristocratic Education in Europe
Infancy of Louis XIII

Mary Niles Maack
University of California, Los Angeles
Children's Libraries

Edith Nye MacMullen
Yale University
Common Schools
Mann, Horace (1796–1859)

Phyllis Magidson
The Museum of the City of New York
Fashion

Shireen Mahdavi
University of Utah
Islam

John Mangan
Yale University
Child Prodigies

Jennifer Marchant
Middle Tennessee State University
Kipling, Rudyard (1865–1936)
Verne, Jules (1828–1905)

James Marten
Marquette University
Soldier Children: Global Human Rights Issues

Waldo E. Martin Jr.
University of California, Berkeley
Brown v. the Board of Education of Topeka, Kansas
Scottsboro Boys

Mary Ann Mason
University of California, Berkeley
Children's Rights
Divorce and Custody
Stepparents in the United States

Susan J. Matt
Weber State University
Jealousy and Envy

Linda C. Mayes
Yale University
Gesell, Arnold (1880–1961)

Velma McBride Murry
Center for Family Research, Athens, Georgia
Teenage Mothers in the United States

Caroline Hinkle McCamant
University of California, Berkeley
Baby Farming
Child Saving
Diapers and Toileting

Alexis McCrossen
Southern Methodist University
Sunday

Patricia A. McDaniel
Public Health Institute, Berkeley, California
Shyness

Ray McDermott
Stanford University
Mead, Margaret (1901–1978)

Chris McGee
Illinois State University
Harry Potter and J. K. Rowling Series Books

Brian Patrick McGuire
Roskilde University, Denmark
Convent Schools (Cathedral Schools)
Desiderius Erasmus of Rotterdam (c. 1469–1536)

Sally G. McMillen
Davidson College
Infant Feeding

Jay Mechling
University of California, Davis
Child-Rearing Advice Literature
Toilet Training

Richard Meckel
Brown University
Infant Mortality

Signe Mellemgaard
University of Copenhagen
Salzmann, Christian Gotthilf (1744–1811)

Bernard Mergen
George Washington University
Street Games

Joav Merrick
National Institute of Child Health and Human Development, Israel
Israel

Laura Mihailoff
University of California, Berkeley
Flappers
Juvenile Court
Youth Gangs

Nara Milanich
University of California, Davis
Latin America: Colonialism

Andrew Thompson Miller
University of Michigan
African-American Children and Youth

Steven Mintz
University of Houston
Parenting

Brian L. Mishara
University of Quebec at Montreal
Suicide

Jeffrey P. Moran
University of Kansas
Sex Education

Steven Noll
University of Florida
Mental Illness

Katharine Norris
American University
Binet, Alfred (1857–1911)

Ellen Nørgaard
The Danish University of Education
Freinet, Célestin (1896–1966)
Neill, A. S. (1883–1973)

Stephen O'Connor
New York, New York
New York Children's Aid Society

Jürgen Oelkers
University of Zürich
Steiner, Rudolf (1861–1925)

James Oles
Wellesley College
Levitt, Helen (b. 1913)

Ole Andkjaer Olsen
Copenhagen, Denmark
Infant Sexuality

Jon Pahl
The Lutheran Theological Seminary
at Philadelphia
Religious Revivals
Youth Ministries

Ulf Palmenfelt
Gotland University, Sweden
Opie, Iona and Peter

Roberta Park
University of California, Berkeley
Gymnastics
Physical Education

Halina Pasierbska
Bethnal Green Museum of
Childhood, United Kingdom
Piggy Bank
Toy Trains

Bissera V. Pentcheva
Columbia University
Madonna, Orthodox

Martin S. Pernick
University of Michigan
Eugenics

Anne-Nelly Perret-Clermont
Université de Neuchâtel, Switzerland
Piaget, Jean (1896–1980)

Anna L. Peterson
University of Florida
*Latin America: Wars in Central
America*

Paula Petrik
George Mason University
Juvenile Publishing
Toy Technology

Mary Anne Pitman
University of Cincinnati
Homeschooling

Hans Pols
University of Sydney
Child Study
Mental Hygiene

Heather Munro Prescott
Central Connecticut State University
Adolescent Medicine

Stephen J. Rebori
West Hollywood, California
Theme Parks

Kimberly A. Redding
Carroll College
Fascist Youth

James W. Reed
Rutgers University
Birth Control

Henrik Reeh
University of Copenhagen
Benjamin, Walter (1892–1940)

William J. Reese
University of Wisconsin, Madison
Education, United States

Richard A. Reiman
South Georgia College
Youth Agencies of the New Deal

Jacqueline S. Reinier
California State University
Breeching
Discipline

John G. Richardson
Western Washington University
Compulsory School Attendance

Benjamin B. Roberts
Free University of Amsterdam,
Netherlands
History of Childhood: Europe

Nathan Roberts
University of Manchester, United
Kingdom
Public Schools: Britain

Stephen Robertson
University of Sydney, Australia
Megan's Law(s)

Rebecca Rogers
Université Marc Bloch—Strasbourg,
France
Girls' Schools

Hugo Röling
University of Amsterdam,
Netherlands
Fear

Don Romesburg
University of California, Berkeley
Baby Boom Generation

Linda W. Rosenzweig
Chatham College
Friendship
Grandparents
Siblings

Mary Logan Rothschild
Arizona State University
Girl Scouts

John L. Rury
University of Kansas
Coeducation and Same-Sex Schooling
Commercial Curriculum

Patrick J. Ryan
University of Texas at Dallas
Hammer v. Dagenhart
Pierce v. Society of Sisters

Ingegerd Rydin
Halmstad University, Sweden
Television

Jon L. Saari
Northern Michigan University
China

Lynn Sacco
University of California, Santa
Barbara
Venereal Disease

Philip Lane Safford
Kent State University
Special Education

Bengt Sandin
Linköping University, Sweden
*Social Welfare: Comparative
Twentieth-Century Developments*

Philippe Savoie
Institut National de Recherche
Pédagogique, Paris, France
Lycée

Inon I. Schenker
Hebrew University of Jerusalem
AIDS

Steven Schlossman
Carnegie Mellon University
Dentistry
Homework

Pia Schmid
Martin-Luther-Universitaet-
Wittenberg, Germany
*Basedow, Johann Bernhard
(1724–1790)*

Kirsten F. Schmidt
Søllerød Museum, Denmark
Dolls

Peter Schouls
Simon Fraser University
Dewey, John (1859–1952)

Kelly Schrum
George Mason University
Bobby Soxers
Teenagers
Teen Magazines

Ellen Schrumpf
Telemark University College,
Norway
Child Labor in the West

Samuel Scolnicov
The Folger Shakespeare Library
Plato (427–348 B.C.E.)

Victoria Sears
Barnard College
Potter, Beatrix (1866–1943)

Anne Elisabeth Sejten
Roskilde Universitet, Denmark
Fénelon, François (1651–1715)

Diana Selig
Claremont McKenna College
Hall, Granville Stanley (1844–1924)
Parents Magazine

Jack L. Seymour
Garrett-Evangelical Theological
Seminary
Sunday School

Peggy A. Shifflett
Radford University
*Homeless Children and Runaways in
the United States*

Wendy Sigle-Rushton
London School of Economics
Foundlings

Shira Silverman
Merchant's House Museum, New
York, NY
Halloween
Indoor Games
Infant Toys
Teddy Bear

Arlene Skolnick
New York University
Beyond the Best Interests of the Child

Linda Smolak
Kenyon College
Anorexia

Claire E. Smrekar
Vanderbilt University
Magnet Schools

Karen E. Spierling
University of Louisville
Protestant Reformation

Margaret A. Spratt
California University of Pennsylvania
YWCA and YMCA

John C. Spurlock
Seton Hill University
Love

Peter N. Stearns
George Mason University
Comparative History of Childhood
Hyperactivity
Posture
Self-Esteem
Sleep

Deborah C. Stearns
Montgomery College
Anger and Aggression
Grief, Death, Funerals
Guilt and Shame

Dionne P. Stephens
Center for Family Research, Athens,
Georgia
Teenage Mothers in the United States

Richard Stevens
The Open University, United
Kingdom
Erikson, Erik H. (1902–1994)

Traian Stoianovich
Rutgers University
Eastern Europe: Balkans

Norbert Störmer
University of Applied Sciences
Zittau/Görlitz, Germany
Comenius, Johann Amos (1592–1670)

Martha Ellen Stortz
Pacific Lutheran Theological Seminary
Christian Thought, Early

Victor L. Streib
Ohio Northern University College of Law
Juvenile Justice: United States

Frank J. Sulloway
University of California, Berkeley
Birth Order

Jan Susina
Illinois State University
Children's Literature

Sonja L. Taylor
George Mason University
International Organizations

Mark Tebeau
Cleveland State University
Accidents

Deborah Thom
University of Cambridge
Isaacs, Susan (1885–1948)

Joseph T. Thomas Jr.
California State University, Northridge
Twain, Mark (1835–1910)

Barrie Thorne
University of California, Berkeley
Sociology and Anthropology of Childhood

James T. Todd
Eastern Michigan University
Watson, John B. (1878–1958)

Kim Tolley
Los Altos, California
Academies

Melissa Geisler Trafton
University of California, Berkeley
ABC Books
Homer, Winslow (1836–1910)

Daniel Tröhler
Research Institute for the History of Education, Zurich, Switzerland

Pestalozzi, Johann Heinrich (1746–1827)

William H. Tucker
Rutgers University—Camden
Burt, Cyril (1883–1971)

George W. Tuma
San Francisco State University
Lord of the Rings and J. R. R. Tolkien

Kathleen Uno
Temple University
Japan
Mothering and Motherhood

Hendrika Vande Kemp
Clinical Psychologist, Annandale, Virginia
Baumrind, Diana (b. 1927)

René van der Veer
Leiden University, Netherlands
Bowlby, John (1907–1990)

Abigail A. Van Slyck
Connecticut College
Children's Spaces
Summer Camps

Pier Paolo Viazzo
University of Turin, Italy
Abandonment

JoEllen McNergney Vinyard
Eastern Michigan University
Parochial Schools

Andrew Wachtel
Northwestern University
Tolstoy's Childhood in Russia

Diane Waggoner
The Huntington Library, Art Collections, and Botanical Gardens, San Marino, California
Carroll, Lewis (1832–1898)
Greenaway, Kate (1846–1901)

Glenn Wallach
Horace Mann School, New York
Student Government

Sheldon Watts
Cairo, Egypt
Epidemics

Harold S. Wechsler
University of Rochester
SAT and College Entrance Exams

Lynn Y. Weiner
Roosevelt University
La Leche League

Eric Weisbard
Experience Music Project
Rock and Roll

Jessica Weiss
California State University, Hayward
Fathering and Fatherhood

Susan B. Whitney
Carleton University, Canada
Communist Youth

Parnel Wickham
Dowling College
Retardation

Jacqueline S. Wilkie
Luther College
Hygiene

David Wolcott
Miami University of Ohio
Police, Children and the Zoot Suit Riots

Jacqueline H. Wolf
Ohio University
Wet-Nursing

Larry Wolff
Boston College
Child Abuse
Oliver Twist
Peter Pan and J. M. Barrie

Roberta Wollons
Indiana University Northwest
Dependent Children

Jackie Wullschlager
Financial Times (London)
Andersen, Hans Christian
(1805–1875)

Jubal C. Yennie
EdSolutions, Inc.
Charter Schools

Geraldine Youcha
Independent Scholar
Child Care: United States

Jeffrey T. Zalar
Valparaiso University
Holocaust

Martin Zerlang
Copenhagen University
Parades
Zoos

Arthur Zilversmit
Lake Forest College
Dewey, John (1859–1952)

Nurith Zmora
Hamline University
Orphanages

Michael Zuckerman
University of Pennsylvania
Spock, Benjamin (1903–1998)

Outline of Contents

Outline of Contents

This topical outline was compiled by the editors to provide a general overview of the conceptual scheme of the Encyclopedia of Children and Childhood: In History and Society. Individual entries along with primary source documents found in Volume 3 are organized by broad category, thereby offering teachers and readers an informed map of the field and an alternate entry point into the content of the encyclopedia.

Many subjects studied in the history of children and childhood cross thematic and disciplinary lines and articles on this list often appear in more than one category. For example, "Abduction" is listed under Law and Institutions; Child Advocacy, Protection, Politics; and Contemporary Childhood. "Hyperactivity" can be found in the categories Education and Schooling and Health, Medicine, and Disease.

The categories below are not listed in alphabetical order. Instead, topics are grouped together by curriculum, an order customary in the fields within the history of childhood. Individual articles are listed alphabetically and documents are listed chronologically. Because topics are not in alphabetical order, please consult the master list of topics that appears directly after this paragraph.

HISTORY AND THEORIES OF CHILDHOOD
CHILDHOOD IN GLOBAL PERSPECTIVE
CHILDREN IN HISTORY
PARENTING AND FAMILY RELATIONS
EDUCATION AND SCHOOLING
PLAY, MUSIC, AND ENTERTAINMENT
MATERIAL CULTURE AND CHILDREN'S SPACES
RACE AND GENDER
PSYCHOLOGY
CHILD ADVOCACY, PROTECTION, AND POLITICS
LAW AND INSTITUTIONS
ECONOMICS AND WORK
INDUSTRIALIZATION AND URBANIZATION
RELIGION, RITUALS, AND CELEBRATIONS
CHILDREN'S LITERATURE
REPRESENTATIONS OF CHILDREN AND CHILDHOOD
ADOLESCENCE AND TRANSITIONS TO ADULTHOOD
HEALTH, MEDICINE, AND DISEASE
BODY AND SEXUALITY
CONTEMPORARY CHILDHOOD

EDUCATION AND SCHOOLING

PLAY, MUSIC, AND ENTERTAINMENT

Abandonment

Child abandonment, mostly in the form of exposing newborn babies either in the wilderness or in public places where they could be noticed, is a widespread theme in religious and imaginative literature. Famous examples include Moses, who was rescued by Pharaoh's daughter, and many gods and heroes of classical mythology, from Zeus and Oedipus to the twins Romulus and Remus, the founders of Rome, who were found and suckled by a wolf. Similar stories have been reported from societies all over the world. The Yaudapu Enga of New Guinea, for instance, have a narrative tradition that includes supernatural beings who take abandoned children and rear them to live privileged lives. Such a pervasiveness in myths and folktales is, however, no proof that abandonment was widely practiced in real life. One may also wonder whether most deserted infants were actually rescued, as the happy ends of legendary tales would seem to suggest. These issues are the subject of intense debate among historians and other scholars.

The Kindness of Strangers

Until the mid-1980s historians and anthropologists broadly agreed that in most premodern societies, including ancient and medieval Europe, infanticide was an important means of population regulation. They also maintained that exposure, rather than outright killing, was the most common method of disposing of unwanted babies, thereby implying that abandonment was tantamount to infanticide. This view was challenged in 1988 by John Boswell in his influential book *The Kindness of Strangers*, which traces the history of child abandonment in Western Europe from late antiquity to the Renaissance. Boswell did not deny that in the ancient world abandonment was widespread. His analysis of a large body of literary, legal, and ecclesiastical sources confirmed that abandonment was not confined to deformed babies or infants born of incestuous and other forbidden relationships; legitimate children, too, were likely to be given up by parents who desired to limit family size. This led him to estimate that in the first three centuries C.E. urban Romans abandoned 20 to 40 percent of their children through exposure. According to Boswell, however, the same evidence also indicated that most of them were rescued. Since in the ancient world there were no institutional arrangements for abandoned children, they owed their survival to what Latin sources called *aliena misericordia*, or the "kindness of strangers" who found and raised the unwanted children. Although some FOUNDLINGS doubtless became slaves, most of them were apparently granted the status of foster children. Childless couples, or parents who had lost some of their offspring, were especially keen to retrieve exposed babies and raise them.

Boswell's picture of child abandonment as an efficient and almost painless mechanism of redistribution, whereby families with a surplus of children surrendered some of them to parents who had too few or none at all, has been criticized on various grounds. It has been argued, in particular, that his contention that most exposed children did not die is too rosy, for survival clearly depended on a combination of lucky circumstances, such as being discovered before harm had been done and being placed with a woman who had fresh milk to give. Nevertheless, Boswell's point that child abandonment should not be conflated with infanticide, whatever its death toll, is supported by ethnographic studies that emphasize that in many cultures it makes a crucial difference that abandoning parents do not actually take the child's life and therefore give the baby a chance to survive. These studies also show that abandonment does not always end in death. Even in supposedly infanticidal societies such as the Netsilik Eskimo society, in which abandonment was frequent, the infant's crying was a message to other members of the group that they might save the infant and adopt it if they wished.

Indeed, in much of Europe as well as in many other societies, abandonment was actually regarded as an alternative to infanticide. This distinction is crucial to understanding

Christian attitudes toward abandonment. Like Jews and Muslims, and in contrast to the Greeks and Romans, Christians believed that infanticide was murder and condemned it resolutely. On the other hand, abandonment was treated less harshly. Sharing the views of philosophers like Epictetus, Musonius, and the Alexandrian Jewish philosopher Philo, who had been the only ancient writers to object to abandonment, early Christian moralists initially had denounced child abandonment as equivalent to infanticide. From the fourth century on, however, early disapproval was replaced by an attitude of resignation and sympathy toward those who abandoned their children as a result of destitution or other misfortune. Whereas infanticide and abortion were strongly condemned throughout the Middle Ages, no councils or ecclesiastical authorities prohibited abandonment. A similar attitude prevailed in medieval Muslim society.

Public Intervention

From about 1000 to 1200 abandonment was less common than it had been previously, but in the thirteenth century it was again on the increase owing to the combined effects of demographic growth and adverse economic circumstances. It was in this period that foundling homes were created in a number of Italian cities, as part of a more general movement by civic institutions, both religious and secular, to handle social problems. Until the nineteenth century foundling homes were regarded as important manifestations of Christian piety. One major reason behind the establishment of these hospices devoted to the care of abandoned children was the fear that infants might be killed by unwed mothers who wanted to avoid social disapproval or by parents made desperate by poverty and hunger.

The appearance of foundling homes was a turning point in the history of child abandonment; the private "kindness of strangers" was superseded by public intervention. The Italian model spread rapidly to Portugal, Spain, and France, though not immediately to the rest of Europe. A new chapter in the history of the care of infants opened during the EN-LIGHTENMENT, when a second generation of foundling homes was established in many European cities, especially in the Catholic countries and in Russia. This institutional development paralleled a dramatic growth in the number of exposures, which in early nineteenth-century Europe reached a height of perhaps 150,000 per year. Such a massive increase was due partly to rising rates of illegitimate births, and partly to the growing tendency of impoverished parents to trust the care of at least some of their offspring to the foundling hospitals. In most parts of Europe admission was supposedly restricted to illegitimate children, but large numbers of unentitled children were smuggled into the hospitals through the "wheels," revolving cradles that were arranged so as to allow people approaching from the street to introduce infants without being seen from within the building. Tokens of various kinds were often left as potential signs of identification, and it was not unusual for abandoning parents to return to

the hospital after a year or two to reclaim their children. However, the chances of finding them alive were slim, since it was rare for more than half the foundlings to survive the first year of life.

Although institutionalized abandonment made some inroads in northwestern Protestant Europe, by the early nineteenth century a striking contrast was clearly discernible between such countries as Prussia, England, Switzerland, and the United States, where newborns were seldom abandoned, and Russia and the Catholic countries of southern and central-eastern Europe, where mass abandonment was exerting a mounting pressure on foundling homes originally intended for a much lower number of children. During the course of the nineteenth century, the closure of the wheels began to be seen as the only way out of an increasingly unbearable situation. French hospitals were the first to make this move. By 1853 most wheels there had been shut, and in the second half of the century the French example was to be followed all over Europe.

The closure of the wheels resulted in a sudden and drastic decline of child abandonment, which helped to curb foundling mortality. In the last decades of the nineteenth century the abandonment of illegitimate children also began to fall, a change partly linked to the spread of contraception. By the beginning of the twentieth century, the classic form of child abandonment had virtually disappeared. The term *abandonment* is nowadays used to designate a different and much wider range of childhood experiences, including the few cases of infants and young children who are exposed, but also the predicaments of street children, victims of war, CHILD PROSTITUTES, children of refugee parents, and runaway children who actually abandon their parents and unhappy homes to escape from troubled environments.

See also: **Foster Care; Homeless Children and Runaways in the United States; Orphanages.**

BIBLIOGRAPHY

Boswell, John. 1988. *The Kindness of Strangers. The Abandonment of Children in Western Europe from Late Antiquity to the Renaissance.* New York: Pantheon.

Fildes, Valerie. 1988. *Wet Nursing. A History from Antiquity to the Present.* Oxford: Blackwell.

Gil'adi, Avner. 1992. *Children of Islam. Concepts of Childhood in Medieval Muslim Society.* New York: St. Martin's Press.

Hrdy, Sarah Blaffer. 1992. "Fitness Tradeoffs in the History and Evolution of Delegated Mothering with Special Reference to Wet-Nursing, Abandonment, and Infanticide." *Ethnology and Sociobiology* 13: 409–442.

Kertzer, David I. 1993. *Sacrificed for Honor. Italian Infant Abandonment and the Politics of Reproductive Control.* Boston: Beacon Press.

Panter-Brick, Catherine, and Malcolm T. Smith, eds. 2000. *Abandoned Children.* Cambridge, UK: Cambridge University Press.

Scrimshaw, Susan C. M. 1984. "Infanticide in Human Populations: Societal and Individual Concerns." In *Infanticide. Comparative and Evolutionary Perspectives,* ed. Glenn Hausfater and Sarah Blaffer Hrdy. New York: Aldine.

Tilly, Louise A., Rachel G. Fuchs, David I. Kertzer, et al. 1991. "Child Abandonment in European History: A Symposium." *Journal of Family History* 17: 1–23.

PIER PAOLO VIAZZO

ABC Books

ABC (or *abécédaire*) books also have been known as *abcee-books*, *absey-books*, *abeces*, and other, similar, variations. In 1596 Shakespeare wrote in *King John* "that is question now, And then comes answer like an Absey booke." In 1751, when Denis Diderot mentioned the word *abécédaire* in his *Encyclopédie*, he defined it as an adjective that applied not only to books but also to people in the process of learning.

From the fifteenth century through the eighteenth century, the teaching of the Roman alphabet was associated with religious instruction. The primer, or book of prayer and religious instruction for students of all ages, often opened with a page of the letters of the alphabet, as well as a short catechism. Although not intended solely for children, these books became associated with simple teachings and those who were just learning. One of the earliest existing primers, published by Thomas Petyt in London around 1538, includes the alphabet, a table of vowels and syllables, prayers, and graces for meals. Petyt was under license to provide "The BAC [*sic*] bothe in latyn and in Englysshe." During this period in England, there was a distinction between the ABC, the first text, and the primer, the second text. *The ABC with the catechisme* (1549), the standard ABC book of its time, sold hundreds of thousands of copies during the next century.

Students also learned their alphabet from hornbooks, or letter boards, which were pieces of wood shaped like a paddle and hung by ribbon or twine threaded through a hole in the handle. To the paddle was affixed a letterpress sheet on which was printed the alphabet in both uppercase and lowercase. Eventually the alphabet was joined by the Lord's Prayer, an invocation to the Trinity, and often, the vowels, a table of syllables, and nine digits. The alphabet was generally preceded by a cross and therefore was called "Criss-Cross Rows." In England and America thin pieces of horn were used to protect the paper, leading to the name *hornbook*. The paddles were used by active school children as rackets and they became known as *battledores*, after the game of battledores and shuttlecocks. In 1746 Benjamin Collins invented a format for a folding cardboard booklet and called it a battledore; these small printed texts quickly replaced hornbooks.

Other forms of teaching the alphabet included needlework samplers and even gingerbread. As early as the fourteenth century, gingerbread, printed with designs like letters, was sold in stalls in open markets. There are many references to *book gingerbread*, and by the eighteenth century

A page from *Noah's Ark ABC* (c. 1872), by Walter Crane, an important and innovative illustrator of the late nineteenth century. In the nineteenth century, ABC books became a way to teach children the alphabet and introduce them to new subjects, such as types of animals or the names of common household items.

gingerbread was shaped like hornbooks and printed with letters.

Initially the alphabet appeared in table form. Eventually, however, illustrations were added to the letters, as a mnemonic aid. The earliest known printed English pictorial alphabet is John Hart's *A methode, or comfortable beginning for all unlearned* (1570). This text paired each letter with a woodcut illustration of an object that began with that letter. From this point on, illustrations became a standard part of ABC books.

In 1658, in Nuremberg, the educational theorist JOHANN AMOS COMENIUS printed in Latin and German the *Orbis sensualium pictus*. In 1659 Charles Hoole printed an English version. This text is thought to be the first picture book designed specifically for children. The text, in both Latin and the vernacular, includes an alphabet in which each letter is illustrated by an animal that makes a sound beginning with that letter (e.g., the letter B is illustrated by a lamb "baaing").

Juvenile literature was given fuel by JOHN LOCKE's *Some Thoughts Concerning Education* (1693) in which he recommended that children learn by enticement instead of fear of punishment. "There may be Dice and Playthings, with the Letters on them, to teach Children the Alphabet by playing; and twenty other ways may be found, suitable to their particular Tempers, to make this kind of Learning a Sport to them."

Eighteenth- and Nineteenth-Century Publications

Eighteenth-century England was a time of immense growth in the publication of children's books, addressing both secular and religious subjects. One London bookshop was even called the "GREAT A, little a AND BIG BOUNCING B." T. W.'s *A Little Book for Little Children* (c. 1702), very different from Thomas White's earlier book by the same name, was an eight-page reading and spelling book that depicts a tiny picture and verse for each letter. It starts with a verse that underwent many variations in later years: "A was an Archer and shot at a Frog, B was a blind Man and led by a Dog." Publisher John Newbery was a key figure in the growth of juvenile literature. He opened a children's bookshop in St. Paul's Churchyard in 1745 and ran it for twenty-two years, during which time he published, sold, and perhaps wrote at least fifty original books for children. One of his first books was *A Little Pretty Pocket-Book* (1744), which included the alphabet (in both uppercase and lowercase) linked with woodcuts and verses about types of children's games. Interestingly, the letters and images have no direct relation; instead, the letters function almost as page numbers. Isaiah Thomas in Worcester, Massachusetts, was responsible for copying many of Newbery's books and introducing them to an American audience.

Toward the end of the eighteenth century, literature for children also flourished in the form of chapbooks. These cheaply produced, small format booklets (about 2 1/2 x 4 inches), with crudely illustrated images, were carried by chapmen or peddlers, in their packs, and sold for a penny or less. Traditionally for adults, by the end of the eighteenth century there were many written for children that included the alphabet.

In America the *New England Primer* (c. 1690) was the most widely used schoolbook during the seventeenth and eighteenth centuries. Compiled by the English bookseller and writer Benjamin Harris during a brief stay in Boston, the exact publication date is uncertain but the earliest known existing copy is dated 1727. It contains an illustrated alphabet with rhymes, an "Alphabet of Lessons for Youth" (which uses sentences from the Bible for each letter), other prayers and religious lessons, and the catechism. Published until at least 1886, it was altered slightly by each publisher.

By the nineteenth century, printing technology made possible complex pictures and color printing in text for children. The purpose of alphabet books changed from using familiar images and verses as mnemonic aids to using the alphabet as a framework to introduce new subjects, including farm animals, exotic animals, birds, children's names, the BIBLE and virtues, vocations, common objects, railways, the seaside, patriotic symbols, and the world's nations. Patriotism was a popular subject in America at the end of the Civil War (*Union ABC*, 1864) and in England at the end of the Crimean War (*Alphabet of Peace*, 1856). Edmund Evans, a London publisher, was especially concerned with improving the quality of children's picture books, and published the works of such authors as Walter Crane, KATE GREENAWAY, and Ralph Caldecott. Nineteenth-century children's magazines serialized alphabets, publishing a few images each month. Although the subjects were extremely varied in the nineteenth century, the formats chosen were relatively simple—generally a single word or rhyming verse accompanying an image for each letter.

Modern Publications

In the twentieth century authors continued to expand the variety of subjects addressed by ABC books and explored the style as much as the subject. Some authors used extended narratives of one sentence per letter, or even one story or book per letter, such as Wanda Gág's *ABC Bunny* (1933) and Angela Banner's *Ant and Bee* (1950) *Richard Scarry's Cars and Trucks from A to Z* (1990) is a whole story that is just one long sentence. Scarry's book is shaped like a car, which demonstrates growing interest in the physical format of books. Pop-up books from this period include Robert Crowther's *The Most Amazing Hide-And-Seek Alphabet Book* (1978) and Robert Sabuda's *A Christmas Alphabet* (1994). Alliterative verses, as seen quite early in "Peter Piper picked a peck of pickled peppers" from *Peter Pipers Principles of Practical Pronunciation* (1813), have found modern versions in Graeme Base's *Animalia* (1986) and MAURICE SENDAK's *Alligators All Around* (1962).

Art was a growing theme toward the end of the twentieth century; it was featured in Lucy Micklethwait's *I Spy: An Alphabet in Art* (1992), museum alphabets by Florence Cassen Mayers, George Mendoza's *Norman Rockwell's Americana ABC* (1975), and in Caroline Desnoëttes's *Le musée des Animaux* (1997). Some other noteworthy twentieth-century alphabets include C. B. Falls's *ABC Book* (1923), Margaret Tempest's *An ABC for You and Me* (1948), Tasha Tudor's *A is for Annabelle* (1954), Garth Williams's *Big Golden Animal ABC* (1957), *Brian Wildsmith's ABC* (1962), *Dr. Seuss' ABC* (1963), and William Steig's *Alpha Beta Chowder* (1992).

The ABC book genre now includes texts that do not instruct but instead provide amusement for an audience already familiar with the alphabet. Some examples are nonsense alphabet books, such as DR. SEUSS's *On Beyond Zebra* (1955) and *Aldiborontiphosskyphorniostikos* (1820), printed by Dean and Munday of London. Books intended for an adult audience include David Hockney's *Hockney's Alphabet* (1991), George Cruikshank's *A Comic Alphabet* (1836), and Man Ray's *Alphabet pour adultes* (1970).

From Hart's 1570 text to recent versions, some common themes emerge. Authors have explored the relation of letter and image and have made decisions about the style and the case of letters. One continual challenge has been some of the difficult letters, especially X. Xerxes is a frequent stand-in, and authors have found ways to evade using it, even omitting the entire letter upon occasion. Hilaire Belloc's explanation for the letter in *A Moral Alphabet* (1899) was: "No reasonable little Child expects / A Grown-up Man to make a rhyme on X."

See also: **Children's Literature.**

BIBLIOGRAPHY

Baldwin, Ruth M. 1972. *100 Rhyming Alphabets in English.* Carbondale: Southern Illinois University.

Carpenter, Charles. 1963. *History of American Schoolbooks.* Philadelphia: University of Pennsylvania Press.

Findlay, James, and Jean Trebbi. 1997. *ZYX: An Exhibition of Selected ABC Books from the Jean Trebbi Collection.* Fort Lauderdale, FL: Bienes Center for the Literary Arts. Also available from <www.co.broward.fl.us/bienes>.

Findlay, James, and Nyr Indicator. 2000. *ABC and Related Materials: Selections from the Nyr Indicator Collection of the Alphabet.* Fort Lauderdale, FL: Bienes Center for the Literary Arts. Also available from <www.co.broward.fl.us/bienes>.

Green, Ian. 1996. *The Christian's ABC: Catechisms and Catechizing in England, c.1530–1740.* Oxford, UK: Clarendon Press.

Klinefelter, Walter. 1973. "The ABC Books of the Pennsylvania Germans." *Publications of the Pennsylvania German Society* 7: 1–104.

McLean, Ruari. 1969. *Pictorial Alphabets.* New York: Dover Publications.

McLean, Ruari. 1976. *Noah's Ark ABC and Eight Other Victorian Alphabet Books in Colour.* New York: Dover Publications.

Ory, Norma. 1978. *Art and the Alphabet: An Exhibition for Children.* Houston, TX: The Museum of Fine Arts.

Roberts, Patricia. 1987. *Alphabet Books as a Key to Language Patterns: An Annotated Action Bibliography.* Hamden, CT: Library Professional Publications.

Roberts, Patricia. 1994. *Alphabet: A Handbook of ABC Books and Book Extensions for the Elementary Classroom.* Metuchen, NJ: Scarecrow Press.

St. John, Judith. 1958. *The Osborne Collection of Early Children's Books, 1566–1910: A Catalogue.* Toronto: Toronto Public Library.

Steinfirst, Susan. 1976. "The Origins and Development of the ABC Book in English from the Middle Ages through the Nineteenth Century." Ph.D. diss., University of Pittsburgh.

Thwaite, Mary F. 1963. *From Primer to Pleasure in Reading.* Boston: The Horn Book.

Tuer, Andrew W. 1896. *History of the Horn Book,* 2 vols. London: LeadenHall Press.

MELISSA GEISLER TRAFTON

Abduction

The abduction of children for various purposes (ransom and extortion, work, sex, power, custody) has historically been a

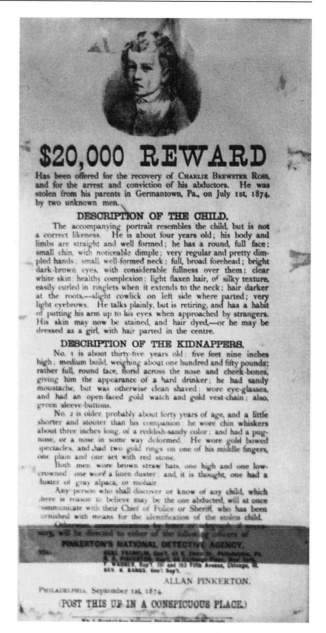

Charley Ross's abduction from his home in Philadelphia in 1874 was the first case of child abduction in the United States to attract widespread national attention. Posters offering a reward for his safe return were distributed as far west as California. Photo by John Lesch.

feature of many societies. In the twentieth century, these abductions became more widely publicized and came to carry very great symbolic power. As childhood itself became an enormously potent focus for social and personal anxieties, child abduction registered as a threat to ordinary people as well as to the prominent individuals to whom it once seemed restricted. The perception of the frequency of such abductions has increased markedly in the late twentieth and early twenty-first centuries, largely because childhood seems to have become more vulnerable and less sheltered while a

The kidnapping of Charles Lindbergh Jr. on March 1, 1932, was the most notorious child abduction in modern history. This photograph, taken on the baby's first birthday, appeared in newspapers around the world in the days after his kidnapping. © Bettman/CORBIS.

number of issues relating to the family have become important public concerns. The mass media have also learned to use child abduction as an issue that evokes strong emotions. In the recent past in the United States and Europe, accelerating divorce, women's growing role outside the home, and public fears about PEDOPHILIA have put a spotlight on child abduction, while dissatisfactions about class disparities in the developing economies of LATIN AMERICA has once again brought ransom abduction into international headlines.

Through most of human history and for the vast majority of people, child ABANDONMENT has been a far more serious social matter than the deliberate abduction of children. Nevertheless, in Europe and many parts of the Mediterranean world, among kings, nobles, and merchants, the abduction of children for reasons of state or alliance could be a serious means to usurp power or force large payments. And even among the general population brigandage, which often involved the threat of theft in property or children, could be a way to challenge power relationships. This kind of abduc-

tion was also practiced, on a group rather than individual basis, among native peoples in North America and Africa. Usually as a part of war strategy, the abduction of women and children was a means to augment population and undermine the strength of competing clan or tribal groups. European colonists in North America experienced some of these abductions in the seventeenth and eighteenth centuries as native peoples sought to defeat their enemies by absorbing their children into their own culture.

Although they also raise questions about cultural and personal identity, modern forms of abduction have been overwhelmingly individual acts that prey on personal sentiments and attachments to children rather than challenges to cultural or political domination. Thus the most common form of child abduction in late-nineteenth-century and early-twentieth-century America were kidnappings for ransom. In these cases, a child's safe return was predicated on the delivery of a large sum of money. The first such well-known abduction was of four-year old Charley Ross in 1874 in Philadelphia. But historically the case most closely associated with this type of crime, because of the enormous publicity it generated, was the abduction and murder of Charles Lindbergh Jr. in New Jersey in 1932. The child's father was aviator-hero Charles A. Lindbergh, the first man to fly solo across the Atlantic (in 1927) and his fame assured that the case would dominate world headlines for months. Ransom abductions exploited the modern Western family's attachments to children and strongly confirmed the cultural elevation of each child to the status of a precious, irreplaceable individual within the family.

Other forms of abduction also became prominent during this time. In the nineteenth century some children were abducted, usually briefly, for the purposes of begging or street entertainment, some ("Black Hand" abductions), as part of extortion demands by one crime group against another. Since the mid-nineteenth century, some abductions resulted from the desire of women to mother children they could not otherwise obtain. In the 1970s and 1980s, the abduction of the children of prominent business figures in Europe and the United States became a part of the operations of left-wing terror groups. (Such abductions also became common in Latin America at the end of the twentieth century.) The most famous of these was the abduction of the twenty-year-old newspaper heiress, Patricia Hearst, in Berkeley, California in 1974. This case lasted for several years, as the group of terrorists who kidnapped her (the Symbionese Liberation Army) engaged in a campaign against American institutions in which cause they enlisted their victim.

The most common modern form of abduction, and certainly the one with the most momentum, has been the abduction of children caught in custody disputes between parents or other family members. In these cases, children are prevented from returning to parents who either share legal custody, or are entitled to visitation rights with the child. Children in such cases are often pawns in a tense battle between parents or other family members, and they are sometimes abducted to protect them from what one parent may believe is abuse or neglect on the part of the other parent. Parental abductions became very numerous in the last third of the twentieth century, as divorce rates skyrocketed in Western societies, but they have been well known and amply documented throughout the century. At their most extreme, such abductions can result in parents not seeing their children for years. But the vast majority of these family disputes usually involve short periods of time during which the child is absent from a parent's life. A recent variant of these family kidnappings has been those which involve international abductions, the consequence of disputes between parents of different nations and cultures. The international cases are often the most aggravated and frequently result in the complete severance of relations between the parent (usually the mother) from the life and activities of the child. The situation has led to a great deal of publicity and diplomatic activi-

ty, and the creation of the Hague Convention on International Child Abduction (1988) in an attempt to both prevent and mediate disputes of this kind among signatory nations.

By the end of the twentieth century, the number of parental abductions in the United States had grown very large (the number of serious parental abductions in the United States has been estimated as close to 150,000 cases each year), and its prominence as a social problem became intertwined with another old, but newly alarming form of child abduction—the abduction of children by strangers for sexual and sadistic abuse. Although such cases had been suspected before (for example, the abduction and murder of Robert Franks by Nathan Leopold and Richard Loeb in 1924), by the 1970s and 1980s, several factors came together to bring these terrifying forms of abduction vividly into the public arena. These included widespread changes in sexual mores; the vastly expanded workplace participation of women with young children and attendant childcare problems; and the prominence of new victims' advocacy groups eager to pass protective legislation. Especially important in this regard were new laws introduced in the 1980s that required doctors and others invested with public authority to report all kinds of suspected CHILD ABUSE. Several cases of child abduction heavily covered by the media brought the issue to the public's attention: the kidnappings of Etan Patz (1979), Adam Walsh (1981), Kevin White (1984), Jacob Wetterling (1989), and Polly Klaas (1993). These cases, which took place in all parts of the country and in small towns as well as big cities, were a source of great alarm as the public discussion merged the various strands of the modern missing-children phenomenon into one public campaign. Children abducted by strangers (always a small number) and children abducted in custody disputes, together with runaways were all counted together as part of a newly hysterical fear about missing children.

The campaign created in the 1980s on behalf of missing children involved private foundations, as well as newly publicly funded institutions (the National Center for Missing and Exploited Children, 1984), and it was monitored by legislative committees, a new FBI registry, and in the media. Together these created elaborate parental fears about the vulnerability of all children in America, fears fanned by proliferating posters and billboards, missing-children advertisements on milk cartons and in home mailings, new kidnapping insurance and public finger-printing efforts, and the massive news coverage of suspected cases and television programming of real and invented kidnappings.

By the 1990s, some of the furor had subsided in the United States as new information gathered by the Justice Department about the actual prevalence of stranger abductions calmed an inflamed atmosphere. But a similar kind of hysteria enveloped a number of European countries, among them Belgium, France, and Germany. In these countries, and others, a new concern with the prevalence of pedophile rings, and gruesome publicity about the discovery of the bodies of missing children spread alarm throughout European culture, hitherto largely unresponsive to the American issues of sexual stranger abductions. In 1996, 300,000 concerned Belgians gathered in a massive demonstration in Brussels to speak out against the perceived threat to their country's children, a threat they believed to have been mishandled by a corrupt police.

In the 1990s, the spread of the Internet and the possibilities that this seemed to offer for strangers to lure children from inside their own homes created a new kind of alarm about the safety of children. By the late twentieth century these fears about the safety of children was gathering in a number of places and around an assortment of issues, most of them centered on sexual exploitation. Child abduction seemed to be only the most fearsome of the many sexual dangers to which children now seemed exposed, such as sex rings in child-care centers, satanic rituals, and pedophilia in churches and other public places. The sexual exploitation of children, which is hardly a new phenomenon, became in the late twentieth century a startling symbol of parents' inability to protect their increasingly vulnerable children. Where in the past, only the rich or powerful were subject to abductions, today, all parents seem helpless before the possibility that their children, to whom they feel a deep emotional attachment, might be exploited, mutilated, or killed. The new fear haunts the early-twenty-first-century imagination, an imagination fed by a news and entertainment industry which has learned over the course of the twentieth century how best to titillate and shock the modern sensibility. Today, the child's place in that sensibility has been secured through the very threat to its well-being that child abduction seems to bring into every home.

See also: **Abduction in Modern Africa; Divorce and Custody; Lindbergh Kidnapping; Mortara Abduction.**

BIBLIOGRAPHY

Best, Joel. 1990. *Threatened Children: Rhetoric and Concern about Child Victims.* Chicago: University of Chicago Press.

Demos, John. 1994. *The Unredeemed Captive: A Family Story.* New York: Knopf.

Fass, Paula S. 1997. *Kidnapped: Child Abduction in America.* New York: Oxford University Press.

Finkelhor, David, Gerald Hoteling, and Andrea Sedlak. 1990. *Missing, Abducted, Runaway, and Thrownaway Children in America. First Report: Numbers and Characteristics,* National Incidence Studies. Washington, DC: United States Department of Justice, Office of Justice Programs, Office of Juvenile Justice and Delinquency Prevention.

PAULA S. FASS

Abduction in Modern Africa

During the last four decades of the twentieth century, the most notorious and widespread abductions of children in Africa have been closely associated with armed conflict in such countries as Angola, Burundi, the Democratic Republic of Congo (formerly Zaire), Mozambique, Rwanda, Somalia, Sudan, Sierra Leone, and Uganda, among others. On the other hand, pervasive poverty, large demands for child labor, and the huge profits to be made by child-marketers have created a massive trade in African children within and outside of AFRICA. Some of the children sold in this network are abducted. Less visible but more persistent and equally deleterious, child abductions thrive in the context of a host of sociocultural practices.

In precolonial Africa, large-scale abductions of children occurred in the course of the trans-Atlantic slave trade in the fifteenth through nineteenth centuries in West Africa, and in the eastern and central African Arab-Swahili slave trade, which peaked in the nineteenth century. In both cases, children were sold into slavery to lands beyond the continent. Traders created intricate conduits for conveying abducted populations from the interior to the coastal trading houses. Perpetrators included individual traders, brokers, royal houses, and European partners, the latter stationed at the coast.

Additionally, localized ethnic conflicts produced limited and intermittent abductions of children as war hostages during the precolonial period. The common practice was to integrate the children into the families and social structures of their captors. The children were looked upon as additional social capital vital for productive and reproductive activities.

As illustrated in the case of Zena (discussed below), the practice of abducting child brides has evolved beyond customary sanction and has increasingly attracted greater attention in judicial circles. There is also an emerging phenomenon of infant abductions traced to desperate childless women. Children of unsuspecting mothers in hospitals and crowded townships become easy targets of such desperate women. It appears also that there is a market for abducted children among childless women who feign motherhood upon returning to their homes. A breakdown of extended family networks has robbed childless women of the benefit of access to communal child-rearing responsibilities. This may have forced the women to child abduction.

Elsewhere, amidst political instability and the emergence of religious cults, there are reports of child abductions associated with ritual sacrifice. Whether the children are targeted for their innocence, and hence ritual purity, for their vulnerability, or as vital social capital, adults, in their efforts to transact political, economic, or social-religious contracts, brutalize children.

Abducted Child Soldiers

At the beginning of the twenty-first century, civil wars constitute the single major cause of child abduction in Africa. The scale, complexity, and brutality of modern, armed-conflict-related child abductions dwarf the precolonial situation by far. Both rebel forces and governments perpetrate the abductions. Abducted children serve as domestics, porters, messengers, and general camp followers. Girls, some as young as ten, become sex slaves for the soldiers. Boys, and some girls, are forced to perform armed combat duties.

While internal precolonial abductions sought to integrate their victims into the captors' society, modern abductions seek to isolate, separate, brutalize, and intimidate the children into malleable errand boys and girls. Thus, in addition to being forced into regular combat, abducted children are also forced to commit rape, torture, and killings, sometimes directed at fellow children. This serves as initiation into a life of violence, and serves as warning of what will befall them should they become recalcitrant, or try to run away. In order to elicit and sustain such criminal responses from the children, some captors are reported to drug the children. Thus children become both perpetrators and victims of violence.

Present-day concentration of settlement has made children more vulnerable to abductions. Schools are popular hunting grounds for rebel armies. For example, between 1994 and 1998, the rebel Lord's Resistance Army (LRA) in northern Uganda abducted about 8,000 children, most of them schoolchildren. In April 2001, the UN High Commission for Human Rights reported that more than one-third of the more than 26,000 abduction cases recorded so far in Uganda were children under the age of eighteen. Some were as young as nine. In 2002, most schools in northern Uganda had been shut down for fear of further abductions. In Angola, child soldiers were as young as eight.

The LRA is also said to sell children in exchange for arms and ammunitions. The resurgence of slavery, and the juxtaposition of child abduction and the trade in weaponry, constitute new variables in the child abduction syndrome. The cordial relations between the LRA and the Sudanese government imply government complicity in the trade in children.

Modern Africa has surpassed other regions in using children to fight its wars. This is a new development. Abducted children comprise an appreciable proportion of child soldiers. In some countries, including Sierra Leone, Angola, and the Democratic Republic of Congo (DRC), child soldiers have played pivotal roles in civil wars. For example, in the DRC, it has been claimed that child soldiers, referred to as *kadogo*, or little ones, constituted the majority of the rebel soldiers used to oust dictator Mobutu Sesse Seko in 1996.

Straddling an international military network, these child soldiers operated among Ugandan and Rwandese soldiers. The new regime in the Democratic Republic of Congo continues to use demobilized child soldiers on street patrols, while in rebel-held sections of the republic continuous child abductions have forced parents to pull their children out of schools. In Angola in 1994, 12 percent of the rebel Unita forces were children.

Trade in Children

The astronomical resurgence of a clandestine trade in children in West Africa is an open secret. Some of these children are abducted. The trade is especially rampant in Benin, Burkina Faso, Cameroon, Côte d'Ivoire, Nigeria, Gabon, Central Africa Republic, Mali, and Togo, countries that are not engaged in civil wars. This is a marked contrast to the era of the trans-Atlantic slave trade, which fuelled wars that in turn provided war captives.

The current trade in children constitutes a wide network of porous, cross-border trade conduits including destinations in Europe, the Gulf states, and Lebanon. Demand for child labor in the domestic, sex, and drug trafficking networks, coupled with massive profits from these circuits, has revived, and massively expanded, child-kidnapping practices.

The majority of the children thus traded are girls, up to 95 percent in the Benin-Nigeria circuit. They are between the ages of seven and seventeen. Storage depots, office markets, and ships for transportation have been established to facilitate the disbursement of kidnapped and other enslaved children. In a 2002 debacle in Côte d'Ivoire, children abducted from Mali for employment in the cocoa sector were set free by the Ivorian government, but not before an international uproar. The government of Côte d'Ivoire was quick to blame immigrant Malian cocoa producers and residents from Burkina Faso for the abductions.

Child Bride Abductions

In the precolonial period, the general practice of forced marriage also involved the abduction of girls below the marriageable age, with or without the knowledge of their parents. In some regions, this practice had the social sanction of the community. In others, the practice was represented as jestful theatrics, implying that there was no forced removal and that the screaming bride was merely joking. While still evident, today the practice has been criminalized and in some cases the abducted child brides, or their parents if they are not party to the abduction, at least in theory have recourse to law. In fact, however, their legal position is ambiguous. This is demonstrated by an ongoing legal battle in Swaziland, which is complicated by the fact that the prospective bridegroom is a man of great social and political standing. In October 2002, eighteen-year-old Zena Mahlangu was abducted from school by two royal messengers to await marriage to thirty-four-year-old King Mswati III. The king is reported to have nine other wives. Zena is a victim of a convoluted practice still sanctioned by customary law but criminal under common law.

While historically the Swazi royal household was expected to consult with the families of prospective brides, this did not happen in Zena's case. More daunting is the fact that under Swazi law neither the king nor the queen can be arrested, sued, or prosecuted. Efforts to make the king a defendant seem unlikely to be successful. In a dramatic turn of events, press releases in late October 2002 stated that Zena Mahlangu had declared that she was ready to be married to the king and that she had settled into her new life. This change will likely bring the litigation to an end.

Modern child bride abduction is often occasioned by males' desire to marry a virgin in the belief that virgins are free from HIV/AIDS. The loss of their virginity upon marriage ensures that even if they flee from their unwanted marriages most of these girls would not return to their homes since this would bring dishonor to their families, and on their ethnic group as a whole. The juxtaposition of a modern scourge and an age-old practice render girl children even more vulnerable than before. So too do child and maternal deaths due to the undeveloped physiology of child mothers. Child marriages also increase school dropout rates among the girls, depriving them of economic independence in the long run.

To the victims, abduction is psychologically traumatic. The torture, killing, and exploitation of abducted children increasingly call into question the conscience and morality of a whole continent. The conniving of a cross-section of global participants, driven by struggles for political power, and by avarice, sexual depravity, and individual inadequacy, have created a horrifying milieu for a large number of African children. All abducted children are robbed of their childhood and most are blatantly exposed to an adult world of senseless killing.

See also: **Abduction; Child Labor in Developing Countries; Juvenile Justice: International; Soldier Children.**

BIBLIOGRAPHY

de Temmerman, Els. 2001. *Aboke Girls: Children Abducted in Northern Uganda.* Kampala, Uganda: Fountain Publishers.

Easy Prey: Child Soldiers in Liberia. 1994. New York: Human Rights Watch Children's Rights Project.

Edwards, Paul, ed. 1996. *Equiano's Travels.* Oxford, UK: Heinemann.

Effah, Josephine. 1996. *Modernized Slavery: Child Trade in Nigeria.* Lagos, Nigeria: Constitutional Rights Project.

Falola, Toyin, and Paul Lovejoy, eds. 1994. *Pawnship in Africa: Debt Bondage in Historical Perspective.* Boulder, CO: Westview Press.

TABITHA KANOGO

Academies

From the revolutionary era to the late nineteenth century, academies were the dominant institution of higher schooling in the United States. Academies generally served students between the ages of eight and twenty-five, providing a relatively advanced form of schooling beyond the elementary level. The Catholic order of the Ursulines founded the first academy for women in French-speaking New Orleans in 1727. Philadelphia's Franklin Academy received a colonial charter in 1753, and the Colonial Assembly introduced a bill to incorporate New Bern Academy in North Carolina in 1766. According to Henry Barnard, by 1850 there existed more than 6,100 incorporated academies across the United States, with enrollments nine times greater than those of the colleges.

Characteristics of Academies

Late eighteenth and nineteenth-century academies can be distinguished from other forms of higher schooling by their corporate structure, legal status, and by the breadth of their curricula. A school bearing the name *academy, seminary,* or *institute* differed from an entrepreneurial venture school by having some form of financial support other than tuition, in addition to articles of incorporation, and the oversight of a board of trustees. The trustees secured land and buildings for the institution, helped with fundraising, recruited and hired teachers, and supervised the public examinations of academy students. Because of this corporate support and governance, academies tended to enjoy a greater degree of financial stability and longevity than venture schools.

Like the many private venture schools in the nation's early years, academies offered a broad range of subjects in response to popular demand. Typically, institutions offered reading, writing, grammar, geography, arithmetic, classical languages, and the higher branches of "English" education, including the sciences, mathematics, composition, history, rhetoric, theology, and philosophy. Most academies also offered applied subjects on a pay-as-you-go basis, such as ornamental needlework, music, painting, drawing, navigation and surveying, and bookkeeping.

In contrast to the early Latin GRAMMAR SCHOOLS, which provided instruction to males and emphasized the classical languages, academies served a broader clientele. Both boys and girls attended academies, either in single-sex or in coeducational institutions where instruction was provided in separate departments. Students hailed from the families of farmers, craftsmen and tradesmen as well as professionals, plantation owners, and wealthy merchants.

Academy Expansion

Religious groups founded many of the earliest academies in both northern and southern colonies and in the southwest. Various teaching orders in the Roman Catholic Church established academies in the early seventeenth century, particularly in the Catholic colony of Maryland and in the French and Spanish territories. The Moravians opened a number of academies for women in the Mid-Atlantic states during the mid-eighteenth century. Irish Presbyterian ministers established more than forty-four academies in prerevolutionary America to train students for the ministry in the middle and southern colonies.

During the decades following the American Revolution, the number of academies in the United States expanded. Many entrepreneurial venture schools were incorporated as academies during this era, and pre-existing academies broadened their curricula in response to community demand. By 1825, the New York Board of Regents had chartered a total of forty-six academies. Ohio incorporated approximately one hundred academies between 1803 and 1840, and Illinois chartered at least one hundred and twenty-five from 1818 to 1848. By the 1830s, there existed as many as twenty-four incorporated academies in Alabama and fifty-five in Virginia, and Texas had ninety-seven academies by 1850.

A number of factors contributed to the expansion of academies and the growth in academy enrollments in the nineteenth century, including Jacksonian politics, population growth, and the Second Great Awakening. Jacksonian political leaders argued in favor of distributing state benefits widely. Legislators in some states facilitated the incorporation process, making corporate charters more widely available. During the same period, state governments also increased the amount of financial support for academies, either in the form of funding or grants of land. Additionally, the first decades of the nineteenth century witnessed an enormous expansion in population, coinciding with a great migration to the western and southern regions of the country. This was the age of canal-building, town-building, and railroad construction; in many communities the establishment of an academy became a traditional feature of a town's internal improvements. Finally, the evangelical fervor of the Second Great Awakening, a period running roughly from 1795 to 1837, gave rise to collaborative educational enterprises among some Protestant denominations. In virtually every community during the 1820s and 1830s, Protestant evangelicals played an important role in the consolidation of free urban schooling and the establishment of academies to provide a form of higher education for women as well as men.

The local communities, individuals, and religious groups that organized and supported academies acted from diverse motivations. Throughout the nineteenth century, various community groups, individuals, and mercantile associations established academies to provide a form of higher schooling for their youth, train a skilled workforce, or increase the property values in their towns. Some communities founded academies as an alternative to the forms of higher schooling provided by dominant cultural groups. For example, the Catholic Institution in New Orleans actively promoted a radical political agenda among free children of color; the academies founded by African Americans in Mississippi provided literacy and racial uplift during the post–Civil War Reconstruction Era; the Chinese Western Military Academy in California—together with its affiliates across the country—sought to empower young Chinese men by providing higher schooling and military training during a period when higher public schooling was denied to Chinese youth in that state.

The Transformation of Academies

In the post–Civil War era, different forms of higher schooling came into intense competition with each other. During the period immediately before and after the Civil War, some independent academies were absorbed into the expanding public education system. In New York, this process began in 1853, when the state legislature passed a law enabling neighboring school districts to unite for the purpose of establishing a local "academical department" or public HIGH SCHOOL. Local districts could establish academic departments either by organizing a new school or by adopting an existing academy. In some communities, the transformation from tuition-driven academy to public high school occurred within the context of a political struggle over the issue of providing tax-support for higher schooling.

Many independent academies continued to exist after 1870, and some communities and religious groups continued to establish new ones. However, as more towns established tax-supported high schools and more families paid the taxes necessary to support them, academies faced increasing pressure either to become public high schools themselves or to transform themselves into some other sort of institution that could continue to attract tuition revenue or other sources of public funding. When states established normal school systems in the 1860s and 1870s, they competed directly with existing academies that had provided much of the regional teacher training up to that time. Some academies met this challenge by successfully applying to become normal schools for their areas. Other academies sought to serve a particular student clientele by remaining independent private schools. Among this group, some institutions transformed themselves into independent colleges or into elite private preparatory schools. Others survived by emphasizing a particular form of schooling, such as religious training, education in the visual and performing arts, scientific and technical training, or compensatory schooling.

The academy movement left many historical legacies. Academies established an infrastructure of capital assets and political and financial support for higher schooling that continues to live on in both public schools and in alternatives to the public system. Academies provide a body of evidence for considering a number of current policy issues in education, including CHARTER SCHOOL and SCHOOL CHOICE policies, as well as broader issues of community-based schooling, teacher autonomy, school funding, local control, and issues of the roles of both church and state in education.

See also: **Common Schools; Convent Schools (Cathedral Schools); Girls' Schools; Latin School; Private and Independent Schools.**

BIBLIOGRAPHY

Beadie, Nancy, and Kim Tolley, eds. 2002. *Chartered Schools: Two Hundred Years of Independent Academies in the United States, 1727–1925.* New York: Routledge.

Kett, Joseph. 1994. *The Pursuit of Knowledge under Difficulties: From Self-Improvement to Adult Education in America, 1750–1990.* Stanford, CA: Stanford University Press.

Miller, George Frederick, 1969. *The Academy System of the State of New York.* New York: Arno Press.

Oats, Mary J. 1994. "Catholic Female Academies on the Frontier." *U.S. Catholic Historian* 12 (fall): 121–136.

Sizer, Theodore. 1964. *The Age of the Academies.* New York: Bureau of Publications, Teachers College, Columbia University.

Whitehead, Maurice. 1996. *The Academies of the Reverend Bartholomew Booth in Georgian England and Revolutionary America: Enlightening the Curriculum.* Lewiston, NY: E. Mellen Press.

Kim Tolley

Accidents

Accidents have been a common feature of childhood in Western and non-Western cultures for much of human history, but their nature and location, as well as whom they affect, have shifted over time. There is a striking amount of continuity in the physical causes of children's mishaps; fire, falls, and being crushed by carriages or other vehicles are hazards that transcend time and place. The family dwelling has remained a common site of mishaps, especially for younger children. Contrary to being a haven—as the nascent middle class defined homes in the nineteenth century—dwellings may have been the site where children faced the most pernicious and intractable risks. Even so, over time, a bevy of new types of accidents have appeared and supplanted older dangers. For example, dangers such as electrical shock, automobile accidents, and accidents involving poisonous chemicals replaced hazards such as "laying over" (or rolling onto children sharing the parental bed) and those associated with caring for animals.

Children, of course, faced many dangers outside their homes, which increased during periods of rapid economic change, such as when the industrial revolution swept Europe and North America in the nineteenth century. By the twentieth century, with the triumph of an urban society and especially the advent of the automobile, the dangers associated with public spaces, including particularly roads, increased in severity. For example, in modern automobile societies, car accidents have become the leading source of accidents to children—especially to TEENAGERS.

The Medieval Period
In medieval Europe, children faced a variety of hazards, including fire, animal bites, falling objects, drowning, scalding, laying over, or being crushed by a passing cart. These dangers appear to have varied little from rural to urban settings, with fire posing perhaps the most dramatic threat, especially for infants. More than one-third of the children listed in coroner's inquests in medieval England died from fires in their cradles, and approximately one-fifth of the children under three died in house fires. To modern audiences, the image of a sow devouring a baby, which appears in Chaucer's "The Knight's Tale," borders on the bizarre, but it almost certainly reflected the common threat that animals posed to children—and one all too frequently recorded in official records.

In a pattern that has remained more or less constant from medieval times through the modern era, the home was the place of greatest hazard, especially for younger children. According to coroner's records from medieval England, most fatal childhood accidents occurred at home. About 49 percent occurred in a child's own home; approximately 20 percent occurred in other people's homes; 20 percent occurred in public places; and 12 percent occurred in bodies of water. Accidents tended to occur during the busiest part of a parents' day—early in the morning or at noon. Nearly half of all fatal accidents happened during the summer months, as families turned their attention toward the fields and their agricultural labors, suggesting that at least part of the cause for such mishaps can be attributed to parental neglect or moments of inattention.

In premodern Europe, most records of accidents come from parish and government records. Accidents constituted only a small portion of childhood mortality, estimated by demographers at between 30 and 50 percent for infants. They are also evidenced in lullabies and songs of the period. Death in childhood was so common in the period and accidents did not represent a chief cause, and thus were probably not of major concern to most families. Even so, basic child-rearing strategies reveal at least some concern about accidental death. SWADDLING was commonly practiced as a way of protecting children from "chills." It also may have been practiced to keep infants safe and immobile—unable to crawl into problems at home, or even out of the house onto streets. Paradoxically swaddling may have facilitated behaviors that actually may have endangered infants. For example, tossing babies from one person to another was a popular form of amusement—something easily accomplished with swaddled children—and one that frequently led to accidents.

As children grew older and stepped outside the protection of their parent's or caregiver's attentions, the dangers facing children changed and new dangers presented themselves. In medieval times, fire accounted for fewer accidental deaths among older children than among their younger siblings. Yet older children's mobility increasingly figured into serious accidents, with PLAY accounting for 65 percent of all fatal accidents. As children aged, they also stepped into the gender roles that would accompany them throughout their lives, and the dangers they faced began to be differentiated. For example, little girls tended to have more accidents in the home and boys were more likely to have fatal mishaps while accompanying their fathers into the fields. Even so, home remained a site of persistent hazard, with 60 percent of boys and 79 percent of girls being injured in or very near the family dwelling. However, by the time that boys reached five or six, the majority of accidents they experienced occurred in the fields, often with tools, animals, and vehicles. By contrast, the home remained the most constant source of danger for girls until at least age eight or nine.

Industrialization

Industrialization brought dramatic changes to Western societies in the nineteenth century, reshaping both childhood and the nature of accidents. The introduction of a cash economy, and of mechanized factories and production processes, exposed everyone in society, including children, to entirely new dangers, as did rapidly changing urban settings, with their poor health conditions. Yet in these new urban and industrial environments, a host of other factors—such as high mortality rates, unprecedented rates of accidents for all workers, and extreme societal dislocation—childhood mishaps did not receive wide attention. When children's accidents did receive reformers' attentions, they did so in the context of broader efforts to address workplace safety, an increased focus on a wide range of issues associated with children's welfare, and concerns about deteriorating health conditions in urban settings.

The new cash economy drove children, and especially boys, into the paid labor force at earlier and earlier ages. For example, in England and the United States, industry made frequent use of children's labor, thus exposing them to new dangers. In Rhode Island, by 1801, one hundred children between four and ten years old worked at Slater's mill, cleaning raw cotton, tending spindles, removing and attaching bobbins, and knotting broken threads. In about the same period, in the coal mines of Lancashire, England, children under twelve accounted for as much as 25 percent of the labor force and suffered the same rash of injuries that struck their parents—fingers cut off by machinery, limbs and skulls crushed by vehicles, and fractures resulting from falls. Yet the presence of children under ten or twelve years of age in factories appears to have been a relatively short-lived phenomenon. By the 1870s, this practice became relatively rare in England and the United States. Reformers' efforts, an increased emphasis on schooling, the influx of adult immigrants, and automation in factories, among other things, all contributed to the decline of CHILD LABOR in manufacturing—and of children's propensity to be victims of factory accidents.

As industrial society emerged in the nineteenth century, children's exposure to dangerous conditions at home and in the community varied with their social class and ethnic or racial origins. The children of relatively poor families faced more hazards because of substandard housing and hazardous conditions, and because their parents had less time to moni-

tor them in the home, neighborhood, or at work—which these children encountered at younger ages than did those of the middle class. Likewise, economic and political refugees migrating to new homes faced dangerous treks to unfamiliar surroundings that exposed their children to a range of hazards. For example, the children of immigrants to New York City at the turn of the twentieth century were pushed outward into the streets from their overcrowded homes. These children discovered a host of delights and dangers; they played in freshly dug tunnels and rode subways. They experienced automobiles at ground level and saw electricity light their world. The streets—full of possibilities and dangers—were their world as much as home, parents, and school were.

At about this time, accidents in childhood slowly began to emerge as a broad societal concern. Individual family homes began to be viewed less as a safe haven from the world than as a place of danger. Already in 1897, Frances Fisher Wood noted in her landmark advice manual, *Infancy and Childhood*, that windows should be barred, open fires shielded, and stairways gated in order to protect children from hazards lurking in family dwellings. Even so, Wood devoted only this brief mention to accidents and as late as 1914 advice guru Dorothy Canfield Fisher made fun of those who took safety precautions in the home. Yet accidents were rapidly replacing disease as the leading cause of death for children early in the twentieth century United States. Indeed, by the 1910s, accidents were the single leading cause of death among children between five and fourteen years old, although among toddlers (one to four year olds) accidents did not eclipse influenza, pneumonia, tuberculosis, and diphtheria as the primary cause of death until the 1940s.

Not surprisingly, in the teens and 1920s, societal clubs, Progressive politicians, and workplace safety organizations, such as the National Safety Council, began to focus attention on dangers in the home. The responsibility for keeping children safe, not surprisingly, emerged in a gendered fashion, as home economists and others argued that women should manage households and their dangers in much the same way that their husbands managed the economy and safety in industry and the public sector.

Efforts to control these hazards shifted, though not completely, away from mothers and families beginning in the 1930s, when the National Safety Council and public health organizations began to collect statistics on accidents in the home and community, including especially the hazards of automobiles. President Herbert Hoover's White House Conference on Child Health and Protection was one of the first explicit recognitions of the rights held by children, including the right to health and to safe dwellings and schools. In 1960, the White House Conference on Children and Youth targeted accidents to children.

Technology

In the twentieth century, technology played a paradoxical role in the history of accidents. As new technologies, such as electricity and a related range of labor-saving appliances, became fixtures in homes and communities, the hazards faced by children and their families changed. Perhaps more than any other innovation, automobiles transformed the landscape of accidents. In Upton Sinclair's muckraking 1906 novel *The Jungle*, an automobile is responsible for killing a young child, and following World War II, fatal motor vehicle accidents became increasingly prevalent, so much so that by the 1970s motor vehicles were the major sources of accidental deaths to children.

Yet, as technology presented new dangers, new safety devices promised protection in a consumer society in which safety increasingly could be purchased in the burgeoning number of shopping malls. Already in the 1950s, consumers could purchase poisons, chemicals, and medicines protected by childproof caps. In the 1960s, safety restraints became common features in automobiles—one mandated in the United States by the federal government. In the 1970s, battery-operated smoke detectors made their way into the marketplace, and their use was also mandated in many legal codes. The United States government pushed these technological consumer solutions through various institutional means, such as the National Highway Safety Bureau (later the National Highway Traffic Safety Administration), which was established by the Highway Safety Act of 1966 and National Commission on Product Safety that resulted from the Consumer Product Safety Act of 1970. Such broad efforts often included a special focus on child safety, which led to the introduction of child car safety seats and labeling on games and toys of potential hazards to children. *Childproofing*—especially the home—became a buzzword as consumer and technological solutions to the problem of accidents in childhood proliferated late in the twentieth century.

By the late twentieth century, accidents remained the leading cause of childhood death in Western industrial countries, but efforts to control them achieved results and the rate of fatal accidents diminished. Even so, in the industrial world, childhood accidents continue to plague poor families significantly more than middle-class and wealthy families, and in the nonindustrial world childhood accidents take a distant back seat to more pressing concerns about disease, poverty, and war.

See also: **Infant Mortality.**

BIBLIOGRAPHY

Burnham, John. 1996. "Why Did the Infants and Toddlers Die? Shifts in Americans' Ideas of Responsibility for Accidents—From Blaming Mom to Engineering." *Journal of Social History* 29, no. 4 (summer): 817–834.

Cooter, Roger, and Bill Luckin, eds. 1997. *Accidents in History.* Amsterdam: Rodopi.

Fass, Paula S., and Mary Ann Mason, eds. 2000. *Childhood in America.* New York: New York University Press.

Hanawalt, Barbara A. 1986. *The Ties That Bound: Peasant Families in Medieval England.* New York: Oxford University Press.

Hiner, N. Ray, and Joseph M. Hawes. 1985. *Growing Up in America: Children in Historical Perspective.* Urbana: University of Illinois Press.

Iskrant, Albert P., and Paul V. Joliet. 1968. *Accidents and Homicide.* Cambridge, MA: Harvard University Press.

Orme, Nicholas. 2001. *Medieval Children.* New Haven, CT: Yale University Press.

Reinier, Jacqueline. 1996. *From Virtue to Character: American Childhood, 1775–1850.* New York: Twayne.

Tarr, Joel, and Mark Tebeau. 1996. "Managing Danger in the Home Environment, 1900–1940." *Journal of Social History* 29, no. 4 (summer): 797–816.

MARK TEBEAU

Acquired Immune Deficiency Syndrome. *See* AIDS.

Addams, Jane (1860–1935)

Jane Addams, social reformer, settlement house director, and international peace activist, was born in Cedarville, Illinois, in 1860. She was the eighth child of John H. Addams, a business entrepreneur and Republican state senator. Her mother, Sarah Weber Addams, died during childbirth when Jane was two years old. As a young woman, Jane Addams aspired toward higher education and she graduated as valedictorian from Rockford Seminary in 1881. She entered Women's Medical College in Pennsylvania but withdrew during her first year due to health problems and emotional distress over her father's unexpected death.

After leaving medical school, Addams traveled throughout Europe as she pondered a suitable career. Like many educated, unmarried women of her era, Addams looked to social reform activities to fulfill her high professional ambitions. These burgeoning charitable and service endeavors allowed women to exercise their professional authority while remaining within the acceptable sphere of "women's work." Following an extended visit to East London's Toynbee Hall social settlement, she returned to the United States to found Hull-House, Chicago's famed social settlement, in 1889. Hull-House became the center of her social and political pursuits for the remainder of her life. She resided at Hull-House with her long-term companion, Mary Rozet Smith, and a cadre of progressive social reformers, activists, artists, and intellectuals who took up residence there.

Addams devoted her personal and professional life to improving the human condition through a blend of public sector activism, published writing, and community service. She committed herself to an array of social issues, including labor reform, juvenile justice, public education, women's suffrage, and international peace. Frequently cited as the "mother of social work," Addams was elected as the first female president of the National Conference of Charities and Corrections in 1909. Her career also carried her far into the national and international political arena, where she advocated for women's suffrage, civil rights, and international peace. Among many major historical achievements, Addams was elected the first chairperson of the Women's Peace Party in 1915. That same year, she presided at the International Congress of Women in The Hague, Netherlands. She also founded the Women's International League for Peace and Freedom and served as its leader from 1919 until her death in 1935. In 1931, Addams's work was honored with the award of the Nobel Peace Prize (which she received jointly with Nicholas Murray Butler).

Addams's ideology and reform activities were anchored in her deep concern for children and her firm belief in children's innate goodness. In her published writings and speeches, Addams insisted that children possessed a unique creative intellect and a spirit of adventure. Her book *The Spirit of Youth and the City Streets* condemned modern industrial society for corrupting children's nascent curiosity by exposing them to modern city vice while failing to provide appropriate recreational venues. Both of her autobiographical works, *Twenty Years at Hull-House* (1910) and *The Second Twenty Years at Hull-House* (1930), document the benefits of after-school clubs and supervised recreational opportunities for children's development and socialization.

Addams routinely voiced a particular set of concerns for working-class immigrant children and families. She believed that immigrant youth faced unjustifiable hardships stemming from poverty, acculturation, and the exploitation of their labor. As a leader in the Progressive CHILD-SAVING movement, she launched fervent state and national campaigns against CHILD LABOR and in favor of compulsory education. She also pressed for labor legislation that would allow working-class parents to spend more time with their children. Her drive to help women and children through protective legislation placed Addams and her colleagues in the center of controversies among the labor movement, the child savers, and some feminist groups.

Addams was also concerned about the plight of modern young women. In stark contrast to her own sheltered upbringing, she believed that the industrial city robbed young women of their innocence. Her work *A New Conscience and an Ancient Evil* (1912) documents her deepest fears that young working-class women's unfulfilling low-wage work in factories or as domestics would eventually launch them into lives of prostitution. To address these concerns, she encouraged working-class girls to seek protection in a traditional domestic life of marriage and motherhood. Although this belief contradicted some of her outspoken feminist principles, her concern for young working-class women reflected her overarching quest to preserve the sanctity and innocence of youth.

Jane Addams's persistent community activism and work for social justice has left a long-standing imprint on American ideology and policies concerning children, youth, and families. The Hull-House museum in Chicago has preserved many artifacts and some of the original structure of Addams's famed social settlement. Her papers on peace and justice are housed at the Swarthmore College Peace Collection in Pennsylvania.

See also: **Juvenile Court; Juvenile Justice; National Child Labor Committee; Social Settlements; Social Welfare; U.S. Children's Bureau.**

BIBLIOGRAPHY

Addams, Jane. 1909. *The Spirit of Youth and the City Streets.* New York: Macmillan.

Addams, Jane. 1910. *Twenty Years at Hull-House: With Autobiographical Notes.* New York: Macmillan.

Addams, Jane. 1912. *A New Conscience and an Ancient Evil.* New York: Macmillan.

Addams, Jane. 1930. *The Second Twenty Years at Hull-House.* New York: Macmillan.

Davis, Allen F. 1973. *The Life and Legend of Jane Addams.* New York: Oxford University Press.

Muncy, Robin. 1991. *Creating a Female Dominion of American Reform.* New York: Oxford University Press.

INTERNET RESOURCES

Bettis, Nicolle. 2003. "Jane Addams 1860–1935." Available from <www.webster.edu/~woolflm/janeadams.html>.

University of Illinois at Chicago. 2003. "Jane Addams Hull-House Museum Home Page." Available from <www.uic.edu/jaddams/hull/hull_house.html>.

LAURA S. ABRAMS

Adolescence and Youth

The term *adolescence* derives from the Latin *adolescere*, "to grow up." The Random House Dictionary defines adolescence as "the process or condition of growing up; the growing age of human beings; the period which extends from childhood to manhood or womanhood; ordinarily considered as extending from fourteen to twenty-five in males, and from twelve to twenty-one in females." As a concept, adolescence has evolved in its biological, social, and psychological implications, but its most consequential evolution has occurred in adult perceptions of the norms and behavior of young people.

Throughout most of history, adolescence was unknown as a stage of life. Native societies have observed RITES OF PASSAGE signifying the emergence of young people from childhood into adulthood, but no concept of adolescence intervened between stages. In the classical world, ARISTOTLE recorded what now is known as adolescent development, that is, the appearance of secondary sexual characteristics in both males and females, but he and other ancients recognized only three distinct periods of life: childhood, youth, and old age. Among Romans the term *child* (*puer*) could be applied almost without regard to age, and through the Middle Ages it served as a demeaning label for any person of low social status. By the Renaissance, the establishment of schools for a somewhat larger proportion of the population helped to extend the period of childhood but still did not define a separate stage of adolescence because neither school attendance nor grade in school was based on age. Other factors inhibiting the evolution of distinct life stages included the brevity of total life span, the necessity for almost all people except elites to work, and the rigid social hierarchies that made most people, regardless of age, dependent on nobility.

The largely agrarian world of early modern Europe kept young people in a condition of semidependence, in which economic and personal status involved important contributions to the family economy but left the individual dependent on parents. Among lower classes in western (though less frequently in southern) Europe, England, and colonial America, many boys and girls in their teens were sent from their homes to work as employees for other families, a practice that served both economic and upbringing functions. Though the French word *adolescence* existed, the term *youth* (or its equivalent) was more pervasively applied to people in this semidependent condition. Some historians have posited that a YOUTH CULTURE, manifested by organizations and activities, existed to some extent in the eighteenth century. Moreover, in Europe and America at this time, adults—particularly religious leaders—expressed concern over presumed emotional and behavioral problems of young people and began to urge their education as preparation for future roles in the family and community.

The Formal Study of Adolescence

During the late eighteenth century and through the nineteenth century, biologists and physicians undertook more formal study of adolescent phenomena. European scientists researched aspects of physical growth such as the onset of MENARCHE in females and seminal emission among males. These works provided scientific and philosophical background when, in the 1890s, psychologists began investigating the abilities, behaviors, and attitudes of young people between the onset of PUBERTY and marriage. Their work marked the first emergence of adolescence as a formal concept.

The notion of youth as a time of sexual awakening and rebellion received particular expression in JEAN-JACQUES ROUSSEAU's philosophical narrative, *Émile* (1762), which described the evolution of a noble boy into a civilized man. At age fifteen or sixteen, according to Rousseau, a boy experiences crisis, and his mind is in such "constant agitation" that he is "almost unmanageable." With proper care and education, however, he learns to enjoy beauty and wisdom so that at the end of adolescence he is ready to marry and raise children.

At the same time as scientists and philosophers were developing the concept of adolescence, the industrialization of Western society placed new pressures on the process of growing up. Industrial capitalism and its attendant mechanization reduced the participation of children in the workforce, thereby diminishing the incidence of APPRENTICESHIP that formerly had characterized the youth of many people. Fewer young persons left home to go to work; more stayed in their parents' homes, often attending school. The removal of work and production from the household made the family more isolated, and, particularly among emerging middle classes, left moral responsibilities in the mother's sphere. Declining birth rates enabled middle-class families to place new values on children, viewing their worth in moral and emotional rather than practical and economic terms. Advances in nutrition and disease control quickened the process of sexual maturation. In the mid-eighteenth century the average age of menarche in America occurred at over sixteen; it dropped to just over fifteen by the end of the nineteenth century, but fell to twelve years and nine months by the end of the twentieth century. Urbanization, with its accompanying employment and entertainment opportunities, was also seen as creating threatening environments from which children needed to be protected. Girls could be sheltered at home, where they prepared for domestic adulthood, while boys were confined to school, where they learned skills needed for professional and community life. As a result, the semidependence that previously had characterized adolescence gave way to even more dependence.

Reacting to these trends, American psychologist G. STANLEY HALL, a pioneer in the study of children and their learning processes, gave adolescence its first full definition in *Adolescence: Its Psychology and Its Relations to Physiology, Anthropology, Sociology, Sex, Crime, Religion and Education*, published in 1904. Widely read in the United States and Great Britain, Hall believed that the stresses and misbehavior of young people were normal to their particular time of life, because human development mirrored the evolution of civilized society. To Hall, just as the human race evolved from savagery to civilization, so too did each individual develop from a primitive to an advanced condition. Adolescence in the individual corresponded to, or recapitulated, the period of prehistory when upheaval characterized society and logical thinking began to replace instinct. Although later theorists rejected Hall's recapitulation scheme, much of his characterization of adolescence as a time of storm and stress endured.

A year after Hall's book appeared, Sigmund Freud published an essay in which he identified adolescence as a period when psychosexual conflicts could cause emotional upheaval, inconsistent behavior, and vulnerability to deviant activity. Freud related much of adolescent behavior to genital developments in puberty, which, he said, induced a need among adolescents to become emotionally independent of parents. This need induced rebellion accompanied by anxiety, moodiness, and aggressive behavior. Concern over self-image, often influenced by social interaction, also comprised one of the challenges of adolescence.

By the mid-twentieth century, the leading theorist of adolescence was the neo-Freudian Erik Erikson, who constructed a staged sequence of lifetime ego development consisting of eight psychosexual, or "identity," crises. How successfully an individual resolves the identity crisis at each stage is determined by the ego strength created in previous stages combined with influences from the cultural environment of the current stage. To Erikson, adolescence, with its marked physiological changes and sexual awareness, is a period of experimentation that creates a crisis between the self concept created in earlier stages and role diffusion, which involves relationships with peers and institutions. The task that an adolescent faces in resolving the crisis requires integrating self-knowledge amid judgments emanating from contemporaries and peers. At various times during this crisis resolution, the adolescent has to decide whether to rebel or submit to prevailing cultural institutions. Throughout the twentieth century, the qualities of anxiety and awkwardness resulting from radical physiological development and sexual awareness that Hall, Freud, and Erikson emphasized pervaded popular as well as scientific definitions of adolescence.

Peer Cultures Resulting from Schooling and Age Grading

In the modern era in both the United States and Europe, adolescence was a middle-class phenomenon, and it received particular impetus from the expansion of secondary schools. Established in part as a means to create a literate work force in industrial society, the American HIGH SCHOOL, English boarding school, and German GYMNASIUM helped construct a new image of youth. Age grading (i.e., grouping students into classes based on their age), which began in lower schools in the mid-nineteenth century, narrowed the age range of students likely to be attending the high school that spread in the late nineteenth century. Though only a minority of youths enrolled in secondary schools until the 1930s, the process of concentrating TEENAGERS in high schools spurred the formation of youth peer groups and enabled adults to attempt the control of young people during their supposedly stormy years. Several Western countries passed COMPULSORY SCHOOL ATTENDANCE laws that kept children in school until they were fourteen or older. Such laws had a strong impact in the United States, where by 1930 nearly half of all youths aged fourteen to twenty were high school students. Enroll-

ment of rural youths and African Americans remained relatively low (only one-sixth of American blacks attended high school in the 1920s). But large proportions of immigrants and native-born whites of foreign parents attended high school. Educational reformers developed curricula to prepare young people for adult life, and an expanding set of extracurricular organizations and activities, such as clubs, dances, and sports, heightened the socialization of youths in peer groups. As a result, secondary school and adolescence became increasingly coincident.

In Great Britain, fewer youths attended high school than in the United States, mainly because a more rigid class structure made state-funded high schools primarily a realm for middle-class adolescents. Working-class youths, especially males, grew accustomed to using the streets to resist institutional means to regulate them. Nevertheless, by 1900 British youth workers were attempting to socialize adolescents into law-abiding, productive adults by herding them into educational institutions and supervised extracurricular activities. The resistance by youths in Great Britain, the European continent, and the United States to adult attempts at control—resistance that galvanized fears of juvenile DELINQUENCY—provoked educators and psychologists to distinguish adolescence even more distinctly as a life stage needing strict supervision.

Beyond the structural changes, the age consciousness of Western society that intensified in the early twentieth century sharpened the distinctiveness and peer socialization of adolescence. By the 1920s, most adolescents spent more waking hours with peers than with family. In the United States, extended opportunities for time and space away from parental eyes, combined with new commercial entertainments such as dance halls, amusement parks, and MOVIES fortified a unique youth culture. These amusements attracted adolescent peer groups in Europe and England as well.

This culture of youths ironically—or perhaps understandably—raised consternation among and conflict with adults who fretted over adolescents' independence in selecting friends, activities, dress styles, and sexual behavior that eluded adult supervision. The American practice of DATING, which by the 1920s had replaced adult-supervised courtship and which was linked to high schools and new commercial amusements, was just one obvious new type of independent adolescent behavior. (Dating was slower to develop in Europe because adolescents there lacked the disposable income generally available to American youths.) The proliferation of automobiles and the opportunities they provided for youthful activity and privacy was another.

Equally important was heightened adult concern over the supposed emotional problems that adolescents experienced, particularly their awakening SEXUALITY and penchant for getting into trouble. Indeed, in the adult mind sexuality stood at the center of adolescence. Male youths especially were seen as having appetites and temptations that lured them into MASTURBATION and HOMOSEXUALITY. Young women's sexuality could allegedly lead to promiscuity and prostitution. In general, adults worried that adolescents were growing up too rapidly. As a result, psychologists and physicians in the 1920s insisted that adolescence necessitated exacting control, not only by the self but also by parents, doctors, educators, social workers, and the police. Moreover, the combination of peer association—sometimes in gangs—with the stresses and challenges to adult authority that characterized adolescence contributed to a rising concern over juvenile delinquency. The street gangs of American cities and rowdy behavior of British hooligans reinforced adult desire to supervise young people's behavior because in theory every adolescent was a potential delinquent. Thus JUVENILE COURTS, reform schools, and other CHILD-SAVING institutions were created to remedy the problems that adolescents, in their unhealthy precocity, allegedly experienced and caused.

Adolescence in the Depression and World War II

During the Depression years of the 1930s, adolescents underwent new strains but also encountered new opportunities. The potential for intergenerational conflict increased as scarcity of jobs and low pay thwarted young people's personal ambitions and delayed their ability to attain economic and social independence. Adult control was challenged, even in Germany where members of the Hitler Jugend (HITLER YOUTH) resisted Nazi party leaders. In the United States, joblessness and lack of income forced many young people to stay in school longer than had been the case in previous generations. By 1940 49 percent of American youths were graduating from high school, up from 30 percent in 1930. Though adolescents in the 1930s had less disposable income than those in the 1920s, they still influenced popular culture with their tastes in music, dance, and movies.

Exigencies of World War II disrupted the lives of European adolescents, but in the United States an expanding war economy brought three million youths between ages fourteen and seventeen, about one-third of people in this age category, into full or part-time employment by 1945. The incomes that adolescents earned helped support a renewed youth culture, one that idolized musical stars such as Glenn Miller and Frank Sinatra and created new clothing styles such as that of the BOBBY SOXER. Their roles in the national economy and mass culture complicated the status of adolescents, who now were caught between the personal independence that employment and war responsibilities provided and the dependence on family and institutional restrictions that the larger society still imposed on them.

Postwar Teen Culture

After the war, the proportion of adolescents in the population in Western countries temporarily declined. Children reaching teen years just after World War II had been born during the Depression, when a brief fall in birth rates resulted in a smaller cohort of people reaching adolescence. Furthermore, a marriage boom followed the war, drastically reducing the age at which young people were entering wedlock, especially in Great Britain and the United States where the median age at marriage for women declined from twenty-six to twenty-three and twenty-three to twenty-one respectively. By 1960, 40 percent of American nineteen year olds were already married.

Soon, the marriage boom translated into the BABY BOOM, which eventually combined with material prosperity to foster an ever-more-extensive teen culture. By 1960, the first cohort of baby boomers was reaching their teen years, and in America goods such as soft drinks, clothing, cars, sports equipment, recorded music, magazines, and toiletries—all heavily and specifically promoted by advertisers to young people with expanding personal incomes—comprised a flourishing youth market that soon spread overseas. At the same time, RADIO, TELEVISION, recording companies, movies, and mass market publications directed much of their content to this segment of the population. Marketing experts utilized long-standing theories about the insecurities of adolescence, along with surveys that showed adolescents tending toward conformist attitudes, to sell goods that catered to teenagers' desires to dress, buy, and act like their peers.

Inevitably, as adolescents began manifesting independent behavior in their tastes and buying habits, they heightened fears among parents and other adults that teenagers were maturing too rapidly. Experts in the helping professions tightened the link between the concept of adolescence as a troubled period of life and uncertainty, crime, and other problems that accompanied the process of growing up. Even before the baby boomers had entered their teen years, social scientists, educators, and government officials were reaching a near-panic state over premarital pregnancy and juvenile delinquency. In the United States, the rate of premarital pregnancy among white women aged fifteen to nineteen doubled from under 10 percent in the 1940s to 19 percent in the 1950s. The rock and roll generation in the United States and teddy boys in England signified a type of rebellion that often included antisocial behavior, which in turn garnered heavy media attention. Much of the concern reflected theory more than reality, however. Especially in America, newspapers eagerly publicized gang wars and other sensational cases of juvenile crime, and police departments created juvenile units to deal with a presumed teenage crime wave.

Though perpetrated by only a minority of youths, antisocial conduct gave adolescence an international flavor by the 1960s and 1970s. In the 1970s in Great Britain, sadistic, mostly working-class skinheads helped generate the punk style of boots, leather outfits, and nihilistic music. Germans accepted the term *Teenagers* into their vocabulary and saw rising numbers of alienated youth engage in destructive acts, some random and others political such as protests over housing policies and police harassment. France and Sweden experienced countercultural uprisings from *blousons noir* (teenage "black shirts") and *raggare* (alienated youths) respectively. In eastern Europe and the Soviet Union as well, industrialization pressed wedges between children and adult society, creating opportunities for adolescents to adopt deviant fads in dress and behavior. Russian sociologists began reporting problems of teenage drinking, assaults, and thievery. A 1973 survey found adolescent alienation in Japan to be the highest among a dozen industrial nations, and problems of juvenile delinquency even reached Communist China by the 1980s.

Remarkably, adolescence of the 1960s and 1970s reflected a quest for conformity that seemed to validate Erikson's theory about identity crisis. In 1961, psychologist James S. Coleman published *The Adolescent Society*, a study of American high school teenagers, in which he noted that youths often sought acceptance among their peers by placing higher value on nonacademic activities, such as sports and social interaction, than on accomplishment in school. They told researchers that their heroes were not teachers or humanitarians but rather athletes, movie stars and musicians. This kind of conformity was at odds with what parents and educators wanted for adolescents, but it reflected both the prevailing peer values and the larger pressures for conformity in an expanding corporate society.

Many postwar trends in adolescence, especially adolescents' influence on the consumer economy, continued to the end of the twentieth century. However, by the late 1960s and early 1970s new attitudes about gender equality and BIRTH CONTROL, aided by increased access to automobiles and generally higher material well-being, helped fashion new sexual values among adolescents. Increasingly, peer groups in American high schools and colleges (in 1970 three-fourths of Americans were graduating from high school and a third were enrolled in college) replaced dating with informal, mixed-gender "going out" and "parties." As well, looser attitudes toward marriage, for which a date had been seen as a first step, and greater acceptance (among adults as well as youths) of nonmarital sex, arose among adolescents in many countries and heightened concern over society's ability to control adolescents' sexual behavior. By 1976 surveys in the United States showed that nearly one-fourth of sixteen-year-old white females and one-half of sixteen-year-old black females had had premarital intercourse. By 1990, 55 percent of women aged fifteen to nineteen had experienced intercourse. Though this figure declined to slightly below half by century's end, the seeming sexual abandon practiced by many young people was prompting some analysts to conclude that marriage was losing its special meaning. A sharp rise in average age of marriage, for men from twenty-three to over twenty-six and for women from twenty-one to over

twenty-three between 1970 and 1990, reinforced such a conclusion.

At the same time a minority—but a vocal and well-publicized minority—of youths began to infuse adolescence with a new brand of political consciousness that seemed to widen the growing "generation gap." Much of the YOUTH ACTIVISM flourished on college and university campuses from Berkeley to Berlin, but enough of it filtered down to high schools that educators and other public authorities faced challenges they had not previously encountered. The civil rights movement and the assassination of President John F. Kennedy in 1963 had caused American teenagers to question the values of adult society, but the Vietnam War ignited them and many of their European cohorts politically. Though the majority of youths did not oppose the war, a number of them participated in protests that upset traditional assumptions about the nonpolitical quality of high school life. This political activity reached as far as the Supreme Court of the United States when, in 1969, the court declared in TINKER V. DES MOINES INDEPENDENT SCHOOL SYSTEM that the right of free speech applied to high school students who wished to wear black armbands in protest of the war. Major protests by young people also occurred in European capitals such as Bonn, Germany, where students stormed and looted city hall in protest over a visit by South Vietnam's president.

After the Vietnam War ended, the alienation of adolescents from society—as well as, in adolescent minds, the alienation of society from adolescents—seemed to intensify rather than abate. Anger over the deployment of nuclear weapons on European soil and dangers to the ecosystem worldwide sparked student protests on both sides of the Atlantic. Moreover, a spreading drug culture, the attraction by teens to the intentionally provocative lyrics of punk rock and rap music, the rise of body art and piercing, the increase in single- (and no-) parent households, and the high numbers of families with two parents employed and out of the home for most of the day—all have further elevated the power of adolescent peer associations. Juvenile crime continued to capture attention as surveys in the 1980s estimated that between 12 and 18 percent of American males and 3 to 4 percent of females had been arrested prior to age twenty-one. To the frustration of public officials, crime-prevention programs ranging from incarceration to aversion to job placement and counseling have failed to stem teen violence and recidivism. As identity politics pervaded adult society, youths also sought havens within groups that expressed themselves through some behavioral or visual (though only occasionally ideological) manner. Neo-nazism attracted youths in Germany and France, but not strictly for its politics. American high school populations contained dizzying varieties of identity groups such as "Goths," "jocks," "nerds," "Jesus freaks," "preppies," "druggies," and many more. All the while, commercial interests in a new global economy, whether they be sneaker and sportswear manufacturers, music producers, or snack-food makers, stayed hot on the teenage trail, eager to capitalize on or guide every new expression of adolescence.

Adolescence as a Universal Concept

In the twenty-first century, multiple models of adolescence bring into question whether or not the historical concept has as much uniformity as some experts implied it had in the twentieth century. Certainly almost all adolescents, regardless of race, class, or nationality, undergo similar biological changes, though characteristics such as the age of menarche have shifted over time. But the social and psychological parameters appear to have become increasingly complex and diverse. Though the most common images of adolescents set them inside the youth-oriented consumer culture of clothes, music, and movies, the variable dark side of growing up has captured increasing attention. Poverty, sexual abuse, substance abuse, learning disabilities, depression, eating disorders, and violence have come to characterize youthful experiences as much as the qualities of fun and freedom-seeking that media and marketers have depicted. Popular theory still accepts that almost all adolescents confront similar challenges of stress and anxiety, but the processes involved in growing up display complexities that confound attempts to characterize it. A continuing rise in age at marriage, which in the United States is approaching the late twenties for males and mid-twenties for females, has made family formation less of an end point for adolescence, and the assumption by preteens of qualities and habits once exclusive to teenagers, such as musical choice, dress (including COSMETICS), hair styles, and even drug and sexual behavior, has challenged the cultural definition of the age at which adolescence begins. Even within adolescence itself, the trend of young people assuming adult sexual, family, social, and economic responsibilities—and their attendant problems—has blurred many of the qualities that previously gave adolescence its distinctiveness.

See also: **Age and Development; Apprenticeship; Baby Boom Generation; Consumer Culture; Flappers; Teen Pregnancy; Victory Girls.**

BIBLIOGRAPHY

Ariès, Philippe. 1962. *Centuries of Childhood.* Trans. Robert Baldick. New York: Alfred A. Knopf.

Bailey, Beth L. 1988. *From Front Porch to Back Seat: Courtship in Twentieth-Century America.* Baltimore, MD: The Johns Hopkins University Press.

Chudacoff, Howard P. 1989. *How Old Are You? Age Consciousness in American Culture.* Princeton, NJ: Princeton University Press.

Coleman, James S. 1961. *The Adolescent Society.* New York: Free Press.

Fass, Paula F., and Mary Ann Mason, eds. 2000. *Childhood in America.* New York: New York University Press.

Gillis, John R. 1975. "The Evolution of Juvenile Delinquency in England, 1890–1914." *Past and Present* 67: 96–126.

Gillis, John R. 1981. *Youth and History: Tradition and Change in European Age Relations, 1870–Present.* New York: Academic Press.

Graff, Harvey J., ed. 1987. *Growing Up in America: Historical Experiences.* Detroit, MI: Wayne State University Press.

Hall, G. Stanley. 1904. *Adolescence: Its Psychology and Its Relations to Anthropology, Sex, Crime, Religion, and Education.* New York: Appleton.

Hine, Thomas. 1999. *The Rise and Fall of the American Teenager.* New York: Avon Books.

Jones, Kathleen W. 1999. *Taming the Troublesome Child: American Families, Child Guidance, and the Limits of Psychiatric Authority.* Cambridge, MA: Harvard University Press.

Kett, Joseph F. 1977. *Rites of Passage: Adolescence in America, 1790 to the Present.* New York: Basic Books.

Macleod, David. 1983. *Building Character in the American Boy: The Boy Scouts and Their Forerunners, 1870–1920.* Madison: University of Wisconsin Press.

Modell, John. 1989. *Into One's Own: From Youth to Adulthood in the United States, 1920–1975.* Berkeley: University of California Press.

Modell, John and Madeline Goodman. 1990. "Historical Perspectives." In *At the Threshold: The Developing Adolescent,* ed. S. Shirley Feldman and Glen R. Elliott. Cambridge, MA: Harvard University Press.

Modell, John, Frank E. Furstenberg, and Theodore Hershberg. 1976. "Transition to Adulthood in Historical Perspective." *Journal of Family History* 1: 7–32.

Sebald, Hans. 1984. *Adolescence: A Social Psychological Analysis,* 3rd ed. Englewood Cliffs, NJ: Prentice Hall.

HOWARD P. CHUDACOFF

Adolescent Medicine

Throughout its history, the field of adolescent medicine has striven to address the needs of the whole person from a variety of psychological, sociological, and physiological perspectives, not simply diseases or disorders that affect adolescents. Currently, the trend in adolescent health care has been to go even further beyond the disease paradigm and examine not only health risks but also assets in the environment that contribute to an adolescent's physical and emotional well-being.

The field began in the early twentieth century with the work of G. STANLEY HALL, a developmental psychologist who firmly established adolescence as a distinct developmental category. Hall was also the first to suggest establishing a field of medicine for adolescents. Yet a new medical specialty dedicated to this age group did not appear until the 1950s, when adolescent medicine first emerged as a branch of PEDIATRICS. The first medical unit in the United States devoted exclusively to adolescents was founded by Dr. J. Roswell Gallagher at Boston Children's Hospital in 1951. The Adolescent Unit represented a major shift in approach to the teenage patient: prior to the 1950s, most physicians who treated adolescents discussed the patient's health problems with the parent, and seldom allowed young people to speak for themselves. In contrast, Gallagher and his staff insisted that teenaged patients needed "a doctor of their own" who would see patients separately from their parents, who would protect their confidentiality, and who would place teenagers' concerns first.

The Boston Adolescent Unit served as a model for other hospitals in North America. By the mid-1960s, there were fifty-five adolescent clinics in hospitals in the United States and Canada, and by 2002 over half of all CHILDREN'S HOSPITALS in the United States had units dedicated to the health care of teenagers. The expansion of adolescent health services led to the creation of a professional organization for adolescent specialists, the Society for Adolescent Medicine (SAM), established in 1968; the founding of a professional journal, *The Journal of Adolescent Health*, first published in 1980; and the decision in 1991 to institute a board-certification examination for physicians interested in becoming subspecialists in adolescent medicine.

Despite this dramatic growth in the field of adolescent medicine, there still is a critical shortage of age-appropriate health services for American teenagers. A report entitled *Partners in Transition: Adolescents and Managed Care*, issued in 2000 by Children Now, a national nonprofit child policy organization based in Oakland, California, provides an overview of the gaps in adolescent health care that still exist in our society. The report states that twenty percent of teenagers surveyed had gone without medical treatment they thought they needed because there were no appropriate services in their community, because they lacked transportation to medical facilities, and/or because they feared their parents would be notified if they sought medical care.

In addition, since the 1960s, adolescents have engaged in behaviors that placed them at risk for new health problems. Changing social norms during this period exposed teenagers to new "social morbidities" such as sexually transmitted diseases, drug addiction, violence, and pregnancy. Although these problems have affected the population as a whole, they appear to affect teenagers disproportionately and may be responsible for the fact that adolescent mortality has risen since 1960, while mortality for other age groups has declined.

Adolescence as a social category also appears to be both disappearing and expanding. Children are exposed to violence, SEXUALITY, and other "adult" themes at ever earlier ages. There is even evidence that children are literally "growing up" faster than ever before, since improved health care and nutrition has caused a steady decline in the age of PUBERTY. At the same time, growing numbers of young adults are living with parents for longer periods of time because of unemployment, divorce, graduate education, loneliness, or the high cost of housing. Since the late 1960s, the number of adult children living with parents has more than doubled from 2 million to 5 million, and it is estimated that nearly 40 percent of all young adults have returned to their parents' home at least once. Therefore, it appears that the period of economic dependency usually associated with adolescence is expanding into the twenties, and for some individuals, the thirties and forties. The Society for Adolescent Medicine responded to these changes in both the biological and social features of adolescence by recently adopting a position statement that declared that adolescent medicine covered the ages of ten to twenty-five, with some members even arguing that the field should be extended to cover the late twenties and early thirties.

Experts in adolescent medicine have also attempted to deal with the complex issues that continue to plague adolescents. One of the major goals of the National Longitudinal Study of Adolescent Health (Add Health), the Search Institute, and other institutions dedicated to improving adolescent health has been to reconceptualize health as more than the absence of disease or risk, but also in terms of assets in family and community that help young people engage in positive behaviors. Researchers involved in these studies have helped communities around the country begin initiatives that bring together families, schools, youth-serving organizations, congregations, and other institutions "to build the foundation of development that all young people in our society need."

Since its inception, the field of adolescent medicine has led the way in helping to ensure that all adolescents have access to quality medical care, regardless of race, gender, sexual orientation, or socioeconomic status. Adolescent specialists argue that giving teenagers age-appropriate care not only helps eliminate the most troubling adolescent health problems, such as pregnancy and substance abuse, but can also prevent adult health problems by educating young people about the importance of lifelong healthy habits.

See also: **Adolescence and Youth.**

BIBLIOGRAPHY

Benson, Peter L. 1998. *Healthy Communities, Healthy Youth*. Minneapolis: The Search Institute.

Brumberg, Joan Jacobs. 1988. *Fasting Girls: The Emergence of Anorexia Nervosa as a Modern Disease*. Cambridge, MA: Harvard University Press.

Brumberg, Joan Jacobs. 1997. *The Body Project: An Intimate History of American Girls*. New York: Random House.

Elkind, David. 1998. *All Grown Up and No Place to Go*. Reading, MA: Addison-Wesley.

Gallagher, J. Roswell. 1982. "The Origins, Development, and Goals of Adolescent Medicine." *Journal of Adolescent Health Care* 3: 57–63.

Hall, G. Stanley. 1904. *Adolescence: Its Psychology and Its Relation to Physiology, Anthropology, Sociology, Sex, Crime, Religion, and Education*. New York: Appleton.

Hall, G. Stanley. 1905. "Adolescence: The Need of a New Field of Medical Practice." *The Monthly Cyclopaedia of Practical Medicine*, n.s., 8: 242.

Halpern, Sydney. 1988. *American Pediatrics: The Social Dynamics of Professionalism 1880–1980*. Berkeley: University of California Press.

Jones, Kathleen W. 1999. *Taming the Troublesome Child: American Families, Child Guidance, and the Limits of Psychiatric Authority.* Cambridge, MA: Harvard University Press.

Lesko, Nancy. 1996. "Past, Present, and Future Conceptions of Adolescence." *Educational Theory* 46: 453–472.

Prescott, Heather Munro. 1998. *"A Doctor of Their Own": The History of Adolescent Medicine.* Cambridge, MA: Harvard University Press.

Resnick, Michael D., et al. 1997. "Protecting Adolescents from Harm: Findings from the National Longitudinal Study on Adolescent Health." *JAMA* 278/10: 823–832.

Schulenberg, John, Jennifer L. Maggs, and Klaus Hurrelmann. 1997. *Health Risks and Developmental Transitions During Adolescence.* Cambridge, UK: Cambridge University Press.

Society for Adolescent Medicine. 1997. "Clinical Preventive Services for Adolescents: A Position Paper of the Society for Adolescent Medicine." *Journal of Adolescent Health* 21: 203.

INTERNET RESOURCES

Children Now. 2000. *Partners in Transition: Adolescents and Managed Care.* Available from <www.childrennow.org>.

Search Institute. 2003. Available from <www.search-institute.org>.

Society for Adolescent Medicine. 2003. Available from <www.adolescenthealth.org>.

HEATHER MUNRO PRESCOTT

Adoption in the United States

Adoption in the United States is a social and legal process whereby a parent–child relationship is established between people not related by birth. American adoption practices have changed radically over the past two and a half centuries. Originally an informal, spontaneous occurrence comparable to APPRENTICESHIP, adoption has become a formalized legal institution governed by a patchwork of statutes in fifty separate state jurisdictions with increasing federal involvement. During the last century the professionalization of social workers emerged, along with uniform standards for regulating adoptions by the U.S. CHILDREN'S BUREAU and the Child Welfare League of America. Adoption has gone through a revolution since World War II, from an elitist institution that restricted who could adopt and who was adopted to one that that is more inclusive and diverse. Moreover, the past fifty years have seen a movement away from secrecy to an embrace of open adoption and legislative mechanisms for uniting adult adopted people with their biological parents. All of these trends toward inclusiveness and openness are likely to continue. In spite of all these changes, however, Americans' cultural bias toward blood ties remains pervasive, and adoption is still viewed by many as a form of second-rate kinship.

Adoption touches upon almost every conceivable aspect of American society and culture and commands our attention by the enormous number of people who have a direct intimate connection to it. Some experts put the number as high as six out of every ten Americans. Others estimate that about 1.5 million children in the United States live with adoptive parents, and that between 2 and 4 percent of American families include an adopted child. According to incomplete and partial estimates in 1992, there were a total of 126,951 domestic adoptions, of which 53,525 (42 percent) were kinship or stepparent adoptions. Because of the dearth of healthy white infants for adoption, 20,099 adoptions in 2002 were intercountry adoptions, slightly more than half coming from Russia and China. In short, adoption is a ubiquitous social institution in American society, creating invisible relationships with biological and adoptive kin that touch far more people than is usually imagined.

Although adoptions took place in the United States before the twentieth century, they were infrequent and achieved through private legislative action. Children who were adopted in the colonial period or more frequently in the nineteenth century typically ranged in age from six to sixteen years of age. Most of them were boys who had been placed out to work on farms. By the mid-nineteenth century, state legislatures began enacting the first general adoption statutes, which were designed to ease the burden legislatures assumed from the many private adoption acts they were forced to enact. The most important of these statutes was called An Act to Provide for the Adoption of Children, America's first adoption statute. It was enacted in 1851 in Massachusetts. The enactment of the Massachusetts Adoption Act marked a watershed in the history of the American family and society. Instead of defining the parent–child relationship exclusively in terms of blood kinship, it was now legally possible to create a family by assuming the responsibility and emotional outlook of a biological parent. In the next quarter century, the Massachusetts Adoption Act came to be regarded as a model statute, and twenty-five states enacted similar laws.

Progressive-Era Reforms

The true beginning of child welfare reform in adoption began during the Progressive Era (1890–1920) as a response to the nation's high INFANT MORTALITY rate, itself a product of the unsanitary conditions in vastly overcrowded industrial cities that lacked medical knowledge of CONTAGIOUS DISEASES. Most infants were born at home, but single mothers often lacked that option, and their babies were born in crowded maternity homes or public infant hospitals where mortality rates reached nearly 98 percent. Galvanized by this knowledge, philanthropic women reformers in New York City founded the first private adoption agencies, such as the Alice Chapin Adoption Nursery (1911) and the Child Adoption Committee (1916, later called Louise Wise Services). Similar institutions, such as the Cradle Society (1924) would soon follow. These private adoption agencies, however, handled only a small minority of adoptions. More typical were institutions such as the State Charities Aid Association of New York or the Children's Home Society of Washington. During this period and in the following years of the Depression, adoptive parents preferred to take in girls, and 50 percent of adoptive parents preferred children above three years of age.

Progressive reformers also lobbied state legislators for measures to safeguard children, which heralded the expanded role of the state in regulating adoptions. In 1917, lawmakers enacted the Children's Code of Minnesota, which became the model for state adoption laws in the next two decades. It was the first state law that required an investigation to determine whether a proposed adoptive home was suitable for a child. The statute also ordered that adoption records be closed to the public, but not to the adoption triad: birth parents, adopted people, and adoptive parents. Three other reforms in adoption practice and law mark the Progressive Era. Child welfare advocates were successful in lobbying many states for the removal of the word "illegitimate" from birth certificates and inventing the amended birth certificate to shield children from public opprobrium of their adoption. Child welfare reformers were also successful in advocating that children should not be separated from the family of origin for light or transient reasons, such as poverty.

Progressive-era social workers institutionalized their reform efforts in two public and private national organizations. In 1912 the U.S. Children's Bureau was established, and until World War II was the leading provider of information about adoption. It was also instrumental in setting standards for adoption agencies and guiding state legislatures, social workers, researchers, and the public in every aspect of adoption. In 1921, the Child Welfare League of America (CWLA), a private, nonprofit institution, was founded; it would become increasingly important in setting adoption standards for public and private agencies. By the 1950s the Children's Bureau had been eviscerated by Congress, and the CWLA emerged as the leading authority in the field of adoption.

Acting as a counterweight to the reform and popularization of adoption practices before World War II was Americans' cultural definition of kinship, which was based on bloodties and stigmatized adoption as socially unacceptable. During the late nineteenth and early twentieth century, a broad segment of the American public believed that adoption was an "unnatural" action that created ersatz or second-rate families. Medical science contributed to popular cultural prejudices against adopting a child by coupling the stigma of illegitimacy with adoption. After 1910 the rise of the EUGENICS movement and psychometric testing led adopted children to be linked to inherited mental defects. Adopted children were thus doubly burdened: they were assumed to be illegitimate and thus medically tainted *and* they were adopted, thus lacking the all important blood link to their adoptive parents. The result was that during the Progressive Era the vast majority of dependent children continued to reside in ORPHANAGES, rather than being placed in FOSTER CARE or adopted.

Post–World War II

The upheaval of World War II was a watershed in the history of adoption. Following the war, social workers and state bureaucrats began for the first time to shroud adoption records in secrecy, preventing adoption triad members from gaining access to adoption records. This was a gradual process that was not completed until the 1980s, because each state legislature acted on its own and adoption agencies sometimes continued informal policies that ignored state statutes mandating secrecy. Another change in the postwar period was adoptive parents' preference for boys rather than girls, wishing perhaps to replace symbolically the men who went off to war. But by the end of the war, the shortage of adoptable children led prospective adoptive parents to be more flexible, and many more would-be adoptive parents were willing to accept children of either sex.

The demand by childless couples for infants also led to radical changes in adoption practices. The baby boom, beginning in the mid-1940s and reaching its peak in the late 1950s, saw a dramatic rise in marriages and births and created an increased demand for adoptable children. Adoption agencies were inundated with requests, and adoptions rose spectacularly: between 1937 and 1945 adoptions grew threefold, from 16,000 to 50,000 annually; a decade later the number of adoptions had nearly doubled again to 93,000 and, by 1965 the number had increased to 142,000.

Although adoptions increased in number and popularity in the twenty years after World War II, the availability for adoption of white, out-of-wedlock infants declined radically in the decades after the 1960s. A number of factors were responsible for the decline, including the sexual revolution of the 1960s, the Supreme Court's legalization of abortion in *Roe v. Wade* (1973), and many unwed mothers' decision not to relinquish their babies. These profound cultural, social, legal, and demographic changes in American society caused a substantial decline in the number of adoptions and precipitated important shifts in adoption policy. First, by 1975 adoption agencies across the nation began to stop taking requests for healthy, white infants. Social workers often informed prospective adoptive parents that they would likely have to wait three to five years for such a child. Second, social workers abandoned the idea of the "unadoptable" child and broadened the definition of adoptability to include any child who needed a family and for whom a family could be found. With the enlarged definition of adoptability, social workers for the first time initiated serious efforts to place children with special needs—individuals with physical or mental disabilities, minority and older children, and children born in foreign countries—in adoptive homes. Third, the shortage of infants available for adoption and the emphasis on minority adoption led social workers to practice transracial adoption. By 1965, transracial adoption had become known as the "little revolution," as adoption agencies all over the nation increasingly placed black babies with white families. Four years later, the CWLA revised its guidelines to reflect the new practice, unequivocally stating that agencies should not use race to determine the selection of an adoptive home. In 1971, transracial adoptions reached their peak, with 468 agencies reporting 2,574 such placements.

Transracial adoption was highly controversial. The first manifestation of discontent emerged in 1972 when the National Association of Black Social Workers denounced transracial adoption as cultural genocide; between then and 1975 only 831 transracial adoptions occurred. In the following years transracial adoptions declined steeply as child welfare workers chose to keep AFRICAN-AMERICAN CHILDREN in foster care rather than place them with a white family, even though repeated studies demonstrated that transracial adoptions were successful. Reaction to social workers' discriminatory practices resulted in Congress enacting the Howard M. Metzenbaum Multiethnic Placement Act in 1994. The act prohibited adoption agencies from denying any person the opportunity to become an adoptive parent based solely on the person's race, color, or national origin.

A fourth consequence of the demographic decline in babies available for adoption was to further redefine the concept of adoptable children to become more inclusive and less concerned with "matching" the physical, mental, racial, and religious characteristics of adoptable children with adoptive parents. Increasingly, the population of children available for adoption was composed of older children, members of minority groups, and children with special needs. In the 1990s, drug-exposed infants, children with AIDS, and infants born HIV positive were added to the special-needs category. Because social workers were often unable to find adoptive homes or unable to free them legally for adoption, these children, numbering some one hundred thousand at the end of the twentieth century, became fixtures in foster care, where they were shunted from one caretaker to another. This situation prompted Congress to pass the Adoption Assistance and Child Welfare Act of 1980, one of the first federal laws to address the problems of adopted children. Congress's landmark legislation mandated that child welfare agencies provide preplacement services, take steps to reunify children with their biological parents, and periodically review cases of children in long-term foster care. "Permanency planning" legislation, as it was called, had as its goal either to return children to their family of origin or place them in an adoptive home. By 1993 the federal government was distributing an estimated $100 million to forty states to fund this program. Consequently, there were an increasing number of older child and special-needs adoptions in the last two decades of the twentieth century.

A fifth consequence of the shortage of infants for couples to adopt was an increase in intercountry adoption. Since World War II, intercountry adoptions have increased tremendously, but they have been denounced by critics as a shameful admission of a nation's inability to care for its own people, exploitative of its poorest class, destructive of children's cultural and ethnic heritage, and riven by baby-selling scandals. Critics' objections were answered by the United States in 2000, when it ratified the Hague Convention, which sets standards and regulates intercountry adoption by placing adoption agencies under the scrutiny of the international community.

A sixth consequence of the demographic decline in infants has been a veritable revolution in the latter half of the twentieth century in adoption agencies' practices toward adoptive parents. In the past, social workers' standards were elitist and rigid. The vast majority of adoptive parents were Caucasian, heterosexual, childless, married couples. African-American couples who wanted to adopt either did so informally or through the few African-American orphanages which had been established; during the first half of the twentieth century they were routinely refused service by mainstream public and private adoption agencies. By 1997, African Americans adopted 38 percent of all children, disproving a popular belief that few African Americans choose to adopt. Caucasians adopt 28 percent of all children adopted, followed by Hispanics, who adopt 12 percent. Adoption agencies have also changed their policies radically to make adoption possible for a broader range of adults, including foster parents, older individuals, families with children (42%), single parents (4 percent), individuals with physical disabilities, and families across a broad economic range. Many of these changes have been controversial. The issue of gay or lesbian adoption did not emerge until 1973; before that, the fields of psychiatry and psychology had defined HOMOSEXUALITY as a mental disorder. And it was not until 1987 that a court allowed a gay adoption to take place. Subsequently, however, there has been an increasing trend toward inclusiveness regarding gay and lesbian adoptions.

A seventh effect of the decline in adoptable infants was open adoption, an innovation in adoption practice that began in the mid-1980s. In an effort to encourage birth mothers to relinquish their babies for adoption, caseworkers began allowing some birth mothers to decide who would parent their child. The result was open adoption, where the identities of birth and adoptive parents were exchanged and, in some cases, continuing contact of varying degrees between the parties was encouraged. It has become increasingly popular, commanding center stage in adoption practice. Between 1990 and 2002, a majority of adoption agencies in the United States had moved toward fully disclosed open adoptions.

Accompanying the revolution in adoption practices during the last three decades of the twentieth century was the birth of the adoption search movement. In 1971, adoption rights became a major social issue when the movement's most vocal and visible leader, Florence Fisher, who searched for twenty years before finding her birth mother, founded the Adoptees Liberty Movement Association (ALMA). ALMA's example sparked the creation of hundreds of other adoptee search groups across the United States, Canada, and the United Kingdom. By 1978, the number of such groups led to the formation in the United States of a national umbrella organization, the American Adoption Congress (AAC). By 1996, complacency within the movement sparked a mini-revolt, resulting in the creation of the Internet-based adoption activist organization Bastard Nation, which successfully challenged the AAC leadership by passing a citizens' ballot initiative, Measure 58, in Oregon that gave adoptees access to their original birth certificates. Research suggests that women make up 80 percent of adult adopted persons who search for members of their birth families.

Adoption rights activists, composed mostly of adopted adults and birth mothers, contend they are entitled to identifying information in the adoption record. Through court challenges, reform of state legislation, and state initiatives, they have pursued their agenda to repeal laws that sealed adoption records. Although only four states, Kansas, Alaska, Oregon, and Alabama, provide for unconditional access to adult adoptees' original birth certificates, the vast majority of other states provide some mechanism—voluntary adoption registries or state-appointed confidential intermediary systems—where adoptees and original family members can meet each other. Nevertheless, this issue remains controversial because the rights of some birth parents, who have been promised confidentiality by adoption agencies, clash with the rights of adopted adults, who want unrestricted access to the information in their adoption records.

See also: **Foundlings; Orphans.**

BIBLIOGRAPHY

Avery, Rosemary J., ed. 1997. *Adoption Policy and Special Needs Children.* Westport, CT: Auburn House.

Babb, L. Anne. 1999. *Ethics in American Adoption.* Westport, CT: Bergin and Garvey.

Bartholet, Elizabeth. 1993. *Family Bonds: Adoption and the Politics of Parenting.* Boston: Houghton Mifflin.

Berebitsky, Julie. 2000. *Like Our Very Own: Adoption and the Changing Culture of Motherhood, 1851–1950.* Lawrence: University Press of Kansas.

Carp, E. Wayne, ed. 1998. *Family Matters: Secrecy and Disclosure in the History of Adoption.* Cambridge, MA: Harvard University Press.

Carp, E. Wayne, ed. 2002. *Adoption in America: Historical Perspectives.* Ann Arbor: University of Michigan Press.

Child Welfare League of America. 1995. *Issues in Gay and Lesbian Adoption.* Washington, DC: Child Welfare League of America.

Fogg-Davis, Hawley Grace. 2002. *The Ethics of Transracial Adoption.* Ithaca, NY: Cornell University Press.

Grossberg, Michael. 1985. *Governing the Hearth: Law and the Family in Nineteenth-Century America.* Chapel Hill: University of North Carolina Press.

Grotevant, Harold D., and Ruth G. McRoy. 1998. *Openness in Adoption: Exploring Family Connections.* Thousand Oaks, CA: Sage.

Hollinger, Joan H., ed. 1998. *Adoption Law and Practice.* 2 vols. New York: M. Bender.

Holt, Marilyn Irvin. 1992. *The Orphan Trains: Placing Out in America.* Lincoln: University of Nebraska Press.

Melosh, Barbara. 2002. *Strangers and Kin: The American Way of Adoption.* Cambridge, MA: Harvard University Press.

Modell, Judith S. 1994. *Kinship with Strangers: Adoption and Interpretations of Kinship in American Culture.* Berkeley and Los Angeles: University of California Press.

Schwartz, Laura J. 1995. "Models for Parenthood in Adoption Law: The French Conception." *Vanderbilt Journal of Transnational Law* 28: 1069–1119.

Simon, Rita J.; Howard Altstein; and Marygold S. Melli. 1994. *The Case for Transracial Adoption.* Washington, DC: American University Press.

Starr, Karla J. 1998. "Adoption by Homosexuals: A Look at Differing State Court Opinions." *Arizona Law Review* 40: 1497–1514.

Zainaldin, Jamil S. 1979. "The Emergence of a Modern American Family Law: Child Custody, Adoption, and the Courts." *Northwestern University Law Review* 73: 1038–1089.

INTERNET RESOURCES

Evan B. Donaldson Adoption Institute. 2002. Available from <www.adoptioninstitute.org>.

Legal Information Institute. 2002. "Adoption: An Overview." Available from <www.law.cornell.edu/topics/adoption.html>.

U.S. Department of Health and Human Resources. 2002. "The National Adoption Information Clearinghouse." Available from <www.calib.com/naic/>.

U.S. Department of State. 2002. "International Adoption." Available from <http://travel.state.gov/adopt.html>.

E. WAYNE CARP

Advertising

Over the course of the twentieth century, child consumers have played an increasingly important role in the economies of developed nations. Children's consumer clout is especially pronounced in the United States, where, according to early-twenty-first-century estimates, children spend or influence the spending of up to $500 billion annually. Advertisers in turn spend hefty sums to capture the consumer allegiance and nagging power of children. Thanks to the power of TELEVISION, advertising to children in the twenty-first century has become a ubiquitous practice across the globe. It is, however, by no means a recent phenomenon.

A market for children's goods—books, TOYS, clothing, and FURNITURE—had existed since at least the eighteenth century, but market awareness of children as consumers first emerged in the United States during the 1870s and 1880s, when national advertisers began supplying retailers with colorful trade cards and advertising jingle books based on parodies of Mother Goose rhymes. Corporations hoped that child shoppers would digest the advertising messages on the backs of trade cards and bring the advertisements to their mothers' attention, but advertisers' primary goal was to stimulate sales at the point of purchase. If a mother had neglected to specify a brand when she sent her child on a shopping errand, an alluring trade card displayed on a store countertop might decide the issue. Children prized trade cards for their luxurious color images—a novelty made possible by advances in chromolithography printing. Collecting the cards in scrapbooks was a favorite childhood pastime, especially among girls. Advertisers encouraged this hobby by producing a set or series of collectible trade cards, and children reveled in the status that an unusual card or fine collection conferred on its owner.

At the turn of the twentieth century, the advertising trade largely dismissed children as members of the buying public, but readily embraced the notion that children constituted the future buyers of tomorrow. Theorists of advertising psychology such as Walter Dill Scott argued that buying was influenced less by rational arguments than by unconscious decision making, including "suggestions" that advertisers implanted in the consumer's mind. The plasticity of young minds, Scott surmised, made children especially valuable targets of advertising. If repeatedly exposed to trademarks and brand names, children could, imperceptibly and unconsciously, acquire brand preferences that would last a lifetime.

Such psychological insights hardly constituted a revolution in children's advertising, but they did suggest, contrary to what some Victorians supposed, that the concept of a sheltered childhood was not inherently at odds with children's exposure to the world of commerce. The whole notion that children possessed a consumer consciousness long before they possessed purchasing power circulated broadly in turn-of-the-century advertising iconography. In magazine advertisements and trade cards read by adults and children alike, admakers depicted children as product endorsers, discriminating shoppers, and voracious consumers. These images traded on new cultural ideals of childhood that prized children as much for their spunk and savvy as their innocence.

These middle-class cultural ideals of the spunky child paved the way for even bolder departures in advertising during the 1920s. By then, advertisers conceived of middle-class children not just as buyers of tomorrow but as buyers of today and selling agents within the home. They recognized children as a more definable and viable group of consumers partly because modern childhood itself had become more organized around peer activities. Compulsory schooling, age-segregated classrooms, and the rise of youth organizations like the BOY SCOUTS and the GIRL SCOUTS all elevated the salience of peer interactions. The fact that the Boy Scouts, Girl Scouts, and Camp Fire Girls published their own magazines provided advertisers a ready means of reaching boys and girls with common interests. Indeed, advertisers frequently capitalized on these peer affiliations by suggesting

that their products could be used to earn scouting merit badges or enhance camping experiences. Transformations within the middle-class family also contributed to advertisers' enthusiasm for cultivating child consumers. Owing partly to their own middle-class backgrounds, admen and adwomen sensed new opportunities in the democratization of the urban middle-class companionate family, which unlike its Victorian predecessor, granted children greater latitude for self-expression and, in many cases, their own allotment of spending money.

Children's magazine publishers such as *St. Nicholas, Boy's Life,* and *American Boy* played an important role in promoting advertising to children as a worthy long-term and short-term investment. *American Boy* placed numerous ads in advertising trade journals, touting the exuberance of boy consumers and their influence over family purchasing, thanks in part to boys' expertise on new consumer technologies such as cars, radios, cameras, and batteries. *American Boy*'s promotional efforts paid off handsomely. During the mid-1910s, *American Boy* began to swell with ads for bicycles, erector sets, rifles, and breakfast cereals. By 1920 annual advertising revenues for the magazine had reached half a million dollars. By the middle of that decade, *American Girl* and *Everygirl's,* magazines published respectively by the Girl Scouts and the Camp Fire Girls, had also attracted advertisers who sought both to cultivate the loyalty of future housewives and to boost present sales.

In the early twentieth century, advertisers and magazine publishers alike initiated numerous games, contests, and educational ventures to teach children an appreciation of advertising and train them in brand-conscious shopping. Publishers' investment in this project was at least as deep as advertisers' because magazines now depended more on advertising revenues than subscription sales for their survival. To gain credibility as a profitable advertising medium, *American Boy* and *Scholastic,* the national weekly for secondary school students, ran a series of columns explaining why their readers should trust in advertisers and the superior economic value of advertised goods over unbranded goods. Juvenile magazine publishers also won advertisers' confidence by sponsoring contests and games that trained children to pay close attention to advertising.

The public schools provided advertisers with another promising venue for raising brand consciousness. Though ostensibly limited by the conventional boundaries of the school curriculum, advertisers spared little effort in getting their messages into the classroom and via the classroom into the home. They offered free booklets, exhibits, charts, and other "enrichment" materials that promised to transform run-of-the-mill lessons into livelier fare. Because restrictive school budgets often curtailed the use of visual aids, teachers and teaching organizations proved remarkably receptive to corporate-sponsored innovations in the curriculum. In the late 1920s, for example, teachers in some 70,000 schools across the country used Cream of Wheat's graded contest devices, prizes, and breakfast charts to encourage regular consumption of hot breakfast cereals. Although editorialists criticized advertisers for diverting "school facilities to its own selfish purposes," schools provided no substantive counterpoint to the claims of modern advertising until the mid-1930s, when the consumer education movement got underway.

Early-twentieth-century juvenile advertisers struggled to strike the right balance in addressing children's desires and parents' concerns. Overt parental appeals that linked children's consumption to nutrition and achievement often appeared in children's advertising. Yet juvenile advertising in the 1920s and 1930s was remarkably bold in its efforts to empower children within a consumer democracy. Advertisements in children's magazines literally instructed children how to lobby their parents for new purchases, supplying them with sales ammunition that appealed to pressing parental concerns. While Canadian broadcast advertising trade guidelines in the 1970s advised advertisers not to "directly urge children to . . . ask their parents to make inquiries or purchases," early-twentieth-century American advertisers exhibited no such compunctions (quoted in Kline 1993). With boldfaced headlines like "Please—Father—Please," advertisements routinely sanctioned begging and the old childhood standby—buttering up mom and dad.

During the interwar years, advertisers also sought to cultivate children's consumer loyalty and interest by addressing their concerns about popularity and personal appearance. As high school enrollments ballooned and adolescents began spending more time in the company of their peers, adjusting to the norms and expectations of age-based peers became an adolescent preoccupation. Even as they presented purchasable solutions to problems of peer approval and image control, advertisers exacerbated adolescent insecurities by reminding teens of their susceptibility to impersonal judgments. Advertisements for products like Postum cereal and Keds shoes encouraged a greater preoccupation with physical appearance in both boys and girls, but advertisers' messages to girls were especially contradictory. They celebrated the athletic girl as emblematic of the post-Victorian gender freedoms modern girls enjoyed, but they narrowed the scope of feminine aspirations and feminine achievement by making peer acceptance and beauty, rather than athletic performance, the ultimate rewards of bodily discipline. If girls purchased their product, advertisers repeatedly counseled, they were sure to garner more dates—a reassuring promise in the newly emerging public culture of DATING, where popularity was measured by the frequency and variety of dates one commanded.

With the advent of children's RADIO programs in the 1930s, advertisers, no longer limited to the typically urban,

middle- and upper-middle-class readers of juvenile magazines, made children's consumer culture a truly national phenomenon. Millions of Depression-era children satisfied yearnings for autonomy and recognition when they joined radio-inspired clubs like Little Orphan Annie's Secret Circle or Post Toasties' Junior Detective Corps and received "free" premiums in exchange for proofs of purchase. Armed with secret passwords, decoding devices, and mysterious languages impervious to adult comprehension, children embraced the privileges of club memberships as a road to empowerment. Membership in such clubs, however, also afforded many children their first lessons in consumer disappointment, when long-awaited premiums failed to live up to advertisers' hype. Children exercised their own limited form of consumer payback in choosing cash contest prizes over dubious premiums and in mocking exaggerated advertising claims. Though some parents complained about broadcasters' advertising excesses, including their practice of inserting ad pitches into story lines, radio paved the way for perhaps even greater advertising intrusions in the television age.

During the postwar years, the spread of affluence and permissive child rearing in the United States gave children greater economic power, while the advent of television gave advertisers new means to reach children en masse. Despite some initial doubts about television's viability as an advertising medium, advertisers enthusiastically took to the airwaves once they became convinced that popular programs like *The Howdy Doody Show* and *The Mickey Mouse Club* could deliver a captivated audience. Radio, however, still had the greater impact on the youth market, as baby boomers accounted for eighty percent of ROCK AND ROLL record sales during the 1950s.

Advertisers' investment in nurturing children's consumer appetites grew along with the expansion of children's own discretionary funds. In 1960, according to a survey by *Seventeen* magazine, the average teenage girl had a weekly income of $9.53. By 1999, the typical weekly allowance for thirteen- to fifteen-year-olds ranged from $30.50 to $34.25, with girls receiving on average three to four dollars more than boys. Supplementary earnings typically doubled the weekly yield for teenage boys and girls. Though younger children aged ten to twelve received only a modest five to six dollar boost to their weekly income from earnings, allowances on average swelled their weekly take by an additional twenty-one to twenty-two dollars. According to one 1996 estimate, ALLOWANCES accounted for more than a third of the $89 billion in spending money at children's disposal. Children's collective consumer clout was weighty, indeed.

In the last two decades of the twentieth century, the barriers between children and the market all but disappeared in the United States. Not only did children's media consumption become more difficult to monitor in families with both parents in the workforce—now the American norm—but parental restraints became more difficult to enforce. Parental acquiescence, of course, also contributed to the commercialization of childhood. Advertisers' work was made easier when many American children enjoyed personal televisions and computers with Internet access in their own private bedrooms. Still, the most vigilant parents could at best exercise limited control over children's exposure to commercial messages. Even in public schools, a morning viewing of the Channel One news service exposed children to a daily dose of commercials along with reports on current events. Indeed, what began as a marriage of convenience between underfunded public schools and advertisers in the 1920s grew into a virtually irresistible collaboration, thanks to the anti-tax movement of the last quarter of the twentieth century and voters' reluctance to approve school bond measures. Cash-strapped public schools welcomed the additional revenues—an exclusive contract with soda companies could net millions, while a restricted arrangement with a computer company could yield a new supply of "free" computers. In return for their largesse, corporations were rewarded with an advertising venue that reached masses of children far more cheaply than television.

Children's advertisers have added some new spices to old recipes for marketing success. The tradition of weaving product endorsements into children's entertainment programming, a technique first perfected on radio, was taken to new lengths with the advent of toy-based television programs like *The Smurfs*, *Strawberry Shortcake*, and *He-Man* in the 1980s—a marketing ploy the toy industry cynically defended by asserting that children needed preformulated story lines to help them play. This strategy also harkened back to the Depression-ridden 1930s, when toymakers revitalized sagging sales by creating licensed character toys that revolved around children's celebrity idols such as Mickey Mouse, SHIRLEY TEMPLE, Buck Rogers, and Superman.

Much like their early twentieth-century predecessors, contemporary marketers judge the effectiveness of children's advertising by the so-called "nag factor"—the aim being to maximize the nag until the parental gatekeeper yields. But where earlier advertisers were more cautious about upsetting the balance of power within the family—winning parental goodwill, after all, was the goal of winning juvenile goodwill—late twentieth- and early twenty-first century advertisers have pushed the limits of those boundaries. The promises of self-improvement and edification that appeased previous generations of parents have given way to a children's advertising culture in which hedonism, antiauthoritarianism, and kid power reign supreme. Today's kids, as Ellen Seiter puts it, are "sold separately," with appeals designed more to increase the nag factor than to placate the parental gatekeeper.

To acknowledge contemporary marketers' greater investment in creating a distinct children's fantasy culture, however, is not to romanticize the early twentieth century

as some utopian moment in children's consumer culture. Far from it. The Pokemon fad of the 1990s, in fact, can be viewed as a direct descendant of the children's radio clubs of the 1930s. Just as the promise of special premiums from Little Orphan Annie and Jack Armstrong got children to pester their parents for more Cocomalt or Wheaties, the Pokemon craze led children to plead for the precious trading cards that would help them capture all 150 Pokemon characters, the mythical "pocket monster" creatures featured in the popular animated kids' television show and video game. While in each case clever market tie-ins with radio idols or popular television shows provided the building blocks for the craze, the appeal of joining a distinct kids' world fueled the fad. Radio club members decoded secret messages to which only their peers were privy, while Pokemon traders became experts in Pokemon lore, memorizing the names, special fighting skills, and point values of each Pokemon.

In the decades since the 1950s, this privileging of children's culture has contributed to greater age segmentation within the children's market. The often fuzzy distinctions between TEENAGERS and children that typified advertising in the interwar years have evolved into clearly delineated categories ranging from toddlers to kids to 'tweens to teens. Marketers also expend more time and money gathering data about their various child audiences. Information formerly gleaned from contest data, children's advertising testimonials, and a smattering of personal interviews now comes to advertising agencies through the more scientific channels of surveys and focus groups. During the 1990s, advertisers found more deceitful means to acquire information about children's tastes by requiring children to provide critical personal data—including name, sex, age, e-mail address, favorite television show, and favorite musical group—before they could enter certain websites. In response to indignant parents and media watch groups, the Federal Trade Commission made it illegal in 1998 to solicit personal information from preteens online without parental permission. Nevertheless, children's advertisers still hold high hopes that the Internet's virtual mall might become as popular a hangout as the neighborhood shopping mall.

Although politicians and consumer advocacy groups have pressured media companies and advertising firms to exercise more restraint and responsibility in promoting violent products and films to children, these limited external controls have done little to rein in a capitalist culture resistant to infringements on free markets and commercial free speech. Indeed, savvy child consumers themselves have discovered avenues of resistance only within the parameters of consumerism itself. One of these avenues is *Zillions*, a magazine for kids published by Consumer Reports that teaches children the basics of product testing and comparative shopping. Children have also turned consumerism into a language of protest, marketing their own anticorporate sentiments through self-styled Internet zines (self-published magazines) and FASHIONS. Yet such protests have not prevented advertisers from extending their global message. Thanks to rapid commercialization and China's one-child-only birth control policy, Shanghai's singletons have become sufficiently acculturated to consumer abundance and global tastes that they readily grasped the moral dilemma of *Toy Story*—a DISNEY tale, told from the perspective of animated toys, about how easily children lose interest in a favorite old toy when a new one arrives. Consumerism paradoxically allows children more control over fashioning independent identities, but it also increasingly binds them to a global commercial culture.

See also: **Consumer Culture; Media, Childhood and the.**

BIBLIOGRAPHY

Cross, Gary. 1997. *Kids' Stuff: Toys and the Changing World of American Childhood.* Cambridge, MA: Harvard University Press.

Davis, Deborah S., and Julia S. Sensenbrenner. 2000. "Commercializing Childhood: Parental Purchases for Shanghai's Only Child." In *The Consumer Revolution in Urban China*, ed. Deborah S. Davis, pp. 54–79. Berkeley: University of California Press.

Forman-Brunell, Miriam. 1993. *Made to Play House: Dolls and the Commercialization of American Girlhood, 1830–1930.* New Haven, CT: Yale University Press.

Garvey, Ellen. 1996. *The Adman in the Parlor: Magazines and the Gendering of Consumer Culture, 1880s to 1910s.* New York: Oxford University Press.

Jacobson, Lisa. Forthcoming. *Raising Consumers: Children, Child-rearing, and the American Mass Market in the Early Twentieth Century.* New York: Columbia University Press.

McNeal, James. 1987. *Children as Consumers: Insights and Implications.* Lexington, MA: Lexington Books.

Palladino, Grace. 1996. *Teenagers: An American History.* New York: Basic Books.

Seiter, Ellen. 1993. *Sold Separately: Parents and Children in Consumer Culture.* New Brunswick, NJ: Rutgers University Press.

LISA JACOBSON

Advice. *See* Child-Rearing Advice Literature.

AFDC. *See* Aid to Dependent Children.

Africa

It is often said that African children face a short, difficult, and brutish existence. Press coverage often stereotypes the sub-Saharan region as a repository of collapse and death. In news reports of civil conflict, plague, and starvation African children are portrayed simply as victims: forever abandoned, turned to fodder by warlords, or buried in endemic calamity. It is tempting to use these pervasive media descriptions to link past and present childhoods in Africa, as if nothing has changed over time. Yet the spotty records that exist from previous centuries do not support this narrow approach. Thus a comprehensive history of African childhood requires a broader analytical view and deeper appreciation of how the most biased sources illuminate the lives of children through the ages.

Rare Historical Perspectives of Childhood in Africa

Beginning in the fourteenth century, "outsider" accounts of sub-Saharan families started to reach wider audiences, offering snapshots that contradicted the images of children's static nightmare existence. In such narratives boys and girls exercised agency, defying notions that they were helpless in the grim tide of history. Even scornful European observers portrayed African children as showing assertiveness or human potential. These eclectic writings, generated by travelers, merchants, missionaries, and colonists, are encumbered by ethnocentrism or, even worse, racist ridicule. Yet on a continent steeped in oral tradition, they also provide rare details of how some adults in Africa perceived childhood, and of how African children influenced governing institutions, sexual mores, environmental sustainability, and religious and political debates.

For example, the trip diary of one fourteenth-century Arab trader, Ibn Batutta, lauded boys in the courts of Mali and Kilwa. They cleverly learned the Qur'an, Ibn Batutta remarked, before assuming posts in Islamic administrations. But he criticized noble girls for sauntering naked in the presence of Muslim suitors. Between the fifteenth and eighteenth centuries, Europeans buying slaves from central and southern Africa noted in shipping logs that drought had periodically ruined crops, compelling children orphaned by famine to sell infant SIBLINGS for grain. Nineteenth-century white missionaries wrote letters home that criticized "heathen" girls on the "Dark Continent" for entering into polygamous marriages and obstructing the spread of Christianity.

In the early 1900s white supremacists justified their subordination of the African "heathen" by asserting they merely ruled over the black "tribal" child. Their ideas, popularized by eugenicists such as Dudley Kidd in *Savage Childhood*, depicted Africans as happy primitives whose development peaked at puberty. Kidd's thesis underpinned a central premise of European rule in Africa, expressed by a British colonial report published in South Africa in 1907: "The treatment of Natives in general must be of an autocratic nature [as the] masses are scarcely out of their childhood. . . . Natives are, in a sense, but children, and should not only be protected from the inherent weaknesses of undeveloped humanity, but guided through the shoals [of] the transition stage" (*Colony of Natal Report*, 11, 12).

The Rise of Scholarship on African Childhood

From the 1920s through the 1960s, anthropologists (and a few missionaries) rejected the pseudoscientific racism permeating colonial administration and instead fostered critical scholarly interest in African childhood. Contrary to Kidd, they recognized Africans as fully realized adults who arrived at maturity in customary ways. For example, the anthropologists Henry Junod, Daryll Forde, and Hilda Kuper conducted fieldwork on RITES OF PASSAGE, marriage, and childrearing in sub-Saharan communities, while Monica Wilson (among others) distinguished between adult attitudes towards children and the children's own viewpoints. Their findings demonstrated variations between childhoods in precolonial periods (pre–nineteenth century) and the colonial era (nineteenth and early to mid-twentieth centuries). From the 1970s onwards, more and more historians adopted anthropological methods and gender analyses to gauge how colonialism and capitalism affected African families, particularly mothers and their offspring.

In the 1980s, research on African childhood gathered momentum with the publication of *Maidens, Meals, and Money*, Claude Meillassoux's anthropological investigations into sub-Saharan relationships between elders and youths. Like Philippe Ariès's *Centuries of Childhood*, a milestone in historical explorations of family and childhood in the West, Meillaissoux's book developed a bold paradigm that outlined distinct age transitions in "precapitalist" domestic settings from agricultural villages to preindustrial states fused by world religion and international trade. Unlike Ariès, Meillassoux downplayed certain questions, such as: When did adults reckon that children succumbed to "original sin"? or When did parents turn childhood into a stage of indulging innocent individuals?

In sub-Saharan regions, rulers and commoners alike, from the Iron Ages through the Middle Ages and into the twentieth century, understood the role of a child differently from their European counterparts (especially the elite monogamous parents Ariès studied). Rather than being cosseted treasures, African children were valued foremost for their obedient work in families and larger communities shaped by polygyny. Meillassoux claimed that children were on the lowest rung of African society. They were part of a larger group of "juniors" that included subordinates with higher status than children, such as unmarried men and women and young wives. This age-based hierarchy rested on ideals of plural marriage—a social system of reproduction sanctioned by "seniors," consisting of both male elders (patriarchs) and older mothers, who controlled the passage of "bridewealth" (cattle or other prestige goods) and brides between households.

Gerontocracy in African Society

A patriarch, or "Big Man," as the historian John Iliffe recently dubbed this figure, was the custodian of an assortment of wives, children, siblings, relations, and dependents. The "Big Man" household originated in equatorial forests and spread south of the Sahara at the start of the first millennium C.E. Big Men and their families used Iron Age tools to clear land for agricultural and pastoral production, instituting polygyny to enlarge their labor force in villages, chiefdoms and, later, states. This pattern of social organization had taken root throughout the continent by 1000 C.E. in West Africa among Yoruba, Hausa, and Ibo communities; in central Africa among Kongo and Gisu peoples; in southern Africa among Pondo, Zulu, and Sotho chiefdoms; and among eastern Africa's Somali, Kikuyu, and Chewa families.

The archetypal Big Man's family depended on unequal reciprocity and the work of juniors, principally his brood of children. Over a period of many years (determined by elders), children carried out tasks according to gender division and senior privilege. A father had rights to the labor of his wives and offspring; older wives had rights to the labor of younger wives and their daughters; young women had rights to the labor of their adolescent sisters; and so forth down the domestic pecking order.

Children understood that this generational hierarchy put older adults into positions of esteem. High-placed members of a household earned reverence for leading rites of passage, sealing marriages, and allocating resources. Unmarried sons and daughters were socialized to offer filial piety in return for the means—usually bridewealth for males and garden land for females—to start their own domestic arrangements. Older children could garner assets (a critical first step before rising in stature) only after they met their responsibilities to elders and their web of kin. Personal accumulation fulfilled certain ambitions, but group belonging superseded individual aims.

As children gained in status, not all could become senior wives and patriarchs—a situation that ignited generational struggles. When thwarted aspirations, natural catastrophe, or colonial rule burdened youths with additional heavy obligations, relationships of respect between the old and young could change dramatically. Indeed, examples from sub-Saharan folklore and archival evidence tell of juveniles avenging their exploitation by elders. One Chewa legend portrays children massacring adults—the young rebels reacted to "toiling endlessly while their elders dined and dozed." A somewhat similar struggle occurred in the modern era. In colonial South Africa in 1906, shortly after a rinderpest epidemic decimated the region's cattle (which was used as bridewealth) and colonialists imposed a tax on single males, Zulu youths attacked their patriarchs for failing to forestall the ensuing hardship.

From Birth to Infancy

Perhaps the first lesson of life learned by the very young was that communal acceptance and nurturance could mean the difference between life and death. Virulent diseases stalked children. Malaria, gastroenteritis, and respiratory infections, to name only a few, kept INFANT MORTALITY high until the middle of the twentieth century, when the advent of modern medical treatments improved the health and life expectancy of newborns. The withholding of clan approval because of severe birth defects, or the arrival of twins, could also prompt infanticide, as these occurrences were considered a harbinger from ancestors that further troubles loomed. Moreover, the mother of a seriously disabled infant might be seen as suffering needlessly if she had to raise an enfeebled child, while a mother of twins might gravely weaken her capacity to survive if she simultaneously nursed two newborns.

Babies less than three years old were typically breast-fed and carried by their mother on the hip or back, with skin-to-skin contact and access to breast milk vital to building immunities. To guard against unforeseen handicaps and illnesses, infants underwent elaborate ceremonies directed by a paternal elder who could administer magical and herbal charms. These special rites strengthened the bonds between young children and their protective network, which included parents, grandparents, uncles, aunts, siblings, cousins, spiritual founders long since passed, diviners, and unrelated guardians. Indeed, a baby's name could be chosen to honor her lifelong defenders from revered ancestors to a saint of the Roman Catholic Church (in the fifteenth-century Christian Kongo kingdom).

From Weaning to Puberty

Weaning could come with unforgiving suddenness. For example, some mothers in southern Africa daubed the sap of hot chilies on their nipples when toddlers reached their second or third year. Newly weaned children were expected to contribute almost immediately to domestic upkeep. They could be assigned to teach infant siblings proper conduct, which barred defiance, jealousy, dishonesty, and unjust violence, or they could impart morals through the recitation of proverbs, such as the Sotho expression: *kgotso ke nala*, (peace is prosperity).

As members of a specially recognized group, some youngsters also taught one another about gender and generational expectations. For example, in Ibo communities boys of the same age and village enrolled in an "age-set" to train to be married men. In twentieth-century Kenya, mission teachers divided Kikuyu children into single-sex school grades and taught them to model themselves on monogamous Christian husbands and wives. Throughout sub-Saharan Africa, boys carrying out collective male tasks took their little brothers along to learn how to build huts and fences, forge metals, carve wood, weave fishnets, hunt game, drill for battle, and tend livestock. Similarly, girls instructed their younger sisters in female duties, such as fetching wood and water, making fires, preparing food, thatching huts, making pots, and cultivating crops. In addition, some African states utilized children to fulfill national obligations. Regents in the nineteenth-century Zulu kingdom enlisted regiments of boys to lug provisions during military campaigns and recruited girls to weed the gardens of the royal family.

Children's responsibilities, of course, became more onerous under coercive labor systems. Girls were taken into mil-

lenniums-old domestic slavery to serve an African master far from their natal kin. Males were kidnapped and shipped to New World plantations from the fifteenth to nineteenth centuries, leaving their younger brothers to fill the void. And twentieth-century European rulers compelled adolescents to travel to find colonial employment (as house servants and commercial farm hands, for example) that brought in money for their family's tax requirements.

Yet such adversity gives an unduly bleak and one-sided picture of African childhoods. Though slavery disfigured many African communities, it scarcely touched others. In parts of central and southern Africa, boys and girls generally lived without fear of raiders, enjoying unfettered PLAY that affirmed family security. Their recreation with peers celebrated the nurturer-mother and warrior-father. Pondo girls, for example, transformed corncobs into DOLLS that they toted on their backs, while boys practiced defensive combat skills by tossing sticks at a branch set upright in the ground.

Even strenuous sacrifices could lead to exploration and benefit. Labor migration, for example, emboldened boys and girls, acquainting them with new cultural possibilities and an economic conduit through which to accumulate their own resources and accelerate their own ascent to seniority. Younger, working sons who bought their own bridewealth did not have to rely on their father's contribution, eroding the generational constraints that prolonged their junior subordination.

Adolescence and Initiation

As children in Africa approached PUBERTY, their games and diversions revealed aspirations to come of age. Not surprisingly, sexual adventuring intensified during adolescence. Various conventions tightly regulated courting, and while romantic interludes could progress to intercourse, this act drew severe censure. The litany of fines and banishments for premarital pregnancy among Yoruba, Kongo, and Zulu people suggests that sexual transgressions occurred with disconcerting regularity. A girl accused of waywardness suffered particularly harsh and lasting punishments, while her male counterpart tended to receive only a firm slap on the wrist. Patriarchal prerogatives dictated this gender discrimination. In many polygynous sub-Saharan societies, a male elder's public pledge that a first-time bride retained her virginity often paved the way for her rites of passage and eventual wedding.

Rites of passage, honored enactments that brought childhood to a close, took place between the ages of twelve and eighteen. In precolonial and colonial times they could entail temporary seclusion from the community, removal of teeth and hair, tattooing, or body incisions. Some coming-of-age ceremonies for boys (that continue to this day) focused on the painful cutting of genitalia, imparting an essential message: achieving adulthood necessitated a sharp separation from childhood and a heightened awareness of the physical and emotional endurance underlying the ancestral commitment to procreate after marriage. At times, initiation practices atrophied, such as when colonial authorities in eastern Africa campaigned to make tribal CIRCUMCISION a crime; when Xhosa migrants living in congested townships of modern Johannesburg had little space to conduct their rituals; or when precolonial leaders such as Shaka Zulu forbade boys' circumcision and replaced it with two decades of military service to the king.

Girls also underwent circumcision (performed principally by their mothers and grandmothers), but this observance was not widespread in Africa and declined in the twentieth century after missionaries, colonialists, and modernizing African leaders urged its banning. However, toward the end of the twentieth century, female circumcision has apparently been revived in western and eastern Africa. Human rights campaigners have targeted the practice as cruel and unusual punishment, calling it "genital mutilation."

Other rites of passage for girls involved less invasive procedures, such as the cleansing of limbs with sacred liquid (i.e., the gall of livestock) and "coming out" feasts and dances that heralded the female initiates' ascent to a marriageable status. After initiation, boys and girls understood that they maneuvered in a society still dominated by elder authority, but one that was now open to their membership as potential seniors, with the enhanced privileges and responsibilities of young adults.

Conclusion

At the beginning of the twenty-first century, two intriguing questions are being explored: (1) Does childhood end at initiation or linger into young adulthood, a liminal stage before marriage and parenthood? and (2) Does childhood begin at birth, weaning, or some other phase before rites of passage? On a continent so vast, with few records (oral traditions far outweigh the keeping of documents), wide social diversity (myriad ethnic groups), and remarkable continuities (e.g., prevalence of "Big Man" families), the main concern is to devise a framework through which to examine variations in children's roles. To date, Meillassoux's model offers a crucial starting point, but like Ariès's ideas, it too will spark more debates than answers. The conceptual approaches that promise to emerge from these discussions will doubtless advance nascent scholarship on the history of childhood in Africa.

See also: **Abduction in Modern Africa; Female Genital Mutilation; Globalization; Soldier Children.**

BIBLIOGRAPHY

Aguilar, Mario, ed. 1998. *The Politics of Age and Gerontocracy in Africa.* Trenton, NJ: African World Press.

Baxter, P. T. W., and Uri Almagor, eds. 1978. *Age, Generation, and Time: Some Features of East African Age Organization.* New York: St. Martin's.

Bledsoe, Caroline, and Barney Cohen, eds. 1993. *Social Dynamics of Adolescent Fertility in Sub-Saharan Africa.* Washington, DC: National Academy Press.

Boothby, Neil, and Christine Knudson. 2000. "Children of the Gun." *Scientific American* 282: 46–65.

Carton, Benedict. 2000. *Blood from Your Children: The Colonial Origins of Generational Conflict in South Africa.* Charlottesville: University Press of Virginia.

Colony of Natal Report Native Affairs Commission 1906–7. 1907. Pietermaritzburg, Natal: P. Davis and Sons.

Comaroff, Jean, and John Comaroff. 1999. "Occult Economies and the Violence of Abstraction: Notes from the South African Postcolony." *American Ethnologist* 26: 279–303.

Forde, Daryll. 1965. "Double Descent Among the Yako." In *African Systems of Kinship and Marriage,* ed. A. R. Radcliffe-Brown and Daryll Forde. New York: Oxford University Press.

Gelfand, Michael. 1979. *Growing up in Shona Society: From Birth to Marriage.* Gwelo, Rhodesia (Zimbabwe): Mambo Books.

Gluckman, Max. 1965. "Kinship and Marriage Among the Lozi of Northern Rhodesia and Zulu of Natal." In *African Systems of Kinship and Marriage,* ed. A. R. Radcliffe-Brown and Daryll Forde. New York: Oxford University Press.

Gottlieb, Alma. 2000. "Where Have All the Babies Gone? Toward an Anthropology of Infants (and their Caretakers)." *Anthropological Quarterly* 73: 121–132.

Guyer, Jane. 1981. "Household and Community in African Studies." *African Studies Review* 24: 86–137.

Iliffe, John. 1995. *Africans: The History of a Continent.* Cambridge, UK: Cambridge University Press.

Junod, Henry. 1927. *The Life of a South African Tribe.* Vols. 1 and 2. London: Macmillan.

Kidd, Dudley. 1906. *Savage Childhood: A Study of Kafir Children.* London: Adam and Charles Black.

Kuper, Hilda. 1965. "Kinship Among the Swazi." In *African Systems of Kinship and Marriage,* ed. A. R. Radcliffe-Brown and Daryll Forde. New York: Oxford University Press.

McClendon, Thomas. 1997. "A Dangerous Doctrine: Twins, Ethnography, and Inheritance in Colonial Africa." *Journal of Legal Pluralism* 29: 121–140.

McKittrick, Meredith. 1996. "The Burden of the Young Men: Property and Generational Conflict in Namibia, 1880–1945." *African Economic History* 24: 115–129.

Meillassoux, Claude. 1981. *Maidens, Meals, and Money.* Cambridge, UK: Cambridge University Press.

Morrell, Robert. 1998. "Of Men and Boys: Masculinity and Gender in Southern African Studies." *Journal of Southern African Studies* 24: 605–630.

Reynolds, Pamela. 1991. *Dance Civet Cat: Child Labour in Zambezi.* New York: St. Martin's.

Richards, A. 1956. *Chisungu: A Girls' Initiation Ceremony among the Bemba of Zambia.* London: Routledge.

Richards, Paul. 1996. *War, Youth, and Resources in Sierra Leone.* Oxford, UK: James Curry.

Schapera, Isaac. 1965. "Kinship and Marriage among the Tswana." In *African Systems of Kinship and Marriage,* ed. A. R. Radcliffe-Brown and Daryll Forde. New York: Oxford University Press.

Seeking, Jeremy. 1993. *Heroes or Villians? Youth Politics in the 1980s.* Johannesburg, South Africa: Ravan Press.

Thomas, Lynn. 1996. " 'Ngaitana (I Will Circumcise Myself)': The Gender and Generational Politics on the 1956 Ban on Clitoridectomy in Meru, Kenya." *Gender and History* 8: 338–363.

Turner, Victor. 1971. "Symbolization and Patterning in the Circumcision Rites of Two Bantu-Speaking Societies." In *Man in Africa*, ed. Mary Douglas and Phyllis Kaberry. New York: Anchor Doubleday.

Vaughan, Megan. 1983. "Which Family? Problems in the Reconstruction of the History of the Family as an Economic and Cultural Unit." *Journal of African History* 24: 275–283.

Wilson, Monica. 1977. *For Men and Elders: Change in the Relations of Generations and of Men and Women among the Nyakusa-Ngonde People, 1875–1971.* New York: Oxford University Press.

BENEDICT CARTON

African-American Children and Youth

Because of the cultural definitions of family that grow out of the traditions of continental AFRICA, and because of the unique histories of the populations of the African diaspora, in African-heritage societies and communities, children often play roles that are distinct from those of children in other social groups. These two factors have produced particular childhood patterns that persist into the twenty-first century to varying degrees among the many contexts and groupings that fall under the cultural generalization *African American*. Together, these two broad categories, heritage and history, reflect the more general way in which all children's lives are defined by the hopes and ideals inspired by new lives, and the constraints of the material conditions in which those lives come to exist and be.

Heritage and History

African cultural heritage is significant because of the way societies throughout continental Africa tend to define families by the presence of children. This stands in contrast to the European tradition of viewing marriage as the moment that defines a new family. Of course, in many situations families contain both a couple and children, but in situations on the margin, when family choices must be made, this difference can lead to a significant variation in outcomes. Because of the emotional role that families play in human life, there is also a contrast in the cultural focus of desire between a partner focus and an intergenerational focus. The partner focus can lead to a contractual orientation, with a sexual component that heightens the private and biological emphasis of relations to children. The generational focus tends to highlight the roles of care provision and dependency, reciprocal obligation, and time- and age-defined stages in relationships that place them more strongly in community.

African-American children have also been affected profoundly by the events, circumstances, and geography of African-American history. Systems of enslavement, displacement, segregation, labor, and formal and informal education, and the distinctions they created and enforced, interact with family systems and the ways children are seen by and interact with communities and society. It is important to emphasize,

Schoolchildren, New Bern, North Carolina, c. 1860s. Because it was forbidden by law to teach slaves to read and write in the pre–Civil War South, after emancipation, one of the chief concerns of newly freed African-American parents was for the education of their children. © CORBIS.

however, that local and individual experiences of cultural interaction and variation, in addition to varied customs, opportunity structures, and legal frameworks, speak against a single timeline or common experience for all African-American children.

The practice of enslaving people to do forced labor, like many systems of migrant labor, had the demographic effect of skewing populations towards a large number of young men. Particularly in climates that allowed for year-round agricultural production, such as the Caribbean and South America, the tremendous profits that built the palaces and treasures of Europe allowed for a constant importation of men who could be exhausted and replaced. Dependents were often an unwelcome expense to the enterprises, while the huge demand for labor developed African-majority societies throughout a region that included southern Louisiana and the South Carolina coast. The sexual exploitation of African women who were dragged into the horror of the middle passage, and the separation of children from parents, which was common in the slave trade, meant that few slaves saw both sides of the Atlantic as children. The harsh conditions in these intensely exploitative economic operations also discouraged the migration of European women, and so these areas quickly saw the emergence of free populations of mixed heritage, along with "maroon" or back-country communities of African heritage that had escaped enslavement.

Boys on Easter Morning, by Russell Lee. Many African-American children followed their parents north or were sent to live with relatives during the Great Migration from the South to the industrial Northern cities of the early twentieth century. These children are dressed in their Sunday best for Easter, April 1941, in their South Side Chicago neighborhood. Rare Books and Special Collections Division, The Library of Congress. © CORBIS.

The household, town, and back country became the most common environments for children and other dependents, and for the few who became elderly. In many cases, children born into SLAVERY were sent both by their enslaved parents and by their purported owners to spend much of their childhood in these communities before being brought into plantation labor. Near enough to be visited by parents but far enough, perhaps, not to be direct witnesses to the immediate traumas of slavery (other than the not-insignificant pain of parental separation), children raised in these collectives experienced some few early years of love and play, while also being schooled by elders and peers in the painful rules of race-associated slavery. Small communities of grannies and children were common in these areas, living on the fringes of plantations and in the alleys of towns, supported by semi-secret religious societies and by the local free African artisans and visiting runaways, who more often than not returned to plantations, as did the children themselves when they came of age to do useful work. In larger plantations, such arrangements of grannies and children were sometimes formalized,

which restricted connections to outside community, but had the advantage of keeping children close to parents for night-time study or Sunday contact.

Because of the limited labor value of children under the age of ten or twelve and the expense of their care during these dependent years, this setup was of some mutual benefit to those who regarded themselves as owners of the children, to the actual parents of the children, and to the children themselves. Except on large plantations, it also meant that there was some mixing and common experience among children who were to be enslaved and those born free or whose freedom would later be purchased. On large plantations, a different sort of mixing occurred, often with the free white children of the plantation owners and employees. The terrifying awakenings of those who were enslaved—the large majority of African Americans—are described in many slave narratives written by those who were enslaved as abrupt and stark ends to childhood at the auction block or in the violence of coerced labor.

Children who were still too young to do the sustained and heavy work of slavery had the important social function of linking groups who often were unable, due to distance, time, exhaustion, or physical restriction, or not permitted, by law or local authority, to visit each other. The children would spend time both off and on the plantation, carry important messages, and travel more than the more closely watched and constrained adults. Children of enslaved people also quickly learned to care for each other and tend the garden plots that provided basic sustenance or a necessary supplement to the unhealthy rations that came through the labor system. Children also could be placed intentionally in situations to their advantage and shielded from witnessing the direct humiliation of parents and parental figures subject to plantation labor. Thus for the majority of African-American children in both towns and on plantations, the notion of family was quickly expanded; a number of adults could play a parental role in their lives, and community responsibilities were an immediate part of their lives. An urgent and elaborate education in operating safely and discreetly within the social system was a part of every child's early experience of responsibility and DISCIPLINE. The pain of constant separations from SIBLINGS, loving adults, and familiar environs made community bonds all the more significant, alienation from dominant whites and elites all the more profound, and early maturity a necessary survival attribute.

Children and the Community

Other regions, where agriculture was more limited by soil and season, relied more openly on African-American communities that could sustain themselves, whether slavery was practiced or not. Being less likely markets for the main slave trade, women, children, and family life quickly became a central part of African-American experience, both as means of surviving urban and rural enslavement and as sites of love, support, and cultural sustenance. Emancipation, formal education, APPRENTICESHIP, and social intermingling came to the northern colonies and were enhanced by the rhetoric and ideals of the U.S. revolutionary period. Inequality and segregation remained significant social factors that children had to learn to negotiate, and the restricted occupations of free African-American adults—domestic workers, sailors, miners, and similar jobs—tended to require frequent separation from children and spouses. This meant that children in the North, a much larger proportion of whom were free after the Revolution than before, also experienced multiple households and served as cultural mediators and connectors between adults and within communities, both free and enslaved. The religious societies that were formed in these communities were often more open and public than those in the Deep South and were likely to include social clubs and betterment organizations, along with specialized schools for children, which often included education about Africa, as Anthony Benezet's school in Philadelphia did in the 1760s. During this time period and into the nineteenth century, the general term of reference for themselves and designation by others was *African*, as in the African Meeting House in Boston, the Free African Society of Philadelphia, and the development of the African Methodist Episcopal (A.M.E.) Church.

Contact between free African communities and Africa was constant throughout the antebellum period (1789–1861) through the whaling and sea trades and through the continued trade in humans where slavery persisted. In addition, the Caribbean trade and the Atlantic world in general were frequently traversed, and so the African diaspora and African heritage were not far from the consciousness of most African Americans, as is illustrated in many slave narratives. The Old Testament stories of Joseph, Moses, Daniel, Gideon, Joshua, and David, which are common to ISLAM and Christianity, held significant messages of God's care and the coming deliverance and were familiar and central texts to African-American children. Because many of the people who were enslaved had origins in the predominantly Muslim populations of West Africa, the transition to another "religion of the book," as Muslims traditionally recognize JUDAISM and Christianity, was not drastic. The innocent and persecuted Jesus of Christianity or Issa of Islam also spoke to the condition of African Americans, and all figured in the music and coded messages of cultural communication in which children participated. Community celebrations involving music and dance, recognized calendar holidays, and claimed holidays, such as the Pinksterfest in New York, were times of reunion and reconnection, as well as places to build networks and a way to place children in living situations with broader opportunity, if possible. Such opportunities were, however, severely constrained for most by geography and enslavement.

Children were regular passengers on the Underground Railroad and its antecedents, and were guaranteed a home in African-American communities in free Canada, Mexico, or Florida, as well as in the northern United States. Union armies entering the South during the Civil War were trailed by large numbers of African-American children who had been sent by their parents and communities to find freedom.

The middle colonies and upper South prior to the Civil War were a blend of the above situations, with a mix of large plantation agriculture, smallholdings, and seasonal change, along with varied urbanization and the differing local presence and numbers of free African individuals. When the religious and secular, white-led African American Abolitionist and Back-to-Africa colonization movements rose in the late eighteenth century and grew in importance in the mid-nineteenth, they had at their center the images of defenseless women and children, which also became the dominant feature of the poetry, novels, and narratives of African-American literature of the period. The mobility of children and the strategic placement of children so they would have opportunities for education and freedom were sometimes enhanced by white patrons and allies but more often were constrained by high mortality, malnutrition, and the violent suspicions of white neighbors and authorities.

Children's TOYS and games in African-American communities were most often homemade and were the hoops, balls, and corn-husk or rag DOLLS typical of the various time periods and locations. Storytelling among children was encouraged by adults and was more distinctively African-American than were toys—as was childhood preaching by both boys and girls. These practices, along with music, dancing, and memory games, were often treated as competitive, while organized outdoor games were somewhat circumscribed until more recent times. Verbal skill and play-acting were essential survival skills for many African-American children. On the occasions they interacted with or were questioned by white authority figures or informers, they needed to be able to protect community secrets, and hide their own possible feelings of fear or resentment.

The distinctive NAMING of children with Africanized or invented names and creative spellings and pronunciations, making each child unique, has always been a part of African-American practice. When resented or disallowed as legal names by whites, such names reemerge as creative nicknames, endearments, chosen names, multiple names for particular circumstances, or names to recognize achievements or social positions. This practice of making a child different and special through a name not only allows for easy identification in a wide community but also gives a child an owned and positive difference in a social context where other experiences of difference will likely have negative impacts. Children are to be both seen and heard in African-American communities, which builds both presence and confidence lest they disappear both literally or figuratively in the discouragement of an oppressive environment. Such naming occurs across the spectrum of education, income, and status up to the present and is one of many strategies used by adults to ensure the normal psychological development of children who will experience discrimination early; it functions as a means to externalize the ignorance of others.

Discipline and Family

Outsiders often regard the disciplining of African American children as demanding or harsh, with an emphasis on minding and respecting elders. In a world of particular danger for African Americans, and in which police and teachers are not necessarily allies or to be trusted, it is important to have children respond immediately to adult warnings or commands. Older children as well as unrelated adults keep an eye out for trouble that might come to African-American youngsters, and responsible adults are prepared to supervise children, whether or not the children are known to them. Such community behavior relies on the kind of strict training that will guarantee a response from children who may need to recognize both subtle and overt warnings and advice from adults.

It also demands clear and frank communication about such situations between adults and children when they are on familiar ground; this often happens through storytelling and relating past experiences. Because many adults feel that the painful realities of contemporary racism must be related to children for their own safety, the painful past, which may not be directly relevant to children, often remains untold. It is typical that the vast majority of children who were born to people who had formerly been enslaved never heard from their parents about the experience of slavery, and many young African Americans have little knowledge of the days of violent legal segregation.

Adolescent rebellion, or self-definition, is normally externalized from family and community so that it is rare for African-Americans to have fraught relationships with their parents as older children or as adults. Children generally understand the situations of their parents and know who their biological parents are, as well as their relationship to the other adults in their lives who may play a parental role. While other cultures may treat the existence of such varied PARENTING as a family secret or as something shameful, it is openly acknowledged to most African-American children from a young age. In this way, children know the vagaries of the world, and also know that their caregivers have chosen them and are doing their best. Children grow up knowing a wide circle of siblings, cousins, aunts, and uncles, many of whom may not be blood relations, and regularly experience large reunions of families and communities. The long postpuberty dependence that emerged in white communities in the twentieth century remained atypical for African Americans, who continued to quickly take on adult earning responsibility and sexual experience.

After the Civil War, some of the main concerns of the Freedman's Bureau were centered around children in the search of lost relatives and the demand for education. Many newly freed African-American citizens rejected other forms of agricultural labor in favor of sharecropping because it allowed them to build a family and community structure where the care of children and the elderly could be pooled and the basic community institutions, church and school, could be supported. In both rural and urban contexts, it was typical for both parents to work outside the home and for the older children to be responsible for managing the household during parental absences with the advice of elderly neighbors or friends. While they were responsible for significant duties within the home, African-American children were much less likely to work for wages outside the home than were white children of similar economic status. When African-American children went to live with other adults, it was most likely for educational or apprenticeship purposes or to leave particularly difficult or oppressive circumstances. This was in contrast to the ways impoverished or orphaned white children would be sent off to work for wages and often encountered even more difficult and oppressive circumstances than those they left.

Aspiration, Connection, and Responsibility

After the Civil War, social distinctions became important within communities where the small but significant free African-American populations often had experienced a high degree of interracial marriage. The descendants of these mixed marriages often assumed leadership roles within the community but also sometimes set boundaries between themselves and those who were recently freed. When intermarriage declined drastically in the late nineteenth and twentieth centuries in the U.S. with the end of Reconstruction and the rise of racism based on "scientific" theories, EUGENICS, legal segregation, and in many places prohibition of intermarriage, the elite of the African-American community developed institutions for their own children. Some were based on distinct church congregations, but specialized SUMMER CAMPS and clubs like the Jack and Jill clubs emphasized class differences among African-American children. The Women's Club movement and the desire for "respectability" helped form the family patterns and aspirations of the elite, and their expectations for their children, while the enforcement of segregation pushed some people toward passing as white and others toward the larger African-American community.

During the Great Migration from the rural South to northern cities, which started before World War I, African-American children continued to play a mediating role, connecting communities and relatives who had become separated. Children would be sent South to friends and relatives to "stay out of trouble" in the summer and North to friends and relatives during the school year to get a decent education. Years and several generations later, these links are still maintained between the cities of the North and the rural South through the exchange of children. Older urban children often remain in charge of significant aspects of home life while all available adults work, just as they did in rural economies. African-American adults and children tend to socialize together to a greater degree than those in other communities, and seek to maintain wide networks of acquaintance and support.

Children and adolescents played a significant role during the civil rights movement, often standing in for parents whose circumstances did not permit their direct participation. The widespread news coverage of the movement led some to criticize this "use" of children, but African-American children have long played significant and strategic social roles in society. As migration and media portrayals led whites to have more and more encounters, both real and virtual, with African-American children, many white adults were critical of the assertiveness of African-American children and of their comfort around adults. This disapproval, along with children's unfamiliar names and family patterns

that appeared disorganized and immoral to outsiders, has often led sectors of the white public to view African-American children negatively.

In the meantime, the channeling of children into avenues where they will have opportunities to be successful and creative continues. When the New York City budget crisis eliminated all arts and music programs, young people took the musical instruments at hand—their parents' stereo systems—and by manipulating the recordings to both sample snippets of music and make new sounds, the rap industry and hip-hop visual, literary, and dance culture were born. When sports became a vehicle for academic scholarships and direct material success, parents and children in African-American communities dedicated themselves to encouraging all kinds of athletic endeavors. When community colleges declared open admissions, youth of color flocked into higher education. Children as entrepreneurs and entertainers are not new to African American communities. They participate both in negative and positive ways, but always as full social participants, following the paths of opportunity. The community generally continues to support unconventional and nonconforming children in unfamiliar endeavors. It is much rarer for African-American children to be written off or completely separated from family and community than it is among other groups.

Immigration and U.S. expansion have brought Latino and Caribbean children of African heritage, as well as African children, to the United States. Some of them resist being labeled African American and see themselves as distinct. Ongoing tensions within black communities, including those involving class differences, people of mixed-race parentage or people involved in mixed-race relationships, gender, rural/urban divisions, and religious differences, have brought with them variation and rich infusions of culture, as well as new social options. Children reflect these interactions even as the social segregation of U.S. society increases in the early twenty-first century, particularly for children. Often the objects of social commentary and research, African-American children remain the central subjects of African-American family and community life.

See also: **Brown v. the Board of Education of Topeka, Kansas.**

BIBLIOGRAPHY

Bennett, Lerone. 1988. *Before the Mayflower: A History of Black America.* New York: Penguin.

Billingsley, Andrew. 1992. *Climbing Jacob's Ladder: The Enduring Legacy of African-American Families.* New York: Simon and Schuster.

Billingsley, Andrew, and Jeanne Giovannoni. 1972. *Children of the Storm: Black Children and American Child Welfare.* New York: Harcourt, Brace, Jovanovich.

Cheatham, Harold, and James Stewart, eds. 1990. *Black Families: Interdisciplinary Perspectives.* New Brunswick, NJ: Transaction.

DuBois, W. E. B. 1909. *The Negro American Family.* Cambridge, MA: MIT Press.

Faust, Drew. 1982. *James Henry Hammond and the Old South: A Design for Mastery.* Baton Rouge: Louisiana State University Press.

Foner, Eric. 1988. *Reconstruction: America's Unfinished Revolution 1863–1877.* New York: Harper and Row.

Franklin, Donna. 1997. *Ensuring Inequality: The Structural Transformation of the African-American Family.* New York: Oxford University Press.

Gates, Henry Louis, ed. 1987. *The Classic Slave Narratives.* New York: Mentor.

Gates, Henry Louis, ed. 1991 *Bearing Witness: Selections from African American Autobiography in the Twentieth Century.* New York: Pantheon.

Gutman, Herbert. 1976. *The Black Family in Slavery and Freedom.* New York: Pantheon.

Harding, Vincent. 1981. *There Is a River: The Black Struggle for Freedom in America.* New York: Harcourt, Brace, Jovanovich.

Hill, Shirley. 1999. *African American Children: Socialization and Development in Families.* Thousand Oaks, CA: Sage.

Huggins, Nathan. 1990. *Black Odyssey: The African American Ordeal in Slavery.* New York: Vintage.

Jones, Jacqueline. 1985. *Labor of Love, Labor of Sorrow: Black Women, Work, and the Family from Slavery to the Present.* New York: Vintage.

Kelley, Robin, and Earl Lewis. 2000. *To Make Our World Anew: A History of African Americans.* New York: Oxford University Press.

Lemann, Nicholas. 1991. *The Promised Land: The Great Black Migration and How it Changed America.* New York: Knopf.

Malone, Ann Patton. 1992. *Sweet Chariot: Slave Family and Household Structure in Nineteenth-Century Louisiana.* Chapel Hill: University of North Carolina Press.

McAdoo, Harriette Pipes, ed. 1981 *Black Families.* Thousand Oaks, CA: Sage.

Miller, Andrew Thompson. 1991. "Looking at African American Families: Recognition and Reaction." Ph.D. diss., University of Pennsylvania.

Miller, Andrew Thompson. 1993. "Social Science, Social Policy, and the Heritage of African American Families." In *The "Underclass" Debate,* ed. Michael Katz. Princeton, NJ: Princeton University Press.

Moody, Anne. 1968. *Coming of Age in Mississippi.* New York: Dell.

Mullings, Leith. 1997. *On Our Own Terms: Race, Class, and Gender in the Lives of African American Women.* London: Routledge.

Nightingale, Carl. 1993. *On the Edge: A History of Poor Black Children and their American Dreams.* New York: Basic Books.

Nobles, Wade. 1978. "Towards an Empirical and Theoretical Framework for Defining Black Families." *Journal of Marriage and the Family* 40: 679–688.

Stack, Carol. 1974. *All Our Kin: Strategies for Survival in a Black Community.* New York: Harper and Row.

Washington, Mary Helen. 1991. *Memory of Kin: Stories about Family by Black Writers.* New York: Anchor.

Zollar, Ann. 1985. *A Member of the Family: Strategies for Black Family Continuity.* Chicago: Nelson Hall.

ANDREW THOMPSON MILLER

Age and Development

Age and development are concepts central to contemporary Western understandings of children's growth and to the way industrialized societies have been organized since approximately the middle of the nineteenth century. If the notion of development offers a map to social and cultural constructions of maturity, the physiological and psychological characteristics accompanying chronological age are the signposts of notable change along its path. By the late twentieth century, the developmental stages of juvenile maturation were thought to proceed in sequence through eight distinguishable but overlapping stages: from early infancy to later infancy; to early childhood and then middle childhood; to pre-, early, middle, and later ADOLESCENCE.

Ariès and the Modern Family

The so-called modern family as described by PHILIPPE ARIÈS in *Centuries of Childhood* was characterized (in part) by the degree to which parents were alive to these phases of their children's growth, as opposed to earlier, more rudimentary, divisions. Overall, the enlarging discernment of predictable chronological and developmental changes in the child reflected the "sentimentalization" of childhood; that is, children were increasingly regarded as requiring special care and attention by adults and were believed to occupy a stage of life precious to their formation individually and collectively as future adults. The sentimentalization of children occurred on a broad scale and was combined with the creation of institutions—notably universal schooling—that were sponsored, with a few exceptions, by the emerging urban middle class of industrialized Europe and North America. They were later applied by the state at all levels of the social structure in these societies.

The dawning concern with children's development can be traced in part to the ancient recognition of the ages of life (or "ages of man"), a concept acknowledged in Western culture from at least the sixth century B.C.E. According to Ariès, Ionian formulations of the ages of man ultimately found their way centuries later into Byzantine writings and, subsequently, into what he called "scientific vulgarizations" of the sixteenth century. During the 1500s the popular understanding of human biology, according to Ariès, derived from the notion of a "universal system of correspondences," that is, the belief that there is a symbolism in numbers that binds natural phenomena into relations or "correspondences" with one another. (Accordingly, the ages of man, of which there were seven, were believed to parallel the number of planets observed in the night sky.)

The Steps of the Ages

The seven ages of man, from birth to death, were depicted iconographically beginning in the fourteenth century as the seven "steps of the ages," which enjoyed popular currency as a means of visualizing human aging. Ascending from the left and descending to the right, these representations begin with a child on a hobbyhorse (the "age of toys"). On the next, boys are depicted as learning to read and girls as spinning

L'Homme commence par l'Enfance, | Si la Jeuneſſe a l'avantage, | A l'Âge de Maturité | L'âge caduc & imbecille
Il y ſouffre beaucoup de maux, | D'être la ſaiſon de. plaiſirs, | L'on commence à ceſſer de vivre, | Ne promet plus de jours heureux
Mais les peines & les travaux, | L'Âge Viril a des deſirs, | Et dans l'âge qui va le ſuivre. | Alors ſont éteints tous nos feux
Le ſuivent dans l'Adoleſcence | Et le goût du libertinage | A peine a-t'on de la ſanté | Et la lampe même faute d'huile

FIG. 316. — LE COURS DE LA VIE OU L'HOMME DANS SES DIFFÉRENTS AGES. D'après une estampe populaire. A Paris, chez Bouché.
* Ce sujet, maintes fois traité, exprime les sentiments de résignation de l'homme devant la vie. C'est la montée et la descente, la succession inéluctable des âges de la vie.

The ages of human development, from the cradle to the deathbed, are depicted in this eighteenth-century French print. © Bettmann/CORBIS.

yarn. This is succeeded by the "age of love"—scenes of boys and girls walking together, or of wedding celebrations. At the summit is the age of war and chivalry, where a man bearing arms is pictured. Then decline: represented on the next (and lower) stair are "men of law, science, or learning"; just below, the "old bearded scholar" sitting by the fire; and finally, infirmity and death.

While children occupied the first two stairs on the steps of the ages, Ariès contended that it was not until the seventeenth century that idea of childhood was recognized as a stage of life in the West, at which point it began commanding particular attention by parents and society's institutions. Ariès argued that this change could be seen in the depictions of children that became common in the 1600s, when they were shown as individuals with characteristic childlike features, clothing, and accoutrements. Indeed, Ariès felt it was the increased effort to differentiate children from adults and the physical separation of children from adult society that defined family life as "modern" and suggested a seemingly permanent departure from child-treatment practices that had been common since ancient times.

Since Ariès, historians have looked much more closely for clues to test the validity of his chief claim, that childhood did not exist before the seventeenth century, or more precisely, that anything like the contemporary fixation on children's well-being and growth flourished before the 1600s. They have discovered a much greater attentiveness to childhood and to the stages of children's emergence from physical, material, and psychological dependence on adults than had been appreciated by Ariès.

Medieval Views on Childhood

Most notably, Shulamith Shahar found that medieval medical works, didactic literature, and moral treatises not only recognized several stages in human life but commonly divided childhood itself into three stages: *infantia*, *pueritia*, and *adolescentia*. Further, most authorities referred to what is now termed the postadolescent phase as *juventus*. Each of these stages implied fairly uniform age groupings.

Infantia lasted from birth to about age seven. Within this stage an early phase lasted from birth to roughly age two—the point when the child has all of its teeth and can walk.

Some writers detected a second substage that ended around age five, when the child's speech is perfected.

Pueritia lasted from age seven to age twelve for girls and to age fourteen for boys, which recognized the differing physiological maturation of girls and boys. The hallmark of this stage, the so-called age of reason, was marked by the capacity of children to distinguish between right and wrong. And yet this potential was accompanied by a supposed proclivity for sin beginning around the age of seven, which was seen as corresponding with the growth of the child's intellect. Still, some religious moralists argued that such reasoning was not commonly accessible to children until the age of ten or ten-and-a-half. Thus, a substage was spliced into *pueritia* that suggested, again, more acute sensitivity to children's aptitudes than was once thought to have been the case. Hence, children under the age of fourteen usually were not considered accountable for crimes, were not liable for oaths, were not subject to penance for sexual sins, and generally performed a lighter penance than adults for sins to which they confessed. Further, young people in this stage of life were observed to be very impressionable, both moody and carefree, to crave sleep and food, to prefer the company, praise, and admonitions of their peers to those of adults, and to be immodest about their bodies. Like moderns, the medieval sages noted the onset of PUBERTY at age twelve for girls and age fourteen for boys.

While there was wide consensus among writers about the initiation of *adolescentia* there was little agreement about when this third stage concluded. Some set its end at the age of twenty-one, others at twenty-five, twenty-eight, thirty, or as late as thirty-five. Many, as intimated by Ariès, divided the ages into multiples of seven, which meant that this stage began straightforwardly at fourteen and ended at twenty-one. Legally, adulthood could include the rights of males and females to marry, own, inherit, and transmit property, bear witness at legal or ecclesiastical proceedings, and to be fully accountable under the laws of the land. While statutes varied dramatically across the European continent, Roman law remained a powerful influence throughout the Middle Ages. Under Roman law, twenty-five was the age of adulthood, the age at which males entailed many rights and responsibilities.

Notable in Shahar's view is that while writers during the Middle Ages addressed themselves to both girls and boys in their musings on the earliest phases of child life, separate treatments are devoted to girls and boys in discussions of *pueritia*. Boys, it was urged, should be schooled. Girls, on the other hand, might be advised to learn how to perform more homely tasks, yet they received decreasing attention in this literature and, according to Shahar, were "almost overlooked in discussions of transitions to full adulthood" (p. 30).

Childhood as Perceived by the Masses

The relative newness of the concept of childhood—the foundation of Ariès's claims about the supposed modernity of family life after the seventeenth century and for the eventual articulation of children's observed physical, mental, moral, and emotional development—was modified if not overturned by Shahar and others. Nonetheless, just as the bases of Ariès's inferences were distrusted for having been drawn from the upper strata of Western culture (think of the seven steps which depicted a child on a hobby horse or boys learning to read, for instance), so also were his critics guilty of invoking the formulations of a social elite in studying the early modern era. Until the nineteenth century the great mass of people were illiterate, therefore recommendations to parents to educate their sons could only be aimed at parents who were themselves literate and who saw the necessity of LITERACY for sons who, too, would circulate among other literate men. Popular literacy would spread in the wake of the PROTESTANT REFORMATION after the sixteenth century, as the individual's ability to interpret scripture was critical to personal salvation in nascent Protestantism. Yet it was presumed at that time and for centuries to follow that parents, especially fathers, would be responsible for instructing their children in the basics of literacy. Therefore, the formation of schools for the masses, so crucial to spreading ideas about age and development, still lay far in the future. How prevalent then was the sensitivity to gradations of chronological age and development in the everyday lives of common people? In other words, how common were these ideas among those who constituted the great bulk of humankind, rather than in the observations and judgments of jurists, moralists, and philosophers?

Certainly in agrarian societies children's physical development was not lost on households that needed the labor of every hand. Work and need were always in greater abundance than the capacity to meet them. The ability of children to do small chores was helpful, but eagerly anticipated was the day when a young person could perform the tasks of an adult. In societies in which child mortality was high, disease shortened the adult life span, and illness, accident, or misfortune truncated so many working lives, the individual physical capacities of children must have been contemplated with the passing of each season. It is reasonable to believe that parents and kin were at least grossly attuned to the bodily and emotional changes of young ones, even if without the kind of sensitivity to children's growth that prevails in modern life. Nonetheless, the arc of children's growth as a social, rather than a physical, phenomenon only faintly resembled what we are accustomed to today.

Maturation in Agrarian Societies

One of the most significant reasons for this is that the productive bases of the household lay in agrarian rather than industrial pursuits. A striking difference between agrarian societies and later industrial ones is that agrarian societies did not recognize adolescence as a separate physical and psychological stage in an individual's advance toward adulthood. The addition of adolescence as a recognized life stage would not become common until the beginning of the twentieth century.

The absence of widespread recognition of adolescence in agrarian societies is arrestingly evident in two descriptions of children's coming of age. The first is historical and is offered by John Demos about children in colonial Massachusetts in the seventeenth century:

Once the child had begun to assume an adult role and style, around the age of six or seven, the way ahead was fairly straightforward. Development toward full maturity could be accomplished in a gradual, piecemeal, and largely automatic fashion. . . . Here was no "awkward" age—but rather the steady lengthening of a young person's shadow, and the whole instinctive process through which one generation yielded imperceptibly to its successor. (p. 150)

The second description is rendered by educator and ethnographer Leonard Covello about attitudes toward young people's development as expressed by southern Italian immigrants to the United States during the 1920s. Notice the similarity to Demos's observations: again, growing up is described as a process of incremental, seamless emergence into adult society:

Under the southern Italian cultural patterns, all children were useful and effective members of their families from an early age [five or six]. As the child became older and increased in physical strength and experience, in judgment and dependability, he performed more numerous and more difficult tasks. . . . There were no sharp age divisions; each shaded into the older and younger. So general was the pattern of life where children fitted into family life and its economy that all people were divided into two groups: children and adults. There was no adolescent group. . . . There were helpless infants and playful tots, young men and women, feeble folk, but there was never a group of adolescents. (pp. 270, 288–289)

As John Gillis points out, until the industrial era relations between the generations within the household were arranged spatially rather than temporally. That is, one's status derived not by achieving a certain age but rather by one's relation to the head of the household. In a very real sense, as Gillis says, until one became the head of one's own household, a man or a woman was ever a boy or a girl. Still, in a functional sense, a boy's or girl's maturation propelled him or her toward full membership in the economy of household relations at a steady rate, and so their subordinate status was also surely provisional and relative.

Children in the Industrial Age

This all began to change, however, with the reorganization of production initiated by industrialization, which in turn stimulated the rapid growth of cities. Cities and their industries were fed by the migration of people, primarily from the countryside—whether the hinterlands from which these migrations issued were local, regional, national, or intercontinental in nature. Swelling nineteenth-century cities revealed two developments relevant here: the growing degree of household dependence on waged labor and the extent to which children's time, in particular, was unstructured. Children on farms were of no concern to anyone except their own households; children present on city streets and underoccupied, however, made apparent the social costs of production's reorganization under burgeoning industrialism.

As capitalist economies grew and their commodities came increasingly from the expansion of mechanized industries, cycles of prosperity and depression became more frequent, making unemployment a recurrent feature of urban working-class life. Cities concentrated unemployment and poverty and so rendered its victims both visible and anonymous. Despite the eagerness of civic leaders in Europe and, especially, the United States to make individual family heads accountable for their own and their children's penury, eventually it was seen that some accommodation must be made for children and youths whose time and activities were underutilized. During the nineteenth century a connection would be drawn between the presumed moral effects of unoccupied time for children and its broader social consequences: a child of tender age enrolled in the "street school" of idleness, it was perceived, would inevitably become a soul-hardened adult due to frequent encounters with poverty and its twin, vice, both familiar escorts on the road to a life of crime. While the histories of social welfare in Europe and North America are variegated and complex, one common solution to children's exposure to idleness and its reputed effects was schooling.

Schooling, of course, owed its beginnings to ancient civilizations, and in the Middle Ages schools were instituted for the purpose of ecclesiastical recruitment and training. But again, the proportion of children (boys) educated for this purpose was miniscule. Popular schooling, which came to be seen as a panacea to the widening plagues of child unemployment and unsupervised time, could only develop if education were free. The establishment of mass schooling, which was to inculcate age consciousness to an unprecedented degree, was contingent upon two occurrences: the first was to gather all children into schools of some kind, and the second was to arrange schools internally so that children would be kept in schools for as long as was desirable for them individually and for the greater social good. The first examples of efforts to attract the great majority of children (typically children of the emerging working class and of the urban poor) into schools for the purpose of instilling morality and the fundaments of literacy were the "charity," "Sunday," and "infant" schools of the late 1700s and early 1800s in Western Europe and the United States.

Grading and Compulsory Schooling

In the United States, each of these examples in its way inspired the creation of the COMMON SCHOOL, which offered education at no or low cost to children of all social (if not racial) backgrounds, of all ages, and both genders. The school class, which sorted pupils by age and achievement into cohorts, was pioneered in early sixteenth-century London. Yet the necessity for widespread adoption of this device (grading) was not realized until it became clear that common schools were problematic for both the working class and the middle class. Working-class parents needed their children to contribute to household income by being employed; middle-class parents desired a greater degree of training that would allow their children to master the skills necessary to become accountants, teachers, clerks, businessmen, or professionals. These skills, which included verbal and quantitative facility, familiarity with the arts and letters and fluency in a foreign language, were transportable from industry to industry. By arranging the public school curriculum sequentially, during the second half of the nineteenth century grading endowed the student who progressed through it with great usefulness in an economy in which proprietorship was rapidly being eclipsed by salaried employment. Because grading tended to standardize the curriculum wherever it was implemented, it also certified a level and range of competency at each grade.

Still, pressure on working-class children to quit school to assist the household's need for income or labor was irresistible, both in times of economic depression and prosperity. Therefore, it was decided that school attendance must be made not only free but also compulsory if the majority of children were to be educated for an extended period of their lives. The establishment of COMPULSORY SCHOOL ATTENDANCE and free, graded schools in the United States took many decades to accomplish. Compulsory school attendance was first instituted by Massachusetts in 1852. The last state to pass a compulsory school attendance law was Mississippi in 1918. Of course, compulsory education legislation was not effective without complementary reinforcement by child labor laws, and most forms of CHILD LABOR were not prohibited throughout the United States until the mid 1930s. Similarly, the grading of schools began in Boston in 1847 and spread throughout the northeastern and midwestern United States but was not pervasive until the 1940s.

Nonetheless, where effectively enforced, compulsory school attendance reversed the "wealth flow" between parents and children. By forcing households to withhold their children's earning power from the sphere of commerce, children's status was altered, and parent-child relations were transformed from a spatial to temporal orientation. That is, in agrarian societies children typically worked for the benefit and well-being of the entire household and of the patriarch in particular; with compulsory school attendance and child labor laws, children could not be legally put to work until the age of fourteen, which curtailed their value as assets to the household economy.

Priceless Children

At the same time, new literary and religious sentiments took hold among the middle class that led to children becoming "sacralized." That is, childhood came to be viewed as a special state, and children were increasingly seen as a resource to be preserved, cherished, and celebrated. When this view was imposed on the working class through school requirements, the value of children within the household shifted from their utility as earners to objects of parental sentiment, and assumed a quality that Viviana A. Zelizer has called "pricelessness." One consequence of this was that at the conclusion of the nineteenth century children's BIRTHDAYS began to be celebrated annually for the first time in history. Some societies in the past had recognized specific chronological markers, such as turning age fifteen or age sixteen, but the habit of commemorating the arrival of each new year in the life of the child betokened a novel, sentimental regard for the passing of time. The accrual of experience and competence, which so enhanced child utility in the family wage economy, came at the expense of innocence and thus was viewed as a bittersweet process in the era of "priceless" children.

At the most basic level, the experience of grading revealed the extent to which children's expanding physical and intellectual aptitudes could be captured statistically and mapped onto entire groups of children. "Child accounting," which included statistics on enrollment, attendance, absenteeism, tardiness, and withdrawal from school were implemented in most northeastern and midwestern urban school systems by the latter decades of the nineteenth century. Age-grade tables, which documented the degree to which children's ages in individual schools corresponded to specified grade levels, were developed by the end of the century as well. All of these indicators implicitly measured the school's pedagogical effectiveness but also betrayed the spreading conviction that children's maturation could be normatively defined and so, too, subjected to corrective management. The peer group, previously more socially porous and tolerant of age span, was tightened to exclude children whose ages were too far above or below those set down by the cohorts created and maintained through the age-graded school class.

Philosophical Foundations

Was this sense of a schedule imposed on children by age-grading straightforwardly internalized by them, or did children's increasing awareness of themselves as being in or out of step with their classmates emerge through a process of give-and-take between the school's reinforcing structure and arising conceptions of development growing alongside of this new apparatus? It is important to recall that the philosophical convictions that undergirded compulsory school attendance, the prohibition of child labor, and a dawning awareness of children's biological and mental development were rooted in ENLIGHTENMENT notions of children's plasticity as growing creatures. English philosopher JOHN

LOCKE's essays on the necessity for parental watchfulness and constant correction of the child's natural instincts were grounded in the idea of human perfectibility, which suggested the opposite possibility—that children unmonitored and untutored would fall well short of this goal. Eighteenth-century French writer and philosopher JEAN-JACQUES ROUSSEAU's writings on child rearing promoted the superiority of yielding to the child's natural proclivities as the best guide to parenting. While Rousseau was effectively an antidote to Locke, the belief in the child's destiny as an unfolding natural phenomenon shared the assumption that children's growth revealed a progression of changes, for ill or good. A scientific basis for this conception was stimulated by Charles Darwin's *The Descent of Man* (1871), which spawned a generation of studies that sketched out parallels between the course of early human history and phases of the child's development. Nineteenth-century English philosopher Herbert Spencer added to this the notion of human progress.

Thus, the course of child study by the end of the 1800s was committed to charting the progressive appearance of cognitive, emotional, and motor functions in children from birth to adulthood. It is possible that novel theories of child development and new opportunities to observe the mass of children arranged in cohorts enabled both educators and the new discipline of psychology to formulate and test the idea of stages of child maturation precisely because children were now sorted in a way that made it possible to generalize about development with some accuracy for the first time.

Adolescence in Human Growth

The arrival of adolescence as a widely acknowledged stage in human growth signaled the successful linkage of ideas about aging and development current by the beginning of the twentieth century; and again it was schooling that provided this connection. For without schooling, the significance of adolescence would always be overshadowed by the imperatives of the family economy in working-class households. American educator and psychologist G. STANLEY HALL, who popularized the "discovery" of adolescence in 1904, when only 7 percent of all seventeen year olds graduated from high school, provided the rationale for this institutionalized cultural space in children's development. HIGH SCHOOL expanded exponentially thereafter: by 1940 almost half of all seventeen year olds earned diplomas nationally.

For the remainder of the century the nascent discipline of academic psychology vacillated on the question of whether nature or nurture is more important to children's development. Behaviorists such as American psychologist JOHN WATSON insisted on the critical place of environmental influence on children's development, while the rival view stressed the significance of biological and genetic blueprints for human maturation. American psychology for the first half of the twentieth century was Watsonian in orientation,

but this perspective was broken by the ascendance of Swiss psychologist JEAN PIAGET, who proposed a more synthetic interplay between genetic endowment and social environment.

Apart from this preoccupying (and ongoing) issue, however, two other trends arose: (1) The stages of development from birth through adolescence were divided and subdivided as specialization within the discipline proceeded; and (2) there was a tendency to privilege one stage of development over others as the "focal period." Infancy, middle childhood, and adolescence have been stressed variously as the periods of development that impart lasting critical effects on later outcomes for the individual. This line of inquiry led developmental psychologists to cast their eyes to later stages of human development and aging to try to untangle cause-and-effect relationships between stages of maturation.

Hall's disciples such as Frederic Thrasher connected observations of boys' development to justify the creation of a host of organizations ancillary to schooling, such as the PLAY-GROUND MOVEMENT, youth athletics, scouting, and other after-school activities to engage children and youths in adult-supervised settings. Child and youth recreational activities adopted the idea of age groupings as an article of faith in organizing athletic competition. It has been reflected in a wide range of activities, from New York's Police Athletic League early in the 1900s to the most popular participatory sport for boys, Little League Baseball, at midcentury. By the 1920s, athletic competition was commonplace in American high schools and they, too, arranged contestants into graduated ability and age groups, typically dividing them into junior varsity and varsity teams.

Progressive Education and Social Promotion

American educator and philosopher JOHN DEWEY and his followers promoted the idea of schooling as preparation for life. The purpose of education was not just to direct intellectual inquiry but to promote "desired social ends" as well (Cahan, p. 157). While the aims of Dewey's philosophy of PROGRESSIVE EDUCATION were varied and only ever implemented in a limited way, the idea of child development was a central feature and enabled school reformers to promote the extension of schooling for virtually all young people through the adolescent years by creating a curriculum that addressed their differentiated educational and social needs.

A by-product of this philosophy was the concept of "social promotion," which solidified the connections between the social and educative functions of schooling by more loosely aligning chronological age, achievement levels, and the cohort through secondary school. Social promotion legitimized promotion from one grade level to the next by demonstrating the positive social affects on child development as compared with the outcomes of promotion based on academic merit. By the early twentieth century the academic-merit system was seen as detrimental to both the educational and social needs of the individual. On the face of it, social promotion, which peaked as an educational policy during the 1970s, would seem to mitigate the heightened consciousness of age induced by age-grading, but it actually reinforced the perceived necessity for taut coordination between chronological age and cognitive and emotional development. The child's, and then adolescent's, concept of self had become so tightly bound up with the progress of his or her age cohort that developmental progress itself was seen as being fostered by keeping up socially if not educationally with one's cohort.

Assessing a Century of Change

Not coincidentally, sociologists and historians during the 1960s and 1970s began to trace the broader outlines of the normative movement from childhood to adulthood in American society. Inspired at least in part by the popular perception that young people were taking longer to come of age—that is, to assume the roles and responsibilities of adult status—they struck out to determine whether social norms involving transitions to adulthood had altered in the period between the mid-1800s and the mid-1900s. What they found was that the age at which the final transition to adulthood (family formation) occurred in the mid-twentieth century was roughly the same as it had been at the midpoint of the nineteenth century. However, the experience of coming of age—the turbulence one felt in moving from childhood to adulthood, especially in adolescence and the postadolescent years—was actually amplified by the rise of institutions to regulate these transitions. Studies by John Modell and others noted that the establishment of universal schooling during the mid-nineteenth century had created a roughly uniform starting line from which children entered and left school, entered the full-time work force, left their parents' household, married, and began their own families. Whereas before the late nineteenth century, a young person could occupy more than one of these states at the same time (i.e., be both at school and working, or working, married, and living in one's parents' household simultaneously), by the early to middle twentieth century, the transitions between them became much more tightly sequenced and separate. Widely observed age norms appeared to coordinate the individual's transition from childhood to adulthood, but the consequences for mixing these states had become (until the 1940s) detrimental to one's life chances. Marrying and remaining in one's parental household, for instance, had come to be regarded as unusual where it had once been an expected condition in agrarian societies in which the first-born male would eventually inherit the property of the household head. This was no longer the case when children were all schooled to the age of fourteen (sixteen by the 1930s) and began working until they could afford to establish their own households, marry, and procreate.

The Late Twentieth Century

By the 1950s, however, this sequencing of transitions began to get jumbled as marriage ages dropped in the wake of

World War II and schooling was extended past the age of sixteen, with larger numbers of young people entering and finishing college. To pay for higher education it was necessary for many college students to work while attending classes, and it was also not unusual for some students to start their own households, marry, and even begin bearing and raising children while enrolled in college. In short, by the 1960s and 1970s a once highly ordered set of transitions to adulthood overlapped extensively. This meant that, on one hand, individuals had wide latitude in the choices they could make about completing school, starting work, and getting married; on the other hand, they experienced greater anxiety both individually and socially about making and ordering these choices.

Since the 1970s several trends affecting the early life course were reversed: ages of first marriage for both women and men returned to their traditional averages, the middle twenties and late twenties, respectively; the average age of women at the birth of their first child increased; the birth rate plummeted; and a new trend, cohabitation, rose steadily during the last quarter of the century, suggesting that men and women no longer felt compelled to remain living with their parents immediately before establishing their own households and could defer both marriage and family formation. By the late twentieth century the early life course of women and men grew more similar. Where previously early life-course transitions were based on the assumption of a male breadwinner, male and female education levels evened out during the last quarter of the century, and wage gaps between them narrowed somewhat.

If the tightly sequenced, non-overlapping set of transitions to adulthood attested to a high degree of age consciousness at midcentury, did their unraveling intimate a loosening concern with age? Historians and social critics see mixed signs. On one hand there appears to be less age segregation than there was earlier in the century when, for instance, universities admitted few undergraduates over the ages of eighteen or nineteen. Increasingly older Americans have reentered the ranks of college students, and educational "retooling" in a rapidly changing economy has become a widely accepted practice for people who may change careers several times in their lives. It has also become more common for women to return to the workforce after bearing and rearing children. On the other hand, in the 1960s a YOUTH CULTURE flourished. It was fed by the expansion of higher education after World War II and the influx of the so-called BABY BOOM GENERATION into U.S. universities, which glorified youthfulness to an unprecedented degree. This preoccupation with the concerns of youth and images of youthfulness were intimately connected with consumer products for a mass audience for the first time and accompanied the abandonment of the previous generation's mortal fear of spending. This trend only gained momentum during the late twentieth century as this large cohort of people has aged, creating new markets for consumers—whether truly young or young at heart—to express their feelings of affiliation with the young.

See also: **Child Development, History of the Concept of; Child Psychology; Life Course and Transitions to Adulthood; Theories of Childhood.**

BIBLIOGRAPHY

Ariès, Philippe. 1962. *Centuries of Childhood: A Social History of Family Life.* Trans. Robert Baldick. New York: Vintage Books.

Cahan, Emily D. 1994. "John Dewey and Human Development." In *A Century of Developmental Psychology*, ed. Ross D. Parke, et. al. Washington, DC.: American Psychological Association.

Caldwell, John C. 1980. "Mass Education as a Determinant of the Timing of Fertility Decline." *Population and Development Review* 6 (June): 225–255.

Chudacoff, Howard P. 1989. *How Old Are You? Age Consciousness in American Culture.* Princeton, NJ: Princeton University Press.

Cole, Michael, and Sheila R. Cole. 2000. *The Development of Children*, 3rd ed. New York: Scientific American Books.

Covello, Leonard. 1967. *The Social Background of the Italo-American School Child: A Study of the Southern Italian Family Mores and their Effect on the School Situation in Italy and America.* Leiden, Netherlands: E. J. Brill.

Cunningham, Hugh. 1990. "The Employment and Unemployment of Children in England, c. 1680–1851." *Past and Present* 126 (February): 115–150.

Cunningham, Hugh. 1995. *Children and Childhood in Western Society since 1500.* New York: Longman.

Demos, John. 1970. *A Little Commonwealth: Family Life in Plymouth Colony.* New York: Oxford University Press.

Elder, Glen H. 1974. *Children of the Great Depression: Social Change in Life.* Chicago: University of Chicago Press.

Fass, Paula S. 1977. *The Damned and the Beautiful: American Youth in the 1920's.* New York: Oxford University Press.

Kessen, William, ed. 1965. *The Child.* New York: John Wiley and Sons.

Labaree, David F. 1997. *How to Succeed in School without Really Learning: The Credentials Race in American Education.* New Haven, CT: Yale University Press.

Lassonde, Stephen. 1996. "Learning and Earning: Schooling, Juvenile Employment, and the Early Life Course in Late Nineteenth-Century New Haven." *Journal of Social History* 29 (summer): 839–870.

Levine, David. 1987. *Reproducing Families: The Political Economy of English Population History.* New York: Cambridge University Press.

Modell, John. 1989. *Into One's Own: From Youth to Adulthood in the United States, 1920–1975.* Berkeley: University of California Press.

Modell, John, Frank F. Furstenberg, Jr., and Theodore Hershberg. 1981. "Social Change and Transitions to Adulthood in Historical Perspective." In *Philadelphia: Work, Space, and Group Experience in the 19th Century*, ed. Theodore Hershberg. New York: Oxford University Press.

Parke, Ross D., Peter A. Ornstein, John J. Rieser, et. al. 1994. "The Past as Prologue: An Overview of a Century of Developmental Psychology." In *A Century of Developmental Psychology*, ed. Ross D. Parke, et. al. Washington, DC: American Psychological Association.

Shahar, Shulamith. 1990. *Childhood in the Middle Ages.* New York: Routledge.

Vinovskis, Maris. 1995. "Historical Development of Age Stratification in Schooling." In his *Education, Society, and Economic Opportunity: A Historical Perspective on Persistent Issues.* New Haven, CT: Yale University Press.

Zelizer, Viviana A. 1985. *Pricing the Priceless Child: The Changing Social Value of Children.* New York: Basic Books.

STEPHEN LASSONDE

Age Grading. *See* Age and Development.

Age of Consent

Traditionally the age at which individuals could come together in a sexual union was something either for the family to decide or a matter of tribal custom. Probably in most cases this coincided with the onset of MENARCHE in girls and the appearance of pubic hair in boys, that is, between twelve and fourteen, but the boundaries remained fluid. In much of classical Greece this was true of both same- and opposite-sex relationships. In Republican Rome, marriage and the age of consent were initially private matters between the families involved. Not until the time of Augustus in the first century C.E. did the state begin to intervene. Marriage then legally became a two-step process, a betrothal which involved an enforceable agreement between the heads of two households, and then marriage itself. Women who were not yet of age could be betrothed with the consent of their fathers, but the woman herself had to consent to marriage.

The Roman tradition influenced peoples and cultures with whom it had come in contact. In the Islamic tradition following Muhammad, betrothal could take place earlier than PUBERTY, perhaps as early as seven, but the marriage was not supposed to be consummated until the girl menstruated and was of age. In medieval Europe, Gratian, the influential founder of Canon law in the twelfth century, accepted the traditional age of puberty for marriage (between 12 and 14) but he also said consent was "meaningful" if the children were older than seven. Some authorities said consent could take place earlier. Such a marriage would be permanent as long as neither party sought annulment before reaching puberty (12 for girls and 14 for boys) or if they had already consummated the marriage. Even if the husband had technically raped his wife before she reached puberty, the marriage was regarded as consummated. It was this policy which was carried over into English common law, and although consent was necessary, force and influence or persuasion seemed to have been permissible elements. Similarly Gratian's ideas about age became part of European civil law.

The age of consent in both English and continental law seemed to be particularly elastic when property was involved or family alliances were at stake. For example in 1564, a three year old named John was married to a two year old named Jane in the Bishop's Court in Chester, England. Though Shakespeare set his *Romeo and Juliet* in Verona, the fact that Juliet was thirteen probably reflects the reality in England. Her mother, who was twenty-six, calls her almost an old maid.

The American colonies followed the English tradition but the law could at best be called a guide. For example in Virginia in 1689, Mary Hathaway was only nine when she was married to William Williams. We know of her case only because two years later she sued for divorce, and was released from the covenant she had made because the marriage had not been consummated. Interestingly, historian Holly Brewer, who discovered the case, speculated that if William had raped Mary, she probably would not have been given the divorce. The only reliable data on age at marriage in England in the early modern period comes from Inquisitions Post Mortem which involved only those who died and left property. It appears that the more complete the records, the more likely it is to discover young marriages. Judges honored marriages based on mutual consent at age younger than seven, in spite of what Gratian had said, and there are recorded marriages of two and three year olds. The seventeenth-century lawyer Henry Swinburne distinguished between the marriages of those under seven and those between seven and puberty. He wrote that those under seven who had said their vows had to ratify it afterwards by giving kisses and embraces, by lying together, by exchanging gifts or tokens, or by calling each other husband or wife. A contemporary, Philip Stubbes, wrote that in sixteenth-century East Anglia, infants still in swaddling clothes were married. The most influential legal text of the seventeenth century in England, that of Sir Edward Coke, made it clear that the marriage of girls under twelve was normal, and the age at which a girl who was a wife was eligible for a dower from her husband's estate was nine even though her husband be only four years old.

The age of consent was more variable than a summary of the law seems to imply. Peter Laslett, for example, used available statistics to argue marriage and child bearing in the late teens was not common in England and marriage at twelve was virtually unknown. The problem is that his statistics might well be skewed because in England only a small portion of marriages were registered, and even on these registrations it is difficult to tell if they recorded first or second or later marriages. A second marriage by a man in his late fifties or a woman in her early thirties skews the data. Not all marriage records even bother to record the participants' ages. Unrecorded are marriages without parental consent and private weddings and the quality of data varies from region to region. For example in the parish of Middlesex County, Virginia, there is a record of fourteen-year-old Sarah Halfhide marrying twenty-one-year-old Richard Perrot. Only in the last sentence of the register does it indicate that she was a widow. Did the compiler read that far? We

simply do not know what her age at first marriage was, or even if it had been consummated. Of the ninety-eight girls on the ten-year register, three probably married at age eight, one at twelve, one at thirteen, and two at fourteen. Historians in the twentieth and twenty-first centuries have sometimes been reluctant to accept data regarding young ages of marriage, holding instead that the recorded age was a misreading by a later copier of the records. Natalie Davis, whose book *The Return of Martin Guerre* became a movie, made her heroine, Bertrande, much older than the nine- to ten-year-old girl she was when she married her missing husband.

In the nineteenth century France issued the Napoleonic Code and many other countries, following France's example, began revising their laws. The Napoleonic Code, however, had not changed the age of consent, which remained at thirteen. When historian Magnus Hirschfeld surveyed the age of consent of some fifty countries (mostly in Europe and the Americas) at the beginning of the twentieth century, the age of consent was twelve in fifteen countries, thirteen in seven, fourteen in five, fifteen in four, and sixteen in five. In the remaining countries it remained unclear. In England and the United States, feminist agitation in the late nineteenth century called attention to the young age of consent and called for changes in the law. By the 1920s the age of consent, a state issue in the United States, was raised in every state and ranged from fourteen to eighteen, with most states settling on sixteen or eighteen.

In the last part of the twentieth century the U.S. public once again took note of age of consent issues. Although sometimes it is not possible to identify a single age of consent since the statutory age varies with the age of the defendant and with the particular sexual activity, in the United States as of 2000 the age at which a person may engage in any sexual conduct permitted to adults within a particular state ranges between fourteen to eighteen. In the vast majority of states the age is either fifteen or sixteen. Most states set the minimum age for marriage without parental approval at eighteen, and there are elaborate provisions governing which parent must give consent and who qualifies as a custodial parent or guardian when marriage under eighteen takes place. There are occasional contradictions since some states will allow a minor to marry with parental permission at an age when the minor cannot engage in legal sexual activity, while others allow a minor to engage in sexual activity years before he or she can marry without parental approval.

See also: **Bundling; Dating; Sexuality.**

BIBLIOGRAPHY

Amundsen, D.W., and C. J. Diers. 1969. "The Age of Menarche in Classical Greece and Rome." *Human Biology* 41: 125–132.

Balsdon, J. P. V. D. 1962. *Roman Women: Their History and Habits.* London: The Bodley Head.

Brundage, James. 1987. *Law, Sex, and Society in Christian Europe.* Chicago: University of Chicago Press.

Bullough, Vern L. 1976. *Sexual Variance in Society and History*. Chicago: University of Chicago Press.

Bullough, Vern L. 1981. "Age at Menarche: A Misunderstanding." *Science* 213: 365–366.

Coke, Edward. 1719. *The First Part of the Institutes of the Laws of England*, 11th edition. London.

Davis, Natalie. 1983. *The Return of Martin Guerre*. Cambridge, MA: Harvard University Press.

Friedlander, L. 1913. *Roman Life and Manners Under the Early Empire*. London: Gough.

Furnivall, Frederick J. 1897. *Child Marriages, Divorces, and Ratification in the Diocese of Chester, A.D. 1561–6*. London: Early English Text Society.

Hirschfeld, Magnus. 2000. *The Homosexuality of Men and Women*. Trans. Michael Lombardi-Nash. Buffalo, NY: Prometheus Books.

Lacey, W. K. 1968. *The Family in Classical Greece*. Ithaca, NY: Cornell University Press.

Laslett, Peter. 1984. *The World We Have Lost: Further Explored*. New York: Scribner.

Percy, William A. 1996. *Pederasty and Pedagogy in Archaic Greece*. Urbana: University of Illinois Press.

Posner, Richard A. and Katharine B. Silbaugh. 1996. *A Guide to America's Sex Laws*. Chicago: University of Chicago Press.

Post, G.B. 1974. "Another Demographic Use of Inquisitions Post Mortem." *Journal of the Society of Archivists* 5: 110–114.

Stubbes, Philip. 1965 [1583]. *Anatomie of Abuses in Ailgna [Anglia]*. Vaduz: Kraus Reprint.

Westermarck, Edward. 1922. *The History of Human Marriage*, 5th edition. 3 vols. New York: Allerton.

VERN L. BULLOUGH

Aggression. *See* Anger and Aggression.

AIDS

AIDS (Acquired Immune Deficiency Syndrome) is the final stage of a lethal infectious disease, beginning with an infection caused by a virus and progressing to a serious and severe damage to the body's immune system. Infection occurs when the virus integrates with the genetic material of a CD4 white blood cell in the immune system. AIDS was first reported on June 5, 1981, in the United States.

The Human Immunodeficiency Virus (HIV), which is the cause of AIDS, attacks key cells in the human immune system and destroys them. This leaves the body exposed to life-threatening infections, specific cancers, and other illnesses. HIV is a latent virus. People infected by it may have no symptoms for many years, while their immune system weakens until they develop AIDS. The first pediatric AIDS cases were reported in San Francisco in 1982.

A laboratory test counting less than 200/ml CD4 white blood cells is the method used by the U.S. Centers for Disease Control to define AIDS. HIV/AIDS is now a chronic and treatable, but not yet curable, disease. Almost all people infected with HIV will progress to AIDS.

Persons who are carriers of HIV may transmit the virus to others, even in the symptom-free period. However, HIV does not spread as easily as many other pathogens (such as those causing tuberculosis or influenza). The virus can be transmitted from an infected individual to others only through four bodily fluids: blood, semen, breast milk, and vaginal secretions. Worldwide, women are infected more frequently than men.

Transmission of HIV is possible when:

Having unprotected anal, vaginal or oral sexual contact with an infected individual. Sexual intercourse is the most common route for HIV transmission from an infected to a noninfected person; 50 percent of cases are youths between fifteen and twenty-four years old.

Through transfusions of blood and blood products (now extremely rare in the United States and other developed countries), needle sharing (e.g., drug use, medical care in developing countries, piercing or tattooing).

Mother-to-child transmission from a pregnant woman to her fetus, via the placenta, at birth or when breast feeding the infant; the most common cause of HIV infection in young children.

Rare circumstances such as accidental needle or laboratory injuries, artificial insemination or through organ donations.

HIV infection is not spread by air, water or by casual contacts, donating blood or organs (in developed countries where sterilized equipment is used), mosquito bites, or during participation in sports.

HIV/AIDS is a public health, social, developmental, and serious humanitarian crisis in many regions of the world. The total number of people infected by HIV from the start of the epidemic was estimated in 2003 to be 60 million. During 2002 alone eight hundred thousand children younger than 15 years old were infected, at a rate of about two thousand per day.

The most affected region is sub-Saharan AFRICA, followed by Asia, LATIN AMERICA, and EASTERN EUROPE. By the year 2010 it is expected that 20 million of the 42 million ORPHANS in Africa will have lost one or both parents due to AIDS. AIDS has led to a dramatic decline in life expectancy in Africa.

Complex biological, psychological, and sociological factors put young people at greater risk for HIV infection. As a result, efforts to prevent infections are focused on this population, with distinctions between in-school, out-of-school and high-risk youth. Curricula, multimedia initiatives, mass media campaigns, games, and role modeling are just a few of the strategies to promote knowledge and skills for HIV/AIDS prevention worldwide. The key prevention messages focus on eliminating or reducing risks for infection by practicing safe behaviors:

Abstaining from sexual intercourse. (Abstinence is the only way to fully prevent sexual transmission of HIV.)

Reducing the number of sexual partners, delaying the initiation of penetrative sex, and correctly using a condom for intercourse in every case where the HIV status of one of the individuals is unknown reduces the risk of infection.

Avoiding any injection of drugs.

Using one-time, nonshared, sterile needle and syringe for injection of medications, blood transfusions or drugs.

For mothers who are HIV-positive, avoiding breast-feeding their infants.

Avoiding direct contact with blood where the HIV status of the bleeding individual is unknown.

Undergoing an HIV test, to determine one's and one's partners' HIV status.

Mother-to-child infection is preventable in most cases by administering medications to the mother before birth and to the infant after birth.

Children with AIDS were able to mobilize enormous public support and attention since the first days of the epidemic. For example, Ryan White (1971–1990) was a hero in his determination to fight both AIDS and AIDS-related discrimination at school. A federal legislation in the United States that addresses the unmet health needs of persons living with HIV was named after him. Nkosi Johnson (1989–2001), South Africa's longest surviving child born with HIV, captured the hearts of thousands when he spoke of his experiences with HIV/AIDS. Ariel and Jake Glaser and their mother, Elizabeth, all infected with HIV, gave rise in 1988 to the Pediatric AIDS Foundation in the United States.

The UN General Assembly Session on HIV/AIDS decided in June 2001 to ensure a massive reduction in HIV's prevalence and a dramatic increase in access of youth education and youth-specific services necessary to reduce their vulnerability to HIV infection globally by 2010.

See also: **Contagious Diseases; Epidemics.**

BIBLIOGRAPHY

Mann, J., D. Tarantola, and T. Netter. 1992. *AIDS in the World.* Cambridge, MA: Harvard University Press.

Schenker, Inon. 2001. "New Challenges for School AIDS Education within an Evolving HIV Pandemic." *Prospects* 31, no 3: 415–434.

Schenker, Inon, G. Sabar-Friedman, and S. S. Sy. 1996. *AIDS Education—Interventions in Multi-Cultural Societies.* New York: Plenum Press.

World Bank. 2002. *Education and HIV/AIDS: A Window of Hope.* Washington, DC: World Bank.

INTERNET RESOURCES

Centers for Disease Control. "Division of HIV/AIDS Prevention." Available from <www.cdc.gov/hiv/dhap.htm>.

Elizabeth Glaser Pediatric AIDS Foundation. Available from <www.pedaids.org>.

Joint United Nations Program on HIV/AIDS. Available from <www.unaids.org>.

The Body. "An AIDS and HIV Information Resource." Available from <www.thebody.com>.

INON I. SCHENKER

Aid to Dependent Children (AFDC)

Aid to Dependent Children (ADC), which the U.S. Congress enacted on August 14, 1935, as part of the Social Security Act of 1935, began as a program limited to dependent children under sixteen who had lost one or both parents, an outgrowth of the underfunded widows' pensions numerous states enacted after 1911. The assistance was cash only. For every two dollars a state provided, the federal government gave one. States mostly set the eligibility rules, and in those states contributing little, difficulties abounded. Even though ADC enrolled double the children in 1939 that it had initially, it never covered more than one-third of the eligible children—and no adults. Because the aged needy had more leverage in Congress than did dependent children, a mother and her child in 1940 received $18 a month, while the elderly needy won $30 a month as individuals. In any event, recipients received very small sums. Until 1950 ADC offered nothing for the caregiver, only the children, forcing many mothers out of the home into the low wage job market. Many states penalized "absent fathers" and mixed moral and economic criteria for ADC. Regional differences in payments and regulations varied widely. Racists, conservatives, and low wage employers manipulated the rules in their favor—and exploited the poor—in many states.

Vastly increased federal spending in the 1940s and 1950s generated enough prosperity to make poverty (apparently) disappear, and to encourage massive movements of peoples of all classes and races around the country, and from farm to city or suburb. By the 1960s ADC and other programs ballooned, and ADC became AFDC, Aid to Families with Dependent Children, with caregivers' stipends added. In 1960 AFDC was the largest federal welfare program, with 3,000,000 enrollees. Even so, only a sixth of those eligible were enrolled in 1960, whereas a third had been in 1939. Support averaged $30 monthly for one dependent or $115 per family in 1960. Well into the early 1970s, the rolls grew at a dizzying pace, due to the growing impoverishment of the lower classes. The age's egalitarianism and individualism encouraged the poor to demand welfare as a right, not merely a privilege, and this, combined with racial tensions, and the growing new conservative movement, led to increasingly fractious criticisms of AFDC. By the early 1990s, AFDC, and the compassionate welfare vision of an earlier era, was increasingly politically out of step with the times. The WELFARE REFORM ACT OF 1996 ended AFDC.

See also: **Great Depression and New Deal; Sheppard-Towner Maternity and Infancy Act; Social Welfare.**

BIBLIOGRAPHY

Altmeyer, Arthur J. 1968. *The Formative Years of Social Security. A Chronicle of Social Security Legislation and Administration, 1934–1954.* Madison: University of Wisconsin Press.

Commager, Henry Steele, ed. 1948. *Documents in American History,* 4th ed. 2 vols. New York: Appleton-Century-Crofts.

Patterson, James T. 1985. *America's Struggle Against Poverty 1900–1980.* Cambridge, MA: Harvard University Press.

HAMILTON CRAVENS

Alcohol. *See* Teen Drinking.

Alcott, Bronson (1799–1888)

Born November 29, 1799, in Wolcott, Connecticut, Amos Bronson Alcott (known as Bronson) was an educator, author, child psychologist, reformer, self-styled conversationalist, lecturer, and transcendental philosopher. He formulated an innovative approach to education and revised traditional assumptions about childhood. However, Alcott's strongest legacy is the formative impressions he made on his better-remembered daughter, Louisa May Alcott, and his many friends, including Ralph Waldo Emerson, Nathaniel Hawthorne, and Elizabeth Palmer Peabody. Often characterized by historians as a dreamy, vague, ineffectual man, Alcott's greatest crime may have been poor writing. Although he was a great conversationalist and public speaker, his intimate companions proved more able to communicate his principles in writing.

Alcott grew up in rural poverty; his schooling began with charcoal letters on the floor and formally ended at age thirteen. Afterward he found employment as a peddler and journeyed to the South before returning to Connecticut to work as a schoolteacher in 1823. His early educational innovations included beautifying the schoolroom with pictures and tree branches, adding physical exercise to intellectual exertions,

and developing his students' reasoning capacities rather than their memorization skills. Alcott found support in the educational reforms proposed by JOHANN PESTALOZZI in Switzerland and Robert Owen in England. Yet his ideas were not well received by local parents, who withdrew their students from his school, forcing him into itinerant teaching after 1827.

In 1830 Alcott married Abigail May, the reform-minded daughter of a socially prominent New England family. At the birth of their first daughter, Anna, in 1831, Alcott started a journal of infant observation. He continued his scrutiny of Anna and her younger sisters for five years, filling over fifty journals. He concluded that children were born with intuitive wisdom and the potential for good; it was the responsibility of parents and educators to elicit children's innate morality and to develop their self-knowledge, self-control, and self-reliance. Alcott's effort to understand child development have earned him a reputation as the first child psychologist.

To put his philosophy into practice, Alcott opened the Temple School in Boston in 1834. The Unitarian minister William Ellery Channing supported the project and persuaded many elite families to enroll their children. Elizabeth Palmer Peabody, who later founded the American KINDERGARTEN movement, assisted. Alcott tried to elicit his students' inner wisdom through silent study, physical exercise, journal writing, and Socratic conversations. He limited corporal punishment; nonetheless, he was a stern disciplinarian, working on his students' consciences rather than their fears—twice he even had students hit him to evoke their contrition. His school was initially popular, but when Alcott published his *Conversations with Children on the Gospels* (1836–1837), many were shocked by his unconventional approach to religion and withdrew their children from his classroom. His admission of a black student the following year lost Alcott the remaining pupils, and the school failed.

In 1840 Alcott moved to Concord to be close to his friends Emerson and Hawthorne. He engaged in many projects before his death in 1888, but few were successful. Alcott's utopian community Fruitlands (1843–1844) attracted many visitors but quickly fell apart. His books had few readers, although his speaking tours were popular. He depended on his wife and daughters for economic support, especially after the success of Louisa May Alcott's *Little Women* (1868), the text that best captures his ideas.

See also: **Child Development, History of the Concept of; Little Women and Louisa May Alcott.**

BIBLIOGRAPHY

Dahlstrand, Frederick C. 1982. *Amos Bronson Alcott, an Intellectual Biography.* Rutherford, NJ: Fairleigh Dickinson University Press.

McCuskey, Dorothy. 1940. *Bronson Alcott: Teacher.* New York: Macmillan.

Strickland, Charles. 1969. "A Transcendentalist Father: The Child-rearing Practices of Bronson Alcott." *Perspectives in American History* 3: 5–73.

RACHEL HOPE CLEVES

Alcott, Louisa May. *See* Little Women and Louisa May Alcott.

Allowances

The practice of giving children allowances developed in the early twentieth century when children's purchases of MOVIE tickets, candy, and TOYS raised concerns about their spending habits. During the Progressive Era (1890s–1920s), allowance advocates recommended giving children a regular but fixed supply of money to inculcate respect for money. Though not the first to advocate allowances—Lydia Maria Child had endorsed allowances to encourage benevolence and fiscal responsibility as early as 1831—Progressive-era child-rearing authorities joined a much larger chorus calling for new money training regimes in women's magazines and parental advice literature.

Allowance proponents believed that lessons in wise spending taught fiscal restraint better than habitual saving. This put them at odds with traditional thrift advocates who valorized saving as a virtue in itself and favored school savings bank programs that made compulsory saving part of the public school curriculum. Nevertheless, allowance proponents and school savings bank enthusiasts both embraced principles of scientific management and behaviorist child rearing that emphasized the importance of system, regularity, and routine to habit formation. Just as advocates of scientific mothering sought to rationalize infants' habits of feeding, sleeping, and toileting, allowance proponents sought to rationalize children's economic habits.

During the 1920s and 1930s, the public culture of DATING and mass recreation intensified family conflicts over spending. Middle-class families faced stepped up demands for spending money, while working-class families found it more difficult to claim their children's wages without granting them a greater share of their own earnings. Child-rearing authorities promoted allowances as a means of modernizing and democratizing the family. Allowances were children's entitlement to their share of the family's resources and psychological compensation for their prolonged dependency.

Viewing allowances as a strictly educational tool, child-rearing authorities criticized using allowance money as a payment for household chores, a reward for good behavior, or a punishment for delinquencies. Doing so, they argued, confounded principles of duty and family obligation with the principles of the marketplace. In place of parental surveillance and parental admonitions, child-rearing experts advised giving children responsibility for their own spending choices as well as their spending mistakes. Granting children such autonomy, they argued, helped children to improve their taste and develop habits of saving as they learned to forgo candy and cheap trinkets in order to purchase more expensive goods. This was in keeping with JOHN DEWEY's idea that education should be molded to the individual child. These child-centered means served adult-approved ends as children learned to spend wisely within a budget.

Allowances continued to garner support during the Great Depression, partly as a means to moderate children's demands on limited family resources, but also because spending itself came to be seen as vital to economic recovery and emotional well-being. Children's consumer desires were now evidence of a well-adjusted personality and excessive thriftiness a sign of a lackluster imagination.

Statistics suggest that parents increasingly used allowances to allocate family resources. According to a 1936 survey, nearly 50 percent of children from professional families received allowances—an impressive increase over the single-digit percentages that typically prevailed at the turn of the twentieth century—while 28 percent of "semi-skilled" workers and 12 percent of "slightly skilled" workers gave their children allowances. The rising standard of living in postwar America made children's allowances both more common and more generous. Allowance rates climbed substantially after 1960, when a *Seventeen* magazine survey indicated that the average teenage girl had a weekly income of $9.53. A 1999 Rand Youth Poll found that the typical weekly allowance for thirteen to fifteen year olds ranged from $30.50 to $34.25.

Although children's economic clout has risen dramatically, the case for allowances has changed little since the GREAT DEPRESSION. Child experts continue to argue that children with allowances learn fiscal restraint while children without master only how to manipulate family breadwinners. It is not clear how much parents are themselves guided by expert opinion. Though an educational tool in theory, children's allowances are commonly viewed as an economic entitlement—a sign that twenty-first-century American children perhaps owe their spending power more to the tenets of family democracy than to concerns about inculcating wise spending.

See also: **Child-Rearing Advice Literature; Consumer Culture.**

BIBLIOGRAPHY

Benson, Susan Porter. 1998. "Gender, Generation, and Consumption in the United States: Working-Class Families in the Interwar Period." In *Getting and Spending: European and American Consumer Societies in the Twentieth Century*, ed. Susan Strasser, Charles McGovern, and Matthias Judt. New York: Cambridge University Press.

Jacobson, Lisa. 2003 *Raising Consumers: Children, Childrearing, and the American Mass Market in the Early Twentieth Century.* New York: Columbia University Press.

White House Conference on Child Health and Protection. 1936. *The Young Child in the Home: A Survey of Three Thousand American Families.* New York: D. Appleton-Century Company.

Zelizer, Viviana. 1985. *Pricing the Priceless Child: The Changing Social Value of Children.* New York: Basic Books.

LISA JACOBSON

American Indian Schools

"You have no education," declared Capt. Richard H. Pratt, founder of the famous Indian Industrial School at Carlisle, Pennsylvania, to a group of Lakota Sioux in 1879 (p. 222). Like generations of white Americans before and after him, this dedicated but ethnocentric educator assumed that because tribal peoples did not educate their children within the four walls of a school building, they were uneducated. Yet education was highly institutionalized in traditional Indian societies. Family members, especially older people such as grandfathers and grandmothers, along with specialists in economic activities, warfare, art, and spiritual matters *systematically* educated boys and girls into responsible tribal adulthood.

Unable to see such apparently unstructured activities as education, from colonial times until well into the twentieth century, European Americans set out to Christianize and "civilize" Indian peoples through the schooling of their children. The term *Indian schools* thus generally refers to establishments designed specifically for tribal boys and girls. "The Apostle of the Indians," seventeenth century Puritan missionary John Eliot, for example, established fourteen "praying towns" in New England. Schools were central to his mission. Initially quarantined from their supposedly deficient family backgrounds, pupils would first be saved themselves, and would then return as cultural brokers—mediators—to carry the Gospel and English culture back to their peoples.

The U.S. government continued this crusade. Employing the "Civilization Fund" of (initially) $10,000 provided by Congress in 1819, the new Office/Bureau of Indian Affairs (BIA) worked alongside missionaries throughout the nineteenth century. Many treaties provided funds in exchange for surrendered lands, and Indian peoples often willingly utilized such money to help sustain schools, becoming active participants in this enterprise. By 1824 there were thirty-two BIA-sanctioned missionary schools among the tribes, enrolling almost 1,000 children. As the decades passed the BIA increasingly came to dominate the campaign. By around 1900 the vast majority of the 20,000 school-going Native Americans attended a government day school, on-reservation or off-reservation boarding school. Some of the latter schools, such as Carlisle, in Pennsylvania, had become beacons of civ-

These Native American students are pictured with their teachers, c. 1900, most likely at the Indian school at Carlisle, Pennsylvania. Although the treatment of students at these schools could be harsh, many students came to identify with the institutions and considered them "our schools." © CORBIS.

ilization, at any one time enrolling hundreds of pupils from tens of different tribes. Most of these boys and girls traveled great distances from their homes to a deep immersion experience. Some lived years at the school in the midst of a white community, without a single return home, and spent part of each summer "outing"—working for—white American families or businesses.

Early in the twentieth century more and more Indian children began to attend state public schools, often with government support. But the BIA campaign also continued, and by 1930 almost 38,000 tribal children attended government Indian schools; with a slightly larger number enrolling in public schools. By then almost all tribal children of school-going age were enrolled in some kind of school. This gradual transfer of Indians from BIA to state public schools has continued throughout the twentieth century. In the year 2002 90 percent of tribal children attended public schools with children of other ethnic groups. Most of the remaining ten percent attended the surviving Indian schools: many were tribal-controlled, often run by their own peoples on BIA grants or contracts. Older Indians attended postsecondary institutes such as the Southwestern Indian Polytechnic Institute (SIPI) in Albuquerque, New Mexico. In addition there were twenty-five tribally controlled community colleges by 2003. Tens of thousands of Indian men and women attended a variety of white American colleges and universities.

In 2003 Indian peoples had vastly more control over the running of specifically Indian schools than in 1903. Yet numbering only around two million in a population of 280 million, they were still at the mercy of majority politics and fashions. A federal government-to-tribal government relationship, grounded in the Constitution, treaties, legislation, and court decisions, still forms the basis of federal responsibility for support of Indian schooling. (The making of treaties with Indian peoples ended in 1871 but ratified treaties remain part of federal law.) Native Americans must constantly struggle, however, to maintain adequate local control over the education of their young people, while simultaneously holding the United States to its historical legal and financial responsibilities.

Indian schools themselves experienced massive changes throughout the twentieth century and into the twenty-first century. Now the BIA cooperates in helping Indian peoples teach both traditional and dominant cultural values, thus contributing to tribal sovereignty and self-determination. It was not always so. Until the 1930s, when, influenced by the PROGRESSIVE EDUCATION movement and the new academic anthropology, a more culturally tolerant approach began in the BIA, the curriculum at government and missionary Indian schools was rigidly ethnocentric. Almost nothing relating to tribal spiritual and cultural values was taught, although some traditional arts and crafts occasionally made the curriculum in the early twentieth century. Instruction at BIA and many missionary schools was *through English*, even for children totally ignorant of the language—producing greater bewilderment in the already disorientated beginner. The "half-and-half" curriculum at Indian schools mixed vocational training supposedly appropriate to the sexes (such as farming for boys, and kitchen work for girls) with forms of academic instruction. Pupils at small schools hardly got much beyond the "three R's," along with a fourth: some form of (Christian) religion. At schools like Carlisle, the curriculum was often as good as that provided for many white children. In addition, big schools encouraged a multitude of extracurricular activities such as football, theater and debating clubs, along with student-produced newspapers (vetted by school authorities, of course). Whether broad or narrow, the goal of this curriculum was to detribalize Indians and turn them into Christian citizens, indistinguishable in anything but skin color from other Americans. BIA education, wrote Commissioner of Indian Affairs William A. Jones in 1903, would "exterminate the Indian but develop a man" (quoted in Coleman, p. 46).

One might expect that ex-pupils who attended Indian schools during the era of assimilation, especially those living in the ethnically conscious later twentieth and early twenty-first centuries, would have decried a system exhibiting such contempt for their own cultural heritage. From letters, reminiscences, interviews, and autobiographies, however, it emerges that children responded in many different ways to this schooling. Even the same individual might express strong ambivalence. Large numbers fled the schools (as runaways); far too many sickened or died at them. Even larger numbers suffered, accommodated, resisted, and used the schools to their own advantage. Perhaps surprisingly, many ex-students left positive recollections of their schooling, even at institutions where corporal and other kinds of punishment were frequently used. Gifted children, especially, and those who quickly learned the language of instruction, sometimes thrilled to the new learning. Although some Indian kinfolk strongly opposed schooling, others saw its advantages for family and group. Thus many children began school with the pragmatic words of tribal adults ringing in their ears: to survive in the modern world, the people need English and the skills of the white man. Learn!

And many did. A combination of factors beyond kin encouragement combined to help tens of thousands of Indian children survive and sometimes thrive in an alien educational environment. The resilience and inventive coping strategies of individual boys and girls, along with the mutually helpful support of peers were crucial. At large schools pupil subcultures developed, with their own rules, rituals, and slang; these helped pupils adapt while allowing a degree of enjoyable resistance to authorities. The sensitivity of gifted teachers must also be acknowledged (although other teachers were harsh or even brutal).

Although tribal identities survived, the Indian schools did achieve a high degree of success by their own assimilationist criteria. For over a century large numbers of children attended, learned English, accepted the alien curriculum (even in retrospect, few adult autobiographers expressed resentment about its content), returned to their peoples, and passed into life on or off the reservation as American citizens of tribal origin. Some consequences were less acceptable from a government perspective. By bringing children from different tribes together the schools probably stimulated pan-Indian identification. Ex-students also used their schooling to resist white encroachments, employing the English language, modern media, American politics and law in defense of tribal rights. In diverse and sometimes unexpected ways, then, these schools did help tribal peoples survive the onslaught of European-American civilization.

Many Indians came to strongly identify with their institutions, and when the BIA closed old boarding schools in the later twentieth century, Indians sometimes agitated to keep them open. For many they had by then become "our schools," and some still exist in the early twenty-first century in different forms, with strong local Indian support. Haskell

Boarding School in Lawrence, Kansas, for example, became the Haskell Indian Nations University (HINU). "Critics dismiss boarding schools as assimilationist institutions whose intent was to destroy Native culture," writes Esther Burnett Horne, a woman of part-Shoshone ancestry who was both a student and a highly accomplished teacher at a number of Indian schools throughout the twentieth century. "While this may be a true generalization, the students and teachers at Haskell will forever be an integral part of who I am as an American Indian." (Horne and McBeth, p. 53).

See also: **Native American Children.**

BIBLIOGRAPHY

Adams, David Wallace. 1995. *Education for Extinction: American Indians and the Boarding School Experience, 1875–1928.* Lawrence: University Press of Kansas.

Bloom, John. 2000. *To Show What an Indian Can Do: Sports at Native American Boarding Schools.* Minneapolis: University of Minnesota Press.

Child, Brenda J. 1998. *Boarding School Seasons: American Indian Families, 1900–1940.* Lincoln: University of Nebraska Press.

Cogley, Richard W. 1999. *John Eliot's Mission to the Indians Before King Philip's War.* Cambridge, MA: Harvard University Press.

Coleman, Michael C. 1993. *American Indian Children at School, 1850–1930.* Jackson: University Press of Mississippi.

DeJong, David H. 1993. *Promises of the Past: A History of Indian Education in the United States.* Golden, CO: North American Press.

Eastman, Charles A. (Ohiyesa). 1977 [1916]. *From the Deep Woods to Civilization: Chapters in the Autobiography of an Indian.* Lincoln: University of Nebraska Press.

Ellis, Clyde. 1996. *To Change Them Forever: Indian Education at the Rainy Mountain Boarding School, 1893–1920.* Norman: University of Oklahoma Press.

Haig-Brown, Celia. 1988. *Resistance and Renewal: Surviving the Indian Residential School.* Vancouver, BC: Tillacum Library.

Holt, Marilyn Irvin. 2001. *Indian Orphanages.* Lawrence: University Press of Kansas.

Horne, Esther B., and Sally McBeth. 1998. *Essie's Story: The Life and Legacy of a Shoshone Teacher.* Lincoln: University of Nebraska Press.

Hoxie, Frederick E. 2002. *A Final Promise: The Campaign to Assimilate the Indians, 1880–1920.* Lincoln: University of Nebraska Press.

La Flesche, Francis. 1963 [1900]. *The Middle Five: Indian Schoolboys of the Omaha Tribe.* Madison: University of Wisconsin Press.

Lomawaima, K. Tsianina. 1994. *They Called it Prairie Light: The Story of Chilocco Indian School.* Lincoln: University of Nebraska Press.

Lomawaima, K. Tsianina. 2002. "American Indian Education: By Indians Versus For Indians." In *A Companion to American Indian History,* ed. Philip J. Deloria and Neal Salisbury, 422–440. Malden, MA: Blackwell.

McBeth, Sally J. 1983. *Ethnic Identity and the Boarding School Experience of West-Central Oklahoma American Indians.* Lanham, MD: University Press of America.

Mihesuah, Devon. 1993. *Cultivating the Rosebuds: The Education of Women at the Cherokee Female Seminary, 1851–1909.* Urbana: University of Illinois Press.

Miller, J. R. 1996. *Shingwauk's Vision: A History of Native Residential Schools.* Toronto: University of Toronto Press.

Pratt, Richard Henry. 1964. *Battlefield and Classroom: Four Decades with the American Indian, 1867–1904.* Ed. Robert M. Utley. Lincoln: University of Nebraska Press.

Prucha, Francis P. 1979. *The Churches and Indian Schools, 1888–1912.* Lincoln: University of Nebraska Press.

Prucha, Francis Paul. 1994. *American Indian Treaties: The History of a Political Anomoly.* Berkeley: University of California Press.

Riney, Scott. 1999. *The Rapid City Indian School, 1898–1933.* Norman: University of Oklahoma Press.

Sekaquaptewa, Helen. 1969. *Me and Mine: The Life Story of Helen Sekaquaptewa. As Told to Louis Udall.* Tucson: University of Arizona Press.

Standing Bear, Luther. 1975 [1928]. *My People the Sioux.* Ed. E. A. Brininstool. Lincoln: University of Nebraska Press.

Szasz, Margaret Connell. 1988. *Indian Education in the American Colonies, 1607–1783.* Albuquerque: University of New Mexico Press.

Szasz, Margaret Connell. 1999. *Education and the American Indian: The Road to Self-Determination Since 1928,* rev. ed. Albuquerque: University of New Mexico Press.

INTERNET RESOURCE

Office of Indian Education Programs (BIA). 2002. "Fingertip Facts." Available from <www.oiep.bia.edu/docs/finger~1.pdf>.

MICHAEL C. COLEMAN

Amusement Parks. *See* Theme Parks.

Ancient Greece and Rome

OVERVIEW
Elise P. Garrison

SELF-FORMATION
Susanna Elm

OVERVIEW

Some contemporary scholarship suggests that adults held children in the Greco-Roman world in small regard, that childhood was simply a period of waiting to grow up, and that what we know today as ADOLESCENCE was unknown in the ancient world. Others argue that the way children were represented in the literary and material arts in ancient times illustrates the LOVE and pride in which family and community held them. In addition, the careful structure society placed on the stages of childhood in this ancient culture, demarcated by very distinct rituals, indicates how much emphasis adults placed on the progress of their children. The clear distinction between childhood and adulthood was felt in all aspects of Greco-Roman society: domestic, civic, sociopolitical, legal, personal, and ritual.

General Considerations and Source Limitations

Typical Greek city-states (*poleis*) shared the values of freedom, competition, individualism, law, commerce, and the use of slaves, and all city-states worshipped the same Olympian gods. Athens and Sparta are two typical city-states, but they each have a uniqueness that makes them of interest, both separately and in conjunction. The majority of ancient written sources that present views or images of children are primarily written by men in classical Athens (fifth to fourth centuries B.C.E.), and none of the sources present evidence for the everyday life of a child or come from the children themselves. Of equal note is the fact that the ancient sources present cultural values on the one hand and social norms on the other. Cultural values are ambiguous. For example, the representation of children in tragedy, though meager, shows the loving care devoted to them by their nurses, tutors, or parents, while the philosophers present a less attractive picture. For PLATO, children belong with women, slaves, and animals, and as animals stand in relation to humans, so too do children to adults. ARISTOTLE likened the physical appearance of boys to women, and also considered them physically weak, morally incompetent, and mentally incapable. He believed that children knew little and were gullible and easily persuaded. The norms, however, are well articulated and unambiguous. For example, a male infant must be accepted into his family through a specific set of ritualistic steps.

In Rome, because of the extent of the power (*patriae potestas*) of the male head of the household (*paterfamilias*), children had few if any rights throughout the Roman Republic and Empire, and surprisingly little attention has been paid to children per se in contemporary scholarship. Most research focuses on the family (which in Rome includes not only the natal family, but also the conjugal, extended, and foster family and slaves) and genealogies and relationships within the family, and scholars have focused on the rich literary evidence supplemented by ample funerary inscriptional evidence. Recent new scholarship on the iconography of children has added a dimension that allows for a broader interpretation of children and their roles, and there is need for more integrated studies of children in the Roman world.

The numerous deaths caused by continuous warfare undertaken by expansionistic Rome and high INFANT MORTALITY and short life expectancies placed a high value on reproduction, and Roman lawmakers and emperors promulgated class-distinct laws to compensate and make this attractive. Indeed, the primary purpose of a Roman marriage was to produce offspring. Generalizations about children in literature tend to be moralistic or comic stereotypes. *Pietas*, or piety, formed the foundation of the relations between generations: parents were expected to bear, rear, and educate children, who in return were to honor and obey their parents and maintain them psychologically and materially in old age. As in all cultures, the ideal could differ dramatically from the real.

From Earliest Infancy to Prepuberty

In the Greek world, births most probably took place in the women's quarters, exclusively in the presence of women and with the help of a midwife. Giving birth could be hazardous to the mothers due in part to inadequate standards of HYGIENE, in part because most first-time mothers had barely passed PUBERTY. To announce the gender of a live birth, the family decorated the doorway with wool to designate a girl, and with a wreath of olive for a boy. The household head, the *kyrios*, had the right to accept the children and could reject them based on gender, size of the family, physical deformity or frailty, economic considerations, legitimacy, or because they were the offspring of slaves. Disposal was arranged through exposure, a process that involved abandoning an infant to its death to the elements. This practice, rather than simply killing the infant, may have developed because it freed the household from bloodguilt, or because parents truly believed that they were placing their exposed infants in the care of the gods. Exposure remains a topic of continuing controversy. In Sparta, exposure of physically weak or sickly infants was demanded by law and determined by the elders of the tribes rather than the household head.

Acceptance of the child by the household head was celebrated in a ceremony on the fifth day after birth called the Amphidromia (literally, a walking around). The ceremony took place in the home, and marked the infant's official entry into the family with the right to live. NAMING the child took place on the tenth day in a ceremony known as *dekate* (tenth), though girls or children of parents of lower economic classes may have been named at the Amphidromia. The Athenian system of nomenclature included three parts: the personal name, which could be an indication of family values (e.g., Philia, friendship or Hegesippos, horse leader); the father's name; and the demotic name, which indicated to which deme (a politically defined subsection of the city-state) the family belonged; for example, Hegesippos, son of Hegesias, from Sounion (Hegesippos Hegesiou Sounieus).

Introduction of the infant to the public world took place at a festival called the Apatouria, held annually in October/November. All male citizens assembled in their hereditary fraternal groups (*phratriai*) and the father or legal guardian was required to swear before the altar of the phratry with his hand on the sacrificial offerings to the legitimacy of the infant. Whether or not girls were also registered in the phratry is unknown. Between the ages of three and four all boys were eligible for participation in a more public spring ceremony called the Choes (pitchers). At this ceremony, which may have marked the end of infancy, each child was presented with a small pitcher from which he had his first taste of wine. The Choes ceremony was confined to Attica (the region around Athens), and marked the first step in the child's progress into the full community.

In the Roman world, births also took place in the presence of a midwife. They generally occurred with the assistance of a birthing chair, in a room with no less than three lights and one entrance, which was guarded by three men and women who inspected everyone who entered or left the room. Upon delivery five nonpregnant free women kept guard and inspected the newborn for health or lack thereof. After delivery, an infant was placed at its father's feet. If he held it up or placed it on his knee, it was fully accepted into the family. If it was not accepted by the father, it was exposed or abandoned.

For girls on the eighth day and for boys on the ninth, a festival of purification (*lustratio*) took place, at which time the child received its name and its *bulla*, a gold charm worn around the neck. Three names were traditional for boys of noble families: the *praenomen*, or personal name (e.g., Marcus); the *nomen*, or clan name (e.g., Tullius, from the clan of Tullii); and the *cognomen*, or family name (e.g., Cicero). First-born sons were often given the same personal name as their fathers or their grandfathers. Other sons were named for other males in the family such as uncles or named in the order they were born (e.g., Sextus, the sixth). There were only about sixteen common personal names during the Republic. In addition to their formal name, boys sometimes earned or were given an *agnomen*, a kind of nickname (e.g., Scipio *Africanus*, given the *agnomen* Africanus because of his victories in Africa). A girl received her name from her clan name (e.g., Tullia, the daughter of Marcus Tullius Cicero). Girls' names were usually feminized versions of boys' names. Because all girls in a family would receive the same clan name, if there was more than one daughter, each would be named in the order she was born (e.g., Julia *Prima*, Julia *Secunda*, Julia *Tertia*). When she married, she assumed the overall clan name and the possessive form of her husband's name (e.g., Terentia *Marci*, wife of Marcus from the clan of Terentius). She was sometimes given a family name. ADOPTION was a common occurrence in Rome, and entailed the transferring of a son from one *paterfamilias* to another. This might happen between close relations when one family lacked a legitimate male heir. Upon adoption, the son lost the rights to his previous family. Legally girls could not be adopted.

Education

In Athens the upbringing and education of children was the responsibility of the parents until the eighteenth year. Boys and girls to the age of six were confined to the women's quarters and were almost exclusively in the presence of women. During this early period little distinction was made between the activities of girls and boys, but boys wore either no clothes or open-fronted tunics, while girls wore long dresses. At age six, boys were usually sent to private schools, called either the GYMNASIUM or the *palaestra*. The curriculum consisted of letters (reading, writing, memorizing Homer), music (learning to play instruments and sing), and athletic training. Girls remained at home acquiring skill at domestic arts like weaving, cooking, and helping their mothers with younger siblings. To aid in discipline, parents would call on such imaginary creatures as Mormo, who ate children, and Empusa, a shape-changing gremlin.

In Sparta, infants of both sexes were taught to be peaceful, fearless, and austere in diet and physical needs. All children were indoctrinated into the service of the state, males knowing that they would become a member of a well-drilled military unit and females learning that their adult goal would be to produce healthy children to perpetuate the system. At age six, boys left the home and entered the educational system (the *agoge*), where they lived communally with other boys. LITERACY was not emphasized, but discipline and athletic/military training were. At age eleven the training program became more demanding, and physical comforts were decreased. Girls also received formal public education, but the degree to which their program differed from the boys' is still uncertain. Recent scholarship has revealed that the typical view of boorish and illiterate Spartans is a result of Athenian propaganda, and, in fact, that literacy played an important role in the management of the Spartan state.

In early Rome, education was more informal and geared toward teaching children how to conduct simple business: children learned reading, writing, and arithmetic at home with their fathers. A great deal of education focused on teaching children respect for tradition and piety (*pietas*). Children were trained to be good citizens. Job skills were taught through APPRENTICESHIPS. But since the Roman government did not oversee education or require that children be educated, a father could decide to let his children grow up uneducated.

As Rome grew in power, it was necessary for education to become more formal. At an early age, guardian tutors or nurturers were hired for male children, be they upper class, poor but free-born, freed, or slaves. A male child-minder (*paedagogus*) was expected to be of serious disposition, trustworthy, reliable, Greek, and learned, and would have a formative influence on the child as well as accompany him outside the house. Occasionally, girls also had chaperons of this sort. These guardians provided education, nurturing, and moral protection of the children, and guardians and their charges could develop strong ties that continued past the child's maturity. Upper-class male children would be encouraged to prepare for a successful life in politics and government; upper-class female children received the same education as boys, and would be inculcated with the values of the Roman *matrona*. Moral education for girls and boys continued at home, but at age twelve boys' formal academic education (music, astronomy, philosophy, natural sciences, and rhetoric) now took place outside the home. Physical punishment by teachers of students who misbehaved or failed to learn their lessons was commonplace. Children of slaves could look forward to earning their manumission in return for faithful service or to earning a livelihood through the skills they acquired. Children of upper-class families would have leisure time for games and study or accompanying their parents in their daily pursuits; children of lower classes or slaves would be put to work at an early age for obvious economic reasons.

Art and Religion

In art until the end of the fifth century B.C.E., children were represented as miniature adults, but artists became increasingly interested in depicting them with the appropriate characteristics of their age, perhaps suggesting that there was concurrently an increased interest in children for their own sake. Greek vase paintings often depict young children at play with PETS and TOYS; terracotta statues show children and their activities: babies in cradles, toddlers carried on adults' shoulders, a young girl learning how to cook. Reliefs on Roman sarcophagi show groups of boys playing roughly and groups of girls at quieter activities with their toys, including wagons and scooters. In religion, children played many significant roles. In public service, their duties ranged from temple servants, choirs dancing and chanting poetry, participating in processions, or serving as priests or Vestal Virgins. Vestal Virgins entered their state service between the age of six to ten and served for thirty years; boys as young as fourteen or fifteen could enter into priestly service. In private religious observances like funerals their participation was prominent. Scholars have suggested that this prominence came about because youth symbolizes purity, or because it was believed that they had been minimally polluted through contact with the dead and therefore did not threaten the Olympian gods with physical corruption. It is interesting to note that specific ritual roles for girls (e.g., their role in the annual festival in honor of Athena's birthday in Athens or for Artemis's birthday at Brauron) in which they performed cult functions in the city-states were more elaborate than those for boys. However, participation was limited to a few girls, probably of aristocratic birth, and it can be argued that the few stood symbolically for young girls as a group. More attention was paid to indoctrinating boys as a group into the civic or sociopolitical structure rather than the religious.

Medicine and Law

PEDIATRICS was a recognized branch of ancient medicine, and we know that at least ten pediatric treatises were written. Childhood diseases were categorized, showing an awareness of childhood vulnerability to certain diseases or infections. From the evidence given by Galen and by Hippocratic writings, common childhood diseases included rickets and anemia, diphtheria, chicken pox, mumps, and whooping cough. Much attention was given to female problems. For example, according to Hippocrates, unmarried girls at MENARCHE frequently grow delirious and try to throw themselves down wells. The problem, in Hippocrates' view, comes from the inability of the menstrual blood to flow properly through an unopened orifice. The solution, he suggests, is intercourse.

In law, an Athenian child was completely under the authority of his father or legal guardian, and until the time of Solon (at the beginning of the sixth century B.C.E.) could be sold into slavery. If they suffered physical abuse at home, they had no legal recourse. Children could be introduced in court by a male plaintiff or defendant for melodramatic attempts to receive pity, although there is no evidence that they actually could testify. In Rome, the law of the *patriae potestas* made children, wives, and slaves subject to paternal authority. Sons were recognized as independent only when their fathers died, regardless of their age, and girls remained dependents. Laws concerning rape did exist. In Crete, a man who raped a free person, male or female, or a female household serf, was subject to a fine. In Athens, a fine would be imposed for rape, whereas death was the penalty for adultery. In Rome, violators of female wards were subject to deportation and confiscation of property.

From Puberty to Adulthood

Greek city-states created rituals to mark the transition from childhood to adulthood, and these rituals were sex specific. Boys went through rituals that were public and civic, focusing on their political life as citizens and socioeconomic status as heads of households, while girls underwent private and domestic rituals, focusing on their biological status as childbearers and social status as wives. Ancient writers agreed that the onset of PUBERTY was in the thirteenth year, but there was no widespread agreement as to the duration of puberty.

A Spartan boy at age fourteen became an ephebe (*ephebos*), and military training became more serious. Between the seventeenth and nineteenth years Spartan ephebes entered a group called the *krupteia*, a sort of secret police organization. They lived isolated from society and probably secretly. After this two-year period of service they were not yet full citizens but were eligible for military service.

In Athens the transitional period lasted from the sixteenth to the twentieth year, during which time the youths were indoctrinated into their social and civic roles. At age sixteen a boy was introduced again to his phratry on the day known as the *Koureotis* during the Apatouria festival. The ceremonial cutting of his hair marked the event. At age eighteen, the Athenian boy was registered in his deme and attained legal majority. He then began a two-year period of compulsory military training as an *ephebos*. During the first year the boys lived in barracks and learned light-armed warfare; in the second year they acted as patrolmen along the Attic borders. At the end of this second year, they reentered the citizen body as young adults. Ephebic service was no longer compulsory by the end of the fourth century B.C.E., and by the beginning of the third century B.C.E. had been reduced to one year.

In Rome, boys at the age of fifteen or sixteen underwent a ceremony to mark puberty at the *Liberalia*, held on March 17th. Young boys with their fathers and other males marched to the temple for sacrifices and then returned home for domestic sacrifices and a family party. At this time they gave up their *bulla* and changed from child's clothing (*toga praetexta*) to adult dress (*toga virilis*). These young males were now free of their guardians, and had to choose a public career in politics or enter a period of military service (*tirocinium*).

In neither Sparta nor Athens nor Rome did the same type of graded initiations occur for girls, suggesting that whereas boys take on a social persona as an adult, girls do not. For girls marriage was the goal, and in marriage a girl passed from GIRLHOOD to womanhood, and from the legal and economic control of her father or guardian to that of her husband. Though a few select girls took part in several ritual activities, like weaving the robe for Athena or serving as a Vestal Virgin, it is still unclear whether the few were symbolic of the many.

Conclusion

In Greco-Roman society the position of children vis-à-vis the family, the government, religious activities, and economic considerations was complex, and the recovery of the nature of childhood by scholars is made more difficult on the one hand by the lack of direct testimony by children and on the other hand by the complexity of the ancient sources at our disposal. Scholars conclude that children's marginality in society is highlighted by a lack of legal rights, infanticide, neglect, and emotional, physical, and sexual abuse. However, the complicated portrayal of children in other literature, including drama, poetry, medical writings, biography, novels, and histories, shows the sincere affection or intense pride that parents may have felt for their children. Many funeral monuments attest to the depth of fondness of parents for their deceased children. Likewise the material evidence of toys, games, and pets shows that serious attention was paid to playfulness in the development of human personality and individual talent.

See also: **Abandonment; Ancient Greece and Rome: Self-Formation; Theories of Childhood.**

BIBLIOGRAPHY

Bradley, Keith R. 1991. *Discovering the Roman Family: Studies in Roman Social History.* New York: Oxford University Press.

Colón, A. R. and Colón, P. A. 2001. *A History of Children: A Socio-Cultural Survey across Millennia.* Westport, CT: Greenwood Press.

Dixon, Suzanne. 1992. *The Roman Family.* Baltimore, MD: Johns Hopkins University Press.

Dixon, Suzanne, ed. 2001. *Childhood, Class, and Kin in the Roman World.* London: Routledge.

Eyben, Emiel. 1993. *Restless Youth in Ancient Rome.* London: Routledge.

French, Valerie. 1991. "Children in Antiquity." In *Children in Historical and Comparative Perspective: An International Handbook and Research Guide*, ed. Joseph M. Haws and N. Ray Hiner. New York: Greenwood Press.

Garland, Robert. 1990. *The Greek Way of Life: From Conception to Old Age.* Ithaca, NY: Cornell University Press.

Garland, Robert. 1998. *Daily Life of the Ancient Greeks.* Westport, CT: Greenwood Press.

Golden, Mark. 1990. *Children and Childhood in Classical Athens.* Baltimore, MD: Johns Hopkins University Press.

Katz, M. A. 1998. "Women, Children and Men." In *The Cambridge Illustrated History of Ancient Greece*, ed. Paul Cartledge. New York: Cambridge University Press.

Lacey, Walter K. 1968. *The Family in Classical Greece.* Ithaca, NY: Cornell University Press.

Lambert, Garth R. 1982. *Rhetoric Rampant: The Family under Siege in the Early Western Tradition.* London, Ontario: Faculty of Education, University of Western Ontario.

Lefkowitz, Mary R. and Maureen B. Fant. 1982. *Women's Life in Greece and Rome: A Source Book in Translation.* Baltimore, MD: Johns Hopkins University Press.

MacDowell, Douglas M. 1978. *The Law in Classical Athens.* Ithaca, NY: Cornell University Press.

Pomeroy, Sarah B. 1997. *Families in Classical and Hellenistic Greece: Representations and Realities.* Oxford, UK: Clarendon Press.

Rawson, Beryl, ed. 1986. *The Family in Ancient Rome: New Perspectives.* Ithaca, NY: Cornell University Press.

Rawson, Beryl, ed. 1996. *Marriage, Divorce, and Children in Ancient Rome.* New York: Oxford University Press.

Rawson, Beryl, and Paul Weaver, ed. 1997. *The Roman Family in Italy: Status, Sentiment, Space.* Oxford, UK: Clarendon Press.

Wiedemann, Thomas. 1989. *Adults and Children in the Roman Empire.* New Haven, CT: Yale University Press.

INTERNET RESOURCES

Bar-Ilan, Meir. 2002. "Bibliography of Childhood in Antiquity." Available from <http://faculty.biu.ac.il/~barilm/bibchild.html>.

Diotima: Materials for the Study of Women and Gender in the Ancient World. 2002. "Bibliography." Available from <www.stoa.org/diotima/biblio.shtmli>.

ELISE P. GARRISON

SELF-FORMATION

Most inhabitants of the Roman Empire saw their world in strictly hierarchical terms and had little reason to do otherwise, even though some thinkers, especially those influenced by Stoic philosophy, posited something akin to the notion that all men were created equal. Daily life in the ancient Mediterranean world provided numerous proofs that a few were created far better than the many: they had more and better food, did not work, were protected from heat and cold, were by law exempt from torture, and as a result looked different and lived longer. Indeed, the superiority of a select few over the many was foundational for a society understood to function just like the human body, dominated by the head (i.e., the mind), which ruled over a well-organized body, in which every member had its preordained place and function. Only the harmonious operation of all members in strict accordance with their place could assure the well being of the community.

The Greco-Roman Cosmologies

The predominant Greco-Roman cosmologies reflected this strictly hierarchical ordering of the world as divinely ordained and natural. Those who belonged to the elites were by nature (i.e., by the very fact of their birth to elite parents) higher up and closer to the divine realm, which in its turn had been created and was guided by the Supreme Good or the Supreme Intellect (i.e., Zeus/Jupiter, etc.). Thus those belonging to the elites (or so the theory went) were intrinsically good and had more intellect by virtue of their good birth (*eugenes*), an inner virtue outwardly manifested by their physical beauty (*kalos kai agathos*).

Intrinsic to this world view, which was widespread throughout the Roman Empire and helped forge unity among elites originating from a wide variety of local backgrounds, were three interrelated concepts.

First, the cosmos was considered an undivided whole and humans but a micro-cosmos mirroring the macro-cosmos. Thus each person (as well as society as a whole) was ruled by the mind, which was of the same essence as the Supreme (divine) Mind/Intellect.

Second, unlike the divine Mind, the human one was intrinsically linked to something ontologically different from the divine realm, namely matter, or the body. This link created an inherent instability, since both matter and the body embodied the opposite of the divine: if the divine was eternal and calm then matter was transient and changing; if the divine was good and just, then the ethical aspects of the physical were the opposite.

Third, since one of the quintessential divine characteristics was the capacity to create and therefore to form matter, so the human mind too created and therefore formed its matter, the physical body and its characteristics (such as desires for food and sex, but also anger, greed, jealousy, etc.), and the physical body in its turn outwardly reflected the inner ruling of the mind (or the lack thereof) through *gestus* and *habitus*. Yet, because everything was essentially one whole, external factors could also imprint the mind; for example, excessive attention to food would leave traces on the mind and incapacitate its ruling facilities. Expressed differently, to be good and beautiful was both the result of good birth and of a lifelong process of self-formation according to the demands of the mind, which were also those of the Supreme Divinity.

Paideia

In practice, this lifelong process of self-formation, also known as *paideia*, was perhaps the single most significant marker indicating elite status in the Roman Empire for the simple reason that it began at birth, continued along a prescribed path of further formation or higher education, and had to be demonstrated at all times throughout the life of an elite male. Each slip in an elite male's behavior—which would be immediately noticed by eyes trained to notice such things since infancy—signified a slip of the mind, which might render the person in question unfit to rule, since who-

ever cannot govern his own body and its desires cannot govern his own household, let alone an empire.

The precondition for this continuing process of self-formation (or self-control) was, of course, wealth. Only those who were rich enough to be free from any pursuit of material gain had the wherewithal to devote themselves to such lifelong formation. Consequently, *paideia* was considered the essential precondition for all forms of governance, since it began at conception and required wealth; those who acquired positions of power by any other than the "natural" way and thus came to *paideia* late in life were never permitted to forget the peculiarities of their accent or gait.

Formation during Pregnancy and Early Childhood

Initiated at conception, the process of formation began in earnest during pregnancy. According to the second century C.E. gynecologist Soranus of Ephesus, who practiced in Rome, elite mothers had to ensure "the perfection of their embryo" through "passive exercise," which consisted of being carried in a large sedan chair and leisurely walks, "fairly warm baths," massages, and the consumption of appropriate food: non-greasy fish and meat as well as "vegetables that are not pungent," and large quantities of water before meals "with a little wine" (book 1.14.46). Birth itself required numerous preparations: a midwife, three female helpers, a soft and a hard bed, a midwife's chair, warm oils, and so on. As soon as the child arrived, "the subject of rearing children" forced issues such as "which of the offspring is worth rearing, how should one sever the navel cord and swaddle and cradle the infant which is to be reared. What kind of nurse should one select, and which milk is best." (Gyn. 2.5.9–10). A child "worth rearing" could be identified by its crying as well as by the fact that "none of its orifices are obstructed, all limbs and joints [are present and] bend and stretch, and it is properly sensitive in every respect" as ascertained by squeezing. Soranus never mentions gender as a criterion. "Unworthy" children were frequently exposed, though Soranus does not suggest this in case of a negative judgment.

If all was in order and the umbilical cord had been properly severed, the newborn had to be swaddled in such a way that all limbs were "molded according to their natural shape" with soft and clean woolen bandages; the aim was to ensure the proper symmetry of limbs and head, considerations which also governed the manner in which the newborn was laid down, bathed, and massaged, as well as the choice of the wet nurse and her milk (Soranus considers the mother's own milk "unwholesome" for the first twenty days, although others did not). A wet nurse (usually a slave) was, ideally, "between 20 and 40 years old, healthy, of good habitus and color. . . . She should be self-controlled, sympathetic, not ill-tempered, a Greek, and tidy" (Gyn. 2.12.19). In short, from the very first, everything had to ensure that the newborn corresponded to the prevailing notions of "beauty and goodness": the child's body should be symmetrical and well-proportioned and its internal "qualities" fostered through correct food, provided by a wet nurse of the appropriate characteristics.

SWADDLING ended when the child had become firm enough to avoid "distortions," at which point all attempts at standing and sitting were to be constantly monitored for the same reasons—the legs might become too bowed, which would affect the adult's gait. At around three to four years of age the constant care of nurses was replaced both for girls and boys by that of a tutor and then a *paidagogos*, slaves in charge of supervising the first steps of literary education, which began inside the house but moved with advancing years into a school setting, where the actual instruction was taken over by a grammarian, though the *paidagogos* would often accompany the pupil.

With the beginning of writing exercises, the child further "wrote himself" or herself into one social class, based again on the underlying notion that the mind is both formed and formative (like a wax tablet): each act of writing, speech, and thought impressed notions of ethics, morals, and social class into the child's mind as well as its body, and thus continuously formed the whole person. In their first exercises (often bilingual, in Greek and Latin), schoolboys wrote and recited their days, beginning with orders to their slaves, greetings to persons according to hierarchy, lists of gods and of distinguished teachers. The pupil's advancement in grammar was also advancement in proper expression through memorization of classical authors (Homer, Hesiod, Plato, the tragedies), each act of writing and its correction reifying the social order and the student's place within it. The more advanced the student, the stronger the formative power of written and recited words.

Higher Education

Higher education always occurred outside the house (and thus was rarer for women) and usually in cities other than the native one under a *rhetor*, a person chosen for his fame and the advancement he could ensure for his students through his own connections. Central to the education under a *rhetor* was a further deepening of the classical readings as well as the so-called declamations, set pieces akin to modern American legal case studies. Confronted with admittedly contrived situations (a soldier deserts but then saves his commander; should he be executed? a young man marries against his father's will and the father kills him, as is his right; did he act justly? a freedman seeks to marry a person above his status, etc.), students learned the intricacies of the law and of forensic speech, but even more importantly practiced being a *paterfamilias* and thus a member of the ruling elite—a *patronus*.

Training to take on an adult persona involved training in persuasion so that those who depended on the patron's advocacy (such as women, who were not persons under the law) could speak through him, or rather he could speak for them, in their voice. Thus the young man learned to speak both in

his master's (i.e., his father's) voice, as a master, and in the voice of his (and his master's) dependents and subordinates without ever being confounded with one of the latter.

Declamatory training in rhetoric and advocacy was the precondition for public office, and most members of the elite received it. A smaller number continued on to more advanced training as legal experts (in the later empire, Beirut was a center for the advanced study in Roman law), physicians (e.g., in Alexandria), or philosophers (in Athens and Alexandria)—but by the time a student had completed his rhetorical training at around age twenty-five he had been sufficiently formed to know how to walk, talk, dress, eat, drink, think, and govern—in short, how to be an elite man and be recognized as such by all at all times.

See also: **Ancient Greece and Rome: Overview; Aristotle; Plato.**

BIBLIOGRAPHY

Dionisotti, A. C. 1982. "From Ausonius' Schooldays? A Schoolbook and Its Relations," *Journal of Roman Studies* 72, no. 1: 83–125.

Gleason, M. 1995. *Making Men: Sophists and Self-presentation in Ancient Rome.* Princeton, NJ: Princeton University Press.

Marrou, H. I. 1982. *A History of Education in Antiquity.* Trans. George Lamb. Madison: University of Wisconsin Press.

Soranus. 1956. *Soranus' Gynecology.* Trans. O. Tempkins. Baltimore, MD: Johns Hopkins Press.

SUSANNA ELM

Andersen, Hans Christian (1805–1875)

Hans Christian Andersen is considered the father of the modern FAIRY TALE. While a few authors before him (such as Charles Perrault in France and the Grimm brothers in Germany) collected folk tales deriving from oral lore, Andersen was the first to treat this peasant form as a literary genre. Many of his original tales, such as "The Ugly Duckling" and "The Snow Queen" entered the collective consciousness with the same mythic power as the ancient, anonymous ones.

Andersen was born in 1805 in provincial Odense, Denmark, the son of an illiterate washerwoman and a poor shoemaker, who died when Andersen was eleven. An important influence during his childhood was his grandmother, who told him folk tales. At fourteen, Andersen went alone to Copenhagen to seek his fortune in the theater. Patrons funded his study, between the ages of seventeen and twenty-two, at a GRAMMAR SCHOOL, where his life was very much like that of the unhappy, over-large duckling of his story.

At a time when children's books were mostly formal, instructive texts, intended to educate rather than entertain, the appearance of his *Eventyr* (Fairy tales) in 1835 marked a revolution in children's literature. The colloquial manner, the humor, the exuberant detail, and the fantastical imaginings in his stories all distinguished them from traditional folk tales, which are generally characterized by an anonymous tone and formulaic structure.

Between 1835 and 1845 Andersen wrote "The Emperor's New Clothes," "The Little Mermaid," "The Nightingale," "The Ugly Duckling," "The Snow Queen," and many other tales whose grace, simplicity, and penetrating insight into the human condition won him a wide following. These tales were translated throughout Europe and in America (they were translated into English in 1846), making him one of the most famous writers of the nineteenth century.

With his use of comedy and fantasy, Andersen determined the course of children's literature right through to the twenty-first century, and his influence as the world's first great fantasy storyteller is inestimable. He created speaking TOYS and animals, and he gave them colloquial, funny voices that children could instantly identify with. Yet he suffused his domestic settings with the fatalism of legend and his own modern sense of the absurd, so that in stories such as "The Steadfast Tin Soldier," "The Fir Tree," and "The Top and the Ball" he became the artist of the idealized world of middle-class childhood. His appeal to a joint audience of parents and children set the standard for the double articulation that has marked all great children's books—as the British *Daily News* said of him in 1875, "it is only a writer who can write for men that is fit to write for children."

Despite his fame, Andersen always remained an outsider: lonely, gauche, sexually uncertain, and socially uneasy. He travelled widely across Europe and had several unhappy, unfulfilled love affairs—with both men and women. His tales are, in fact, often veiled autobiographies: the gawky duckling, the restless fir tree, the poor match girl, the mermaid unable to speak her love; these are self-portraits whose honesty to experience reveals universal truths.

See also: **Children's Literature.**

BIBLIOGRAPHY

Wullschlager, Jackie. 2001. *Hans Christian Andersen: The Life of a Storyteller*. New York: Knopf.

JACKIE WULLSCHLAGER

Anger and Aggression

Definitions of anger vary from theorist to theorist; it has been variously associated with physiological arousal, unpleasant feelings, appraisals of insult, desire for revenge, frustration, and aggressive behavior. Although anger has often been classified as a biologically grounded, universal emotion, it is clear that anger is interpreted, managed, and regulated differently in different social contexts. Cultures vary in their attitudes toward anger, norms regarding its expression, and beliefs about the extent and normalcy of anger in children, all of which contribute to child-rearing patterns and children's experiences. Teaching children to manage anger is one of the important tasks of child rearing and provides vital socialization into local norms.

Variations within and between Cultures

The degree to which anger is sanctioned differs considerably by culture. Some cultures strive to eliminate anger in children, whether by avoiding mention of the emotion or by extensive discussion of anger and its negative consequences. Jean Briggs's work among the Utku (an Inuit group) established that while expressions of anger in infants up to the age of two were tolerated, older children and adults were held to strict emotional standards that forbade explicit manifestations of anger. In general, parental treatment of children's anger ranges from providing angry children with loving attention to shaming them or imposing corporal punishment. Barbara Ward's account of temper tantrums in the children of Kau Sai, China, during the early 1950s indicates that adults simply ignored children's tantrums, leaving children to cry themselves out. Indeed, adults were so unconcerned about these fits of anger that they often instigated them by frustrating children. However, aggressive responses were feared and strictly controlled; children who fought each other were quickly restrained, and even verbal aggression was considered wrong. Some societies abhor physical violence but tolerate verbal expressions of anger. One anthropologist's account of a southern French village in the 1950s indicated a sophisticated pattern of verbal aggression in the village, with ritual insults and epithets, and a simultaneous absence of schoolyard fighting of the sort familiar in the United States. Cultures and historical periods differ, as well, in their acceptance of adult anger directed toward children. Child-rearing advice in Europe and America since the mid-eighteenth century has been fairly consistent in admonishing parents to avoid expressions of anger toward (or even around) their children, but Michelle Rosaldo's research among the Ifaluk tribe in the Philippines found it common for adults to express anger toward children.

However, even within culture, childhood anger norms also differ across social class and gender. Expressions of anger are often prohibited toward those of higher status, as they may constitute a challenge to the social hierarchy. One of the social nuances children must learn is that of deference, and who is considered an appropriate target for anger. This is particularly relevant for children from families explicitly marked as low status, such as those found in slave or caste societies, but it also applies to children from peasant or working-class backgrounds. Indeed, children must attend to status markers even within their own families; these include age differences among children and the status differences between children and adults. Although expressions of anger toward those of higher status may be limited, stereotypes of the working class (for example, in the United States) have often assumed that they are less in control of base emotions, including anger.

Gender and Anger

In patriarchal societies, where males are accorded higher status, girls are often more restricted in their expressions of anger than boys are. In many cases, the degree of appropriate anger is regarded not merely as a normative component of sex roles but also as a natural difference between males and females. In early modern Europe, for example, girls and women were taught that references to anger as a basis for making demands was simply inappropriate, although similar demands could be grounded in other emotions, such as jealousy. Anger, which was associated with responses of honor, was a male emotion. This differential carried over strongly to the nineteenth century in both Europe and the United States. U.S. standards of femininity argued that anger was unladylike, that a "real" woman would simply not experience the emotion. Since, in fact, girls and women often did feel angry, great effort was urged to keep the emotion in check, and angry feelings often provoked negative self-evaluation and concerns regarding femininity. Novels like LITTLE WOMEN detailed how hard girls worked to live up to these expectations, and American girls today still report more self-regulation of anger than do boys.

Ideologies regarding anger have changed over time in Western cultures. While girls were still expected to be free of anger, anger in boys and men (even among dominant males) began to be of greater concern in European society by the eighteenth century, as part of what Norbert Elias has called the civilizing process. In particular, as part of a growing idealization of a loving family, anger was increasingly viewed as inappropriate in the domestic sphere; anger seemed to violate the emotional ties that should positively unite family members. Prescriptive literature also began to warn against anger toward inferiors, such as servants. It is not clear how much this advice altered children's experiences of anger, but some effect seems likely. Growing concern about dueling by upper-class young males in the eighteenth century, which extended into debates throughout the nineteenth century, expressed new ambivalence about anger and aggression.

By the nineteenth century in the United States, a complex anger formula had evolved for middle-class boys. Boys should be taught to avoid anger in the home because it would contradict the loving relationships that should build family life, and anger toward superiors continued to be considered inappropriate. However, anger was an important part of masculinity, so it should not be completely eliminated in boys, but rather channeled to useful purposes. A boy without the capacity for anger might grow up to be a man without competitive fire or without the ability to fight injustice. Par-

ents were urged to provide boys with experiences that would help them retain their anger but direct it constructively. The popularity of SPORTS, including BOXING lessons, for boys at the end of the nineteenth century was in part related to their role in maintaining but channeling anger. Many uplifting stories for boys involved the expression of righteous anger against bullies, often in defense of weaker children, including sisters. The standards for boys and men were highly complicated, in that boys were simultaneously warned against lack of anger and against angry outbursts.

The actual culture of nineteenth-century American boys seems to have embodied these directives, albeit in ways that were rougher than some parents would have recommended. Boys were expected to stand their ground in fights without becoming gratuitously angry. Boys who fled, rather than summoning up anger and courage, were derided by their peers. Between the 1840s and the 1880s in the United States, the word *sissy* (originally a British term meaning girl, or sister) evolved to cover boys who could not display appropriate anger and who cowered in fear. *Sissy* came to mean a boy who lacked the emotional apparatus that would prepare him for manhood, of which appropriately channeled anger was a central fixture.

Discouraging Anger

By the 1920s in the United States, multiple forces resulted in a challenge to the belief in the value of anger. Growing concern about juvenile DELINQUENCY contributed to an emerging belief that anger should be discouraged among boys, not merely channeled. Child-rearing experts in the 1930s were less convinced of the positive purposes of anger and began to use the term *aggression* instead. These shifts in anger norms coincided with broader changes in socialization and patterns of labor. As more and more men headed toward occupations in the service sector or in corporate management, the importance of smooth, anger-free professional relationships intensified. Channeled anger lost its function. Anger was now a bad, even dangerous, emotion, pure and simple. At the same time, the intense focus on anger-free femininity eased, creating a bit more leeway for expressions of moderate anger among girls.

As anger and aggressiveness emerged as dangerous elements, adults became increasingly concerned about children's exposure to aggressive or angry behavior in the media. The belief that COMIC BOOKS, RADIO, MOVIES, and TELEVISION might provide a stimulus to unhealthy emotions and antisocial behavior instigated recurrent efforts to censor children's media. The advent of aggressive lyrics in adolescent music, particularly by the 1990s, and the graphic violence of video and Internet games continued to raise questions about access to aggressive impulses. Children's ongoing fascination with this fare, however, elicited varied interpretations: did this indicate (or even cause) unhealthy aggressiveness, or could media representations provide safe outlets for anger and aggression? Other possible avenues for venting anger, such as punching bags, were suggested by some experts, but many others believed this would only exacerbate the child's anger. There was more widespread support for encouraging children to identify and talk out their anger so that it would not seem to generate any problematic results and at the same time would not fester.

Even amid the growing concern about children's anger, many of the earlier themes persisted to some degree. Fathers were more likely than mothers to worry about their sons being sissies if they lacked the capacity to stand up for themselves. Girls worried more about anger than boys did, on average, and were more likely to cry when placed in anger-generating situations. The term *sissy* went out of fashion, partly because it was no longer appropriate to encourage boys to be aggressive; but new words, like *wimp*, conveyed some of the same meaning.

As efforts to constrain anger increased, aggressive behavior became a central concern. Schoolyard fighting declined due to adult supervision and changes in boys' culture. By the 1990s in the United States, school violence declined statistically. But individual cases of horrific mass violence, abetted by the availability of lethal weapons, kept adult anxiety high. Early in the twenty-first century, a new concern about bullying reflected the substantial adult consensus that aggressiveness was now bad for children individually and collectively. Building on research pertaining to delinquency, authorities and experts debated the crucial causal factors in aggressive behavior and the possibility of identifying potentially violent adolescents. Childhood aggression increasingly fueled adult anxieties regarding the physical and psychological health of youth, both perpetrators and victims.

See also: **Discipline; Emotional Life; Gendering; Guns.**

BIBLIOGRAPHY

Averill, James R. 1982. *Anger and Aggression: An Essay on Emotion.* New York: Springer-Verlag.

Briggs, Jean. 1970. *Never in Anger: Portrait of an Eskimo Family.* Cambridge, MA: Harvard University Press.

Elias, Norbert. 1982. *The Civilizing Process.* Trans. Edmund Jephcott. New York: Pantheon.

Rosaldo, Michelle. 1980. *Knowledge and Passion: Ilongot Notions of Self and Social Life.* Cambridge, UK: Cambridge University Press.

Rotundo, E. Anthony. 1993. *American Manhood: Transformations in Masculinity from the Revolution to the Modern Era.* New York: Basic Books.

Russell, J. A., and B. Fehr. 1994. "Fuzzy Concepts in a Fuzzy Hierarchy: Varieties of Anger." *Journal of Personality and Social Psychology,* 67: 186–205.

Sabini, John, and Maury Silver. 1982. *Moralities of Everyday Life.* New York: Oxford University Press.

Solomon, Robert. 1984. "Getting Angry: The Jamesian Theory of Emotion in Anthropology." In *Culture Theory: Essays on Mind, Self and Emotion,* ed. Robert A. Shweder and Robert A. LeVine. New York: Cambridge University Press.

Stearns, Carol Z., and Peter N. Stearns. 1986. *Anger: The Struggle for Emotional Control in American History.* Chicago: University of Chicago Press.

Stearns, Peter N. 1994. *American Cool: Constructing a Twentieth-Century Emotional Style.* New York: New York University Press.

Trumbach, Randolph. 1978. *The Rise of the Egalitarian Family: Aristocratic Kinship and Domestic Relations in Eighteenth-Century England.* New York: Academic Press.

Underwood, M. K., J. D. Coie, and C. R. Herbsman. 1992. "Display Rules for Anger and Aggression in School-Age Children." *Child Development* 63: 366–380.

Ward, Barbara E. 1970. "Temper Tantrums in Kau Sai: Some Speculations upon Their Effects." In *Socialization: The Approach from Social Anthropology,* ed. Philip Mayer. London: Tavistock.

Wylie, Laurence William. 1974. *Village in the Vaucluse.* Cambridge, MA: Harvard University Press.

DEBORAH C. STEARNS

Anorexia

As defined by the American Psychiatric Association's Diagnostic and Statistical Manual, fourth edition (DSM-IV; 1994), anorexia nervosa is an eating disorder marked by four major symptoms. First, the patient must be less than 85 percent of ideal weight for age, height, and gender. Second, there must be a morbid fear of fat. Third, the person must believe himself or herself to be normal weight or even fat despite emaciation. Finally, the victim should be amenorrheic (i.e., have no menstrual periods) or, in the case of men, show abnormally low levels of testosterone. Anorexia nervosa is considerably more common in women than in men with 80 to 90 percent of the cases diagnosed in adolescence or adulthood being females. The gender difference is somewhat less pronounced in childhood cases, with girls being approximately five times more likely than boys to suffer from the disorder. Less than 1 percent of the postpubertal female population suffers from anorexia nervosa. It is more common among white than African-American girls and women.

Anorexia nervosa has two ages of peak onset: around age fourteen, and at about age eighteen. The frequency of adolescent onset has led theorists to suggest that the developmental transitions to ADOLESCENCE and to adulthood present special risks for girls, making them more vulnerable than boys are not only to anorexia nervosa but also bulimia nervosa and depression. The combination of age and gender factors has also led theorists to suggest that cultural variables, such as the thin body ideal for females and the relative lack of power among women, contributes to the disorder. Finally, it is clear that anorexia nervosa typically starts in a pattern of either dieting or excessive exercise which itself is probably rooted in an attempt to achieve a particular body shape.

There are at least two paths that lead to the modern definition of anorexia nervosa. The first is self-starvation. The second is a history of defining adolescence and young adulthood as problematic for women. These historical trends meet in the eighteenth century to define anorexia nervosa.

Self-Starvation

Walter Vandereycken and Ron van Deth (1994) suggest that self-starvation is a pervasive phenomenon in human history. Given the cross-cultural and cross-historical presence of self-starvation, it is not surprising that it has many motivations. Perhaps the best-known motives are political and religious. For example, Mahatma Gandhi's lengthy hunger strikes in defiance of British domination of India in the 1930s are well known. Less dramatically, fasting is required of Roman Catholics on certain holy days during Lent and even today, devout Muslims participate in a month-long fast during Ramadan.

The link between religion and self-starvation has received the most attention from students of anorexia nervosa. The link between self-denial, including of food, and spirituality, dates at least as far back as the Egyptian pharaohs. During the fourth and fifth centuries C.E., men went into the Egyptian and Palestinian deserts to dedicate themselves to the worship of Jesus Christ. Self-starvation was part of this dedication. As religious practice was largely limited to men at this time, most of those engaging in religious self-starvation were men.

Of greater interest in terms of anorexia nervosa is the medieval practice of self-starvation by women, including some young women, in the name of religious piety and purity. By the twelfth century, it was increasingly common for women to participate in religious life and to even be named as saints by the Catholic Church. Many women who ultimately became saints engaged in self-starvation, including St. Hedwig of Silesia in the thirteenth century and Catherine of Siena in the fourteenth century. By the time of Catherine of Siena, however, the Church became concerned about extreme fasting as an indicator of spirituality and a path to sainthood. Indeed, Catherine of Siena was told to pray that she would be able to eat again, but was unable to give up fasting.

While there is a long-standing link between self-starvation and piety, there is also a historical relationship between self-starvation and demonic possession or witchcraft. For example, Catherine of Siena ate something everyday so that she would not be labeled a witch. After the middle ages, numerous "fasting saints" were accused of witchcraft under the Inquisition. In some places, women could prove they were not witches if they weighed a sufficient amount on government-designated scales. Again, the relationship between self-starvation and religion was particularly pronounced for women.

The virtually simultaneous designation of self-starvation by women as pious and demonic raises interesting issues concerning the cultural meaning of women's bodies, issues that are still debated in terms of anorexia nervosa. In the calculus of the early twenty-first century, the ideal body type for women is thin. "Supermodels," actresses, and even singers are typically substantially below the weight of the average American woman. Research indicates that this image is so pervasive that even elementary school-age children are aware of it. Studies routinely find that 40 percent of girls in fourth and fifth grade wish they were thinner or worry about getting fat. Yet, if girls take this message too much to heart, dieting severely and actually becoming as thin as the models, they are considered "mentally ill."

Early Adolescent Girls and Illness

Anorexia nervosa is not the first disorder in history marked by unusual eating and amenorrhea that is found predominantly in adolescent or young adult women. According to Brett Silverstein and Deborah Perlick (1995), a paper by Hippocrates, known as *On the Disease of Young Women*, describes an anorexia nervosa-like disorder. This treatise suggests that the dramatic weight loss is caused by problematic menstrual cycles and recommends marriage and pregnancy as the best treatment.

Similarly, *hysteria*, a disorder made famous in SIGMUND FREUD's Anna O. case but that was also diagnosed earlier in the nineteenth century, was marked by loss of appetite, depression, and amenorrhea. *Neurasthenia* was another late nineteenth century "female disorder" involving disordered eating and amenorrhea.

Probably the best known of these disorders of adolescent girls is *chlorosis*. Chlorosis was made famous by Joan Jacob Brumberg's book *Fasting Girls*. Brumberg argues that chlorosis, like anorexia nervosa, was a disease of middle-class American girls who were fulfilling the expectations of their culture in an extreme manner. In both the nineteenth and twentieth centuries, such girls developed exaggerated behaviors concerning food. Chlorosis was a form of anemia, found only in girls, that was linked to both the onset of menstruation and physical attractiveness. Oddly, these ill girls were considered particularly attractive, just as the most "beautiful" women in the United States of the early twenty-first century have an anorexic appearance. Chlorotic girls, like those with anorexia nervosa, were likely trying to exercise some control over their own lives and, like anorexic girls, were considered to be suffering from a "nervous" or "psychological" disorder rather than from a primarily physical illness.

By the early twentieth century, chlorosis was no longer being diagnosed in the United States. While it is possible that improved nutrition led to the decline of this form of anemia, it is more likely that culture changes affected the expression of eating-related pathology among adolescent girls. The belief that women were fragile and physically weak generally declined as opportunities for women in jobs, education, and even politics increased. However these changes were not quickly or universally accepted, setting up a clash between images of the "traditional" and the "modern" young woman. Young girls received and internalized these conflicting messages about womanhood and may have sometimes felt unable to control their own destinies or to even know want they wanted to do. One thing they could control, however, was their own eating. This culture-based model resonates with current explanations of the causes of anorexia nervosa.

Anorexia Nervosa

Neither the "fasting saints" nor the "chlorotic girls" were anorexic in the sense that the term is used today. Their self-starvation and "nervous" illness reflected beliefs and women's roles during their historic periods. Although Richard Morton described a case of tuberculosis that resembled anorexia nervosa in 1694, current definitions of the disorder are routinely traced to the work of Sir William Withey Gull and Dr. R. Lasègue, in 1874 and 1873 respectively.

Both Lasègue and Gull describe cases marked by self-starvation and high levels of activity or restlessness. Both note that the problem is particularly pronounced in young women; indeed, Gull suggests that adolescent and young adult women are unusually susceptible to MENTAL ILLNESS. Lasègue notes that these young women are pleased with their food restriction, do not wish to eat more, and do not believe that they are abnormally thin. Lasègue referred to this condition as *hysterical anorexia* while Gull used the term *anorexia nervosa*.

Although Gull and Lasègue considered anorexia to be a "nervous" disorder, both treated it medically. Gull in particular seemed to have remarkable success, at least by today's standards, in gradually re-feeding the girls. He reported that his clients recovered their eating habits, weight, and health. Lasègue had more pessimistic reports, noting that patients often went many years without recovering.

It is important to recognize that neither Gull nor Lasègue considered anything resembling a "drive for thinness" as key in the etiology of anorexia nervosa. This focus is a product of the twentieth century, probably instigated by the work of Hilde Bruch. Some practitioners are now questioning the wisdom of the twentieth and twenty-first century emphasis on the role of drive for thinness in anorexia nervosa. They note that in some Asian cultures, particularly Hong Kong and China, drive for thinness does not seem to be part of what otherwise looks like anorexia nervosa. Others note that Gull's success in using medically based treatments ought to encourage us to re-examine the efficacy of such an approach.

Historians have raised a number of issues concerning the emergence of modern anorexia nervosa, which was a trans-Atlantic phenomenon involving both the United States and Western Europe from the mid-nineteenth century onward. The basic issues involve sorting out the "real" disease from its specific historical cause—why the disease emerged when it did— and the fact that it appears so disproportionately in females. The first outcroppings of the modern disease occurred before thinness was widely fashionable, which has prompted consideration of the dynamic of loving, middle-class families in which some young women chose food refusal as a method of rebellion that could not be explicitly articulated. Obviously, the rise of concern for slenderness from about 1900 onward as a fashion standard particularly bearing on women, helped sustain the disease. But the incidence of anorexia was not constant through the twentieth century in the Western world, raising questions about causation and about fluctuations in medical attention. By the 1970s, societal and parental concern about anorexia was widespread, sometimes working against efforts to limit children's food intake in a period when the incidence of childhood obesity was rising more rapidly than anorexia nervosa.

In its current form, anorexia nervosa dates from the mid-nineteenth century. Yet, it grows out of a long history of self-starvation and female-specific pathologies. As such, it likely is a disorder that can tell us much about the role of young women in today's society and why they opt to wage war against their own bodies.

See also: **Gendering; Girlhood.**

BIBLIOGRAPHY

Andersen, Arnold E. 1985. *Practical Comprehensive Treatment of Anorexia Nervosa and Bulimia.* Baltimore, MD: The Johns Hopkins University Press.

Brumberg, Joan Jacobs. 1982. "Chlorotic Girls, 1870–1910: An Historical Perspective on Female Adolescence." *Child Development* 53: 1468–1474.

Brumberg, Joan Jacobs. 1988. *Fasting Girls: The Emergence of Anorexia Nervosa.* Cambridge, MA: Harvard University Press.

Silverstein, Brett and Deborah Perlick. 1995. *The Cost of Competence: Why Inequality Causes Depression, Eating Disorders, and Illness in Women.* New York: Oxford University Press.

Vandereycken, Walter and Ron van Deth. 1994. *From Fasting Saints to Anorexic Girls: The History of Self-starvation.* New York: New York University Press.

LINDA SMOLAK

Anthropology of Childhood. *See* Sociology and Anthropology of Childhood.

Antiquity. *See* Ancient Greece and Rome.

Apprenticeship

In a formal sense, apprenticeship is a contractual agreement between an expert practitioner of a trade, art, or profession and a novice in which, for a fixed period of time, the latter exchanges labor for training. Widely associated with the crafts, apprenticeship traces its origins in the West to the household economies of medieval Europe.

Origins and Practice

Until the separation of work from home that began in Europe and North America around 1800, households were also sites of production and reproduction. Since most families needed their children to contribute to their own support, the young nearly always worked alongside their parents in the home and on the land. In the process, they acquired their parents' vocational skills, learned responsibility, and internalized the values of their society. The practice of apprenticeship extended this family-centered model of work and learning to households not necessarily related by blood. It transferred children or adolescents from natal households to interim, external ones for a set period of time—typically four to seven years.

Throughout the early modern period, two distinct types of apprenticeship coexisted side by side. The first, a predominately instructional form, originated in the guilds of the Middle Ages. Practiced by prosperous merchants, professionals, and artisans, it placed sons in the households of prominent counterparts. Since guild oversight and the influence of parents protected the interests of the young, these apprenticeships generally resulted in genuine training. They were especially useful to large families, which sought to diversify the activities of their sons.

In places where guilds were strong, they exercised strict oversight over training. This permitted them to maintain prices by restricting entry into the trades. Good training mattered too, for it diminished guild exposure to competition from less skilled, nonsanctioned producers. When training became too restrictive, however, government officials and powerful consumers worked to weaken guild authority.

At the opposite end of the social spectrum, apprenticeship took a predominately economic form. Modest artisans and small landholders apprenticed out their children primarily for financial reasons. These groups generally lacked the capacity, due to limited land or capital, to employ the labor of all their children productively. Thus, they contracted out their "surplus labor" to families typically without children or with grown ones. Since food, shelter, and heat consumed most of most families' incomes, shifting older children to other households brought meaningful economic relief.

In turn, apprentices provided masters with needed labor at a marginal cost. In this context, however, training was a by-product of work, not the primary object of the exchange. Although masters promised to instruct their charges in a trade, they had an economic incentive to maximize work and skimp on training. Further, they often withheld crucial trade secrets from apprentices in order to prevent future competi-

tion. In the absence of guild regulation or influential parents, apprentice exploitation was widespread.

Neither form of apprenticeship was universal, however. Young women were only occasionally indentured to learn a trade, although they frequently served in extrafamilial households to acquire the so-called domestic arts and relieve their families of extra mouths to feed. In agricultural regions where primogeniture was practiced, the eldest son rarely left the household he was destined to inherit. Further, in areas where families typically pooled their labor, as in cottage industries or viniculture, apprenticeship outside the family household was uncommon, since parents could productively employ the labor of all their children.

Despite its variety (all manner of intermediate forms existed) apprenticeships shared several characteristics. First, both economic and educational forces were always at work, though the relative importance of each varied greatly. Further, whatever the context, apprentices acquired knowledge and skill inductively through work. Much like children who acquire language without formal study, apprentices learned through observation, imitation, practice, and interaction with experienced practitioners. Finally, all apprentices learned more than practical skills and the meaning of hard work; they also acquired their community's norms of moral and professional behavior. As teacher and role model, the master served a public function—one in which the community as a whole had a vested interest. Within individual households and shops, however, private interests always mediated this public function. As these grew more legitimate and openly pursued, the practice of apprenticeship shed its public purpose, metamorphosing into a private contract.

Modern Development

Apprenticeship experienced a steep, and apparently permanent, decline in the wake of industrialization. Insofar as it functioned as an economic exchange, its transformation into a wage relationship had several benefits. Wages greatly enhanced the freedom of the young, permitting them to limit their hours of work, bring an end to onerous household chores, escape the master's household and round-the-clock surveillance, and change employers freely. They also permitted poorer families to keep their older children at home by pooling incomes. Masters, too, were often happy to rid their homes of unruly and unreliable adolescents. Moreover, wage relations allowed them to hire and fire young workers as the need arose. However, since employment relations implied no training, employers had no obligation to instruct the young beyond what was required to perform the work at hand. Learning continued as a by-product of work, but as the division of labor grew within centralized factories, the scope of learning shrank.

It is easy to overstate the decline of apprenticeship, however. In rural areas it lingered on well into the 1900s. More significantly, firms throughout the industrializing regions of

Europe and North America began to experiment with modern forms of apprenticeship after 1880. As workforce composition shifted from the low-skill textile, leatherworking, and needle trades to metals production, machine building, and metalworking, apprenticeships grew sharply. Employers in the most dynamic and technologically sophisticated sectors of the economy discovered that in-house training offered the only way to provide skilled labor in a period of breakneck expansion. By 1910 nearly all of the world's leading firms had established expensive apprenticeship programs, often accompanied by corporation schools. Few firms captured returns on these training investments, however.

Because of the way modern work conditions transformed work, the initial year of apprenticeship involved costly full-time training, divorced from productive labor. Firms sought to capture these costs during the final year of a three-year indenture, when apprentices produced more than they were paid for. In a period of growing demand for skills, however, apprentices often abrogated their contracts for higher wages elsewhere. This experience taught firms that it was cheaper to poach than to train. But when everybody poached and nobody trained, the global production of skills fell.

Two distinct responses to this quandary emerged. The first, pursued most systematically by U.S. firms, dispensed with apprenticeship. Rapid productivity gains associated with mass production in the 1920s permitted output to expand without a corresponding growth in the labor force. As average job tenure grew and the ratio of green to experienced workers declined, firms found it possible to dispense with preservice training and make do with on-the-job learning. Further contributing to this informal training regime, elaborate divisions of labor, narrow job definitions, and job ladders permitted a stepwise acquisition of experience and skill. Finally, U.S. firms turned decisively to high schools and colleges after 1920 for the recruitment of their white-collar personnel. Thus, apprenticeship survived primarily in the building trades, the one sector of the U.S. economy in which mass production strategies have limited application and unions have remained strong enough to regulate training.

The second strategy, typified by Germany, involved the collective regulation of apprenticeship, a solution built upon a social partnership between organized groups of employers and workers. Germans found it difficult to adopt American mass production strategies in the face of American competition, especially since their historic strength was in the production of custom-made industrial equipment and high-quality consumer goods. Moreover, the importance and modernization of Germany's crafts between 1890 and 1913 made the transition to highly regulated, instructional forms of craft, industrial, and commercial apprenticeship easier.

Gradually, Germany built an elaborate system of vocational training, testing, and certification that forced apprentices to honor their contracts and imposed public training standards on private training firms. In effect, the practice of apprenticeship professionalized most German occupations, while also providing an appealing educational alternative to full-time schooling for two out of every three Germans.

The great advantage of apprenticeship as an instructional device derives from the way it ties learning to real-world applications, imbuing the process with intrinsic motivation and rewards. In view of the general disaffection throughout the industrialized world with the shortcomings and inequities of school-based educational regimes, government officials, employers' organizations, and unions have developed a renewed interest in apprenticeship. Nowhere has this been greater than in Europe, where nearly all the major European countries (e.g., Germany, Austria, Denmark, France, the United Kingdom) have active vocational programs in which apprenticeship plays a central part. Americans, in contrast, generally consider vocational education to be second class and unworthy of a democratic society. Arguably, this has had more to do with how vocational programs evolved in the United States than with their intrinsic merits. Where apprenticeship programs have been well regulated, rigorous, and led to good jobs, they have proven popular, motivated students to learn, and enhanced social and economic equality.

See also: **Child Labor in the West; Early Modern Europe; Economics and Children in Western Societies; European Industrialization; Medieval and Renaissance Europe; Vocational Education, Industrial Education, and Trade Schools.**

BIBLIOGRAPHY

Ainley, Patrick, and Helen Rainbird, eds. 1999. *Apprenticeship: Toward a New Paradigm of Learning.* London: Kogan Page.

Douglas, Paul. 1921. *American Apprenticeship and Industrial Education.* New York: Columbia University.

Hajnal, John. 1965. "European Marriage Patterns in Perspective." In *Population in History: Essays in Historical Demography,* ed. D. V. Glass and David E. Eversley. London: Arnold.

Hamilton, Stephen. 1990. *Apprenticeship for Adulthood: Preparing Youth for the Future.* New York: Free Press.

Land, Joan. 1996. *Apprenticeship in England, 1600–1914.* London: UCL Press.

Rorabaugh, W. J. 1986. *The Craft Apprentice: From Franklin to the Machine Age in America.* New York: Oxford University Press.

HAL HANSEN

Architecture. *See* Children's Spaces; School Buildings and Architecture.

Ariès, Philippe (1914–1984)

The French historical demographer and pioneering historian of collective mentalities Philippe Ariès is best known for his *L'Enfant et la vie familiale sous l'Ancien Régime* (1960, published in English in 1962 as *Centuries of Childhood*), the seminal study that launched historical scholarship on childhood and family life in the Western world. Born into a middle-class professional family with Catholic religious convictions and sentimental attachments to the traditions of old France, Ariès earned his *licence* in history and geography at the University of Grenoble and his *diplôme d'études supérieures* at the University of Paris (Sorbonne) in 1936 with a thesis on the judicial nobility of Paris in the sixteenth century. During the late 1930s, he was also a journalist for the student newspaper of the royalist Action française and was active in allied right-wing intellectual circles, notably the Cercle Fustel de Coulanges, through which he became acquainted with Daniel Halévy and other old-fashioned men of letters. During the war years, he taught briefly at a Vichy-sponsored training college, then accepted a post as director of a documentation center for international commerce in tropical fruit, where he worked for most of his adult life. But history was his passion, and he led a parallel life as a researcher and independent scholar in a new kind of cultural history.

Ariès's ideas about the history of childhood and family were inspired by the public debate under Vichy about the crisis of the French family. While initially sympathetic with the proposals of Vichy's leaders for the family's rehabilitation, he disputed their claims about its moral decline and their fears about the biological decay of the French population. He embarked on his research in historical demography to challenge such notions. His book *Histoire des populations françaises* (1948), inquired into the secrets of family life, where he discovered what he claimed was a "hidden revolution" in the mores of conjugal life during the early modern era, made manifest in the widening use of contraceptive practices among well-born married couples, the key element of a cluster of medical and cultural "techniques of life" that encouraged calculation and planning in family life. The emerging family that Ariès identified in his demographic research was distinctly modern in its mentality and became the subject of his following study of the rise of the affectionate family, *L'Enfant et la vie familiale sous l'Ancien Régime.*

In this book, Ariès examined the emergence of a new kind of sentiment among well-born families of the early modern era, made manifest especially in the rising value they attached to companionate marriage, their greater concern for the well-being of their children, and their newfound sentimentality about the vanishing mores of the traditional family. The new attitudes toward children, he argued, were not so much about simple affection (which is timeless) but rather solicitude for their proper development. Once relegated to the margins of family life, children increasingly became the center of its attention, and their particular needs for nurture and direction were openly acknowledged. Schooling, institutionalized first under religious and later under secular auspices, furthered this process. Such thinking presaged the elaboration of a developmental conception of the life cycle,

delineated over time in an ever more elaborate demarcation of the stages of life—first childhood, then youth, later ADOLESCENCE, and finally middle age.

L'Enfant et la vie familiale elicited widespread interest during the 1960s, especially among the helping professions in the United States, where its argument spoke to worries about the loosening ties of family life and an emerging crisis of adolescence in contemporary society. It also accorded well with the current vogue of ego psychology as epitomized in ERIK ERIKSON's theory about the lifelong psychosocial growth of the individual. Among historians Ariès's book was initially received appreciatively and stimulated much new historical research on childhood and the family, until then surprisingly neglected.

While historians in the English-speaking world, such as Lawrence Stone, eventually grew disenchanted with the broad cast and imprecision of Ariès's thesis, Ariès himself by the mid-1970s was gaining newfound respect among younger French historians for the bold new directions of his research. By then he had turned to the study of historical attitudes toward death and mourning, published what some consider his greatest work, *L'Homme devant la mort* (1977, published in English in 1991 as *The Hour of Our Death*) and participated in a much-publicized running debate on the topic with a friendly rival, the left-wing historian Michel Vovelle. In 1978 Ariès was elected to the faculty of the Ecole des hautes études en sciences sociales, a research center for new approaches to history. Admired as one of the most original minds in late-twentieth-century French historiography, he designed but did not live to see the publication of the five-volume *Histoire de la vie privée* (1985–1987, published in English in 1987–1991 as *The History of Private Life*), a synthesis of twenty-five years of scholarship in the history of collective mentalities.

Today, nearly a half century after its publication, Ariès's *L'Enfant et la vie familiale* remains a point of departure for the study of the history of childhood and family, although most often as a target for scholars who dispute his thesis about a revolution in sentiment in the early modern era (e.g., Steven Ozment), one that his earlier critics of the 1970s for the most part had accepted. It is interesting to note that late in life, Ariès returned to the topic of childhood and family, publishing articles on long-range changes in attitudes toward SEXUALITY and marriage, as well as on the crisis of adolescence and changing parent/child relationships in the contemporary age.

See also: **Comparative History of Childhood; History of Childhood.**

BIBLIOGRAPHY

Ariès, Philippe. 1960. *L'Enfant et la vie familiale sous l'Ancien Régime.* Paris: Plon.

Hutton, Patrick H. 2001. "Late-Life Historical Reflections of Philippe Ariès on the Family in Contemporary Culture." *Journal of Family History* 26: 395–410.

Hutton, Patrick H. 2004. *Philippe Ariès and the Politics of French Cultural History.* Amherst: University of Massachusetts Press.

Ozment, Steven. 2001. *Ancestors: The Loving Family in Old Europe.* Cambridge, MA: Harvard University Press.

Vann, Richard T. 1982. "The Youth of Centuries of Childhood." *History and Theory* 21: 279–297.

PATRICK H. HUTTON

Aristocratic Education in Europe

In order for a person to play an aristocratic role in society, education is of tremendous importance. The Shakespearean figure Orlando in *As You Like It* (1599–1600) is bitter in his grievance that his brother, Oliver, has undermined his gentility by training him as a peasant. Aristocrats since Homeric times have been men of honor who want to be the best and keep well ahead of the others; they must be educated to be strong and able to play a prominent role in the world. Our knowledge about the education of kings and noblemen begins to become coherent in the twelfth and thirteenth centuries, which saw the emergence of the important genre of didactic courtesy books giving advice on etiquette as well as treatises addressing the education of children in general.

The Middle Ages

The European aristocrats of the Middle Ages were the land-owning nobility, whose members were privileged by fiefs from the king in return for services in war. Although their prestige was increased by the deeds they exercised as armored knights on horseback, their honor as nobles was thought to be hereditary. In the eleventh century and especially in the twelfth, the upper nobility gained power at the expense of the lower and developed a refined set of manners and lifestyle with which to stage their prestige in great halls and at the kings' courts. Court life became the model of good behavior, and the word *courteous* came into the language.

Aristocratic children were brought up to be courteous knights and chatelaines—even aristocrats who became ecclesiastics learned to handle weapons. Parents made great efforts to organize the education of children by choosing masters, mistresses, and servants and planning marriages and careers. Babies had wet nurses, who fed them, and dry nurses, who took care of them in other ways—for example, rockers to rock the cradles. Aristocratic parents often had a noble lady who surveyed the upbringing of the infants. Royal children could have their own courts governed by noble persons appointed by the king. As soon as they could speak, children were introduced to the adult code of good manners and morality. In the great halls they listened together with the adults to tales about King Arthur and his knights of the Round Table with their ideals of virtue, bravery, loyalty, comradeship, courage, and determination to sacrifice life for something higher, pride deriving from acknowledgment of

proven superiority as well as competition among themselves to exceed the greatest deeds. The children learned proper table manners along with dancing, singing, and playing music. Games were a feature of daily life for both children and adults. Playing chess seems to have been used for educative purposes. Some children were raised by relatives, a custom which strengthened kinship, or they were sent to nobles of higher rank or if possible to the royal court, which gave them opportunities to learn more refined manners and to be educated by more erudite masters.

When children were six or seven years old a transition occurred. They continued to progress in the earlier mentioned topics, but the boys got male tutors, who taught them reading and writing as well as some Latin. Only a few nobles continued their studies at the university. Girls also learned to read and write, but their teaching was less formal and intensive. Boys began to participate in the prestigious sport of hunting, where they learned horsemanship and the management of weapons. Between the ages of twelve to fourteen they began the necessary physical training to become knights, learning to wear armor, handle swords and lances, and joust at tournaments. At age eighteen they entered knighthood. Girls did not learn to fight, but they learned to ride. Mistresses taught the young girls housekeeping and how to sew, weave, and spin. Needlework by aristocratic women, including exquisite embroideries and tapestries, was appreciated all over Europe.

Renaissance and Early Modern Times

During the sixteenth century armored knights lost their military significance, and kings and princes began to rely on mercenaries with firearms. At the same time, Renaissance humanism challenged the nobles' notion of inherited superiority and proclaimed the idea of a spiritual aristocracy deriving from a more refined control of bodily instincts as well as extensive literary skills. Aristocrats therefore needed a better education in order to compete with the learned bourgeois in obtaining the influential offices at the king's government. The image of the knight was still a symbol of nobility as shown in the persistent use of coats of arms and armored portraits, and knightly games continued in derivative forms such as riding at the ring. However, the physical exertions of the aristocratic male were formalized as these were transformed into a ceremonialized lifestyle that culminated in the Baroque and Rococo periods in an emphasis on look and manner, such as the donning of powder and wigs. It became a matter of extreme honor to act in accordance with the correct manners at court. In *Il cortegiano* (1528) the Italian writer Baldassare Castiglione put words to the new aristocratic ideals: the outer refined and carefully choreographed staging of the courtier reflected true inner nobility.

These new features influenced education. Dance, for example, became increasingly significant and attracted the interest of educational writers. Good dancers were more easily taught the look, the posture, and the gait necessary for success in aristocratic life. Music education continued, but now attention was also given to drawing and painting, which developed the visual sense. Aristocratic children continued to be brought up in the manor houses of their parents, by other noblemen, or at court. The formal literary education of boys was upgraded and now led by professional schoolmasters; such teaching became an occupation regulated by clock time and distinct from everyday life. Latin was the subject given most attention; some boys learned Greek and even Hebrew. As Italian and, later, French succeeded Latin as the lingua franca, it became important to learn these languages.

Boys also began to frequent educational institutions where they mixed with the bourgeoisie. Some, mostly in England, attended LATIN SCHOOLS, and aristocratic boys extended their presence at the universities as well. However, from an aristocratic point of view, universities could not teach the important qualities of honor, virtue, and taste. In 1594 Antoine de Pluvinel opened an *académie d'équitation* in Paris. Here young aristocrats learned horsemanship and fencing but also good manners, playing the lute, painting, mathematics, classical as well as modern languages, poetry, literature, and history. The academy emphasized the teaching of the mind as well as development of the body, which was to be hardened as well as refined according to aristocratic norms. Pluvinel's initiative attained royal support, and when aristocratic academies during the seventeenth century spread throughout Europe they were often founded by kings and princes. Most of the academies were boarding schools and taught Pluvinelian subjects to which later in the eighteenth century were added economics, agriculture, and *Staatswissenschaft* (statecraft). Schoolmasters were competent and sometimes called in from foreign countries.

Another feature of aristocratic education was the grand tour, during which a young man and his tutor traveled around Europe for some years studying at academies and universities. By associating with foreign members of their own rank young men learned refined cosmopolitan manners, eloquence, and languages. When they returned they were able to serve the state as officers, ambassadors, chancellors, counselors, governors, and judges.

The literary education of girls was also expanded. In addition to reading and writing they were now taught Italian and French. Many sixteenth-century writers presented such famous women of learning as Plato's Diotima and Queen Zenobia of Palmyra as models for contemporary women and urged the parents of girls to let their daughters study Latin and Greek as well as literature. Some women became famous in Europe for being learned, but in general the teaching of girls was still second to that of boys; the main emphases were still housekeeping and needlework.

The Decline of Aristocratic Education

The romantic-naturalistic educators who emerged in the eighteenth century saw the polite behavior of the aristocracy as fraudulent, without true virtue. The ideal was that infants should be brought up according to what was explained as their own inner natures. Thus they should not be polished by courteous manners. As the bourgeoisie took over power in society in the late-eighteenth and nineteenth centuries, its culture obtained a position of hegemony, and the old aristocratic education became ridiculous and eroded away. Stories from eighteenth-century Eton about well-born children fighting each other with a strong sense of honor were made fun of by the Victorians, and bourgeois ideals also took over at the aristocratic academies. In the patriotic and nationalistic education of the people, however, some fragments of aristocratic values did survive, such as the ideas of virtue, deeds, heritability of honor, and determination to sacrifice oneself for a higher purpose.

See also: **Education, Europe; Infant Rulers.**

BIBLIOGRAPHY

Andersen, Birte. 1971. *Adelig opfostring: Adelsborns opdragelse i Danmark 1536–1660.* Copenhagen: Gad.

Conrads, Norbert. 1982. *Ritterakademien der frühen Neuzeit: Bildung als Standesprivileg im 16. und 17. Jahrhundert.* Göttingen, Germany: Vandenhoeck and Ruprecht.

Hammerstein, Notker, ed. 1996. *Handbuch der Deutschen Bildungsgeschichte.* Vol. 1. Munich, Germany: C. H. Beck.

Hexter, John H. 1961. "The Education of the Aristocracy in the Renaissance." In *Reappraisals in History.* London: Longmans.

Marrou, Henri-Irénée. 1948. *Histoire de l'éducation dans l'antiquité.* Paris: Éditions du Seuil.

Motley, Mark. 1990. *Becoming a French Aristocrat: The Education of the Court Nobility, 1580–1715.* Princeton, NJ: Princeton University Press.

Orme, Nicholas. 1984. *From Childhood to Chivalry: The Education of the English Kings and Aristocracy 1066–1530.* London and New York: Methuen.

Wallbank, M. V. 1979. "Eighteenth Century Public Schools and the Education of the Governing Elite." *History of Education* 8: 1–19.

Woodward, William Harrison. 1906. *Studies in Education during the Age of the Renaissance 1400–1600.* Cambridge, UK: Cambridge University Press.

THOMAS LYNGBY

Aristotle (384–322 B.C.E.)

The Greek philosopher and scientist Aristotle was born in Stagira, a town in Chalcidice. For twenty years he was a member of Plato's school. He then taught philosophy at Atarneus in Asia Minor, in Mytilene on the island of Lesbos, and tutored the future Alexander the Great. In 335 to 334 he founded a school called the Lyceum in Athens.

Like Plato, Aristotle departed from the prevailing idea of childhood in Greek antiquity, according to which children were treated as miniature adults and schooled in adult literature as if their minds were able to function like those of adults. Aristotle's ideas on childhood are found, for the most part, in the *Nicomachean Ethics* and *Politics*, in which the aim is to strive for the highest good, happiness, in a city-state. His ethical and political writings are interrelated parts of a whole: because human beings are by nature political (we would say *social*) animals, one cannot become happy apart from a community. People become individuals as participating members of a social context by sharing certain ends with others and working with them to realize those ends.

Aristotle insists that the conduct by which we strive for the highest good is learned; it is not inborn. That conduct comes about as the consequence of growing, as experienced adults attempt to acknowledge (1) the nature of children who are to be educated toward the best conduct of which they are capable, and (2) the nature of educated adults who have gained some measure of that conduct. Children, Aristotle holds, are incapable of happiness inasmuch as they have not developed the ability to use their intelligence to guide their actions. Children live as their desires impel them; as their development is incomplete, so their desires may lead them to harmful consequences. The behavior of children is akin to that of licentiousness in adults, Aristotle says; but while adults are capable of knowing that they are licentious, children are not.

Children should be trained in the direction of virtuous conduct but cannot engage in such conduct until their intellects develop in such manner that they can determine which means to employ in the pursuit of moral and social ends. This is why children need teachers who conduct themselves according to high moral principles. Training children's desires is not just for the sake of their desires; the training is ultimately for the sake of their developing intellects. As a corollary, one may say that training their bodies is not just for the sake of their bodies, but ultimately for the sake of the souls that are being shaped.

The difficulties in educating children's desires for the sake of their intellects, and in educating their bodies for the sake of their souls, are many. For one thing, the intellects of children's teachers can miss the highest principles of morality, with the result that children may be trained incorrectly. For another thing, certain desires of children, if left unattended by wiser adults, get in the way of proper growth. Aristotle generalizes this difficulty in a memorable passage in the *Eudemian Ethics*, saying that while the good is simple, the bad comes in many shapes. With these difficulties in mind, it is clear that training children's desires and bodies so that they may be enabled to gain some measure of virtuous conduct is a difficult undertaking, fraught with many obstacles stemming from children's desires as well as from the shortcomings of their teachers. In one passage, Aristotle calls learning a *painful* process.

While Aristotle departed from the idea that children may be viewed as miniature adults and thus cannot be expected to engage meaningfully in adult intellectual activities, he was not "permissive" in a modern sense. He did not believe that it should be left to children to determine what they are to do; rather, educated adults, even if they have missed the highest principles of morality, should have some sense of what children can and should do. With this in mind, Aristotle argues that the kind of games children play, as well as the stories appropriate for them, are to be determined by educational officials. Most games, Aristotle holds, ought to be imitations of serious occupations of later life; while children cannot reason as adults are expected to do, they can imitate certain activities without knowing why they are engaged in them. If their education succeeds in realizing the moral aims of their teachers, they can understand the reasons for those activities when they become adults. Their training in childhood is for ultimate happiness, even though children are incapable of happiness: the aim is to enable them to *become happy*.

Private education prevailed in the Greek states in Aristotle's time. Aristotle opposed this practice, arguing that it is an injustice for states to punish citizens who had not been educated in the ways of right conduct. He insisted that states should be responsible for educating their citizens. Pointing out that the state is a plurality that should be made into a community by education, Aristotle argued that public education should strive to work toward common ends to be sought by all citizens, and that the inseparability of the individual and the community constitutes an essential condition requiring public education. Thus the social and moral unity that Aristotle encompassed in his *Nicomachean Ethics* and *Politics* is to be forged and maintained as a *public* responsibility. In this context, the educational officials responsible for determining children's games and stories serve to establish and maintain the public good.

Aristotle connects the pursuit of philosophy with the musical education of children by pointing out that the tunes and modes of musical education must have *ethical* value. He closes the *Politics* by holding that we must be mindful of three aims of education—the happy mean, the possible, and the appropriate. In keeping with his idea that while children are incapable of happiness, education should strive for them to become happy as adults, Aristotle reminds us that what is possible and appropriate for adults is not so for children. What is possible and appropriate for children is for the sake of what they are capable of becoming.

See also: **Ancient Greece and Rome; Plato.**

BIBLIOGRAPHY

Aristotle. 1932. *The Politics.* Trans. H. Rackham. Cambridge, MA: Harvard University Press.

Aristotle. 1934. *Nicomachean Ethics.* Trans. H. Rackham. Cambridge, MA: Harvard University Press.

Burnet, John, trans. and ed. 1967. *Aristotle on Education: Being Extracts From the Ethics and Politics.* Cambridge, UK: Cambridge University Press.

Chambliss, J. J. 1982. "Aristotle's Conception of Childhood and the Poliscraft." *Educational Studies* 13:33–43.

Curren, Randall R. 2000. *Aristotle on the Necessity of Public Education.* Lanham, MD: Rowman and Littlefield.

Randall, John Herman, Jr. 1960. *Aristotle.* New York: Columbia University Press.

J. J. CHAMBLISS

Artificial Insemination

Artificial insemination is the mediated use of sperm to impregnate a woman. The term has historically been used in cases where this procedure is done under medical supervision, socially legitimized as a medical treatment for infertility. It has required medical legitimization because in most cases the sperm used is from a man who is not the woman's partner (artificial insemination by donor, or AID). Artificial insemination, likely practiced outside the medical setting for much of history, was first reported in the medical literature by John Hunter in 1790. In the early twentieth century, its popularity grew, and its moral and social implications were debated in both the medical and popular press in the United States starting in 1909, and in Europe by the 1940s. Supporters pointed to the joy of parents who were able to bear children thanks to the procedure. Critics believed that AID was a form of adultery, and that it promoted the vice of MASTURBATION. The Catholic Church objected to all forms of artificial insemination, saying that it promoted the vice of onanism and ignored the religious importance of coitus. Other critics were concerned that AID could encourage EUGENIC government policies.

As popular concerns about AID faded in Europe and the United States, the demand for donor sperm increased tremendously. In 1953, the first successful pregnancy from frozen sperm was reported, leading to the development of a thriving sperm-bank industry starting in the 1970s and the commercialization of AID. While a 1941 survey estimated that 3,700 inseminations had been performed in the United States, by 1987 U.S. doctors performed the procedure on about 172,000 women in a single year, resulting in 65,000 births. The growing number of AID pregnancies has raised new concerns, and in many places sparked new regulation. Because fresh sperm can be a source of sexually transmitted diseases, including HIV, testing of donors and donations has become routine in many clinics, and is required by many local and national governments. In addition, because the privacy of the donor is generally protected and it is physically possible to donate semen many times, in many places clinic policies and/or government regulations tightly restrict the number of times a single donor's semen may be used, in order to diminish the chances of unknowing marriage of biological siblings among AID children.

Legal and social questions surrounding AID in many countries reflect cultural concerns with biological paternity and the maintenance of the heterosexual, married couple as the basis of the family. The Catholic Church and many interpreters of ISLAM consider AID to be adulterous, and as of 1990, it was banned in BRAZIL, Egypt, and Libya. Ireland, ISRAEL, Italy, and South Africa restricted its use to married couples and many more countries have not approved its use by lesbian couples. While a number of European countries have instituted regulations legitimizing AID children as the offspring of the mother's husband or partner, providing he had given written consent, in many places the law remains ambiguous. While many clinics and some governments deny clinical AID services to single women and lesbians, some feminists have organized to demedicalize AID and provide services to women creating nontraditional families. Debates rage about what to tell AID children about their biological parentage. AID is one of several new reproductive technologies which challenge the "naturalness" and inevitability of identifying social kinship with biological kinship.

See also: **Adoption; Conception and Birth; Egg Donation; Fertility Drugs; Obstetrics and Midwifery; Surrogacy.**

BIBLIOGRAPHY

Arditti, Rita, Shelley Minden, and Renate Klein. 1984. *Test-Tube Women: What Future for Motherhood?* Boston: Pandora Press.

Meyer, Cheryl L. 1997. *The Wandering Uterus: Politics and the Reproductive Rights of Women.* New York: New York University Press.

Pfeffer, Naomi. 1993. *The Stork and the Syringe: A Political History of Reproductive Medicine.* Cambridge, MA: Polity Press.

Strathern, Marilyn. 1992. *Reproducing the Future: Essays on Anthropology, Kinship, and the New Reproductive Technologies.* New York: Routledge.

LARA FREIDENFELDS

Asia. *See* China; Japan; India and South Asia.

Attention Deficit Disorder. *See* Hyperactivity.

Australia

Perceptions of childhood in Australia have long been dominated by the notion that there used to be and perhaps still is something special, precious, and distinctive about the Australian child. Yet it is difficult to reconcile this generalized national child with the exceptionally broad range of actual childhood experience. In fact, what has been more distinctive about Australian childhood may be the profound and pervasive influence of this nationalist ideal on child-raising concepts and welfare policies, helping to justify and rationalize a broad range of interventions between parent and child.

Colonized at the end of the eighteenth century, largely by British emigrants, it was almost inevitable that the Australian continent would be seen not just as another New World but as an ideal environment in which to rear the young. Sentimental and economic investment in childhood merged with concurrent ideals of individual liberty and egalitarianism to produce a particularly trenchant version of the prevailing cult of childhood innocence and malleability. Every child was a potential citizen, and the seedbed of all that the individual and the nation might become. And such was the opportunity to realize this potential, and the freedom from the dictatorial Old World constraints of father, church, or crown, that childhood could not but be joyous, mischievous, and free. Thus, as early as the 1820s, it was said that the children of people who arrived as convicts flourished in Australia to the point where they overcame both the vices and disadvantages of their parents.

The Nationalist Ideal

By the late nineteenth century, growing nationalist sentiment stepped in to foster these ideals. The separation and elevation of the child's world became imbued both with patriotic fervor and with EUGENIC concerns, so that the white Australian child, and particularly the adolescent, was seen to epitomize the vitality and resources of nation and race. This was true elsewhere but was especially the case in Australia, where the new nation was perceived as an innocent, energetic, and independent offshoot of the old. Idealistic and young, it was represented as eager to equal and impress the wily old mother country, though not throw off all of the maternal bonds.

This construction of a nationalist child was all the more pervasive in Australia because of its particular identification with the land, or bush. In the lead-up to Federation, nationalists created an influential rural ideology postulating that special spiritual, mental, and physical qualities were fostered by the white Australian's battle to explore, cultivate, and tame the inland. This ideology was soon applied to the young, especially boys. The result was a stream of journalism, ballads, stories, paintings, photographs, and later films celebrating a hardy little bush-bred (white) boy whose potential manhood was honed in helping to fight bushfires, blacks, floods, and drought, then tested and proved on the battlefields of World Wars I and II. This lively little Australian male was a miniature pioneer, fairly rebellious, even a larrikin, but always heterosexual, innocent, and never the moral cripple that social reformers imagined inhabited the city slum.

Viewed through this nationalist lens, the ideal Australian child was also exceptionally healthy, always provided he was reared in the wide sunny spaces of the bush, or failing that, the beach. Even in the days of convict colonization, tallness in the native-born was taken as a measure not just of physical health but of moral rectitude, and by the 1880s the measurement and medical inspection of school children was seen as crucial for assessing how well the white population might fill up the nation's vast interior and people its tropical north. A falling birthrate and rising rates of INFANT MORTALITY lent fuel to these concerns, the more so since the first generations of "currency" children (the first generations of white children born in Australia) had been isolated by sheer distance from the main infectious diseases that elsewhere afflicted the young. But rising family immigration, peaking during the gold rushes of the 1850s, and the concentration of the child population in the growing ports and towns, meant that mortality rates soon approached those of the main European centers. The presence of more prolific and supposedly expansionist nations to the north lent a special urgency to public health initiatives to reduce mortality and improve the physique of the white Australian child.

This nationalist ideology rested uneasily with the modernization of the family, feminism, and the elevation of women as "mothers of the race." In Australian nationalist cultural products, younger children, mothers, and girls were more often associated with urban life, and even with the perceived disease and corruption of the city. If they strayed into the male realm of the bush, they were routinely depicted as lost in it, or driven mad by it, or even more misogynistically, as spoiling male freedom and camaraderie by venturing there at all. Mothers were invisible, peripheral, or heavily criticized as spoiling the development of their sons, while the ideal father became defined as boyish and egalitarian—a mate. The application of nationalist ideals to girls was seen as doubtful in the extreme. Sisters rarely appeared in the nationalist ideal, and if they did they had to be much more obedient than males, and fairly athletic. Sometimes thought of as "little Aussie battlers," above all they had to be good sports.

State Involvement

This ideology operated not merely to obscure the numerous departures from the ideal, but to justify a broad range of interventions in other patterns of child life that were thought to threaten the nationalist ideal. These departures were not intrinsically different from similar initiatives elsewhere, and were similarly liberal, justified in terms of the need to realize the rights of the child. In Australia, however, they were particularly trenchant, owing to the early and powerful role of the state in constructing and refining family life.

Beginning in the earliest settlements, the lack, for most families, of a network of supportive kin, coupled with the paucity of established, well-endowed charities, meant that the nascent state was forced to provide both food and clothing for impoverished mothers and children and construct a network of ORPHANAGES and asylums to house them. Arguably the penal nature of the earliest societies and the prejudice against women convicts began a tradition whereby it was perceived as mandatory to remove the vulnerable infant from mothers deemed unfit, sending them either into institutions or to families who would take over their upbringing.

During the colonial period, the idea that Australia was a healthy place to send British orphans and juvenile offenders meant that approved families in Australia became accustomed to receiving other people's children, who were both a labor source and a future population resource. And though the extremes of child labor characteristic of industrialized cities in Britain were not a feature of Australian child life, the ongoing demand for domestic and especially rural labor meant that children removed from the care of relatives and parents were exploited, even into the early twentieth century and beyond. Cases of cruelty and sexual abuse in the various children's institutions themselves were not unusual but normally went undetected until a change in legislation or in personnel caused a government enquiry, followed by a reshuffling of staff.

Another factor making for high rates of child removal in Australia was the early demographic imbalance. The colonial convict system, followed by waves of gold rush immigration, favored a predominance of males, which was not corrected by the efforts of moral reformers to import shiploads of pauper women and girls. It was not until the 1860s that sex ratios began to level out and rates of marriage and family formation began to increase, and by that time concerns about illegitimacy, prostitution, male HOMOSEXUALITY, and VENEREAL DISEASE further seemed to justify removal of the "innocent" child.

Patterns of male employment further weakened the family life of children at risk. Even as late as the 1950s, the bush provided opportunities for men, single and married, to eke out a living, usually as itinerant bush workers—fencing, mustering, droving, and shearing—and sometimes as goldseekers, or fossickers, after the main alluvial deposits had been won. Coupled with the fact that Australia was largely an immigrant society, the result was high rates of family desertion, especially during the nineteenth century, with husbands and fathers slipping away, either up the country or back to families left behind in Britain. Efforts by the state to force men to provide maintenance were largely unsuccessful, and it was the state that assumed the role of father, further creating a tradition of bureaucratic control over family life.

Intervention and Aboriginal Children

This pattern of intervention in child life undoubtedly had its most severe and prolonged effect on the continent's indigenous children. The practice of taking in Aboriginal children who appeared to be ORPHANS dated from the earliest days of settlement at Sydney, when Nanbaree and Booron, left homeless by the first smallpox epidemic, were placed as servants in the homes of two prominent officials. But even this initial act was not entirely charitable. The children were expected to become servants, and within a decade a phrenological report on their "progress" towards "civilization" had appeared in an American scientific journal. Both children were considered failures, beginning a pattern that was to be re-

peated thousands of times around the continent as children whose families had been killed, had died of disease, or simply could not be found at the moment were taken away, first informally by settlers, whalers, sealers, and pastoral workers, either for labor or sexual purposes or both, and later by authorized agents of the state. The fact that these children, if they survived, usually tried to find their way back to their own people was taken as a further indicator of their nomadic habits, and hence of their need to be removed.

While the state never officially condoned cruelty or the sexual exploitation of indigenous children, as was true of all the other Australian children removed "for their own good," the cruelty of the act of removal was not seen as an issue. For non-Aboriginal children, from the early twentieth century on, new theories of the importance of mothering, plus the sheer cost of institutionalizing so many, forced an increasing emphasis on monitoring impoverished children or juvenile offenders in their own households. For Aboriginal children, however, archaic policies of wholesale removal and long-term separation continued to be applied. This racial edge in state policy became apparent as early as the 1880s, when Aboriginal children began to be excluded from compulsory primary education. In this period, spates of new legislation specified precisely where Aboriginal families might live and work, and in some cases legislation also sought to control Aboriginal marriage. These policies continued into the 1960s, and in some states even later. Meanwhile, Aboriginal living conditions remained appalling, and infant mortality and child removal and incarceration rates remained extraordinarily high.

Conclusion

For many children, Australia has undoubtedly been a place to grow up happy and contented. The absence of a rigid, hereditary class structure and of extreme exploitation in factories and mines, the early provision of facilities for education, and even the ever-present bush and beach have all made for equality of opportunity as well as freedom and fun. The down side has been the narrow, interventionist, and in some cases racially motivated agenda that has always underlain the otherwise well-intentioned rhetoric of the rights of the child.

See also: **New Zealand; Placing Out.**

BIBLIOGRAPHY

Kociumbas, Jan. 1997. *Australian Childhood: A History*. St. Leonards, NSW, Australia: Allen and Unwin.

JAN KOCIUMBAS

Autobiographies

Children from the past have not left autobiographies in the strict sense of the word. Most writers working in the genre tend to come to it around the age of fifty. That, at least, was the age at which JEAN-JACQUES ROUSSEAU wrote his *Confessions*, a work that was to be an influential example over the following two centuries. As the writers of diaries, children under the age of fifteen have left more traces, although even these were initially quite rare. There are only seven known children's diaries from England and the United States written prior to 1800. In the Netherlands, systematic research yielded six surviving diaries by children written before 1814. Among them was that by Otto van Eck, who filled over 1500 pages in seven years, starting in 1791 when he was ten. He wrote his diary at the behest of his parents, in keeping with an educational strategy recommended by pedagogues since the late eighteenth century. The writing of a diary was meant to increase the child's self-knowledge. Parents were to read their children's diaries in order to closely follow their development. In the nineteenth century, the writing of diaries became especially popular with young women, as Philippe Lejeune established. The best-known diary from this period is by the Russian-born Marie Bashkirtseff, who started writing when she was fifteen years old. Her diary was published in 1887, following her early death. The book caused a sensation, first in France, and after being translated also in England and even more so in America. Never before had a young woman openly claimed to have ambitions as an artist, been so hungry for fame and so egotistical. But in another respect it conformed to a more common pattern—it was published by her father who had edited the text. Many children's diaries survived only to serve as a memorial because of an early death; this was also the case with Otto van Eck, who died at seventeen. *The Diary of Anne Frank*, the most famous diary written by a young person, also fits this pattern. ANNE FRANK kept her diary while hiding in Amsterdam during World War II. She and her family were discovered and deported, and only her father survived. The first edition of Anne's diary was published in 1947 through the initiative of her father.

In the twentieth century, the writing of diaries was still being encouraged by educators. Moreover, such texts were now used as sources for their studies. In Germany, for instance, this was done by CHARLOTTE BÜHLER. Educators now saw writing as an aid to the development of self-consciousness, not as a means of control. The diary developed into the ultimate form of private writing, and even parents had to respect this privacy. Teachers encouraged the writing of diaries to promote writing skills. The writing of a fictional diary often became part of language lessons. Later, some children would keep diaries on the Internet, which again stimulated debate about the private or public character of children's diaries.

Beginning with Rousseau autobiographies written in adulthood began to focus on childhood as a formative stage in the writers' lives. The way in which autobiographers recalled their memories also changed. Associative memories became important, and details once seen as trivial were now regarded as meaningful. In the nineteenth century a specific genre of childhood memories developed. A new literary genre was the *Bildungsroman*, a narrative of the development of a child into adulthood. This genre in turn influenced the lives of its young readers. One of the first examples was published by the German novelist Heinrich Jung-Stilling in 1777. According to Richard N. Coe, poets and novelists were especially able to conjure up their childhood in creative ways. Outside Europe, childhood memories as a genre developed in the twentieth century; with the Japanese writer Ju'ichro Tanizaki as an early example. Thus, the western view of childhood was exported to the rest of the world in literary form. As a literary form, childhood memories are today written in every part of the world, but content and form can vary in different cultures. Psychological research has made clear that there are significant differences in the working of what is called *long-term autobiographical memory*. Scholars and scientists still have many questions to answer about the act of recalling childhood years and transforming memories into literature.

See also: **Children's Literature.**

BIBLIOGRAPHY

Baggerman, Arianne. 1997. "The Cultural Universe of a Dutch Child, Otto van Eck and his Literature." *Eighteenth Century Studies* 31: 129–134.

Bashkirtseff, Marie. 1980. *The Journal of Marie Bashkirtseff.* Trans. Mathilde Blind. London: Virago.

Coe, Richard N. 1984. *When the Grass Was Taller: Autobiography and the Experience of Childhood.* New Haven, CT: Yale University Press.

Dekker, Rudolf. 2000. *Childhood, Memory and Autobiography in Holland from the Golden Age to Romanticism.* New York: St. Martin's.

Wang, Qi, and Michelle D. Leichman. 2000. "Same Beginnings, Different Stories: A Comparison of American and Chinese Children's Narratives." *Child Development* 71: 13–29.

ARIANNE BAGGERMAN
RUDOLF M. DEKKER

Automobiles. *See* Cars as Toys.

B

Baby Boom Generation

Born between 1946 and 1964, the baby boomers represent the largest generational birth cohort in U.S. history—nearly 76.5 million in total. Following World War II, a fertility surge coincided with rapid economic expansion. Government, industry, and society all fueled the boom. Governmental policies encouraged particular models of suburban family life, from expanded veterans' benefits and easy housing loans to the replacement of many women in wartime jobs with men in peacetime employment. From 1950 to 1970, the suburban population doubled, from 36 to 72 million, becoming the largest single sector of the nation's population. Though suburbanization was a predominantly white, middle-class phenomenon, the boom crossed nearly all categories of race, class, ethnicity, and religion. Liberalized immigration policies also contributed to increases in the birthrate, especially for Mexican and Chinese people in the United States, throughout the late 1940s and 1950s.

The Early Boomers

As Cold War anticommunism and pro-corporatism merged with the suburban ideal, the nuclear family became charged with symbolic and practical meanings for the health of the individual, community, and nation. Those who did not fit into the ideal suburban, middle-class, married, white family structure faced stigmatization. Black female household heads were frequently held accountable for their own poverty, and their children were marginalized. Such attitudes made it possible to formally and informally deny young, poor women of color access to a variety of health and social services throughout the 1950s and 1960s.

Community displacement due to wartime and postwar mobility and suburbanization decreased the role of extended family networks in providing parenting advice and support. In an age of technological innovation, parents turned to experts such as Dr. BENJAMIN SPOCK, who encouraged positive reinforcement and full-time parental devotion to affection-

ate child-raising. Throughout the 1950s and 1960s, critics grew concerned with the potential lack of limits that could result from what scholar Richard Hofstadter called "the overvalued child."

Boomer childhoods were filled with vast institutional, social, and media attention. During the 1950s and early 1960s, elementary schools could not be built fast enough to keep up with demand, and membership in Little League and the Boy and Girl Scouts exploded. Churches enjoyed a rise in membership from 64.5 million in 1940 to 114.5 million in 1960 and especially in the suburbs churches developed recreational and youth programs.

The media quickly recognized the potential to reach the boomer child market via the new phenomenon of TELEVISION. The growth of children's programming, such as *The Mickey Mouse Club*, which began in 1955, allowed direct toy advertising to children, cutting parents and educators out of the loop. TOYS also shifted from parent-directed play to advertiser-led consumption. BARBIE, for example, introduced in 1959, just as older boomers headed into adolescence, modeled a teenage lifestyle of carefree consumerism rather than an idealization of motherhood or family.

In their teens, boomers continued to transform institutions and culture. HIGH SCHOOL enrollment rose due to both the sheer quantity of TEENAGERS and an increasing pressure to keep all teenagers in school through graduation. Perhaps most significantly, boomers experienced the rewards and strains of school integration, which gradually followed BROWN V. BOARD OF EDUCATION in 1954. Questions of racial integration and equality were concerns for most young people. Little practical change occurred until the decade after the Civil Rights Act (1964–1968), when 75 percent of African-American students still attended segregated schools. For later boomers, experiences of mandatory integration through the busing of students to various districts were common. By 1976, only 17 percent of black students still attended formally segregated schools.

Youth DATING culture changed significantly throughout the 1950s and 1960s. In the early postwar years, the previous system of dating many different people was replaced by the ideal of "going steady" with a single partner. Premarital intercourse became more common, although long after the advent of the BIRTH CONTROL pill in 1960, and even the legalization of abortion with *Roe v. Wade* in 1973, young people tended to be critical of "going all the way," or having sexual intercourse.

Like their parents, boomer teens eagerly embraced consumerism as a means of personal fulfillment, although they rejected the corollary of familial security. Marketing expanded to meet their desires for "self-expression," with everything from mod clothes to rock music. By the late 1960s, anti-materialist youth aesthetics were conjoined with teens who had higher disposable incomes and greater recreational expenditures than any previous generation. As such, the combination of consumerism and the linked belief in the therapeutic self came to define the baby boom generation. Together, they fueled young people's insistence on free expression, from boys wearing long hair in high school to the purchasing of "alternative" clothing, rock music, and drugs, to protesting against the Vietnam-era military draft.

Protest they did. In the late 1960s, high school students fought for a say on dress code regulations, textbook selection, and club management, engaging in sit-ins and publishing underground newspapers. They received validation from the more extensive and radical boomer college battles about free speech, the war, civil rights, and women's issues. They also found support in such institutional high places as the U.S. Supreme Court, which, in TINKER V. DES MOINES in 1969, ruled that high school students had a right to free speech. Young people also found inspiration in a countercultural movement for personal liberation that was geared toward universal love and a rejection of such mainstream values as monogamy and careerism.

While the way for part-time, discretionary-fund teen employment was paved by the rise of suburban shopping malls and fast-food restaurants, nonwhite and lower-income teens, especially young men in inner cities, needed jobs. For them, opportunities to work became scarcer throughout the 1960s and 1970s. Young people participated in a wave of urban uprisings throughout the mid- to late-1960s. They also organized to attack systems that failed to address their needs. In March 1968, for example, Chicano and Chicana youth organized a boycott of five East Los Angeles high schools to protest overcrowding, discriminatory practices, and related high drop-out levels.

The Late Boomers

Unlike early boomers, who were born between 1946 and 1955 and were collectively named *Time*'s Man of the Year in 1967, late boomers (born 1956 through 1964) were in many ways the generation's forgotten members. American society

was less invested in raising them as "ideal" children than it was in simply managing them. Many youth-related institutions were prepared to accommodate them. To further facilitate the gradual transition from childhood to adolescence, the 1970s saw the rise of the middle school. In 1966, only 499 existed, but by 1980 there were over 6,000.

Teenagers in the 1970s, in large part, retreated from political activity into a consumer-based exploration of peer-based belonging. Recreational drug use rose dramatically, and due in part to the women's movement and sexual liberation, teens experienced a gradual shifting away from formalized steady courtship toward heterosexual group socializing with more informal dating and sexual relations. Nevertheless, for some late boomers the 1970s were a time of involvement within the growing movements for people of color, women, gay people, and the environment.

Baby boomers redefined the meanings of childhood and youth in the United States. YOUTH CULTURE and institutions will continue to feel their presence for decades to come.

See also: **Campus Revolts in the 1960s; Drugs; Twenty-Sixth Amendment; Rock and Roll; Youth Activism.**

BIBLIOGRAPHY

Bailey, Beth L. 1988. *From Front Porch to Back Seat: Courtship in Twentieth-Century America.* Baltimore, MD: Johns Hopkins University Press.

Chafe, William H. 1981. *Civilities and Civil Rights: Greensboro, North Carolina, and the Black Struggle for Freedom.* New York: Oxford University Press.

Chávez, Ernesto. 1998. "'The Birth of a New Symbol': The Brown Berets' Gendered Chicano National Imaginary." In *Generations of Youth: Youth Cultures and History in Twentieth-Century America,* ed. Joe Austin and Michael Nevin Willard. New York: New York University Press.

Echols, Alice. 1989. *Daring to Be Bad: Radical Feminism in America, 1967–1975.* Minneapolis: University of Minnesota Press.

Gutiérrez, David G. 1995. *Walls and Mirrors: Mexican Americans, Mexican Immigrants, and the Politics of Ethnicity.* Berkeley: University of California Press.

Jackson, Kenneth T. 1985. *Crabgrass Frontier: The Suburbanization of the United States.* New York: Oxford University Press.

Jones, Jacqueline. 1986. *Labor of Love, Labor of Sorrow.* New York: Vintage Books.

Jones, Landon Y. 1980. *Great Expectations: America and the Baby Boom Generation.* New York: Coward, McCann and Geoghegan.

May, Elaine Tyler. 1988. *Homeward Bound: American Families in the Cold War Era.* New York: Basic Books.

Miller, James. 1994. *"Democracy Is in the Streets": From Port Huron to the Siege of Chicago,* 2nd ed. Cambridge, MA.: Harvard University Press.

Palladino, Grace. 1996. *Teenagers: An American History.* New York: BasicBooks.

Solinger, Rickie. 1992. *Wake Up Little Susie: Single Pregnancy and Race Before Roe v. Wade.* New York: Routledge.

Sugrue, Thomas J. 1996. *The Origins of the Urban Crisis: Race and Inequality in Postwar Detroit.* Princeton, NJ: Princeton University Press.

DON ROMESBURG

Baby Farming

In the latter half of the nineteenth century, the practice of baby farming came under scrutiny in both Britain and the United States. *Baby farming* referred to a system in which infants were sent away to be nursed and boarded by private individuals for either a flat, one-time fee or a weekly or monthly charge. Baby farmers, usually middle-aged women, solicited these infants through "adoption" advertisements in newspapers, and through nurses, midwives, and the keepers of lying-in houses (private houses where poor, unwed women could pay to give birth and arrange for the transfer of their infants to baby farmers).

In 1868, the *British Medical Journal* published allegations that baby farming was just a form of commercial infanticide, that the infants in the care of baby farmers were deliberately and severely neglected, leading to their deaths. A very large percentage of the infants entrusted to the care of baby farmers did die, but the extent to which those deaths were intentional is less clear. According to historian Linda Gordon, babies sent to orphan asylums were as likely to die as those cared for by baby farmers. Some baby farmers seem to have done the best they could to raise healthy children but were restricted in their ability to provide basic care for the infants by poor parents who could afford only minimal payments and did not even necessarily pay those.

Equally nebulous are the intentions of the parents who turned their babies over to the care of baby farmers. Benjamin Waugh, a British reformer writing in 1890, claimed that most mothers were snared by seemingly respectable procurers who then turned the infants over to nefarious baby farmers. Some mothers, however, "infamous creatures, mere she-things," according to Waugh, looked to baby farmers to rid them of the problem of an unwanted, sometimes illegitimate, infant. Extreme poverty caused some well-meaning women to seek the help of respectable-seeming baby farmers, sometimes hoping to maintain contact with the child and the child's caregivers. The same poverty brought other parents to clearly disreputable baby farmers as a means of committing infanticide indirectly, with the promise of infant death sometimes being openly discussed by the parents and the baby farmer. Other infants were sent to baby farmers so that the mother could attain a job as a wet nurse, a relatively easy and well-paid job. Infanticide was very difficult to prove, particularly in cases of neglect. Nonetheless, in Central Middlesex, England, in 1867, 94 percent of all murder victims were under one year old.

The attention given to baby farming, in part through some sensational cases of mass infanticide, helped to build the SOCIETIES FOR THE PREVENTION OF CRUELTY TO CHILDREN in the United States and the Infant Life Protection Society in Britain. Reformers fought for laws requiring the registration of all births and of baby farmers. Britain passed the Infant Life Protection Act in 1872 requiring the registration of those boarding more than one infant. In the United States, Massachusetts passed an act requiring the registration of all boarding homes and of any illegitimate children given to board in 1882, but there were still cases of large-scale infanticide through baby farming operations revealed in the press in the first decade of the twentieth century.

See also: **Infant Feeding; Infant Mortality; Wet-Nursing.**

BIBLIOGRAPHY

Gordon, Linda. 1988. *Heroes of their Own Lives: The Politics and History of Family Violence, Boston 1880–1960.* New York: Penguin.

Rose, Lionel. 1986. *The Massacre of the Innocents: Infanticide in Britain, 1800–1939.* London: Routledge and Kegan Paul.

Waugh, Benjamin. 1890. "Baby-Farming." *Contemporary Review* 57: 700–714.

Zelizer, Viviana A. 1985. "From Baby Farms to Black-Market Babies: The Changing Market for Children." In *Pricing the Priceless Child: The Changing Social Value of Children,* ed. Viviana A. Zelizer. Princeton, NJ: Princeton University Press.

CAROLINE HINKLE MCCAMANT

Baby-Sitters

According to the *Oxford English Dictionary*, the earliest use of the term *baby-sitter* was in a 1937 publication that described "two high-school girls in the neighborhood who hire out for twenty-five cents an evening as baby-sitters when the family wants to go to the movies." Up until the 1940s, however, the phrase *minding the children* was more widely used to describe the temporary care of children, which was principally done by family, kin, neighbors, and friends. Generations of American parents—especially those with few resources—often relied on their older children to care for younger SIBLINGS, despite attempts by reformers' to decrease child labor and increase school attendance. Typical of Depression-era child-care arrangements (in which children of both sexes played a principle part) is a 1935 episode of the *Little Rascals* in which Spanky is expected to "mind the baby" while his mother goes out. Declining birth rates, however, began to limit this option.

The disruptions caused by conscription, migration, and female employment during World War II challenged these traditional child-care patterns. As mothers and teenage girls worked for wages in the defense industries, retail trades, and the service sector, grandmothers, in addition to landladies and unrelated children, often baby-sat. At 25 cents a night, they were often burdened with housekeeping responsibilities along with caring for all the children of several families. With mothers at work and domestic servants scarce, home-front girls of all ages were expected to "keep house" as well as baby-sit. For all the work they did, wages were low—and sometimes paid only in part, or not at all.

Postwar prosperity, a gender ideology that promoted maternity and domesticity, sharply rising birth rates (with children being born closer together), and a new leisure culture all contributed to a surging demand for baby-sitters in the years following World War II. War-weary couples disrupted long-standing family and kin networks when they relocated to developing suburban communities largely populated by young parents like themselves. Parents—especially housewives and mothers eager for a "day off" and a "night out"—looked to teenage girls to baby-sit. By 1947, baby-sitting had become the principal form of part-time employment and the nearly exclusive domain (called the "petticoat monopoly") of teenage girls who had been both forced out of the economy and stimulated to consume by a burgeoning commercial teen culture. Empowered by their wartime autonomy, however, teenage girls protested poor working conditions (e.g., housekeeping, low wages), issued manifestos, devised labor codes, and organized baby-sitter unions in communities in the Northeast and Midwest.

During the 1950s, the politicization of baby-sitters gave way to their professionalization when "experts" established baby-sitter courses in schools and communities. The aim of these courses was to contain the subversive girls' culture that inspired baby-sitters to contest the working conditions they disliked. While it would not be until the early 1950s that dictionaries would include the term *baby-sitter*, teenage girls of the period often referred to this occupation as "bratting," a reference to the sometimes unruly children who were raised according to DR. SPOCK'S permissive methods of child rearing.

That there were too few reliable and responsible teenage girls in the population generally, and in the suburbs in particular, led experts to promote (and parents to employ) teenage boys as baby-sitters. While most boys in the 1950s delivered newspapers, mowed lawns, or did odd jobs, *Life* magazine reported in 1957 that nearly one-quarter of all boys worked as baby-sitters. Lionized in popular magazines, educational journals, and etiquette manuals by adults anxious about "momism," boy baby-sitters were widely praised for their professionalism and masculinity. In the absence of breadwinning fathers during the day, boy sitters were believed to instill virile virtues critical to the healthy development of little boys' gender identity.

The representation of the pleasure-seeking baby-sitter of the 1950s yielded to a highly sexualized one in the 1960s. The eroticized baby-sitter in high culture, folk culture, popular culture, and pornography was shaped by the sexual revolution, women's liberation, and the counterculture. Although baby-sitting largely continued as a mundane exchange of patience for pennies (about 75 cents per hour), teenage temptresses easily aroused husband-employers disenchanted with postwar suburban life. In MOVIES, TELEVISION sitcoms, and urban legends, the often vulnerable (yet implicitly voluptuous) teenage baby-sitter expressed the fears and fantasies of adults anxious about rapidly changing gender roles, girls' culture, the breakdown of the family, and community instability.

By the mid-1980s, when there were fewer teenagers in the population once again (and in the midst of a backlash against feminism), demonized baby-sitters in popular and made-for-TV movies threatened children, destabilized marriages, and destroyed families. At the same time, increasing employment opportunities for teens enabled many girls and boys to seek out jobs where they could make more money and meet people. The expanding retail trade and service industries provided greater remuneration, status, and sociability than did the often solitary job of "sitting." Beset by last-minute calls, cancellations, bounced checks, uncertain hours (generally later than expected), drunk drivers, and sexual harassment, teenage girls increasingly relinquished baby-sitting jobs to inexperienced preadolescent girls.

Though postwar parents had been warned by experts not to hire a baby-sitter who was younger than her mid-teens, preadolescent girls began to be hired in the mid-1980s by new parents whose increased rates of childbirth were reversing a fifteen-year demographic trend. Often educated in "safe sitting" training courses offered by local schools and hospitals, preadolescent girls have since been acculturated by *The Baby-sitters Club* book series (written by Ann M. Martin) and movie spin-offs that idealize the preadolescent "Super Sitter" and an emergent "girl power" ideology that: (1) reinforces the belief that determination, ambition, individual achievement, competence, and hard work enables girls to realize their dreams; (2) encourages girls' economic role in the consumer market; and (3) fosters empowerment through pleasure, style, FASHION (e.g., makeup), and attitude.

See also: **Adolescence and Youth; Child Care: In-Home Child Care; Consumer Culture.**

BIBLIOGRAPHY

Forman-Brunell, Miriam. Forthcoming. *Get a Sitter! Fears and Fantasies about Babysitters.* New York: Routledge.

Margolin, Leslie. 1990. "Child Abuse by Baby-Sitters: An Ecological-Interactional Interpretation." *Journal of Family Violence* 5, no. 2 (June): 95–105.

Neus, Margaret. 1990. "The Insider's Guide to Babysitting: Anecdotes and Advice from Babysitters for Babysitters." Master's thesis, Emerson College, Boston.

MIRIAM FORMAN-BRUNELL

Baden-Powell, Robert (1857–1941)

Robert Baden-Powell created the BOY SCOUTS which grew rapidly into an international educational youth movement before 1914. He wrote *Scouting for Boys* in 1908, and also co-authored the Girl Guides manual, *How Girls Can Help Build Up the Empire*, with his sister Agnes in 1910.

The Boy Scout scheme was a system of character development and citizenship training that, while based on a manual of military scouting, was firmly grounded in both contemporary psychological theory and educational methods. The aim was to create model adolescents and ultimately model adult citizens through Boy Scout training—complete with its own moral code (encapsulated in the Scout Promise and Scout Law)—and by its public service roles in ambulance, fire fighting, and lifesaving. Boy Scouts were to be replete with the skills and virtues of backwoodsmen and frontiersmen by taking a whole series of scout tests such as cooking without utensils, shelter building, and knots and lashings.

Scouting was designed as an "all-embracing game" by Baden-Powell to be pursued all year round both indoors and out, that contrived to mold boys' character and moral values. For younger boys scouting could provide an adult-inspired "escape" from the suffocating domestic conventions of childhood combined nonetheless with custodial supervision. For fourteen year olds it was intended as a diversion from adult recreational forms (notably smoking and gambling) widely adopted by precocious school leavers in Edwardian Britain.

Major-General Baden-Powell, the Boer War's "hero of Mafeking," had an upbringing with a Progressive educationalist mother. Following public school Baden-Powell did so well in the entrance exam that he bypassed officer training and went straight to his regiment. He was to prove an unconventional and unorthodox regular soldier who advocated the use of irregular volunteer forces and wrote the military manual *Aids to Scouting*—subsequently adapted as the core theme for citizenship training in the Boy Scouts. Later RUDYARD KIPLING's *Jungle Book* was used as the basis for his Wolf Cub program for boys below scout age.

Prior to the publication of *Scouting for Boys*, Baden-Powell developed scouting for the Boys Brigade at the invitation of its founder, W. A. Smith. Scouting then grew largely by being adopted by existing youth organizations like the Boys' Clubs, SUNDAY SCHOOLS, and church choirs, who would establish a scout troop so as not to lose their members completely to the new fashionable movement.

Baden-Powell's concept of scouting was shaped by an eclectic blend of influences and ideas. He borrowed the idea of self-governing clubs from American Charles Stelzle, who helped operate boys' clubs starting in the 1880s; the scout's secret handshake and notion of a scout brotherhood came from Freemasonry; the Scouts Farm schools and emigration policy imitated the Salvation Army plan. Baden-Powell also drew heavily from MARIA MONTESSORI's ideas on PLAY and G. STANLEY HALL's biogenetic psychology—including the idea that children recapitulated the cultural history of the race in their development and play as they grew up. Accordingly, the Wolf Cub program was designed for those in Hall's "Savage or Barbaric stage" and the Boy Scouts, for

those over ten years in the "Tribal or Clan stage." The six-boy Scout Patrol was meant as a "fraternity gang." Maria Montessori greatly admired the Scout movement and saw it as an invaluable preparation for "going out."

Despite being a product of Edwardian England's intellectual and cultural climate and its socioeconomic preoccupations, scouting had widespread appeal and proved equally applicable in many diverse national contexts. By 1914 it had spread to fifty-two other countries, dominions, and colonies including France, Germany, Austria, Japan, Russia, the United States, Peru, Australia, and Canada. Baden-Powell actively encouraged this by making a six-month world tour to promote his brain child in 1912. In 1918 there were 750,000 Boy Scouts overseas and 155,000 in Britain.

Scouting has been modified and kept up to date since then (for example, the Beavers were started for the pre–Wolf Cub age group) and the uniform altered to accommodate changes in fashion (short trousers were abandoned). Nevertheless, the Scout movement's aims, objectives, and most of its activities are fundamentally the same at the start of the twenty-first century as they were in 1908.

See also: **Boyhood; Child Development, History of the Concept of; Girl Scouts.**

BIBLIOGRAPHY

Aitkin, W. Francis. 1900. *Baden-Powell, the Hero of Mafeking*. London: S. W. Partridge and Co.

Dedman, Martin J. 1993. "Baden-Powell, Militarism and the 'Invisible Contributors' to the Boy Scout Scheme 1904–1920" *Twentieth Century British History* 4, no. 3: 201–23.

MARTIN J. DEDMAN

Baptism

For Christians, baptism is one of the three rites of initiation which incorporate an individual into the Body of Christ—that is, into membership in the Christian church (see 1 Cor. 13). The others are CONFIRMATION and Eucharist. Baptism takes place when an individual is immersed or sprinkled with water while the baptizer recites this formula: "I baptize you in the name of the Father, the Son, and the Holy Spirit" (Matt. 28:19). As a sacrament, baptism removes the sins of the newly initiated, which is in itself an unmerited gift from God. Christian baptism may be traced back to the baptism of Jesus Christ by John the Baptist in the river Jordan. Most Christian denominations require infant baptism because of Jesus' injunction, "Amen, amen, I say to you, no one can enter the kingdom of God without being born of water and Spirit" (John 3:5), as well as the authority of St. Peter (Acts 2:38–39).

By the third century, the early church began to administer baptism, confirmation, and the Eucharist to infants immediately after birth. The church recognized the spiritual equality of all of its members, whether children or adults. Writing about 80 C.E., Irenaeus of Lyons underscored this point: "For he [the Lord] came to save all of them through himself; all of them, I say, who through him are born again in God, the infants, and the small children, and the boys, and the mature, and the older people" (*Adversus Omnes Haereses*, Book 5).

The *Traditio Apostolica* (c. 217), which is attributed to Hippolytus of Rome, provides a third-century description of the rite of baptism and implications for children. The document notes that children are to be baptized before adults and that parents or relatives are to answer the prescribed questions if the children are unable to do so. Origen, a third-century theologian in the East, mandated infant baptism in his *Commentarii in Romanos*. Moreover, the Nicene Creed, which was drafted in the fourth century, acknowledged "one baptism for the remission of sins" and continued to associate confirmation and the Eucharist with baptism. By the time of Augustine of Hippo in the fifth century, the baptism of infants was widespread in the West. He recommended that children were to be baptized as soon as possible because of the high rate of infant mortality. According to St. Augustine, baptism removed both the original sin of Adam and Eve as well as any other sins. But the Fourth Lateran Council (1215) rejected both the early tradition of administering Eucharist to infants after baptism and the fifth-century custom of delaying confirmation and Eucharist for several years after baptism, and forbade infants from receiving the Eucharist until they had reached the age of discretion (i.e., seven). They equated spiritual readiness with reason.

After 1525, Anabaptists shared the view that physically immature children were also spiritually innocent, but they became the only Christian sect to deny the efficacy of infant baptism. Anabaptists insisted that preadolescent children could not be admitted into the church because they lacked faith. At the same time the Anabaptists comforted distraught parents by maintaining the belief that unbaptized children who died before adolescence were assured salvation because they were incapable of deliberate sin.

In the 1960s, the second Vatican Council authorized a ritual for the baptism of children (*Ordo Baptismi Parvulorum*, 1969) that discourages private baptisms. It prescribes that baptism is to take place in the parish church either within the Sunday celebration of the Eucharist or at least preceded by the Liturgy of the Word. The members of the parish are enjoined to assist the parents and the godparents in the education of children in the truths of the faith. Finally, the new rite stresses the inherent link between the three sacraments of initiation, even though in practice they are administered over an extended period of time (age eight for Eucharist and sixteen for confirmation).

See also: **Catholicism; Christian Thought, Early; Communion, First; Protestant Reformation.**

BIBLIOGRAPHY

Cullmann, Oscar. 1978. *Baptism in the New Testament.* Trans. J. K. S. Reid. Philadelphia: Westminster Press.

DeMolen, Richard L. 1975. "Childhood and the Sacraments in the Sixteenth Century." *Archiv für Reformationsgeschichte* 66: 49–71.

Nocent, Adrian. 1997. "Christian Initiation." In *Sacraments and Sacramentals*, ed. Anscar J. Chupungco. Collegeville, MN: The Liturgical Press.

Osborne, Kenan B. 1987. *The Christian Sacraments of Initiation: Baptism, Confirmation, Eucharist.* New York: Paulist Press.

Searle, Mark. 1980. *Christening: The Making of Christians.* Collegeville, MN: The Liturgical Press.

RICHARD L. DEMOLEN

Barbie

The origins of Barbie—the most popular DOLL in the world in the last half of the twentieth century—can be traced to Lilli, originally a *Das Bild* comic strip character of a saucy blonde, later produced as a pornographic doll popular among bachelors in postwar Germany. While on a trip to Europe, Mattel co-founder Ruth Handler discovered Lilli, the prototypical doll she believed would enable girls like her daughter, Barbie, to imagine their future selves in roles other than that of mothers. (Baby dolls dominated the postwar American toy market.) Male designers at Mattel modified the German sex toy into a teenage doll they encoded with the prevailing feminine ideals of both purity and prurience and a CONSUMER CULTURE ethos. The eleven-and-a-half inch Barbie doll and her extensive miniaturized haute couture wardrobe were marketed to stimulate consumer desire among America's youngest shoppers. In turn these shoppers proceeded to make Barbie the most successful product in the history of the toy industry.

Although one billion Barbie dolls had been sold by the early twenty-first century, the doll was not immediately popular with consumers and social critics. Controversy developed shortly after the doll's marketing debut in 1959 at the New York Toy Fair. Mattel's claims about the doll's "educational value" did not convince many mothers at the time who detested the doll's exalted femininity and scandalous sexuality. Barbie's seductive figure, suggestive look, and provocative wardrobe designed to attract the attention of men like her boyfriend Ken led feminists to condemn the doll for its sexual objectification of women. Social critics denounced the doll's materialism—as exemplified by her lavish lifestyle and shopping sprees—and the slavish consumerism it fostered in daughters of hard-working breadwinners. Although Barbie changed with the times from fashion model to career woman, many still pointed to the preoccupation with body image in girls whose beauty ideal was defined by Barbie's unrealistic physique. (She would be ten feet tall if she were real.) On the other hand, scholars and others have shown that girls and boys, children as well as adults, play with Barbie dolls in ways that contest gendered norms.

As a quintessential icon of American femininity, the Barbie doll has served as the focus of countless satirical artistic works, many of which, like *The Distorted Barbie* website, Mattel has tried to censor. A Barbie doll starred in *Superstar* (1987), a movie by Todd Haynes that traced the anorexic life and death of singer Karen Carpenter. The iconic Barbie has been printed on faux prayer cards and has been crucified on the cross. In 1993, the Barbie Liberation Organization switched the voice boxes of three hundred Barbies with those of G.I. Joes, leading the Barbies to bellow, "Eat lead, Cobra! Vengeance is mine!" and the perky G.I. Joes to chirp: "Let's go shopping!"

By the early twenty-first century the average American girl between the ages of three and eleven was said to own ten Barbie dolls (purchased at a rate of two Barbies every second). However, a high-priced market developed for the dolls among adult collectors. Among the numerous collectors and dealers who specialized in Barbie dolls, the Barbie Hall of Fame in Palo Alto, California, with its ten thousand Barbies, was the largest collection in the world.

See also: **Girlhood; Toys; Theories of Play.**

BIBLIOGRAPHY

Boy, Billy. 1987. *Barbie: Her Life and Times.* New York: Crown.

Lord, M. G. 1994. *Forever Barbie: The Unauthorized Biography of a Real Doll.* New York: William Morrow.

McDonough, Yona Zeldis, ed. 1999. *The Barbie Chronicles: A Living Doll Turns Forty.* New York: Touchstone.

MIRIAM FORMAN-BRUNELL

Bar Mitzvah, Bat Mitzvah

The bar/bat mitzvah ceremony is an important RITE OF PASSAGE for contemporary Jewish youth, marking the end of childhood and the beginning of ritual adulthood. The term *bar mitzvah* can be found in Talmudic literature, but the rite itself is a relatively recent development, probably dating from the late Middle Ages. The *bat mitzvah* was not mentioned until the nineteenth century.

The Talmud, a compendium of legal and narrative discourse completed about 500 C.E., based legal maturity on PUBERTY, which was declared to occur at thirteen and a day for a boy and twelve and a day for a girl. At that point, a male became a "bar mitzvah" (literally, "son of the commandment"), responsible for his own ritual and moral behavior. (The term refers also in common parlance to the rite itself.) Most importantly, the bar mitzvah was a full-fledged adult in matters of communal religious status, though not necessarily in all legal matters. He was counted in the *minyan*, the quorum of ten males necessary for public prayer, and could be called up for the public reading of the Torah in religious services. The change in a girl's status was less noticeable. Although the bat mitzvah too became responsible for her ritual and moral behavior, a female, whether a minor or an adult, was not counted in a *minyan* nor eligible for the honor of being called up for the reading of the Torah. She was under the authority of her father, and later her husband, and did not enjoy the moral or legal autonomy of the adult Jewish male.

The ceremony of bar mitzvah that developed in the Middle Ages—there was no ceremony at that time for the bat mitzvah—was a ritual in which the boy reaching maturity would be called up for the reading of the Torah on the Sabbath following his birthday, or, often in Eastern Europe, on the following Monday or Thursday morning. If his bar mitzvah took place on the Sabbath, he would chant the *haftarah*, a selection from the prophets. There were local variations. In some places the bar mitzvah boy would lead the congregation in prayer or, on the Sabbath, also read the weekly Torah portion in the traditional chant. In synagogues that followed both the Ashkenazi (northern European) and Sephardi (Iberian and Levantine) rites, boys were tutored to deliver a special Talmudic discourse to display their learning and reflect well on their families. After becoming a bar mitzvah, the boy was required to put on *tefillin* (phylacteries) in daily morning prayer. The bar mitzvah celebration itself, while accompanied by special blessings and often a festive meal, was generally a modest affair.

As Jews in Western Europe and the United States acculturated to the mores of the larger society in the nineteenth century, the bar mitzvah ceremony was diminished in significance. Group confirmation ceremonies generally accorded well with Christian customs and had two additional benefits: they allowed Jews who were sensitive to charges that JUDAISM disparaged the female sex to incorporate girls in the ceremony and they could be scheduled in mid-adolescence, permitting a longer period of study of Judaism than did the bar mitzvah rite. Reform, or Liberal, synagogues particularly in Germany and the United States, virtually eliminated the bar mitzvah ceremony in favor of CONFIRMATION.

The twentieth century witnessed the reemergence of the bar mitzvah, even in Reform synagogues, especially in the United States. One Jewish historian even pointed out in 1949 that "the bar mitzvah has become the most important milestone in a Jew's life in America" (Levitats, p. 153). The children of the large number of East European Jews who immigrated to the United States between 1880 and 1924 were eager to retain the custom, even as many affiliated with the Reform movement. The bar mitzvah ritual also enabled economically successful American Jews, from the 1920s on, to combine consumerism with their child's rite of passage. The festive meal that sometimes accompanied the bar mitzvah ritual in traditional Jewish societies became the occasion for a catered celebration, often complete with band and dancing, that marked not only the child's, but also the parents' new status. Gift-giving accompanied the modern bar mitzvah and also added a commercial element to the day. From the 1930s on, rabbis and communal leaders criticized the excessive lavishness of the bar mitzvah "affair" and its subordination of spirituality to secular celebration.

The ritual celebration of a girl's becoming a bat mitzvah is essentially a twentieth-century American phenomenon that reflects growing concern in America with gender egalitarianism. Although girls were included in group confirmations in the nineteenth century and there are references to bat mitzvah ceremonies in Italy and France, the first documented individual bat mitzvah took place in the United States in 1922. Conservative Rabbi Mordecai Kaplan, later the founder of Reconstructionist Judaism, decided to celebrate his daughter Judith's religious majority with an innovative ceremony in his new synagogue in New York City. However, the bat mitzvah rite did not become common in America until after World War II. It flourished first in the Conservative movement and, once the Reform movement reestablished the importance of the rite of bar mitzvah, in Reform synagogues as well. Under pressure, Orthodox Jews in America began marking a girl's religious majority, within the constraints of their understanding of Jewish law, in the 1970s. In Israel a girl's bat mitzvah is generally celebrated only with a party, outside the synagogue and with no religious elements.

In the modern period, as adolescence became a newly recognized period of life, the bar/bat mitzvah ritual became a rite of passage, not from childhood to adulthood but from childhood to adolescence. The popularity of the rite in the United States reflects the child-centeredness of American and especially American Jewish society as well as the continued strength of religious tradition in America. The bar/bat mitzvah ceremony, which takes place in a communal setting, enables Jews to link an event centered in their family with the celebration of group survival, a central concern of post-Holocaust Jews.

See also: **Adolescence and Youth.**

BIBLIOGRAPHY

Geffen, Rela M. 1993. *Celebration and Renewal: Rites of Passage in Judaism.* Philadelphia: Jewish Publication Society.

Hyman, Paula E. 1990. "The Introduction of Bat Mitzvah in Conservative Judaism in Postwar America." *YIVO Annual* 19: 133–146.

Levitats, Isaac. 1949. "Communal Regulation of Bar Mitzvah." *Jewish Social Studies* 10, no. 2 (April): 153.

PAULA E. HYMAN

Barnardo, Thomas. *See* Placing Out.

Barrie, J. M. *See* Peter Pan and J. M. Barrie.

Baseball

Baseball, an American invention, is part of American culture and national identity and for many boys, playing baseball is a male RITE OF PASSAGE. Although the game of baseball as it is known today is uniquely American, it derives from the popular English children's bat-and-ball game called rounders. In the American colonies various versions of bat and ball games—chiefly popular with boys—evolved such as round ball, goal ball, one old cat, town ball, and base.

As early as the 1700s there are also references to men playing forms of baseball. A diary entry of a soldier from the American Revolution, who served under General George Washington at Valley Forge in 1778, talks about exercising in the afternoon by playing at base. A 1787 notice forbids Princeton College students from playing stick and ball games on the common.

Credit for the game of baseball as it is known today, however, goes to Alexander Cartwright, a bank clerk, who established the Knickerbocker Base Ball Club of New York in 1845 and wrote down the first official set of rules. These rules also became know as "New York rules." By 1857 there were almost fifty clubs within and around Manhattan. These baseball clubs were organized around occupational, ethnic, and neighborhood affiliations. That year, the Knickerbocker Club with fifteen other New York area clubs formed the National Association of Base Ball Players (NABBP). Many of these New York City area clubs also formed junior boys' teams. By 1860 there were enough junior boys' teams to form a national association. The era of informal boys' games had evolved into the era of formally organized clubs. Boys continued to play informal pick-up games of baseball in rural areas in open fields, in urban areas in vacant lots, and in the street.

The Civil War, rather than curtailing the development of baseball, became instrumental in democratizing and spreading the game throughout the country. Veteran soldiers, having played the game during the war, brought the game back to their hometowns. At the end of the war in 1865 the National Association of Base Ball Players membership included ninety-one clubs from ten states. The upper-class amateur gentlemen's club game of the Knickerbockers had evolved into the people's game. However, this democratization had its limits. In 1867 the NABBP banned black players, setting a precedent for segregated teams that remained in place for eighty years.

As baseball became more popular, rivalries between city and town teams placed greater emphasis on winning than sportsmanship, leading to an influx of gamblers and to star players being paid off the record. The first professional team, the Cincinnati Red Stockings, was formed in 1869. In 1869 and 1870, the team barnstormed across the country playing against local amateur teams, winning 130 of the 132 games they played. Their popularity led to the formation of other professional teams. In 1871 the National Association of Professional Baseball Players was formed and in 1881 the American Association followed. The 1880s mark the golden age of baseball and by 1890 there were seventeen white and two black professional leagues. The era of professional baseball had arrived. Although professional baseball was confined primarily to urban areas, every town and city had amateur and semi-professional teams that drew large crowds. Watching baseball games became a major form of entertainment. Professional team owners even encouraged women to come to the games in the belief that the presence of ladies would attract more male fans and curtail their rowdy behavior.

Baseball was also flourishing in the public schools. Grammar school boys often played at recess and high schools were developing their own teams. At private boys' boarding schools baseball was a part of the athletic program. By the end of the century boys at Exeter, Andover, Groton, St. Marks, and other elite schools were playing interscholastic ball. Boys also played baseball at private military academies such as the Virginia Military Institute. Even though baseball was considered a boys' game, some girls at Miss Porter's, an elite private girls' school in Connecticut, as early as 1867 also played the game.

With the development of the PLAYGROUND MOVEMENT first in Boston in 1885 and then in other cities, baseball became a popular playground sport. Settlement houses, boys clubs, and the YMCA developed baseball programs to keep boys off the street and out of trouble. Through playing baseball it was hoped that boys would learn sportsmanship and would become good citizens. Baseball was also seen as a way to Americanize immigrant groups.

Although baseball-type games had been played at men's colleges as early as the late 1700s, it was in the 1850s and 1860s that baseball became an integral part of men's college life. The first intercollegiate game was played between Williams and Amherst Colleges in 1859. Although the general belief was that strenuous physical exercise was unhealthy for women, a few women's colleges such as Vassar, Smith, Mount Holyoke, and Wellesley allowed girls to play baseball as early as 1866. However, by the 1930s, softball had replaced baseball in girls' sports programs. By the 1980s, there were 1,600 college men's baseball programs associated with the National Collegiate Athletic Association.

In the 1900s, in the public's mind baseball represented all that was good about America. Baseball served as a model for children's moral development. Therefore the Black Sox Scandal of 1919, over the fixing of the World Series, was a national disgrace. The scandal so deeply affected the Ameri-

can public that when Judge Kennesaw Mountain Landis became Commissioner of Baseball in 1921, the *St. Louis Globe-Democrat* wrote that if Landis could keep baseball on a high ethical plane, it would be more important than anything he could do on the federal bench.

The golden era of sport in the 1920s produced baseball's first superstars, Babe Ruth, Ty Cobb, and Lou Gehrig. Games were broadcast over the RADIO to millions of people. It was during this time that organized youth baseball got its start. In 1925 the American Legion started their junior baseball program to give more boys an opportunity to play and as a means of teaching them good sportsmanship and citizenship. With the financial support of major league baseball, American Legion baseball competition began in 1926. In 1928 the issue of girls playing became an explosive one when it was discovered that Margaret Gisolo was a member of the Blanford, Indiana, team. Although Margaret was allowed to finish the season, the next year the rules were changed to allow boys only to play. Later leagues were careful to specify that only boys could join. In 1939 Carl Stotz founded Little League Baseball with the purpose of developing citizenship, sportsmanship, and manhood. PONY (Protect Our Nation's Youth) Baseball, Inc. was formed in 1951 and the Babe Ruth League in 1952. Not until 1974 after a lengthy court battle were girls allowed to play Little League baseball. After that the other leagues also permitted girls to play. Even with that change relatively few girls play baseball today.

American Legion and Little League Baseball continue to be popular programs. In 2000 American Legion Posts sponsored 5,300 baseball and other athletic teams throughout the United States. By 1999 Little League baseball was being played in 100 countries. Baseball became an Olympic sport in 1992.

See also: **Interscholastic Athletics; Organized Recreation and Youth Groups; Sports; Title IX and Girls Sports.**

BIBLIOGRAPHY

Berlage, Gai. 1994. *Women in Baseball: The Forgotten History.* Westport, CT: Praeger.

Crepeau, Richard. 1980 *Baseball: America's Diamond Mind.* Orlando: University Presses of Florida.

Rader, Benjamin. G. 1999. *American Sports: From the Age of Folk Games to the Age of Televised Sports,* 4th ed. Upper Saddle River, NJ: Prentice Hall.

Seymour, Harold. 1990. *Baseball: The People's Game.* New York: Oxford University Press.

Ward, Geoffrey, and Ken Burns. 1994. *Baseball: An Illustrated History.* New York: Knopf.

GAI INGHAM BERLAGE

Basedow, Johann Bernhard (1724–1790)

Johann Bernhard Basedow was the leading representative of the first generation of philanthropinists, as German pedagogues of the late ENLIGHTENMENT referred to themselves. He was born on September 11, 1724, in Hamburg, Germany. After a childhood spent in poverty as the son of a Hamburg wig-maker, he studied theology and then successfully tutored the son of a nobleman. Basedow used the *confabulatio* for language learning, which consisted of a constant dialogue between pupil and teacher in the foreign languages, including Latin. He described his new teaching method in his 1752 dissertation and also introduced it to the public in a German-language publication. After teaching for some years he devoted most of his energies to writing on theological, philosophical, and pedagogical themes. Because of his critiques of revealed religion he was persecuted by the orthodox clergy. Under the protection of the enlightened Prince of Anhalt-Dessau, Basedow was able to open his first school, the Philanthropinum, in 1774 with three pupils, including two of his own children. Even if it never had more than fifty pupils at one time, this school, run along reformist principles, enjoyed extraordinary public attention, especially because of Basedow's playful and vivid teaching methods and the relaxed atmosphere among the pupils and teachers. The waning interest of the public and the prince, as well as conflicts with colleagues, caused Basedow to withdraw from the directorship. The Dessau Philanthropinum closed once and for all in 1793.

Other philanthropin, of which there were more than sixty in the German-speaking world by 1800, existed for considerably longer. Unlike Basedow, the next generation of philanthropinists, including Joachim Heinrich Campe, Ernst Christian Trapp, CHRISTIAN GOTTHILF SALZMANN, and Friedrich Eberhard von Rochow, no longer placed their hope on princely protection, but rather tried to push through educational reforms by creating a pedagogically interested public. To this end they published an *Allgemeine Revision des gesammten Schul- und Erziehungswesen* (General Revision of the Entire School and Educational System, 16 vols.,1785–1792, ed. J. H. Campe).

Basedow's programmatic *Vorstellung an Menschenfreunde und vermögende Männer über Schulen, Studien und ihren Einfluß in die öffentliche Wohlfahrt* (Presentation to friends of humanity and men of means regarding schools, studies, and their influence on public welfare, 1768) marks the birth of philanthropic pedagogy. In conventional schools, according to Basedow, the pupils spent far too much time learning far too little, and all the wrong things. In his *Vorstellung an Menschenfreunde* Basedow developed his pedagogical program of social reform through school reform, for he believed that only human beings trained to be useful could guarantee their own happiness and thus the happiness (i.e., the welfare) of the state as a whole. For that reason it was in the interest of the authorities to set up a special government department to oversee the schools. Basedow argued here in favor of a separation between the church and the schools, and this process of a growing autonomy of educational institutions would continue through the nineteenth century. Basedow assumed that the authorities were virtuous and enlightened and thus in harmony with their subjects, and argued within the framework of the corporate order, which he also took as the basis for the educational system, with its division into small schools for the cultivated classes and large schools for the common horde.

Basedow is important for the history of childhood because he was one of the first educators to stress that children could enjoy school and learning, and that it was the duty of pedagogy to ensure that children learned with ease and pleasure. He placed great emphasis on vivid and playful teaching methods, but also on incentives to learning. One example was the so-called merit boards, on which teachers publicly recorded their pupils' moral and cognitive achievements in order to infuse them with competitive zeal.

See also: **Education, Europe.**

BIBLIOGRAPHY

Basedow, Johann Bernhard. 1965. *Ausgewaehlte paedagogische Schriften.* Besorgt von A. Reble. Paderborn: Ferdinand Schoeningh.

Kersting, Christa. 1992. *Die Genese der Paedagogik im 18. Jahrhundert. Campes Allgemeine Revision im Kontext der neuzeitlichen Wissenschaft.* Weinheim: Deutscher Studien Verlag.

Pinloche, A. 1914. *Geschichte des Philanthropinismus.* German edition by J. Rauschenfels and A. Pinloche. 2nd ed. Leipzig: Brandstetter.

PIA SCHMID

Basketball

In December 1891, James Naismith, a Canadian-born instructor at the Young Men's Christian Association (YMCA) training school in Springfield, Massachusetts, introduced the game of basketball. The YMCA soon published rules for the game, which spread rapidly throughout settlement houses, colleges, and high schools. In March 1892 Senda Berenson adapted the game for her Smith College students by restricting the players to zones, thus limiting their running to allay concerns about female debility. By the end of the year girls in West Coast schools eagerly took to the game. The YMCA promoted state and regional competitions and offered a national championship in 1896.

Professional teams appeared by the late 1890s and high school students, both boys and girls, organized their own leagues for competition. High school play became particularly intense in certain regions of the country, such as Indiana and Kentucky, where the game took precedence in the sporting culture as it fostered communal pride and identity. In Iowa the girls' game even superceded the boys' in popularity, despite its adherence to the divided court system until the 1993–1994 season. In the South historically black colleges developed particularly strong female contingents, and their white counterparts, company teams composed of young females, barnstormed the country, often playing and defeating men's teams.

The game retained a strong presence in urban areas, however, where social clubs, churches, schools, and companies sponsored teams. Leagues in northern cities featured integrated games and African-American teams proved among the best by the World War I era. Colleges began sponsoring competitions to attract the best players to campus, such as the national invitational tournament started by the University of Chicago in 1918. Racial, ethnic, and religious rivalries spurred the formation of teams and fostered greater assimilation in the process. Organizations originally founded to preserve ethnic cultures, such as the German Turners, Czech Sokols, and Polish Falcons, acquiesced to the interests of second-generation youths in American sports, such as basketball. Both the B'nai B'rith Youth Organization and the Catholic Youth Organization (CYO) aimed to counteract the Protestant influences of the YMCA. The latter conducted its own National Catholic Interscholastic Basketball Tournament at Chicago's Loyola University after 1923. By the 1930s the CYO claimed the largest basketball league in the world, as its Chicago archdiocese accounted for more than 400 teams.

The best youths earned college scholarships or graduated to semipro or professional units that proliferated throughout American cities. Others joined barnstorming teams, like Chicago's Savoy 5 (later renamed the Harlem Globetrotters). Girls, too, found similar opportunities, particularly on employer-sponsored teams in the South.

The international scope of the game resulted in its inclusion in the 1936 Olympic Games. Nationally, basketball prospered throughout the latter half of the twentieth century, gradually assuming a primary role in inner-city playgrounds and urban community recreation programs. Like past sponsors, entrepreneurs initiated basketball camps, tournaments, and traveling teams that promised training, continuous competition, and offered hopes of recognition by high school, college, and professional coaches. By the late twentieth century the best high school boys eschewed college play, opting for direct employment in the National Basketball Association. Most, however, honed their skills on thousands of community teams that offered age group competition or played recreational basketball on city playgrounds or rural spaces.

See also: **Sports; Title IX and Girls Sports; YWCA and YMCA.**

BIBLIOGRAPHY

Axthelm, Pete. 1970. *The City Game: Basketball, from the Playground to Madison Square Garden.* New York: Harper's Magazine Press.

George, Nelson. 1992. *Elevating the Game.* New York: Harper Collins.

Hult, Joan S., and Marianna Trekell, eds. 1991. *A Century of Women's Basketball: From Frailty to Final Four.* Reston, VA: American Alliance for Health, Physical Education, Recreation, and Dance.

GERALD R. GEMS

Bastardy

Writing the first comparative history of bastardy in 1980, Peter Laslett introduced the phenomenon by stating that it had been called a social problem for the last two centuries and a moral problem from time immemorial. In 1980, however, bastardy had long ceased to be a common term—in France, for example, it had been abandoned in 1793 during the Revolution. At the threshold of the twenty-first century, not only bastardy but also illegitimacy are words in rare use, which should serve as a reminder that these are legal, social, and cultural constructions. The most common definition of illegitimacy is to be born out of wedlock, but throughout history, the legal and social status of children in that position has changed. Differences can be found also between canon and secular law and between and within states and continents. The following contains a brief survey on some legal aspects, the main issue, however, being the social and cultural significance of illegitimacy in the Western world.

Levels of Illegitimacy

Giving a general overview of levels of illegitimacy is not easily done. As several authors have discussed, the disparity in definitions poses a problem and the reliability of the registration varies according to time as well as place. Nevertheless a few main tendencies have been established.

The rate of extramarital births during the sixteenth century is generally perceived to be quite high, but it later sank during the age of absolutism. It is stipulated that only 2 to 3 percent of all births in the mid-1700s were extramarital, but a century later numbers hovered between 7 and 11 percent in the Nordic countries and around 7 percent in France and England. Certain countries and regions had higher figures; in Iceland more than 14 percent of all births occurred outside of marriage, and in the Basque Country the illegitimacy rate was exceptionally high. The following century or so, from the 1840s to 1960, witnessed a new decline of illegitimate births, particularly conspicuous around the turn of the century. Regional differences, however, were still to be found.

Comparing western and northern European countries to those in the South and East, the overall pattern at the beginning of the twentieth century seems to be that the former had a lower level of illegitimacy than southern and eastern areas. In America it has been claimed that illegitimate births during colonial times were relatively rare, and that the ratio remained low at the beginning of the twentieth century. However, all slave children were considered illegitimate, and there were large disparities. In 1938, 11 percent of black children and only 3 percent of white were born by unwed mothers.

A high level of tolerance for extramarital births has been found to characterize some societies with high illegitimacy ratios. This tolerance can be connected with morals, religion, and culture but not least with economic conditions and household structures. Lola Valverde has explained the high portion of illegitimate births found in the Basque Country is explained by the lack of shame appending to such births and the fact that engagement was perceived as the same as marriage. Thus a legally illegitimate child could be socially legitimate. Further, irregular unions, as between priests and unmarried women, were widely accepted, and a father had economic responsibilities for his children even though he was not married to the mother.

On the other hand, abrupt economic changes and reduced means of livelihood have led to fewer marriages and an increase in the number of illegitimate births. The increase after 1750 has in some countries, though far from in all, been seen in this perspective.

Legal Status

Illegitimacy is connected with the parents' legal obligations toward their children not only with regard to maintenance but also to the right to family name and inheritance. Such rights have been limited, even quite absent in some places. Illegitimacy could also dictate the nature of the individual's relation to society. A career in the Roman Catholic Church for illegitimate children, for instance, was only feasible through papal dispensation, and a person of illegitimate birth had limited or no access to several guilds. However, there are no absolute rules, and stories of illegitimate heirs who managed to fight their way to European thrones are well known.

The criteria for being recognized as legitimate differed before and after Christianity, but according to canon law the status of illegitimate children changed if the parents married. This was the usual principle in the Nordic countries, but in England and Iceland, later in the United States, the principle was not immediately acknowledged. Furthermore, the Pope had the ability to change a child's status.

In many European countries, particularly Catholic ones, illegitimate births were first and foremost a matter for the church. The church and charitable institutions established several large ORPHANAGES in major cities, especially in southern Europe. However, the fact that many legitimately born children were also brought to these orphanages illustrates that problems of familial connections were not restricted to children born of unwed parents. In the Nordic countries illegitimate births were handled by the state and could lead to criminal persecution. In early modern times the persecution of unwed mothers especially became more severe.

Population Policies

Toward the end of the nineteenth century the question of illegitimacy versus legitimacy was closely linked with population policies. International rivalries combined with a decline in birthrates led several states to become interested in INFANT MORTALITY. Demographic statistics showed that mortality rates were far higher among illegitimate children than among those born within wedlock. Political leaders with a stronger interest in the power of the state than the morals of its population combined forces with philanthropists in order to better the conditions for illegitimate children. In some countries, such as Great Britain and Germany, experiences from World War I were decisive in making the issue a subject for debate at high political levels.

According to Edward R. Dickinson, radical feminists in Germany had argued for state maintenance and paternal contributions in addition to a right for the child to the father's name and limited inheritance since the turn of the century. German fathers already had a certain legal obligation to contribute economically, but more than half of them sought reprieve from these obligations. Furthermore, fathers were only obliged to pay until the child reached sixteen years of age, and the amount was to be in compliance with the mother's standard of living. Accordingly the children were more often than not raised in poverty with no means of receiving further education. All over Europe unwed mothers and their children faced similar problems.

New legislation was in Germany strongly opposed by Christian politicians in defense of family values and female sexual morality, and legal equality was in many countries long in coming. The disparities between culturally similar areas could be significant. A law giving illegitimate children the right to inheritance and name after the father was passed in Norway as early as in 1915, while legislation in Denmark and Sweden was based on principles of differentiation until the 1960s.

In Norway the economic rights appending to the legal ones were for a long period of time limited. The German state took a certain economic responsibility, while France appeared among the most liberal and generous states by placing a great deal of importance on equal rights for all children to welfare and health benefits. On the other hand, the legal rights of illegitimate children were especially limited in France.

Social Inclusion and Exclusion

The law and practice have not always been in sync with each other, and many children born out of wedlock were socially included within families and local communities: their parents married, their mothers married someone else, or the children were taken in by extended family. That leaves those children who were not integrated by family or local community. The size of this group has varied, but it has been large enough to ensure that illegitimacy throughout history has been connected with poverty, shame, and cultural exclusion from local communities. These children more often than others risked being abandoned in orphanages and institutions or becoming foster children. They were also put up for ADOPTION more often than other children when this became an option in several countries in the early twentieth century.

As the twentieth century advanced, the idea that a child belonged with its mother, married or unmarried, became gradually more dominant. The conflict between the mother as caretaker and the mother as breadwinner has nevertheless seemed particularly strong with unwed mothers, since in most countries they were granted economic support for their children much later than widows. The differentiation was based on moral judgments. Widows were regarded as worthy, unwed mothers as unworthy.

The intertwining of the legal, cultural, and economic aspects can be clearly identified in the Western world after 1960. The number of children born of unwed parents increased dramatically as public and private economies improved, public welfare programs were expanded, and the state inflicted economic responsibilities upon the fathers. Another vital factor was the increase in couples living together without being married. Legal equality has since then in most countries been established between children born within or out of wedlock, and the profound cultural, economic, gender, and social changes of Western society has made differentiating between children on the basis of their parents' marital status irrelevant.

The most disquieting feature in the early twenty-first century seems to be that children with single parents, whether born within or outside of wedlock, generally have a lower standard of living than children in a two-parent family. This is the situation in Europe as well as the United States.

See also: **Children's Rights; Fertility Rates; Inheritance and Property; Law, Children and the.**

BIBLIOGRAPHY

Anderson, Michael, ed. 1996. *British Population History from the Black Death to the Present Day.* Cambridge, UK: Cambridge University Press.

Dickinson, Edward Ross. 1996. *The Politics of German Child Welfare from the Empire to the Federal Republic.* Cambridge, MA: Harvard University Press.

Gordon, Linda. 1994. *Pitied But Not Entitled: Single Mothers and the History of Welfare 1890–1935.* New York: Free Press, Macmillan.

Hansen, Lars Ivar, ed. 2000. *Family, Marriage and Property Devolution in the Middle Ages.* Tromsø, Norway: University of Tromsø.

Henderson, John, and Richard Wall, eds. 1994. *Poor Women and Children in the European Past.* London and New York: Routledge.

Klaus, Alisa. 1993. *Every Child a Lion: The Origins of Maternal and Infant Health Policy in the United States and France, 1890–1920.* Ithaca, NY, and London: Cornell University Press.

Laslett, Peter, Karla Osterveen, and Richard M. Smith, eds. 1980. *Bastardy and Its Comparative History.* London: Edward Arnold.

Løkke, Anne. 1998. *Døden i barndommen.* Copenhagen, Denmark: Gyldendal.

Valverde, Lola. 1994. "Illegitimacy and the Abandonment of Children in the Basque Country, 1550–1800." In *Poor Women and Children in the European Past*, ed. John Henderson and Richard Wall. London and New York: Routledge.

ASTRI ANDRESEN

Baum, L. Frank. *See* Wizard of Oz and L. Frank Baum.

Baumrind, Diana (b. 1927)

Diana Blumberg Baumrind is best known in the PARENTING and socialization literature for identifying and describing four basic parenting styles that have defined the field for researchers and practioners for more than four decades. In 1960 the psychologist Diana Baumrind joined the Institute of Human Development at the University of California, Berkeley, where she became the principal investigator for the Family Socialization and Developmental Competence Project. Baumrind has published numerous articles and book chapters on family socialization, parenting styles, developmental competence, moral development, adolescent health and risk-taking, and research ethics.

Baumrind identified and described four basic parenting styles that constitute variations in the values and practices of normal (i.e., nonabusive, non-neglectful) parents seeking to socialize and control their children. Parents, she wrote, hope their children and adolescents will have an identity grounded in both agency and communion, "validating *simultaneously* the interests of personal emancipation and individuation, and the claims of other individuals and mutually shared social norms" (1991, p. 747). The four parenting styles she identified involve different combinations of demandingness (confrontation, monitoring, consistent discipline, and corporal punishment) and responsiveness (warmth, friendly discourse, reciprocity, and attachment).

1. *Indulgent or permissive* parents, whether they are democratic or nondirective, are more responsive than demanding. They avoid confrontation and allow self-regulation. Their children are friendly, sociable, and creative, but may also be verbally impulsive, aggressive, and resistant to limit-setting.

2. *Authoritarian* parents are highly demanding, direc-

tive, and nonresponsive. They are obedience- and status-oriented, and they create well-ordered, structured environments with clearly stated rules. They are often highly intrusive, modeling aggressive modes of conflict resolution. Their children are typically moody, fearful of new situations, and low in self-esteem.

3. *Authoritative* parents are both demanding and responsive. They monitor behavior, impart clear standards, and are assertive without being intrusive or restrictive. Their disciplinary methods are supportive rather than punitive. This style is generally regarded as optimal for the development of social competence, which includes assertiveness, social responsibility, self-regulation, cooperation, and respect for parents.

4. *Uninvolved* parents are low in both responsiveness and demandingness. At the extremes, these parents may be rejecting-neglecting and neglectful. Their children often engage in deviant and high-risk behaviors and are vulnerable to substance abuse.

Parenting styles also differ in the extent to which they are characterized by psychological control, which involves guilt induction, withdrawal of love, or shaming that lead to both internalized and externalized problems in children and adolescents. Authoritative and authoritarian parents are equally high in behavioral control, but authoritative parents are generally low in psychological control, whereas authoritarian parents are generally high in such control.

Baumrind's best-known single work is her 1964 article, "Some Thoughts on the Ethics of Research: After Reading Milgram's 'Behavioral Study of Obedience.'" The publication of this article brought Baumrind numerous invitations to reflect on research ethics. Baumrind's work on research design, socialization, moral development, and professional ethics is unified by her belief that individual rights and responsibilities cannot be separated, her conviction that moral actions are determined "volitionally and consciously," and her assertion that "impartiality is not superior morally to *enlightened partiality*" (1992, p. 266).

See also: **Child Development, History of the Concept of.**

BIBLIOGRAPHY

Barber, Brian K. 1996. "Parental Psychological Control: Revisiting a Neglected Construct." *Child Development* 67: 3296–3319.

Baumrind, Diana B. 1964. "Some Thoughts on the Ethics of Research: After Reading Milgram's 'Behavioral Study of Obedience.'" *American Psychologist* 19: 421–423.

Baumrind, Diana B. 1991. "The Influence of Parenting Style on Adolescent Competence and Substance Use. *Journal of Early Adolescence* 11: 56–95.

Baumrind, Diana B. 1992. "Leading an Examined Life: The Moral Dimension of Daily Conduct." In *The Role of Values in Psychology*

and Human Development, ed. William M. Kurtines, Margarita Axmitia, and Jacob L. Gewirtz. New York: Wiley.

HENDRIKA VANDE KEMP

Bellotti v. Baird

In *Bellotti v. Baird* (*Bellotti* II), the Supreme Court addressed the issue of whether a dependent, unmarried minor can be required to obtain parental consent before undergoing an abortion. In a decision that recognized that minors can possess the competency and maturity to make the important decision of whether to obtain an abortion, the Court ruled that a state law can require a pregnant, unmarried minor to obtain parental consent for an abortion if the law also provides a bypass procedure that allows her to obtain judicial permission for the abortion without parental notification.

The 1974 Massachusetts law in question required an unmarried, pregnant minor to provide proof of her consent and her parents' consent to obtain an abortion. If either or both of her parents withheld consent, the young woman could obtain a judicial order to permit her to have an abortion. Alleging that the law created an undue burden for minors seeking abortions, opponents of the law brought a "test-case" class-action suit in the Federal District Court of Massachusetts to enjoin the operation of the statute. This legal action reached the U.S. Supreme Court in 1976, but the Court declined to consider the merits of the case because of a procedural error. Instead, the Supreme Court vacated the judgment of the District Court and remanded the case for a final determination of the statute's meaning by the Supreme Judicial Court of Massachusetts.

The case again reached the U.S. Supreme Court in 1979, at which time the Court fully addressed the issue of whether the law's parental consent requirement placed an undue burden on an unmarried, pregnant minor seeking an abortion. The Court stated that persons under age eighteen are not without constitutional protection; however, their constitutional rights and individual liberty must be balanced against considerations such as a minor's possible inability to make an informed decision and the important parental role of child rearing. Although the Court recognized that parental advice and consent could be important in helping a minor decide whether she should obtain an abortion, in an 8–1 decision, the Court invalidated the Massachusetts statute.

As Robert H. Mnookin and D. Kelly Weisberg have suggested, Justice Powell's plurality opinion sets forth guidelines to assist states in determining the extent to which a state can permissibly limit a minor's right to an abortion. According to the decision in *Bellotti v. Baird*, a state can require a minor to obtain consent to undergo an abortion, but it cannot solely require parental consent. Instead, the law must provide an alternative to parental consent—a "bypass" procedure. This procedure must satisfy four requirements: first, the minor must be permitted to demonstrate to the judge that she is mature and adequately well-informed to make the abortion decision with her physician and without parental consent; second, if she cannot demonstrate the requisite maturity, she must be permitted to convince the judge that the abortion would nonetheless be in her best interest; third, the bypass procedure must assure her anonymity, and; fourth, the bypass procedure must be sufficiently expedient to allow her to obtain the abortion.

See also: **Adolescence and Youth; Children's Rights; Law, Children and the; Teenage Mothers in the United States.**

BIBLIOGRAPHY

Davis, Samuel M., and Mortimer D. Schwartz. 1987. *Children's Rights and the Law.* Lexington, MA: D.C. Heath and Company.

Dembitz, Nanette. 1980. "The Supreme Court and a Minor's Abortion Decision." *Columbia Law Review* 80: 1251.

Harrison, Maureen, and Steve Gilbert, eds. 1993. *Abortion Decisions of the United States Supreme Court: The 1970s.* Beverly Hills, CA: Excellent Books.

Mnookin, Robert H. 1985. *In the Interest of Children: Advocacy, Law Reform, and Public Policy.* New York: W. H. Freeman and Company.

Mnookin, Robert H., and D. Kelly Weisberg, eds. 1995. *Child, Family and State: Problems and Materials on Children and the Law,* 3rd ed. Boston: Little, Brown and Company.

Ramsey, Sarah H., and Douglas E. Abrams. 2001. *Children and the Law in a Nutshell.* St. Paul, MN: West Group.

Shapiro, Ian, ed. 2001. *Abortion: The Supreme Court Decisions, 1965–2000,* 2d ed. Indianapolis, IN: Hackett Publishing Company.

Veerman, Philip E. 1992. *The Rights of the Child and the Changing Image of Childhood.* Boston: Martinus Nijhoff Publishers.

AMY L. ELSON

Benjamin, Walter (1892–1940)

Walter Benjamin was a German philosopher, literary critic, and writer who worked in exile in Paris after 1933. Besides being the author of *Berlin Childhood around 1900 (Berliner Kindheit um neunzehnhundert)* which was written throughout the 1930s, Benjamin published book-length studies on the Romantic concept of criticism, on Goethe, and on allegory and melancholy in the German mourning play, along with influent critical essays on authors such as Kafka, Proust and Baudelaire, as well as a seminal essay on art in the age of technical reproduction. As part of his research for the Frankfurt Institute of Social Research, Benjamin worked until his death on the *Passagen-Werk* (his so-called *Arcades Project*), studying the glass covered passages of nineteenth-century Paris as a microcosm of urban modernity.

Resulting from Benjamin's passion for children's books and Russian toys as well as his activity as a radio narrator for children around 1930, his urban childhood memoir *Berlin Childhood* reflects upon the experiences of children in private and public spaces of the metropolis. Originally conceived by Benjamin as a way of writing on contemporary Berlin issues, his childhood recollections soon turned away from chronological narrative in order to explore a deliberately fragmented mode of literary presentation. Focusing on the spaces and images through which childhood becomes mentally accessible to the adult writer, aged forty, in the light of his present situation, *Berlin Childhood* is composed of more than thirty minor chapters that may be read separately or arranged in various configurations. Detailed descriptions of bourgeois interiors as (uncannily) experienced by a child join renderings of the child's encounters with public places such as the Tiergarten park or a market hall as well as with urban characters inhabiting the real and imaginary world of urban childhood. In this way, modern urban childhood is represented in a series of enigmatic and intimate miniatures.

Benjamin's *Berlin Childhood* provides insight into a variety of private, semi-private, and public spaces, all of which prove important to the amnesia of an intellectual adult living an insecure life after having fled the Nazi regime of Germany in early 1933. As a modern literary critic and intellectual, Benjamin was trying to understand what was fundamental about childhood as a contemporary urban experience. Although the narrator's childhood was indeed socially privileged, the young individual's entire experience is recalled under the sign of what Benjamin terms *"entstellte Ähnlichkeit"* (disfigured similitude). The child identifies fully with the things, images, and words surrounding him; on the other hand, this mimetic approach takes the elements of the world for granted to such an extent that reality appears as magic or at least as inhabited by many forces—contradicting the idea of an autonomous individual mastering his own life. In this way, a powerful constellation of mimesis and "misunderstandings" (from the adult point of view) is laid bare at various situations of everyday life that seem to anticipate and even outline the adult urban life of the narrator in exile. With a description of the particular approach to life provided by the backyard "Loggias" of his childhood apartment, Benjamin establishes a literary self-portrait of an extraterritorial child, neither fully inside the family apartment nor successfully integrated into the society of the metropolis. With all its contradictions, this Berlin childhood seems to point out the cultural and social sphere of the city as the adequate place for addressing the essential issues of modern life, private and public alike.

A preface by Benjamin, found in the only version of *Berlin Childhood* to provide a table of contents indicating the order of the individual chapters, also outlines some of the basic methodological assumptions informing the book. Writing his urban childhood memories first in order to limit nostalgia in exile, the narrator further suggests to leave out individual details, focusing, instead, on "the images . . . in which the experience of the metropolis settles in a child of the bourgeois class," as Benjamin terms it (1989, p. 385). In this way, the author hopes to contribute to a new literary and historiographic genre, capable of providing a language that may successfully articulate the experiences of childhood in the modern city.

See also: **Autobiographies.**

BIBLIOGRAPHY

Barlyng, Marianne, and Henrik Reeh, ed. 2001. *Walter Benjamins Berlin: 33 laesninger i* Barndom i Berlin omkring år 1900. (Walter Benjamin's Berlin: 33 readings into *Berlin Childhood around 1900*.) Hellerup, Denmark: Spring Publishers.

Benjamin, Walter. 1972–1989. *Gesammelte Schriften*, vol. I–VII. Frankfurt am Main: Suhrkamp Verlag.

Benjamin, Walter. 1985. "Berliner Chronik." In *Gesammelte Schriften*, vol. VI, pp. 465–519.

Benjamin, Walter. 1989. "Berliner Kindheit um neunzehnhundert [Fassung letzter Hand]." In *Gesammelte Schriften*, vol. VII, pp. 385–433.

HENRIK REEH

Beyond the Best Interests of the Child

The term *psychological parenthood* was first introduced in 1973 through an influential book entitled *Beyond the Best Interests of the Child*. A psychological parent refers to a person who has a parental relationship with a child, whether or not the two are biologically related. The term is used mainly in legal discourse, in the context of custody disputes. A prime example of the concept would be a dispute between an adoptive parent who has raised a child since infancy and biological parent who later claims the child, although this is not the most common kind of situation in which claims of psychological parenthood might be made. Such claims might also be made in the following circumstances: divorce, disputes between a stepparent and a biological parent, between two biological parents not married to one another, or between same-sex partners who have raised a child together. At the start of the twenty-first century an increasing number of custody disputes have involved foster parents who want to adopt a child they have been raising and state agencies who want to shift the child to a biological parent or to relatives of the biological parent.

Traditionally, the law has had a presumption in favor of biological parents in disputes with other people. In many states today, unless a parent has abandoned a child or been declared to be "unfit" to raise the child, the rights of biological parents are all but inviolate.

In 1973 *Beyond the Best Interests of the Child* challenged this biological emphasis. The first volume of a trilogy, the book was a collaboration among a law professor (Joseph Goldstein), a child analyst (ANNA FREUD), and a child psychiatrist (Albert Solnit). Goldstein, Freud, and Solnit argued that whether or not the psychological parent was biologically related to the child or not, courts should preserve this bond because normal development depends on its continuity. They also stressed that for a child, being caught up in a custody battle is a psychological emergency. Since harm has already been done and the child is still at risk, the best the courts can do is resolve matters quickly. Above all, judges and lawyers should base their decisions on the child's immature sense of time and steady need for a continuing relationship with the person who has provided ongoing, loving care.

Psychological parenting is a legal term, not a psychological one. Although psychoanalytic theory has traditionally stressed the importance of early parent-child relationships, the ideas put forth in *Beyond the Best Interests of the Child* differ from later research and theory in developmental psychology. Attachment theory, based on the work of JOHN BOWLBY, has become the major conceptual framework in the early twenty-first century for understanding parent-child relationships. The most controversial aspect of Goldstein, Freud, and Solnit's book was the recommendation that in a typical divorce, the court should determine whether the mother or the father is the psychological parent and give that person sole custody of the child. In addition, they recommended that the chosen parent should be able to regulate or even put an end to visits between the child and the other parent.

More recent research has shown, by contrast, that a young child is capable of becoming emotionally attached to more than one person. Although one parent may be the primary attachment figure, children typically become emotionally attached to both, as well as to others who provide loving, attentive care. Despite these and other criticisms, the concept of psychological parenthood has been influential in drawing attention to the child's needs and perspectives in determining custody.

See also: **Adoption in the United States; Children's Rights; Divorce and Custody; Law, Children and the; Same-Sex Parenting.**

BIBLIOGRAPHY

Goldstein, Joseph, Anna Freud, and Albert Solnit. 1973. *Beyond the Best Interests of the Child*. New York: Free Press.

ARLENE SKOLNICK

Bible, The

The Bible has connoted different texts within different religious communities. For literate laypeople in the later Middle Ages it meant the edited Bible stories of Petrus Comestor's *Historia scholastica*, first published around 1170 and later translated into the vernacular all over Europe. After the Reformation the Bible could connote the canonical Bible in any of its many translations, with or without the Apocrypha; Bible excerpts in prose or verse; single books such as Ecclesiasticus or Psalms; children's Bibles; the Hebrew Scriptures for Jewish readers; or from the nineteenth century onward, often the New Testament by itself. Bible reading in the Middle Ages and sixteenth and seventeenth centuries was carefully guided by richly interpretive marginal glosses, which aided the understanding of texts of early publications of Luther, Geneva, and King James translations. This entry uses the text of *The New English Bible with the Apocrypha*, first published in 1970 by Oxford University Press.

Before the advent of nineteenth-century textual criticism, Bible readers commonly understood the Bible as a single coherent text manifesting the word of God. The Bible as we know it today, however, is a compilation of texts of varying antiquity, some of which are themselves based on older oral or written traditions. The Bible's most ancient components reflect the values of nomadic herding cultures and their conflicts with settled agrarian communities (e.g., God's preferring Abel's animal offering to Cain's vegetable ones). As Israelites became urbanized, Biblical texts excoriated their continuing service to alien gods such as Ba'al and Molech, as well as their devotion to city fleshpots such as Sodom and Gomorrah. Late mystical texts used striking end-of-days imagery that lived on in the writings of early Christian writers who were well-versed in the Hebrew Scriptures.

Children's Bibles and the Invention of Bible Children

With an eye to fostering Biblicity among young readers, early modern editors of the Bible's histories revised children's ages downward. Noah's grown son Ham became a disrespectful child, and Isaac was gradually made younger, from a medieval thirty-seven (derived from Josephus's estimate) to a frightened but obedient child of seven or eight.

Petrus Comestor altered Bible narratives significantly in his Latin *Historia scholastica*. In his telling, Ham's report to his brothers of their father's drunken nakedness became punishable filial impiety by the addition of the adjective *ridens* ("laughing"). Later redactors of Bible histories for children attempted to account for Absalom's rebellion by transforming his Biblical handsomeness into an external ugliness that automatically connoted internal sinfulness, despite the fact that David's paternal neglect and personal failings accounted for many of Absalom's rebellious acts. In a reverse direction, the "fine" baby Moses, Israel's heroic leader, took on ever greater handsomeness in children's Bibles between the seventeenth and twenty-first centuries.

Obedience gradually emerged as the primary virtue among children in children's Bibles, joined by hard work from 1750 onward in Bibles for children of the laboring classes; Bible stories were changed or invented to accommodate obedience and industry. In the nineteenth and twentieth centuries, Catholic authors of devotional literature for children created biographies describing Mary's (Biblically nonexistent) childhood and vastly expanded the few facts of Jesus' early years. School religious dramas also expanded popular acquaintance with Biblical figures' fictive childhoods. Such dramas existed in the Middle Ages, but the genre gained impetus as a form of educational exercise in France in the seventeenth century and in England in the eighteenth.

The descriptions of children and childhood that are widely believed to exist in the Bible are largely the product of Bible stories in prose or dramatic form, each of which reflects the values of the age that produced it: nineteenth-century awareness of a child such as Samuel, for example, resembles a nineteenth-century childhood as its author envisioned it.

Girls and Boys in the Canonical Bible

Childhood in the canonical Bible presents different images altogether. Biblical girls were married to close relatives to form advantageous alliances that consolidated family networks by marrying a daughter to a close relative. Outside the family, fathers used daughters' marriages to forge political bonds, as when Solomon betrothed his daughter to "Pharaoh King of Egypt" (1 Kings 3:1). Beauty, modesty, and virginity comprised a daughter's most valuable attributes. A Biblical girl appeared in the role of sister only rarely and then problematically: Lot's daughters cooperated actively to carry out their plan to perpetuate their father's lineage by intoxicating him, lying with him, and mothering the Moabites and Ammonites (Gen. 19). Dinah and Tamar, each of whom suffered a sexual assault, were both avenged by a full brother for the sake of family honor and personal outrage respectively (Gen. 34; 2 Sam. 13).

Biblical boys are far more numerous than Biblical girls, consistent with the Bible's predominant male-centeredness. Generational succession followed male lineage, hence a son's name lived on far more often than a daughter's. For example, Adam (and Eve) had Cain, Abel, Seth, and "other sons and daughters" (Gen. 5:3–4). That listing heralds the Bible's numerous genealogical listings through male lines, which continue into the New Testament Gospel of the Jewish evangelist Matthew.

A dark side of generational succession appeared in Old Testament scriptures of more ancient provenance, namely that Jehovah would punish "sons and grandsons to the third and fourth generation for the sins of their fathers" (Exod. 34:7); the illness and subsequent death of the son born of David's adultery with Bathsheba (2 Sam. 12) provides a dramatic example. The secular world pragmatically adopted the same ethic, when seven grandsons of Saul (some of them no doubt adolescent or younger) were hurled to their deaths to appease the anger of the Gibeonites against Saul (2 Sam. 21), and "Zedekiah's sons were slain before his eyes" after Nebuchadnezzar defeated him (2 Kings 7; Jer. 52:10). The ethic of transferring a father's guilt to his issue shifted in later prophetical literature: Ezekiel preached that "a son shall not share his father's guilt" (Ezek. 18:20).

The stages of a Biblical boy's early life—birth, CIRCUMCISION, and weaning—provided occasions for rejoicing, and in Isaac's case, "for a great feast" (Gen. 20:8). A strict hierarchy among sons granted primacy to the first born, which—according to Deuteronomy 21:16–17—had to be respected even if that son had been born to an unloved wife. Occasionally, however, primogeniture was overridden by emotion, as when Sarah forced Abraham to drive out his first-born son Ishmael (Gen. 21:9–21), when Jacob exploited Esau's hunger and Isaac's blindness to secure his brother's birthright for himself (Gen. 25:29–34; Gen. 27), or when Jacob knowingly conferred his blessing on the younger of Joseph's two sons (Gen. 48:14–20). Predictably, the Bible enjoins a son to pay attention to his father's instruction, as well as to his mother's teaching (Prov. 1:8–9; Prov. 4:1–5). Earlier texts had harshly prescribed death for such physical disobedience as striking a father or mother (Exod. 21:15, 17).

The Old Testament is filled with dramatic instances of adult fraternal strife, but only two take place between certifiable boys: Ishmael taunted Isaac (Gen. 21:9), and seventeen-year-old Joseph's brothers cast him into a pit from which he was sold into Egyptian servitude (Gen. 38:28–30). All other episodes detail strife between brothers who had attained the full or semi-independent status of economic production (herding, farming) or separate domicile: Cain versus Abel, further strife between Jacob and Esau, and Absalom versus his half-brother Amnon. Even the friendship of David and Jonathan was an adult one, as Jonathan already was a father at the time and David was long gone from the protection of his parental home.

The Bible's few sustained narratives of children and childhood—particularly those of Moses, Samuel, and David—are told quickly. Moses' infancy was recorded in emotive language: "When [his mother] saw what a fine child he was, she hid him for three months" (Exod. 2:1–2). Afterward his older sister Miriam guarded him until Pharaoh's daughter found the crying child. "Filled with pity for it, she said, 'Why, it is a little Hebrew boy.'" "Thereupon the sister," devising a clever ruse to protect her brother, "said to Pharaoh's daughter, 'Shall I go and fetch one of the Hebrew women as a wet-nurse to suckle the child for you?'" (Exod. 2:4–8). Directly afterward, Moses was "grown up" (Exod. 2:11). A small detail from the life of the boy Samuel communicates maternal care: Samuel was "a mere boy with a linen ephod fastened round him. Every year his mother made him a little cloak and took it to him. . . ." (1 Sam. 2:18–19). We further learn that "the child Samuel was in the Lord's service under his master Eli" and that God spoke to him (1 Sam. 3:1–4). The boy David lives on as "handsome, with ruddy cheeks and bright eyes" (1 Sam. 16:11–12; 1 Sam. 17:43), a "lad" (1 Sam. 17:56) who served Saul as armor-bearer and

harp-player (1 Sam. 16:21–23). When he hung around the battlefield, however, his older brother called him an "impudent rascal" (1 Sam. 17:28).

In a variety of texts, irresistible adolescent urges push aside the Bible's general sobriety. "Will a girl forget her finery?" Jeremiah asked rhetorically (Jer. 2:32). Worse was Ezekiel's inculpation of Oholah and Oholibah, two sisters who "played the whore in Egypt, played the whore while they were still girls; for they let their breasts be fondled and their virgin bosoms pressed" (Ezek. 23:3). In the New Testament Herodias's daughter danced before Herod and gained John the Baptist's head for her efforts (Mark 6:21–28), another testimony to the effective power of an adolescent girl's SEXUALITY.

Boys' sexuality, though castigated, seems to have been more part of the daily scene. A foolish lad was easy prey for a practiced prostitute, who seduced him at twilight (Prov. 7:6–29). Paul's warning to Timothy to "turn from the wayward impulses of youth" (2 Tim. 2:22) seems part of an early warning system that included freewheeling sexuality among other dangers to adolescent virtue.

In the seventeenth century Ecclesiasticus, a now largely forgotten apocryphal book of the Bible, counted as a child-rearing manual. Often published separately for children's use, it was equally often the only part of the Bible known by the young. Ecclesiasticus offered a wealth of practical advice for living a safe and sober life. It began by urging a son to respect his parents and continued by recognizing parents' fears for their daughters' virtue and well-being (Ecclus. 22:3–5 and passim).

Differences between Old and New Testament Imagery of Children and Childhood

In a New Testament reprise of Old Testament ferocity, Herod massacred "all children in Bethlehem" (Matt. 1:16) just as Pharaoh had instigated an indiscriminate murder of Jewish boys (Exod. 1:15–22). Similarly present in both testaments were child healings. The Old Testament prophets Elijah and Elisha each had restored a boy to life (1 Kings 17:17–23; 2 Kings 4:18–37). In the New Testament, however, Jesus cured and revived girls and boys alike: the twelve-year-old daughter of the synagogue president Jairus (Matt. 9:25; Mark 5:42; Luke 8:40–42, 49–56), a "young daughter" possessed by an unclean spirit (Mark 7:25–30), a "boy" possessed by a "deaf and dumb" spirit (Mark 9:17–27), and an officer's son in Capernaum (John 4:43–53), while Paul and Silas together cured an Israelite slave girl possessed by an oracular spirit (Acts 16:16–18).

Jesus repeatedly used the word "children" to mean "adherents" (as in "children of the Kingdom," Matt 13:38) and to indicate spiritual advancement ("the Kingdom of God belongs to children," Mark 10:14–15). Jesus identified himself as a little child and proclaimed that whoever received "one of these children in my name . . . receives me" (Mark 9:36–37; Luke 9:46–48). Jesus also treated children as representations of innocence, simplicity, and helplessness in some of his preaching (Matt 18:1–6; Matt 19:14).

New Testament writing assumed that parents would lovingly nurture their children (Luke 11:11–13). Paul, for instance, referred allegorically to providential parenting to represent the relationship between divinity and followers of Jesus: "Parents should make provision for their children, not children for their parents" (2 Cor. 12:14). The first letter of John actually addressed one verse to real rather than metaphorical "children" (1 John 2:13), a rarity in the New Testament and in John's own letters, where "my children" generally refers to adults who are spiritual children.

In most respects New Testament depictions of and references to childhood differ fundamentally from those in the Old Testament. Portrayed overwhelmingly in their vulnerability, Old Testament children fall victim to war and oppression and communicate Jewish suffering as men and women also experienced it. The seventy children of Ahab who remained behind in Samaria with their tutors were beheaded, their heads transported in baskets to Israel and dumped on the ground at the city gate (2 Kings 10:1–11). Equally savage, "the Medes . . . have no pity on little children and spare no mother's son" (Isaiah 13:17–18). Suffering the effects of siege, "children and infants faint in the streets of the town and cry to their mothers, . . . gasping out their lives in their mothers' bosom" (Lam. 2:11–12); "the sucking infant's tongue cleaves to its palate from thirst; young children beg for bread but no one offers them a crumb" (Lam. 4:4). Doing Saul's bidding, Doeg "put to the sword every living being, men and women, children and babes in arms" (1 Sam. 22:19).

Even within their own families danger lurked. Abraham was prepared to sacrifice his son Isaac to demonstrate his fidelity to Jehovah (Gen. 22), and later fathers returning from Exile dismissed the children they had fathered with foreign wives (Ezra 10). Even a grandmother might turn murderous, although six-year-old Joah escaped Athalial's wrath by hiding with his nurse in the house of the Lord for six years (2 Kings 11:1–3).

Old Testament children were parental possessions of the father who had sired them; they comprised his personal worth and added to his individual wealth. This understanding echoes in Jacob's declaration that his two grandsons Ephraim and Manassah counted as his own (Gen. 48:5). Ownership implied the right of disposal: on occasion hungry parents pledged their children to pay their own debts (Neh. 5:1–6). In the worst case, children became food for their starving parents. The statement that "tender-hearted women with their own hands boiled their own children, their children became their food in the day of my people's wounding" (Lam. 4:10) was followed by the anguished cry, "Must women eat the fruit of their wombs, the children they have

brought safely to birth?" (Lam. 2:20). Of all children, ORPHANS who lacked familial protection were the most vulnerable. Hence, already in the Pentateuch the people of Israel were adjured not to ill treat "a fatherless child" (Exod. 22:23).

Various prophetical authors of the Old Testament drew on metaphors of childhood to describe Israel's eventual restoration: Israel would suck the milk of nations (Isa. 60:16) and be fed from the breasts that give comfort (Isa. 66:11). In Isaiah's vision, "a little child shall lead [the calf and the lion] . . . the infant shall play over the hole of a cobra, and the young child shall dance over the viper's nest" (Isa. 11:6, 8). Isaiah's infantine image was meant to communicate safety within a mortally threatening environment, but it also communicates a sense of utter vulnerability among the young. Prophetical authors often used metaphors of childhood to convey devastating fear: death "sweeps off the children in the open air" (Jer. 9:21), while the people of Israel were characterized as the most vulnerable of the young, "fatherless children" (Jer. 49:11; Jer. 51:22) and "babes [who] will fall by the sword and be dashed to the ground" (Hos. 13:16).

Joseph and his brothers generated an enormous literature, both fictional (e.g., Thomas Mann) and scholarly, including linguistic analysis. The sacrifice of first-born sons in the context of Mediterranean Moloch rituals and requirements in later texts to dedicate a child to God, as well as investigations of BIRTH ORDER comprise the principle research subjects addressed to date.

See also: **Theories of Childhood.**

BIBLIOGRAPHY

Bottigheimer, Ruth B. 1996. *The Bible for Children: From the Age of Gutenberg to the Present.* New Haven, CT: Yale University Press.

Daube, David. 1942. "How Esau Sold his Birthright." *Cambridge Law Journal* 8: 70–75.

Hayward, R. 1981. "The Present State of Research into the Targumic Account of the Sacrifice of Isaac." *Journal of the Study of Judaism* 32: 127–150.

Heider, George C. 1985. *The Cult of Molek: A Reassessment.* Sheffield England: JSOT Press.

Levenson, Jon. 1993. *The Death and Resurrection of the Beloved Son: The Transformation of Child Sacrifice in Judaism and Christianity.* New Haven, CT: Yale University Press.

Longacre, Robert E. 1989. *Joseph: A Story of Divine Providence. A Text Theoretical and Text Linguistic Analysis of Genesis 37 and 39–48.* Winona Lake: Eisenbrauns.

Mendelsohn, Isaac. 1959. "On the Preferential Status of the Eldest Son." *Bulletin of the American Schools of Oriental Research* 156: 38–40.

Weinfeld, Moshe. 1972. "The Worship of Molech and of the Queen of Heaven and Its Background." *Ugarit-Forschungen* 4: 133–154.

RUTH B. BOTTIGHEIMER

Bicycles and Tricycles

Bicycles and tricycles are both children's riding toys. As distinct types of pedal-driven motion they both appeared for the first time in the 1880s. The tricycle was conceived and produced especially for children from the outset, however bicycles for children were derived by a simple reduction of the scale of the adult counterpart.

After the invention of the modern bicycle with rear wheel chain-driven transmission and a diamond-shaped frame in the 1880s, it quickly entered into widespread use for transportation, work, and leisure purposes. In America, due to the development of private automobiles as the principal form of adult transportation, the bicycle became primarily a child's toy or youth transportation option after the 1920s.

In Europe motorization was slower and the bicycle has been in use for transportation, work, leisure, sport, and play for longer and to a greater extent but with considerable national variation. The use of bicycles for transportation purposes is most pronounced in northern Europe, particularly in Holland and Scandinavia.

Bicycle frames constructed for children appeared immediately after its invention, but it did not become a mass-production item until well into the 1950s. Until this point, children in general were precluded from cycling until an adult frame of small size was manageable in youth. Today the availability of a range of smaller frame sizes enables children from age three or even younger to cycle with training wheels. With further private and public motorization and institutionalization, children's cycling is generally turning into an activity solely of leisure and play. A recent development of significance is the drive towards reduction of risk through safety campaigns and technological innovation, mainly resulting in a range of typically compulsory accessories, such as reflective devices, lighting, and helmets. On the urban scale it has led to the establishment of bicycle lanes in several cities in northern Europe.

Before the invention of the modern bicycle the velocipede enjoyed an enthusiastic following in the late 1860s. Its principle of gearing by upsizing the driving front wheel, has survived among children's riding toys in the tricycle, where this simpler principle of construction has allowed for a cheap product. The element which sets the tricycle apart from the velocipede is the rear transverse two-wheel shaft that provides stability. This eliminates the need for balancing, eases mounting, simplifies starting and stopping and allows children as young as one year old to ride. Tricycles are produced in an extensive number of different forms, materials and qualities; ranging from inexpensive and short-lived indoor plastic models to expensive and durable outdoor models in steel, some with pneumatic tires. Tricycles are typically one-size models for children aged one to three. Until the 1960s tricycles were available in several larger sizes; it was the prin-cipal bike of the preschool period. However, in the late twentieth century, bicycles began to cut into this market, as younger children began to purchase two-wheeled bikes.

See also: **Cars as Toys; Play.**

BIBLIOGRAPHY

Dodge, Pryor. 1996. *The Bicycle.* New York: Flammarion.

HANS-CHRISTIAN JENSEN

Bilingual Education

On June 2, 1998, California voters approved Proposition 227, a measure designed to eliminate bilingual education, the use of another language along with English, in their public schools. In the preceding two decades there had been many other efforts to do away with bilingual education. The subject is a lightning rod of controversy and one of the most recognizable issues in what commentators have termed the nation's "culture wars." Its history is as controversial as its practice. One central question is whether or not the United States had a true "bilingual tradition." Another is to what degree bilingual education represented movements toward either assimilation or ethnic maintenance.

Bilingual education goes back as far as the colonial period in the United States. Franciscan missionaries from California to Texas systematically used indigenous languages in translating and teaching the Catholic catechism to Native Americans. In the English-speaking colonies before the American Revolution and up through the early Republic, a myriad of ethnic groups, especially Germans, patronized bilingual schools, although influential thinkers and nationalists such as Noah Webster and Benjamin Franklin opposed them because they feared linguistic heterogeneity.

The nineteenth century witnessed the rise of significant pro-bilingualism legislation, particularly for German speakers. In the 1830s, for example, the state of Ohio constitutionally guaranteed German-English bilingual education to local communities that wanted it. States such as Indiana, Illinois, Michigan, and Wisconsin also protected German bilingual education through statutory or constitutional means. Cities such as Baltimore, Cincinnati, Cleveland, Indianapolis, Milwaukee, and St. Louis operated large, public bilingual programs for German Americans. Historian Heinz Kloss links the bilingual education of the past with that of today and sees it as evidence of a national bilingual tradition. Several historians defend this interpretation through focused, regional studies. Other scholars criticize this contention, holding instead that it was a disorganized phenomenon and not representative of a true bilingual tradition.

While German Americans were certainly the most influential nineteenth-century practitioners of bilingual education, many other groups were also involved. Though often relegated to private bilingual schools due to their lack of political influence, Czechs, Italians, Poles, Mexicans, and others established bilingual programs when they deemed them necessary, usually because of a belief that the public schools were culturally intolerant. Most immigrants wanted their children to speak English, and preferred bilingual to completely non-English schools. In the middle of the nineteenth century, Mexican Americans utilized both public and private bilingual schools, particularly in New Mexico and Texas, which had recently been acquired from Mexico. At this time the state of Louisiana constitutionally protected bilingual instruction for its native French speakers. Chicago's Catholic schools implemented bilingual education for Poles at the turn of the century, with Americanization as the goal. Indeed, one of bilingual education's most important rationales among non-ethnic educators was the belief that it furthered Americanization by making public schools more desirable to ethnic parents and by ensuring some level of English instruction.

This varied, hard-to-define bilingual tradition in nineteenth-century America was the product of a Jeffersonian society committed to principles of local, limited government and undertaken at the behest of the ethnic communities themselves. These ethnic epicenters, sometimes called island communities, were targeted by both the Progressive and Americanization movements in the twentieth century. Progressives advocated centralized control of educational decision making and wanted to standardize the teaching of non-English-speaking children using an English-Only pedagogy. Traditional bilingual methods depended upon literacy in a foreign language for the ultimate acquisition of English. However, English-Only entailed all-English instruction for non-English speakers; not one foreign language word could be used in the lessons. Violation of these rules meant physical punishment and possibly expulsion for students. For teachers it entailed incarceration, fines, and loss of certification. The Americanization movement during the hysteria of World War I resulted in the criminalization of bilingual education. Though the Wilson administration discussed outlawing all German in the nation's public schools, it settled for federal directives to the states urging replacement of bilingual education with English-Only. States pursued this to extremes. But in *Meyer v. Nebraska* in 1923 the U.S. Supreme Court grudgingly overturned a Nebraska law banning all foreign languages in private institutions.

English-Only pedagogy and IQ testing became key legal and educational justifications for segregated schools. Despite a brief flirtation with foreign languages during World War II, English-Only remained the nation's official pedagogical approach for non-English speakers well into the 1960s. By then scholars had begun to question English-Only's pedagogical assumptions. Also, ethnic activists, especially Mexican Americans, brought increasing legal and political pressure to bear against English-Only's segregating effect on their children. These unrelated forces culminated in the modern bilingual education movement.

The Bilingual Education Act—passed in late 1967 and signed early in 1968—represented bilingual education's rebirth in the United States. It was signed by Lyndon Johnson, the only American president with experience in teaching non-English-speaking children: during the 1928–1929 academic year, the young Johnson taught impoverished Mexican Americans in Cotulla, Texas (ironically he taught his children using English-Only). Bilingual education's growth during the 1970s was aided by its utility as an affirmative curricular tool in desegregation cases. In 1970 the Office of Civil Rights in the Nixon Justice Department ruled that grouping children in so-called "special" or "educationally retarded" classes on the basis of language was a violation of their civil rights. Spurred by Chinese-American parents, the Supreme Court ruled four years later in *Lau v. Nichols* that schools were obligated to offer non-English-speaking children equal educational opportunity, in this case bilingual education.

However, bilingual education was never uniformly accepted. By the late 1970s a significant backlash against it developed among serious intellectuals and nativist groups. The Reagan administration actively sought to discredit bilingual education by promoting English as a Second Language (ESL) as a better option. This politicization escalated in the 1990s, culminating in California's Proposition 227. In the early twenty-first century, bilingual education remains a hot-button political issue with an indisputably rich and meaningful history in the United States.

See also: **Education, United States; Literacy.**

BIBLIOGRAPHY

Crawford, James. 1999. *Bilingual Education: History, Politics, Theory, and Practice*, 4th ed. Los Angeles: Bilingual Educational Services.

Davies, Gareth. 2002. "The Great Society after Johnson: The Case of Bilingual Education." *Journal of American History* 88: 1405–1429.

Finkelman, Paul. 1996. "German American Victims and American Oppressors: The Cultural Background and Legacy of *Meyer v. Nebraska*." In *Law and the Great Plains: Essays on the Legal History of the Heartland*, ed. John R. Wunder. Westport, CT: Greenwood Press.

Heath, Shirley Brice. 1981. "English in Our National Heritage." In *Language in the U.S.A.*, ed. Charles A. Ferguson and Shirley Brice Heath. New York: Cambridge University Press.

Kloss, Heinz. 1977. *The American Bilingual Tradition*. Rowley, MA: Newbury House.

Leibowitz, Arnold H. 1971. *Educational Policy and Political Acceptance: The Imposition of English as the Language of Instruction in American Schools*. Washington, DC: Center for Applied Linguistics.

San Miguel, Guadalupe, Jr. 1984. "Conflict and Controversy in the Evolution of Bilingual Education in the United States—An Interpretation." *Social Science Quarterly* 65: 508–518.

Schlossman, Steven L. 1983. "Is There an American Tradition of Bilingual Education? German in the Public Elementary Schools, 1840–1919." *American Journal of Education* 91:139–186.

Tamura, Eileen H. 1994. *Americanization, Acculturation, and Ethnic Identity: The Nisei Generation in Hawaii.* Urbana: University of Illinois Press.

Wiebe, Robert H. 1967. *The Search for Order, 1877–1920.* New York: Hill and Wang.

CARLOS KEVIN BLANTON

Binet, Alfred (1857–1911)

Alfred Binet is perhaps best remembered for his role in elaborating the first numerical scale of intelligence, but his contributions to individual psychology, experimental science, and applied pedagogy transcended the confines of intelligence testing. Binet was a pioneering scholar whose diverse and eclectic research interests fundamentally transformed the scientific study of the child in France as well as abroad.

Binet was born in Nice but moved to Paris at age twelve to study at the prestigious Lycée Louis le Grand; he spent the rest of his life in the capital region. Descended from at least two generations of medical doctors, Binet hesitated in choosing a career, passing his *licence* in law in 1878 but abandoning legal studies in favor of the emerging field of psychology; he earned a doctorate in natural sciences in 1894. Fascinated by the work of English associationists, particularly John Stuart Mill, Binet began an exceptionally prolific publishing career with an 1880 *Revue philosophique* article on the psychology of sensations; under the direction of the embryologist E. G. Balbiani (whose daughter, Laure, he would marry in 1884), he soon launched an equally prolific experimental career. In 1883 Binet joined the laboratory of the preeminent Parisian neurologist Jean-Martin Charcot at the Salpêtrière hospital. During his seven-year tenure at the laboratory, Binet became embroiled in the controversies surrounding Charcot's studies of hypnosis, loyally defending Charcot against charges that his demonstrations had been tainted by experimenters' unintentional suggestions to the patients.

In 1891, chagrined by his experiences in Charcot's laboratory, Binet joined the Sorbonne's new Laboratory of Experimental Psychology; in 1894, he was named director of the laboratory and became cofounder of the *Année psychologique*, a journal he would edit until his death. In the mid-1890s Binet became increasingly fascinated with the higher mental faculties, breaking with the preoccupation of the first generation of scientific psychologists; he also devoted substantial attention to questions of experimental method. Perhaps most significant, his interest in children's mental faculties, first evident in a trio of 1890 articles about his two daughters, combined with his search for suitable experimental subjects to produce a research agenda that would dominate the rest of his career. The pupils of public primary schools in several working-class districts of Paris became important research subjects, and Binet quickly became the pre-eminent member of the Société libre pour l'etude psychologique de l'enfant, established in 1899. Elected president in 1902, Binet became a tireless advocate for rigorous experimentation in numerous educational and developmental domains.

At a time when the French governing elites were preoccupied with problems of juvenile DELINQUENCY and educational inefficacy, Binet's work soon attracted legislative attention. When, in 1904, the French government established a commission to explore ways of diagnosing and educating children who were described as "abnormal" and "backward," Binet was invited to become a member; it was in this context that he and Théodore Simon developed the first version of their metric intelligence scale. Meanwhile Binet received permission in 1905 to open a laboratory of experimental pedagogy at the public primary school in Paris's rue de la Grange-aux-Belles. He soon transferred the bulk of his activities to this laboratory. Until his sudden death in 1911 he pursued an ambitious research agenda, equally eager to improve the condition of "abnormal" children and to trace the contours of "normal" child development. Although contemporaries were skeptical about his insistence that education be adapted to the individual needs of all children, such ideas attracted additional interest after World War I, and in the late twentieth century French scholars began to grant Binet overdue recognition as one of the founders not only of scientific pedagogy but also of French experimental psychology.

See also: **Child Development, History of the Concept of; Child Psychology; Intelligence Testing.**

BIBLIOGRAPHY

Avanzini, Guy. 1969. *La Contribution de Binet à l'élaboration d'une pédagogie scientifique.* Paris: Vrin.

Avanzini, Guy. 1999. *Alfred Binet.* Paris: Presses Universitaires de France.

Binet, Alfred. 1890. "Perceptions d'enfants." *Revue philosophique* 30: 582–611.

Binet, Alfred. 1900. *La Suggestibilité.* Paris: Schleicher.

Binet, Alfred. 1909. *Les Idées modernes sur les enfants.* Paris: Flammarion.

Binet, Alfred, J. Philippe, and V. Henri. 1894. *Introduction à la psychologie expérimentale.* Paris: Alcan.

Binet, Alfred, and Théodore Simon. 1907. *Les Enfants anormaux. Guide pour l'admission des enfants anormaux dans les classes de perfectionnement.* Paris: Colin.

Binet, Alfred, and N. Vaschide. 1898. "La Psychologie à l'école primaire." *Année psychologique* 4: 1–14.

Vial, Monique. 1990. *Les Enfants anormaux à l'école. Aux origines de l'éducation spécialisée, 1882–1909.* Paris: Armand Colin.

Wolff, Theta H. 1976. *Alfred Binet.* Chicago: University of Chicago Press.

Zazzo, René. 1993. "Alfred Binet (1857–1911)." *Perspectives: Revue trimestrielle d'éducation comparée* 23, nos. 1–2: 101–112.

KATHARINE NORRIS

Birth. *See* Conception and Birth.

Birth Control

Human beings have sought to avoid child bearing since ancient times and have used many methods to prevent conception or to kill a developing fetus. Religious and secular authorities usually discouraged the separation of sexual intercourse from procreation because they believed that it violated natural law or deprived the state of human capital. Thus, while individuals pursued their self-interests through such practices as coitus interruptus or inducing abortion, they usually acted in flagrant violation of official standards of sexual conduct.

Falling Birth Rates and the Social Environment

The English economist and cleric Thomas Malthus brought reproductive behavior into public debates over the nature of poverty through his *Essay on Population* (1798). He argued that rapid population growth forced down the living standards of the working classes, whose only hope for amelioration lay in "moral restraint" or the prudent postponement of marriage. In the early nineteenth century, English labor organizer Francis Place and other champions of the poor advocated family limitation as a tool in the struggle for social justice and sometimes published descriptions of how to prevent conception. These neo-Malthusians found a growing audience during the nineteenth century as birth rates began to decline in many countries that were actively involved in the developing market economy of the Atlantic world. These secular declines in fertility resulted from the private efforts by the sexually active to avoid pregnancy and were routinely denounced by political leaders, who attempted to suppress information on fertility control techniques. The term *birth control* was coined in the June 1914 issue of *The Woman Rebel*, a militantly feminist journal published in New York by Margaret Sanger (1879–1966), who became the preeminent champion of reproductive autonomy for women through her campaigns to abolish the legal and social obstacles to contraceptive practice. Eventually the term *birth control* became a synonym for *family planning* and *population control*, but the term *family planning* was originally adopted by those who wished to disassociate the movement to control fertility from Sanger's feminism, and the phrase *population control* was largely a post–World War II movement led by social scientists and policy-making elites, who feared that rapid population growth in the non-Western world would undermine capitalist development.

The precise timing and social determinants of the demographic transition in western Europe and North America from a vital economy of high birth rates and high death rates to one of low fertility and low mortality is still much in dispute among demographers, perhaps because of class and geographical differences in motivation and behavior. While French peasants seem to have been pioneers in fertility restraint during the eighteenth century, a broad spectrum of native-born Protestants in the United States led the turn to family limitation during the nineteenth century. In the United States the average native-born white woman bore seven or eight children in the late eighteenth century, but by the middle of the nineteenth century she was the mother of five, by the early twentieth century the mother of three, and by the middle of the Great Depression of the 1930s the mother of two. One of the remarkable aspects of the American demographic transition is that there were no sustained declines in INFANT MORTALITY before 1900. Several generations of American women had fewer children than their mothers despite high infant mortality and vigorous attempts by social leaders to encourage higher fertility.

The fertility decline is best understood as a response to a changing social environment. As the home ceased to be a unit of production, and as the manufacture of clothing and other goods moved to factories, children no longer provided necessary labor in the family economies of the emerging middle and white-collar classes. Rather, they became expensive investments, requiring education, capital, and an abundance of "Christian nurture" from mothers who measured respectability by the ability to stay home and efficiently manage the income won by their husbands in a separate, public sphere of work. Marriage manuals, some containing instructions for contraception, were prominent among the self-help books that became a staple of American culture after 1830. Romantic love became the rationale for marriage and religious leaders gave new prominence to the erotic bonds between husbands and wives. Thus, socially ambitious married couples bore the burden of reconciling sexual passion with a manageable number of children, whose socialization required more expensive and permissive nurture.

Historians now attribute the fertility decline to restrictive practices—contraception, abortion, and abstention from coitus—rather than biological changes or shifts in the percentage of individuals who married or their age at marriage. The efforts by individuals to control their fertility for personal reasons inspired the first self-conscious attempts to suppress birth control. Between 1840 and 1870, leaders of the medical profession organized successful campaigns to criminalize abortion through new state laws. The culmination of the campaigns against abortion in state legislatures coincided with the passage of the Comstock Act (1873) a strengthened national obscenity law in which no distinctions were made between smut, abortifacients, or contraceptives—all were prohibited.

During this period of legislative repression of contraception, Catholic theologians debated the moral implications of claims by experimental physiologists that there might be a naturally occurring sterile period in the female menstrual cycle. Church authorities quietly accepted the legitimacy of limiting coitus to periods of natural sterility, but the effectiveness of this "rhythm method" proved limited, and the Church's ancient prohibition on "artificial" contraception was reaffirmed by Pius XI in the encyclical *Casti Connubi* (December 1930).

Margaret Sanger

By the second decade of the twentieth century women in both Great Britain and the United States had begun to challenge the taboos on fertility control. Margaret Sanger won her place as the charismatic leader of the birth-control movement in the United States through her ability to develop a compelling rationale for the acceptance of contraception as an alternative to illegal abortion, since an appalling number of women died from septic abortions. Although she was influenced by the anarchist Emma Goldman and by trips to Europe, during which she was impressed by the sexual know-how of ordinary French women and by the birth-control advice stations operated by feminist physicians in the Netherlands, Sanger claimed that the death of one of her nursing clients from a self-induced abortion led her to focus all her energy on the single cause of reproductive autonomy for women. Sanger opened the first birth-control clinic in the United States in October 1916, in the Brownsville section of Brooklyn, New York. A police raid closed the clinic after ten days, but Sanger's trial and brief imprisonment made her a national figure, and in appealing her case she won a 1919 clarification of the New York State obscenity law that established the right of doctors to provide women with contraceptive advice for "the cure and prevention of disease."

Sanger interpreted this decision as a mandate for doctor-staffed birth-control clinics. Spurred by the emergence of an English rival, Marie Stopes, who opened a birth-control clinic in London in 1921, Sanger played down her radical past and found financial angels whose support allowed her to organize the American Birth Control League in 1921 and the Birth Control Clinical Research Bureau in New York City in 1923. The first doctor-staffed birth-control clinic in the United States, it provided case histories that demonstrated the safety and effectiveness of contraceptive practice and served as a model for a nationwide network of over 300 birth-control clinics by the late 1930s. In 1936 Sanger won an important revision in federal law with *U.S. v. One Package* (1936), which established the right of physicians to receive contraceptive materials. In 1937 the American Medical Association recognized contraception as an ethical medical service.

On the eve of World War II, the limits of the birth-control movement seemed to have been realized. A majority of Americans practiced some form of fertility control, but there was widespread concern about the low birth rate and little support for public subsidy of the services. Many social leaders were disturbed by the more permissive standards of sexual behavior that emerged during the first decades of the twentieth century as young women became increasingly visible as wage earners and as participants in an eroticized consumer culture. Alfred Kinsey and other pioneers in the survey of sexual behavior documented increases in premarital sexual activity that convinced some social conservatives that sexual liberation had gone too far. After World War II, however, influential social scientists such as Frank Notestein of Princeton University's Center for Population Research provided a new rationale for birth control by drawing attention to rapid population growth in the Third World and by arguing that the United States risked losing the Cold War because economic development compatible with capitalism might be impossible if the means were not found to curb birth rates.

Birth Control after World War II

John D. Rockefeller III became the leader of a revived movement to promote population control by founding the Population Council in 1952, after he failed to convince the directors of the Rockefeller Foundation that his interests warranted major new initiatives. The Population Council subsidized the development of academic demographic research in the United States and foreign universities and by the late 1950s was providing technical assistance to India and Pakistan for family planning programs. Concerned over the failure rates of the conventional barrier contraceptives such as condoms and diaphragms, the council invested in the clinical testing, improvement, and statistical evaluation of intrauterine devices (IUDs), that is, objects placed in the uterus to invoke an immune response that inhibits conception. A second major advance in contraceptive technology came with the marketing of an oral contraceptive by J. D. Searle and Company in 1960. "The pill" depended on recent advances in steroid chemistry, which provided orally active, and inexpensive, synthetic hormones. Margaret Sanger ensured that these new drugs would be exploited for birth control by recruiting Gregory Pincus of the Worcester Foundation for Experimental Biology for the work and introducing him to a feminist colleague, Katharine Dexter McCormick, who provided the funds Pincus needed to realize their dream of a female-controlled form of birth control that did not require specific preparation before sexual intercourse and thus made spontaneous sexual activity possible. The pill's rapid acceptance by the medical community and its female clients was enhanced by the growing use of synthetic hormones to treat a wide range of gynecological disorders so that contraception now appeared to be divorced from the "messy gadgets" of the past and was place in the context of modern therapeutics. In 1963 the Roman Catholic gynecologist John Rock, who had led the clinical trials of the first oral contraceptive, proclaimed, in *The Time Has Come*, that contraception was, thanks to the pill, now compatible with Catholic natural law theology. Rock's optimism proved false when Pope Paul VI's encyclical *Humanae Vitae* (July 1968) confirmed traditional teachings that prohibited artificial contraception, but by then a majority of married Catholics in the United States were practicing birth control.

A series of federal court decisions and new welfare policies reflected the changed status of birth control in public opinion. In 1965 the U.S. Supreme Court, in *Griswold v. Connecticut*, struck down a statute that prohibited contraceptive practice. The court continued to expand the rights of individuals to defy outdated restrictions in *Eisenstadt v. Baird*, (1972), which established the right of the unmarried to contraceptives. As President Lyndon Johnson's War on Poverty emerged from Congress, the Social Security Amendments of 1967 specified that at least 6 percent of expanding maternal and child health care funds were to be spent on family planning services. The Foreign Assistance Act of the same year provided aid for international programs, and contraceptives were removed from the list of materials that could not be purchased with Agency for International Development funds.

By the late 1960s feminists and population control advocates were successfully challenging state laws that limited access to abortion. In 1973 the U.S. Supreme Court attempted to forge a new consensus in *Roe v. Wade*, which recognized the right of abortion on demand during the first trimester of pregnancy. The Court's decision simply added fuel to an escalating firestorm of controversy as Roman Catholic leaders found common cause with Protestant fundamentalists and social conservative critics of the welfare state in a "right-to-life" and "family values" movement. From the left, groups such as the Committee to End Sterilization Abuse (founded in 1974) charged that minority women were being coerced by government maternal health programs that they viewed as genocidal. Revelations that disproportionate numbers of Hispanic and African-American women were sterilized in government programs that lacked adequate ethical guidelines supported complaints by such organizations as the National Women's Health Movement and the International Women's Health Coalition that the American health-care establishment had gone radically wrong in its high-tech, top-down, paternalistic approach to reproductive health issues.

At the 1974 United Nations World Population Conference, held in Bucharest, Rumania, John D. Rockefeller III recognized the criticisms of conventional family planning programs that had been mounted by feminists and the Population Council was reorganized to emphasize holistic approaches to women's health issues. New ethical guidelines were developed for federally sponsored maternal health programs as well, but deep social divisions remained between "pro-choice" and "pro-life" advocates, with the Democratic Party embracing the former and the Republican Party embracing the latter. Despite numerous challenges in state and federal courts and legislatures, *Roe v. Wade* remained the law of the land. In the late 1990s federal and state expenditures for subsidized family planning, including contraception,

sterilization, and therapeutic abortion, exceeded $700 million annually, while the birth rate among the native-born was below the level needed to maintain the population, which continued to grow because of liberal immigration laws and mass immigration to the United States.

The birth rate was even lower in Europe, where in countries such as Spain and Italy reproduction was not at a rate high enough to maintain their populations. In many other parts of the world, including China, India, and the Middle East, previously high birth rates were also in decline.

See also: **Conception and Birth; Eugenics; Fertility Rates; Obstetrics and Midwifery; Sexuality.**

BIBLIOGRAPHY

Brodie, Janet Farrell. 1994. *Contraception and Abortion in Nineteenth-Century America.* Ithaca, NY: Cornell University Press.

Chesler, Ellen. 1992. *Woman of Valor: Margaret Sanger and the Birth Control Movement in America.* New York: Simon and Schuster.

Critchlow, Donald T. 1999. *Intended Consequences: Birth Control, Abortion, and the Federal Government in Modern America.* New York: Oxford University Press.

Critchlow, Donald T., ed. 1996. *The Politics of Abortion and Birth Control in Historical Perspective.* University Park: Pennsylvania State University Press.

Dixon-Mueller, Ruth. 1993. *Population Policy and Women's Rights: Transforming Reproductive Choice.* New York: Praeger.

Garrow, David J. 1994. *Liberty and Sexuality: The Right to Privacy and the Making of* Roe v. Wade. New York: Macmillan.

Gordon, Linda. 1990. *Woman's Body, Woman's Right: A Social History of Birth Control in America.* New York: Grossman. 1976. Revised, New York: Penguin.

Hull, N. E. H., and Peter C. Hoffer. 2001. Roe v. Wade: *The Abortion Rights Controversy in American History.* Lawrence: University Press of Kansas.

McCann, Carole R. 1994. *Birth Control Politics in the United States, 1916–1945.* Ithaca, NY: Cornell University Press.

McLaren, Angus. 1990. *A History of Contraception: From Antiquity to the Present Day.* Cambridge, MA: Blackwell.

Mohr, James C. 1988. *Abortion in America: The Origins and Evolution of National Policy, 1800–1900.* New York: Oxford University Press.

Reagan, Leslie J. 1997. *When Abortion Was a Crime: Women, Medicine, and Law in the United States, 1867–1973.* Berkeley: University of California Press.

Reed, James. 1984. *The Birth Control Movement and American Society: From Private Vice to Public Virtue.* New York: Basic Books. 1978. *From Private Vice to Public Virtue: The Birth Control Movement and American Society since 1830.* Reprint, Princeton NJ: Princeton University Press.

Tone, Andrea. 2001. *Devices and Desires: A History of Contraceptives in America.* New York: Hill and Wang.

JAMES W. REED

Birthday

The celebration of the anniversary of one's birth is a phenomenon of modern industrial society. It is connected to the rise of a scientific way of thinking and to new attitudes about children and childhood. Perfection of the calendar by the Egyptians and Mesopotamians enabled people to reckon exact birth dates, but ancient and classical cultures rarely celebrated birthdays, except for those of royalty. The early Catholic Church deemed birthday festivities to be pagan; more important was the name day, the commemoration of the patron saint whose name was attached to a child upon BAPTISM. After the PROTESTANT REFORMATION, Western cultures celebrated birthdays of royalty, presidents, and war heroes, but common folk seldom used the occasion of their own birth for special notice. Native societies in Africa and America rarely kept records of age, and therefore did not observe birthdays except for special RITES OF PASSAGE, usually from childhood to adulthood. In the East, Chinese families often recognized birthdays, though mainly for adults; the Japanese, on the other hand, often collapsed all birthdays to New Year's Day, which they made into a common celebratory event.

By the mid-nineteenth century, the official collection of demographic data, most notably birth certification, decennial censuses, and other public surveys that listed exact date of birth, as well as the recording of birth and baptismal dates in family bibles, prompted more ordinary people to identify and observe their birthday. Still, the occasion seldom involved special ritual. Diaries and reminiscences of American children either omitted recognition of birthdays or mentioned them only in passing without reference to gifts or parties. Certain customs, however, were taking hold. German families, for example, feasted on *Geburtstagtorten*, birthday cakes, usually eaten at a party.

New attitudes about the worth and special qualities of children helped to transform birthdays into elaborate rituals in the late nineteenth century. Influenced by the Romantics, who emphasized feeling over reason, along with a decline in infant and child mortality, writers and parents began to dote on and cherish children as well as treat them in ways separate from adults. Such treatment often meant indulgences that formerly had not existed. Birthdays presented occasions for such indulgence. By the 1870s, wealthy families were holding elaborate children's birthday parties, and birthday books, in which children listed the birthdays of friends and relatives, circulated widely. Parties and cakes became common among rural and working-class families as well. Customs such as birthday spankings for good luck and wishing on the candles of the birthday cake before blowing them out became customary. Perhaps more importantly, new attitudes about measurement and time induced people to begin using the birthday to measure their experiences and accomplishments relative to peers and to social expectations. A child who had not lost all baby teeth or contracted certain childhood diseases by a particular birthday was said to be "behind schedule"; one who was in an advanced school grade or had grown taller than peers by a certain age was "ahead of schedule."

As the twentieth century progressed, commercial interests increasingly responded to the new popularity of birthday celebrations, especially for children. Birthday cards, adapted from Christmas and greeting cards of the nineteenth century, contained ever more elaborate messages and later included representations of characters in children's popular culture such as Mickey Mouse and the Peanuts comic strip characters. Decorations, hats, party favors, and gift wrap became birthday staples, and "Happy Birthday to You" by the sisters Mildred J. Hill and Patty Smith Hill became the most commonly performed song in the English language. For children, a birthday remains one of the most anticipated celebrations of the year, a rite fraught with expectations of privilege and indulgence that reflect their special status in the family and society.

See also: **Age and Development; Child Development, History of the Concept of; Theories of Childhood.**

BIBLIOGRAPHY

Ariès, Philippe. 1962. *Centuries of Childhood: A Social History of Family Life.* Trans. Robert Baldick. New York: Knopf.

Chudacoff, Howard P. 1989. *How Old Are You? Age Consciousness in American Culture.* Princeton, NJ: Princeton University Press.

Linton, Ralph and Adelin Linton. 1952. *The Lore of Birthdays.* New York: Schuman.

HOWARD P. CHUDACOFF

Birth Defects

About 3 percent of babies born alive have serious birth defects. Some defects are genetic; others may result from damage to a growing fetus caused by infection, chemicals (including fertilizers, alcohol, or drugs), diet, X rays, or a mixture of these. They can also be caused by direct damage, as in a failed abortion. Interest in damaged children, who were once known as "monsters," goes back at least to ancient Egypt. The study of birth defects is now known as *teratology* and the damaging agents as *teratogens.*

For many centuries birth defects were seen as warnings or divine omens and children with birth defects were often confused with mythological beings. It was an ancient Jewish custom to put a beautiful child at the door of public baths to help women to "have children as fine as he." In ancient Carthage it is said that alcohol was forbidden to a bridal couple in case a fetus was damaged by it. Later monsters became objects of interest, to be collected and described. Most museums of pathology still possess a collection of them, although recently this has come to be regarded as inappropriate.

Definition of defects depends also, of course, on time and place. In Western Europe around 1700, babies born "with the cowl" (a piece of placenta attached to the head) were viewed as defective, marked by the devil. In some societies twins were seen as defective, again marked by evil. Generally, with the rise of modern science and global contacts, these particular definitions of defects have declined.

In the eighteenth century there was much interest in maternal impressions; a fright, for example, was believed to cause birth defects. In the mid-nineteenth century it was believed in the English-speaking world that heredity could be altered by external circumstances at any point between conception and weaning. Physicians warned against sexual intercourse under the influence of drugs or alcohol as they believed that these could affect the constitution of a child. In 1870 the medical profession was criticized for its prevalent belief in the ability of maternal impressions to cause any degree of malformation.

In the late nineteenth century this kind of belief was falling into disrepute because it was linked with magic and "unscientific" thinking. This connection may be a reason the subject was rejected and ignored for so long. As medicine became more scientific, magic was increasingly despised. The placenta was steeped in myth and mystery, so no one working with humans thought to analyze it scientifically. It remained in a kind of quasi-magical limbo, vulnerable to the social fantasies of the time. Moreover, in the late nineteenth century there was little medical interest in the well-being of pregnant women, newborn babies, or older children. So many babies and children died from infection that the smaller number who were afflicted with birth defects was not seen as important. It was widely acceptable to drop them into a bucket of water as soon as they were born.

Belief in the placenta as a perfect barrier against damaging influences in the environment was reinforced by the Victorian tendency to put woman on a pedestal. This led to the idealization of the womb as well as of the woman. Women's reproductive organs were regarded as different and special and also as the source of all symptoms and ills that were not visibly due to something else.

By the 1930s there was more serious interest in teratology but, typically, as late as 1937 a popular textbook discussed the diagnosis of fetal abnormalities but not their causes. In 1941, when it was shown that rubella in pregnancy caused birth defects, the peculiarity of the infection was emphasized but it was not taken as a general warning about the vulnerability of fetuses. Today one can still find examples of residual idealization of the womb, perhaps describing it as a perfect environment or an ideal convalescent home.

Another possible reason little notice was taken of environmental dangers in pregnancy was that fetuses, stillbirths, and newborn babies had long been regarded as expendable, or at least as not very important. Few doctors were interested in them for their own sake. Unborn children created danger for their mothers at a time when maternal mortality was

Boy with a Clubfoot (c. 1642–1652), Jusepe de Ribera. In early modern Europe, children born with birth defects often had to rely on charity for their care. Ribera's subject holds a paper in his hands that reads "Give me alms, for the love of God." The Art Archive/Musée du Louvre Paris/Dagli Orti.

high. By the 1930s the maternal mortality rate was falling, BIRTH CONTROL was spreading, families were smaller, and there was greater interest in infants and their survival. Also, decline in mortality from infection and improved prenatal care meant that congenital defects became more prominent as a cause of death and debility, which at least provided a reason for studying them.

Still, the subject interested few doctors and scientists. Medical students were taught that the placenta was a perfect barrier protecting the fetus from the outside. All this was changed by the discovery, in 1962, that the drug thalidomide was causing horrifying defects in fetuses. Suddenly many people had to change their views.

Thalidomide changed the way in which the medical profession regarded drugs taken in pregnancy. It also played a part in breaking down the alternate idealization and denigration of women and the idealization of the placenta that has been so prominent in Western medical history. However, thalidomide was a useful and effective drug and recently it has been used again in some parts of the world in the treatment of leprosy, with the inevitable result that "thalidomide babies" are once again being born. Meanwhile pregnant women today are discouraged from taking drugs or exposing themselves to other teratogens and there are much more enlightened attitudes toward birth defects.

See also: **Conception and Birth.**

BIBLIOGRAPHY

Ballantyne, John W. 1904. *Essentials of Obstetrics.* Edinburgh: Green.

Dally, Ann. 1998. "Thalidomide: Was the Tragedy Preventable?" *The Lancet* 351: 1197–1199.

Huet, Marie-Hélène. 1993. *Monstrous Imagination.* Cambridge, MA: Harvard University Press.

Moscucci, Ornella. 1990. *The Science of Woman: Gynaecology and Gender in England, 1800–1929.* Cambridge, UK: Cambridge University Press.

Paré, Ambroise. 1982. *On Monsters and Marvels.* Trans. Janis L. Pallister. Chicago: University of Chicago Press.

Porter Dorothy, and Roy Porter. 1989. *Patient's Progress: Doctors and Doctoring in Eighteenth-Century England.* Stanford, CA: Stanford University Press.

Rosenberg, Charles. 1967. "The Practice of Medicine in New York a Century Ago." *Bulletin of the History of Medicine* 41: 223–253.

Wilson, James G., and Josef Warkany, eds. 1965. *Teratology: Principles and Techniques.* Chicago: University of Chicago Press.

ANN DALLY

Birth Order

Throughout recorded history, birth order has affected diverse aspects of social, political, and economic life, and this influence continues to manifest itself today in many traditional societies. Especially in previous centuries and in non-Western portions of the world, societies have generally sanctioned practices whereby parents favor some offspring over others. Such patterns of parental favoritism are often associated with birth order. For example, when a child is deformed or when an older child is still breast-feeding, most traditional societies permit infanticide; but no society condones the killing of the older of two SIBLINGS.

Through differences in parental investment, birth order sometimes affects the general health and well-being of offspring. Laterborns, for example, are less likely than firstborns to be vaccinated, and in developing countries laterborns tend to be shorter and to suffer higher rates of childhood mortality than do their older siblings. Birth order

also appears to influence intelligence and personality, doing so through differences in parental investment, as well as through sibling interactions. These intellectual and behavioral differences affect various aspects of life achievement.

Social and Political Influences

One study of the role of birth order in thirty-nine non-Western societies found that the birth of the first child generally has special significance, stabilizing the marriage and raising the status of the parents. In these same non-Western societies, firstborns were typically found to receive more elaborate birth ceremonies than laterborns, to have power over their younger siblings, to acquire and control more parental property in adulthood, and to carry greater authority with nonfamily members.

INHERITANCE practices have often been linked to birth order. The system of primogeniture has generally been followed in societies where wealth is largely dependent on land ownership and where land is a scarce resource. Under this system, firstborns or eldest males inherit the bulk of the parental land and property—a practice that limits the subdivision of estates and thereby helps to preserve the patrilineal family and its patronymic. James Boone's 1986 genealogical study of the leading families of medieval Portugal found that eldest sons were 1.6 times more likely than younger sons to leave descendants over a period of two centuries, whereas younger sons were 9 times more likely than firstborns to father offspring out of wedlock. Among daughters, laterborns were often destined for convents and, as a consequence, left fewer descendants than did earlierborn daughters.

Some countries, including Portugal, recognized landless younger sons as a potential threat to political stability. Expansionist military campaigns as well as the Crusades were in part undertaken as a means of exporting these younger sons to distant lands. There, while attempting to distinguish themselves, these younger sons often died in combat or from diseases.

Male primogeniture has long been the custom in the transfer of political power among royalty. Instituted in feudal times, this practice helped to curb the sometimes bloody conflicts among siblings that had previously punctuated royal succession. Although leaders of the PROTESTANT REFORMATION—in the spirit of egalitarian reform—successfully called for the abolition of primogeniture in parts of Germany, this practice remains the accepted succession policy in those European countries that still have monarchies.

Other discriminatory systems of inheritance are also known, including secondogeniture (whereby the secondborn child or son inherits the majority of the parental property), and ultimogeniture (the practice of leaving property to the youngest child or son). This last inheritance practice is most commonly found in societies that impose heavy death taxes, because ultimogeniture lengthens the period between taxa-

During the French Revolution, the 893 deputies to the National Convention turned on one another in a seemingly fratricidal manner, with firstborn and laterborn deputies allying themselves with different political parties and voting in disparate manners. Mary Evans Picture Library.

tions. Sometimes parents have opted for an equitable distribution of their assets to progeny. In medieval Venice, where wealth was based on commercial speculation and where prosperity was often a matter of unforeseeable circumstances, parents generally subdivided their estates in order to maximize the likelihood that at least one offspring would achieve commercial success. In short, although inheritance practices associated with birth order have exhibited considerable historical and geographic variability, the specific form chosen by each family and society has usually made local economic sense.

Birth Order, Intelligence, and Personality

One of the most remarkable discoveries in the field of psychology during the last several decades has been the finding that siblings who grow up together are almost as different as people plucked at random from the general population. Behavioral geneticists have shown that only about 5 percent of the variance in personality from one individual to another is associated with the shared family environment—that is, growing up in the same home. About 40 percent of the vari-

ance in personality appears to be genetic in origin, and another 20 percent is associated with errors in measurement. The remaining 35 percent of the variance is attributable to the nonshared environment (unique experiences that are not shared by siblings).

One important conclusion from this behavioral genetic research is that, for the most part, the family is not a shared environment. One possible source of such nonshared experiences is birth order, since children of different birth orders vary in age, size, and family roles. In addition, siblings compete with one another for parental investment (including love, attention, and scarce resources), and parents sometimes favor one child over another even when they try not to do so.

Darwinian theory predicts such competition among siblings, which has been widely documented among animals, fish, insects, and even plants. The principles of genetics help us in understanding this particular form of Darwinian competition. On average, siblings share only half of their genes, so they are twice as related to themselves as they are to another sibling. Based on the theory of kin selection, siblings are expected to act selfishly toward one another unless the benefits of sharing scarce resources are greater than twice the costs. Siblings therefore tend to develop context-sensitive strategies for optimizing parental investment—sometimes at the expense of other siblings—and these strategies are influenced by differences in age, size, power, and status within the family. Birth order is an excellent proxy for these differences.

Prior to about 1800, fewer than half of all human offspring ever reached adulthood, so even slight differences in parental investment, or in the competitive advantages developed by siblings, were sufficient to tip the balance in determining who survived and who did not. By cultivating unique and useful family niches, siblings increase their value within the family system. Firstborns have customarily adopted the role of a surrogate parent, which causes them to be more parent-identified and conservative than younger siblings. Because laterborns cannot baby-sit themselves, they generally seek to develop alternative and unoccupied niches within the family system, a process that seems to involve a predilection for experimentation and openness to experience.

Birth-order research, which encompasses more than two thousand studies, has established a consistent pattern of birth-order differences in personality. These differences can be usefully summarized by the Five Factor Model of personality, which encompasses the dimensions of conscientiousness, openness to experience, agreeableness, extraversion, and neuroticism. As reflected by their frequent role as surrogate parents, firstborns tend to be more conscientious than laterborns. By comparison, laterborns tend to be more open to experience than firstborns, especially in those facets of this personality dimension that involve the questioning of family values or the authority of their elders. Laterborns are also somewhat more agreeable than firstborns, since they generally adopt low-power strategies, including cooperation and acquiescence, that accord with their lesser age, power, and physical size. In addition, laterborns are more extraverted than firstborns in the specific sense of being fun-loving, excitement seeking, and sociable. Finally, firstborns and laterborns both manifest aspects of neuroticism, but in different ways. Firstborns are more neurotic in the sense of being anxious about loss of power and status, whereas laterborns are more neurotic in the sense of being self-conscious—an attribute that probably stems from their tendency to compare themselves with older and more accomplished sibling models.

Compared with birth-order differences in personality that are measured within the family, those documented in extrafamilial contexts tend to be less pronounced. Still, there is considerable evidence that birth-order differences in personality and behavior manifest themselves in nonfamilial contexts—especially when these behavioral contexts resemble those previously encountered within the family. To cite an example documented by Catherine Salmon, firstborns and laterborns respond differently to political speeches that use the terms *brother* and *sister* as opposed to *friend*.

Extensive research indicates that firstborns tend to have higher IQs than laterborns, although this difference is small (IQ is reduced about one point with each successive birth rank in the family). Explanations for these findings have generally focused on the consequences of increasing family size, since children from large families have lower IQs than children from small families. According to Robert Zajonc's confluence model, the addition of younger siblings impoverishes the family's intellectual environment because children are less intellectually proficient than adults. This theory predicts that firstborns will tend to have higher IQs than laterborns because firstborns spend more time alone with their parents, and more time in smaller sibling groups.

Birth Order and World History

Differences in personality and behavior related to birth order sometimes reflect themselves onto the stage of world history. The tendency for firstborns to receive greater parental investment than laterborns, and in turn to be more conscientious and have higher IQs, fosters greater achievement and has led to an overrepresentation of firstborns among people listed in *Who's Who* and other biographical encyclopedias. Similarly, firstborns have tended to be overrepresented among world leaders, successful writers, and famous scientists (including Nobel Prize winners). By contrast, laterborns have been historically prominent as explorers and as leaders of radical political and social upheavals, including the Protestant Reformation, the French Revolution, and other noteworthy episodes of radical social and political change. The expression of these birth-order differences is generally context sensitive—that is, dependent on local circumstances. For example, in Catholic countries during the Reformation, laterborns were more likely than firstborns to undergo martyrdom for supporting the Reformed faith; but in Protestant countries such as England, firstborns were more likely than laterborns to be martyred for their resistance to Protestant reforms.

In the history of science, birth order has often played a role during times of radical theory change. Laterborns such as Nicholas Copernicus (the youngest of four children) and Charles Darwin (the fifth of six children) pioneered revolutions in science that challenged both the scientific status quo and associated religious dogma. Other laterborns, such as Francis Bacon and René Descartes, led the seventeenth-century assault on scholastic learning and Aristotelian dogma, culminating in the Scientific Revolution. Even when firstborns have initiated major revolutions in science—such as those led by Isaac Newton, Antoine Lavoisier, and Albert Einstein—the earliest supporters of these revolutions have tended to be laterborns. Laterborns nevertheless possess a decided Achilles heel when it comes to initiating and supporting revolutionary science. They have generally promoted radical but failed revolutions such as phrenology (the nineteenth-century notion that bumps on the head reveal character and personality) just as eagerly as they have endorsed successful revolutions such as Darwinism, quantum mechanics, and plate tectonics. For this reason, there is no evidence that laterborns are more creative than firstborns. Rather, firstborns and laterborns are each capable of creativity, but in different ways. In particular, firstborns tend to create within the system, whereas laterborns are more likely to create by questioning the status quo.

Conclusion

Owing to its influence on inheritance practices as well as social and political life, birth order appears to have exerted greater impact on people's lives in past centuries than it does today. Still, birth order continues to shape personality and behavior by influencing parental investment, as well as by affecting sibling strategies for increasing parental investment. In large part through behavioral genetic studies, psychologists have learned that the family is not primarily a shared environment. Most environmental influences on personality appear to owe themselves to nonshared experiences, including some that are attributable to birth order. In addition to shaping personality and behavior, birth order also exerts an influence on familial sentiments. Individual differences in family sentiments mediate loyalties to the family, degree of contact with parents and other close relatives, and attitudes toward parental authority. In past centuries, these birth-order differences have often played themselves out during radical revolutions, providing a link between the formative experiences of childhood and the course of world history. Even today birth order continues to shape differences in personality and behavior that, in meaningful ways, affect overall life experience.

See also: **Family Patterns.**

BIBLIOGRAPHY

Boone, James L. 1986. "Parental Investment and Elite Family Structure in Preindustrial States: A Case Study of Late Medieval–Early Modern Portuguese Genealogies." *American Anthropologist* 88: 859–78.

Costa, Paul T., Jr., and Robert R. McCrae. 1992. *NEO PR-R Professional Manual.* Odessa, FL: Psychological Assessment Resources.

Daly, Martin, and Margo Wilson. 1988. *Homicide.* Hawthorne, NY: Aldine de Gruyter.

Dunn, Judy, and Robert Plomin. 1990. *Separate Lives: Why Siblings Are So Different.* New York: Basic Books.

Fichtner, Paula Sutter. 1989. *Protestantism and Primogeniture in Early Modern Germany.* New Haven: Yale University Press.

Herlihy, David. 1989. "Family and Property in Renaissance Florence." In *The Medieval City,* ed. David Herlihy and A. L. Udovitch, pp. 3–24. New Haven: Yale University Press.

Hertwig, Ralph, Jennifer Nerissa Davis, and Frank J. Sulloway. 2002. "Parental Investment: How an Equity Motive Can Produce Inequality." *Psychological Bulletin* 128: 728–45.

Hrdy, Sarah Blaffer, and Debra Judge. 1993. "Darwin and the Puzzle of Primogeniture." *Human Nature* 4: 1–45.

Rosenblatt, Paul C., and Elizabeth L. Skoogberg. 1974. "Birth Order in Cross-Cultural Perspective." *Developmental Psychology* 10: 48–54.

Salmon, Catherine. 1998. "The Evocative Nature of Kin Terminology in Political Rhetoric." *Politics and the Life Sciences* 17: 51–57.

Salmon, Catherine, and Martin Daly. 1998. "Birth Order and Familial Sentiments: Middleborns are Different." *Human Behavior and Evolution* 19: 299–312.

Sulloway, Frank J. 1996. *Born to Rebel: Birth Order, Family Dynamics, and Creative Lives.* New York: Pantheon.

Sulloway, Frank J. 2001. "Birth Order, Sibling Competition, and Human Behavior." In *Conceptual Challenges in Evolutionary Psychology: Innovative Research Strategies,* ed. Harmon R. Holcomb III, pp. 39–83. Boston: Kluwer Academic Publishers.

Zajonc, Robert B. 2001. "The Family Dynamic of Intellectual Development." *Psychological Review* 82: 74–88.

FRANK J. SULLOWAY

Bobby Soxers

By the mid-1940s, ankle socks and saddle shoes symbolized teenage girls. Neither teenage girls as a fashion group nor the socks and shoes were new, though. Throughout the 1920s and 1930s, media, manufacturers, and marketers made uneven attempts to understand teenage girls as a separate group with unique demands and interests. The story of bobby soxers provides a window into these attempts to follow girls' trends and to shape their emerging identity.

In the late 1920s, female tennis players first adopted a "stockingless mode," wearing only socks. This created an uproar culminating in efforts to ban women from wearing socks at Wimbledon in 1929. Despite opposition, the spread of socks was unstoppable. Teenage girls abandoned stockings for socks as the teenage FASHION market emerged, bare legs gained acceptance, and HIGH SCHOOL fashions shifted from dresses to more informal skirts and sweaters.

Most girls wore stockings to high school in the 1920s and early 1930s, prompting yearbook complaints of "runs" and other inconveniences. Socks first appeared in yearbooks with athletic uniforms, worn over tights. By 1935, ankle socks appeared throughout yearbooks, outside of the gym, with saddle shoes or loafers. National marketers, such as the Sears catalog, demonstrated some awareness of this trend, although with continued uncertainty. Sears advertised ankle socks for ages four to forty in 1934, but by 1936 were marketing them only to children. By 1938, Sears was targeting girls aged ten to sixteen.

Fashion historians often credit stocking shortages during World War II with the rise of ankle socks, but by the late 1930s the practice was already widely accepted. Adapted from a college trend, bobby socks and saddle shoes soon distinguished teenage girls from other age groups. While college interest waned, high school yearbooks and girls' writings confirmed that the trend spread quickly among high school students. Saddle shoes and anklets pleased parents because of their comfort, durability, and low heels. But they also provided a perfect palette for expressions of teenage culture. Girls wore socks in bold or plain colors; folded, pulled up, or pushed down; decorated with gadgets and charms; over stockings; or held up with boys' garters. They decorated saddle shoes with everything from flowers to friends' names to favorite songs, creatively using nail polish, shoe polish, or paint.

While high school yearbooks pictured girls in ankle socks with saddle shoes or loafers almost exclusively by the 1940s and the term *sox* appeared frequently, the media, not girls themselves, largely used the phrase *bobby soxer*. Many girls rejected the nickname and the associated stereotypes. Major national publications, such as *Time* and the *New York Times*, described bobby soxers as mindless worshipers of Frank Sinatra or crazed followers of adolescent fads. While many followers of Benny Goodman or Frank Sinatra did wear bobby socks, others did not. The term *bobby soxer* did not accurately represent high school girls or pop music fans, but the linkage among these was perhaps an effort to grapple with public displays of sexual energy from an emerging social group, especially one increasingly recognized as a viable, even powerful consumer market.

The rise of ankle socks and saddle shoes were linked more to the establishment of casual clothing as high school fashion than to musical taste. And ankle socks and saddle shoes proved a platform for creative expression and differentiation among girls at least as much as they served to unify or identify.

See also: **Adolescence and Youth; Flappers; Media, Childhood and; Rock and Roll; Teenagers; Youth Culture.**

BIBLIOGRAPHY

Kahn, E. J., Jr. 1946. "Profiles Phenomenon: II. The Fave, the Fans, and the Fiends." *The New Yorker* November 2: 35–48.

Palladino, Grace. 1996. *Teenagers: An American History.* New York: Basic.

"What Is a Bobby Sock?" 1994. *The New York Times Magazine* March 5: 23.

KELLY SCHRUM

Body Modification. *See* Tattoos and Piercing.

Bowlby, John (1907–1990)

John Bowlby was born on February 26, 1907, and studied medicine in Cambridge, England and psychology in Lon-

don. While still a student, he volunteered at a progressive school and began his training at the British Psychoanalytic Institute. After graduation, he began working at the London Child Guidance Clinic.

Bowlby's experiences outside academia were at least as formative as his academic training. His supervisors at the progressive school convinced him that the maladaptive behavior of some children was a result of their primary caregivers having abandoned them. His psychoanalytic training made him aware of the importance of affective relationships in the first years of life. Finally, his work at the Child Guidance Clinic brought him into contact with juvenile delinquents whose behavior Bowlby believed to be rooted in unsatisfactory emotional relationships.

Starting in about 1940 Bowlby elaborated his conviction that children's socioemotional problems originate in a lack of consistent parental love. This led him to formulate his attachment theory. In its ultimate form, attachment theory incorporated elements of psychoanalytic theory, cybernetics, Piagetian theory, and ethology. In line with ethology, for example, Bowlby believed that crying and smiling are proximity-seeking behaviors that trigger parental intervention and love and thus promote the infant's survival.

Empirical support for Bowlby's ideas originally came from maternal deprivation and hospitalization studies. The invention of two measurement instruments, and their accompanying classifications, gave the empirical study of attachment behavior new impetus. These instruments were the Strange Situation (SS) procedure invented by psychologist Mary Ainsworth and the Adult Attachment Interview (AAI) invented by psychologist Mary Main.

The SS is a standardized laboratory procedure during which a one-year-old child and her caregiver are twice briefly separated. The child's behavior as she is reunited with the caregiver is believed to betray essential elements of their relationship. On the basis of these reunions, children's attachment patterns are characterized as secure (B), avoidant (A), ambivalent (C), or disorganized (D).

The SS and the classification into attachment patterns led to an avalanche of empirical studies, including investigations into the factors that contribute to specific attachment patterns (e.g., child characteristics, parental behavior, life events), ways to modify unsatisfactory attachment patterns, and long-term effects of attachment patterns as measured by the SS.

The AAI is a semistructured interview devised to assess adults' views of their own childhoods with respect to attachment. The ways the adults reflect on their childhood experiences are believed to be indicative of the ways they have coped with these experiences. Different styles of coping lead to an A, B, C, or D classification, similar to the one used in the SS.

The AAI has been used in numerous studies to investigate how attachment patterns are transmitted across generations, thus testing Bowlby's belief that, for example, parents' unresolved conflicts are played out in the interactions with their own children. Although attachment theory and its measurement instruments have been criticized, the number of investigations inspired by Bowlby's theory is still growing. The practical implications of attachment theory for the way we raise our children are potentially enormous.

See also: **Age and Development; Child Development, History of the Concept of; Child Psychology; Freud, Anna; Freud, Sigmund; Klein, Melanie.**

BIBLIOGRAPHY

Bretherton, Inge. 1992. "The Origins of Attachment Theory: John Bowlby and Mary Ainsworth." *Developmental Psychology* 28: 759–775.

Holmes, Jeremy. 1993. *John Bowlby and Attachment Theory.* London: Routledge.

Van Dijken, Suzan, René van der Veer, Marinus H. Van Ijzendoorn, et al. 1998. "Bowlby before Bowlby: The Sources of an Intellectual Departure in Psychoanalysis and Psychology." *Journal of the History of the Behavioral Sciences* 34: 247–269.

RENÉ VAN DER VEER

Boxing

Boxing, traditionally a sport of the least advantaged, proved a requirement for working class youth, who often settled ethnic, religious, and racial rivalries with their fists. African-American slaves who fought for the pleasure of their masters were among the first professional prizefighters. Even after Emancipation black youths were often forced or coerced into battles royal or group fights, sometimes blindfolded, while a surrounding cordon of white onlookers offered money to the winner.

By the latter nineteenth century boxing gained a slight measure of respectability as the sport became more organized with weight class championships under the sponsorship of Richard Kyle Fox, publisher of the National Police Gazette. More importantly, boxing offered a cloak of masculinity for men during this period who perceived an increasing feminization of American culture.

Working class youths saw the sport as an opportunity for social mobility as middle-class athletic clubs, newspapers, and even religious groups supported amateur teams and tournaments in the twentieth century. Successful fighters often progressed to the professional ranks where a series of ethnic immigrant groups enjoyed success. Irish, Jewish, and Italian champions won fame and symbolized a greater degree of assimilation in American culture.

Boxing was a controversial sport, and for a time was banned in many states. New York only legalized the sport in 1920. Three years later the Chicago Tribune sponsored a major boxing tournament, eventually known as the Golden Gloves, to challenge the New York team. Both cities became centers for the sport. By 1930 the Catholic Youth Organization (CYO) joined the ranks of national boxing enterprises. The CYO team proved especially popular during the Depression, as it supplied its members with a full suit of clothes as well as medical and dental care. CYO fighters who opted for the professional ranks received guidance from program affiliated management teams. Others got jobs through the Catholic social and commercial network.

While the CYO and individual municipalities invoked age restrictions, usually age sixteen, professional boxing had (and still has) no age limitations. Wilfredo Benitez won a world championship at age seventeen. Teenage boys became heroes on local, civic, national, and international teams, often finding the esteem and recognition denied them in other spheres of life. The amateur bouts produced members of the Olympic teams and the professional ranks for the remainder of the twentieth century.

By the 1930s African-American boxers began to displace the white ethnics atop the ranks, joined by Hispanic fighters at mid-century. Girls, too, joined the amateur boxing ranks by the 1980s in training programs offered by park districts, police athletic associations, and private gyms. While most engaged in the activity in pursuit of personal fitness, a very visible minority joined the annual Golden Gloves tournaments for competition, with a select few attaining professional status in televised bouts. Though few have found material success in the pastime, boxing has assumed both historic and symbolic value in the physicality and toughness required and admired by working-class youth.

See also: **Organized Recreation and Youth Groups; Sports.**

BIBLIOGRAPHY

Gorn, Elliott J. 1986. *The Manly Art: Bare Knuckle Prize Fighting in America.* Ithaca, NY: Cornell University Press.

Sammons, Jeffrey T. 1990. *Beyond the Ring: The Role of Boxing in American Society.* Urbana: University of Illinois Press.

GERALD R. GEMS

Boyhood

Boyhood is a difficult word to define, in part because definitions of boyhood have changed over the centuries and in part because they continue to differ depending on culture and region. Boyhood is definitely associated with boys, and with a bounded time period between infancy and young adulthood.

Boyhood and Popular Advice Literature

In the United States during the late 1990s, an ongoing interest in defining boyhood was reflected in the publication of

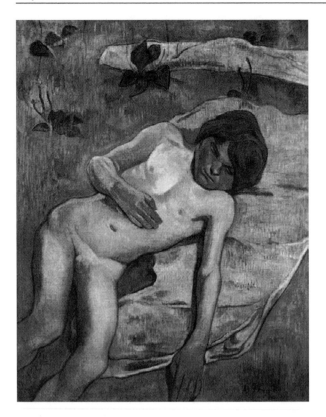

Paul Gauguin's *Naked Breton Boy* (1889) is portrayed as a simple, primitive being, unfettered by the trappings of civilization. Wallraf-Richartz-Museum, Köln; photo courtesy of Rheinisches Bildarchiv, Köln.

many texts about boys that were marketed to the general reader. Many of these texts explore what the authors saw as the problems boys would have in the twenty-first century. Titles include Michael Gurian's 1996 *The Wonder of Boys*, which uses history and other textual evidence to resist the idea that gender is a social construct and to insist on the validity of biological differences. William Pollack's 1998 *Real Boys: Rescuing Our Sons from the Myths of Boyhood* critiques the presence of women in the workplace and suggests that mothers and women teachers do not allow boys enough time and space to express their emotions or to be what he calls "real boys." Not all of these books about boys and the problems caused by cultural treatment and view of boys are by men. Angela Phillips's 1994 *The Trouble with Boys: A Wise and Sympathetic Guide to the Risky Business of Raising Sons* explains how mothers can help boys to experience less painful and more rewarding boyhoods, while Christine Hoff Sommers' 2000 *The War against Boys: How Misguided Feminism Is Harming Our Young Men* suggests problematically that feminists should allow boys to be boys. For Hoff Sommers, boys are boys when they are more aggressive, more competitive, and more physical in their play than girls.

In "Boyology in the Twentieth Century," Kenneth Kidd responds to these texts that treat the "problem" of boys and finds that in the early twentieth century there was a similar proliferation of manuals that addressed the nature/nurture components of boyhood and the best methods of raising boys. These earlier manuals often point to literary and cultural myths that construct boys as wild, savage, and in a state of rebellion against social norms. Like the late-twentieth-century popular manuals about boyhood, the handbooks written in the early twentieth century focus on how the "proper" treatment of boys can build a civilization of middle-class white men who are productive and prosperous citizens. Kidd points out that the term *boyology* is used by Henry William Gibson in 1916 but that the idea of discussing both the biology and social culture of boys had been well established by the circulation of such books as William Byron Forbrush's *The Boy Problem* (1901) and Kate Upson Clark's *Bringing Up Boys* (1899). The early-twentieth-century manuals suggest that adults who work with boys can, with additional knowledge about boys' physical, emotional, and educational needs, intervene in boyhood experience so that dangerous behaviors are curtailed and safer, more productive ones are promoted. Late-twentieth-century manuals return to this theme but focus on the current state of boyhood as one that causes trouble for boys and for other members of society. Nearly all of the late twentieth-century help-for-boys manuals claim to explain and then propose to fix what they see as the serious problems with boyhood. One way to challenge these narratives is to closely examine the cultural context of those boyhoods that are considered representative, and also those of boyhoods that have been ignored.

Creating Boyhood

How did these constructions of boyhood as inherently fraught with problems get put into place? Since the 1960s, much work has been done to understand childhood and the changing definitions of childhood. Perhaps the best-known work on this topic is PHILIPPE ARIÈS' *Centuries of Childhood: A Social History of Family Life*, which focuses mostly on boyhood. Using Ariès's text as a starting point, it could be argued that the first children (as they are now understood through the lens of European history and imperialist expansion) were boys. That is, because more boys were taught to read and write, and because boys became men who helped maintain patriarchal systems of power in a wide variety of cultures, published records of boys' childhoods are easier to obtain, and therefore many of the examples of childhood that emerge from the thirteenth century on are actually examples of boyhood. Ariès suggests that what we now understand as boyhood was in fact difficult to distinguish from manhood, with boys either ignored or regarded as small men. In part, this lack of interest in boyhood as a separate state stemmed from high mortality rates among children.

The emergence of the idea of boyhood can be traced by examining art that shows the emergence of distinct costumes for childhood (a time when boys and girls were dressed in long gowns) and then for boyhood (a time when boys were breeched, or given pants). This costume gave boys more physical freedom than girls and contributed to boyhood cultures that took place outdoors, away from the house, with other boys. This tradition of BREECHING continued through the nineteenth century, although it became less formal towards the end of the century.

In addition to being defined by dress, changes in education also helped to shape boyhood. One means of marking boyhood was with the beginning of primary school and the first departure from the house of the parents. Before educational systems became formalized, boyhood lasted a long, indefinite period of time, and its ages for beginning and ending were not clear until the nineteenth century. With the implementation of an educational system that was divided into classes, stages of boyhood were created. Boys were expected to reach physical and cultural milestones that coincided with the progression of their lessons. Ariès points out that in the seventeenth century, before the graded educational system was put into place, boys as old as twenty-four might be in classes with children as young as eleven. In France during the seventeenth century, boyhood was marked by a time set aside for education at the ACADEMIES; boyhood occurred between the first years at GRAMMAR SCHOOL and then APPRENTICESHIP, the finishing tour of Europe, or a few years spent in army life.

During the seventeenth century, girls were raised very differently from boys, since it was not customary for them to attend the same academies or to be apprenticed at a distance from their homes. Girls' costumes stayed closer to the childhood gowns that both young boys and girls wore. When coeducational primary schools became common and more girls began to learn basic reading and writing, they were able to establish relationships with peers in ways that had not been possible when they were isolated at home with mothers and relatives.

Boyhood in the United States
In the United States, boyhood has been shaped by costume, education, and attitudes toward work. Regional economics have also shaped boyhood. During the 1830s, laws for COMMON SCHOOLS were put into place in Massachusetts, and the schoolroom served to gather boys together and reshape boyhood. Children's texts published by Jacob Abbott in the late 1830s show boys working with their fathers to develop courses of study. By the 1850s, Oliver Optic's texts about boys, especially his texts about boys living in small towns, show boys organizing clubs with elaborate rule systems and uniforms that mark out those who belong and those who do not. In contrast to the cities and towns on the eastern seaboard, the Midwest and the southwest territories developed common school educational systems at different rates, and the boyhoods in these regions were shaped less by urban street culture than were those in the increasingly urban Northeast. In these territories, land separated boys from

their peers, and the work of farming and ranching demanded that the boys labor alongside adults. Before emancipation in 1863, boys who were slaves were kept near their mothers until they reached about age seven. At this age, they were often sold and forced to begin the work of men. Frederick Douglass's autobiographical narrative indicates that some boys kept in slavery used affiliations with educated free boys to gain access to literacy and to freedom.

Boyhood, then, is both a time period and a term used to define a variety of behaviors. In the late twentieth and early twenty-first centuries, some American boyhoods last until the boys are in their late twenties. In the 1890s, upper-middle-class and middle-class boys in England and the United States experienced a similar kind of extended boyhood, with marriage and property ownership not being achieved until the boys had reached their late thirties. Even though it can vary in length, boyhood is, in most constructions of the term, finite, and therefore somehow precious.

Nostalgia for Boyhood
This preciousness of boyhood provides part of the impetus to write texts about boyhood: as something lost, it is also something that can be recaptured nostalgically through texts and images. In *Being a Boy Again*, Marcia Jacobson points out that this move toward nostalgia about boyhood was particularly strong in the late nineteenth century. Jacobson discusses the nostalgic boyhoods found in Hamlin Garland's 1899 *Boy's Life on the Prairie* and Stephen Crane's 1900 *Whilomville Stories*. She notes that some of the authors used children's magazines as a forum for their pieces about boyhood. Howells, for example, published *A Boy's Town* in *Harper's Young People* in 1890. These publications, which were read by both children and adults, helped to shape ideas about boyhood in profound and lasting ways. MARK TWAIN's 1886 *Adventures of Huckleberry Finn* is still used to idealize boyhood.

When boyhood is defined in fiction and nonfiction, it is often seen as shaping behaviors to be wielded later in manhood. Boys, then, are the participants in boyhood, while authors of texts about boys are former boys, or observers of boys, but not usually ongoing (contemporary) participants in boyhood. The written commentaries on boyhood reflect memories and reshape boyhood in the retelling.

Varieties of Boyhood
When histories of boyhood are considered, it is also important to remember that the kinds of boyhood that have been recorded and put into histories often leave out or ignore the shape of other boyhoods. The popular 1990s treatises about the problems with boys focus, for the most part, on white, middle-class boyhoods; however, these boyhoods were not the only ones discussed during those years. J. M. Coetzee's 1997 *Boyhood Scenes from Provincial Life* stands out as a depiction of white boyhood in South Africa during the 1940s and 1950s, while Nega Mezlekia's 2001 *Notes from a Hyena's Belly: An Ethiopian Boyhood* provides details about boyhood in Ethiopia during the 1960s and 1970s.

Partly because boyhood continues to provide powerful material for social commentary and because the entrenched idea that "boys will be boys" continues to provide excuses for behavior that is disturbingly violent and misogynistic, expanding the boyhoods studied will provide ways to question those constructions that have gone unchallenged for too long.

See also: **Gendering; Girlhood.**

BIBLIOGRAPHY

Ariès, Philippe. 1962. *Centuries of Childhood: A Social History of Family Life.* Trans. Robert Baldick. New York: Alfred A. Knopf.

Clark, Beverly Lyon, and Margaret Higonnet, eds. 1999. *Girls, Boys, Books, Toys: Gender in Children's Literature and Culture.* Baltimore: Johns Hopkins University Press.

Coetzee, J. M. 1997. *Boyhood: Scenes from Provincial Life.* New York: Viking.

Gurian, Michael. 1996. *The Wonder of Boys: What Parents, Mentors, and Educators Can Do to Shape Boys into Exceptional Men.* New York: Penguin.

Hoff Sommers, Christina. 2000. *The War against Boys: How Misguided Feminism Is Harming Our Young Men.* New York: Simon and Schuster.

Jacobson, Marcia. 1994. *Being a Boy Again: Autobiography and the American Boy Book.* Tuscaloosa: University of Alabama Press.

Kidd, Kenneth. 2000. "Boyology in the Twentieth Century." *Children's Literature* 28: 44–72.

Kotlowitz, Alex. 1991. *There Are No Children Here: The Story of Two Boys Growing Up in the Other America.* New York: Random House.

Mezlekia, Nega. 2001. *Notes from a Hyena's Belly: An Ethiopian Boyhood.* New York: Picador.

Nelson, Claudia. 1991. *Boys Will Be Girls: The Feminine Ethic and British Children's Fiction, 1857–1917.* New Brunswick, NJ : Rutgers University Press

Pollack, William. 1998. *Real Boys: Rescuing Our Sons from the Myths of Boyhood.* New York: Random House.

Rotundo, E. Anthony. 1993. *American Manhood: Transformations in Masculinity from the Revolution to the Modern Era.* New York: Basic Books.

LORINDA B. COHOON

Boy Scouts

In January 1908, a program for young boys was launched in Britain by the Boer War hero ROBERT BADEN-POWELL. It adapted army scout and applied it to the training of young people in citizenship. The scheme proved so popular that before World War I the program was to be found throughout the British Empire, in the United States, and in many other countries.

Formation and Influences

In this early period several controversies arose. One of these was over authorship of the scheme. In spite of worldwide acclaim for Baden-Powell, other individuals also claimed to be founders of Boy Scouting. The controversy arose because the elements that made up Baden-Powell's scheme were not unique. Even the name was not of Baden-Powell's devising. The phrase *Boy Scout* was used toward the end of 1899 by authors writing for the Aldine Press, first in the Buffalo Bill Library magazines to describe Harry White, Buffalo Bill's assistant, then in the True Blue War Library magazines of 1900 to 1906 to describe a young man serving in the colonies. Other elements of Scouting, including moral codes, self-government, mottoes, secret signs, patriotism, woodcraft, uniforms, and rituals, could also be found in kindred youth schemes of the period.

Schemes similar to the Scouts had gained modest success: in Britain, the Boys Brigade was founded in 1884 by William Smith and the Boys Life Brigade in 1899 by John Paton; in the United States, the Woodcraft Indians was founded in 1902 by Ernest Seton and the Sons of Daniel Boone/Boy Pioneers in 1905 by Daniel Beard; in South Africa, the Boys' Guide Brigade was founded in 1902 by Edward Carter; in Germany, the Wandervogel was founded in 1901 by Alexander Lion.

Baden-Powell felt that the application of Scouting to the program of the Boys Brigade of Britain would enhance its attraction. In 1906, Baden-Powell proposed using an adaptation of his army manual of 1900, *Aids to Scouting*, in the organization. While the Boys Brigade awarded badges for proficiency in various subjects, no badge was awarded for Scout training, and therefore boys had no incentive to undertake the training. The introduction of the Boys Brigade Scout Badge and Certificate only came in 1909, a year after the general publication of Baden-Powell's scheme in the wake of popularity of the Scout Movement.

The British-born Ernest Thompson Seton, who lived in the United States, proved a decisive influence on Scouting. In 1902, he had founded an organization called the Woodcraft Indians. In 1906, Seton sent Baden-Powell a copy of his latest woodcraft manual, *The Birch Bark Roll of the Woodcraft Indians*, which provided a model for a complete training scheme. With help from newspaper owner Arthur Pearson, Baden-Powell was able to launch both a handbook and a boys' paper, *The Scout*. Baden-Powell also gained assistance from the Young Men's Christian Association in launching a national tour. He held an experimental camp from July 25 to August 9, 1907, on Brownsea Island, Poole, which proved a success.

Baden-Powell's borrowings were not restricted to Seton and *Aids to Scouting*. He may also have been influenced by Andrew Burnham, an American Scout working in South Africa in the late 1800s. Other influences are also detectable in the pages of *Scouting for Boys*.

So well chosen were the ingredients that made up Baden-Powell's scheme, however, that it had a universal appeal and

Robert Baden-Powell addresses over 5,000 scouts at an early-twentieth-century rally in Perth, England. Scouting was extremely popular in the early years of the twentieth century and by 1914, the Boy Scouts organization had spread to dozens of countries. © Bettman/ CORBIS.

struck a chord with so many people that the Boy Scout empire was able to attract and incorporate other organizations or their leaders. In 1910 the Woodcraft Indians, the Boy Pioneers, and various independent Scout troops and patrols formed the Boy Scouts of America. Also in that year, Dr. Lion of the Wandervogel formed the German Boy Scouts, and a number of Canadian Boys Brigade Companies became Boy Scout troops. In 1911 Carter's Boy Guides had joined the British Boy Scouts.

Robert Baden-Powell was the son of an Anglican priest, and the Scout promise, which was the basis of membership, required religious belief, thus disqualifying atheists. This enhanced Scouting's attraction to churches, which with their access to young people provided a ready market for the expansion of Scouting.

Some authors have concluded that the defense of the British Empire formed a very important motive for the foundation of the Boy Scouts. Baden-Powell was impressed by the Military Mafeking Cadet Corps, which gained fame, as

Baden-Powell did, through its work during the Boer War. In 1905, Elliot E. Mills published a pamphlet anonymously, *The Decline and Fall of the British Empire*. It encapsulated the xenophobic fears of England in that period. Baden-Powell treated the readers to excerpts of the pamphlet's themes in his book *Scouting for Boys*, reinforcing the belief that national defense was a prime motive.

A severe schism occurred in 1909, leading to the creation of the pacifist British Boy Scouts (BBS), led by Barrow Cadbury and Sir Francis Vane. Within two years the BBS had formed or allied to counterpart organizations in the British Empire as well as France, Italy, and the United States. In November 1911 they formed the Order of World Scouts, which was led by Sir Francis Vane.

By the early 1920s, there had been a detectable shift toward a more pacific and educational role in response to severe criticism and to the presence of a pacifist alternative.

Initially Baden-Powell had offered his scheme to other agencies as a means of youth work, almost as a public domain youth activity. This offer was taken up enthusiastically, especially by churches, which sponsored up to 70 percent of the troops. In reaction to direct competition from Vane's Order of World Scouts, however, Baden-Powell's organization and its counterparts developed a proprietary rights view, vesting its authorship firmly in Baden-Powell, who could then pass on rights to use the scheme. Vane's Order of World Scouts collapsed in 1912, following his bankruptcy, but many member organizations persisted in their home countries. In a New York court case lasting two years and ending in 1919, the Boys Scouts of America, supported by Baden-Powell, established a firm monopoly against its competitor, the United States Boy Scout. The idea of a monopoly was institutionalized in the World Organization of Scout Movements (WOSM), which began modestly in 1920 and which offers recognition to national associations or federations. Despite the early controversies, the Scout movement has made an overwhelming contribution to the nurture of young people.

The minimum age of Baden-Powell's Boy Scouts was not defined at first, but it was eventually set at around eleven, with eighteen as an upper limit. Junior Scouts existed in the British Boy Scouts in 1909 for boys under eleven and were later mirrored in Baden-Powell's scheme, renamed Wolf Cubs, or Cubs in 1916. Boys over seventeen were retained by the movement by the creation of Rover Scouts by 1918. Various titles were developed for older sections in different countries, including Explorers and Venture Scouts.

The success of the scheme was not restricted to boys, and Girl Scouts began to appear unofficially as early as 1909. In 1910 the Girl Guides Association was created in the United Kingdom. Some counterparts abroad, such as the United States, maintained the word *Scouts*. The World Association of Girl Guides and Girl Scouts was formed in 1928, with a purpose similar to the WOSM's.

The Challenges from the Twentieth Century On

Despite losses in 1914 to 1918 due to World War I and further losses due to totalitarian regimes, Scouting grew worldwide until it had four million participants in 1950. Both Communist and Fascist governments in Europe banned Scouting. Russia substituted the Pioneers; Italy substituted the Black Shirts; and Germany substituted the HITLER YOUTH. During World War II, Japan also disbanded its Scout organization.

Postwar reconstruction saw a rapid rise in membership with the restoration of Scouting in Germany, Italy, and Japan, offsetting losses due to the suppression of Scouting when eastern Europe became part of the Communist bloc. By 1985 the tally stood at 16 million.

By the 1960s, the relevance of the Scouts' frontiersman image had diminished. From that period onward, various national associations sought to recast the image, updating the uniform and training scheme. Some of the changes were in

reaction to falling numbers, especially among eleven to eighteen year olds. This led to the formation of independent associations, which had small memberships but maintained the traditional image.

Society's increasing pluralism and liberalism from the 1960s on put pressure on the Scouts to create an entirely inclusive organization, which would admit homosexuals and atheists as members. In June 2000 the U.S. Supreme Court allowed the Boy Scouts of America to deny membership to homosexuals. The U.K. association set in place an Equal Opportunities Policy. However, the organization retains the right to exclude any individual on grounds of unsuitability, which is acceptable under the European Convention on Human Rights.

Public awareness and legislation covering safety and the protection of children from abuse have brought added pressures to the various Scout organizations. This has led to further training for volunteer leaders. Recruitment varies within each national association. For example, in the United States, the various sponsoring organizations are responsible. In England, the association itself undertakes national advertising.

Western societies have seen a decline in the volunteer culture, which has led to increasing difficulties in finding adult leaders and helpers and has affected membership. A more positive challenge has been brought about by the expansion of the Scout movement to countries in the former Communist bloc in the 1990s and early twenty-first century. In January 2003, the only countries without Scout organizations were Afghanistan, Andorra, the People's Republic of China, Cuba, the Democratic People's Republic of Korea, the Lao People's Democratic Republic, and Myanmar. Caution must be applied to any comparison with figures from earlier periods, however, as some of the decline in England and the United States is masked by the inclusion of new categories (e.g., auxiliary members—adult helpers and young people whom Scouting has helped but who have not taken the Scout promise), who were not previously part of the census. It is a tribute to the success of the Scout movement that in 2003 the Boy Scouts had 28 million members worldwide and the Girl Guides/Scouts had 10 million.

See also: **Boyhood; Communist Youth; Fascist Youth; Girl Scouts; Organized Recreation and Youth Groups; Summer Camps; Youth Ministries.**

BIBLIOGRAPHY

Adams, William Scovell. 1957. *Edwardian Portraits.* London: Secker and Warburg.

Baden-Powell, Robert. 1910. *Scouting for Boys: A Handbook for Instruction in Good Citizenship.* London: C.A. Pearson.

Foster, Michael. 1987. *The Complete History of the British Boy Scouts.* Aylesbury, UK: British Boy Scouts.

Jeal, Tim. 1989. *Baden-Powell.* London: Hutchinson.

MacDonald, Robert H. 1993. *Sons of the Empire: The Frontier and the Boy Scout Movement, 1890–1918.* Toronto: University of Toronto Press.

Macleod, David I. 1983. *Building Character in the American Boy: The Boy Scouts, the YMCA, and Their Forerunners, 1870–1920.* Madison: University of Wisconsin Press.

Morris, Brian. 1970. "Ernest Thomson Seton and the Origins of the Woodcraft Movement." *The Journal of Contemporary History* 5, no. 2: 183–194.

Reynolds, E. E. 1950. *The Scout Movement.* New York: Oxford University Press.

Rosenthal, Michael. 1986. *The Character Factory: Baden-Powell and the Origins of the Boy Scout Movement.* New York: Pantheon.

Springhall, John. 1971. "The Boy Scouts, Class, and Militarism in Relation to British Youth Movements 1908–1930." *International Review of Social History* 16, no. 2: 125–158.

Springhall, John. 1977. *Youth, Empire and Society.* London: Croom Helm.

MICHAEL J. FOSTER

Brace, Charles Loring (1826–1890)

Founder in 1853 of the NEW YORK CHILDREN'S AID SOCIETY (CAS)—an early child-welfare organization that provided a variety of programs for impoverished city children—Charles Loring Brace was an important proponent of the CAS's "Emigration Scheme." Widely known today as the ORPHAN TRAINS, Brace's emigration program transported more than 100,000 persons, mostly children, from the burgeoning city of New York to rural homes and farms—in various, mostly Midwestern states, some as far away as Texas. During its seventy-five year history, the program was widely copied by other child-saving philanthropies and is still viewed as a significant precursor to the modern FOSTER CARE system.

Biography

Cousin to the Beecher clan, intimate friend of Frederick Law Olmsted (designer of Central Park), student of theologian Horace Bushnell, and admirer of Hungarian revolutionary Louis Kossuth, Charles Loring Brace was born into a privileged social network in his New England hometown of Litchfield, Connecticut, though his family itself was not particularly wealthy. His father, John, was the head teacher at the well-regarded, progressive Litchfield Academy and later served at Catharine Beecher's Hartford Female Seminary. His mother, Lucy Porter, aunt to the Beecher children, met John Brace while he was renting a room in the Beecher home during his first years as a teacher in the Academy. They married in 1820, and had two children, a daughter, Emma, and their son, Charles.

Brace attended Yale University from 1842 to 1846, graduated from Yale, and then, after a brief stint teaching in rural Connecticut, returned to Yale for a year in divinity school. He was ordained in 1849 as a Congregational minister. In Hartford, Brace first met his mentor Horace Bushnell, who, in his popular work *Christian Nurture* (1847), asserted ideas about the malleability of the human soul under "Unconscious Influences," particularly in childhood—ideas that were considered radical in evangelical Protestant circles of that time. These notions about the long-term effects of even tiny, everyday actions on those whose lives intersect with ours remained critical to Brace's philosophy that independent spirits must be carefully nurtured in childhood to create healthy adults. This care, he came to believe, could only be found in "family" settings.

Brace set off on his own in 1848 by moving to New York City at a time when that city's population was soaring, primarily due to waves of immigration and the increasing urbanization of the U.S. population. Although he was attending Union Theological Seminary in training for the ministry, during this time he also taught Latin to schoolboys and volunteered for various city-based missions, particularly Louis Pease's Five-Points Mission, located in one of the worst early slums in the country. He began to dabble in journalism, creating a regular column for the *New York Times*, entitled, "Walks Among the New-York Poor," which provided sensational portraits of "poverty and vice" for mostly middle-class readers. Both Brace and Pease were eventually disappointed in their attempts to work with impoverished adults, who struck their middle-class eyes as intractably "poisoned" by a life of poverty. As a result, both men turned their attention to poor children, who seemed to offer genuine hope for change.

Brace traveled to Europe in 1851 to visit experimental social-welfare programs being developed there. While in Hungary, he was imprisoned for several weeks for purportedly revolutionary activity. After returning to the United States, Brace published two books and various articles on his experiences and the new European social experiments. His writing, speaking engagements, and philanthropic activity drew the attention of a group of civic leaders and businessmen who were gathering to form the CAS; they immediately selected him to lead the new organization, which he did, almost until his death.

The organization solicited both public and private funding to create educational and religious Sunday meetings, industrial schools for boys and girls, reading-rooms, and, one of Brace's favorite projects, the Newsboys Lodging Houses. Not only were these lodging houses one of the most successful of Brace's programs, but they also inspired several of Horatio Alger's stories of young, orphaned boys whose independence, pluck, hard work and perseverance are rewarded by great wealth.

From the first, the CAS also planned to send these "STREET ARABS" to rural, "Christian homes" as a way to "drain the city" of its unwanted child population and simultaneously provide much needed labor for the newly settled

Western regions. Although not the first of its kind, Brace's emigration scheme soon became the largest and most influential child outplacement program in the United States. Its lack of binding indentureship contracts and formal ADOPTION agreements represented a radical, if somewhat naïve attempt to maintain a fundamental respect for the independence of children, whom Brace believed needed to have the opportunity to leave any placement that did not suit them. Although he believed that the best outcome would be at least informal adoption, Brace wanted children and family to work out for themselves whether their relationship would be primarily economic or more familial.

Not surprisingly, the experiences of orphan train riders varied widely. Less than half of the children were truly ORPHANS; many were taken from at least one parent, if not two. Some encountered horrific conditions approaching child slavery, while others were treated like family. At least one was convicted of murder, while two others were elected as state governors. Meanwhile, some critics complained that New York was using the program to dump its juvenile delinquents onto other states, and some Catholic charities suspected that the program was designed to place Catholic children into Protestant homes for conversion. Brace vigorously contested all these claims, and conducted several internal investigations. Still, it gradually became clear that, as the frontier closed, rural life declined, and social welfare programs were increasingly formalized and governmentalized, the Brace's program was doomed. The last "orphan train" arrived in Texas in 1929.

Brace's Legacy

Brace worked for the CAS almost until his dying day in 1890, and the CAS remained an important city-based child-welfare institution throughout the twentieth and early twenty-first centuries. Brace's firm belief in family-based settings, as well as a deep respect for the personhood of all children, had a lasting effect on child-welfare practices in the United States. Although ORPHANAGES survive to this day, most abandoned the factory-like dormitory settings that were typical of the early nineteenth century, and now incorporate cottage-style dwellings with only a few children per supervising adult. Most importantly, the modern foster care system is clearly a direct descendent of Brace's vision of a family home for every needy child.

See also: **Child Saving; Placing Out.**

BIBLIOGRAPHY

Askeland, Lori. 1998. "'The Means of Draining the City of These Children': Domesticity and Romantic Individualism in Charles Loring Brace's Emigration Plan, 1853–1861." *American Transcendental Quarterly* 12, no. 2: 145–162.

Bellingham, Bruce. 1983. "The 'Unspeakable Blessing': Street Children, Reform Rhetoric, and Misery in Early Industrial Capitalism." *Politics and Society* 12: 303–330.

Brace, Emma. 1894. *The Life of Charles Loring Brace Told Chiefly in His Own Letters.* New York: Scribner.

Holt, Marilyn. 1992. *The Orphan Trains: Placing Out in America.* Lincoln: University of Nebraska Press.

O'Connor, Stephen. 2001. *Orphan Trains: The Story of Charles Loring Brace and the Children He Saved and Failed.* Boston: Houghton Mifflin Company.

LORI ASKELAND

Brazil

HISTORY
Ana Cristina Dubeux Dourado
CONTEMPORARY
Tobias Hecht

HISTORY

In spite of advances in anthropological and ethnographic studies, historians' chances of discovering a range of sources on the history of indigenous children prior to the arrival of the Portuguese in Brazil are slim. Information on the treatment of children and adolescents by the Indians generally comes from observations made by people far removed from indigenous culture. For this reason, we begin our account of the history of children in Brazil in the year 1549, when Jesuit priests took on the mission of catechizing indigenous children along various parts of the Brazilian coast. Their broader objective was to bring about a change in customs and beliefs among indigenous societies, opening the path for the teaching of Christian principles through the children.

The first school for indigenous children was opened in Bahia in 1552. A number of studies show that the Indian children in Jesuit schools studied with white orphan children who were brought to Brazil to teach the local children Portuguese and Christian customs. The use of children in the catechism of Indians created a favorable environment for activities typical of the child's universe, such as games, theater, and music. But these schools were also characterized by a rigid sense of discipline, and indigenous children who tried to escape the daily activities suffered corporal punishment, at times being tied for hours to tree trunks or to chains prepared for this purpose.

The Jesuit schools were few and their influence on the indigenous children's education was limited. Contact between whites and Indians was usually the result of not-always-peaceful encounters that, in addition to dramatically reducing the indigenous population through extermination or disease, destroyed many of the original expressions of religiosity and indigenous culture. In spite of the controversies about the size of the indigenous population in the period immediately prior to the arrival of the Portuguese in Brazil, conservative estimates suggest that there were at least one million Indians in 1492, and that one hundred and fifty years later, this population had been reduced to around two hundred thousand people. Other studies indicate the existence of over five million Brazilian Indians in 1500, of which 95 percent were decimated by sickness and armed conflicts with the European conquerors.

The few records made by European travelers on the daily lives of children in the villages show the diversity of customs among the various indigenous nations. But they also had customs in common, such as washing and painting newborn children. A practice of the Tupinambas, who inhabited the entire Brazilian coastline, was to wash and paint a newborn child. The boys received a small tomahawk, a bow, and parrot-feather arrows from their father, so they would become great warriors. The girls wove cotton from the age of seven; in addition to weaving they made manioc flour and prepared food. In the passage to adult life, both boys and girls experienced rituals that were aimed at testing their courage. The girls' bodies received cross-shaped cuts, and they were isolated for days following their first periods. The boys also had their bodies cut and their lips pierced, and lay on anthills to build up the courage they would need in intertribal wars. All these practices were common to various indigenous nations living on the Brazilian coastline.

Childhood under Slavery

Before the end of the sixteenth century, the Portuguese began to bring slaves on ships from Africa to work in the fields and in other occupations that formed part of the colonization system. The slaves were treated as merchandise and the conditions they lived under were terrible. Men, women, and children were thrown into dark and filthy holds with scarcely any food and water, and many died in the crossing, which could last for months in periods of calm. When they arrived on the continent, the children, often separated from their parents, were taken to slave markets to be sold cheaply, since merchants preferred strong men who could work on the plantations harvesting sugarcane. The high mortality rate for children during the crossing tended to discourage the importation of children directly from AFRICA. Nonetheless, around 4 percent of the slaves who disembarked in Valongo Market in Rio de Janeiro were children, even in the nineteenth century.

When children were born in the slave quarters, they were treated as merchandise from an early age. Their value increased from the age of twelve onward, when they were assumed to have developed the necessary strength for hard labor in the fields. However, younger children also worked at a number of lighter occupations, above all in the domestic sphere on the big sugar plantations. In the country, the smaller children moved easily between the slave quarters (*senzala*) and their master's mansion, known as the *casa grande*, and they only began to work with a more defined routine from the age of seven or eight. The girls would sew and some learned lace making as well. They also served as domestic servants for the ladies and looked after young children. The

boys worked as pages, looked after the horses, and washed their masters' feet and those of their visitors. They would also serve at the table and help with cleaning.

The unit formed by the sugar mill, the sugarcane fields, the property-owners' residence, and the slave quarters was known as the *engenhos* (plantation). This productive unit, of such significance for Brazil's colonial history, is perhaps the most expressive example of the confusion between the public and private spheres that characterize the country's social history. Authoritative studies on the history of daily life and thought analyze the various ways in which the social relations generated in the *engenhos* ended by influencing how politics have functioned in Brazil. In the *engenhos* the relative intimacy shared by whites and blacks eventually created a hybrid cultural universe, based on the interchange of myths, symbols, art, religious beliefs, and other forms of expression common to both European and African culture. This coexistence between blacks and whites did not occur without conflict. From an early age, the children of the elite saw their fathers reacting violently towards rebellious attitudes from the slaves. Thus, although they could experience moments of equality when fun and games were shared, white children soon learned to discriminate against the slaves, even repeating patterns of violent behavior learned from their parents. And in spite of black children's access to the domestic sphere, their future chances of social mobility were inevitably linked to personal favors that the representatives of the elite might be inclined to offer. In colonial Brazil, education was allotted to very few, and poor children had to work from a tender age.

A Rehearsal for Public Policies

Direct welfare provision for needy children used to be provided almost exclusively by the Catholic Church. In the eighteenth century, asylums for foundlings were created to receive the large number of children abandoned in public places or at the gates of the wealthy. Children were abandoned for a variety of reasons: slave mothers left their children in the asylums so that they could live in liberty; needy families sometimes made use of charitable institutions for short periods, collecting their offspring when they could afford to raise them; and there was a high level of ABANDONMENT triggered by the birth of illegitimate children. The lack of adequate hygiene and care for children was denounced by several doctors and jurists in the nineteenth century. These professionals hoped to mold Brazil to the civilized standards imported from modern European nations.

In 1888 and in 1889, Brazil experienced two significant events: the abolition of slavery and the proclamation of the republic. These new times encouraged a discussion of social and welfare policies that could contribute to the organization of the urban centers, which were undergoing rapid population growth. Frightened by the presence of a large number of children roaming the streets, Brazil's governors adopted welfare measures that aimed to offer some form of occupation to children most in need. Even though these initiatives represented a first attempt at creating specific public policies for children in Brazil, their practical application did not always result in real benefits for underprivileged children. While the speeches of those who defended modernization in Brazil exalted the school as the efficient answer to backwardness and ignorance, in practice the Brazilian educational system was based on a discriminatory structure that separated rich from poor. The majority of the schools built in this period offered neither good equipment nor adequate methods to address children's needs. There was a distinct separation between schools catering to the poor that prioritized training for work and the schools for the elite that, in spite of the use of traditional teaching methods, included a greater range of educational opportunities, such as the teaching of music, art, and sports. Many children found on the streets, on the other hand, were taken to shelters and "'corrective' schools, which were organized around a rigid disciplinary system that conceived of education as a training process rather than an opportunity for developing the pupils' cognitive potential.

In the process of constructing the Brazilian nation, many authorities believed that the simple transposition of European ideas and practices would make Brazil an essentially modern country, free of the slave legacy and monarchical past that, in the social imagery of the period, represented backwardness. However, in terms of children's education, the aspirations of a small number of politicians, jurists, and teachers who managed to see beyond their time eventually lost their strength in the face of an economic structure based on the concentration of wealth and social exclusion.

A Light at the End of the Tunnel

Over the course of the twentieth century, there have been a few attempts at creating good state schools and effective welfare policies to benefit children. However, the results were limited to brief periods or to well-defined geographical areas. Only after the 1990s, with the passage of the Statute on the Child and Adolescent, did Brazil seriously begin the process of building public policies to provide full attention to children. Distinct among the many legal measures and public policies that have been envisioned or implemented throughout Brazil's history, this new legislation makes children and adolescents national priorities, considering them citizens whose rights should be respected. In this new concept of citizenship, society is seen as a participatory element in the struggle for the effective guarantee of human rights. This participation also occurs through the individual actions of each citizen, but chiefly by means of specially designed institutions to act as a bridge between society and the state, in the task of transforming what exists by law into reality.

See also: **Latin America.**

BIBLIOGRAPHY

Goldstein, Donna M. 1998. "Nothing Bad Intended: Child Discipline, Punishment, and Survival in a Shantytown in Rio de Janeiro, Brazil." In *Small Wars: The Cultural Politics of Childhood*, ed. Nancy Scheper-Hughes and Carolyn Fishel Sargent. Berkeley and Los Angeles: University of California Press.

Hecht, Tobias. 1998. *At Home in the Street: Street Children of Northeast Brazil.* Cambridge, UK: Cambridge University Press.

Hecht, Tobias. 2002. *Minor Omissions: Children in Latin American History and Society.* Madison: University of Wisconsin Press.

Kenny, Mary Lorena. 2002. "Orators and Outcasts, Wanderers and Workers: Street Children in Brazil." In *Symbolic Childhood*, ed. Daniel T. Cook. New York: Peter Lang.

Scheper-Hughes, Nancy, and Daniel Hoffman. 1998. "Brazilian Apartheid: Street Kids and the Struggle for Urban Space." In *Small Wars: The Cultural Politics of Childhood*, ed. Nancy Scheper-Hughes and Carolyn Fishel Sargent. Berkeley and Los Angeles: University of California Press.

ANA CRISTINA DUBEUX DOURADO

CONTEMPORARY

With a population of 170 million in a territory larger than western Europe, Brazil is home to some 61 million people under the age of eighteen. Not surprisingly, the lives of Brazilian children are anything but uniform.

Wealth and Poverty

One aspect of Brazilian social life that makes childhood so diverse is the staggering inequality in the distribution of national wealth. According to the World Bank's *1999/2000 Development Report*, the richest 10 percent of the population are responsible for 47 percent of consumption, while the poorest 10 percent account for only 0.8 percent. Children who grow up in tall, guarded apartment buildings and watch MTV, play video games, shop in air-conditioned malls, and vacation at Disney World can gaze out their windows at the shacks where other children suffer from malnutrition. In the poorest areas of Brazil, such as the northeast, even the physical size and appearance of poor children tends to be markedly different from those of their richer peers; children growing up in middle-class condominiums are likely to be considerably taller and heavier than age-mates residing in rural areas or in precarious shacks just down the street. Contemporary researchers are far less likely than previous generations of scholars to accept the notion that Brazil has something like a racial democracy; even the casual observer cannot help but notice the correlation between whiteness and wealth and blackness and poverty. While there are certainly destitute white children in Brazil, the bulk of poor Brazilian youngsters are descendants of African slaves and Amerindians; most rich children are light skinned.

Although the proportion of all Brazilian children attending primary school has risen dramatically in recent years to about 90 percent, poor children cannot attend the better private schools and are more likely to drop out along the way;

of the population as a whole, according to the World Bank, only 20 percent of high-school-age children were attending secondary institutions in 1996. Free university education serves mostly those whose families had the means to send them to expensive private schools.

Deemed to be of great sentimental value but something of an economic liability for their families, rich children in Brazil are unlikely to work inside, much less outside, the home. In this sense, their status is similar to that of children in advanced industrial countries. Poor Brazilian children, on the other hand, while usually cherished sentimentally, often contribute to household income, be it in agriculture in the rural areas or through the informal sector in the cities. According to Brazil's official Institute of Geography and Economy, 9 percent of children aged ten to fourteen are "economically active," and of these 32 percent work more than forty hours per week. Such figures say nothing about the prevalence of poor children working in the home, minding younger siblings so that their parents can be employed outside, for instance, or how many children are involved in illegal forms of work, such as the drugs trade. With 44 percent of Brazil's population living on 2 dollars or less per day (as indicated in World Bank figures from 1990), the survival of millions of households almost certainly depends on child labor in one form or another. Unfortunately, careful studies of this phenomenon in Brazil are remarkable for their absence.

Infant and Childhood Mortality

Rates of INFANT MORTALITY have fallen dramatically, from 70 per 1,000 live births in 1980 to 34 in 1997. Still, the prevalence of infant death among the poorest populations in Brazil remains high and is largely attributable to malnutrition in combination with easily treatable childhood diseases. In a controversial 1992 ethnography of infant death in a Brazilian shantytown, anthropologist Nancy Scheper-Hughes argued that mothers living in conditions of extreme poverty and chronic hunger exhibited a sort of indifference to the deaths of their offspring, not unlike that reported by some historians studying preindustrial societies; this indifference, she contended, was both a reasonable coping strategy given the reality of pervasive child death and a contributing factor to it. Other scholars have refuted the contention about maternal detachment, yet the debate has drawn needed attention to the social consequences of malnutrition and infant mortality.

Brazil has one of the highest rates of violent death of any country not at war, with children figuring prominently as both victims and perpetrators. According to a study by Tom Gibb, 4,000 children and adolescents under the age of eighteen were killed by firearms in a single and by no means anomalous Brazilian city, Rio de Janeiro, between 1987 and 2001—eight times the number of all Palestinian children killed in the conflict with ISRAEL during the same period.

The massacre of a group of children sleeping in the street in Rio de Janeiro in 1993 led to international protest (in 1996 a member of the military police was convicted for his participation in the crime). Still, the preponderance of violent crimes carried out by young people and the ineptitude and corruption of the Brazilian police and judiciary have been accompanied by considerable tolerance of vigilante justice.

Street Children

In the late 1980s and early 1990s, Brazilian street children became the focus of media attention the world over. For a time, international advocacy institutions were estimating the presence of some 7 million children living in the street. These claims—wildly exaggerated, as carefully gathered census data later demonstrated—were also partially responsible for the emergence of a vibrant social movement on behalf of children. With intensive lobbying by the National Movement of Street Children and other organizations, Brazil adopted in 1990 the Children and Adolescents Act, an ambitious piece of legislation guaranteeing children the right to attend school, access to leisure activities, special treatment at the hands of the police and judiciary, and many other entitlements and protections. Few would contend that the implementation of this law has been successful, however.

Whereas most research on contemporary Brazilian children has focused on a small minority living in extraordinary circumstances—for instance in the street or working as prostitutes—scant attention has been paid to rural children or to the conditions of the vast majority of urban children who live and stay at home.

See also: **Latin America; Sociology and Anthropology of Childhood; Violence Against Children.**

BIBLIOGRAPHY

Hecht, Tobias. 1998. *At Home in the Street: Street Children of Northeast Brazil.* Cambridge, UK: Cambridge University Press.

Scheper-Hughes, Nancy. 1992. *Death without Weeping: The Violence of Everyday Life in Brazil.* Berkeley: University of California Press.

Sheriff, Robin E. 2001. *Dreaming Equality: Color, Race, and Racism in Urban Brazil.* New Brunswick, NJ: Rutgers University Press.

INTERNET RESOURCES

Gibb, Tom. 2002. "Rio 'Worse than a War Zone.'" Available from <http://news.bbc.co.uk/2/hi/americas/2247608.stm>.

Instituto Brasileiro de Geografia e Economia. Available from <www.ibge.gov.br/>.

World Bank. 2003. "1999/2000 Development Report." Available from <www.worldbank.org/wdr/2000/>.

TOBIAS HECHT

Breast-feeding. *See* Infant Feeding; La Leche League.

Breeching

In early America an important RITE OF PASSAGE in the lives of small boys was the moment they wore breeches or trousers for the first time. In infancy and early childhood, boys and girls were relegated to the feminine domestic circle and were dressed alike in petticoats, gowns, pinafores, and caps. Sometime between the ages of four and seven, however, boys were encouraged to acquire a masculine identity as they donned clothing that set them apart, gave them physical freedom, and indicated their dominant social position. Although the ritual of breeching died out in the nineteenth century, changes in clothing designed for boys continued to mark stages in their growth and development.

In the seventeenth century, little children wore linen shifts covered by petticoats and ankle-length robes, protected by a bib and apron or pinafore, and tight white caps. As boys grew, their long robes resembled those worn by adult men in the Middle Ages, for children were relegated to outfits resembling clothing that adults had abandoned. Ribbons, which hung down the back and symbolized childhood, recalled the adult robes of the sixteenth century with hanging sleeves. Such ornamental ribbons were different from leading strings, cords also attached to the shoulders which an adult held to help a child learn to walk. When boys reached the age of six or seven, they put on the breeches, frock coats, waistcoats, and hats worn by adult men. David Mason of Massachusetts, for example, was painted in 1670 at the age of eight, holding gloves and a silver-headed walking stick, and wearing a waistcoat with slashed sleeves, a shirt with a square collar, full breeches, long gray stockings, and black leather shoes.

As the eighteenth century progressed, children's dress was influenced by the child-rearing advice of JOHN LOCKE and other physicians, who recommended building the strong constitution with fresh air, physical exercise, and loose clothing. Locke approved the dress of sturdy children from farming and artisan families, who wore long frocks as toddlers and later changed to shirts with trousers or breeches for boys and petticoats and dresses for girls. But families of means continued to dress their children in ways that indicated gender and social dominance. The long robes worn by little boys resembled fashionable gowns with low-cut necks and full skirts over petticoats. When boys were breeched, they assumed the outfit of adult males: breeches, frock coat, waistcoat, soft ruffled shirt, long stockings, leather shoes, and even a tricorne hat. Yet their loose hair tied with a ribbon in a queue instead of a wig and a black ribbon around the neck in place of a cravat signaled their juvenility. Boys were delighted when they donned masculine outfits for the first time. Elizabeth Drinker remarked on the breeching of her grandson in 1799: "Sally has a Young woman at work . . . making a little man of Henry—he is very pleas'd . . . one of the happiest days of his life" (quoted in Reinier, p. 56).

By the late eighteenth and early nineteenth centuries, the androgynous clothing of little children—muslin frocks, soft shoes, and short hair with bangs—minimized gender differences and symbolized the increasing value placed on childhood. Yet boys between the ages of three and nine still were distinguished from girls when they donned hussar or skeleton suits—long trousers buttoned to a short jacket over a shirt with a square collar. Rather than copying the dress of their fathers, this costume expressed their subordination to men, for trousers were the dress of laborers and sailors when their social betters still wore breeches. Not until the age of about ten would boys acquire a relaxed version of adult dress. In the 1830s middle-class girls acquired the freedom of trousers when pantaloons were introduced from Europe. Soon little children of both sexes were dressed alike in knee-length frocks over white pantaloons. When men adopted trousers at about the same time, eight-year-old boys gave up their frocks and pantaloons for knee-length knickers or short pants. Throughout the nineteenth century, little boys continued to wear dresses or tunics, graduating as they grew to sailor suits, military uniforms, short jackets, or frock coats. Not until the 1920s were creepers and rompers designed to distinguish toddler boys from girls. Age distinctions in older children's clothing have declined in the twentieth century as parents have selected parkas, sweatshirts, sneakers, and baseball caps for both sexes. Since the 1970s, gender distinctions have declined as well, as notions of nonsexist child rearing have encouraged parents to dress children of all ages androgynously in T-shirts and jeans.

See also: **Boyhood; Fashion; Gendering.**

BIBLIOGRAPHY

Ariès, Philippe. 1962. *Centuries of Childhood: A Social History of Family Life.* Trans. Robert Baldick. New York, Vintage Books.

Brant, Sandra, and Elissa Cullman. 1980. *Small Folk: A Celebration of Childhood in America.* New York: Dutton, in association with the Museum of American Folk Art.

Calvert, Karin. 1992. *Children in the House: The Material Culture of Early Childhood, 1600–1900.* Boston: Northeastern University Press.

Paoletti, Jo B. 2001. "Clothing." In *Boyhood in America: An Encyclopedia,* vol. 1, ed. Priscilla Ferguson Clement and Jacqueline S. Reinier. Santa Barbara, CA: ABC-CLIO.

Reinier, Jacqueline S. 1996. *From Virtue to Character: American Childhood, 1775–1850.* New York: Twayne.

JACQUELINE S. REINIER

British Colonialism in India

Colonialism is a distinct form of imperialism in which a colonizing nation exerts direct controls over a colonized state by military, economic, and political means. The forceful widespread intrusion of a colonizing nation naturally causes an ir-

The Children of Edward Holden Cruttenden with an Indian Ayah (1759–1762), by Joshua Reynolds. Ayahs were commonly employed to take care of British children in India and often developed close bonds with them. The Cruttenden family's ayah reportedly saved the children's lives in an uprising, yet here she is pictured in the background, as if to emphasize her relationship of servitude to her lighter-skinned charges. © Alinari/Art Resource, NY. Museu de Arte, Sao Paulo, Brazil.

reversible change in all dimensions of the colonized state, the lives of the people, and the social architecture. To achieve the primary objective of colonialism, creating wealth for the colonizing nation and its people, many different groups, including women and children acting synergistically,

must contribute. India forms an excellent case study, beginning with the children of imperial officials themselves.

During the period between 1830 and 1880 a large number of British children either went to India with their parents or were born there. The exact number of British children in India at any given time during that period is unclear, as sources of information about British children in the Indian subcontinent are scanty. The accounts of children's lives are in parents' letters and diaries, and in contemporary domestic manuals. If all of these writings are read as a corpus, a picture emerges about British childhood in India. The available documents relate the experiences of children from British families ranging from lower-middle class to upper-middle-class.

Infant Mortality

A major anxiety for British families in colonized India was the high rate of INFANT MORTALITY. In the Bengal presidency between 1860 and 1869, the average death rate was about 148 per thousand British children under the age of five, while in England during the same period the mortality rate was about 67 per thousand. The grief of losing children was expressed time and again by British mothers. Maria Amelia Vansittart, wife of a Civil Session judge in northern India, noted in her diary on March 26, 1846, that between eight and nine in the evening a very little girl was born, and in the entry of April 13 she described her daughter's burial. Theon Wilkinson, who studied tombstones in India, documented the repeated misfortunes of some families. The rate of infant mortality decreased as the century progressed, but it was still high enough to create anxiety and perceived helplessness among British mothers.

Wet Nurses, Ayahs, and Bearers

In the subcontinent, British mothers generally depended on Indian wet nurses to nurse their children, as European wet nurses were not available and British physicians advised mothers not to breast-feed their own children since the climate was thought to be too debilitating. The wet nurses, commonly called *ammahs*, were low-caste Hindus or Muslims. Many memsahibs (British married women in India) hired an Indian wet nurse for the infants and Indian ayahs (nurses) for the other needs of their children, although many greatly disliked the idea. Besides having an ayah, many Anglo-Indian parents hired a male servant, or *bearer*, for their male children. Anglo-Indian children spent most of their waking hours with Indian servants. These domestics, serving frequently as playmates, taught the children Hindi words like *bhaia* (brother) and *baba* (infant), and often "papa" and "mama" as well. Children generally developed a close attachment to their ayahs and bearers and the close bond served to provide comfort to the children when the families were in transit. As the time came for the Anglo-Indian mothers to take their children to England, some took their children's ayahs or bearers with them.

Racial Barriers

The need to have help to raise infants forced memsahibs to hire Indian servants, but they were always apprehensive about the intimate bond between the ayah and the infant and attempted to maintain a distance between their children and the servants. Authors of prescriptive literature discouraged any closeness between British children and the Indian servants, fearing that the children would imitate "native" habits, mannerisms, and language. This fear clearly surfaced in the mind of Julia Thomas Maitland, wife of a district judge at Rajahmundry in Madras, when she emphasized in a letter that she did not want her daughter to learn Indian languages and grow up "like a little Hindu" (Jan. 9, 1839).

Mothers were not often successful in shielding their children from learning the local language. When little Eric Bailey's mother Florence wrote to her husband that Eric could say a few words in Hindi and imitated making *chappatis* (Indian bread), her husband became quite upset. To check the infusion of Indian influence on their children, many memsahibs employed English women in addition to ayahs as nurses for their babies. Some tried to assuage the problem by hiring Indian ayahs who could speak English. The British nurse and the Indian ayah were sometimes at odds with each other about their authority over the child; not surprisingly, the white nurse was usually the winner. The underlying reason for Anglo-Indian parents' fear of close bonds between their offspring and their native servants was undoubtedly tied to the attitude of racial exclusiveness that accompanied imperialism. While Anglo-Indian parents were maintaining a social distance from the Indians, however, their children, through their close relationships with the servants, were dismantling the barrier between the colonizers and the colonized. This cross current from the children ultimately acted to erode the foundations of the empire.

Education

Emma Roberts reported in 1837 that schools were established in every regiment for the children of European soldiers. Boys were educated to become noncommissioned officers, regimental clerks, and so on. The girls were trained to be wives for men of higher ranks. Information on Anglo-Indian children's education is often quite sketchy. The letters of Sarah Terry described the education of her eight-year-old daughter and five-year-old son. During their first year in India, Sarah taught English and math to her children at home in the morning. In the second year, both of them went to school at the Bombay Fort at 7:30 in the morning and returned at 4:00 in the afternoon.

Transient Life of Anglo-Indian Children

During the summer it was quite common that British infants suffered from heat stroke, boils, and diarrhea. To protect children from heat-induced diseases they were taken to the hill stations by their mothers from March to October, while their fathers remained at their jobs in the plains. Most Anglo-Indian parents believed that if their children stayed in India for too long the Indian climate and environment would weaken their constitutions, perhaps for all their lives. Even an English nurse was not a sufficient protection from this danger, so British parents sent their children to England at a very early age. Boys usually left India by the time they were five years old, and girls normally went back at the age of seven or eight.

Colonialism influenced the texture of British family life in India. Anglo-Indian children lived in the Indian subcontinent without a lasting home base. Soon after their birth, many children had to be separated from their fathers for six to seven months to avoid the summer heat. Their daily routines were disrupted by their fathers' recurrent job transfers. By the time these children reached the age of seven, many of them returned to Britain without their parents. Thus, unlike their contemporaries in Britain, the Anglo-Indian children seldom had a stable home life with both parents around. Although it was common for upper- and upper-middle-class children in Victorian Britain to go away to boarding school for months at a time, the Anglo-Indian children were often not able to see their parents for periods extending over many years.

Sometimes it became difficult for parents to send their children back to England. Often Anglo-Indian men did not get the leave to take their families home or lacked the money to send them back. They frequently had difficulty finding someone to take their children home. For example, following the death of his wife in 1871, a Mr. Wonnacott sought to send his three-year-old daughter to Britain. He was not able to find her a woman escort until 1874. (Female children under age seven were not considered old enough to travel with unrelated and often unknown adults; boys could go home at the age of five with unrelated and often unknown army personnel.) Because of the great distance and high cost of the journey between India and England, parents and children could see each other only at lengthy intervals, sometimes as long as nine to ten years. At times children never saw their parents again. The Metcalfe children's mother died in India while they were in Britain. The Wonnacott children's father died on his way back to Britain and their mother died in India.

Victorians placed the need for a strong family at the center of their lives. The family disruptions caused by long separations between parents and their children commonly seen in Anglo-Indian families were not in tune with the Victorian emphasis on creating a stable home and family that would provide what historian Anthony Wohl called moral, ethical, religious, and social standards of good citizenship. Still, colonialism sometimes created a repetition in the pattern of parent–child relationships within Anglo-Indian families as the young men returned to India as civil servants or members of the armed services and the young women returned to marry and again create a family life in a colonial atmosphere.

Effects of Colonialism on Indian Children

Colonial governments generally did little to change the lives of local children, particularly in rural areas. There were some attempts to regulate what imperial authorities regarded as abuses. For example, colonial officials frowned on marriages that were contracted for young girls, though they did not usually press their concerns very vigorously. While colonial officials often criticized "natives" for working children too hard, the colonial economy usually depended on continued child labor, so there was little change here. Gradually, colonial administrations did introduce some new educational opportunities, supplemented often by missionary efforts. So some children were exposed to formal schooling, which in some cases pulled them away from family traditions and into new contact with Western values. Schools for girls might also influence socialization for women's roles, again pulling away from tradition. Educational opportunities were limited, however, so the impact of this aspect of colonialism was only gradually felt.

BIBLIOGRAPHY

Bayley, Emily. 1980. *The Golden Calm: An English Lady's Life in Moghul Delhi: Reminiscences by Emily, Lady Clive Bayley, and by Her Father, Sir Thomas Metcalfe*, ed. Mary M. Kaye. Exeter, UK: Webb and Bower.

Chaudhuri, Nupur. 1988. "Memsahib and Motherhood in Nineteenth-Century India," *Victorian Studies* 31, no. 4: 517–535.

Fayrer, J. 1873. *European Child-Life in India*. OIOC Tract 820. London: J. A. Churchill.

Maitland, Julia. 1846. *Letters from Madras: During the Years 1836–1839*. London: J. Murray.

Roberts, Emma. 1837. *Scenes and Characteristics of Hindostan, with Sketches of Anglo-Indian Society*. London: W. H. Allen.

Wilkinson, Theon. 1976. *Two Monsoons*. London: Duckworth.

NUPUR CHAUDHURI

Brown v. the Board of Education of Topeka, Kansas

On May 19, 1954, the Supreme Court outlawed separate public schools for black and white schoolchildren in the celebrated *Brown v. Board of Education* decision (*Brown* I), one of the most important high court rulings in American history. A year later the same court ruled in its implementation decree (*Brown* II) that the process of creating integrated schools out of formerly all-white and all-black public schools had to go forward "with all deliberate speed." The *Brown* decision (parts I and II) was the culmination of a series of concerted legal battles against Jim Crow schools and other forms of American apartheid, such as separate public transportation and separate public accommodations. Spearheaded by the National Association for the Advancement of Colored People's legal team and its head lawyer Thurgood Marshall these legal battles were crucial to the growing mid-twentieth-century civil rights movement.

Brown proved crucial to the assault on the entire edifice of separate black and white worlds in the Jim Crow South

Watson Grandchildren (also known as *Black Children with White Doll*, 1942), Gordon Parks. Reformers such as psychologists Kenneth and Mamie Clark argued that the "separate but equal" doctrine of *Plessy v. Ferguson* was anything but equal. The Clarks' work showed that segregation reinforced notions of white supremacy to the point that black children preferred playing with white dolls over dolls of their own color. © CORBIS.

and beyond. At the end of the nineteenth century, *Plessy v. Ferguson* (1896) had established the legal fiction of separate black and white worlds as equivalent and, thus, constitutional. Separate was rarely equal, as evidenced in the woeful and systemic underfunding of black schools and discriminatory pay for black teachers. By overturning the guiding legal precedent as established in *Plessy*, *Brown* promised a new day: a fully integrated society beginning with the nation's schools.

A key line of argument in the case against Jim Crow generally, and Jim Crow schools specifically, was their negative impact on black self-esteem, especially that of black children. In other words, the invidious distinction imposed by legally mandated segregation promoted white supremacy and, in turn, enforced notions of black inferiority. A famous piece of evidence in particular in the original case relied upon the controversial doll test of Kenneth and Mamie Clark, pioneering black social psychologists. When the Clarks asked a series of black children whether they preferred a black or white doll, most preferred the latter. While social scientists have debated the viability and meaning of these kinds of tests their central argument curried wide favor with both contemporary and later audiences. The Clarks argued that the black child's preference for the white doll reflected the dehumanizing impact of white supremacy on the young black psyche.

One step toward remedying this damage was to underscore notions of equality, sameness, and oneness by replacing Jim Crow with an integrated society.

Another argument against segregated schooling was that legally mandated racial separation braced white perceptions of white superiority and informal as well as institutionalized forms of white supremacy. In effect, Jim Crow also harmed white schoolchildren as well as white adults. Integrated schools where black and white children learned that they were fundamentally alike would not only erode racial fears and antipathies early on, but also lay the necessary groundwork for future generations of more racially enlightened citizens. As learned behavior, then, racial prejudice could be unlearned and a more racially egalitarian society created. The half-century after Brown witnessed both the dismantling of *de jure* segregation and a measure of racial progress. Unfortunately, it also witnessed the persistence of institutionalized patterns of racial inequality as reflected in the increasing resegregation of public schools in the early twenty-first century.

See also: **African-American Children and Youth; Education, United States; Law, Children and the.**

BIBLIOGRAPHY

Kluger, Richard. 1975. *Simple Justice: The History of Brown v. Board of Education and Black America's Struggle for Equality.* New York: Knopf.

Martin, Waldo E., Jr., ed. 1998. *Brown v. Board of Education: A Brief History with Documents.* Boston: Bedford Books.

Patterson, James T. 2001. *Brown v. Board of Education: A Civil Rights Milestone and Its Troubled Legacy.* New York: Oxford University Press.

WALDO E. MARTIN JR.

Bühler, Charlotte (1893–1974)

Twentieth-century developmental psychologist Charlotte (Malachowski) Bühler was born in Berlin, Germany, on December 20, 1893. Her comprehensive investigations of infants' and young children's motor control, mental performance, and social development broke new ground by documenting individual levels of mastery, providing data for establishing norms, and confirming that very young children are active, intentional beings. Bühler is best known for her developmental theory that emphasizes growth and purposeful activity throughout the lifespan. She investigated adolescents' quest for self-determination, a quest that generally marks the transition from ADOLESCENCE to healthy adulthood. Bühler designed an autobiographical method that provides insight into an individual's path towards fulfillment. She also collaborated with like-minded psychologists to establish humanistic psychology in North America.

Charlotte Malachowski's interest in human development first became evident in high school as she investigated adolescent thinking. Later she pursued a Ph.D. at the University of Munich under Oswald Kulpe, an expert in thought processes. After Kulpe's untimely death, she continued her university studies with his chief assistant, Karl Bühler, whom she married in 1916, before completing her Ph.D. in 1918.

In 1922 the Bühlers accepted positions at the University of Vienna, which became their research base until 1938. In Vienna, Charlotte Bühler founded a child-study laboratory devoted to comprehensive, innovative, and often naturalistic investigations of the development and familial relationships of infants and children. During that period, she also served as Rockefeller Fellow at Columbia University (1924 to 1925), as Guest Visiting Professor at Barnard College (1929), and as child-study consultant in several Western European countries, including England and Norway.

Like American developmentalist ARNOLD GESELL, whom Bühler respected, she stressed rigorous observation of infants' and children's unique, biologically rooted patterns of attaining sequentially attained competencies—such as sitting and walking—that all healthy children achieve. Bühler also admired psychoanalyst SIGMUND FREUD for clarifying the complexities of everyday human activity by providing a fresh way of thinking about them. She applauded Sigmund and ANNA FREUD's recognition of the importance of the early years, which Anna Freud studied firsthand while striving, like Bühler, to improve the lot of children.

In 1940, following the Nazi takeover of Vienna, Bühler moved to the United States. She found the first few years after her move extremely difficult. However, a happy, fruitful period dawned after Bühler settled in Los Angeles, California, and became a naturalized American citizen. From 1945 to 1953 she served as clinical psychologist at the Los Angeles County General Hospital. She taught during the same period at the medical school of the University of Southern California. From 1953 to 1972 she maintained a private practice in Los Angeles. Her close friendship with Abraham Maslow and their collaboration with other psychologists led in 1962 to founding the Association of Humanistic Psychology, which launched the humanistic movement in North America.

In later life, Bühler continued to improve and revise her theory of lifelong development. According to Bühler, healthy human beings actively strive toward fulfillment and growth from infancy onwards. Four basic tendencies (the need for satisfaction, self-limiting adaptation, creative expansion, and upholding the internal order) work together to foster the finest fulfillment outcome that a person is able to achieve.

Bühler returned to Germany in 1972 and died in Stuttgart on February 3, 1974. The Archives of the American Psychiatric Association in Washington, D.C., and the Archives of the History of American Psychology in Akron, Ohio, contain additional information about her.

See also: **Child Development, History of the Concept of; Child Psychology; Child Study; Life Course and Transitions to Adulthood; Theories of Childhood.**

BIBLIOGRAPHY

Bühler, Charlotte. 1930. *The First Year of Life.* Trans. Pearl Greenberg and Rowena Ripin. New York: John Day Company.

Bühler, Charlotte. 1937. *From Birth to Maturity: An Outline of the Psychological Development of the Child.* Trans. Esther and William Menaker. London: Kegan Paul, Trench, Trubner and Co.

Bühler, Charlotte, and Herbert Goldenberg. 1968. "Structural Aspects of the Individual's History." In *The Course of Human Life,* ed. Charlotte Bühler and Fred Massarik. New York: Springer.

Bühler, Charlotte, and Marianne Marschak. 1968. "Basic Tendencies of Human Life." In *The Course of Human Life,* ed. Charlotte Bühler and Fred Massarik. New York: Springer.

Gavin, Eileen A. 1990. "Charlotte M. Bühler (1893–1974)." In *Women in Psychology,* ed. Agnes N. O'Connell and Nancy Felipe Russo, pp. 49–56. Westport, CT: Greenwood Press.

EILEEN A. GAVIN

Bundling

Historically, bundling was a courtship practice in which, as a part of an ongoing courtship process, a couple spent a night together, usually in bed, dressed or half dressed. During the night, the young couple got to know each other intimately and sexually through various kinds of stimulation and mutual gratification. However, these were supposed to fall short of penetrative sex that could lead to pregnancy. The custom was practiced with either parental permission or at least tacit knowledge, and took place mostly in the female partner's home. Most of the surviving evidence for the practice is from eighteenth-century New England. However, variations of premarital nonpenetrative sex customs similar to bundling are known from earlier times in many parts of Europe as well as other parts of the world. It is probable that bundling increased in Europe in the sixteenth and seventeenth centuries, partly reflecting a high average age at marriage (mid- to late twenties) and a growing emphasis on affection.

Variations of Bundling

Essentially, bundling was a social mechanism that helped to insure the stability of sacred matrimony. In traditional societies, where divorce seldom took place, minimizing the risk of broken marriages was one aim of the courtship period. It was therefore accepted that the courtship, as a kind of trial period, included some sexual acquaintance, though amid constraints. It has also been argued that the custom of bundling in premodern times had a circumstantial cause, namely that the harsh climate as well as poor housing was conducive to the growth of physical intimacy. Even the supposed widespread existence of bundling in New England is usually explained as due more to the harsh climate and the long distances between the dwellings of early settlers than to the alleged economic and moral independence of young couples.

The young courting mate, having traveled a long way to visit his woman, perforce stayed the night in her home, usually in the same one large room where the rest of her family slept. These sleeping arrangements surely helped to control the intimacy of the couple and minimized the risk of abusing the privilege. An eighteenth-century New England ballad emphasized this practical aspect of the custom: "Since in bed a man and maid/ may bundle and be chaste/ it does no good to burn out wood/ it is needless waste."

Like many other popular European practices concerning courtship and marriage, prenuptial nonpenetrative sex is also believed to be rooted in pre-Christian culture, especially in Germanic societies. Henry Reed Stiles, whose 1871 *Bundling: Its Origins, Progress, and Decline in America* remains one of the most cited books on the practice, traced its origin back to ancient rural Wales and parts of Scotland. Stiles also gave examples of what he viewed as bundling in medieval Holland, as well as in central Asia. Not all scholars are in agreement with Stiles about the exact time of the custom's appearance, but most recognize the validity of evidence on bundling variations at least from late medieval and early modern Europe. The evidence comes mostly from Wales, Scotland, the Netherlands, and Scandinavia, and less so from Germany, Switzerland, and parts of France. Evidence of nonpenetrative sexual courtship practices also exists for Eastern Europe.

The Swiss-German customs that shared the characteristics and purposes of bundling were *Kiltgang, Fenstreln,* or *Nachtfreien.* In early modern times in southern Germany these customs included young men climbing through the window of young women's rooms at night with the intention of gratifying mutual desires, but without incurring the risk of pregnancy. In the Netherlands *queesten* was probably comparable to bundling. It is described as a custom of wooing in which lovers sit in an open room, the man sitting on top of the bed covering, wooing the girl who is underneath. A New England equivalent was tarrying, in which a young man who wanted to marry a woman was allowed, with her parents' consent, to tarry with her for one night.

In most cases involving premarital nonpenetrative sex customs, the defining structures of class and geography were significant. Usually, but not exclusively, bundling was more common among people of the lower classes of society and in rural areas. It was also in these social classes and geographical settings that youngsters enjoyed greater freedom in choosing their spouses.

Youth Sexuality

By creating an accepted social space for practicing bundling, adult authorities gave young people in the medieval and early modern periods a socially legitimized framework for their sexual desires. As in other youth customs, such as the European CHARIVARI, young men and women used bundling to express their SEXUALITY in a specific time and place within the boundaries of social consent. Although marriage rather than sociability was the premise of bundling, the youngsters received a space where their urgent sexual adolescent needs were tolerated. However, the unwritten behavioral code of bundling, which excluded penetrative sex, left the expression of the couple's sexuality controlled, supervised, and restrained by society. The restraints usually implied a gender bias. Young women were at much greater risk while negotiating their sexuality during courtship, not just of pregnancy, but also of damaging their matrimonial prospects.

In eighteenth-century New England bundling was often condemned as immoral. Washington Irving, in his *Knickerbocker's History of New York,* argued that a large number of pregnancies outside of marriage were a result of bundling. Other religious authorities, however, defended the practice. They even occasionally used examples of "religious" bundling or tarrying, such as that of the biblical Boaz and Ruth at the threshing floor ("Tarry the night . . . " Ruth 3:13). One material clue that points to the prevalent as well as conservative aspect of bundling is the Pennsylvanian centerboard. This was a wide board running through the length of the bed in which a courting couple lay, preventing too close a physical intimacy. A contemporary ballad in favor of bundling, called "The Whore on the Snow Crust," encouraged youngsters to practice it rightly: "Since bundling is not a thing/ that judgment will procure/Go on young men and bundle then/ But keep your bodies pure."

Bundling was declining in America around the time of the Great Awakening in the early 1700s, due to a combination of material as well as moral factors. The improvement in living conditions, which meant less isolated dwellings and larger homes in which there was more than one heated room, reduced the necessity of providing a couple with a warm bed to court in. The decline of bundling was also due to the changing climate of ideas regarding female sexuality around 1800. The nineteenth-century ideal of the pure asexual woman further limited the theoretical as well as the practical scope in which men and women could express their sexuality within accepted social norms.

In America as in other parts of the world such as Russia or Scotland evidence of the persistent customs of premarital nonpenetrative sex exists well into the nineteenth century. The balance between sexual expression and sexual restraint continued to be the rule in these encounters. Secularization and modern BIRTH CONTROL rendered penetrative sex less threatening. In time the back seats of cars in drive-in theaters and dark city street corners replaced in many ways the traditional bundling bed.

BIBLIOGRAPHY

Adair, Richard. 1996. *Courtship, Illegitimacy, and Marriage in Early Modern England.* Manchester, UK: Manchester University Press.

Beck, Rainer. 1983. "Illegitimität und voreheliche Sexualität auf dem Land: Unterfinning, 1671–1770." In *Kultur der einfachen*

Leute: Bayerisches Volksleben vom 16. bis zum 19. Jahrhundert, ed. Richard Van Dulmen. Munich, Germany: C. H. Beck.

Caspard, Pierre. 1974. "Conceptions prénuptiales et développement du capitalisme dans la Principauté de Neuchâtel (1678–1820)." *Annales ESC* 29: 989–1008.

Engel, Barbara Alpern. 1990. "Peasant Morality and Premarital Sexual Relations in Late Nineteenth Century Russia." *Journal of Social History* 23: 695–708.

Fischer-Yinon, Yochi. 2002. "The Original Bundlers: Boaz and Ruth and Seventeenth-Century English Practices." *Journal of Social History* 35: 683–705.

Flandrin, Jean-Louis. 1977. "Repression and Change in the Sexual Life of Young People in Medieval and Early Modern Times." *Journal of Family History* 2: 196–210.

Rothman, Ellen K. 1950. *Hands and Hearts: A History of Courtship in America.* New York: Basic Books.

Shorter, Edward. 1975. *The Making of the Modern Family.* New York: Basic Books.

Stiles, Henry Reed. 1999 [1871]. *Bundling: Its Origins, Progress, and Decline in America.* Sandwich, MA: Chapman Billies.

YOCHI FISCHER-YINON

Burt, Cyril (1883–1971)

Sir Cyril Lodowic Burt was perhaps the most controversial figure in the history of psychology. Trained in philosophy and the classics, Burt was a polymath who eventually turned to psychology, becoming a pioneer in the field. He was the first psychologist to function in the profession outside a university; the first educational psychologist; the author of a number of important books and articles on juvenile DELINQUENCY, child development, INTELLIGENCE TESTING, factor analysis, and the heritability of mental abilities; and the first psychologist to be honored with knighthood for his contributions. Appointed to the London County Council early in his career, Burt had the opportunity to study children with various backgrounds and abilities, resulting in such classic works as *The Young Delinquent* (four editions from 1925 to 1957) and *The Backward Child* (five editions from 1937 to 1961). He also pioneered in the development of group tests of ability, many of which remained in use for decades. Offered the position as chair of the psychology department at University College, London, in 1931, he turned his prodigious abilities to more technical issues, producing *Factors of the Mind* in 1940, a landmark work in the history of factor analysis, and a number of elegant, theoretical papers on models of heritability, published in the *British Journal of Statistical Psychology,* which Burt edited.

It was his empirical studies of heritability, however, that damaged Burt's reputation after his death. A furious opponent of those who failed to recognize what he regarded as the obvious importance of genetic influence on intelligence, Burt sought to silence the "environmentalists" with studies of kinship correlations of IQ scores. In particular, his 1966 study reporting the similarity in IQ of separated monozygotic twins was recognized as the most important of its kind— the largest ever at the time and the only one that could confirm the model's key assumption of no relationship between the socioeconomic status of the homes in which the separated twins had been raised.

Yet only months after Burt's death, Princeton psychologist Leon Kamin noted a number of anomalies in the data that not only rendered the study worthless but raised accusations of fraud. At first the subject of vigorous debate, these charges were eventually accepted with the appearance of Burt's biography (containing a list of his publications and information about archival material) by the British historian of science L. S. Hearnshaw (1979), who had previously praised Burt's work and delivered the eulogy at his funeral. Provided access to Burt's diaries and personal papers, Hearnshaw concluded that, among many breaches of scientific ethics— including the pseudonymous authorship of a large number of articles and reviews supporting his position—Burt had indeed fabricated the test scores of the monozygotic twins some time after publishing the correlation between their IQs. Although publication of the biography seemed to settle the issue, a decade later two new, independent investigations by British social scientists Robert Joynson (1989) and Ronald Fletcher (1991) sought to reverse the earlier judgment and present Burt as unfairly maligned, the victim of "left-wing" influence on Hearnshaw.

A subsequent study by William Tucker (1997), comparing the characteristics of Burt's sample of twins with those from other well-documented studies, strongly suggests that his data were fictional. However, the debate over Burt has become a surrogate for the nature/nurture controversy, in which neither side is likely to provide evidence the other will find persuasive.

See also: **Age and Development; Child Development, History of the Concept of; Child Psychology; Education, Europe.**

BIBLIOGRAPHY

Burt, Cyril L. 1925. *The Young Delinquent.* London: University of London Press.

Burt, Cyril L. 1937. *The Backward Child.* London: University of London Press.

Burt, Cyril L. 1940. *The Factors of the Mind.* London: University of London Press.

Burt, Cyril L. 1966. "The Genetic Determination of Differences in Intelligence: A Study of Monozygotic Twins Reared Together and Apart." *British Journal of Psychology* 57: 137–153.

Fletcher, Ronald. 1991. *Science, Ideology, and the Media: The Cyril Burt Scandal.* New Brunswick, NJ: Transaction Publishers.

Hearnshaw, L. S. 1979. *Cyril Burt: Psychologist.* Ithaca, NY: Cornell University Press.

Joynson, Robert B. 1989. *The Burt Affair.* London: Routledge.

Tucker, William H. 1997. "Re-reconsidering Burt: Beyond a Reasonable Doubt." *Journal of the History of the Behavioral Sciences* 33:145–162.

WILLIAM H. TUCKER

C

Campus Revolts in the 1960s

A complex set of issues originating in the 1950s formed the background of the most extensive and influential decade of campus revolts in recent history. Cold War militarism, authoritarianism, and colonialism in East and West collided with democratic ideas well in advance of the democratizing potential of even the most open societies. At the same time, social and cultural trends that once concerned a tiny vanguard now became part of mass YOUTH CULTURE. Intellectual liberation was accompanied by sexual trends in conflict with the traditional structure of the family. The scene was set for an assault on conformism and intolerance in its many guises. The coming of age of the BABY BOOM GENERATION, and university institutions ill-accustomed to mass enrollment by students from a variety of social (and in the United States also ethnic) backgrounds provided the context. The momentum necessary for mass mobilization came from a continuous series of confrontations occasionally sparked by minor issues and culminating in the worldwide events of 1967 and 1968.

The United States

Even when universities were not the sites for actual rebellions in this period, they were the sites for organizing mass actions carried out elsewhere. In the United States, student radicalism first focused on the problem of nuclear disarmament; and the Student Peace Union, formed in 1959, staged a march on Washington in 1962. Meanwhile, students participated in the Greensboro sit-ins in February 1960, which helped bring racial segregation in the South to national attention. In the spring the same year, students at the University of California at Berkeley demonstrated against local hearings of the House Committee on Un-American Activities, clarifying the divide between conventional politics and student politics. While the Kennedy administration attempted to tap some of the energy of student activism, in 1960 the more radical students formed Students for a Democratic Society (SDS) led, for a time, by Tom Hayden.

Civil rights and the Vietnam War headed the agenda of the student movement in subsequent years. The Student Nonviolent Coordinating Committee collaborated with the Congress of Racial Equality in the mass registration of African-American voters in Mississippi and other Southern states in summer of 1964. Some of these students, returning to the University of California at Berkeley that fall, rebelled against university administration attempts to curtail political activities on campus. The rebellion, which went on through the end of the term and involved mass meetings, tense negotiations with university and city officials, and clashes with police, set the pattern for similar rebellions elsewhere. While the Berkeley revolt was in progress, SDS began to organize an antiwar march on Washington, D.C., for the following year.

The escalation of the war effort in Vietnam was accompanied by a corresponding increase in the incisiveness of the protest. The 1967–1968 academic year opened with a sit-in at the University of Wisconsin to protest chemical weapons, soon followed by a siege of the Oakland military induction center near Berkeley and a massive march on the Pentagon. In February, demonstrations for civil rights and better facilities to accommodate black students ended in violent confrontations at the University of South Carolina at Orangeburg. Howard University students protesting police violence at Orangeburg demanded a "black university" and other changes at the University of South Carolina at Orangeburg. Similar actions on campus soon afterwards at Bowie State in Maryland were repressed by the police. A combination of civil rights and antiwar issues characterized the April 23, 1968, uprising at Columbia University, the second largest after Berkeley. In August, students demanding troop withdrawal and supporting the antiwar candidacy of Eugene McCarthy for the Democratic nomination staged demonstrations in Chicago, where the party's national convention was being held. Confrontations with police there reached unprecedented levels of violence, helping to guarantee public support for Richard Nixon in the next presidential elections.

Even before the war ended, the tragic showdown between students and police at Kent State in May 1970, where four students were killed, served to discourage further violent confrontations for a time.

Europe

From a European perspective, the Vietnam War seemed to symbolize the worst effects of Western militarization and colonialism, while U.S. student actions off- and on-campus showed the potential for mass mobilization. The pattern of confrontation spread rapidly from place to place. European protests also involved concerns about crowded, impersonal universities and about shaky job prospects, along with ideology that attacked the shallowness of consumer societies and continuing class barriers to university access.

In France, the rift between the De Gaulle regime and student politics had begun to grow in 1960, when the National Students Union (UNEF) declared its support for Algerian independence. In 1963, rumblings of discontent culminated in the Sorbonne explosion, ostensibly sparked by the breakdown of university structures in the face of growing enrollments. After a day of struggle between 10,000 Sorbonne students and 4,500 police, some 300,000 students in the nation's twenty-three universities went on strike, along with half the professors. The following year, on the occasion of a university tour by the Italian president, who was accompanied by the intransigent French education minister Christian Fouchet, University of Paris students and the UNEF organized protests calling for democratic reforms within the universities.

In Britain, protests in 1965 at the London School of Economics were concentrated against white rule in Rhodesia. In Italy, the first protests, centered at the University of Turin in 1965, began with the question of official recognition for a degree in sociology and spread out to include student governance, curricular reform, and the relevance of instructional programs to contemporary affairs. Likewise at Turin, a seven-month occupation of the university buildings in 1967 began by focusing on university issues and broadened out to include social issues of national concern.

In German universities, student anger reached critical mass in June 1967, when students protesting a state visit by the Shah of Iran were subjected to a previously planned police attack involving brutal beatings and the execution of a bystander. About 20,000 students from throughout West Germany attended the bystander's funeral in Hannover on July 9. The Hannover meeting produced a manifesto connecting police brutality to the authoritarian and exclusionary structure of the German government as well as to the general crisis of the university. The meeting and its outcome propelled the student leader Rudi Dutschke and the Sozialistische Deutsche Studentenbund (SDS) into prominence. The same year, students formed the Kritische Universität in West Berlin as an alternative to the increasingly bureaucratized Free University, offering student-taught courses.

The 1968 season of student unrest opened in Czechoslovakia. In January, an unpopular neo-Stalinist secretary of the Czech Communist Party was replaced by Alexander Dubček, who introduced far-reaching reforms, including democratization within the party, freedom of movement, and freedom of expression. Students played an important role in the Prague Spring of discussion and protest that followed, with calls for a continuation of the reforming line and the dissolution of Communist Party rule. Encouraged by the Prague movement, students in Warsaw, Poland, took the occasion of the banning of a nationalist drama to demonstrate for more freedoms and democratization. The brutal repression of both movements would be a point of reference for student leaders in 1989.

In the West, the power of the student movement in Prague inspired actions chiefly motivated by such issues as NATO demands on Europe, the Vietnam War, and the effects of U.S. policies in the Middle East. In Rome, the via Giulia riots led to 250 student arrests. Next came Germany, where Rudi Dutschke was shot and severely wounded during the suppression of the Easter riots in April, crippling the movement. The same month, University of Copenhagen students demonstrated. In France, expulsion of the student leader Daniel Cohn-Bendit from the University of Paris at Nanterre for his organizational activities moved the center of protest once more to the Sorbonne in early May. Police brutality and government intransigence brought the workers over to the side of the demonstrators, and by the end of the month some 10 million French workers were on strike, joining labor issues to the political ones. Only quick concessions by De Gaulle on labor issues, weakening the workers' support for the student movement, avoided political disaster. Inspired by the May events in Paris, outbreaks occurred from June 3 through 10 in Zagreb and Belgrade, Yugoslavia; in Zurich, Switzerland, and in London later that month; and still later in Warwick, United Kingdom, where students discovered documents showing university administrators' investigations into student political activity. Outside Europe, parallel events occurred at the universities in Dakar, Tokyo, Venezuela, Mexico City, and elsewhere.

Significance

The significance of the two-year period of protest is still a matter of debate among social historians. Most agree that the immediate results were less important than the long-term consequences. The movements produced few concrete gains besides more open enrollments (in Europe, vastly expanded enrollments), fewer entrance requirements, and greater accountability of universities toward students as consumers. Over the long term, some studies have blamed the movement for driving the radical leftist fringe toward a drastic change in tactics. Disappointed by the failure of the movement to bring about a general revolution, these studies say, some organizers resorted to forming a tiny vanguard of violent operatives dedicated to subverting the system. Examples include the Red Army Faction in Germany, Direct Action in France, the Red Brigades in Italy, and groups like the Symbionese Liberation Army and the Weather Underground in the United States. On the positive side, studies have suggested that the movement drew attention to the persistent class divisions that seemed to prevent realization of the democratic dream, while the postwar political parties began to abandon ideology in the general enthusiasm that accompanied the economic boom. It drew attention to the negative side of capitalist development and modern technology, emphasizing the limits to economic growth and highlighting environmental concerns.

See also: **Youth Activism.**

BIBLIOGRAPHY

Erikson, Erik H. 1968. *Identity, Youth, and Crisis.* New York: Norton.

Feuer, Lewis S. 1969. *The Conflict of Generations: The Character and Significance of Student Movements.* New York: Basic Books.

Keniston, Kenneth. 1971. *Youth and Dissent: The Rise of a New Opposition.* New York: Harcourt Brace Jovanovich.

Lipset, Seymour Martin, and Philip G. Altbach, eds. 1969. *Students in Revolt.* Boston: Houghton Mifflin.

Statera, Gianni. 1975. *Death of a Utopia: The Development and Decline of Student Movements in Europe.* New York: Oxford University Press.

BRENDAN DOOLEY

Canada

Canada occupies the northern half of the continent of North America. The forty-ninth degree of latitude between the Pacific Ocean and Lake of the Woods forms its southern boundary with the United States. This border follows a series of lakes and rivers through the Great Lakes to the St. Lawrence River. The eastern portion follows an irregular path across the state of Maine to the Bay of Fundy. On the coast of the Pacific Northwest, the state of Alaska separates the northern portion of its most western province, British Columbia, from the Pacific Ocean. In terms of area, Canada is the second-largest country in the world. In terms of population, however, it ranks only thirty-third. The vast majority of Canadians live along the southern edge of the country, in the Great Lakes–St. Lawrence region where Toronto and Montreal, the two largest cities, are located.

The French first colonized Canada, a name derived from the Huron-Iroquois *kanata*, meaning a village or settlement, in the early seventeenth century. Known as New France, it occupied a small territory around the Gulf of St. Lawrence. From the founding of the city of Quebec in 1608 until the ceding of Canada to Britain in 1763, France placed its stamp upon the history of the continent. Canada came into its own in 1791 when the Constitutional Act (or Canada Act) divided

Quebec, then considerably enlarged, into the provinces of Upper Canada and Lower Canada. In 1841 they were joined to form the province of Canada and in 1867 the British North America Act united the province of Canada (divided into Ontario and Quebec) with Nova Scotia and New Brunswick to form "one Dominion under the name of Canada." The remaining provinces and territories followed suit between 1870 and 1999.

The history of Canada's children follows the varied paths of the country itself. Although we do not have any physical evidence, the first child born in what would become Canada was likely a son or daughter of Canada's first inhabitants, who are believed to have come from Asia some 18,000 years ago over a temporary land bridge that joined Siberia and Alaska. The children of the First Nations peoples, the eventual successors of these anonymous early settlers, had to learn the ways of complex societies. The nature of childhood, like adulthood, varied greatly among aboriginal peoples, depending on their location and means of survival. The rhythm of life for fishing people like the Kwakiutl on the western coast, hunters like the Blackfoot on the prairies, or farmers like the Huron in central Ontario differed from each other and, in turn, shaped the unique nature of childhood among First Nations peoples.

First Nations: Kwakiutl and Huron

On the central West Coast, for example, Kwakiutl lived in *numaym*, extended households of up to one hundred people. Midwives assisted at births. Four days after birth the infant was given its first name, and it spent its first year in a cradle carried by its mother. At about a year the child acquired a new name, and boys had their hair singed and holes pierced in their ears and nose. High-status children were later given other names owned by the family. Families marked each new name with a potlatch, or gift-giving ceremony.

Each *numaym* in Kwakiutl society moved several times a year to one of the five to seven resource sites owned by the chief. In a society highly conscious of property rights, children learned the precise locations of fishing and food-gathering sites and winter village locations. By observation and practice, children gradually mastered some of the skills employed at each site: making wood, stone, bone, and metal tools; constructing longhouses, canoes, and watertight wooden boxes; preserving and storing food; carving poles and masks; and weaving aprons, capes and blankets.

By contrast, the Huron in southern Ontario lived in longhouses consisting of an average of six nuclear families. Families had on average three children. Since the Huron were a matrilineal society, girls were particularly prized. Newborn children usually had their ears pierced, and later, beads and other trinkets were hung about the child's neck. The Huron had a large supply of names available to give their children. It is possible that particular names were the property of different clans.

The training of Huron children followed a gendered script. Boys were encouraged to refuse domestic chores and instead were trained to use the bow and spend much of their time outside shooting arrows, hunting and trapping small game, and playing ball games. Girls received a much different training that focused almost exclusively on domestic tasks, such as pounding corn.

As the process of colonization took increasing hold, First Nations families would struggle to adapt to, and often resist, the encroachments of settler society. After an initial period of cooperation with Europeans, First Nations peoples found their way of life increasingly questioned and threatened by notions of European Christianity and racial superiority. This long period of contact and conflict forever altered the ways in which aboriginal peoples raised children and their expectations for the future.

The Colonial Period: New France

When Samuel de Champlain founded a tiny trading post at Quebec in 1608, the colony of New France began to take shape. In New France, *sage femme* (midwives) assisted women in childbirth. During the first few months of life, babies were bound tightly in SWADDLING clothes believed to help straighten their legs and backs. In the absence of either mother's milk or a wet nurse, some infants were given raw cow's milk diluted with river or well water.

As Jacques Henripin's studies show, as many as one in four children in New France died before they celebrated their first birthday. This high rate of INFANT MORTALITY was countered somewhat by an equally astounding birth rate. Peter Moogk has demonstrated that after the birth of her first child and until the age of about thirty-five, a married *Canadienne* bore one child every two years. Families in the colony averaged six children. As infants, children slept in wooden cradles and were often given rattles. At night, a mother would tie a rope to the cradle so she could rock her baby from the warmth of her bed. By around the age of seven, children entered the period known as *tendre jeunesse*, a time in which they were believed to begin to reason for themselves. Along with *tendre jeunesse* came added responsibilities, such as helping with family chores.

The inhabitants of New France, including its children, were constantly ravaged by EPIDEMICS of smallpox, by war, and by infections brought ashore from visiting ships. Nearly half of the adolescents in the colony lost a parent. Illegitimate children were seen as a particular problem in New France, reflecting, in the watchful eyes of church officials, the breakdown of communal social restraints. Between 1701 and 1760, some 1,112 illegitimate children were baptized in what would become the province of Quebec. Guardianship and foster parentage were often the only recourse for single mothers who could not bear the burden of looking after many fatherless children. Often, children as young as five or six were indentured as domestic servants to merchants or to wealthier families. The colonial administration, far from regretting such private arrangements, enforced children's indentures.

In general, few children in the colony were strangers to work. Well before adolescence, children were expected to engage in productive labor. The youngest children helped their mothers amuse infants or took younger siblings for walks. Older children could be expected to help plant crops, cut firewood, or rake hay. In village settings, stables had to be cleaned, chamber pots emptied, firewood gathered and piled, dirty boots scraped, and water fetched. Children generally reached a certain level of competency in their domestic skills, reflected in the fact that, theoretically, those who reached PUBERTY were eligible for marriage (legally twelve for girls and fourteen for boys). Few, however, actually entered into marriage at such a young age.

Childhood among the English-speaking settlers in the eighteenth and early nineteenth centuries was similar to that described for New France. In particular, children were highly valued for the work they performed in settler families. European commentators remarked on the independent and self-reliant character of North American settler children—characteristics more highly developed, they argued, than in children back home.

The Importance of Schooling in the Nineteenth Century

By the nineteenth century, schooling began to slowly overshadow work as the dominant experience in the lives of many children. Most children attended publicly supported schools for a certain number of years, and by around 1900 many children between the ages of five and sixteen years attended consistently. The increasing importance of schooling in the lives of children reflected shifting attitudes emerging in Western Europe and North America regarding childhood as a separate and special stage of life. Children were increasingly seen as needing protection, special attention, and training. This attitude was reflected also in the care of dependent children, for this was the period in which Canadians began to build special institutions to care for ORPHANS and for children whose parents could not, or would not, care for them. Other economic and demographic changes, such as increasing urban populations, improved roads, and innovations in standardized and mechanized work, also had a considerable impact on the changing character of Canadian children's lives.

By the 1920s, professional interest in the quality of CHILD CARE and child rearing brought these private concerns more firmly into the public domain. In anglophone Canada (and somewhat later in francophone Canada), social workers, social activists, public health reformers, and education reformers, predominately white and middle class, worked to shape the nature of childhood. Sometimes for better, but occasionally for worse, they intervened in the home and nursery in order to advocate for more hygienic feeding methods, better public health, safer milk supplies, better outdoor play space, and a more inclusive school curriculum. More often than fathers, mothers were the target of this advice and admonishment.

In order to promote ideal middle-class families, social reform advocates in the early years of the twentieth century outlawed child labor, made school attendance compulsory, and worked for the appointment of truancy officers. They tried to provide support for families that had suffered the loss or incapacitation of a male breadwinner by agitating for workers' compensation and mothers' pensions. The work of mothers in factories or sweatshops was more closely monitored, and hot lunch programs at schools were set up. In the larger cities, such as Toronto, "fresh air" funds were initiated to provide poorer children with a chance to escape the city environment during summer vacations.

The turn of the twentieth century also saw a significant change in the way reformers viewed the efficacy of institutional care—a feature of the nineteenth century—for dependent or troubled children. In an effort to ameliorate the worst evils of the BABY FARMING system, they began ADOPTION services to place illegitimate children into family homes rather than in FOUNDLING institutions and to legitimize children whose parents subsequently married. The Federal Juvenile Delinquents Act set up a system of JUVENILE COURTS, detention homes, and probation officers to focus detection and treatment efforts on the needs of troubled children.

Despite these successes, many other children continued to live under institutional care well into the 1940s and 1950s. Across the country, First Nations children in state-cosponsored residential schools, so-called delinquent children, and children with disabilities often languished in poorly run and supported institutions. As historians continue to discover, many of these children, whether due to racism, powerlessness, official incompetence, or a combination of these and other factors, suffered horrible abuses.

The hardships endured by many children, particularly those outside the dominant white middle class, temper the notion that the history of childhood in Canada has represented an uncomplicated march toward success and improvement. Clearly, however, over the course of the nineteenth century, Canadians by and large strove to improve the lives of the children in their midst.

See also: **Australia; Native American Children; New Zealand; Placing Out.**

BIBLIOGRAPHY

Henripin, Jacques. 1954. *La population canadienne au début du XVIIIe siècle: nuptialité, fécondité, mortalité infantile.* Paris: Presses universitaires de France.

Moogk, Peter C. 1982. *"Les Petits Sauvages*: The Children of Eighteenth-Century New France." In *Childhood and Family in Canadian History,* ed. Joy Parr. Toronto: McClelland and Stewart.

Sutherland, Neil. 1976. *Children in English-Canadian Society: Framing the Twentieth-Century Consensus.* Toronto: University of Toronto Press.

Sutherland, Neil. 1997. *Growing Up—Childhood in English Canada from the Great War to the Age of Television.* Toronto: University of Toronto Press.

Trigger, Bruce G. 1969. *The Huron—Farmers of the North.* New York: Holt, Rinehart and Winston.

MONA GLEASON

Carroll, Lewis (1832–1898)

The English writer, mathematician, Oxford don, and photographer Charles Lutwidge Dodgson is best known by his pen name Lewis Carroll. The eldest son of the Anglican minister Charles Dodgson and Frances Lutwidge, Dodgson spent his early childhood in Cheshire and later in Yorkshire. Educated as a boy away from home at Richmond School and at Rugby, he matriculated in 1851 at Christ Church College, Oxford, which would prove to be his home for the remaining forty-seven years of his life. Dodgson excelled in mathematics and gained a studentship (equivalent to a fellowship at other colleges), which he kept for life, fulfilling the double requirements of remaining unmarried and taking orders in the Church of England, although he proceeded to ordination only as a deacon. He served as a mathematical lecturer at Christ Church from 1855 to 1881 and published mathematical works as C. L. Dodgson. He was also a distinguished photographer. Dodgson achieved fame as Lewis Carroll upon the publication of *Alice's Adventures in Wonderland* in 1865 and its sequel, *Through the Looking-Glass, and What Alice Found There,* six years later. After his two Alice books, Dodgson, as Lewis Carroll, wrote several more books for children, including *The Hunting of the Snark: An Agony in Eight Fits* (1876), *Sylvie and Bruno* (1889), and *Sylvie and Bruno Concluded* (1893).

Although Dodgson has been described often as a retiring Oxford don who only liked the company of children, Dodgson's surviving diaries and letters attest to the strong adult, as well as child, friendships that he cultivated. His adult life followed a steady routine. Dodgson spent term times at Christ Church, where he kept busy with college and mathematical affairs. During holidays he visited the family home, and he spent summers at the seaside. Dodgson made several trips to London every year. While there, he led a busy social life, avidly attending the theatre and art exhibitions and visiting with friends. He also traveled widely around England, again visiting friends and acquaintances. In 1856 Dodgson took up photography, still a nascent technology, and for the next twenty-four years of his life, until he stopped taking pictures in 1880, it played a major role in his social activities. He specialized in portraiture, taking pictures of any adult and child acquaintances whom he could persuade to sit for his camera.

Dodgson was one of a number of Victorian men, such as John Ruskin and George MacDonald, who turned to GIRL-HOOD for creative inspiration and for emotional solace. Some scholars have suggested that Dodgson's fascination with girlhood stemmed from feelings of nostalgia for his domestic childhood home after being sent away to the masculine environment of school. In the twentieth and twenty-first centuries, shifting ideas concerning the relationship between childhood and sexuality have led scholars to debate whether or not Dodgson was in fact sexually interested in young girls. This speculation is fueled, in part, by the uncertain number of photographs he took later in his life of children in the nude. As he grew older, however, Dodgson's "child-friends," as he often termed them, tended more and more to be young women in their teens and twenties.

The Alice Books

The Alice books are seminal to the history of CHILDREN'S LITERATURE, for they liberated the genre from the didactic and moral children's books fashionable at the time. Replete with wit, humor, nonsense verse, and parodies of the illogical conventions of everyday life, the books were immediately popular upon publication, amusing and delighting both children and adults. They have never gone out of print, have been translated into many languages, and have been dramatized and filmed countless times since their first appearance on the London stage in 1886.

The character of Alice originated in Dodgson's close friendship with Lorina, Alice, and Edith Liddell, the eldest daughters of Henry George Liddell, the dean of Christ Church. Dodgson first narrated the adventures of his heroine Alice during a boating trip with the Liddells. Following the trip, Dodgson wrote and illustrated the manuscript *Alice's Adventures Under Ground*, which he gave to Alice Liddell as a Christmas gift. The book chronicles seven-year-old Alice's dream of entering a world populated with bizarre characters, from the March Hare and the Mad Hatter, to the Queen of Hearts and the White Rabbit. Alice went against the grain of previous literary child heroes and heroines. In her, Dodgson created a modern child. She is "curiouser and curiouser" and, throughout her adventures, progresses through many moods, sometimes cheerful, sometimes peevish, as she attempts to make sense of the nonsensical world in which she finds herself.

Dodgson's portraits of children also hold a place in the history of childhood. Rooted in the sentimental bonds of friendship between Dodgson and particular children he knew and entertained, such as the Liddells, both his children's books and his photography depict childhood as playful, informal, intimate, and, above all, separate from adult experience. Dodgson's model has proved relevant throughout the twentieth century and into the twenty-first.

See also: **Photographs of Children.**

BIBLIOGRAPHY

Cohen, Morton N., ed., with the assistance of Roger Lancelyn Green. 1979. *The Letters of Lewis Carroll*, 2 vols. New York: Oxford University Press.

Cohen, Morton N. 1995. *Lewis Carroll: A Biography*. New York: A. A. Knopf.

Kincaid, James R. 1992. *Child-Loving: The Erotic Child and Victorian Culture*. New York: Routledge.

Knoepflmacher, U. C. 1998. *Ventures into Childland: Victorians, Fairy Tales, and Femininity*. Chicago: University of Chicago Press.

Leach, Karoline. 1999. *In the Shadow of the Dreamchild: A New Understanding of Lewis Carroll*. London: Peter Owen.

Mavor, Carol. 1995. *Pleasures Taken: Performances of Sexuality and Loss in Victorian Photographs*. Durham, NC: Duke University Press.

Robson, Catherine. 2000. *Men in Wonderland: The Lost Girlhood of the Victorian Gentleman*. Princeton, NJ: Princeton University Press.

Smith, Lindsay. 1999. *The Politics of Focus: Women, Children, and Nineteenth-Century Photography*. Manchester, UK: Manchester University Press.

Taylor, Roger, and Edward Wakeling. 2002. *Lewis Carroll: Photographer*. Princeton, NJ: Princeton University Press.

Waggoner, Diane. 2002. "Photographing Childhood: Lewis Carroll and Alice." In *Picturing Children*, ed. Marilyn R. Brown. Aldershot, UK, and Burlington, VT: Ashgate.

Wakeling, Edward. 1993–2000. *Lewis Carroll's Diaries, the Private Journals of Charles Lutwidge Dodgson*, 6 vols. Luton, UK: Lewis Carroll Society.

DIANE WAGGONER

Cars as Toys

At sales and auctions of old TOYS, a prominent part is played by cars, vans, buses, and trucks in a variety of shapes and sizes. It is striking how soon after the invention of the motorcar it became the subject of—mostly boys'—fantasies and PLAY. The famous tin toy factories in Nuremberg in Germany produced toy cars in the early 1900s that, because of their delicate nature, did not last very long if used for their intended purpose. They did, however, represent the look of the motorcars of the day very well, producing high, carriagelike vehicles with narrow, spidery wheels and often with a driver and a passenger perched on top. Very soon more detailed products began to be made. Although these were even less suited for the hardships of boys' play in a sandpit, they were very satisfactory from the point of view of correct representation of specific cars, with details such as steering and brakes.

Cars have remained popular toys and over the last century have gone through a number of design phases, from primitive wooden blocks with four wheels to model cars with opening doors and interior details, cars not fit for playing with and out of bounds for younger sisters and brothers. The invention of plastics was a boon to toy producers, enabling them from the 1950s to manufacture relatively strong, correct-looking toy cars in seconds at very low costs. In the early twenty-first century only very young children are willing to accept toy cars that do not look like a specific make and model. Any three-year-old boy will recognize his grandparents' car, and mothers are constantly amazed when their very young sons lecture them on the differences between the various cars they encounter when shopping.

It has long been observed that cars seem largely to belong to the realm of boys, while only a few girls show the same interest. Even if mothers drive as much as fathers, the "car bug" does not seem to infect girls to anything like the same degree as it does boys. While playing with toy cars, boys dream of driving real cars, not in order to move from A to B but just for the sake of driving.

A child's first vehicle—apart from a PRAM—usually is a tricycle, often followed by a pedal car. Before World War II such pedal cars rarely tried to represent any particular model, except for a few very expensive examples, the most prominent of which was the toy car built by the luxury automobile producer Bugatti in about 1930 as a scale model of one of its racing cars. Such cars were powered by a small combustion engine. Since the 1990s producers have tried to make their pedal cars at least recognizable as particular models. The use of plastics has made this easier, just as modern electronic developments have made it possible to build and sell small children's cars powered by electric motors and small, rechargeable batteries at very competitive prices.

For a number of years building model cars was popular with many boys. Some very ambitious characters embarked upon the creation of a model from a piece of raw wood or from sheets of cardboard, but by far the most popular way of doing it was to buy a plastic assembly set to be glued together and painted. Only the most enthusiastic ever finished the project or achieved the desired standard, and it appears that computers have won the battle for children's minds. When model cars are sold today they are mostly finished products. Some are produced to a very high standard and at a comparable price, while mass producers have shown themselves capable of producing and selling model cars of a fairly high quality at fairly low prices. These cars are, however, not really meant as toys for children. The same applies to the small electric-powered cars running along slots in sections of miniature roadway. Like model trains, this increasingly has become the realm of hobby clubs for adults.

Even if many children today spend many hours in front of a video screen, the car is still with them. It now takes the shape of various games. There are countless games on the market in which players can drive cars or motorcycles. Most popular are the ones in which players compete on one or several famous racing circuits or rally courses. To enhance the illusion, joysticks in the shape of a steering wheel are available along with the necessary pedals and gearchange. Only the youngest children prefer the pedal car to a computer thus equipped.

While many children dream of driving their own cars, their practical experience with cars often bores them. Most parents are familiar with hearing the question from the backseat, "Are we there yet?" From the time they are very young, children are placed inside a car and strapped in, unable to do much and confined to looking out of windows that are often too high. Each spring magazines and newspapers swell with good advice to parents planning a driving vacation about how best to keep the children occupied during the many hours of forced inactivity in the backseat.

Since their invention, cars have posed risks for children. They are in a vulnerable position when walking or playing near traffic. Small children are not able to judge the speed of an oncoming car and are generally not in a position to survey what is going on in the street. In many countries much energy is spent on trying to teach children the necessary skills to navigate traffic. In a number of countries, school patrols of older children have been in operation since the 1950s. By creating these patrols authorities tried to solve the problem of not having the manpower to use policemen to guide young children when leaving school. Despite their vulnerability, until they become drivers themselves, most children are involved with cars as consumers of toys and fantasy.

See also: **Boyhood; Construction Toys; Toy Technology.**

BIBLIOGRAPHY

Bloemker, Larry, Robert Genat, and Ed Weirick. 1999. *Pedal Cars.* Osceola, WI: MBI.

O'Brien, Richard. 2000. *Collecting Toy Cars and Trucks.* Iola, WI: Krause.

NIELS JONASSEN

Cassatt, Mary (1844–1926)

Mary Cassatt's paintings of mothers and children revolutionized the genre at the end of the nineteenth century. Cassatt employed formal devices such as pattern and color to explore the sensual nature of the mother-child relationship, and in doing so rejected the overly sentimental approach to the subject taken by many of her contemporaries.

Mary Cassatt was born on May 22, 1844, in Allegheny City, Pennsylvania, the daughter of a wealthy banker. As a child, she spent five years traveling in Europe with her family, living in Paris, Heidelberg, and Darmstadt. At sixteen, she began her art studies at the Pennsylvania Academy of the Fine Arts. After this initial training, Cassatt traveled to Paris where she studied with Jean-Léon Gérôme, Charles Chaplin, Paul Soyer, and Thomas Couture. From 1870 to 1874 she also studied and painted in Italy and Spain. By 1877 Cassatt had settled definitively in Paris, where she remained for most of the rest of her life. Because of her innovative manipulations of space, deft painting technique, and modern subject matter, Cassatt was asked to exhibit with the Impressionists. At the beginning of her career, Cassatt created paintings of independent, modern women much like herself. She also painted several perceptive representations of children, such as *Little Girl in a Blue Armchair* (1878). However, by 1885 Cassatt was painting scenes of mothers and children almost exclusively. Art historians have speculated that Cassatt turned to this theme because of a changing social climate, which encouraged women to paint what were considered appropriate feminine subjects. However, her paintings of mothers and children made Cassatt famous. She was no doubt eager to capitalize on this success by recreating similar compositions. At the same time, Cassatt's most penetrating depictions of mothers and children were contemporaneous with new theories about CHILD PSYCHOLOGY and the relationship between mother and child.

Cassatt's best-known painting of maternal devotion is *The Bath* (1891), which depicts a mother washing her child's foot. Absorbed in this intimate moment, neither mother nor child are aware of the viewer's presence. Cassatt uses an elevated vantage point, dramatic cropping, and contrasting patterns to accentuate the physical closeness of mother and child, as well as to draw attention to the child's naked flesh. In other pictures, such as *Maternal Caress* (1896), bold strokes of paint knit together the child's tiny hand and the mother's cheek, suggesting the organic unity of the two figures. Cassatt also created a series of technically innovative color prints, showing women bathing, dressing, and playing with children. In paintings such as *Mother and Child (The Oval Mirror)* (c. 1899), Cassatt positioned her models in the conventional pose of the Madonna and Child, the mirror behind the figures standing in as a halo. Modern motherhood is therefore equated with divinity in Cassatt's late works.

After falling out of fashion, Cassatt's work was rediscovered by feminist art historians in the 1970s. This initial scholarly reappraisal of Cassatt has led to her increased visibility in museum displays and art history textbooks. Cassatt's images of mothers and children are particularly popular with the general public and are reproduced on a variety of items from posters and note cards to tea towels and tote bags. A 1998 retrospective of Cassatt's work was one of the most well-attended museum exhibitions of that year.

See also: **Images of Childhood; Madonna, Secular; Mothering and Motherhood.**

BIBLIOGRAPHY

Mathews, Nancy Mowll. 1987. *Mary Cassatt.* New York: Abrams, in association with the National Museum of American Art, Smithsonian Institution.

Nochlin, Linda. 1999. "Mary Cassatt's Modernity." In *Representing Women*, pp. 180–215. London: Thames and Hudson.

Pollock, Griselda. 1980. *Mary Cassatt.* London: Jupiter Books.

A. CASSANDRA ALBINSON

Catholicism

The Catholic nature of childhood is often elusive, changes across time and place, and often reflects the broader culture of which it is part. In addition, historians of Catholicism have only recently turned their attention to childhood experiences. Given these important cautions, however, there are some important distinctive ways in which Catholicism has shaped childhood experiences.

The Early Church

Early church sources contain repeated favorable references to people who chose the church over their families, of parents who abandoned their children to lead devout lives themselves, or who gave their children to the church to help build monastic populations. But it is not clear whether this indifference to children reflected more the Christian or the Roman cultural influence. Some historians suggest that these attitudes reflected the dualistic thought of early Christians that contrasted the perfect sacred with the profane secular. Theologians and church officials often characterized things of the world, such as the body and material goods, as inherently evil. Attachment to biological families reflected the power of the world to sway individuals. Christian literature characterized those who chose marriage and parenthood as weaker and more prone to their passions and desires than those who chose childlessness. Christianity clearly praised the latter over the former. But for those Christians who bore and raised children, little evidence suggests a powerfully distinct experience from that of non-Christian families.

The emphasis on the duality of thought did appear to provide a theological or philosophical foundation for child-rearing practices, however. Many debated whether children, and especially "infant" children (those under seven years of age), were capable of sin. Did they suffer from the same earthly passions and enticements that plagued adults? The introduction and adoption of infant BAPTISM during the fourth century suggests that church officials believed that children could sin, and that they inherited original sin. Evidence of severe corporal punishment for childhood transgressions abounds, and suggests a special fervor aimed at ridding children of their proclivity to sin. But here again it is not so clear that these Christian child-rearing practices differed significantly from those of non-Christians. The Christian reasons for severe child-rearing practices might differ, but the practices themselves seem more widely shared. Moreover, some historians see the Church as a strong child advocate. Historian Richard Lyman Jr., for example, writes that the Church insisted that "children had souls, were important to God, could be taught, and should not be killed, maimed or abandoned, and that they were very useful to the self-image of the parents" (p. 90). In short, the Church championed children's interests against cultural pressures to kill, abandon, or devalue them.

Infant baptism had other implications for church sacraments and children. The early Church initiated adults with a process that required great preparation and instruction, and culminated with a ceremony incorporating what Roman Catholics today know as baptism, FIRST COMMUNION, and CONFIRMATION. By the fourth and fifth centuries, however, Roman churches began to baptize infants (relative newborns), and delay the other ritual sacraments until later in childhood. This separation of the sacraments did not spread universally until the eleventh century, however, and did not receive official sanction until the Council of Trent in 1562 asserted that small children need not receive the Eucharist. Throughout the medieval period, the Church stressed Christ's divinity more and more, and therefore discouraged children from receiving communion for fear that they might not fully comprehend the distinction between the Eucharist and normal bread and wine. Catholic theology teaches that the bread and wine actually transform into Christ's body and blood during Mass, and so communion reception is a powerful sacred act. Delaying communion reception until children become older was a recognition that young boys and girls would likely not appreciate the gravity of the ritual. Some places forbade children from receiving communion until age fourteen.

Pope Pius X sought to increase communion reception among all Catholics, and so decreed in 1910 that children should receive first communion at age seven. Only in the twentieth century has this become the common age at which Catholic children receive their first communion. Confirmation too has changed a great deal over the years. Eastern churches continued to link baptism and confirmation, so that Eastern-rite Catholic children were confirmed in their infancy. Western churches saw a variety of practices over time and from place to place, with a more uniform practice emerging only in the twentieth century. Pope Pius X's 1910 decree *Quam singulari* had the effect of making confirmation a sacrament that children received in their ADOLESCENCE, as a mark of spiritual maturity.

Despite the universal practice of infant baptism during the Middle Ages, the Church came to see children younger than seven years old as largely incapable of sin. Manuals for confessors began to focus on the sins of older children. These manuals suggested a great concern for two kinds of sin: theft and sexual activity. One presumes that the church stressed these to parents as well, and urged them to discourage their children from stealing (especially food) and having sex. Italian Catholic child-rearing manuals in the mid-sixteenth to the early eighteenth century recognized the important role that parents played in shaping their children,

First Communion (1896), Pablo Picasso. For Roman Catholics, first communion is not only a sacrament of initiation but a rite of passage signifying attainment of the age of reason. © Estate of Pablo Picasso/Artists Rights Society (ARS), New York. The Art Archive/Museo Picasso Barcelona/Dagli Orti.

and for this reason struggled with two somewhat opposed positions. The first supported and encouraged parents as the surest teachers of their children to help in resisting the allure of sin. The second worried about the parents' roles in discouraging children of mature age from choosing a religious vocation. These guides, commissioned largely for powerful bishops who sought to guide their flocks in their roles as parents, concentrated on urging parents to take on nurturing rather than repressive roles in moving children toward a virtuous life. They saw within children the seeds of virtue, and not primarily the weeds of sin, and they instructed parents to support virtue's growth within their children. Catholic parents following these manuals would have created a nurturing and affectionate environment for their children.

Catholic childhood experiences varied so widely throughout Europe during the nineteenth and twentieth centuries, and the state of research is so young, that it is difficult to make broad and accurate generalizations. But it is reasonable to suppose that as the international Church became more tightly controlled by Rome, and as the local Bishops sought to establish their own power more firmly, the emphasis on obedience to authority heightened. Catholic child-rearing practices may have reflected the greater stress on hierarchy within the family. Some social scientists have suggested as much, though the empirical data are not so strong here. It is clear that many Catholic children felt the difficult transition to industrialization through first-hand experience with mechanized work. Even Catholic ORPHANAGES embraced child labor as a means of covering institutional costs. It is also quite clear that many Catholic children embarked on overseas voyages as their families sought economic improvement in the developing United States.

American Catholicism and Childhood

American Catholic children in the revolutionary and early national period grew up in what historian Jay Dolan has termed the "republican" church. American Catholics in this period sought to align themselves culturally, politically, and socially with the democratic ideals of the emerging nation. Catholics sought less to separate themselves from prevailing norms than to embrace the new ideals that guided social and cultural behavior. Because so few priests and nuns labored in America during this time, the laity provided most of the institutional, community, and liturgical structures for themselves. Children would have grown up experiencing their religious lives in their homes primarily, rather than in a separate sacred space. Their parents provided religious instruction and the opportunities for prayer, reflection, and ritual practices, and they would have emphasized very similar social and cultural ideals to their Protestant neighbors. Though still clearly patriarchal, Catholic families moved with Protestant Americans toward a more democratic family structure that emphasized affection over duty.

Once European Catholics began immigrating to America in large numbers during the early nineteenth century, the nature of American Catholic childhood experiences changed dramatically. Catholics in this immigrant church constructed and lived within a church suffused with a hierarchical and formal institutional presence that sought to shape children's lives profoundly. The family remained the most powerful influence on Catholic children, of course, but the institutional church sought to shape Catholic children much more powerfully than in the republican church. The rise of the separate Catholic school system and the devotional culture that immigrants brought with them and then adapted to the new nation shaped Catholic childhood indirectly through its influence on parents and directly by its pervasive contact with children themselves. With the masses of lay Catholic immigrants to America came thousands of Catholic priests and nuns as well, so that a church that had developed largely independent of clerical presence saw the dramatic growth of the formal institutional structure.

The Catholic school system grew tremendously throughout the nineteenth and early twentieth centuries as an alternative to the emerging public school system. For many Catholics, their experiences in PAROCHIAL SCHOOLS constituted their most extensive immersion in the Catholic world. Catholic bishops stressed to their priests from the middle of the nineteenth century onward the importance of developing parish schools, with the result that parishes built their schools before even their churches. Until the latter half of the twentieth century, Catholic children often sat in classes of fifty to seventy students taught largely by women religious whose own education often ended with the eighth grade. Students learned discipline, deference, obedience, and respect for hierarchy.

Despite extraordinary efforts to educate all Catholic children in parochial schools, at no point in American history did more than half of Catholic children actually attend such schools. Throughout the nineteenth and twentieth centuries, most Catholic children attended public schools with their Protestant, Jewish, and other neighbors. For these Catholics, the most significant institutional encounters came when they joined the Catholic school children in the extensive devotional culture that immersed Catholic children in an extensive array of formal rituals. This powerful devotional experience most distinguished Catholic childhood from others.

Historian Jay Dolan has characterized devotional Catholicism for the century between 1850 and 1950 as exhibiting four key features: a strong sense of sin, a heavy emphasis on ritual, a firm belief in the miraculous, and a keen sense of hierarchy and deference within that hierarchy. Catholic children experienced this culture in the churches when they attended weekly—and sometimes daily—Mass, confession, any of the regularly sponsored novenas (special rituals typically dedicated to particular saints offered each of nine consecutive weeks), benedictions, and adorations. Parishes also sponsored "missions" offered by orders of priests who specialized in generating enthusiasm among the faithful or fallen away. Children here learned of the dangers that the temporal world posed for them, that God would intervene to help deserving believers in their crises, and that they should respect church—and by extension all—authority. Wedded to each other through a vast array of distinctive behaviors, Catholic children developed powerful identities as a unique and religiously privileged group. Though historians disagree on whether these experiences aided or hindered adult Catholic social and cultural success in America, they generally agree that Catholics developed a very powerful Catholic identity with strong boundaries that limited social interaction with others. They lived within an extensive Catholic social and cultural (though not geographical) ghetto that prized otherworldly salvation above all else, and saw as the only means to that aim a life lived apart from the evil influences of the broader materialist society.

In the schools and churches, Catholic institutional representatives had direct and powerful contact with Catholic children. Priests and nuns sought to shape childhood experiences according to religious norms defined largely by church officials. But the children came from families with varying commitments to these ideals, and embraced or resisted the institutional influences accordingly. The Catholic family more than any official church institution most profoundly shaped Catholic childhood, and the Catholic family did not always embrace official church ideals. Because Irish Catholics dominated the clergy, for example, families from other ethnic backgrounds often resisted the institutional influence resolutely.

Immigrant Catholics came to America from a number of different nations and cultures even within their nations of origin. Catholic families often differed from each other in the values that they prized and passed on to their children. It is difficult therefore to make precise conclusions that apply to all Catholics in this period, so readers should be mindful of the great variety of American "Catholic" experiences throughout the period. Some generalizations are warranted, however. In general, Catholic immigrant families in the late-nineteenth and early-twentieth centuries tended to have more children than their native counterparts, and they tended to be quite poor. Catholic children often grew up in large families that suffered great economic hardship. They understood want and deprivation, and they went to work at young ages to help support their families. At a time when middle-class American culture prized domesticity and a pronounced and prolonged childhood experience apart from the emerging market economy, American Catholic children experienced the market intrusion into their lives at very young ages. Catholic parents worked long hours in the mills and mines, and their children filled the tenements and alleys of America's emerging slums. Catholicism both challenged and ameliorated these experiences.

American church officials and the parochial schools by and large emphasized deference to authority, and this included civic and economic authority. In this way the Church pushed children to work within established social structures rather than challenge them. Yet the late nineteenth century saw increasing sanction for social justice efforts that condemned exploitation of the poor and their families. Pope Leo XXIII's 1893 encyclical *Rarem novarum* officially endorsed social justice work and supported demands for family wages, unions, and a just economic order. For the most part, Catholic families remained largely working class through the early decades of the twentieth century. The real changes in Catholic family size and child-rearing strategies came in the latter decades of the twentieth century, and coincided with Catholics' movement to the middle classes.

Social scientists in the twentieth century tell us that American Catholic families in the early decades of the century had more children than Protestants. Catholic FERTILITY RATES then converged briefly with Protestant in the 1930s

before diverging during the baby boom decades of the 1950s and 1960s. The Catholic rate declined faster than the Protestant during the 1970s, however, so that they were largely indistinguishable by the 1980s. Not surprisingly, Catholic attitudes toward BIRTH CONTROL followed similar patterns, so that by the 1970s they differed insignificantly from Protestant attitudes even as church officials persisted in forbidding their use.

A similar pattern seems to have existed for Catholic child-rearing strategies. Social scientists suggest that Catholic parents more than Protestants valued obedience highly and devalued intellectual autonomy in their children throughout much of the twentieth century. The evidence for these claims is less firm than for the birth rate patterns, however. The conclusions depend upon the logical extension of a hierarchical church model into the family, and interpretations of responses on social surveys. Catholic parents presumably discouraged their children from creative explorations of intellectual challenges and from pursuing challenges to authority. By the early 1980s, however, Catholic PARENTING values converged with mainline Protestant perspectives, and conservative Protestant parents appear to have adopted the positions once held by Catholics. At the end of the twentieth century, American Catholic parents differed very little in their child-rearing attitudes and practices from their Protestant neighbors. But the Church continued to support a separate school system, mark childhood milestones with sacraments, and prize child rearing as a laudable vocation. The latter two actions characterized Catholic practices throughout the rest of the world as well. The Catholic influence on childhood experience throughout the western world matters less than socioeconomic class, race, and geography, but it continues to mediate responses to these forces. It does not do so uniformly, though, nor with the same power.

See also: **Islam; Judaism; Protestant Reformation.**

BIBLIOGRAPHY

Alwin, Duane F. 1986. "Religion and Parental Child-Rearing Orientations: Evidence of a Catholic–Protestant Convergence." *American Journal of Sociology* (September): 412–440.

Ariès, Philippe. 1962. *Centuries of Childhood: A Social History of Family Life.* Trans. Robert Baldick. New York: Knopf.

Burns, Jeffrey M. 1978. "The Ideal Catholic Child: Images from Catholic Textbooks 1875–1912." Working Paper Series, Center for the Study of American Catholicism, University of Notre Dame. Spring. Notre Dame, IN: The Center.

deMause, Lloyd, ed. 1974. *History of Childhood.* New York: Psychohistory Press.

Dolan, Jay P. 1985. *American Catholic Experience.* Garden City, NY: Doubleday.

Ellison, Christopher, and Darren Sherkat. 1993. "Obedience and Autonomy: Religion and Parental Values Reconsidered." *Journal for the Social Scientific Study of Religion* 32, no. 4: 313–329.

Hyde, Kenneth E. 1990. *Religion in Childhood and Adolescence: A Comprehensive Review of the Research.* Birminghan, AL: Religious Education Press.

Lyman, Richard B., Jr. 1974. "Barbarism and Religion: Late Roman and Early Medieval Childhood." In *The History of Childhood*, ed. Lloyd deMause. New York: Psychohistory Press.

Martos, Joseph. 1982. *Doors to the Sacred: A Historical Introduction to the Sacraments in the Catholic Church.* Garden City, NY: Image Books.

Mosher, William D., David Johnson, and Marjorie Horn. 1986. "Religion and Fertility in the United States: The Importance of Marriage Patterns and Hispanic Origin." *Demography* August: 367–380.

Shahar, Shulamith. 1990. *Childhood in the Middle Ages.* Trans. Chaya Galai. London: Routledge.

Walch, Timothy. 1996. *Parish School: American Catholic Parochial Education from Colonial Times to the Present.* New York: Crossroad.

Wood, Diana, ed. 1994. *Church and Childhood: Papers Read at the 1993 Summer Meeting and the 1994 Winter Meeting of the Ecclesiastical History Society.* Oxford, UK: Blackwell.

TIMOTHY KELLY

Century of the Child

Ellen Key's (1849–1926) two-volume work *Barnets århundrade* (Century of the child) was published on New Year's Eve 1900. Publication on this date was a conscious choice, for Key believed that the status of children in Western society would undergo a dramatic change in the century to come. Education and upbringing, she believed, would become the focal point of both family life and society.

The book attracted practically no attention in the Swedish press when it was published, though two review articles of some length were written, one of them quite critical. Ellen Key had many enemies—due to her opinions on free love, she was seen as a "seducer of young people." But she also had important friends active in the adult education movement, which was very strong at that time in Sweden. *Barnets århundrade* was incorporated into study circles and lecture series throughout Sweden and its neighboring countries. Key's ideas on upbringing and education soon garnered a growing number of supporters, particularly in Germany. The book was translated into some thirteen European languages, and in Germany it was published in seventeen editions between 1902 and 1926, the year of Key's death.

Barnets århundrade is not only about upbringing and education; it also deals with family structure, gender roles, child labor, and class. It betrays utopian leanings, like most of Key's other writings and lectures. In her analysis, every child has a right to its childhood, which she defines as a period in an individual's early life when he or she bears no economic responsibility. Like many contemporary liberals, Key was very critical of the existence of child labor on a large scale, and her book presents statistical materials about child labor in various European countries. Key saw a close relationship between child raising and gender, and she believed the child's natural place is at home with its mother. She preached that women of all classes must be allowed to stay at home while their children are small, advocating for a kind of home school consisting of children from several families and taught by a female teacher. Older children, she wrote, should attend a common school open to children from all social classes.

A common school and ideas about the "right to childhood" for all children regardless of class were in conflict with the Swedish legal provisions, as well as the economic necessities, of the day. However, Key's ideas anticipated the reforms introduced by the Swedish welfare state established in the mid-twentieth century. In this and many other respects, the twentieth century did indeed prove to be the century of the child, at least in the Western world.

The ideological arguments that motivated Key are significant. Collectivism does not, according to Key, contradict individualism. A school system common to all classes is open to all variety of influences, which in turn stimulates individuality. The ultimate aim of bringing up children is to create "personalities." As its motto, *Barnets århundrade* features a quotation from the German philosopher Friedrich Nietzsche, the prophet of the "superman," a term that Key often employed.

Aside from Nietzsche, Key's ideological individualism can also be traced to her early studies of JEAN-JACQUES ROUSSEAU, whose ideas about the worth of self-made experience, put forward in his book *Émile*, had a significant effect on Key. She was also well acquainted with reformist pedagogy, especially the German educator FRIEDRICH FROEBEL's ideas on "free play" (even though she herself did not care for KINDERGARTEN). She believed that teachers should be mentors, not supervisors. For Key, school was not primarily an exponent of society's rules and morality, but a way of creating individuals who can build a better society.

See also: **Children's Rights; Key, Ellen; Social Welfare.**

BIBLIOGRAPHY

Key, Ellen. 1900. *Barnets århundrade.* Stockholm. Reprint, 1996; New York: Arno Press, 1972.

Lengborn, Thorbjörn. 1976. *En studie i Ellen Keys tänkande främst med utgångspunkt från* Barnets århundrade. (A study in Ellen Key's thought from the perspective of the *Century of the Child.*) Stockholm.

INTERNET RESOURCE

Key, Ellen. *Century of the Child.* Available from <www.socsci.kun.nl/ped/whp/histeduc/ellenkey/key03_b.html>.

RONNY AMBJÖRNSSON

Charivari

Charivari was a ritual used by medieval and early modern Europeans to chastise community members who failed to conform to social expectations, especially sexual ones. Examples included a widow who remarried, a wife who beat her husband, or a couple who failed to have children. In France, where this term originated, teenage boys and young unmarried men usually led such rituals. The youths would parade through the streets, making rough music by banging pots and pans, shouting mocking insults, and sometimes threatening violence. If the victim of the charivari handled the situation effectively by paying off the youths with wine or money, the ritual usually ended peacefully and the matter was laid to rest.

Until the nineteenth century, most Europeans thought charivari was a legitimate and effective means to curb social deviance. It allowed the community to vent complaints against the victims publicly, but it also provided the opportunity for a peaceful resolution of a potentially explosive situation. In premodern communities, the pressures on individuals to conform to social conventions was high, and failure to conform could lead to long-standing feuds between families or among neighbors. Charivari could diffuse such tensions before they became disruptive. The loud and discordant music, the costumes, and the use of effigies to mock the victim signaled that charivari, like the traditional celebration of Carnival each year just before Lent, was a special "time-outside-of-time" in which everyday taboos about speaking out against one's neighbor were temporarily lifted. There was an element of teasing playfulness in charivari, which made it more difficult for the object of the joke to take offense and helped to diffuse the hostility of the shouted insults. For some, the ritual may have also had magical power to eliminate evil spirits from the community. Although the victims of charivari were shamed by the ritual, it also served to re-integrate them into the community. Only in the mid-seventeenth century did some victims begin to see charivari as inherently abusive, and to lodge formal complaints against it with church or city officials.

Charivari offered youths the opportunity to assert some authority over the community expectations about courtship and marriage. By chastising those who deviated from the norm, young men reminded everyone who was allowed to marry whom and under what circumstances. In Sardinia, informal groups of teenage boys often harassed adulterers and remarried widows. They were encouraged to do so by married women, who often provided the boys with the pots and pans needed for the noisy procession. During the seventeenth and eighteenth centuries, English youths participated in rough music rituals against women who beat their husbands and led attacks on local brothels during Lent. Male rivals were also victims of charivari: in 1590, all the male youths living in the German community of Burglen confronted a young man who had just moved into the village with loud music and insults because the outsider threatened their marriage prospects. On occasion, the victims refused to accept the sanction of the charivari, and the situation could get violent. Such was the case in 1668 when Florie Gallo, a Lyon widow who had just remarried, publicly insulted the employer of the young journeymen who had made her the victim of a charivari. Gallo refused to be shamed by her remarriage, and her audacity sparked a second charivari against her, during which her young husband was shot and killed. Overall, charivari encouraged youths to feel that they had a role in enforcing social norms, specifically those that maintained a favorable male marriage market, even as they transgressed everyday norms of violence and propriety while undertaking the ritual.

As early as the sixteenth century, both church and secular authorities formally outlawed charivari. In practice, however, local authorities were often reluctant to prosecute male youth groups that performed the ritual. Unlike gangs in modern cities, early modern youth groups were often sanctioned by city officials to organize Carnival festivities and to participate in Christian religious processions. That these same groups also initiated charivari after a night of drinking at the local tavern did not lead city officials to outlaw them. Even when youths did cross the line and transformed charivari into gang rape or violent assault, judicial officials were often quite lenient when sentencing them. The youths might be kept in prison for a few days or sent to a house of correction to reform their morals, but they were rarely condemned to the usual sentences for assault. Instead, the authorities preferred to turn a blind eye to youthful infractions whenever possible. By not punishing these youths severely, the authorities avoided creating a sub-class of delinquent young men fundamentally alienated from the values of the community.

During the eighteenth and nineteenth centuries, the practice of charivari gradually declined in Europe, first in the cities and then in the countryside. Whereas in the sixteenth century, charivari was both a shaming and a healing ritual, three centuries later state officials and middle-class city dwellers saw the practice as fundamentally disruptive and uncivilized. Literate Europeans began to draw sharper lines between church activities and popular culture and no longer sanctioned youth groups that participated in both. There was also less need for the community to regulate sexual norms because marriage was now unequivocally administered by the state, whose officials reached into every town and village. By the late nineteenth century, newly established police forces patrolled the city streets of Europe, preventing youths from ritually harassing victims but also replacing them as the upholders of social norms.

See also: **Early Modern Europe; Medieval and Renaissance Europe; Rites of Passage; Youth Culture.**

BIBLIOGRAPHY

Boes, Maria R. 1996. "The Treatment of Juvenile Delinquents in Early Modern Germany: A Case Study." *Continuity and Change* 11: 43–60.

Burgière, André. 1980 "The Charivari and Religious Repression in France during the Ancien Régime." In *Family and Sexuality in French History*, Robert Wheaton and Tamara K. Hareven. Philadelphia: University of Pennsylvania Press.

Cashmere, John. 1991. "The Social Uses of Violence in Ritual: Charivari or Religious Persecution?" *European History Quarterly* 21: 291–319.

Davis, Natalie Zemon. 1984. "Charivari, Honor, and Community in Seventeenth-Century Lyon and Geneva." In *Rite, Drama, Festival, Spectacle: Rehearsals Toward a Theory of Cultural Performance*, ed. John MacAloon. Philadelphia: Institute for the Study of Human Issues.

Hammerton, A. James. 1991. "The Targets of 'Rough Music': Respectability and Domestic Violence in Victorian England." *Gender and History* 3: 23–44.

Ingram, Martin. 1984. "Ridings, Rough Music, and the 'Reform of Popular Culture' in Early Modern England." *Past and Present* 105: 79–113.

Schindler, Norbert. 1997. "Guardians of Disorder: Rituals of Youthful Culture at the Dawn of the Modern Age." In *A History of Young People in the West, Vol. 1, Ancient and Medieval Rites of Passage*, ed. Giovanni Levi and Jean-Claude Schmitt, trans. Camille Naish. Cambridge, MA: Belknap.

SARA BEAM

Charter Schools

One of the most popular school restructuring strategies in the early 1990s was the emergence of charter schools. In 1991, Minnesota became the first state to pass legislation enabling the establishment of charter schools. In the ensuing decade, many states crafted charter school laws by taking advantage of unusual bipartisan support in the governor's offices and state legislatures. The schools quickly became popular and the number of charter schools grew from two schools in 1992 to more than 2300 public charter schools in thirty-four states and the District of Columbia serving over 500,000 students by the fall of 2001.

A charter school is a public school that is established by writing a charter, or contract, between a public authorizing entity and an interested party. Depending on the state charter school legislation, authorizing entities could include local education agencies, institutions of higher education, or special chartering agencies formed for the purpose of awarding charters. Charter schools receive public funding based on the number of children enrolled and operate as an independent, legal entity for a specified period. Charter operators must attain predetermined results or the charter may be revoked. In exchange for this level of accountability, charter schools request waivers from many state regulations that may inhibit the attainment of the educational goals set out in the charter.

Charter schools were founded to realize an alternative vision for schooling, to serve a special target population of students, or to gain flexibility and autonomy from local school districts. Charter developers maintained that charter schools could accomplish educational goals more effectively than conventional schools, if they were given the opportunity to operate free from restrictive regulations and had stable financing that could be tied directly to the attainment of educational goals. Waivers were requested for state and local testing mechanisms, personnel regulations, or state or local curriculum mandates; however, regulations for discrimination, health, or safety of children could not be waived.

The initial success of charter schools depended primarily on the accountability that charter authorizing entities placed upon the school. Most charter schools reported that they had measurable goals as part of the charter, and the primary means for accountability included standardized tests and attendance. Charter schools that were closed or lost their charter often did so as a result of financial mismanagement or governance issues rather than deficient academic results. Charter school operators had primary control over most areas critical to school operations, including purchasing, hiring, scheduling, and curriculum in order to achieve measurable results. Charter schools also had a positive impact on school districts where they were implemented. Many districts implemented new educational programs, and/or created new schools with programs that were similar to those in the local charter schools. They also improved public relations and customer service orientation.

The charter schools created during the 1990s tended to be smaller than conventional schools, had grade configurations that were unique, frequently serving students K–8, and generally served a similar demographic of students; however, in some states charter schools served significantly higher percentages of minority or economically disadvantaged students. Charter school developers experienced many start up problems including resource limitations for facilities and operating expenses, and negotiating the extent of legal autonomy from the chartering agency. The federal government assisted the growth of charter schools with the Public Charter Schools Program established in 1994, which provided funding to offset some of the start up limitations including planning and early implementation costs. The federal authorization for charter schools increased from the initial $6 million in 1995 to over $200 million in fiscal year 2002. With continued federal dollars alleviating start up burdens, charter school development increased as proponents replicated successful models and encouraged greater autonomy and accountability of charter schools.

See also: **Education, United States; Magnet Schools; School Choice.**

BIBLIOGRAPHY

Hassel, Bryan C. 1999. *The Charter School Challenge: Avoiding the Pitfalls, Fulfilling the Promise.* Washington, DC: Brookings Institution Press.

Office of Educational Research and Improvement. 2000. *The State of Charter Schools: Fourth-year Report.* Washington, DC: U.S. Department of Education.

JUBAL C. YENNIE

Child Abuse

Child abuse, as a historical subject, is deeply problematic, since the concept of abuse is inevitably relative and can be only very tentatively applied across cultures and across centuries. Parental conduct that would be considered battering abuse in contemporary America might be practiced as routine parental DISCIPLINE in other parts of the world, and would certainly have been regarded thus in past centuries in America itself. Furthermore, by today's Scandinavian standards even limited corporal punishment, as practiced in some American families, might seem abusive, and there is debate about the acceptability of such punishment within the American medical establishment. Without doubt, judging across cultures, Americans would consider as abusive the female circumcision practiced in parts of the contemporary Islamic world or the foot binding that was once practiced in CHINA. The history and sociology of child abuse thus inevitably involve a recognition of relativism in identifying and describing the practice of abuse, inasmuch as abuse can be best understood within a particular social and cultural context.

Defining Abuse in Historical Context

The watershed in the history of child abuse must be dated as recently as 1962, when child abuse received its modern formulation by the American medical establishment as the battered-child syndrome. The mistreatment of children was certainly common in earlier centuries, indeed timelessly imprinted upon European folklore as recorded, for instance, in the tales of the brothers Grimm. Yet that very prevalence ruled out any consensus about what constituted an abusive divergence from the social norm. The article "The Battered-Child Syndrome," by C. Henry Kempe, Frederic N. Silverman, and colleagues thus marked the end of the ancien régime in the history of child abuse, separating the epochs before and after 1962. Thereafter it was the medical establishment, with its scientific credentials, that defined child abuse according to the evidence of medical examination, including the evidence of radiology, revealing the battered bones of young children. At the same time, the scientific conclusions of "The Battered-Child Syndrome" further implied a set of sociological revelations: first, the general prevalence of abuse in a supposedly enlightened society, and second, the hitherto unacknowledgable circumstance that abuse was not usually the work of evil strangers, or even evil stepparents, but was largely practiced by natural parents upon their own children.

Crucial for the theoretical understanding of the history of child abuse was the history of childhood itself. In 1960 the

French historian PHILIPPE ARIÈS proposed the controversial theses that the concept of childhood varied and developed in different historical contexts and that modern childhood was, in some sense, "discovered" in the Renaissance; only then, according to Ariès, did European culture and society become fully attuned to the distinctive character of childhood, to its fundamental difference from adulthood. The notion of fundamental difference between childhood and adulthood is essential for understanding child abuse, since the concept of child abuse assumes that there is a distinctive standard for the treatment of children and the violation of that standard defines abuse.

The relevance of the battered-child syndrome for the centuries before 1962 concerns not only the prevalence and intensity of corporal punishment but also the changing norms of punishment that might have made beating seem excessive to contemporaries. Historians such as Lawrence Stone and Philip Greven have described a culture of corporal punishment in early modern England and colonial America that is extreme by modern standards but seemingly normal in the contemporary contexts. Beatings at school constituted routine pedagogical discipline in EARLY MODERN EUROPE, England, and the United States, and this continued into modern times, while the punishment of children during the Reformation and Counter-Reformation was prescribed according to differing religious perspectives on the fundamental innocence or sinfulness of children. The well-known principle of not sparing the rod for fear of spoiling the child was not evidence of widespread abuse, but indicated rather that beating was considered an appropriate measure in the rearing of children. In fact, the Protestant culture of corporal punishment still flourished in America in the late twentieth century, prescribed in such fundamentalist publications as *God, the Rod, and Your Child's Bod: The Art of Loving Correction for Christian Parents* (1981).

While social practice in early modern families generally involved some degree of corporal punishment and some variation in judging the appropriate degree of intensity, landmark ideological developments in the writings of such philosophers as JOHN LOCKE and JEAN-JACQUES ROUSSEAU began to transform the earlier religious controversy concerning children's sinfulness and the application of the rod. Locke, in *Some Thoughts Concerning Education* (1693), advocated less beating and preferred a penal strategy of inducing shame, while Rousseau, who celebrated the innocence of humanity in the state of nature, was correspondingly convinced of the innocence of children. "Love childhood," he enjoined his readers, in *Émile* in 1762, outlining a new pedagogy so sensitive to the child's supposed nature that conventional education appeared almost in itself to be something abusive. Rousseau believed that childhood could be violated by inappropriate treatment, and that the child could be accordingly robbed of childhood; such ideas were essential to the formulation of a modern concept of abuse. Stone argues that a whole new culture of child rearing emerged in eighteenth-century England, a culture of coddling, based on indulgence of children and childhood. The controversy surrounding SWADDLING was characteristic of the century, for Rousseau declared this conventional practice to be cruel and oppressive, in some sense abusive of the child's freedom of the limbs; therefore he called for liberation from swaddling and enlightened parents heeded his appeal.

Locke's preference for shame over corporal punishment eventually pointed the way toward a modern conception of punishment for children in which excessive beating would appear as abusive. Yet considering the twentieth-century French philosopher Michel Foucault's argument on the historical transition from the exemplary punishment of criminals to a social system of discipline and surveillance, one might conclude that children too were subject to the pressures of more comprehensive discipline even when they were ultimately spared the rod. In this sense the crystallization of the concept of child abuse would have occurred at the historical crossroads when beating was no longer regarded as the most efficacious method of pedagogy or discipline.

Innocence and Abuse

The secular standard of children's innocence, dating from the late eighteenth century, suggested whole new arenas for reconsidering what was appropriate treatment of children. The attribution of innocence implied the possibility of violation, and the necessity of protection. The British Parliament passed legislation to protect chimney sweeps in 1788, and in 1789 the poet William Blake conjured their condition in his *Songs of Innocence*. During the nineteenth century child labor laws were enacted in England, America, France, and Germany, with rhetorical emphasis on the need to protect children from exploitation. That concept of exploitation implicitly suggested the notion of child abuse.

Innocence also implied the need for sexual protection, and beginning in the late eighteenth century, according to the research of historian Georges Vigarello, the prosecution of rape in France began to reflect a new and particular disapproval of the rape of children. Though in the eighteenth century Casanova had sex with girls as young as eleven and cheerfully boasted about it in his memoirs, by the late eighteenth century in Casanova's Venice, sexual relations between adult men and prepubescent girls could also be formulated with emphatic disapproval as the violation of innocence. Nevertheless there was neither a legal nor a sociological framework for identifying such conduct as sexual abuse.

A public breakthrough occurred in the late nineteenth century when the London journalist W. T. Stead exposed the prevalence of CHILD PROSTITUTION in the Maiden Tribute scandal of 1885, publishing his revelations, for instance, under the headline, "A Child of Thirteen Bought for Five Pounds." In response to this scandal, the age of sexual consent in England was raised from thirteen to sixteen. Public horror at child prostitution pointed toward the eventual public recognition of sexual abuse, and, in the late nineteenth century, psychiatry further focused on the issue by diagnosing the perpetrators. The nineteenth-century German psychiatrist Richard von Krafft-Ebing, in his *Psychopathia Sexualis* described the "psycho-sexual perversion, which may at present be named erotic paedophilia (love of children)," which he defined, according to German and Austrian law, as the "violation of individuals under the age of fourteen" (p. 371).

The recognition of sexual abuse in its domestic context was almost achieved by SIGMUND FREUD when he arrived at the "seduction theory" in 1895, ascribing hysteria to the sexual victimization of children by adults, especially their fathers. In 1897 Freud reconsidered this theory, and decided that his patients suffered only from fantasies of sexual violation as children. This conclusion suggests how difficult it was for even the most intellectually adventurous Victorians to confront the concept of child abuse as a common sociological syndrome. In 1919, when Freud wrote the article "A Child is Being Beaten," he discussed this scenario entirely as a matter of fantasy.

Yet in the late nineteenth century, there were established philanthropic societies for intervention on behalf of children neglected or mistreated by their parents. The model, ironically, was the Society for the Prevention of Cruelty to Animals, founded in America in 1866 and followed afterwards by SOCIETIES FOR THE PREVENTION OF CRUELTY TO CHILDREN in America and England in the 1870s and 1880s. A "Children's Charter" in England, in 1889, attempted to formulate the rights of children. Inevitably, the philanthropic societies became the agents of Victorian middle-class intervention in the family life of the poorer classes, for the mistreatment of children was more readily attributed to the poor.

Throughout the Victorian age, dating from the first serial installments of Charles Dickens's OLIVER TWIST in 1837, at the very beginning of Victoria's reign, the figure of the menaced and mistreated child became a sentimental totem, and the brutalization of childhood's innocence exercised an almost prurient fascination upon the Victorian public. The preservation of innocence became such an obsession in nineteenth-century society that the consequences were often oppressive to the children themselves, and indeed abusive by the modern standard. The most striking instance was the medical preoccupation, all over Europe, with the prevention of MASTURBATION, as parents were encouraged to employ with their children painful precautions, contraptions, and punishments. In 1855 a French governess, Celestine Doudet, was discovered to be torturing five English sisters, with the approval of their father, in order to prevent them from masturbating. She was tried and imprisoned when one of the children died. Similarly, in Vienna in 1899, sensational cases of battering abuse came before the public only when mistreatment actually brought about the children's deaths.

The crucial technological development that brought about the twentieth-century revolution in the recognition of battering abuse was the X ray. Radiology played a pioneering role in exploring the hidden presence of abuse in American families, beginning in 1946 with an article by John Caffey entitled "Multiple Fractures in the Long Bones of Infants Suffering from Chronic Subdural Hematoma." With such crucial discoveries being made in the medical profession, it was, eventually, in the field of PEDIATRICS that the evidence of radiology was synthesized and assimilated, culminating in the publication of "The Battered-Child Syndrome" in 1962. Recognition of the prevalence of a child abuse was a challenge both for the medical profession and for society at large. The authors of "The Battered-Child Syndrome" remarked, "There is reluctance on the part of many physicians to accept the radiologic signs as indications of repetitive trauma and possible abuse. This reluctance stems from the emotional unwillingness of the physician to consider abuse as the cause of the child's difficulty" (pp. 18–19). Yet, by the end of the decade, child abuse laws were adopted in all fifty states, and departments of social services all over America were receiving reports and making interventions in domestic scenarios for the protection of children. In the 1970s the national incidence of child abuse was estimated at 500 cases annually for every million Americans. In 1977 an International Society for the Prevention of Child Abuse and Neglect was established, with backing from the United Nations Children's Fund (UNICEF) and the World Health Organization, for promoting and coordinating awareness of these issues all over the world.

Preventing and Prosecuting Child Abuse

Recognizing the problem has not led to automatic or simple solutions. The most emphatic interventions—that is, the removal of children from the parents' home and sometimes even the complete termination of parental rights—may have disastrous consequences for the child. Depriving the child of parents, even violent and abusive parents, can only be vindicated by the provision of compassionate FOSTER CARE, which is always, inevitably, in short supply. Indeed, institutional foster care sometimes exposes abused children to new forms of abuse. In December 2002 the *New York Times* interviewed an adult who had been victimized as a child: "He spent six months with his mother, months when he was abused and beaten again, he said, before being sent to another foster home. . . . He said he was sexually and physically abused in several foster homes."

Even the mandated reporting of suspected abuse has turned out to be an unreliable instrument. Especially the category of neglect, which, according to one pediatric account, encompasses "lack of supervision" and "chaotic life styles,"

encourges social workers to make rather subjective judgments, especially concerning poor families (Cantwell, p. 183). Child abuse in the middle classes, however, remains more easily concealed and less readily suspected. In 1987, New York City, and most of America, was rocked by the sensational coverage of the savage abuse, resulting in death, of Lisa Steinberg, age seven, the daughter of Joel Steinberg, a lawyer, and Hedda Nussbaum, an editor.

Because some of the categories of abuse are inevitably vague, and because American consciousness of abuse changed so rapidly in the course of a generation, it became more and more common in the 1980s for adults to define themselves as victims of abuse in their own childhoods. The category of emotional abuse was considered alongside physical abuse, and some spankings, in memory, seemed like batterings. Furthermore some therapists encouraged their patients to "recover" memories of abuse that had been forgotten or repressed. This was often sexual abuse, sometimes satanic sexual abuse, and in some therapy practices it turned out, implausibly, that 100 percent of patients had been victims of childhood abuse. Issues of sexual abuse also led to devastating legal tangles in the great day care scandals of the 1980s, at the McMartin Preschool in California and the Fells Acre Day Care Center in Massachusetts. At first these cases seemed to suggest hitherto unsuspected depths of child abuse hidden away in the world of institutional day care, but the questionable legal procedure surrounding the children's testimonies led to doubts about their reliability, resulting in mistrials and overturned convictions.

Following the rape and murder of seven-year-old Megan Kanka in New Jersey in 1994, and the subsequent revelation that the crime had been committed by a man who had previously been convicted, a national movement emerged to establish a registry of sex offenders. The determination to identify convicted sexual criminals in local communities, culminating in the passage of "Megan's Law" in New Jersey in 1996, reflected the anxiety in American society about child abuse. Though the abused child can sometimes be identified through bruises or burns by a doctor or a teacher, the abusive adult can rarely be distinguished from others in the community.

A full generation after "The Battered-Child Syndrome" was first published, there is general public recognition that various forms of child abuse are pervasive—but also an awareness that abuse may remain largely concealed within the domestic walls that protect family privacy. Furthermore, just as treatment of children in the historical past may appear abusive by current standards, so there is also a divergence of perspectives within contemporary society about what exactly constitutes abuse. For all these reasons, child abuse is a social problem that has been recognized but by no means resolved. This was emphatically demonstrated at the very beginning of the twenty-first century with the scandalous revelations of pedophile predation by Catholic priests in American parishes during the previous several decades. It was discovered that the church hierarchy had been willfully looking the other way, suppressing the scandal of abuse and reassigning pedophile priests who simply continued their abusive conduct in new communities. Public outrage, which eventually resulted in the resignation in December 2002 of Cardinal Bernard Law, the archbishop of Boston, marked a new level of American commitment to the prosecution of child abuse as an unmitigated social evil.

See also: **Age of Consent; Child Labor in the West; Children's Rights; Incest; Megan's Law(s); Pedophilia; Recovered Memory; Violence Against Children.**

BIBLIOGRAPHY

Ariès, Philippe. 1962. *Centuries of Childhood: A Social History of Family Life.* Trans. Robert Baldick. New York: Knopf.

Behlmer, George. 1982. *Child Abuse and Moral Reform in England, 1870–1908.* Stanford, CA: Stanford University Press.

Cunningham, Hugh. 1995. *Children and Childhood in Western Society Since 1500.* London: Longman.

DeMause, Lloyd, ed. 1974. *The History of Childhood.* New York: Psychohistory Press.

Greven, Philip. 1977. *The Protestant Temperament: Patterns of Child-Rearing, Religious Experience, and the Self in Early America.* New York: Knopf.

Greven, Philip. 1990. *Spare the Child: The Religious Roots of Punishment and the Psychological Impact of Physical Abuse.* New York: Knopf.

Kantwell, Hendrika. 1980. "Child Neglect." In *The Battered Child,* 3rd edition, ed. C. Henry Kempe and Ray Helfer. Chicago: University of Chicago Press.

Kempe, C. Henry, and Ray Helfer, eds. 1980. *The Battered Child,* 3rd ed. Chicago: University of Chicago Press.

Kempe, C. H., F. N. Silverman, B. F. Steele, W. Droegemueller, and H. K. Silver. 1962. "The Battered-Child Syndrome." *Journal of the American Medical Association* 181: 17–24.

Krafft-Ebing, Richard von. 1998. *Psychopathia Sexualis.* Trans. Franklin Klaf. New York: Arcade.

Masson, Jeffrey. 1984. *The Assault on Truth: Freud's Suppression of the Seduction Theory.* New York: Farrar, Straus, Giroux.

Miller, Alice. 1984. *Thou Shalt Not Be Aware: Society's Betrayal of the Child.* Trans. Hildegarde and Hunter Hannum. New York: Farrar, Straus, Giroux.

Shorter, Edward. 1975. *The Making of the Modern Family.* New York: Basic Books.

Sommerville, C. John. 1982. *The Rise and Fall of Childhood.* Beverly Hills, CA: Sage.

Stone, Lawrence. 1977. *The Family, Sex, and Marriage in England, 1500–1800.* New York: Harper and Row.

Vigarello, Georges. 2001. *A History of Rape: Sexual Violence in France from the 16th to the 20th Century.* Trans. Jean Birrell. Malden, MA: Polity Press.

Wolff, Larry. 1988. *Postcards from the End of the World: Child Abuse in Freud's Vienna.* New York: Atheneum.

LARRY WOLFF

Child Care

IN-HOME CHILD CARE
  Amy Harris-Solomon
INSTITUTIONAL FORMS
  Kerstin Holmlund
UNITED STATES
  Geraldine Youcha

IN-HOME CHILD CARE

The phrase *child care* is a broad term used to describe any number of arrangements or settings in which the primary responsibility is caring for a young child. There are as many different settings as there are definitions of quality in child care. The number of young children under the age of five who were cared for a portion of their day by adults other than the custodial parents increased dramatically from the early 1980s to the early 2000s largely because of the increase in the number of mothers who had joined the workforce. According to the 2002 Quality Counts survey conducted by *Education Week* newspaper, approximately six out of every ten children, or 11.9 million children, ages five and younger were being jointly cared for by parents and early childhood educators, other child-care providers, relatives, or others.

While many parents may prefer to stay home with their infants or young children, this is not a financial option for most. Whether by choice or necessity, the majority of mothers are now working. Approximately one out of four young children are in a single parent home. Parents are forced to make choices for their children, and all too often choices are driven by the financial resources of the family, the availability or location of child care, hours of operation, or other factors not necessarily associated with either quality of care or parent's preference for care. In addition to paid care both in and out of the home, many families rely on the assistance of family members, older siblings, neighbors, or friends to help care for their young children.

There are several types of child care available to families of young children. In-home care is one type of care families choose that allows the child or children to remain in their home environment. In this model of care the provider either comes to the home or lives part- or full-time in the child's home with the family. Frequently a relative is the person providing the care, and in this situation it is not required that a child-care license be obtained. In-home day care is one of the only unregulated forms of child care in existence today. Other forms of child care, such as family day homes, center care, and corporate child-care centers, have become highly regulated systems with states determining how programs are evaluated and monitored and by whom.

Historical View of In-Home Child Care

Mothers have not always had the primary role of caring for their children in their home. Over the years children have been cared for at home by a variety of caregivers including, but not limited to, servants, slaves, wet nurses, and mammies. Even in recent history the more modern views of mothers staying at home to care for the children while the fathers work was largely a myth. Many homes of middle income or above continued to have black domestic servants as late as the 1950s.

Society's views on childhood have changed over the years as well, making it difficult to compare and contrast care provided in the home. In today's society children are cared for at least until they reach the legal adult age of twenty-one, sometimes even beyond that while they attend college or graduate school and get settled into a career. Dating back to the colonial times some children worked in the fields as early as age seven. Their childhood ended at this time, and they began to take on adult-like responsibilities of APPRENTICE-SHIPS, working in the home or in the fields. Wealthier families could pay for their children to study according to their inclinations, whereas children who came from poor environments had little say in where they went. Regardless of whether a parent paid for their child to go study with someone or a child was sold into an apprenticeship, the overall responsibility for their care at that time was with the caregiver or master. There was little formal schooling for young children outside of the home, therefore the work they learned through their apprenticeships was critical for their future livelihood.

Servants and Slaves

According to Geraldine Youcha, author of the 1995 book *Minding the Children*, it is hard to detail accurately what the day-to-day child-care arrangements were like in the United States during the days of SLAVERY and the colonial period. The slave mother was not expected to take care of her children, as she was required to work in the fields or on the plantation. Children were the property of the plantation owners, and many of the children of slaves were thought to have been fathered by the masters. Children of slaves were sometimes cared for by the wife of the plantation owner, older slave children, or older slaves, or were left to fend for themselves during the long day when the mother was working. Those children who were born to slaves became slaves themselves.

Some black mothers became what were termed *mammies*. These women cared for the white children on the plantation and were in charge of many household domestic matters. These women upheld the high standards of the family and enforced the values and beliefs of the family with the children. The mammy's duty of caring for the children and the home is similar to the current role of the day nanny, with a major difference being that the mammies sometimes served as wet nurses to the white infants as well.

Domestic service was a common occupation for young girls during the nineteenth century. The number of servants a household had was generally related to the family's income. Those who had more income had more servants and a wider variety of servants. The servants who took care of young children were considered lower servants, and these included the nursemaids and children's maids.

The Impact of Industrialization

For many urban families, the Industrial Revolution raised new issues regarding child care in the home. Most obviously, some families depended on work by mothers as well as fathers outside the home, which greatly complicated child care. Most mothers, even in the working class, ceased outside work upon marriage or the birth of the first child, but this was not always possible. Children were often cared for by other relatives. The number of grandmothers living with younger kin increased, in part because of the need for child care.

The spread of educational requirements also changed child-care patterns. Schools provided care for children, reducing the focus on the home after infancy. But schools also removed SIBLINGS who might help with child care in the home—though some groups tried to keep girls out of school in part because of their child-care potential. Falling birthrates, by the later nineteenth century, also reduced siblings as a source of in-home care.

In the twentieth century, some of these arrangements continued, although the emphasis on a single wage-earner household by labor unions and other social policies allowed a period in which women most frequently took care of their own children, at least at times when their husbands were fully employed. During World War II (1939–1945), when women with young children took many jobs associated with war industries, employers and even the federal government sometimes provided child-care facilities.

Twentieth- and Twenty-First-Century Options for In-Home Child Care

After the 1970s, as women moved strongly into the labor force, families with low to moderate income levels often chose in-home care with grandparents caring for multiple children of varying ages at one time. Higher income families had the added option of hiring an au pair or a nanny to provide in-home care. While there are no licensing requirements for being an au pair or a nanny, there are interview processes and agencies that can assist with the hiring of these types of child-care workers.

An au pair is a foreign national living in a country specifically to experience life in that country. According to the American Institute of Foreign Policy, a legal au pair is a person who has contracted to come to the United States from a foreign country for a set amount of time, often one year. The term *au pair* means "equal" or "on par." An au pair lives with a family, receives room and board in exchange for child-care or baby-sitting services. The au pair may or may not be a person with any background in child development.

Nannies also provide child care in the family home, generally as live-ins. Typically these people provide more than routine child care, as they often assist in the daily routines of running a household—running errands, shopping, doing laundry, fixing meals, cleaning house, and performing other duties. The term *nanny* comes from the term used to describe a woman who lived with a wealthy British family and cared for the children. Nannies in British families were strictly to provide child care, as other servants took care of routine household chores. Nannies in the United States are generally young women, are often illegal immigrants, and typically have simple household responsibilities in addition to the primary role of caring for the children. The majority of larger cities in the United States have agencies that assist families in locating nanny care that meets their particular needs. Nanny care, like other types of in-home care, has recently been challenged by the growth in center care and other forms of out-of-home child care that are now available.

A growing number of GRANDPARENTS are taking care of their young grandchildren. Data from the U.S. Bureau of the Census from 2002 indicated that grandparents were taking care of approximately 21 percent of all preschoolers who were in some type of child-care arrangement. This type of care may provide more economic advantage for the family because there may be minimal or no cost associated with it. The grandparent provides an emotional connection for the child and is in the position to support the values of the family, provide enriching family history, share stories, and pass traditions down from one generation to the next.

Families are also becoming more creative in their work schedules, with fathers and mothers often splitting their days so they work alternate shifts in order to continue caring for their children in the home. This dependence on family members continues a long tradition of assistance from among kin and children. If the mother works during the day, the father becomes the primary caregiver in the home, and the roles are reversed once the mother returns home from work, with the father working an alternate shift.

BABY-SITTERS differ somewhat in their role as in-home caregivers. Often a baby-sitter provides short-term care for a specified number of hours and is not the primary caregiver outside of those specified hours or days. Many are still students who work part-time. They may be one of many baby-sitters a family calls on, and often their care depends on their own activities, school schedules, and time. Their influence on children can nevertheless be significant. Baby-sitters can range in age from a young TEENAGER to an elderly acquaintance, and their skills and experiences are as varied as their ages. There are baby-sitting courses available through local agencies such as the Red Cross, the YMCA, local colleges, and other youth or civic organizations.

The care of the child or children is dependent on the provider in much the same way as that of a parent. There are no overall standards related to fee structure, roles, and responsibilities especially in the case of relative caregivers. Payment for services is dependent on such factors as whether the person providing care is also receiving room and board, whether the person is a family member doing child care as a favor or as a family obligation, and what other benefits the caregiver is receiving. Commercial in-home care requires licensing if more than one family of children is being cared for. But some families create cooperative care arrangements with an exchange of services in a given rotation.

BIBLIOGRAPHY

Berry, Mary Francis. 1993. *The Politics of Parenthood: Child Care, Women's Rights, and the Myth of the Good Mother.* Harmondsworth, UK: Penguin.

Bredekamp, Sue, ed. 1987. *Developmentally Appropriate Practice in Early Childhood Programs Serving Children from Birth through Age Eight*, expanded ed. Washington, DC: National Association for the Education of Young Children.

Cooper, Sonja. 1999. *Child Care: A Parent's Guide.* New York: Checkmark Books.

Ehrich, Michelle. 1999. *The Anxious Parent's Guide to Quality Childcare.* New York: Penguin Putnam.

Fein, Greta, and Alison Clarke-Stewart. 1973. *Day Care in Context.* New York: Wiley.

Gardner, Marilyn. 2002. "Meet the Nanny—'Granny'." *Christian Science Monitor* August 1. Also available from <www.csmonitor.com/2002/0801/p01s01-ussc.html>.

Helburn, Suzanne, and Barbara Bergmann. 2002. *America's Child Care Problem: The Way Out.* New York: Palgrave Publishing.

Lally, J. Ronald, Abbey Griffin, Emily Fenichel, et al. 1995. *Caring for Infants and Toddlers in Groups: Developmentally Appropriate Practice.* Washington, DC: Zero to Three.

National Research Council. 1990. *Who Cares for America's Children?* Washington, DC: National Academy of Sciences.

Peisner-Feinberg, Ellen S., Margaret R. Burchinal, Richard M. Clifford, et al. 1999. *The Children of the Cost, Quality, and Outcomes Study Go to School: Executive Summary.* Chapel Hill: University of North Carolina, Frank Porter Graham Child Development Center.

Quality Counts 2002 Executive Summary. 2002. "In Early Childhood Education Care: Quality Counts." *Education Week* 17: 8–9.

Youcha, Geraldine. 1995. *Minding the Children: Child Care in America from Colonial Times to the Present.* New York: Scribner.

INTERNET RESOURCE

Carnegie Corporation of New York. 1994. "The Quiet Crisis." Available from <www.carnegie.org/starting_points/startpt1.html>.

AMY HARRIS-SOLOMON

INSTITUTIONAL FORMS

Preschools are an inherent aspect of welfare policies in many countries, but from time immemorial the upbringing of children of preschool age has been deemed a duty for the family. The formation of child-care strategies has been influenced by the social position of men and women, as well as societal value judgements, norms, and regulations. Any history of child care services should, therefore, consider the varying social situations of which it has been a part. The history of child care varies as well according to the social structures in different countries. Nevertheless, two distinct paths of development can be traced. The first has a social focus (care) and is linked to charity, while the second emphasizes pedagogical activities (education). The differences between these two types of institutions are still evident in the early twenty-first century.

Child Care Becomes an Issue for Poor Relief

Society faced a radical change as it underwent the transition from an agricultural to an industrialized capitalist society during the 1800s, and this affected people's living conditions. Wage earning became common and production was moved from the homestead to factories and workshops. This, in turn, created a need for child care on the part of working parents. Many children were left to look after themselves or each other because of a lack of organized child care. According to accounts beginning in the early 1800s, social unrest was an established factor in the social fabric of countries such as Germany, France, England, Sweden, and the United States. Women were actively involved in finding solutions for the problems society faced, and this also affected the social scene.

In the public debate on social problems, the working class and their families were the prime target. The wealthier classes agreed that the prevalence of street children was a central problem. Private initiatives, associations, and authorities did their best to solve these SOCIAL WELFARE problems. In England, for example, the Infant School Society was started in 1821; in Germany the KINDERGARTEN movement developed; in the United States the NEW YORK CHILDREN'S AID SOCIETY was established in 1850; and in Sweden members of the bourgeoisie organized themselves to establish infant schools, asylums, and crèches.

Child Care for the Workers' Children

During the 1800s, in many parts of Europe and the United States, there emerged institutions whose goal was providing care for workers' children. These went under different names, including child crib, crèche, cradle-school, infant school, and workhouse, but had similar ambitions, including training and reform for young offenders and activities to keep children out of trouble in their free time.

The infant school. Robert Owen was known as the creator of infant schools, which started in 1816 in Scotland. The infant school was designed as a disciplinary measure for street children, and looked after children until the age when the compulsory education system could take over. They spread rapidly throughout Europe and the United States, where people committed to social change tried to incorporate them into their respective social systems. These schools were supposed to help solve urban problems. In England, infant schools were viewed as an ideal means of dealing with the vicious effects of industrialization. Infant schooling took a different turn in the United States. During the 1830s and 1840s an internal division arose within the movement, resulting in its decline. In France, Johann Friedrich Oberlin had already established schools for infants at the end of the 1700s, based on a social welfare perspective. The first French infant school was opened in 1828, and was eventually incorporated into the French *école maternelle*.

The workhouse. For the poor and their children throughout Europe and the United States, there was always the alternative of the workhouse. These institutions were established at various times in different countries, depending largely on when industrialization emerged there. In England, this occurred at the end of the 1700s and beginning of the 1800s. In the United States it took place during the first half of the nineteenth century, and in Sweden it did not occur until the second half of the same century. It was assumed that children in workhouses could be isolated from the unsuitable influence of their impoverished parents. The children were to be provided with moral upbringing, a simple form of education, and above all, they were to be put to work. By working, they would learn to take responsibility for their own upkeep. Critics of these institutions have seen their activities as a means of class control.

The crèche. In France, Firmin Marbeau established a crèche in 1844 as an alternative to the inadequate care provided by unaware babysitters. In 1846 he published a work entitled *Cradle schools, or the means of lessening the misery of the people by increasing the population* and was rewarded with the Monthyon prize by the French Academy. The French crèche became a model and spread rapidly to Scandinavia, Belgium, Holland, Italy, Spain, Austria, China, and the United States. Its advocates claimed they produced better results than providing financial assistance to individual parents. But critics stated that those who were in favor of letting society take responsibility for impoverished children were, in fact, also benignly accepting the licentious behavior that was thought to be the underlying cause of poverty.

The role of the crèche, also called nursery or cradle school, was to look after the children of working mothers. The crèche was a full-day institution for the supervision of children of poor parents where the mother had to go out to work, either because she was a single parent or because she had to contribute to the livelihood of the family The children were to be provided with nutritious food, good care, and sound moral training. From the beginning they were run under private management, through an association, or supported by local authorities, church boards, and poor relief bodies. The emphasis in the crèche was on the day-to-day supervision and care of children. Very simple materials were used for this and often the groups were large and the buildings unsanitary. The staff of the crèches consisted of poorly paid untrained working-class women. But upper-class men and women, sitting on their committees, carried out an extensive and sometimes painstaking supervision of the staff and activities provided.

A Kindergarten with an Educational Aim

The kindergartens were started by private initiative and with other motives than those of the infant schools, workhouses, and crèches. The first kindergarten was founded in Germany 1837 and emanated from the pedagogy and philosophy of FRIEDRICH FROEBEL. Froebel was inspired by JEAN-JACQUES ROUSSEAU and JOHANN PESTALOZZI. He did not believe in punishment as a force for upbringing and described the child as a plant in need of nourishment, light, and care. The term *kindergarten* (German for "children" and "garden") can be seen as a symbol of his main ideas. Its activities spread to many countries due to Froebel's writings and, above all, though the efforts of middle-class women. The growth of the kindergarten went hand-in-hand with the needs of bourgeois women to find an opportunity to establish a profession and career. For example, Margarethe Meyer and Elisabeth Peabody pioneered the kindergarten movement in the United States in the 1850s; and Bertha Meyer, Margarethe's sister, went to England and continued the kindergarten movement there. From the middle of the 1800s onward, kindergartens were adopted all over Europe. A number of Swedish kindergarten pioneers qualified as teachers at the Pestalozzi-Froebel Haus in Berlin and on finishing their training returned to Sweden where, on a private basis, they established kindergartens, institutions for staff training (at the end of the 1800s), and a few years later, their own journal. The female pioneers within the kindergarten movement were good examples of how successfully the ideal of maternity could be combined with an interest in preschool pedagogics.

In the kindergarten the focus was on education. The staff were trained teachers or monitors, whose methods and materials constituted a part of their educational view. The activities of the kindergarten were restricted to a few hours every day. Many different interests had a stake in the kindergartens. They were financed by private individuals, companies, churches, immigrant societies, foundations, and municipalities. The kindergarten movement itself had internal contradictions. One issue was the question of which children would have access to the kindergartens. Some thought they should only be available to upper-class children, but most upper-class mothers were housewives and did not require child care. Representatives of the public kindergartens expressed the view that these institutions should be open to children from all walks of society, in order to reconcile class differences. In the United States so-called charity kindergartens were established. The first charity kindergarten was opened in St. Louis by Susan E. Blow during the winter of 1872–1873. Other women followed her example and it was not long before charity kindergartens were found in many of the towns and cities of the country.

Conclusion

Organized child care has focused its activities either on care or education. This dichotomy has reflected the institutional needs of different groups within society, either based on child care for working parents or the child's educational process. Children have been treated differently within these dichotomous infant institutions, and the division has been an obstacle to providing an integrated program of care and education for young children. Still, in the majority of European countries and in the United States, the preschool is integrated into the school system and provides an important role in the education, upbringing, and care of children.

In the twentieth century, most traditional forms of child care have continued to serve working mothers, but the ideas underlying the workhouse or crèche have largely disappeared. In the first half of the century, they were replaced by mothers' pensions, which allowed poor women to remain at home with their children, or by family subsidies. Since the 1970s, as more middle-class women have gone into the workplace, out-of-home child care has largely been left up to private business initiatives in the United States, while it is both provided by the state and closely supervised in most European countries.

See also: **Nursery Schools.**

BIBLIOGRAPHY

Allen, Ann Taylor. 1991. *Feminism and Motherhood in Germany 1800–1914.* New Brunswick, NJ: Rutgers University Press.

Barnard, Henry. 1884. *Kindergarten and Child Culture Papers: Froebel's Kindergarten, with Suggestions on Principles and Methods of Child Culture in Different Countries, Republished from the American Journal of Education.* Hartford, CT: Office of Barnard's American Journal of Education.

Bloch, Marianne N. 1987. "Becoming Scientific and Professional: An Historical Perspective on the Aims and Effects of Early Education." In *The Formation of the School Subjects,* ed. Tom Popkewitz. New York: Falmer Press.

Brannen, Julia, and Peter Moss, eds. 2003. *Rethinking Children's Care.* Philadelphia: Open University Press.

Crowther, Margaret A. 1981. *The Workhouse System 1834–1929: The History of an English Social Institution.* Athens: University of Georgia Press.

David, Miriam. 1980. *The State, the Family, and Education.* London: Routledge and Kegan Paul.

Duchatel, Tanneguy, and Francois Marc Louis Naville. 1842. *Fattigvården i alla dess riktningar såsom Statsanstalt och Privaträttning samt dess nuvarande tillstånd i civiliserade stater inom och utom Europa, svensk översättning* (Poor relief in all its forms, from government to private institutions; its present state in civilized country within and outside of Europe, Swedish translation). Stockholm, Sweden: Norstedt and Söner.

Hareven, Tamara K., ed. 1977. *Family and Kin in Urban Communities, 1730–1930.* New York: New Viewpoint.

Holmlund, Kerstin. 1996. "Låt barnen komma till oss: Förskollärarna och kampen om småbarnsinstitutionerna"(Let the children come to us: Preschool teachers and their struggle for the child-care institutions). Ph.D. diss, Umeå Pedagogiska institutionen.

Holmlund, Kerstin. 1999. "Cribs for the Poor and Kindergartens for the Rich: Two Directions for Early Childhood Institutions in Sweden, 1854–1930." *History of Education* 28, no. 2: 143–155.

Holmlund, Kerstin. 2000. "Don't Ask for Too Much! Swedish Pre-school Teachers, the State, and the Union, 1906–1965." *History of Education Review* 29, no. 1: 48–64.

Klaus, Alisa. 1993. *Every Child a Lion. The Origins of Maternal and Infant Health Policy in the United States and France, 1890–1920.* Ithaca, NY: Cornell University Press.

Michel, Sonya, and Rianne Mahon, eds. 2002. *Child Care Policy at the Crossroads: Gender and Welfare State Restructuring.* New York: Routledge.

Moberg, Ellen. 1947. "Barnträdgårdens uppkomst och dess utveckling i Sverige" (The rise and development of the kindergarten in Sweden). In *Barnträdgården*, ed. Maria Moberg, Stina Sandels. Stockholm, Sweden: Natur och Kultur.

O'Connor, Sorca M. 1995. "Mothering in Public: The Division of Organized Child Care in the Kindergarten and Day Nursery, St. Louis, 1886–1920." *Early Childhood Research Quarterly* 10: 63–80.

KERSTIN HOLMLUND

UNITED STATES

A look at child care in the United States today is a look back at the past. It has all been tried before, and the systems society has tended to support are the ones that have met its needs. These systems have been rejected and replaced by others that fit the ethos of a particular time, then resurrected in slightly different form. Group care away from home, day care, FOSTER CARE, the schools as BABY-SITTERS, and nanny care have all had previous incarnations, and twenty-first century debates about them are echoes of the heated discussions of earlier times. There is a long legacy of shared motherhood, with more than one mother in the center of the picture; there is also a little-known tradition of men as nurturers.

The Apprenticeship System

Colonial APPRENTICESHIP, imported from England, was to a large extent male child care. Designed to train adolescent boys in trades such as carpentry and printing and girls in housewifery, it was, for the poor, an early form of foster care. More than half the eleven hundred poor apprentices in Boston between 1734 and 1805 were five to nine years old. The master was responsible for children barely out of toddlerhood as well as those in their teens, and he served as "father" until the children were old enough to be on their own—usually twenty-one for boys and sixteen to eighteen for girls, or until they were married. Apprenticeship in the early teens was more common in Europe where up to a third of all adolescents were apprenticed in rural or craft households—in a combination of child care with service and training. In the United States the system began a slow decline with the American Revolution and with growing industrialization, and by the Civil War (1861–1865) it persisted only in pockets here and there.

Slavery

While apprenticeship flourished and faded, SLAVERY, that "peculiar institution," evolved its own innovative child-care practices. To free able-bodied women to work in the fields, most slave children were cared for, usually in groups, by other slaves (typically those too old to work). Sometimes the group care was day care that foreshadows more contemporary patterns; sometimes it was a system anticipating the communal child rearing of the Israeli kibbutz, with children living in a separate house. Infants were usually nursed by their mothers or by another slave. But there were instances in which the mistress acted as wet nurse to free the mother to return to more productive labor.

As for the white children on the plantation, the fabled Mammy of *Gone with the Wind* fame often served both as wet nurse and then dry nurse of the white master's child. But she existed for the most part only on large plantations. Many white children were cared for by black children hardly older than they were.

Nineteenth-Century Developments

A contagion of reform swept through the United States in the mid-nineteenth century, challenging the sanctity of the cult of motherhood. This generated a few, relatively small experiments in child care. Utopian communities, dedicated to the idea that the road to a perfect world would be paved with perfect children, included the celibate Shakers who provided what were essentially ORPHANAGES for neglected and dependent children and the controversial Oneida Community in upstate New York in which everything—human beings as well as property—was shared. Both groups cared round the clock for children who came to or, in the case of Oneida, were born into the community. The Shaker communities lasted longer than any others—from 1776 to remnants of one in the early 2000s. The Oneida Community, started by the visionary John Humphrey Noyes (1811–1886) in 1848, lasted forty years and included as many as three hundred men, women, and children. Children were reared together from the time they were weaned (at one point this was as early as seven months) and were the responsibility of the community, not their parents. This horrified outside society but freed women for work, education, and love of both men and God.

In the midst of the immigrant slums of the late nineteenth century, science, philanthropy, social conscience, and practicality coalesced in the settlement house—a "settlement" of do-gooders. JANE ADDAMS (1860–1935) was a key figure in the movement. She cofounded Hull-House, which opened in Chicago in 1889 and soon became the most famous and the most influential example.

The day nurseries at the settlement houses provided for young children from the time a mother went to work until she came back at night. There was drop-off care for a few hours, care for sick children, and twenty-four-hour care, if necessary. Children were fed hot, nutritious meals. Babies as young as two weeks old were accepted if there was real need, parents were involved as teaching assistants and in parent education classes, and caretakers made home visits to provide continuity in the child's life. These day nurseries, supported by private contributions, were criticized as the condescending meddling of well-meaning women. But they now seem to have been an effective, humane way to deal with the children of working mothers.

The KINDERGARTEN arose initially in Germany as a way of providing early education and also, particularly for the lower classes, as improved child care. Spreading to the United States, the idea of the kindergarten, where very young children could be cared for by trained professionals, fit neatly with the theoretical concepts of the influential pioneering American psychologist G. STANLEY HALL (1844–1924). Child rearing, Hall believed, was a science and too difficult to be left to bumbling mothers.

The kindergarten (run by private, charitable organizations at first, and then picked up by the public schools) was seized on as a way of assimilating the children of immigrants now crowding the American shores. By 1862 the word had come into the language, and the number of kindergartens grew along with the number of immigrants. Society had once again approved what it needed to care for its children. And as had happened with day nurseries, strategies to improve the lives of the poor trickled up to the rich and middle class. By 1920, about 10 percent of U.S. children, poor or not, attended kindergartens. For many mothers, child care for at least half the day could be assured.

Various ethnic groups brought with them the conviction that the extended family must care for its own children. Children who were ORPHANS or half orphans, or those in families in which there were simply too many children for their parents to handle, were parceled out to relatives. The ravages of death and desertion made shared mothering necessary. Many nineteenth-century families had an older relative, most commonly a grandmother, living in, mainly for assistance in child care. This residential pattern began to diminish starting in the 1920s.

In black families, too, the extended family played a large role in caring for children of unmarried mothers and women who had to work, but this safety net extended beyond blood relatives to "fictive kin," neighbors or close female friends of the mother, or people who had come into the family constellation so long ago that no one remembered when or why. Such care lasted for a few hours, a week, or the rest of the child's life.

Even in the early twenty-first century, 50 percent of the children whose working mothers had less than a high school education were cared for by relatives. Relatives cared for 30 percent of the children of mothers with a high school diploma and 16 percent of those whose mothers had graduated from college. According to the U.S. Census Bureau, the number of fathers staying home and caring for children increased dramatically since the 1990s.

By the mid-nineteenth century, ORPHANAGES, caring for large groups of children, were widely hailed as ideal institutions. They were established for the best of reasons to nurture children in the worst of times. Industrialization and immigration had cut families off from earlier supports. Epidemic disease and later the carnage of the Civil War (1861–1865) made it urgent to find a new way to care for children set adrift.

Historians have recently emphasized the extent to which working-class families often used orphanages as places to put children temporarily, when the family was financially destitute or disrupted by illness, with the parents maintaining contact with the children and later taking them back. For other children, orphanages sometimes doubled as child-placement schemes, with the goal of placing children in the homes of other families. Many authorities supported this system as the best way to provide a home environment and work training for children of the poor. It was often exploited, however, by foster parents themselves, who sought cheap labor.

A noninstitutional method to deal with orphans—the ORPHAN TRAINS—focused on individuals. In the seventy-five years between 1854 and 1929 a mass displacement rivaled only by the Children's Crusade of the thirteenth century transported more than two hundred thousand orphaned, neglected, and abandoned children from the crowded, filthy streets of New York and other eastern cities to the salubrious air of the midwestern countryside. Most of them were in the care of the NEW YORK CHILDREN'S AID SOCIETY, whose founder, CHARLES LORING BRACE (1826–1890), was determined to rescue "uncared for waifs before the evil environment has done its deadly work." Although the older children were essentially indentured servants, the farm families sometimes legally adopted the younger ones they took in. The system was criticized for tearing children from their homes or from familiar streets and for turning Catholics into Protestants in the Midwest. Yet many children prospered in homes far from home.

Trends in the Twentieth Century

The very rich, particularly before and after World War I (1914–1918), imported nannies to care for their children within the home. Preferably English or French or German and bringing with her an overlay of aristocracy on top of her own working-class origins, Nanny (or Mademoiselle or Fraulein) sometimes completely replaced parents, who made only brief state appearances. Some nannies were horrors—others lifesavers. Middle-class families, meanwhile, often gained some child care from day servants, though their quality was widely distrusted.

During the mid- and late twentieth century, with mothers with young children entering the labor force in increasing numbers, the nanny became a fixture in middle- and upper-middle-class families. The word has now come to be a generic term for a full-time or part-time home-based childcare worker. In 2001, 11 percent of young children of college-educated working mothers were cared for by nannies or baby-sitters; the percentage drops to 5 for mothers with a high school education.

Between the two world wars, rich and not-so-rich parents who could not or chose not to care for their children themselves found another solution. Elite boarding schools took the boys (and sometimes the girls) and helped their parents avoid many of the upheavals of ADOLESCENCE. The schools themselves, and the concept of adolescence as a separate period of life, were both born in the nineteenth century. Throughout this period, convents and other religious institutions continued to care for young children as they had done for centuries.

In the wider culture, after 1909 when the first WHITE HOUSE CONFERENCE ON CHILDREN concluded, "The carefully selected foster home is for the normal child the best substitute for the natural home," foster family care came to be seen as ideal in place of the orphanage. SOCIETIES FOR THE PREVENTION OF CRUELTY TO CHILDREN (based on the Society for the Prevention of Cruelty to Animals and sometimes combined with it) pioneered in investigating CHILD ABUSE and removing children from unsuitable homes starting in 1874. Slowly the focus began to shift to foster care or preserving the family rather than removing the child.

With the GREAT DEPRESSION of the 1930s, the focus shifted again. Faced with massive unemployment, the Works Progress Administration began a system of day nurseries meant to give jobs to out-of-work teachers, nutritionists, nurses, and custodians, among others. The program, available only to the poor, was the first comprehensive support for and funding of child care by the federal government. When those make-work day-care centers were discontinued on March 1, 1943, most of them became Lanham Act centers for the children of mothers working in vitally important war-related industries. For the first time day care lost the stigma of "for the poor or unwanted only."

Under the Lanham Act, approximately 1.6 million American children were in federally funded NURSERY SCHOOLS and day care centers by July 1945, the peak of the war effort. The centers often operated in schools or on the grounds of factories, providing day care, before- and after-school care, and vacation coverage. A total of about six hundred thousand different children received care through Lanham Act funds during the two and a half years of the program's existence. More young children were cared for away from their mothers than ever before. The centers closed six months after the war ended when women were told firmly to go back home and make room for returning servicemen.

The success of the Lanham Act centers was largely forgotten in the 1950s as women were viewed as the only effective nurturing figures. After the 1960s, however, increasing numbers of American women with young children were ignoring the conventional wisdom as they chose to work or were forced by circumstances to do so. In 2002, 72 percent of women with children under eighteen years of age were in the labor force. Day-care centers spread haltingly in the United States in response to these patterns, with some state-run institutions for the urban poor and often-expensive private centers for others.

In other cultures day care is built permanently into the national SOCIAL WELFARE system. In France, nearly 90 percent of children aged three to five are served in a program that blends education, health care, and child care in all-day centers and licensed private care homes, largely funded with tax dollars. The Israeli government provides kindergarten for all five-year-olds, and 50 percent of all three- to four-year-olds are in public child care. In China almost all children, starting at the age of fifty-six days, have government child care available, and five-day-a-week boarding care is offered in the large cities.

The widespread conviction that only a mother (preferably perfect) or her exemplary substitute can provide what a child needs to thrive is not supported by a body of respected research. Children have been helped and hurt by any system, whether orphanages, foster care, communal care, nanny care, or mother care. What matters is the quality of care and the quality of caring. And in each case much depended on the age and resilience of the child. Every era has had to find its own way of caring for the children it has produced, supported by psychological understanding that is, itself, a product of that time.

See also: **Placing Out.**

BIBLIOGRAPHY

Baltzell, E. Digby. 1964. *The Protestant Establishment: Aristocracy and Caste in America.* New Haven, CT: Yale University Press.

Cott, Nancy, and Elizabeth H. Pleck, eds. 1979. *A Heritage of Her Own: Toward a New Social History of American Women.* New York: Simon and Schuster.

Klaw, Spencer. 1993. *Without Sin: The Life and Death of the Oneida Community.* New York: Viking Penguin.

Langsam, Miriam Z. 1964. *Children West: A History of the Placing-Out System of the New York Children's Aid Society.* Madison: State Historical Society of Wisconsin.

Lerner, Gerda. 1973. *Black Women in White America: A Documentary History.* New York: Vintage.

NICHD Early Child Care Research Network. 2001. "Nonmaternal Care and Family Factors in Early Development: An Overview of the NICHD Study of Early Child Care." *Journal of Applied Developmental Psychology* 22, no. 5: 457–492.

Rawick, George P., ed. 1972. *The American Slave: A Composite Autobiography,* 19 vols. Westport, CT: Greenwood.

Steinfels, Margaret O'Brien. 1973. *Who's Minding the Children? The History and Politics of Day Care in America.* New York: Simon and Schuster.

Youcha, Geraldine. 1995. *Minding the Children: Child Care in America from Colonial Times to the Present.* New York: Scribner.

GERALDINE YOUCHA

Child Development, History of the Concept of

The notion that children "develop" seems an intuitive, obvious, and even self-evident idea. Children are born small, knowing the world in limited ways, with little or no understanding of other people as separate from themselves in body or mind, and no understanding of social relations or morality. They grow larger, learn about the physical and social worlds, join different cooperative social groups, and cultivate a more and more complex sense of right and wrong. Psychologists, teachers, and others who deal with children constantly invoke the term *development* as a way to understand the child's status and to rationalize practice. The language of development permeates CHILD PSYCHOLOGY and the child-centered professions. Practitioners in these areas speak of such things as "developmentally appropriate practices" for early childhood education, developmental "readiness" for reading, and "stages" of cognitive, moral, and social development. Policymakers often turn to developmental psychologists to help justify social programs on behalf of children. If "high-quality" CHILD CARE enhances a child's development, then providing such care is good public policy.

The idea of development is used extensively to give order and meaning to changes over time in children's physical, cognitive, psychosocial, and moral development. Development provides the rationale for myriad practices and policies related to children. There are, however, several concepts embedded in the idea of development that, upon closer inspection, may not be quite so obvious. What is not as obvious as the idea of development itself are the mechanism(s), direction(s), and end(s) of development. When one thinks about development in these terms and considers more deeply the origins and meaning of the idea of development, the obvious does not appear quite so obvious any longer.

Development is a teleological concept—it must have a direction and an end. The presumption is that later stages build on earlier stages and are more developed and "better" than earlier stages. The Swiss psychologist JEAN PIAGET (1896–1980) proposed formal operations as the universal end of cognitive development. For Piaget, formal operations provided the most comprehensive and logically powerful organization of thought. Extending Piaget's work, Lawrence Kohlberg elaborated a stage-based theory of moral development. He too invoked a universal end based upon increasing-

ly abstract conceptions of justice. Both Piaget and Kohlberg have been criticized for their initial presumptions about universality: more differences across cultures and between genders exist than either expected. These variations have rattled the bones of those seeking a universal, timeless developmental psychology but, at the same time, opened the doors to a more pluralistic notion of development. Still, typical notions of development (universal or not) presume that development proceeds in a specific direction and that later stages are "better" and more comprehensive than early stages. Direction and end are axiomatic to development.

At the very core of the idea of development are values and ideas about the "good" for individuals and societies. Later stages are not only more comprehensive, they also represent better ways of being because the end is highly valued as a good for human existence. If development is going somewhere, if later states are "better" or "higher" than previous states, then the "end" must represent some pinnacle of human excellence; the end must be Good. On what bases are these ends grounded? These questions are critical for any inquiry into the meaning of development. The idea of development is as much grounded in values as in empirical facts. Can science provide values? (It should be noted that this entry does not address development in domains that are highly "canalized"—domains that are highly driven by genetics and physiology, for example, aspects of perceptual or motor development.)

This entry explores the meaning of development by first introducing the historical context out of which the idea of development in children arose in American thought. Second, the entry briefly explicates the work of two prominent American thinkers whose ideas about development were founded upon dramatically different assumptions about the source, mechanisms, and ends of development. James Mark Baldwin elaborated an enormously complex notion of natural development under a thinly disguised divinity. For Baldwin, the direction and end of development inhered in nature itself, conceived as good, true, and beautiful. In stark contrast, JOHN DEWEY resisted the temper of the times and rested his ideas about development on a set of explicitly chosen values. The contrast illustrates the fundamental difference between conceiving development as a natural or as a socially guided process—the child as a natural or as a cultural being.

The Historical Origins of the Idea of Development in Children

The idea of development did not begin or end with children. The idea of development in children arose from a set of older ideas about natural and human history. By the mid-nineteenth century, ideas about evolution, development, and progress formed a virtual trinity. Evolutionary history (phylogeny), individual development (ontogeny), and social change (history) all illustrated and revealed development. When systematic child study began in the United States, it entered through an ideological prism of evolution, progress, and development.

Although arguments for development in both natural and human history were not new, the nineteenth is most famously known as the century of "history," "development," and "progress." Prior to the publication of the theories of the English naturalist Charles Darwin (1809–1882), the Scottish publisher and author Robert Chambers (1802–1871), in his influential 1844 anonymously published book, *Vestiges of the Natural History of Creation*, maintained that alongside gravitation there was one great law of life—the law of development. Just as inorganic matter was governed by the principle of gravitation, so all of life was governed by the principle of development. The English philosopher Herbert Spencer (1820–1903) captured the optimistic spirit of the times when he wrote that the ultimate development of the ideal man (in his words) was logically certain; progress was not an accident for Spencer, it was a necessity. Civilization, Spencer wrote, was not artificial, but part of nature and all of a piece of a developing embryo or the unfolding of a flower. This was no mere analogy for either Spencer or the American culture that so warmly welcomed him.

Amidst the din of development, Darwin remained (arguably) neutral. Darwin's theory of evolution by natural selection, as set forth in his seminal work, *On the Origin of Species* (1859), served not only as a radical secular theory of the origin of humans; it also provided a new scientific sanction for a set of older beliefs. Though Darwin himself was not committed to the notion that the evolutionary record implied development or progress—that human beings are necessarily more "developed" than other species, or that species perfect themselves through evolutionary change—many of his predecessors and proponents were just so committed. Darwin's theory of gradual, nonprogressive evolutionary change was assimilated into a culture that was ideologically prepared to receive and transform Darwin into a spokesman for development in general. Armed with the authority of science, developmental zealots seized upon the new and secular science to confirm and extend a set of older ideas. Biologists, philosophers, historians, and many of the blossoming new social and political scientists seized Darwin's theory of evolution as a platform for demonstrating development in fields far and wide. So-called evolutionary theists worked hard at reconciling the Biblical account of human origin with the new science. Many solved the dilemma by assimilating natural law as a visible demonstration of God's work. Riots of analogies were drawn between the development of different animal species, human races, civilizations, and children. The idea of development, broadly construed and expressed in fields as divergent as evolutionary theory, philosophy, anthropology, and history formed, the dominant intellectual context for the systematic study of development in children. The child's development served to demonstrate the connection between development in evolution and the development of civiliza-

tion. The child became a linchpin—a link between natural and human history.

Development: The Natural, the Social, and the Good

Both James Mark Baldwin (1861–1934) and John Dewey (1859–1952) were distinguished philosophical psychologists. Baldwin was a brilliant theorist whose theory is now recognized as an anticipation of Piaget's work. More recently, Baldwin's work has inspired a number of both historical and empirical inquiries. His psychology was complex, comprehensive, and brilliant in many ways. Baldwin rested much of his work on a platform of evolutionary theory to explain development in general, across natural and human history. John Dewey was a first-rate philosopher who focused his many lines of inquiry around education.

Both men wrote about evolution, child development, and history but in profoundly different ways. Baldwin found natural lines of development in evolution, child development, and historical change. Nature governed and directed these developmental processes toward truth, beauty, and goodness. Dewey saw no inevitable, automatic, or general development in any of these passages of change over time. He believed that the direction and ends of individual and social development were based on culturally negotiated values. The contrast between Baldwin and Dewey is powerful. It illustrates the vastly different implications of understanding child development as a naturally occurring process in which the end resides in nature or in culture and history. Both theories are anchored in values, but the source of those values differs.

James Mark Baldwin. Baldwin entered Princeton University (then the College of New Jersey) in 1881 and soon fell under the influence of minister, professor, and college president James McCosh. McCosh was one of many liberal clergy who struggled to reconcile science and scripture. He taught the young Baldwin that human beings were fundamentally good and that just as science revealed divine handiwork in nature so moral philosophy demonstrated moral purpose and design in human affairs. Moral law was as real and inexorable as gravity, and both indicated the presence of a divine governor of the world. When Baldwin elaborated a thinly empirical but richly theoretical account of child development, he maintained his professor's conviction that to describe normal social practice was also to prescribe ethical behavior. Through his many written volumes Baldwin specified ends of development founded upon presumably natural causes. In so doing, Baldwin proposed a basic concurrence between the natural and the good. People are good because God directs nature toward the good.

Baldwin acknowledged evolutionary biology as the "handmaiden" to individual development. Darwin identified natural selection as the mechanism of evolutionary change. Jean-Baptiste Lamarck (1744–1802) proposed that animals may, through effort, modify their form to better adapt to the environment and transmit these adaptations to progeny. Without resorting to simple Lamarckian theory, Baldwin, by a series of rather ingenious moves, invented a second mechanism of evolutionary transmission, *organic selection*, in order to explain apparently inherited acquired characteristics. (The notion of organic selection, also known as the *Baldwin effect*, is still recognized by evolutionary biologists as a mechanism that can account for various kinds of local adaptations in species.) Baldwin elaborated and transposed principles of evolutionary development onto wider and wider platforms to include both the child and society. He depicted children's social development as a dialectical process in which notions of self and other developed concurrently toward an increasingly comprehensive understanding of both. Moral development was part and parcel of social development. As one of the late-nineteenth-century idealist thinkers, Baldwin maintained that a sense of self that is good and law-abiding must be a public self in which private ends and social ideals were one and the same. The naturally developing social self is good, and it demonstrates the unfolding of more highly developed forms of self-realization, or Mind. The source, direction, and end of development are thus transcendent, beyond the reach of ordinary human experience.

In 1884 Baldwin declared that the embryology of society is open to study in the nursery, and that any theory of social organization and social progress must be consistent with individual psychology. The individual and society are two sides of a naturally growing whole; the dialectic of individual development must hold true on the level of social organization. Thus, social progress occurs through a dialectic process strictly analogous to the dialectic of personal growth in the child. Human history cannot move in a direction that violates those states of mind—the ideal, social, and ethical states—that have enabled the individual to come into social relationships. Baldwin was convinced that social progress proceeded toward the pursuit of moral and social ends because "this is the direction that nature itself pursues in social evolution" (Baldwin, p. 163). The child and society both develop by means of natural law expressed in traditional Christian values. Naturally occurring "facts" or descriptions of development reveal values because values are inherent in nature. Mind, when fully revealed, is true, good, and beautiful. Development leads naturally to God made manifest in nature.

John Dewey. There were skeptics, however, who did not believe in the trinity among development in evolution, child development, and social progress. They were minority voices barely heard above the din of development. Dewey was one of those skeptics, and he too wrote about the meaning of changes over time in evolution, child development, and history. Highly critical of those around him who found the source and end of development in nature, Dewey once remarked that the idea that everything develops out of itself

was an expression of *consummate juvenilism*—a relic of an older mode of thinking made obsolete by Darwin.

Dewey's ideas about development are most visible in his writings on education, his philosophical center. In a direct assault on Spencer, Dewey found false the common analogy between a child's development and the unfolding of a flower. Dewey remarked that the seed's destiny is prescribed by nature, whereas the growth and destiny of the more plastic child is open and variable. More flexible outcomes are possible for richly endowed human beings than for a seed. The child may possess "germinal powers," according to Dewey but, playing on the analogy of the child as seed, he asserted that the child may develop into a sturdy oak, a willow that bends with every wind, a thorny cactus, or even a poisonous weed. Dewey rejected any idea of development that suggested or invoked the unfolding of latent powers from within toward a remote goal. Development does not mean just getting something out of the child's mind; development is manifested through lived experience. Dewey recognized the need to specify direction and ends to growth. He understood that one cannot know what development is desirable without antecedent knowledge of what is good. It is just this presumed antecedent knowledge on which those purporting "natural" development depend.

Dewey's philosophical psychology is, first and foremost, a social psychology. He acknowledged a rapidly changing American landscape and lived through a period of extraordinary social change. He contended that ideas and institutions must change with social change. He urged philosophers to stop worrying about the problems of philosophers and worry more about the problems of people. In response to the complex nature of the American industrial social order, Dewey leaned most heavily on schools to provide an institutional setting for children's development. He proposed that education serve as a lever of social change and charged schools with a mandate to become places that set development in the right direction. Dewey maintained that teachers should strive to provide a designed environment in which particular ideals of development are fostered through lived experience. Specifically, Dewey found those ideals in democratic governance and scientific inquiry, the latter broadly construed and akin to the term *critical thinking*.

If the classroom could become a miniature model of a community based upon democratic governance and critical inquiry rather than arbitrary authority or sentiment, then that would provide, Dewey maintained, the best guarantee of a good society. Children arrive at school with certain native interests or curiosities. These dispositions are beginning points for teachers to guide children toward particular socially desired ends. It is the business of school to set up environments that make possible the creation of small cooperative groups; the task of the teacher is to direct natural tendencies toward systematic inquiry and democratic governance. Systematic inquiry into the biology of plants may thus emerge from the children's collectively designed and cultivated garden. From a class trip to the ZOO might emerge shared inquiry into the history or ecology of zoos or to the natural habitats of different zoo animals. Growth occurs through lived experience. Dewey hoped that transforming social experiences in classrooms would guide children to grow "in the right direction." The classroom becomes a place in which the conditions of democratic governance and inquiry free from arbitrary authority or sentiment can and must exist to ensure that democracy and science thrive in the wider society. Education, growth, and experience thus become synonymous with one another. Knowledge and politics become one, as science in the classroom becomes democracy in action. Schools thus become agents of both individual development and social progress.

Dewey thought of schools as laboratories in which scientists can learn about the possibilities of human development. In 1896 he began one such "laboratory" school at the University of Chicago. In schools, Dewey maintained, citizens may project the type of society they want. Dewey wanted schools to become places in which children would grow and carry intelligence into a social democracy. Science and democracy demand one another, because science is the most democratic means of knowing and democracy is the most objective means of governance.

Dewey promoted science and democracy as ideal ends for both the child's individual development and society's progress as well. In this sense, he resembles Baldwin and others in yoking individual development to social progress. While not inscribed in nature, science and democracy approach the status of absolute goods because they are, in Dewey's judgment, the best ways of solving an enormous range of problems. Science and democracy are not inevitable ends of history; they demand constant nurture and reformulation. The solution to the problem of values, endemic to the idea of development, lies not in natural law for Dewey but in socially agreed-upon values. Natural law conceptions of development avoid the problem of specifying values because the ends of development, the good, are presumed to be inherent in nature itself.

Having rejected development as a natural process, Dewey posed and answered just the sorts of questions demanded by the idea of development. Rather than postulating development as a natural unfolding of latent powers, Dewey maintained that development is a function of socially acknowledged goods for self and society. In his judgment, democratic governance and objective thinking were the best guarantees of a good, just, and experimenting society. Like the nineteenth-century English philosopher John Stuart Mill, the German physiologist and psychologist Wilhelm Wundt (1832–1920), the American psychologist Hugo Münsterberg (1863–1916), and others, Dewey sought a so-

cial and developmental psychology based upon understanding people in relation to their cultural circumstances. In this view, culture itself becomes a mechanism of development. He thought that this social psychology could stand beside the older and more entrenched experimental psychology and become a "second psychology." By the early 2000s, "ecological," "sociocultural," or sociohistorical developmental psychologists perhaps best represented Dewey's perspective. Following on the heels of the great Russian psychologist LEV VYGOTSKY (1896–1934), contemporary psychologists such as Urie Bronfennbrenner, Michael Cole, Barbara Rogoff, and Jerome Bruner have all proposed models of and mechanisms for a cultural-historical approach to development. These are developmental psychologists who situate development in a social context and understand development as incumbent upon culturally valued goals and social practices.

Theories of the Late Twentieth Century and Beyond

From the mid-1970s to the early 2000s, a persistent string of philosophers, historians, and psychologists have argued again that psychology traffics in values in spite of its persistent hopes to be a value-free, objective science. Development is a value-laden idea, sometimes derived not as closely from empirical data as some might like to believe. Dewey illustrates how once one renounces natural ends to development, one must become politically and morally engaged in a process to determine that which shall constitute good development and how it might be achieved. Science cannot identify what those goods are, but it can suggest different ways to achieve different ends. Once one renounces fixed and naturally determined ends, development becomes historically contingent. The philosopher Marx Wartofsky wrote that there are no values in nature; people create them. In this view, development does not lurk directly in the people studied but resides in the perspective used. Jerome Bruner has argued that theories of development require a metatheory of values about the good person and the good society. If developmental psychologists fail to examine those values and hide behind the veil of nature, developmental theory risks becoming a mere handmaiden of society's implicit values rather than a consciously implemented goal. Sheldon White has suggested that while the idea of development may be proposed in the context of analysis, it becomes the idea of the Good in practical affair; and that while the idea of development is a systematic idea, it is likely to be treated as an ethical ideal. Bernard Kaplan (1983) and William Kessen (1990) have also drawn our attention to the value-laden nature of the idea of development. The "end" of development reflects that which people value and toward which people steer their children's development. These developmental values have varied tremendously across history and cultures. If development points the way to the good, then it is good to help development. In the midst of his youthful struggles to reconcile religion with science, the young Piaget wrote that "to hasten evolution is to do good" (p. 29). Developmental psychology began as a search for values and continues to do so today.

See also: **Bowlby, John; Bühler, Charlotte; Burt, Cyril; Freud, Anna; Freud, Sigmund; Froebel, Friedrich Wilhelm August; Gesell, Arnold; Hall, Granville Stanley; Isaacs, Susan; Klein, Melanie; Watson, John B.**

BIBLIOGRAPHY

Baldwin, James M. 1911. *The Individual and Society or Psychology and Sociology.* Boston: Richard G. Badger.

Bruner, Jerome. 1986. "Value Presuppositions of Developmental Theory." In *Value Presuppositions in Theories of Human Development,* ed. Leonard Cirillo and Seymour Wapner. Hillsdale, NJ: Lawrence Erlbaum.

Dewey, John. 1981. "The Need for a Philosophy of Education." In *John Dewey: The Later Works, 1925–1953,* ed. Jo Ann Boydston. Carbondale: Southern Illinois University Press.

Kaplan, Bernard. 1983. "Value Presuppositions of Theories of Human Development." In *Value Presuppositions in Theories of Human Development,* ed. Leonard Cirillo and Seymour Wapner. Hillsdale, NJ: Lawrence Erlbaum.

Kessen, William. 1990. *The Rise and Fall of Development.* Worcester, MA: Clark University Press.

Kohlberg, Lawrence. 1981. *The Psychology of Moral Development: The Nature and Validity of Moral Stages.* San Francisco: Harper and Row.

Piaget, Jean. 1977. "The Mission of the Idea." In *The Essential Piaget,* ed. Howard E. Gruber and J. Jacques Vonèche. New York: Basic Books.

Spencer, Herbert. 1850/1864. *Social Statistics.* New York: Appleton.

Wartofsky, Marx. 1986. "On the Creation and Transformation of Norms of Human Development." In *Value Presuppositions in Theories of Human Development,* ed. Leonard Cirillo and Seymour Wapner. Hillsdale, NJ: Lawrence Erlbaum.

White, Sheldon H. 1983. "The Idea of Development in Developmental Psychology." In *Developmental Psychology: Historical and Philosophical Perspectives,* ed. Richard M. Lerner. Hillsdale, NJ: Lawrence Erlbaum.

EMILY D. CAHAN

Child Guidance

Child guidance in the United States began with an idealistic mission characteristic of Progressive reform: prevention, first of juvenile DELINQUENCY and then of MENTAL ILLNESS by identifying the first signs of problems in children. Over the years, the goal of prevention faded, and child guidance came to treat mild behavior and emotional problems in children. The child guidance movement began in 1922 as part of a program sponsored by a private foundation, the Commonwealth Fund's Program for the Prevention of Juvenile Delinquency. The movement established community facilities, called child guidance clinics, for treating so-called maladjusted children, school-aged children of normal intelligence exhibiting slight behavior or psychological problems.

The Program for the Prevention of Juvenile Delinquency introduced eight demonstration clinics in cities across the country, which sparked the creation of some forty-two clinics by 1933. Child guidance clinics employed clinical teams made up of newly established professionals: a psychiatrist, a psychologist, and a psychiatric social worker. Members of these clinical teams pooled their different perspectives to provide treatment sensitive to all aspects of the child's situation. Established as facilities to treat all maladjusted children in a community, the new clinics cooperated with existing social welfare, educational, and medical services to reach the widest range of children.

The child guidance movement of the early 1920s embodied the optimism and vigorous outreach of the MENTAL HYGIENE movement—psychiatry's early-twentieth-century push into the community, to educate the public about mental illness, identify its early signs, and it was hoped, to prevent it. The very term *guidance* suggests something between education and nurture on the one hand, and medical models of treatment and cure, on the other. By the 1930s, however, child guidance was a clearly delineated medical endeavor, aimed at treating a population of children with mild behavioral and emotional problems within the confines of clinic offices. Gone was the practice of early intervention in children, the broad local outreach linking clinics to networks of child-helping services, and identifying problems in children appearing in a variety of locations throughout the community, especially immigrant and poor children.

Nevertheless, child guidance continued to direct itself toward the same at-risk population: treatment of the so-called problem child. Child guidance defined the problem child as a child of normal intelligence, exhibiting a range of behavior and psychological problems, which were lumped together in a category called *maladjustment*. Indications of such maladjustments ranged from thumb sucking, nail biting, enuresis, and night terrors, in younger children, to personality traits such as sensitiveness, seclusiveness, apathy, excessive imagination, and fanciful lying. Also included was a category of undesirable behavior in older children such as disobedience, teasing, bullying, temper tantrums, seeking bad companions, keeping late hours, and engaging in sexual activities.

The problem child in the early movement was a social problem; its definition signified nonconformity to socially defined norms of behavior. The clinics were invested with social importance, responsible for enforcing norms of behavior and preventing social deviance. By 1930, child guidance began to help individual children whose problems were seen as important only to themselves and their families. The focus of problems had changed from an aggressive, extroverted, misbehaving child, to the internal psychological and emotional states of children. Child psychiatrists, psychologists and psychiatric social workers, saw their work as medical; diagnosing psychological disorders in children. This shift brought about a marked change in the *social characteristics* of the problem child. The social agenda of child guidance in the

1920s reached poorer, immigrant children, on whom it imposed middle-class standards of conformity. By the 1930s, child guidance treated an increasingly middle-class, native born population: the children of anxious, educated parents. With this profound change in focus, child guidance clinics became centers of research and treatment for the continually shifting population of problem children in the community.

See also: **Child Psychology; Child Saving; Juvenile Court.**

BIBLIOGRAPHY

Horn, Margo. 1989. *Before It's Too Late: The Child Guidance Movement in the United States 1922–1945.* Philadelphia: Temple University Press.

Jones, Kathleen. 1999. *Taming the Troublesome Child: American Families, Child Guidance, and the Limits of Psychiatric Authority.* Cambridge, MA: Harvard University Press.

MARGO HORN

Child Labor in Developing Countries

Exploitation of working children in developing countries has been reported since the 1800s. However, political awareness of the effects of working on children's physical and psychological well-being has gained substantial momentum in the international community only since the start of the 1990s.

Child Labor in International Law

The UN CONVENTION ON THE RIGHTS OF THE CHILD (1989) was a landmark in international law. It became an unprecedented success as it reached almost universal acceptance with 190 state ratifications in less than ten years. Although the question of child labor was dealt with in only a few of the convention's provisions, the massive political support for CHILDREN'S RIGHTS, as such, also enhanced the commitment to working children. In international law, labor issues have been reserved for the International Labour Organization (ILO). In the traditional perspective of the ILO, child labor must be eradicated from the labor market. Hence, from its establishment, the ILO strategy to combat child labor was to secure international agreements on a minimum working age for children. During the 1920s and 1930s a series of international treaties covering different sectors urged states to set a minimum working age. In 1973 these instruments combined into the Convention concerning Minimum Age for Admission to Employment. The overall aim, as stated in Article 1, was to "ensure the effective abolition of child labour."

Parallel to the endeavors to regulate the (adult) labor market, the League of Nations and later the United Nations (UN) strived to abolish slavery and forced labor. Children were not dealt with specifically until the UN's Supplementary Convention on the Abolition of Slavery (1956), which included children "delivered . . . to another person . . . with a view to the exploitation of the child" in a list of slavery-like practices (Article 1). Ten years later children were mentioned in one of the fundamental UN human rights treaties, the International Convention on Economic, Social and Cultural Rights (1966), which obliges state parties to criminalize employment of children under conditions "harmful to their morals or health" (Article 10). The perspective of the human rights treaties of the UN differed from that of the ILO: the former addressed the well-being and development of the child, and thus adopted the protective approach that had long prevailed in philanthropy and welfare legislation throughout the industrialized world.

With the Convention on the Rights of the Child of 1989 a child-centered approach became popular. In line with the Convention on Economic, Social and Cultural Rights, it demands protection of the child against economic and social exploitation (Article 32). Furthermore, the 1989 convention included new aspects of protection against sexual and other forms of exploitation (Articles 34 and 36) and against recruiting children to any form of war activities (Article 38).

The tremendous support for the children's rights convention influenced the approach to child labor. In the ILO the traditional trade union perspective was gradually revised to correspond more closely with the protective orientation. In 1999 the ILO adopted for the first time a purely child-oriented treaty: the Convention concerning the Prohibition and Immediate Action for the Elimination of the Worst Forms of Child Labour. The new strategy and instrument proved to be the greatest success in the history of the organization, with more than 130 states ratifying the treaty in three and a half years.

Child Labor in Practice

The overall figures of children at work show a decreasing trend; the ILO provides a very cautious benchmark of 1995 with approximately one out of four children, ages five to fourteen, working, against one out of five in 2000. In its more detailed analysis the ILO refers to three categories of child labor: nonhazardous work, hazardous work, and unconditional worst forms of child labor. Their estimates, from 2000, are that 186 million children under fifteen years of age undertake nonhazardous work. The definition of this category allows up to fourteen hours of work per week for children over five and below twelve years of age, and up to forty-three hours of work per week for children age twelve years and above. Hazardous work includes working hours that exceed these figures, or work that has or leads to adverse effects on the child's health or moral development. The estimate is that 111 million children fall under this category, almost 60 percent of economically active children (estimated to include 211 million children ages five to fourteen). More boys fall within these two categories than girls. The unconditional worst forms of child labor include forced and bonded labor, armed conflict involvements, prostitution, pornography, and illicit activities. A conservative calculation by the ILO estimates that eight million children below eighteen years of age are involved in these types of activities.

The largest single group of working children are those active in their parent's business, farm, workshop, or other endeavor. They are not represented in any of the statistics above and are rarely included in macro studies.

Even with a narrower focus on children employed in paid labor, research is still difficult and relatively scarce for the developing world. The growth of children's rights movements from the 1990s, however, has facilitated new research institutions and programs, such as the Innocenti Research Centre, which operates under the auspices of the United Nations Children's Fund (UNICEF).

Distribution and conditions of child labor vary from region to region. Comparative studies based on rather large samples from the World Bank household or living standard surveys around 1990 indicate that children, and in particular boys, in some countries contribute substantially to their families' income: one-third of household earnings in Ghana, one-fourth in Pakistan, and only one-tenth in Peru, in families in which children were working and not attending school. Such families are highly dependent on their working children and thus vulnerable to reduction in their children's access to jobs.

In families in which children are going to school in addition to working, the families are generally better off and less dependent on the child's income. There seems to be no clear relation, however, between child labor and school attendance. In some regions the prevailing tradition is that children combine work and school, whereas in other regions girls in particular do neither—generally because they are busy with domestic duties. Latin American countries most markedly have children in the former category, Asian countries the latter, with African countries placed in between.

Socioeconomic factors that influence the rate of child labor include economic growth (though not always with a decreasing effect on child labor); the adult labor market (for women in particular); parents' level of education; access to school as well as other community facilities; and household composition. Culturally, it is widely accepted in the developing world that children engage in work. Taking a share in the family income generation or in household duties is not only vital for survival or comfort but also an integral aspect of the child's moral and physical education.

Children's health is influenced by their work in many ways. Statistics in this field are most often poor or lacking, and in macro studies it is not possible to point to clear and unambiguous relationships. Work may have positive effects on children's health in some situations, for the poorest children by contributing to the mere means of subsistence. On the other hand, children are more sensitive to influences of noise, heat, certain chemicals, and toxics, and they are more prone to ACCIDENTS than adults. Furthermore, children tend to work in the most unsafe sectors. By far the largest group, over two-thirds, of economically active children is found within primary production, particularly in agriculture. Manufacture, trade, and domestic services are less hazardous but also count a smaller proportion of laboring children, with a total share of one-fourth. Children employed in construction, transportation, and mining are exposed to very high health and safety risks, but the proportion of children in these business sectors is relatively small, below 10 percent. The unpaid work that most children undertake within the family does not generally appear to be safer or more favorable to their health than paid work. Finally, although long-term effects of child labor cannot be clearly identified, there seems to be a correlation between inferior health standards in adulthood and child labor, particularly for women.

Combating Child Labor

Among the major international agents in the field, in particular the ILO, UNICEF, and the World Bank, a consensus has been reached to focus efforts to curb the worst forms of child labor. All three organizations assist governments in developing policies and strategies, and they also support implementation programs.

Though only a very small share of working children is involved in export businesses, trade mechanisms including sanctions are prominent in the public debates on the issue. In the World Trade Organization (WTO), however, binding statutes against trade involving child labor are being strongly opposed, particularly by developing countries that see protectionism as the underlying motive.

There is a broad consensus that trade sanctions are a double-edged instrument that may have adverse effects on children. Collaborative initiatives between the human rights and business sectors are on the other hand a fast-expanding field. In 2000 the UN launched a program, Global Compact, to work directly with companies, with "effective abolition of child labour" as one of the nine goals.

Regionally, under the North American Free Trade Agreement (NAFTA) there is a mechanism to monitor labor rights within member countries. The United States has a long tradition of unilaterally applying certain labor standards, encompassing prohibition of child labor, to trade agreements. In the early 2000s, both the United States and the European Union (EU) have a so-called General System of Preferences granting trade benefits to countries that live up to certain labor standards. While the U.S. system focuses solely on import goods, the EU system, installed in 1998, also focuses on applicant state policy to abolish child labor more broadly.

Other measures to combat child labor have been developed by individual companies as well as business sectors, often in cooperation with nongovernmental organizations. These initiatives include the promotion of investment and trade principles, demands on suppliers in developing countries, and the labeling of products.

Despite these efforts, given the many and complex interests embedded in child labor issues, strategies to combat the adverse effects of child labor must operate at many different levels and include all stakeholders, including children themselves.

See also: **Child Labor in the West; Globalization; International Organizations; Work and Poverty.**

BIBLIOGRAPHY

Boyden, Jo, Birgitta Ling, and William Myers. 1998. *What Works for Working Children.* Stockholm, Sweden: Rädda Barnen and UNICEF.

Cullen, Holly. 1999. "The Limits of International Trade Mechanisms in Enforcing Human Rights: The Case of Child Labour." *International Journal of Children's Rights* 7, no. 1: 1–29.

Cunningham, Hugh, and Pier Paolo Viazzo, eds. 1996. *Child Labour in Historical Perspective, 1800–1985: Case Studies from Europe, Japan, and Colombia.* Florence, Italy: UNICEF.

Grootaert, Christiaan, and Harry Anthony Patrinos, eds. 1999. *The Policy Analysis of Child Labor: A Comparative Study.* New York: St. Martin's Press.

International Labour Organization. 2002. *Every Child Counts: New Global Estimates on Child Labour.* Geneva, Switzerland: International Labour Organization, International Programme on the Elimination of Child Labour and Statistical Information and Monitoring Programme on Child Labour. Also available from <www.ilo.org/public/english/standards/ipec/publ/policy/>.

Maitra, Pushkar, and Ray Ranjan. 2002. "The Joint Estimation of Child Participation in Schooling and Employment: Comparative Evidence from Three Continents." *Oxford Development Studies* 30, no. 1: 41–62.

O'Donnell, Owen, Furio C. Rosati, and Eddy van Doorslaer. 2002. *Child Labour and Health: Evidence and Research Issues.* Florence, Italy: Innocenti Research Centre. Also available from <www.ucw-project.org/resources/pdf/childlabour_health.pdf>.

INTERNET RESOURCES

Child Rights Information Network. Available from <www.crin.org>.

International Labour Organization. International Programme on the Elimination of Child Labour. Available from <www.ilo.org/public/english/standards/ipec/index.htm>.

Understanding Children's Work: An Inter-Agency Research Cooperation Project at Innocenti Research Centre. Available from <www.ucw-project.org>.

UNICEF. Innocenti Research Centre. Available from <www.unicef-icdc.org>.

ANETTE FAYE JACOBSEN

Child Labor in the West

Children have always worked. In preindustrial times peasant children aided both parents in their work as soon as they could make themselves useful, and they contributed to supplement the income of the household. Children's access to work was regulated by their strength and work ability. Industrialization promoted changes concerning children's wagework. Children at work became a political and social issue.

Child labor is employment of children who are less than a specific legal age. The specific minimum age for when children were allowed to work in certain trades varied from nation to nation. A limit was, however, often set at twelve or thirteen years around the turn of the twentieth century. Legislation had actual and cultural consequences. Age—more than body and physical strength—shaped the conceptions of children's identity.

Child Labor in Western Societies: Development and Change

The history of child labor in Western societies is a history of how children were partners in the family economy. In a household economy the condition of children was strongly shaped by the family's status and labor requirements. Whether the nature of the family enterprise was agricultural production, industrial employment in an artisan or putting-out system, or some combination, children were expected to begin contributing to the work at a young age. As participants in a family enterprise, children were incorporated into adult roles early on. Socialization centered on the gradual introduction of children into the household economy.

As early as the eighteenth century, industrialization led to the employment of very small children in British textile mills, and in the nineteenth century children played an important role in key industries such as textiles and coal mining. In the British coal industry in the mid-nineteenth century, 13 percent of the labor force was under the age of fifteen. In Belgium, the percentage was even higher: in the coal and coke industry, children under sixteen constituted 22.4 percent of the total workforce of forty-six thousand in 1846.

Child labor was gender divided. Whereas boys worked in industries such as sawmills and coal mines, girls worked in the textile and garment industries. According to the censuses of 1871 from Lancashire, England, one girl in four aged between ten and fifteen worked in cotton manufacture. In the 1870s nearly one in three of Bedfordshire's girls between the ages of ten and fifteen were employed in straw plait trades, whereas one in nine of the Buckinghamshire girls in the same age group worked as pillow lace-makers.

In the United States rapid industrialization after the Civil War (1861–1865) increased the child labor force and introduced new occupations for children. According to the nationwide census of 1870 about one out of every eight children in the United States was employed. By 1900 approximately 1,750,000 children, or one out of six, had wagework. Sixty percent were agricultural workers, and of the 40 percent in industry over half were children of immigrant families.

Child labor in the West was often divided along gender lines. Boys worked in saw mills and coal mines but most textile mill workers, such as this girl photographed by American photographer Lewis Hine at the start of the twentieth century, were female. The Library of Congress.

Life imposed heavy burdens of work on all members of immigrant farm families in North America. Life was even harder for a huge contingent of single immigrant children who migrated from the United Kingdom to Canada between 1869 and 1919. Seventy-three thousand neglected children from urban areas, "unaccompanied by parents and guardians," were transferred to Canadian families, often on remote farms. Ten times as many families as could be provided with a British child volunteered to take one into their homes. The reason for this was that in preindustrial and rural Canada families needed children for the work they could do. The immigrant children worked as farm laborers and domestic servants.

How were the conditions for child laborers in industry compared with agriculture? In France, research shows that industrialization intensified work for some children, as workdays in factories were long and more structured. On the other hand, rural life in late-nineteenth-century France was rigorous and primitive, and young men from certain rural areas were more often rejected for military service than young men from cities, challenging the "misery history" of industrial child labor.

Another historical myth is that industrialization broke down traditional family ties and dissolved working-class families. A case study of what was the world's largest textile plant at the turn of the twentieth century—the Amoskeag Manufacturing Company in New Hampshire—dispels the myth and illustrates how families adapted to changing work patterns and survived. In a sharecropping village outside Bologna, Italy, a local textile mill strengthened family unity by promoting coresidency of children and parents. Rather than passing their childhood as apprentices and servants in the houses of relatives or strangers, children of peasant families now had the opportunity to live at home with their parents while working in manufacturing.

Children's contributions to family income varied in amount and as a percentage of the total across the family's life cycle, becoming greatest after adult male earnings had peaked. Figures from the United States indicate that children were likely to contribute about one-third of family income by the time the adult male was in his fifties. In Europe, children's contributions were even greater; about 41 percent when the head was in his fifties, and in some cases even higher. In a textile town in Catalonia, Spain, when the head of household was in his late fifties children were contributing just under half the family income, and when he was over sixty, more than two-thirds. In France, a study of family incomes noted that the contribution of children's wages to family income actually rose from 10 percent in 1907 to 18.5 percent as late as in 1914. The male breadwinner norm was hardly an actuality in these areas. Children, primarily boys, were considerable wage earners. Girls were needed as domestic workers in the households.

By the late nineteenth century British children for the most part no longer participated in key industries such as mining and textiles. In 1911 over one-quarter of employed males under age fifteen worked in service industries in Britain. This was work that was marginal to the economy. In Norway statistics show a similar change in the child labor market. In 1875 children worked in such major industries as agriculture, tobacco, and glass manufacture. Of a total of forty-five thousand industrial workers, about three thousand were children. By 1912, however, their role had been sharply restricted, and, typically, boys were distributors of newspapers and girls worked in domestic service. Thus by the early twentieth century, the essential role of children's labor was on the decline.

Child Labor Revisited: New Perspectives

Why did child labor decrease around the turn of the twentieth century in Western societies? An increase in children's school attendance is part of the explanation. Research from Sweden, Denmark, and Chicago indicates that one of the key motives for the introduction of compulsory schooling laws was to control and abolish child labor. In Norway the number of days at school increased by 50 percent from 1880 to 1914. At that time children were schoolchildren and part-time workers.

A crusade against child labor developed in most Western countries in the late nineteenth century. The modern order of childhood demanded actions against the "social evil" and for child labor laws. The child labor laws were hardly effective, as they did not provide for sufficient enforcement. Compulsory schooling laws were more effective, and the debates on child labor had an educative impact as well. States, educationalists, politicians, and philanthropists joined in the efforts to get children out of the factories and into school. In the United States, the NATIONAL CHILD LABOR COMMITTEE (NCLC) was organized in 1904. The committee helped organize local committees in every state where child labor existed, held traveling exhibits, and was the first organized reform movement to make wide use of photographic propa-

William Blake's "The Chimney Sweeper" from his *Songs of Innocence and Experience* (c. 1802–1808) details the misery of a young chimney sweeper's plight. In the eighteenth century, childhood was increasingly seen as a time of innocence that needed to be protected. Child labor, which had been considered a necessity for the family's survival, began to seem like abuse. Fitzwilliam Museum, University of Cambridge, UK/Bridgeman Art Library.

ganda. In 1915 the NCLC published 416 newspapers and distributed more than four million pages of propaganda materials. The propaganda promoted—here and elsewhere—changing attitudes and practices regarding childhood. The well-known photographer LEWIS HINE was one of the NCLC's crusaders. In 1908 Hine resigned from his job as a teacher and devoted his full career to photography and to his work as a reporter for the NCLC.

Whereas child labor was considered both economically valuable and ethical in preindustrialized societies, it was increasingly understood as uncivilized as industrialization progressed. Traditionally, the history of child labor is inscribed within this framework of progress and morality. E. P. Thompson, writing in 1963 about the Industrial Revolution in Britain, concluded that child labor was interpreted as "one of the most shameful events in our history," a reminiscence of a barbarian and dark past. In later years, however, a broader cultural perspective on child labor has opened up various nuances. One crucial question challenged the traditional perspective on child labor: because work is an important component of the human identity, why should children at work not experience the value of their efforts?

Within a cultural perspective, working children and their families moved from the periphery to the center of study. Child labor was interpreted as a meaningful activity in which children made themselves self-reliant and responsible for the support of the family. Working children were sometimes, but not always, victims. According to a new regime that condemned child labor, children were supposed to PLAY and go to school. The schoolchild as norm was gradually perceived as "natural" and "universal." As history is a way of seeing the past through the filters of the present, the complexity of child labor in the past turned out to be difficult to depict.

On the societal level, changing family strategy from "all hands at work" to a male breadwinner strategy, state action for compulsory schooling, and change of employment from paternalism to capitalism profoundly changed the conditions of child labor. Nevertheless, children continued to work as part-timers and as full-time laborers in many parts of the non-Western world. In the late twentieth century, child labor expanded enormously in the world as industry globalized, and child labor also reemerged in Western societies. The history of child labor is hence a history of continuity, and child labor remains an issue in the early twenty-first century.

See also: **Economics and Children in Western Societies: From Agriculture to Industry; European Industrialization; Placing Out; Work and Poverty.**

BIBLIOGRAPHY

Bremner, Robert H., ed. 1971. *Children and Youth in America: A Documentary History: Vol. II: 1866–1932.* Cambridge, MA: Harvard University Press.

Coninck-Smith, Ning de, Bengt Sandin, and Ellen Schrumpf, eds. 1997. *Industrious Children: Work and Childhood in the Nordic Countries, 1850–1990.* Odense, Denmark: Odense University Press.

Cunningham, Hugh. 2000. "The Decline of Child Labour: Labour Markets and Family Economies in Europe and North America since 1830." *Economic History Review* 53, no. 3: 409–428.

Hawes, Joseph M., and N. Ray Hiner, eds. 1991. *Children in Historical and Comparative Perspective: An International Handbook and Research Guide.* New York: Greenwood Press.

Parr, Joy. 1980. *Labouring Children: British Immigrant Apprentices to Canada, 1869–1924.* London: Croom Helm.

Schrumpf, Ellen. 2001. "The Working Child—Enslaved or Privileged? Changing Perspectives on Child Labour." *Brood and Rozen* 6, no. 4: 35–53.

Sutherland, Neil. 1976. *Children in English-Canadian Society: Framing the Twentieth-Century Consensus.* Toronto: University of Toronto Press.

ELLEN SCHRUMPF

Child Pornography

Child pornography refers to visual representations of children that are considered obscene. It is both a cultural issue and a legal definition. Child pornography is a problem about which North Americans, and to some extent Europeans, have been acutely concerned since about 1980, but overtly sexual images and texts involving children have always been made. Cupid, for instance, a mythological figure who incites lust, has always been represented as a child or adolescent. Prior to about the eighteenth century, childhood SEXUALITY was considered normal—one among many natural traits education was supposed to discipline in order for a child to attain adult social status—and therefore pictures of sex involving children were considered to be only one among many types of pornography. With the advent of a modern ideal of absolute childhood sexual innocence in the eighteenth century, however, explicitly sexual representations of children became socially unacceptable.

Many respectable Victorian images of and stories about children contain sexual overtones or betray unconscious sexual desires. These implications, however, were not apparent to anyone who was utterly convinced of childhood innocence at any time between the early nineteenth century and the late twentieth century. Charles Dodgson (better known by his pen name of LEWIS CARROLL), for instance, made photographs of semi-dressed or nude children, and would have been sincerely shocked by the innumerable late-twentieth-century allegations of child pornography that now plague his reputation. By the 1960s and 1970s, however, novels such as LOLITA, as well as other aspects of popular culture, had begun to stir a public sense of apprehension about the literary or visual abuse of children for sexual purposes. Shortly thereafter, the growing focus on CHILD ABUSE, child ABDUCTION, and other concerns about child safety turned public attention to the potential problems of pornography.

Legally, child pornography was first distinguished from adult pornography in the United States in 1982, with the case of *New York v. Ferber.* Over the course of the next fourteen years, a succession of legal decisions or government reports broadened the definition of child pornography until it meant any photographic image, of real children or not, that in any one person's opinion might seem "lewd." Key cases, government reports, and legislation include the 1986 Attorney General's Commission on Pornography (the Meese Report), *Massachusetts v. Oakes* (1989), *Knox v. the United States* (1991–1994), and the 1996 Child Pornography Prevention

Brooke Shields was only fifteen years old at the time she posed for a notoriously provocative jeans ad for Calvin Klein in 1980. Although the ad campaign focused public attention on the issue of child sexuality, there was no significant backlash against Calvin Klein as a result. AP/WIDE WORLD PHOTOS.

Act. The production, distribution, or consumption of child pornography became punishable under federal law by prison terms of up to twenty years. In addition, most states passed laws requiring all photographic film processors to report any pictures they found suspicious to the police.

Only photographic images, analog or digital, were implicated, for only photographic images seemed sufficiently real and documentary to warrant prosecution. The link that child pornography was thought to forge between artificial images and the realities of sexual child abuse informed the logic behind child pornography law. Lawmakers and the American public feared not only the abuse of children during the making of child pornography, but also its effects on later viewers. Child pornography was believed to lower the sexual inhibitions of both child victims and adult perpetrators, as well as haunting children throughout their lives. In 2002, the legal trend of child pornography law was altered by *Ashcroft v. the Free Speech Coalition.* Rejecting the claim that child pornography should include all images of children, regardless of whether any real children had been involved in its making, the Supreme Court ruled that digitally artificial images were

exempt, because they did not document any actual child abuse.

Child pornography law developed in a climate of high anxiety about the sexualization of children throughout Western culture. This anxiety, and reactions to it, can be charted by three successive scandals about advertising campaigns by the Calvin Klein company, a successful clothing manufacturer. In 1980, Calvin Klein launched a series of magazine and television advertisements for jeans showing child star Brooke Shields, in the guise of a sexually attractive woman, uttering the slogan, "What comes between me and my Calvins? Nothing." The campaign made the phenomenon of the child-woman a public issue, but incurred no reprisals. Sales of the jeans soared. In 1995, Calvin Klein again produced an ad campaign for jeans that shocked many consumers and generated widespread comment. The ads featured several models in suggestive poses, some with their underwear exposed, who appeared to be close to the legal AGE OF CONSENT (eighteen). This time, a legal investigation was initiated. Although the models proved to be adults, the ad campaign did not last long. By 1999, tolerance for any hint of child pornography had vanished. That year, yet another troubling Calvin Klein ad campaign, featuring children gamboling in underwear, elicited outrage so vociferous it forced the withdrawal of the campaign within a day.

The growing accessibility of the Internet has raised new concerns about child pornography. Pictures of children involved in sex acts can now be circulated much more rapidly and widely than ever before. Because children use the Internet, the risk of their exposure to child pornography is correspondingly increased. The crime of child molestation can be strongly correlated to the consumption of child pornography, although no cause and effect relationship had ever been conclusively proved. It is much more likely that consumption of child pornography and violence against children are both effects of far more complex causes.

Anxiety over criminal child pornography both expresses and conceals a much deeper and more pervasive anxiety over ordinary images of ordinary children. As fears escalate about children becoming too sexual too young, attention focuses on pictures. Children posed or attired according to the codes of adult sexuality appear constantly in every mass medium, in advertisements for products completely unconnected to childhood, among young entertainers, in beauty pageants, and in many sports. The sexualization of childhood is a mainstream phenomenon, not a marginal one. It affects the image of girls much more than the image of boys, possibly because the image of adult femininity tends to be more sexualized than the image of adult masculinity.

Images of children made within families receive as much new scrutiny as images of children in the public domain. Legislation requiring photo processors to report suspected child pornography to the police was intended to catch parents or parental figures as much as, or even more than, it was designed to stifle a commercial child pornography market. Many cases of parents apprehended by police when they came to pick up processed film, and of artist parents whose work about their children was seized by police during exhibitions, have received wide press attention. These cases serve as a warning about the perils of engaging in one of the most common representational practices of modern culture: taking photographs of one's children. Whether the warning is perceived to be against indiscriminate photographing that observes no limits, or against the excesses of judicial vigilance, the result is the same. Intimate photographs of children are dangerous to make, no matter how close to the child the photographer might be. Any legal allegation of child pornography can be extremely psychologically and financially damaging, even if an investigation leads nowhere, because child pornography is now considered a heinous moral offense.

In the late twentieth and early twenty-first centuries, a growing and increasingly successful number of professional artists have nonetheless tackled the subject of the child body, and especially the awakening, troubled, and sometimes violent physicality of ADOLESCENCE. In the wake of the pioneering work of SALLY MANN in the 1980s and early 1990s, artists such as Anna Gaskell, Marcel Dzama, Dana Hoey, Malerie Marder, Amy Cutler, Anthony Goicolea, Justine Kurland, and Katy Grannan made images of children that challenged ideas of absolute childhood innocence not only by asserting children's sexuality, but by associating sexuality with a range of other attributes both positive and negative, such as confidence, strength, imagination, and beauty as well as anger, escapism, doubt, and malice. The intention of these artists is hardly to objectify children, but rather to endow them with a rich and varied subjectivity. It remains to be seen whether or not this work can be understood according to its intentions, for the essential problem of child pornography is perceptual. Sexuality, and especially the representation of sexuality, is in the eye of the beholder.

See also: **Law, Children and the; Photographs of Children; Theories of Childhood.**

BIBLIOGRAPHY

Edwards, Susan H. 1994. "Pretty Babies: Art, Erotica or Kiddie Porn." *History of Photography* 18, no. 1 (spring): 38–46.

Fisher, William A. and Azy Barak. 1991. "Pornography, Erotica, and Behavior: More Questions than Answers." *International Journal of Law and Psychiatry* 14: 65–73.

Geiser, Robert L. 1979. *Hidden Victims: The Sexual Abuse of Children.* Berkeley: University of California Press.

Ginsberg, Allen and Joseph Richey. 1990. "The Right to Depict Children in the Nude." In *The Body in Question*, ed. Melissa Harris. New York: Aperture.

Goldstein, Michael J. and Harold Stanford Kant. 1973. *Pornography and Sexual Deviance.* Berkeley: University of California Press.

Heins, Marjorie. 2001. *Not in Front of the Children; "Indecency," Censorship, and the Innocence of Youth.* New York: Hill and Wang.

Higonnet, Anne. 1998. *Pictures of Innocence: The History and Crisis of Ideal Childhood.* London: Thames and Hudson.

Marks, Laura U. 1990. "Minor Infractions: Child Pornography and the Legislation of Morality." *Afterimage* 18, no. 4 (November): 12–14.

Stanley, Lawrence. 1991. "Art and Perversion: Censoring Images of Nude Children." *Art Journal* 50, no. 4 (winter): 20–27.

Strossen, Nadine. 1995. *Defending Pornography: Free Speech, Sex, and the Fight for Women's Rights.* New York: Scribner.

ANNE HIGONNET

Child Prodigies

Child prodigies are characterized by extraordinary ability in a given sphere of human endeavor often creative, quantitative, spatial, or lingual in composition. Their mastery, usually evident well before the age of ten, can appear without assistance, or in spite of it, and their achievements can provoke wonder and at times disbelief and are generally viewed as amazing for a person of any age. Through the nineteenth century, the traditional Western view of prodigies held that they were exclusively phenomena of nature, a view largely revised over the twentieth century through findings in the behavioral and biological sciences, which argue for a synthesis of both natural and environmental factors in shaping prodigies. In JAPAN and CHINA, where Confucian ideology is widely influential, exceptional accomplishments in children are linked more directly to motivation and hard work, with less emphasis placed on innate ability.

Child prodigies tend to emerge in fields that are ordered and integrated, where components can be manipulated in unambiguous ways, and where outstanding achievement is readily recognized and measured, such as in music or mathematics. The internationally competitive game of chess is another forum where prodigies have made their mark, and they frequently find themselves called upon to demonstrate in some public way the range and depth of their gift. In 1958 American television audiences were introduced to a supremely talented thirteen-year-old, Israeli-born violinist, Itzhak Perlman, on *The Ed Sullivan Show*.

The intermittent historical record of child prodigies includes THE BIBLE, with its portrayals of David in the Old Testament and the young Jesus Christ in the New Testament, to medieval tales of human calculators displayed as public oddities, to the life of visionary Joan of Arc in the early fifteenth century. The medium most famously pursued by prodigies in recent centuries is music, and the most celebrated exemplar is Wolfgang Amadeus Mozart, who in the eighteenth century performed in European capitals and composed symphonies before the age of nine. Noted twentieth-century child prodigies include violinist Yehudi Menuhin, visual artist Pablo Picasso, and chess player Bobby Fischer.

Institutional support for child prodigies begins with the family and often a master teacher. Prodigies have also been known to enroll in colleges, universities, and at music conservatories before adolescence, though sociocultural impediments coupled with the rare nature of their ability make for unpredictable outcomes. As child prodigies mature, their attention often becomes more dispersed, which may account in part for why their developmental trajectory can plateau in later adolescence and adulthood. Gender bias and related factors appear to have slanted the identification of and limited research on child prodigies in favor of males. Anecdotal evidence suggests, however, that this trend is changing, as evidenced by the emergence in the 1980s of Japanese violinist Midori, in the 1990s by Korean-American violinist Sarah Chang, and the success of Welsh soprano CHARLOTTE CHURCH in the late 1990s and early 2000s. The accomplishments of Hungarian chess player Judit Polgar were revealingly chronicled in *The New York Times* in a 1992 front-page headline, "Youngest Grandmaster Ever Is 15, Ferocious (and Female)."

BIBLIOGRAPHY

Feldman, D. 1991. *Nature's Gambit: Child Prodigies and the Development of Human Potential.* New York: Teachers College Press.

Feldman, D. 1994. "Prodigies." In *Encyclopedia of Human Intelligence,* ed. Robert J. Sternberg. New York: Macmillan. vol. 2: 845–850.

Gardner, Howard. 1997. *Extraordinary Minds: Portraits of Exceptional Individuals and an Examination of our Extraordinariness.* New York: Basic Books.

Smith, S. B. 1983. *The Great Mental Calculators: The Psychology, Method, and Lives of Calculating Prodigies.* New York: Columbia University Press.

JOHN MANGAN

Child Prostitution

Social problems that are difficult to deal with are in fact often not dealt with effectively and remain submerged beneath a reluctance to recognize the distasteful underside to society. Moral issues are perhaps the most subject to this. The involvement of children and young people in commercial sex exposes many sensitive areas of the culture, in particular its ideals regarding childhood, the family, and SEXUALITY. The unequal power relations that tend to make children and young people vulnerable to adult influence and control have enabled their prostitution from both inside and outside of the family. ECPAT, which became prominent in the late twentieth century for its work toward the elimination of child prostitution, CHILD PORNOGRAPHY, and trafficking of children for sexual purposes, defines child prostitution as "the use of a child in sexual activities for remuneration or any other consideration."

The Mythology of the "White Slave Trade"

Unfortunately, obtaining historical or indeed contemporary evidence about the phenomenon of child prostitution is difficult. Historically, what is available must usually be filtered through the ideologies and perceptions of both the many who had heard of it only in its most dramatized form as the "white slave trade" and the few who both encountered it and recorded its existence. Thus even where evidence is available, it is fragmented, sporadic, and often encased in the language of morality. The voices of the children and young people themselves are very rarely discernible above the clamor of adult judgment and rhetoric. Historically, little has been published on the subject and information is particularly scarce before the late nineteenth century. In the late twentieth century, research in this area expanded considerably.

Until the end of the twentieth century, discussion about the prostitution of those under the AGE OF CONSENT was largely restricted to medical or political circles or to volunteer organizations. However, the involvement of young people in commercial sex also emerged in a dramatized version, distanced from connections with recognizable daily existence. The story dramatized as the white slave trade in Britain, Europe, and the United States was of the forced ABDUC-TION of innocent young white girls and women, usually by foreigners, to work in brothels overseas. While this story says a great deal about racism and social fears regarding the increased freedoms enjoyed by women, changing sexual mores, migration, and new locations of leisure activity, it tells us little about the prostitution of children and young people. Indeed, in the early twenty-first century, when Western governments are becoming increasingly concerned about human trafficking and the supply of girls and women by this means, the mythology of the white slave trade often serves to obscure the real experiences behind the sex trade.

The terminology of trafficking and of slavery remains a part of the debates on child prostitution, but the imperialist and racist emphasis upon the victims being white has largely been dropped. After the mid-twentieth century, trafficking became defined in terms of movement and exploitation rather than color. The movement of children for the purposes of prostitution has historically tended to reflect the economic disparities between rural and urban areas and between richer and poorer regions and countries. However, other factors, including gender, age, and market factors are clearly important in that they exacerbate the vulnerability of the young especially. Thus, in the late twentieth century, social and economic instability and war in EASTERN EUROPE increased the flow of both women and children into the commercial sex industries of the European Union. However, child prostitution can also be influenced by a perception, supported by global mass marketing and commercialization, that more can be obtained elsewhere.

One of the first and possibly the most notorious of national media exposés of child prostitution was in July 1885 in the London newspaper the *Pall Mall Gazette*. This series of articles claimed to have uncovered a trade in young girls for brothels in London. The sensational and salacious "Maiden Tribute of Modern Babylon" stories, which contained subheadings like "Buying Girls at the East-End" and "Strapping Girls Down," excited one of the first national moral panics on the subject of child prostitution. This kind of account entrenched for the next century or more the depiction of children and young people involved in commercial sex as abducted and betrayed innocents. These "Maiden Tribute" articles and the events surrounding them provided the crucial force in Britain to ensure the final passage of the Criminal Law Amendment Act 1885, which increased the age of consent from thirteen to sixteen and augmented police powers to deal with vice. The balance between control and protection was to become an enduring feature of the debates on child prostitution and on the subject of youthful DELINQUENCY in general. The "Maiden Tribute" furor did at least help to highlight that the commercial sex market was no respecter of age.

The late nineteenth century panics in both Britain and America concerning the abuse of children resulted in the establishment of numerous charitable organizations, which thereafter continued to highlight the plight of poor and exploited children. Indeed, one of the best sources of evidence on child prostitution is the archives of children's charities. The work of such charities operated to define and separate "delinquent" from "normal" children and associated concepts of dirt, independence, and in particular sexual knowledge and experience with the former. Children who were believed to have sexual experience, even as a result of abuse, were in some cases taken from their families and placed in institutions for children with "knowledge of evil." Paradoxically, once a girl had crossed the line into being sexually experienced, many contemporaries perceived her to be tainted and blameworthy. In Britain, it was not until the period between World Wars I and II that many feminist and child welfare organizations consistently sought to explain sexual precociousness in young girls as an outcome of sexual abuse, in opposition to the narrow portrayal of immoral girls inviting and seducing older men.

Trafficking in Children and Young People

Historically, the international traffic in children and young people has attracted the most official action. Following several conferences in the early twentieth century and an international agreement of 1904 for the Suppression of the White Slave Traffic, the League of Nations in 1919 set up a committee to gather information regarding the trafficking in prostitutes. In 1921 a League of Nations conference was held at Geneva on the Traffic in Women and Children. The work of this committee was taken over by the United Nations in 1946. In 1953 the United Nations amended the League of Nations Slavery Convention of 1926, which highlighted the human rights issues of slavery and "slavery-like practices," including the slave trade, sale of children, child prostitution, and the exploitation of CHILD LABOR.

Trafficking can occur within a country, often from rural to urban areas, or across national borders. During the twentieth century, agencies working to combat the exploitation of women and children in its many forms multiplied and the problem of child prostitution became part of the work of INTERNATIONAL ORGANIZATIONS such as the United Nations Children's Fund (UNICEF), the International Labour Organization, as well as various nongovernmental organizations. Article 34 of the 1989 UN CONVENTION ON THE RIGHTS OF THE CHILD calls for appropriate action to prevent the inducement or coercion of a child to engage in unlawful sexual activity. In the late twentieth century, extraterritorial legislation sought to enable countries to prosecute their citizens for sexually abusing children while overseas. This was enacted in the wake of increased CHILD ABUSE carried on through a commercial sex trade catering to tourists. This was a major theme of the 1996 First Congress against the Commercial Sexual Exploitation of Children, which was organized by ECPAT, UNICEF, and the nongovernmental Group for the Convention on the Rights of the Child.

One consequence of the continued sensitivity of the subject of children and young people involved in commercial sexual activity has been that the meaning of child prostitution has historically been created from a series of negative beliefs. Child prostitutes have been perceived as not being asexual, dependent, and moral, and therefore as not being real children, but also as not being adults. This tendency for negative abstraction has led to assumptions about what child prostitutes are, so that they have been seen as sexually assertive, independent, and immoral—as representing a distorted or perverse form of childhood, of something "other." Hence over the twentieth century, as discourses about child sexual abuse were being constructed, those relating to child prostitution took a distinct journey, one likely to lead to condemnation of the child and even to criminalization. These negatives were not seriously challenged until the late twentieth century, when child prostitution increasingly was placed within the realm of child abuse and the clients came to be considered child abusers and pedophiles who should be subject to child protection legislation.

See also: **Incest; Pedophilia.**

BIBLIOGRAPHY

Barrett, D. 2000. *Youth Prostitution in the New Europe: The Growth in Sex Work.* Lyme Regis, UK: Russell House.

Brown, A., and D. Barrett. 2002. *Knowledge of Evil: Child Prostitution and Child Sexual Abuse in Twentieth Century England.* Cullompton, Devon, UK: Willan.

Ennew, J. 1986. *The Sexual Exploitation of Children.* Cambridge, UK: Polity Press.

Gibbens, T. N. C. 1957. "Juvenile Prostitution." *British Journal of Criminology* 8: 3–12.

Gorham, D. 1978. "The 'Maiden Tribute of Modern Babylon' Re-Examined. Child Prostitution and the Idea of Childhood in Late-Victorian England." *Victorian Studies* 21: 353–79.

Smart, C. 2000. "Reconsidering the Recent History of Child Sexual Abuse, 1919–1960." *Journal of Social Policy* 29, no. 1: 55–71.

INTERNET RESOURCE

ECPAT International. Available from <www.ecpat.net/eng/index.asp>.

ALYSON BROWN

Child Psychology

Although parents and students of human development have been observing children for millennia, researchers in America and Europe began to conduct systematic studies of childhood behavior around the turn of the twentieth century. Prior attempts to codify normal development had been published as diaries that described the behavior of a single child, usually the son or daughter of the author. In 1787, for example, German psychologist Dietrich Tiedemann documented the growth of a child's intellectual abilities; a century later,

German psychologist William Preyer authored elaborate essays that described the development of both the embryo and the young child. In 1887, even British naturalist Charles Darwin published the observations he had gathered during his son's first two years.

During the late nineteenth century, American psychologists conducted the first objective evaluations of large groups of children. These researchers were committed to egalitarianism; that is, they held the idealistic hope that most children could become responsible adults if their early family experiences had been optimal. Yet the psychologists' studies revealed dramatic variation among children in their intellectual ability, school achievement, and character. The troubling results motivated the researchers not only to document the magnitude of the variation, but also to attempt to explain why so many children had not attained a minimum proficiency level.

Most psychologists working during this first phase of systematic inquiry held five implicit premises that were consistent with scientific thought during the eighteenth and nineteenth centuries. For example, they believed that any changes in the psychological properties of children occurred gradually rather than abruptly. This belief was consonant both with the views of eighteenth-century mathematicians and philosophers as well as with Darwin's conviction that evolution was a gradual process.

The second premise was that a child's psychological traits were due in large part to the profile of rewards and punishments administered by adults, especially parents. This assumption rested on the belief that children acted in order to maximize pleasure or to minimize pain, a view asserted two hundred years earlier by philosopher JOHN LOCKE and promoted in the 1920s by the American behaviorist JOHN WATSON. According to this premise, actions that brought the child pleasure would be strengthened and repeated while actions that brought pain would be weakened and discontinued. American parents were told, and many believed, that their treatment of their child would determine his or her personality, talents, and character.

At the end of the nineteenth century, however, the American psychologist James Mark Baldwin represented the views of a growing minority of researchers who recognized the importance of reasoning, language, and symbolism in a child's development. He suggested that the influences of pleasure and pain were only ascendant during infancy. As children matured after age two, Baldwin asserted, they began to distinguish between right and wrong and implicitly asked, "What should I do?"

During the early decades of the twentieth century, however, Watson's behavioristic principles continued to be favored over Baldwin's theories. Scientists and journalists published accounts that described the inferior academic achievements of European immigrants to the United States. These authors attributed the immigrant children's poor school performance and deviant behavior to their inherited propensities. Not only did this fatalistic explanation trouble the egalitarians, it also motivated other researchers to deny the importance of biological factors and enthusiastically emphasize the role of social experience.

Besides political tensions related to immigration, a second reason for the continuing popularity of behaviorism was psychology's status as a new scientific discipline. Psychologists wanted to present their field to biologists and physicists as an experimental and rigorous science, distinct from philosophy and pruned of all metaphysics. Theories that emphasized the conditioning of habits demonstrated elegant empirical science and appealed to young faculty who were beginning careers in developmental psychology. Thus, by the late 1920s, the learning of new habits through conditioning and the proper application of reward and punishment had become the primary way to explain both the appearance of universal characteristics as well as the variation in these and other features. This behavioristic view persisted until the middle of the twentieth century.

The third premise favored a strong connection between childhood habits and moods and those of adulthood, asserting that behavior and emotions acquired during the first years of a child's life could be preserved indefinitely. Intellectual retardation that hampered the acquisition of reading and arithmetic, as well as asocial habits that led to a delinquent career, were two symptoms that caused societal concern. Some commentators claimed that the intellectual profile of every adult had its origins in infancy. Others warned parents not to take their young children to the movies because the film's scenes might be overly stimulating and thus produce an undesirable trait years later. A faith in connectedness was consistent with egalitarian principles, however, for it implied that if one could arrange similar growth-enhancing experiences for all infants and young children, every citizen could attain an ideal profile of abilities, beliefs, and emotions. Both the premises of gradual change and connectedness were consonant with eighteenth-century scientists' attraction to historicism, the belief that in order to understand any phenomenon, one had to know its complete history.

The fourth premise was that the mother represented the most important influence on the child's growth. Although ancient Roman, medieval, and Renaissance scholars all believed that the father played the more important role, John Locke and subsequent thinkers insisted that it was the mother's relation to the child, and her socialization practices, that had greater potency. This assertion appealed to Americans because of the enhanced significance of American women in the families that had left the East Coast to settle in the Appalachians and the Midwest. Middle-class women in European cities were less necessary than those among the pioneers who were settling throughout Tennessee, Kentucky, Ohio, Indiana, and Illinois. These isolated families required a woman's labor, loyalty, and affection in order to survive.

The final premise, an affirmation of John Locke's declaration that children love liberty, assumed that a child's freedom was the most important quality to nurture. This imperative was hidden in psychological essays on the importance of PLAY and the encouragement of personal autonomy. One commentator suggested that an infant who protested the mother's removal of a nursing bottle was showing the first sign of a defiance of authoritarian control that should be encouraged. The most popular developmental textbooks of the 1930s stated that children should be emancipated from parental control and allowed to free themselves from a close emotional attachment to their family. The eroticization of individual freedom was one reason why children's play was a popular topic of research. It seemed obvious to many that when a child was playing he was maximally free, and according to one expert, child's play was the foundation of American democracy.

Phases in Developmental Study

It is possible to discern five historical eras in the study of children over the last century. The first, from approximately 1900 to 1925, is distinguished by the study of differences among children in intellectual ability and character, motivated largely by concern for the many immigrant children who were failing in school and committing crimes. Chicago established the first JUVENILE COURT for delinquents in 1899, and in the following decade, the Judge Baker Children's Center in Boston was the first institution to attempt a scientific study of the causes of DELINQUENCY.

The second phase, which occupied the next twenty-five years and was theoretically consonant with the first, was marked by the influence of Freudian theory. Psychoanalytic ideas seemed to be intuitively correct to large numbers of psychiatrists, psychologists, and educated parents. The latter brooded over whether they should breast- or bottle-feed, when to wean their nursing infant, how to TOILET TRAIN, whether to SLEEP with the child, and how to handle the child's sexual curiosity. SIGMUND FREUD's notions were popular with the public because he left intact most of the nineteenth-century views of human nature, altering only the less essential features.

For example, nineteenth-century scientists believed that humans varied in the amount of energy available for psychic activity. Each person's brain was supposed to possess a fixed amount of energy, and psychological symptoms could appear if the individual depleted this resource. Charles Beard, a neurologist, coined the term *neurasthenia* in 1869 to describe individuals who experienced tension, depression, and insomnia because their brains ran out of energy. Freud accepted the popular understanding that each person inherited a fixed amount of energy, but he attributed the depletion of energy to the repression of libidinal instincts rather than to excessive mental work. A person who used energy to repress sexual impulses would therefore have less energy available for adaptive work.

Another popular belief Freud exploited was that early experiences influenced personality development and, therefore, the possibility of acquiring symptoms. Freud accepted the significance of early childhood, but he made the improper socialization of sexual impulses, rather than obedience, the major cause of symptoms. Freud took advantage of the popular belief that excessive bouts of sexual pleasure were dangerous and frequent MASTURBATION or an obsession with sex could cause insanity or mental retardation.

The final feature of nineteenth-century thought was that physical therapeutic interventions—such as cold baths, herbs, and electrical stimulation—could alleviate psychological problems. Freud substituted psychological therapies instead, insisting that patients could gain insight into the causes of their repression by telling their therapist their deepest thoughts.

The third phase is characterized by the cognitive revolution, which was initiated by American linguist Noam Chomsky's radical critique of the behaviorist's interpretation of language acquisition and continued by Swiss psychologist JEAN PIAGET's extensive research. The growing dissatisfaction with the demonstrated limitations of conditioning theory rendered child psychologists receptive to Piaget's rejection of the conditioning assumptions and his emphasis on the child's autonomous behavior. Piaget replaced Watson's passive child with one who is cognitively active in acquiring knowledge, initially through manipulations of objects and, later, through the manipulations of ideas. Echoing Baldwin, Piaget insisted that the child was continually trying to construct the most coherent understanding of an event. Surprisingly, even though he adopted a stage theory, Piaget was loyal to the doctrines of gradualism and connectedness, and he minimized the importance of brain maturation. Although Piaget acknowledged that each infant was born with some sensory motor functions, he wished to award biology as little power as possible. Some scholars have speculated that Piaget made encounters with the environment, rather than biology, the primary sculptor of growth because he wanted to base human morality on a history of experiences.

The fourth phase is defined by the research of British psychiatrist JOHN BOWLBY, who introduced the concept of infant attachment. The sense meaning of attachment is an emotional connection to a person who cares for the infant, created by the infant's pleasant experiences in the presence of the caretaker and a reduction in distress when she returns. The broad interest in Bowlby's speculations on infant attachment was partially due to the large numbers of American mothers who had begun placing their infants and young chil-

dren in surrogate care in order to join the work force after World War II. This new social arrangement violated the normative nineteenth-century conception of a mother who remained at home to care for her brood of children. The public was receptive to a wise scholar who believed that the young infant should develop an emotional attachment to a single caretaker. Bowlby's presumption that these early attachments represented the hub around which a person's life revolved promised to reduce the tensions caused by greater geographic mobility, a higher percentage of working mothers, and the increasingly strained relationships among people and between citizens and their community.

Although many nineteenth-century observers would have understood his theories, and probably agreed with Bowlby, few would have written three books on attachment because this idea seemed to be as obviously true as the fact that the sky is blue. Bowlby's conclusions became newsworthy in the last half of the twentieth century, however, because historical events had led many to question the inevitability of maternal devotion to the child and children's love for their parents. Newspaper headlines that described parental abuse and adolescent children killing their parents undermined the nineteenth-century faith in the naturalism of parental love. Citizens were saddened by these new conditions and were eager to hear a psychiatrist declare that the love between child and parent was a requisite for psychological health.

Every society needs some transcendental theme to which its citizens can be loyal. In the past, the existence of God, the beauty and utility of knowledge, and the sanctity of faithful romantic love were among the most sacred ideas in the American ethic. The facts of modern life had made it difficult for many Americans to remain loyal to those ideals. The sacredness of the bond between mother and infant persisted as one of the last beliefs that remained unsullied. The large number of books and magazine articles on the attachment of infant to mother, and the necessity of skin bonding to the mother in the first postnatal hours, generated strong emotion, suggesting that something more than scientific fact was prompting the discussion. If an infant could be cared for by any concerned adult, the biological mother was expendable, and one of the few remaining ethical imperatives would be at risk.

Contemporary Developmental Psychology

Biology has returned to the study of children during the last two decades as a result of elegant discoveries in genetics, molecular biology, and neuroscience. The enthusiasm for biological influences assumes two forms. It is represented first by descriptions of the biologically prepared competencies of infants and young children in the opening years of life. These include infants' attentional preferences for certain kinds of stimuli (e.g., an attraction to contour, motion, and curvature); the enhancement of memory and the appearance of imitation later in the first year; and the emergence of language, a moral sense, and self-consciousness in the second year. Each of these developments is inevitable as long as children live in a world of objects and people. None requires the regimen of rewards and punishments that behaviorists had described as essential a century earlier.

A second form of biological influence involves the study of human temperaments, which the American psychiatrists Alexander Thomas and Stella Chess reintroduced to researchers during the late 1950s. Neuroscientists speculated on the reasons for variation among infants in traits such as irritability, activity, or fearfulness. These speculations center on inherited variation in the neurochemistry of the brain. The social environment was assumed to influence each infant's temperament to produce the personality of the older child.

With these advances, developmental psychology has come full circle; the early researchers' diaries also emphasized the common psychological properties that emerge in all children who grow up exposed to people and objects. We have learned, however, that the time of emergence of each of these competencies corresponds closely to maturational events in the brain. Both biological and experiential influences contribute to growth; consequently, an attempt to synthesize both forces, necessary for complete understanding, will dominate research and theory in the decades to come. This synthesis will require one vocabulary to describe the biological events and another to describe the psychological phenomena. A behavior, thought, or feeling is the final product of a series of cascades that begins with an external event, thought, or spontaneous biological change. The forms that comprise each succeeding cascade have to be described with a distinct vocabulary. Genes, neurons, and children require distinct predicates because each has unique functions: genes mutate, neurons inhibit, and children act. Developing an understanding of these issues will dominate the future of child psychology.

See also: **Child Development, History of the Concept of; Parenting; Theories of Childhood.**

BIBLIOGRAPHY

Bowlby, John. 1969. *Attachment and Loss: Vol. 1. Attachment.* New York: Basic Books.

Cairns, R. B. 1998. "The Making of Developmental Psychology." In *Handbook of Child Psychology: Vol. 1*, 5th edition, ed. R. M. Lerner and W. Damon. New York: Wiley.

Freud, Sigmund. 1957. *A General Selection From the Works of Sigmund Freud.* New York: Liveright.

Kagan, Jerome. 1983. "Classifications of the Child." In *Handbook of Child Psychology: Vol. 1*, 4th edition, ed. W. Kessen and P. H. Mussen. New York: Wiley.

Piaget, Jean. 1951. *Play Dreams and Imitation in Childhood.* New York: Norton.

JEROME KAGAN

Child-Rearing Advice Literature

The very appearance of printed advice literature meant to help parents rear a child signals a profound historical change in the social distribution of knowledge. In most cultures, across space and time, child-rearing advice is an oral genre found in face-to-face groups. GRANDPARENTS and other members of the extended family living with or near young parents are available to dispense advice and, often, to participate actively in the rearing of children. The oral culture of child-rearing advice still thrives, even in modern industrialized societies, where mothers might seek and offer advice in a conversation with other women, or where fathers might have conversations with male friends about how to rear a boy in today's world.

A number of historical forces, however, gave rise to published advice literature in Europe and the British American colonies in the seventeenth century. Initially written by physicians and eventually by ministers and others who extended the advice to matters of morality and character, the appearance of this printed genre suggests the increased physical mobility of families (who might move away from the extended family), the rise of certain professions with legitimated "expertise," and certain social conditions (e.g., social class aspirations) that would lead parents to distrust their own instincts and to seek professional advice on matters as seemingly commonsensical as child rearing. The ENLIGHTENMENT, with its emphasis on reconstructing humanity and creating a reasonable citizen, also encouraged advice-giving and -seeking in child-rearing matters.

The emergence of this advice literature also required a conceptualization of childhood as a distinct and separate stage in life. The material culture of the seventeenth and eighteenth centuries in the American colonies, for example, supports the account from written evidence of the historical transition from viewing the child as a little adult to the Enlightenment portrait of the child as an innocent creature with unique needs for nurturance and guidance. Children began to have their own rooms in houses, their own dishes and chamber pots, and more durable TOYS. The invention of childhood in this period in many ways required the parallel invention of motherhood and fatherhood.

Child-rearing advice literature may have been a prime mover in these inventions, and historians read it for evidence of changing conceptions of the child, of the mother, and of the father. As historical evidence, printed child-rearing advice has some limitations. It is not at all clear, for example, whether the advice given during a historical period was actually followed by the parents who received it. Not every social class has access to printed advice, even in the present, as differences in both disposable income and literacy limit the expert knowledge available to a segment of the society.

Still, historians are drawn to the child-rearing advice literature not merely because the advice signals a social class's conception of the child and of parental duties. One way or another, most historians share the belief that "the child is father of the man," or (to switch aphorisms) that "the hand that rocks the cradle rules the world." In short, historians are eager to reconstruct the child-rearing practices of a society or of a segment of a society in order to understand what sorts of adult men and women that rearing would be likely to create—or at least the kinds a society would like to create. From the mid-eighteenth century, scientific psychology provided a number of theories of child development aimed at linking childhood experiences with adult thought and behavior, and the history of child-rearing literature charts the history of these ideas. But some historians also attempt to use developmental psychologies (most often psychoanalytic theory) to explain a society's patterns with reference to child rearing. For some historians, then, the psychologies linking child rearing and adult personality are both subject matter and analytical tool.

Seventeenth and Eighteenth Centuries

Physicians were among the first to put into print their advice on how to rear children. The first advice manuals in the American colonies and in the early national period came from England and include William Cadogan's 1749 *Essay on Nursing* and William Buchan's 1804 *Advice to Mothers*, which went through many American editions. Books like these mark the beginning of the "medicalization of motherhood," as the historian Julia Grant put it in 1998, but these physicians did not limit their advice to the purely medical. For physicians in the seventeenth and eighteenth centuries, the socialization of children's feeding, TOILET TRAINING, crying, sleeping, ANGER, and independence implied issues of character. While these physicians wrote primarily from the Enlightenment view (inherited from JOHN LOCKE, JEAN-JACQUES ROUSSEAU, and others), which saw the child as an innocent creature of nature, they were quite aware of the popular Calvinist view that rearing a child was a battle of wills between the inherently sinful infant or child and the parent. The physical punishment of children in order to shape their behavior and character, for example, had deep religious roots and meanings for Americans. It was not until the middle of the nineteenth century that mainstream Protestant ministers, such as Horace Bushnell, provided their congregants with sermons that urged them to see young children as capable of being gently molded toward the good and not innately sinful. By then, middle-class parents had already begun to mellow their regimens and disciplinary devices under the tutelage of physicians.

Advice to parents softened in the eighteenth century, and the general trend across time has been toward recommending increasingly permissive, child-centered approaches to socializing the child. Scientific thinking and advice was slowly replacing purely moral advice about rearing children, though the moral and the scientific have always been tangled in American approaches to rearing children. Historians working on the history of emotions note, for example, the eighteenth-century campaign against anger as an emotion to be eradicated in children. Physical punishment declined, and the authors of advice manuals recommended guilt rather than shame as a way to motivate good behavior. Experts writing in the eighteenth century tended to see the family as a microcosm of society, so what children learned of human relationships in the family was important to their future interactions as adults in a society increasingly moving from a rural social organization and agrarian values to more mobile, urban, commercial patterns.

Nineteenth Century

With the industrialization and urbanization of life in western Europe and the United States came the increasing separation of life into two spheres, the public and the private, which also came to be associated with gender roles. The public, masculine sphere demanded certain qualities in young men, which were suited to the competitive individualism of a commercial culture. The literature on child rearing in the early national period made it clear that this public figure was created in the private, domestic sphere belonging to women. A cult of motherhood developed, recognizing the crucial role of mothers in creating independent (male) citizens for the new nation.

Advice manual writers in the antebellum period put new emphasis on self-control and self-discipline. Emotions like anger and JEALOUSY were unproductive in this social world, and parents were advised to help their children learn ways to control their tempers. Writers advised against parents' expressions of anger, since Victorians saw the home as, in Christopher Lasch's phrase, a "haven in a heartless world." Among the public activities of white, middle-class antebellum women was the creation of maternal organizations, usually associated with churches, and the 1830s through 1840s saw the publication of new monthly magazines and books aimed at sharing information on mothering.

The Enlightenment-based psychology of the child so common early in the eighteenth century gave way after 1859 (the publication date of Charles Darwin's *The Origin of Species*) to a Darwinian, evolutionary psychology that acknowledged instincts and unconscious drives as features to be reckoned with in rearing children. Psychologist G. STANLEY HALL, a powerful figure in the creation of scientific psychology in the United States and a key inventor of the idea of ADOLESCENCE as a period of life distinct from both childhood and adulthood, was instrumental in founding the CHILD-STUDY movement, which provided scientific foundations for advice to parents and teachers about how to rear children. The child was no longer the "blank slate" of Enlightenment thought but was the inheritor of instincts and traits forged by evolution. Advice literature based on Darwinian psychology urged parents, teachers, and youth workers (a growing professional group) to channel these powerful instincts into positive activities rather than attempt to eradicate or suppress them.

Early Twentieth Century

By 1909 enough experts on the scientific rearing of children existed that the first WHITE HOUSE CONFERENCE ON CHILDREN could be convened, and in 1912 the federal government created the U.S. CHILDREN'S BUREAU, which would soon become a primary source of scientific information about children, from diet and health to socialization. The authorship of advice manuals shifted, accelerating the decline of the morally based advice manual in favor of those making some claim to science. By the early twentieth century, PEDIATRICS and CHILD PSYCHOLOGY were established specialties with expertise about the child. Through the Children's Bureau and other venues, the government published books and pamphlets and established infant-welfare stations meant to provide the most current scientific information about children's health, safety, and well-being. Research universities, especially land grant public universities honoring their mission to serve the citizenry, established home economics extension services to help disseminate the most current scientific knowledge about rearing children. By 1920 an extensive institutional network existed, offering expert advice, which was supposed to be scientifically grounded, on understanding children.

The women's movement was also having effects on child study and parent education. The National Congress of Mothers, the Child Study Association, and the American Association of University Women, for example, generally supported a scientific (as opposed to religious) approach to understanding modern motherhood.

The behaviorism of JOHN B. WATSON and others provided the scientific psychology behind most ideas about child rearing in the 1920s and 1930s, though Freudian and other psychoanalytic ideas also enjoyed some popularity in these circles. Both approaches considered the first two or three years of life to be critical to child rearing. The behaviorist approach assumed that behavior could be fashioned entirely through patterns of reinforcement, and Watson's ideas permeated the Children's Bureau's *Infant Care* bulletins and PARENTS MAGAZINE, which was founded in 1926. As historians and others have observed, this approach to programming and managing children's behavior suited a world of rationalized factory production and employee management theories rationalizing industrial relations. Watson explicitly criticized "too much mother love," advising parents to become detached and objective in their child-rearing techniques so as to develop self-control in the child.

Many experts in the late nineteenth and early twentieth centuries expressed concern about the large number of immigrant mothers raising children in the United States.

These mothers became the target audience for efforts by parent education associations to Americanize the huge immigrant population. Similar political motives impelled efforts to teach African-American mothers what were considered modern, scientific approaches to child-rearing. It has also been suggested that changes in generational relations and the decline of advice within the family made even middle-class parents more dependent on advice. Certainly child-advice book sales and the number of titles in print soared by the 1920s.

While the behaviorist approach continued to have great strength through the 1930s, there were also signs of a growing realization that children have individual natures which must be taken into account. The growth of a child-centered approach redirected the problem of child rearing from the training of children to the training of parents to be more sensitive to the needs of the child. At the same time, the economic circumstances of the GREAT DEPRESSION tended to disrupt gender roles, placing more women (and children) into the workforce and leading experts to elevate the importance of the father in child rearing. The language of the advice to parents in the 1930s became more therapeutic, stressing the need for a family culture that was more egalitarian and more sensitive to the individual needs of children, mothers, and fathers. The gentle management of emotions, especially anger, became a central topic in this advice.

ARNOLD GESELL and Francis L. Ilg's enormously popular 1943 book, *Infant and Child Care in the Culture of Today*, put an end to the behavioral approach and popularized a developmental approach that recognized the power of biology in the child's physical and psychosocial growth. In the midst of World War II, this book made explicit the ideology of their developmental approach. Whereas regimented behaviorism resembled fascism, a developmental approach aimed at maximizing the growth of the unique individual child was suited to a democratic family and a democratic society. The child-centered approach recommended relaxed approaches to feeding, toilet training, and independence training.

Mid- to Late Twentieth Century

Dr. BENJAMIN SPOCK's 1946 book, *The Commonsense Book of Baby and Child Care*, guided the child rearing of the BABY BOOM GENERATION's parents (1946–1964). Spock's aim, he said, was to get mothers to trust themselves again, to take a more relaxed approach that recognized the qualities of individual children. The book, however, and Dr. Spock himself, became a central topic in the culture wars of the 1980s and 1990s, as some conservatives blamed society's woes on the effects of his permissive, child-centered approach. Dr. Spock's own high visibility as a critic of the Vietnam War helped cement the impression that he had helped create a generation of rebellious children and adolescents who mocked authority.

By the 1970s other physicians were vying with Spock to be the most visible and most trusted dispenser of advice on rearing babies and children. Dr. Lendon H. Smith was among the most successful of these. Beginning with his 1969 book *The Children's Doctor* and continuing in his radio and television shows in the 1970s, Smith pointed to the diet and resulting body chemistry of children to explain their behavior. His message that children's health and behavior could be managed through diet suited the 1970s and 1980s trend, which looked toward biology, rather than learned behavior, for the cause of behavioral problems. In contrast, Dr. Thomas Gordon, a clinical psychologist, took a management training approach in his 1970 book, *Parental Effectiveness Training: The No-Lose Program for Raising Responsible Children*, which became the foundation for Parental Effectiveness Training Seminars and programs around the country.

A new baby boom (sometimes called a "boomlet" or an "echo boom") of births began around 1982, creating a demand for books on baby and child care, parenting, and related matters. The bookstores began stocking large numbers of titles as physicians, psychologists, and others raced to claim the increasing readership.

Physician William Sears and his wife, Martha Sears, a nurse, came the closest in the mass market of the 1990s and early 2000s to duplicating Dr. Spock's wide influence. Beginning with their 1993 *The Baby Book: Everything You Need to Know about Your Baby from Birth to Age Two*, the Sears couple, sometimes with a coauthor, have written a series of books offering advice on topics ranging from basic health care to moral education for older children, as in their 1995 *The Discipline Book* and their 2000 *The Successful Child: The Proven Program for Raising Responsible Children*. Like their predecessors, these books emphasize the earliest period of a child's life as the most fundamental. Recent studies of early brain development have reinforced this trend. At the center of the Sears couple's advice is "attachment parenting," whose origins in JOHN BOWLBY's theories of attachment make it a somewhat controversial approach. It counsels nursing for as long as both mother and child enjoy the relationship; responding promptly to the infant's cries; being responsive to the baby's preferences in sleeping arrangements (including sleeping with the baby in a king-size bed); and carrying the baby in a sling that keeps him or her in touch with the mother's or father's body. Attachment parenting, insist the authors, makes it more likely that parents will be sensitive to their particular child's needs and will trust their own responses to those needs; consequently it increases the child's skill at giving the parents cues. The trust developed in this relationship, argue the authors, sets the foundation for a child's self-esteem, for the child's bonding with other people throughout his or her life, and for a disciplinary relationship based on trust and the growth of a "healthy conscience."

The rapid development of the Internet in the 1990s and the early 2000s multiplied the range of resources parents could turn to in search of child-rearing advice, though the class issues of the digital divide still affect access to this information. Parents who have access to the Internet can find all books in print through Internet bookstores and finding services. Perhaps more important, hundreds of websites dispense information and advice on children's health and personality training. Dr. William Sears has his own website, for example, as do many other well-known authors of baby-care and child-rearing books. Often these websites feature questions from online readers, with answers provided by the experts. Parents of children with special needs—which includes physical disabilities, emotional problems, attention deficit problems, and developmental problems—can find websites full of advice and resources for parents dealing with these challenges.

Conclusion

Child-rearing advice provides useful historical evidence of changing conceptions of the child and of the proper roles of mothers, fathers, family members, and other care givers. As the advice has moved from oral to written to electronic means of communication, the source of expertise has moved from family to religious leaders to physicians and psychologists. The general trend in the written advice proffered by authors over the past four hundred years has been toward more permissive child-rearing practices (feeding on demand, relaxed toilet training, reduction of frustrating experiences, and so on), with an occasional swing back in the direction of rigid scheduling and control (e.g., the behaviorism of the 1920s and 1930s).

In the last decade of the twentieth century, stricter demands about toilet training and feeding have returned, together with a reduction in strictures against physical correction. This has resulted from both a new view of parental nurture as less significant than the natural internal development of the child's emotional and cognitive life and in response to growing concerns about children's misbehavior. The heightened visibility of the evangelical religious right in public disputes about the family has clearly affected this development as well.

Child-rearing advice has always carried ideological weight. Advice reflects the religious, scientific, and broadly political ideas of a period, even if what they reflect is a profound conflict over and discomfort with the tension between the current ideas. Political and economic ideologies work their way into child-rearing advice in the United States as experts and parents debate which child-rearing approaches are compatible and incompatible with current thinking about the nature of American democracy and its institutions, including the family. This was as true in the early national period as it was in the twentieth-century debates, but a heightened public discourse about culture wars in the 1980s and 1990s has again put debates about the proper rearing of children at the center of deeply felt debates about the nature and future of American democratic institutions. Sociolinguist George Lakoff shows how many differences about the political and moral meanings of the United States are rooted in two different conceptualizations of the family, one hierarchical and authoritarian, the other egalitarian. Similarly, in concluding her historical account of the education of parents for child rearing, Julia Grant notes how a number of current, highly visible experts on child rearing (among them T. Berry Brazelton, Penelope Leach, and David Elkind) are promoting the view that there is a biological foundation for gender differences in parenting. Public arguments over the role of fathers and other care givers in raising children has been particularly fierce. Child-rearing advice, it seems, speaks to some of the largest issues and tensions experienced by a society, and that is unlikely to change soon.

See also: **Fathering and Fatherhood; Mothering and Motherhood; Parenting; Scientific Child Rearing.**

BIBLIOGRAPHY

Deetz, James. 1996. *In Small Things Forgotten: An Archaeology of Early American Life*, rev. and expanded ed. New York: Anchor Books/Doubleday.

Grant, Julia. 1998. *Raising Baby by the Book: The Education of American Mothers.* New Haven, CT: Yale University Press.

Greven, Philip. 1990. *Spare the Child: The Religious Roots of Punishment and the Psychological Impact of Physical Abuse.* New York: Knopf.

Hulbert, Ann. 2003. *Raising America: Experts, Parents, and a Century of Advice about Children.* New York: Knopf.

Hunter, James Davison. 1991. *Culture Wars: The Struggle to Define America.* New York: Basic Books.

Lakoff, George. 1996. *Moral Politics: What Conservatives Know That Liberals Don't.* Chicago: University of Chicago Press.

Lasch, Christopher. 1977. *Haven in a Heartless World: The Family Besieged.* New York: Basic Books.

Mechling, Jay. 1975. "Advice to Historians on Advice to Mothers." *Journal of Social History* 9: 44–63.

Stearns, Carol Zisowitz, and Peter N. Stearns. 1986. *Anger: The Struggle for Emotional Control in America's History.* Chicago: University of Chicago Press.

Stearns, Peter N. 1989. *Jealousy: The Evolution of an Emotion in American History.* New York: New York University Press.

Stearns, Peter N. 2003. *Anxious Parents: A History of Modern Child-rearing in America.* New York: New York University Press.

Wishy, Bernard. 1968. *The Child and the Republic: The Dawn of American Child Nurture.* Philadelphia: University of Pennsylvania Press.

JAY MECHLING

Children's Defense Fund

The Children's Defense Fund (CDF) was founded in 1973 as an outgrowth of the civil rights movement of the 1950s and 1960s. The CDF quickly became a powerful advocacy agency for impoverished and at risk children, more effective than the U.S. CHILDREN'S BUREAU ever was. Marion Wright Edelman, its founder and vigorous leader, was born June 6, 1939, in Bennettsville, South Carolina, the daughter of an African-American Baptist minister, Arthur Bennett, who taught that Christianity necessitated service to the world. The elder Bennett idolized A. Philip Randolph, president of the Brotherhood of Sleeping Car Porters and a hero of the civil rights movement. Edelman studied at Spelman College, in Atlanta, and abroad, including in the Soviet Union. When she returned to Spelman in 1959, she abandoned her Foreign Service plans for the law, and threw herself into the civil rights movement. She took her law degree at Yale in 1963. She then worked for the NAACP Legal Defense Fund in New York, then Mississippi, where she worked on civil rights issues and established a Head Start program. When U.S. Attorney General Robert Kennedy was touring Mississippi, she met Peter Edelman, a Kennedy assistant, and moved to Washington, D.C. a year later to marry him. In 1968 she helped found the Washington Research Project, Inc., a private, not for profit institution that helped poor people investigate and monitor the federal programs that Congress had designed for them. Marian Wright Edelman developed a double-barreled style: vigorous, no-nonsense public advocacy and investigatory research.

In 1973, Edelman and her allies in the Washington, D.C. area organized the Children's Defense Fund using the personnel and knowledge that had accrued in the Washington Research Project. Edelman eschewed direct dependence on government agencies, budgets, and officials. Instead she and her associates organized the CDF as a private, not for profit organization of lawyers, monitors of federal policy, researchers, and community liaison persons, all of whom were dedicated to long-term systematic advocacy and reform on behalf of the nation's children. An early CDF project probed why children of varying ages and backgrounds were not in school. Between July 1973 and March 1974, forty-two part time and summer staffers, plus Edelman and three full time associates knocked on 8,500 doors in thirty areas of nine states, and talked to over 6,500 families. From this interviewing came the first of many hard-hitting, often shocking, reports of how many poor children fall between society's cracks. Often CDF surveys were more thorough than the United States Census in investigating these problems and issues.

When Bill Clinton became President in 1993, CDF staffers hoped for child-friendly policies. Instead Clinton terminated Aid to Families of Dependent Children (AFDC), and other similar programs. Edelman vigorously attacked these actions. By 2003 the CDF employed a staff of 130, raised and spent about $25 million a year from private corporations as it continued its advocacy work for the most needy and underserved children.

See also: **Aid to Dependent Children (AFDC); Law, Children and the; Social Welfare; Welfare Reform Act (1996).**

BIBLIOGRAPHY

Children's Defense Fund. 1974. *Children Out of School, a Report by the Children's Defense Fund of the Washington Research Project, Inc.* Cambridge: Children's Defense Fund.

INTERNET RESOURCE

About Women's History. "Marian Wright Edelman." Available from <http://womenshistory.about.com/library/bio/blbio_marian_wright_edelman.htm>.

HAMILTON CRAVENS

Children's Hospitals

Pediatric hospitals began in the United States with the establishment of Nursery and Child's Hospital in New York City in 1854. Children's Hospital of Philadelphia opened its doors the following year. During the 1860s three other hospitals for children opened: Chicago Hospital for Women and Children (1865), Boston Children's Hospital (1869), and the New York Foundling Asylum (1869). Over the next thirty years most of the major cities in America created a children's hospital.

The establishment of children's hospitals paralleled the explosion of hospitals in the rest of the country. As historian Charles Rosenberg has pointed out, the rapid growth of American hospitals between the 1860s and the 1930s reflected changes in American cities as well as in the medical profession. The development of children's hospitals reveals as much about society's evolving perception of children as about the changing role of medicine in America. Many major cities still rely on children's hospitals as centers for care, not merely for inpatient services but also for outpatient care.

Children's Hospitals and Nineteenth-Century Reforms

Early children's hospitals began as coalitions between elite physicians, who sought the experience and prestige of hospital appointments, and influential laypersons, who sought to improve the lives of poor children. Antebellum reformers believed that poverty, disease, and morality were closely linked and therefore that hospitals should instill moral values as well as offer medical care. Because of their youth and innocence, children seemed particularly amenable to this form of social meliorism. Thus it was no accident that early children's hospitals espoused overtly religious missions.

CHILD SAVING was a prominent feature of many late-nineteenth-century reforms, including the movement to abolish CHILD LABOR and the KINDERGARTEN movement, and optimizing child health played an integral role in these reform efforts. Hospitals were part of a larger societal move that turned to institutions and professions to solve social problems. PEDIATRICS and children's hospitals were typical of Progressive-era reforms.

In addition to appealing to charitable and religious motives, the movement to establish children's hospitals was a reaction to fundamental changes occurring in American cities. Historian Morris Vogel demonstrated how urbanization, industrialization, and immigration strained American cities and created a growing need for hospital services for poorer citizens. Families crowded into cramped tenements lacked both extended family members and space to care for seriously ill family members. As poor mothers entered the workforce, they too were unavailable to care for sick children. For many desperate families, the hospital was the only place for health care. Like other hospitals of the era, pediatric hospitals were designed specifically to care for the children of the "worthy poor." In reality, however, children were only turned away if they were deemed contagious or incurable. Wealthy families could afford private physician care in their homes; only the most destitute families brought their children to the hospital.

The hospital was not simply a response to societal changes. During the late nineteenth century, medicine was becoming increasingly cognizant of the unique medical needs of children. Doctors with a particular interest in children's diseases argued that sick children merited medical care separate from adults. Children were not little adults, these doctors argued. Not only did children react differently to common diseases, but they suffered from distinct diseases and presented unique diagnostic and therapeutic challenges. The appalling INFANT MORTALITY rates witnessed in late-nineteenth-century American cities lent a sense of urgency to the issue of child health care. Blaming this atrocity on a combination of moral laxity among the poor, inadequate city resources, and the relative inability of babies to resist disease, doctors and reformers alike felt called to attack this serious problem.

The young field of pediatrics took the pressing health care needs of children seriously. Pediatrics formally began in the 1880s with the creation of the American Medical Association's Section on the Diseases of Children (1880) and the American Pediatric Society (1888). These early pediatricians witnessed first hand the benefits of separate hospital care for children. Their efforts at professionalization legitimized the young field of pediatrics, created a community of like-minded doctors, helped elaborate a scientific rationale for the field, and publicized the advantages of specialized care for children. The concentration of sick children in pediatric hospitals also provided a fertile training ground for young doctors interested in pediatrics. By working on pediatric hospital wards, these ambitious doctors refined surgical techniques, tested new therapies, and conducted research on childhood diseases.

Early Models of Children's Hospitals

Most nineteenth-century general hospitals occasionally admitted children. Typically, these youngsters were placed on adult wards, where they were cared for by nurses and doctors who lacked special training in children's health. Shortly after the turn of the twentieth century, general hospitals began to acknowledge the benefits of separate care for children and created pediatric wards. Typically, however, general practitioners—and not pediatricians—treated these children.

Although early hospitals for children promised distinct advantages over general hospitals, these institutions varied considerably in philosophy and services. Some evolved from older institutions for children, especially ORPHANAGES and FOUNDLING homes for abandoned infants. Others began as babies' hospitals, concentrating on the health problems of infancy. Their medical mission focused on providing nutritious infant formula and treating diarrhea, the predominant disease responsible for the inordinate infant death rate. Because medicine could do so little to counteract infant mortality, most early children's hospitals limited their clientele to children over two. As urban sanitary conditions improved after 1900, however, infant mortality declined and babies' and children's hospitals merged into the modern institution that treats children of all ages.

The humble beginnings of children's hospitals reflected not only their meager financial resources but also their philosophy. The founders typically procured a small house, assigning separate wards for female and male patients. If space allowed, patients were further divided onto surgical and medical wards. Because contagion could close a hospital and threaten the lives of already weak children, an isolation room was commonly included. The hospital matron lived in the hospital and oversaw daily patient care. In this homelike environment the trustees believed that sick, poor children would receive the warmth, nurture, and comfort of a Christian home. Toward the end of the nineteenth century, as physicians began to play influential roles in hospital management, a more medical model of pediatric care emerged, and many children's hospitals expanded to freestanding buildings with up-to-date hygienic designs.

Hospitalizations frequently lasted weeks, even months. Despite an attempt to bar chronic and CONTAGIOUS DISEASES, many early hospital wards were filled with children with these complaints. A large number of children suffered from tuberculosis, a major and indolent killer of nineteenth-century Americans. Many children who entered the hospital were severely malnourished or near death's door; their recovery, if it occurred, was protracted. Because so much hospital care was supportive, nursing was critical. Members of religious sisterhoods often acted as nurses in early hospitals; by 1900 professionally trained nurses had replaced these volunteers.

Hospitals severely limited visiting hours, making it difficult for working parents to visit their sick children. These visiting hours reflected practical concerns that families would worsen homesickness, create behavior problems on the wards, introduce new infections and unsanctioned food, and adversely affect recovery. In addition, poor families were often held responsible for their children's illnesses and therefore frequent contact with parents was considered detrimental. Attention was paid, however, to entertaining sick children; photographs show rocking horses and dolls in the wards.

After discharge, children were either sent to a convalescent home or followed in the hospital's outpatient department. Because recovery from disease and surgery was often protracted, many pediatric hospitals established convalescent homes in the country, where recuperating children spent several weeks receiving fresh air and nutritious food. Beginning in the 1890s hospitals assigned social workers and nurses to visit convalescing children at home in order to teach families the principles of adequate home care.

One of the most unusual early pediatric hospitals was the floating hospital. Modeled in part after military hospital ships, the floating hospital took sick children and their families into the harbor, where they could breathe the supposedly salubrious sea air. While on board, children would be given carefully prepared formula and parents would be taught the benefits of proper nutrition and HYGIENE. Initially, the trips were day excursions; by the 1920s the sicker children stayed overnight as well.

A Unified Pediatric Model

Throughout the nineteenth century, pediatric hospital care largely consisted of nursing, nutrition, dressing changes, and general supportive care. As pediatrics became more professional and scientific in its approach, children's hospitals shed their image as supportive care providers and began to stress the acute medical and surgical services they could perform, as well as the medical research they conducted. As a result, these hospitals evolved into institutions with obvious benefits for rich as well as poor children. During the 1920s and 1930s these hospitals began to woo paying patients, especially for surgical procedures.

By the 1930s the diversity of pediatric hospitals had evolved into a fairly unified model of pediatric hospital care in which children from all walks of life received up-to-date medical and surgical care. Within the children's hospital, young medical graduates pursued advanced training in pediatrics and learned the latest medical and surgical techniques for children.

See also: **Children's Spaces.**

BIBLIOGRAPHY

Evans, H. Hughes. 1995. "Hospital Waifs: The Hospital Care of Children in Boston, 1860–1920." Ph.D. diss. Harvard University.

Golden, Janet, ed. 1989. *Infant Asylums and Children's Hospitals: Medical Dilemmas and Developments 1850–1920.* New York: Garland.

Halpern, Sydney A. 1988. *American Pediatrics: The Social Dynamics of Professionalism, 1880–1980.* Berkeley: University of California Press.

Rosenberg, Charles E. 1987. *The Care of Strangers: The Rise of America's Hospital System.* New York: Basic Books.

Vogel, Morris J. 1980. *The Invention of the Modern Hospital: Boston, 1870–1930.* Chicago: University of Chicago Press.

HUGHES EVANS

Children's Libraries

Inspired by Progressive social reform movements in the late nineteenth century, public librarians in the United States and Britain established children's services that emphasized outreach and programming as well as the creation of special collections of books for young readers. These collections and services are meant to complement those in school libraries whose goal is to support the curriculum. Although children's collections in public libraries do attempt to meet educational needs, public librarians have always focused on promoting the joy of reading as well as fostering the emerging LITERACY skills of children. Scholars note that over the late nineteenth and twentieth centuries American children's librarians have developed a number of "articles of faith." These include: a belief in the uniqueness of each child; a belief in the crucial importance of each child's personal selection of reading materials; a belief in the children's room as "an egalitarian republic of readers;" and a belief in literature as a positive force for understanding, not only between individuals, but also between groups and nations. Similar ideals have been articulated in the United Kingdom where the Library Association's guidelines for service to children identify four areas of child development in which libraries are vitally important: intellectual development, language development, social development, and educational development.

In many countries the national library association has a special section for children's librarians, and it is often this group that advocates for both the improvement and extension of services; among children's librarians in Japan there is a popular slogan: "Like lampposts in town, we need children's libraries on every corner." Although children's libraries are found throughout the world, their development is quite varied and is influenced by educational priorities, funding, and legislation. The general development of public libraries and the availability of children's books in the local languages are also important.

By the 1890s many public libraries in the United States began to set up special sections with books for children, but it was not until 1895 when the first library was constructed with a specially designed room for children—a practice that became the norm during the period of widespread library construction in the early 1900s. American librarians also took the lead in establishing the first round table for children's librarians in the American Library Association (ALA) in 1900 and in 1901 a special two-year training program for children's librarians was opened in Pittsburgh. The American tradition of children's librarianship that emphasized school visits, book talks, story telling, and other programs had a great influence on the development of children's work in other parts of the world. Prior to World War I a number of European librarians came to the United States for special training, but interest in American practices dramatically increased when children's libraries were given to the cities of Brussels (1920) and Paris (1923) by a group of wealthy American women who wished to promote postwar "educational reconstruction"; they chose a model children's library as their philanthropic focus because they viewed it as "a truly American creation . . . contributing to the program of self-education." Following World War II the *Amerika-Gedenkbibliothek* in Berlin was likewise credited with having great influence on the development of youth services in Germany.

While most countries integrate children's services into their public library systems, other models also exist. In India a number of university libraries have children's sections, and some developing nations, such as the Ivory Coast, offer children's services as one of the functions of the national public library. In contrast, Iran provides children's services through an extensive system of free-standing children's libraries. France, Germany, Japan, Jordan, and Russia serve children through their public libraries, but also have a number of free-standing children's libraries. Among the most notable children's libraries are the International Youth Library in Munich, *L'Heure Joyeuse* in Paris, and the Library of the Children's Book Trust in New Delhi. Development of children's services has been promoted by the United Nations Educational, Scientific, and Cultural Organization (UNESCO) through the construction of model public libraries in developing countries and through its publications and conferences. UNESCO also works closely with the International Federation of Library Associations and Institutions (IFLA), which has an active subsection on Library Work with Children, organized in 1955.

During the last half of the twentieth century, public library services to children spread throughout the world, along with the expansion of primary and secondary education and the growth in children's book publishing. Nonetheless, children's librarians faced challenges obtaining adequate funding for audio-visual materials and access to Internet resources as well as books. Librarians also faced challenges in maintaining the child's right to access information and in adapting their services to changing social conditions. Virginia Walter, past president of the Association for Library Service to Children, emphasizes the importance of person-to-person outreach and calls on children's librarians to design services for "the child in the community" as well as providing appropriate Internet access and communicating "the importance, the relevance, and the excitement of reading" (p. 93).

See also: **Children's Literature; Children's Spaces.**

BIBLIOGRAPHY

Elkin, Judith, and Margaret Kinnell, ed. 2000. *A Place for Children: Public Libraries as a Major Force in Children's Reading.* London: Library Association.

Hearne, Betsy, and Christine Jenkins. 1999. "Sacred Texts: What Our Foremothers Left Us in the Way of Psalms, Proverbs, Precepts and Practices." *Horn Book* 75: 556–558.

Maack, Mary Niles. 1993. "*L'Heure Joyeuse*, the First Children's Library in France: Its Contribution to a New Paradigm for Public Libraries." *Library Quarterly* 63: 257–281.

Walter, Virginia. 2001. *Children and Libraries: Getting It Right.* Chicago: American Library Association.

MARY NILES MAACK

Children's Literature

Like the concept of childhood, children's literature is very much a cultural construct that continues to evolve over time. Children's literature comprises those texts that have been written specifically for children and those texts that children have selected to read on their own, and the boundaries between children's literature and adult literature are surprisingly fluid. John Rowe Townsend once argued that the only practical definition of a children's book is one that appears on the children's list by a publisher. Contemporary publishers are not making that distinction any easier; for example, MAURICE SENDAK's *Outside Over There* (1981) was published as a picture book for both children and adults, and J. K. Rowling's HARRY POTTER series is available in adult and children's versions with the only difference being the book's cover art. While folk and FAIRY TALES were not originally intended for children, they have become a staple of children's literature since the early nineteenth century. On the other hand, many books written for and widely read by children during the seventeenth and eighteenth centuries are considered historical children's literature today and are read almost exclusively by adult scholars of children's literature. Children's literature has been written, illustrated, published, marketed, and purchased consistently by adults to be given to children for their edification and entertainment. Generally speaking, it is the intended audience rather than the producers of the texts who define the field. Children's texts written by child or adolescent authors, such as Daisy Ashford's *The Young Visiters* (1919) or ANNE FRANK's *Het Achterhuis* (1947; *The Diary of a Young Girl*, 1952), are exceptions to the rule. Many famous children's authors, such as Louisa May Alcott and LEWIS CARROLL, produced family magazines as children, and bits of their juvenilia were reworked into published children's books. More often, children's books result from the collaboration or direct inspiration of a specific child or group of children with an adult author. James Barrie's friendship with the Lewelyn Davies boys resulted in the play *Peter Pan, or The Boy Who Would Not Grow Up* (1904) and the novel *Peter and Wendy* (1911). The bedtime stories that A. Milne told his son Christopher Robin were revised into *Winnie-the-Pooh* (1926).

Although children's literature is intended primarily for children, it is more accurate to view such texts as having dual audiences of children and adults. Adults, particularly parents, teachers, and librarians, often function as gatekeepers who identify appropriate texts for children. Since children's literature has been marketed and purchased by adults who, in turn, present it to children, authors and publishers have attempted to produce children's texts that appeal to the desires of the actual adult purchaser, if not the child reader of the text. In the picture book and chapter book genres especially, an adult reads to a child or children in a group. It is only with the advent of the paperback book that adolescents, and in some cases younger children, have been able to select their books independent of adult supervision or funds. Prior to the development of public education and free libraries in the late nineteenth century, children's literature tended to be limited to the middle and upper classes. A children's book reflects the ideologies of the culture in which it was written and embodies that period's assumptions about children and appropriate behavior. Consequently, children's literature more often embodies adult concerns and concepts of childhood rather than topics children might choose for themselves. This gap between children's and adult's attitudes toward children's literature is often revealed in the difference between the top-selling children's books, which are frequently series books, and the books chosen annually by the American Library Association as the outstanding picture book (winner of the Caldecott Medal) and the outstanding book of prose (winner of the Newbery Medal).

Early History

In order for a society to produce a substantial body of children's literature it must recognize the existence of children as an important and distinctive category of readers with separate needs and interests. Despite PHILIPPE ARIÈS's much debated assertion that childhood was discovered in the seventeenth century, children's texts with limited circulation have been located from earlier periods of history. Manuscripts for religious education and courtesy books intended to teach rules of conduct were circulated among the wealthy in the Middle Ages. Harvey Darton has suggested that there were no children's books in England prior to the seventeenth century; however, he limits children's books to those printed texts that appeared after Johannes Gutenberg's fifteenth-century invention and includes handmade as well as printed texts that were concerned primarily with instruction, thus excluding educational textbooks or religious primers.

The twin purposes of instruction and delight have long been accepted as the primary goals of children's literature. John Newbery, a London bookseller, published at least thirty children's books and is recognized as the first British publisher to make children's books a permanent and profitable branch of the book trade. Newbery's *A Little Pretty Pocket-Book* (1744) is the first significant commercial children's book published in English. Greatly influenced by JOHN LOCKE's *Some Thoughts Concerning Education* (1693), the frontispiece of *A Little Pretty Pocket-Book* features the motto "*Delectando Momenus*: Instruction with Delight," which Newbery borrowed directly from Locke. Locke modified the concept from Horace's *Ars poetica* (c. 19 B.C.E.; *On the Art of Poetry*), which recommended, "He who combines the useful and the pleasing wins out by both instructing and delighting the reader." What Locke theorized, Newbery put into practice. Locke recommended that to encourage reading, a child should be given an "easy pleasant book suited to his capacity." While Locke rejected fairy tales, he felt fables, because they often were coupled with a moral, were appropriate texts for children. He specifically recommended both *Reynard the Fox* (1481) and *Aesop's Fables* (1484), noting "If his *Aesop* has pictures in it, it will entertain him much the better." *A Little Pretty Pocket-Book* is a compendium, including an illustrated alphabet, a selection of proverbs, and an illustrated group of Aesop's fables.

Darton was too limiting when he excluded didactic books from his definition of children's literature. Townsend considered the material published prior to Newbery as the prehistory of children's literature. These books were not intended for children, but eventually reached them, particularly chapbooks that featured folk tales or the legends of Robin Hood. Educational texts such as *The Babees Book* (1475), a conduct book for young gentlemen, also contribute to the prehistory of children's literature. William Caxton, the first English printer, published several texts that were not intended specifically for children, but his printings did appeal to them, notably *Aesop's Fables*, *Reynard the Fox*, and Thomas Malory's *Morte Darthur* (1485).

An early form of didactic children's literature was the hornbook in which a single sheet of printed text, generally consisting of an alphabet and a prayer, was shared by a group of young scholars. The printed text was attached to a wooden frame and protected by a bit of flatted horn attached to a wooden handle. A later innovation was the battledore, which used parchment or heavy paper instead of wood and therefore allowed for printing on both sides. The Czech theologian and educator JOHANN COMENIUS recognized that children learn both visually and verbally. He published *Orbis sensualium pictus* (1658) in Hungary, and the textbook was translated into English by Robert Hoole as *Visible World* (1659). The first illustrated textbook, *Orbis sensualium pictus* includes simple captions in Latin and in the common language as well as woodcuts that provide a visual encyclopedia of the world. This integration of visual and verbal elements has remained a significant design feature of children's literature, particularly in information and picture books. Another influential children's textbook was the *New England Primer* (c. 1689), compiled by Benjamin Harris. (While no copy of

John Tenniel's illustration of Alice holding a bottle labelled "Drink Me" from the first edition of Lewis Carroll's *Alice's Adventures in Wonderland* (1865). Every generation has remade the image of Alice, thereby constantly renewing her relevance. © Bettman/CORBIS.

the first edition has been located, a second edition was advertised in 1690 and the earliest surviving American copy is dated 1727.) It also combined significant visual and verbal elements; its most famous section is the illustrated alphabet, which begins "A, In Adam's Fall We Sinned All," linking the teaching of literacy with religious education. The *New England Primer* became the most frequently used schoolbook in North America during the seventeenth and eighteenth centuries.

Puritan children's literature was intended to provide children with religious and moral education. The most extreme example is James Janeway's *A Token for Children: Being an Exact Account of the Conversion, Holy and Exemplary Lives and Joyful Deaths of Several Young Children* (1672) in which multiple deathbed scenes present children who are physically weak but spiritually strong. While the Puritans were one of the first groups to create a large body of children's books, their doctrine of original sin assumed that all children were damned until they were converted to Christianity. A less harsh version of Puritan theology for children is found in John Bunyan's *A Book for Boys and Girls* (1686), a collection

Stories about animals, such as Beatrix Potter's *The Tale of Peter Rabbit* (1902), were popular during the Victorian era, when children's literature reached a cultural peak. Potter's books were especially renowned for their charming illustrations.

of poems or divine emblems drawn from nature. Bunyan's religious allegory *Pilgrim's Progress* (1678) was not written specifically for children but was quickly produced in abridged versions for younger readers along with Daniel Defoe's *Robinson Crusoe* (1719) and Jonathan Swift's *Gulliver's Travels* (1726). The enduring popularity of *Pilgrim's Progress* with children can be observed in the March sisters "Playing Pilgrims" in the first half of Alcott's LITTLE WOMEN (1868).

Newbery's children's books were less overtly religious than those produced by the Puritans. Instead his children's texts appealed to parents drawn to economic and social advancement. Directly aimed at the emerging urban middle classes, these books showed how literacy led to financial success. The most overt example is *The History of Little Goody Two-Shoes* (1765), which is thought to have been written by Oliver Goldsmith, who wrote other children's texts for Newbery. The story features the poor but hard working orphan, Margery Meanwell, who becomes a tutoress and eventually impresses and marries a wealthy squire. Newbery's children's books support a middle-class ideology.

Newbery's genius was not as an author or illustrator but as a promoter and marketer of children's books who was skilled at convincing middle-class parents of the value of this new product category. His frequent advertisements in the press and his habit of inserting other titles and specific products into the texts of his children's books is a practice that continues in children's publishing. He also developed the custom of coupling children's books with non-book accessories. *A Little Pretty Pocket-Book* was available at a slightly higher price when accompanied by either a "Ball and Pincushion, the Use of which will infallibly make Tommy a good Boy and Polly a Good girl."

The development of children's literature in England occurred simultaneously with the rise of the English novel. It is worth noting that the first children's novel, *The Governess, or Little Female Academy* (1749) by Sarah Fielding, was published in the same year as *Tom Jones*, which was written by her brother Henry Fielding. *The Governess* introduced the popular genre of the school story, the most celebrated example being Thomas Hughes's *Tom Brown's School Days* (1857). This enduring fascination with the genre is echoed in J. K. Rowling's Harry Potter series.

Another major educational theorist to have a profound influence on children's literature was JEAN-JACQUES ROUSSEAU, whose *Émile* (1762) was published in France and quickly translated into English. In *Émile* Rousseau rejected the Puritan concept of original sin and maintained that children were born innocent but were later corrupted by society. Ironically for a text that was to inspire the publication of many children's books, Rousseau thought children should learn by doing rather than by reading. He argued that children should only be taught to read at age twelve and then be limited to the book *Robinson Crusoe*. The best-known English follower of Rousseau, Thomas Day, wrote *History of Sandford and Merton* (1783–1789), a three-volume comparison between the virtues of Harry Sandford, the poor but virtuous son of a farmer, and Tommy Merton, the spoiled son of a wealthy merchant, who are educated under the constant moralizing of their tutor, Mr. Barlow. Mary Wollstonecraft's *Original Stories from Real Life* (1788), illustrated by William Blake, is a similar story for girls, with the rational Mrs. Mason finding object lessons from nature to inform her two charges, Caroline and Mary. Rousseau's belief in the ability to reason with children rather than using physical punishment is exemplified in Anna Laetitia Barbauld's *Lessons for Children* books (1778) as well as in Richard Edgeworth's *Practical Education* (1798), written in collaboration with his daughter, and in Maria Edgeworth's *The Parent's Assistant* (1796). Maria Edgeworth, daughter of Richard, was one of the finest writers of moral tales, which were those short domestic stories that encouraged children to focus on self-improvement. Such moral tales were one of the dominant forms of children's literature during the eighteenth century.

Fairy and Folk Tales

At the beginning of the nineteenth century, fairy and folk tales were considered inappropriate reading material for children, especially among the middle class. Puritans viewed them as a form of witchcraft, and both Locke and Rousseau warned against their frightening aspects, preferring stories of daily life. Mary Sherwood was the most strict writer of the moral tale and the author of the popular *The History of the Fairchild Family* (1818–1847), which was intended to provide the reader with religious education. At one point in the book, after the Fairchild children quarrel, to teach them a lesson their father takes them to a gibbet on which hangs the decaying body of a man who was executed for killing his brother. Sarah Trimmer's *Fabulous Histories* (1786) is a tale in which a family of robins teaches moral values. Trimmer also edited *The Guardian of Education* (1802–1806), a journal for parents and tutors, which was one of the first to evaluate children's books and to attempt a history of children's literature.

Attitudes toward fairy tales as children's literature changed during the nineteenth century when Jacob and Wilhelm Grimm published their two-volume collection *Kinder- und Hausmärchen* (1812–1815) in Germany. The Grimms were part of the German romantic movement and, with other writers for adults—including Ludwig Bechstein, Clemens Brentano, and E. T. A. Hoffmann—championed the folk tale and the literary fairy tale. The Grimms were attempting to collect and preserve German folklore for other scholars, but when Edgar Taylor translated the tales into English as *German Popular Stories* (1823–1826), he revised and redirected the tales for children. George Cruikshank illustrated the volumes, and his humorous designs were praised by John Ruskin. The popularity of the Grimm's fairy tales as children's literature was buttressed by the 1697 publication of Charles Perrault's *Histories, ou contes du temps passé, avec des Moralitez* (1697). Perrault's artful and moral collection of eight fairy tales was translated as *Histories, or Tales of Past Times* in 1729 by Robert Samber. The literary fairy tales written by Perrault are often referred to as *The Tales of Mother Goose* or simply *Mother Goose's Tales*. The phrase *Contes de ma mere l'oye* appeared in the engraving of an older woman telling stories to a group of children that served as the frontispiece of Perrault's collection; the phrase was translated by Samber as "Mother Goose's Tales."

Fairy tales became fashionable among adults in the French court at the end of the seventeenth century as a result of Perrault's publication and of Marie-Catherine Aulnoy's publication in the same year of *Contes de fées* (Stories of the fairies). Aulnoy's collection of literary fairy tales was translated into English in 1699 as *The History of Tales of the Fairies*. Another influential French writer of literary fairy tales was Marie Beaumont, who immigrated to England in 1745, where she published *Magasin des enfans* (1756), which was translated into English as *The Young Misses Magazine* (1757). The work features the conversations of a governess with her

The original teddy bear that inspired A. A. Milne's *Winnie-the-Pooh* (1926). The bear was given as a present to Christopher Robin Milne by his father and was immortalized in Milne's text, as well as Ernest Shepard's illustrations and later Disney's. AP/World Wide Photos.

pupils and includes a number of fairy tales, the best known being her version of "Beauty and the Beast."

Perrault's fairy tales gradually were adopted as children's texts known collectively as tales of Mother Goose. Aulnoy's fairy tales were identified as the tales of Mother Bunch and became the basis for many pantomines, a Victorian family theatrical entertainment.

Henry Cole, under the pseudonym Felix Summerly, edited the influential series of children's books, *The Home Treasury* (1843–1847), which helped rehabilitate the reputation of fairy tales as appropriate children's fare. Cole wanted the series to develop imagination in children and also to counteract the attacks on fairy tales by writers such as Trimmer and Sherwood. Moreover, the series was intended as an alternative to the enormously popular information books written by Peter Parley. Parley was the pen name of Samuel Goodrich, a prolific American writer of information books who considered fairy tales and nursery rhymes coarse and vulgar. *The Home Treasury*, with its numerous fairy tales and works of imaginative literature, was conceived by Cole as anti-Peter Parleyism. The constant battle over fairy tales, an impulse that pits the value of stories of ordinary life against imaginative and fantastical texts, is a debate that regularly appears in the history of children's literature.

"I know it is wet
And the sun is not sunny.
But we can have
Lots of good fun that is funny!"

7

Dr. Seuss's classic *The Cat in the Hat* (1957) was written as a reading primer for younger children, using a vocabulary of just over 200 words. The most popular of Dr. Seuss's books, *The Cat in the Hat* sold over 7 million copies by the year 2000. Geisel, Theodor, illustrator. TM and copyright © 1957 and renewed 1985 by Dr. Seuss Enterprises, L.P. Reproduced by permission of Random House, Inc.

With the publication of HANS CHRISTIAN ANDERSEN's *Eventyr, fortalte for børn* (Tales, told for children; 1835, 1843, 1858, 1861) into English in 1848, the triumph of the fairy tale as legitimate children's literature was complete. Shortly thereafter, collections of folk tales and literary fairy tales, which were written in the manner of folk tales by a specific author, tended to dominate children's literature until the end of the Victorian period. The most popular literary fairy tale of the Victorian period was Lewis Carroll's *Alice's Adventures in Wonderland* (1865), which was followed by its sequel *Through the Looking Glass* (1872); both were illustrated by John Tenniel. Carroll's imaginative novels are often credited with changing the emphasis of children's literature from instruction to delight. When compared with the majority of the children's books that preceded the Alice books, Carroll's works are remarkably free of religious or social lessons. Carroll even gently parodied Isaac Watts's poem "Against Idleness and Mischief" from *Divine Songs* (1715), yet the allusion also confirms the continued popularity of Watts's religious

work. Religious lessons, such as those found in George MacDonald's *At the Back of the North Wind* (1871), or social lessons, as those emphasized in Christina Rossetti's *Speaking Likenesses* (1874), remained significant features of children's literature during the Victorian period.

Carroll's Alice books did not single-handedly cause a shift in children's literature. Catherine Sinclair's *Holiday House* (1839), which describes the frolicsome adventures of Laura and Harry Graham, reintroduced noisy, mischievous children into the world of children's books. Heinrich Hoffmann's *Lustige Geschichten und drollige Bilder* (Merry stories and funny pictures) was published in Germany in 1845 but since the third edition, which appeared in 1847, was known as *Struwwelpeter*. It featured illustrations and poems that mocked the excesses of Puritan cautionary tales for children. Edward Lear's *Book of Nonsense* (1846) is another celebrated collection of nonsense verse with comic illustrations that rejects the impulse to be morally improving or didactic. Lear specialized in the limerick although he also was skilled at writing longer poems, such as "The Owl and the Pussy-cat" and "The Dong with a Luminous Nose," which are tinged with melancholy. Carroll and Lear are often paired as the two great writers of nonsense literature. Both authors were influenced by those anonymous comic verses known in England as nursery rhymes and in the United States as Mother Goose rhymes. There have been countless publications of collections of Mother Goose rhymes. One of the most notable is *Mother Goose's Melodies* (1833), published by Munroe and Francis of Boston, in which Mother Goose proudly announces herself to be one of the great poets of all ages and on a first name basis with Billy Shakespeare. James Orchard Halliwell's *Nursery Rhymes and Tales of England* (1845) provided the respectability for nursery rhymes that fairy tales had already achieved.

Victorian Children's Literature

Victorian children's literature reflected the culture's separate spheres for men and women with different types of books written for girls and boys. Stories for girls were often domestic and celebrated the family life, such as Alcott's *Little Women* or Kate Douglas Wiggin's *Rebecca of Sunnybrook Farm* (1903). Stories for boys, such as MARK TWAIN's *The Adventures of Tom Sawyer* (1876) and its sequel *Adventures of Huckleberry Finn* (1884), encouraged boys to have adventures. While Victorian children's literature developed the character of the good and bad boy, female characters were allowed less flexibility. Adventure stories—such as R. M. Ballantyne's *The Coral Island* (1858), Robert Louis Stevenson's *Treasure Island* (1883), and RUDYARD KIPLING's *Kim* (1901)—became a popular genre for boys. Girls were encouraged to read moralistic and domestic fiction such as Charlotte Yonge's *The Daisy Chain* (1856) and the extremely popular girls' school stories by L. T. Meade, begun with *The World of Girls* (1886). Animal tales, such as Anna Sewell's *Black Beauty* (1877) and Kipling's *The Jungle Book* (1894) and

An illustration by Clement Hurd for Margaret Wise Brown's *Goodnight Moon* (1947). Intended for children under the age of six, Brown's book has become a bedtime classic for generations of children. Harper & Row, Publishers, 1975. Illustrations copyright renewed 1975 by Edith T. Hurd, Clement Hurd, John Thacher Hurd, and George Hellyer.

Second Jungle Book (1895), were thought to appeal to both sexes. This tradition continued into the twentieth century with BEATRIX POTTER's *The Tale of Peter Rabbit* (1902), Kenneth Grahame's *The Wind in the Willows* (1908), and E. B. White's *Charlotte's Web* (1952) as some of the most memorable animal stories. Stuffed animals became the characters in A. A. Milne's *Winnie-the-Pooh* (1926) and *The House at Pooh Corner* (1828), which are illustrated admirably by Ernest Shepard.

The second half of the nineteenth century saw an explosion of children's literature, both in terms of quantity and quality. Children's literature historically has been more open

to women as authors and illustrators because it has been considered less significant than adult literature and because publishers have regarded women as more capable of teaching and raising children. Children's literature also began to segment itself in terms of social class as penny dreadfuls, or dime novels, were produced for the working class and more high-minded literature was produced for the middle and upper classes.

The Victorian era is considered a golden age for book illustration and picture books. In the first half of the nineteenth century most children's books were illustrated with woodcuts or printed on wood blocks and then hand-colored,

Hilary Knight's whimsical illustrations helped make *Eloise,* Kay Thompson's story about a little girl living in a hotel in New York City, a favorite among children since the mid-twentieth century. Simon & Schuster, 1983. Copyright © 1955 by Kay Thompson. Copyright renewed © 1983 by Kay Thompson. Reproduced by permission.

but later innovations in printing allowed for the widespread use of color. By the 1850s the master color printer Edmund Evans worked with some of the most capable picture book illustrators of the age—including Randolph Caldecott, Walter Crane, KATE GREENAWAY, Beatrix Potter, and Richard Doyle—to produce brilliant picture books and illustrated texts.

Contemporary Children's Literature

Twentieth-century children's literature was marked by increased diversity in both characters and authors. Earlier popular children's books—such as Joel Chandler Harris's *Uncle Remus, His Songs and His Sayings* (1880); Helen Bannerman's *The Story of Little Black Sambo* (1899); Hugh Lofting's *The Story of Dr. Dolittle* (1920); Jean de Brunhoff's *Histoire de Babar, le petit éléphant* (1931), translated by Merle Haas from the French as *The Story of Babar, The Little Elephant* (1933); and Roald Dahl's *Charlie and the Chocolate Factory* (1964)—have since been judged racist. Most children's literature prior to the twentieth century embodied a white ideology that was reflected in both the text and illustrations. From the 1920s on, there have been attempts to provide a more multicultural approach to children's literature. W. E. B. Du Bois's *The Brownies Book* (1920–1921) was the first African-American children's magazine. It featured stories, poems, and informational essays by authors such as Langston Hughes and Jessie Fauset. Over time publishers became more concerned with multiculturalism and issues of diversi-

ty. Notable African-American writers—such as Arna Bontemps, Lucille Clifton, Mildred Taylor, Virginia Hamilton, and John Steptoe—and Asian-American writers—including Laurence Yep, Allen Say, and Ken Mochizuki—have forever changed the once all-white world of children's literature.

On the other hand, children's literature has become more segmented in terms of age appropriateness. In the 1940s Margaret Wise Brown, inspired by the education theories of Lucy Sprague Mitchell, the founder of the Bank Street College of Education, began to produce picture books intended for children under age six. Brown's best-known picture books for the very young are *The Runaway Bunny* (1941) and *Goodnight Moon* (1947), both illustrated by Clement Hurd. Mitchell also promoted stories that reflected the real world in collections such as her *Here and Now Storybook* (1921). This newfound interest in age-specific material led to the creation of the widely used Dick and Jane readers (1930–1965) developed by William S. Gray and Zerna Sharp and distributed by Scott Foreman and Company. DR. SEUSS's *The Cat in the Hat* (1957) was written as a creative alternative to such basal readers, although it was also designed as a controlled vocabulary book.

While Lothar Meggendorfer developed the movable picture book at the end of the nineteenth century with tabs and pullouts, pop-up books, shaped books, and tactile books did not achieve widespread popularity until the twentieth century. The best known of these books is Dorothy Kunhardt's interactive *Pat the Bunny* (1940). More contemporary texts, such as Jan Pienkowski's pop-up books *Haunted House* (1979) and *Robot* (1981), blur the distinctions between book and toy. Board books are available for infants and toddlers; some of the most imaginative are the series of Rosemary Wells's Max books, beginning with *Max's Ride* (1979), which provide compelling stories for preschoolers.

While many twentieth-century children's texts appealed to and explored the lives of older children, most critics point to Maureen Daly's *Seventeenth Summer* (1942) and J. D. Salinger's *The Catcher in the Rye* (1951) as the beginning of adolescent literature as a genre separate from children's literature. More recently, middle school literature has emerged as a distinctive category. Texts such as Beverly Cleary's Ramona series, which began with *Beezus and Ramona* (1955), Louise Fitzhugh's *Harriet the Spy* (1964), and Judy Blume's problem novels, such as *Are You There God? It's Me, Margaret* (1970), have attracted readers too old for picture books but not ready for the adolescent novel.

SERIES BOOKS remain a larger, but contested, segment of children's literature. Books that follow the same set of characters or repeat an established formula have been an important part of children's literature since the nineteenth century with the publication of Horatio Alger's novels, which feature plucky boys who go from rags to riches, or Martha Finley's series on the pious but popular Elsie Dinsmore. Early in the twentieth century Edward Stratemeyer's syndicate of anonymous writers wrote books for multiple series under various pseudonyms, including the Nancy Drew series as CAROLYN KEENE, the Hardy Boys series as Franklin W. Dixon, and the Tom Swift series as Victor Appleton. While librarians and critics have tended to dismiss the repetitive nature of series books, some series books—such as Laura Ingalls Wilder's Little House series, begun with *Little House in the Big Woods* (1932), and C. S. Lewis's collection *Chronicles of Narnia* (1950–1956), which started with *The Lion, the Witch, and the Wardrobe* (1950)—have been recognized as outstanding works of literature. Nonetheless, most series fiction—such as L. Frank Baum's Oz series, begun with *Wonderful Wizard of Oz* (1900); R. L. Stine's Goosebumps series, begun with *Welcome to the Dead House* (1992); and Anne Martin's Baby-Sitters Club series, begun with *Kristy's Great Idea* (1986)—have been embraced by older children but generally dismissed by adults and critics as insubstantial.

Media adaptation of children's books as films or as TELEVISION series has become an increasingly important aspect of children's literature. Popular television series have been based on books such as Wilder's Little House series and Marc Brown's Arthur Adventure series, begun with *Arthur's Nose* (1976). Walt DISNEY has dominated the field of film adaptation of children's texts into cinema, beginning with *Snow White and the Seven Dwarfs* (1937), the first feature-length animated film. Best known for animated films based on fairy tales, Disney has produced a number of live-action films, such as *Mary Poppins* (1964), based on P. L. Travers's *Mary Poppins* (1934), as well as animated features based on Carlo Collodi's *Le avventure di Pinocchio* (1882) and T. H. White's *The Sword in the Stone* (1939). As is the case with Victor Fleming's film *The Wizard of Oz* (1939), based on L. Frank Baum's 1900 novel, or Alfonso Cuaron's film *A Little Princess* (1995), based on Frances Hodgson Burnett's 1905 novel, film adaptations often change, if not revise, the original text. This complicates the meaning of a children's text when children are more familiar with a text through viewing a media adaptation than through reading the book.

Since the 1960s, an increasing number of well-designed picture books have been produced. Such book illustrators as Maurice Sendak with *Where the Wild Things Are* (1963), Chris Van Allsburg with *Jumanji* (1981), and Anthony Browne with *Gorilla* (1983) have created highly imaginative picture books. Talented graphic designers—such as Eric Carle with *The Very Hungry Caterpillar* (1969), Leo Lionni with *Swimmy* (1963), and Lois Ehlert with *Color Zoo* (1989)—have provided bold new approaches to creating picture books.

Despite the recent trend of categorizing children's literature by age, an increasing number of adults have begun reading children's books, blurring the boundaries between children's and adult texts. J. K. Rowling's Harry Potter series, begun with *Harry Potter and the Sorcerer's Stone* (1997), has wide appeal with both child and adult readers. Francesca Lia Block's postmodern fairy tales, such as *Weetzie Bat* (1989), and the darkly ironic A Series of Unfortunate Events series by Lemony Snicket, which began with *The Bad Beginning* (1999), both have strong adult readership. Picture books have always been a showcase for designers and illustrators to display their talents. Increasingly sophisticated picture books—such as David Maccaulay's *Black and White* (1990) or the postmodern revisions of fairy tales written by Jon Scieszka and illustrated by Lane Smith in *The Stinky Cheese Man and Other Fairly Stupid Fairy Tales* (1992)—appeal as much to adults as to children. Contemporary children's literature continues to be a highly innovative and challenging field. As children's literature has become an increasingly financially profitable business, more successful writers who have first established themselves as writers for adults, such as Carl Hiassen (*Hoot* [2002]) and Michael Chabon (*Summerland* [2002]), are choosing to write for children.

See also: **ABC Books; Comic Books; Juvenile Publishing; Movies.**

BIBLIOGRAPHY

Avery, Gillian. 1965. *Nineteenth Century Children: Heroes and Heroines in English Children's Stories 1780–1900.* London: Hodder and Stoughton.

Avery, Gillian. 1994. *Behold the Child: American Children and Their Books.* Baltimore: Johns Hopkins University Press.

Bader, Barbara. 1976. *American Picturebooks from Noah's Ark to the Beast Within.* New York: Macmillan.

Carpenter, Humphrey, and Mari Prichard, eds. 1984. *The Oxford Companion to Children's Literature.* Oxford, UK: Oxford University Press.

Darton, F. J. Harvey. 1932. *Children's Books in England: Five Centuries of Social Life.* Cambridge, UK: Cambridge University Press.

Green, Roger Lancelyn. 1964. *Tellers of Tales: British Authors of Children's Books from 1800 to 1964.* New York: Franklin Watts.

Hunt, Peter, ed. 1995. *Children's Literature: An Illustrated History.* New York: Oxford University Press.

Hunt, Peter, ed. 1996. *Intentional Companion Encyclopedia of Children's Literature.* New York: Routledge.

Hürlimann, Bettina. 1959. *Three Centuries of Children's Books in Europe.* Trans. and ed. Brian Alderson. Cleveland, OH: World Publishing Company.

Jackson, Mary V. 1989. *Engines of Instruction, Mischief, and Magic: Children's Literature in England from Its Beginning to 1839.* Lincoln: University of Nebraska Press.

Muir, Percy. 1954. *English Children's Books.* London: B.T. Batsford.

Silvey, Anita, ed. 1995. *Children's Books and Their Creators.* Boston: Houghton Mifflin.

Thwaite, Mary F. 1963. *From Primer to Pleasure in Reading.* Boston: The Horn Book.

Townsend, John Rowe. 1974. *Written for Children: An Outline of English-Language Children's Literature.* New York: J. B. Lippincott.

Watson, Victor, ed. 2001. *The Cambridge Guide to Children's Books in English.* Cambridge, UK: Cambridge University Press.

JAN SUSINA

Children's Rights

Over the course of American history, obligations and rights between children, their parents, and the state have evolved in response to the dynamic changes of the growing nation. Most prominently, the nearly absolute rights of parents have contracted as the state has taken an increasingly powerful role in protecting and educating children. Children's rights, however, have not emerged as a full-blown independent concept. Only pockets of law, primarily in the areas of criminal justice and reproductive rights, have evolved to consider children's rights discretely from those of their parents.

In early American history, the law viewed the child as an economic asset or liability, whose value was perceived in terms of labor capacity rendered to parents and other adults. During the colonial period and the early years of the republic, the father as the head of the household exercised unquestionable rights to the custody and control of his children both during the marriage and in the then-rare event of divorce. A father could hire out a child for wages or apprentice a child to another family without the mother's consent. Education, vocational training, and moral development were also the father's responsibility.

Only in certain circumstances did the state assume responsibility for children: in the event of illegitimate birth and thus the absence of an acknowledged father's duties, in the event of the death of a father or both parents, and in the event of the incompetence or financial inability of parents to care for or train their offspring. In such instances, the fate of the child was determined by the primary considerations of the ability of the adults to exercise proper maintenance and supervision, and the child's labor value. A child born out of wedlock was known as *filius nullius* or "child of no family" and the town's poor law official was authorized to place out the child with an unrelated family. Widows often lost their children when they became unable to support them. Before ORPHANAGES or ADOPTION became common, such children were usually apprenticed or placed out to a family that would provide subsistence in exchange for labor.

During the 1800s as the nation grew more urban and industrial, emphasis on the child's value as a laborer diminished and more interest developed in child nurture and education. The new industrial age required fathers to leave their farms or home-based shops and work elsewhere. Mothers, who remained at home, replaced fathers as the main figures in the child's world. In addition, the new industrial order required a managerial middle class with skills that could be taught and learned not in the fields but in the classroom. Public school teachers began to replace parents as the primary educators of children. With this shift, children for the first time were looked upon as having some rights of their own.

The first recognition that children had rights independent of their parents' became embodied in the legal concept expressed as the "best interest of the child." Mothers gained favor as the parent better able to nurture the emotional needs of children of tender years. Following the increasingly more common event of divorce, mothers became more likely to prevail over fathers in custody disputes. Orphanages arose as a more child-centered alternative to PLACING OUT children whose parents were dead or unable to care for them. At the same time, public education rapidly took the place of HOMESCHOOLING. The state replaced the parents in shaping the intellectual and vocational life of the child.

A variety of reforms designed to protect children from exploitation and mischief was advanced at the beginning of the twentieth century by a coalition of civic-minded adults, popularly known as child-savers. Groundbreaking measures included restrictive CHILD LABOR laws, COMPULSORY SCHOOL ATTENDANCE, and JUVENILE COURTS that adjudicated children who were neglected by their parents or delinquent in their own behavior. These initiatives placed the state in a decisively more active role, irreversibly reducing parental authority and laying the foundation for the modern American child welfare and educational structures.

Legal recognition of children's civil rights apart from their parents, however, began to develop only much later, in the context of the 1960s civil rights movements. In 1965 in Des Moines, Iowa, three Quaker children were suspended from school for symbolically protesting the Vietnam War in their classroom. In an important freedom of speech decision, the U.S. Supreme Court proclaimed that children "did not leave their constitutional rights at the school house door" (TINKER V. DES MOINES, 1969).

In the more conservative 1970s, the Supreme Court allowed censorship of school newspapers and gave school authorities wide discretion to search student lockers. Later judicial rulings continued limiting the prerogatives of minor students. In the early twenty-first century the Court gave public school officials much wider latitude to test students for drugs. In *Board of Education v. Lindsay Earls* (2002), the Supreme Court permitted districts to require random tests of any student who takes part in extracurricular activities such as band, chorus, or academic competition. It had already upheld mandatory testing of student athletes.

Courts have accorded most serious consideration to rights for children in the procedural arena of JUVENILE JUSTICE. In 1965, the same year as the incident underlying *Tinker v. Des Moines*, a fifteen-year-old Gila County, Arizona, boy allegedly made an anonymous obscene phone call to an elderly neighbor. Without benefit of an attorney or a trial, Gerald Gault was sentenced to incarceration in a juvenile correctional institution until age twenty-one. The ensuing landmark Supreme Court decision, IN RE GAULT (1967)—later expanded by several subsequent decisions—gave minor defendants in juvenile court criminal actions nearly all the due process protections that adult defendants receive in the regular criminal courts, including lawyers and the right against self-incrimination. However, by the end of the century rights to a speedy trial, bail, or a jury had not been established.

In the 1990s, in response to highly touted reports of increases in juvenile crime, most state legislatures adopted measures to bring ever younger juvenile offenders to trial in adult courts, and to subject them to adult sentencing rules. By the beginning of the twenty-first century a fourteen-year-old could be tried for murder as an adult, and a sixteen-year-old could be sentenced to execution in most states.

Although a partial array of rights for children vis-à-vis schools, courts, and other governmental institutions were recognized by the Supreme Court, it was reluctant to grant children rights that were traditionally exercised by parents. Some of the most contested of these rights concerned areas of reproductive decision-making. Soon after *Roe v. Wade*, the Court ruled that an adult woman's right to choose to end a pregnancy via abortion extended to adolescent girls as well. However, in holding that individual states could enact parental consent laws, the Court reserved substantial authority to parents. With the ambivalence typical of its earlier decisions on children's rights issues, the Court also held that a girl could bypass her parents' withholding of consent by petitioning a judge. If the judge found that she was a mature minor, she would be permitted her own choice (BELLOTTI V. BAIRD II, 1979). Parents, public opinion, and states continue to be seriously divided on the issue of minors' access to abortion, and challenges to varying legal precedents are likely to continue.

More latitude has been allowed on the less controversial issue of adolescent consent to other sensitive medical procedures, such as the treatment of sexually transmitted diseases and drug and alcohol abuse. In many states a doctor who cannot give an adolescent an aspirin without parental consent can treat the minor for a VENEREAL DISEASE. Contrarily—and in sharp contrast to the due process protections provided children who face possible criminal incarceration—the Supreme Court has ruled that parents may commit their minor child to a mental health facility upon the recommendation of a physician, with no judicial review (*Parham v. J. R.*, 1979). A child thus volunteered by his parents need not be a "danger to self or others"—the adult standard for commitment—but only deemed in need of medical treatment.

In courts of family law, the child's best interest remains the standard in determining custody between divorced or separated biological parents. In practice, however, the child is rarely granted a representative in judicial custody proceedings and, in most states, the preference of a child who has attained adolescent age is only one consideration among many factors to be considered by the court. Thus, the best interest standard is seldom informed by direct or even indirect input from the child herself.

In key respects, the United Nations has surpassed the progressive reforms of the American legal system in clarifying and expanding the rights of children. The framework of principles articulated in the 1989 UN CONVENTION ON THE RIGHTS OF THE CHILD provides that children have a right to a nurturing environment in accordance with their developmental needs; the right to have their voices heard in accordance with their ages; the right to independent representation in legal proceedings, and the right to economic and emotional support from their parents and from the state. By 2003, only Somalia and the United States had not signed this convention.

See also: **Beyond the Best Interests of the Child; Child Saving; Divorce and Custody; Law, Children and the.**

BIBLIOGRAPHY

Ladd, Rosalind Ekman. 1996. *Children's Rights Revisioned: Philosophical Readings.* Belmont: Wadsworth.

Mason, Mary Ann. 1994. *From Fathers' Property to Children's Rights: A History of Child Custody in America.* New York: Columbia University Press.

Mnookin, Robert H., and D. Kelly Weisberg. 1994. *Child, Family, and State: Problems and Materials on Children and the Law.* Boston: Little, Brown.

MARY ANN MASON

Children's Spaces

There have always been children's spaces, in the sense that every culture has understood some spaces to be more appropriate than others for children and their activities. However, the practice of providing purpose-built spaces exclusively for the use of children became widespread only in the nineteenth century, coincident with the conceptualization of childhood as a special phase of human existence. While much of the historical literature has interpreted the creation of child-centered spaces as a boon to the young, scholars of contemporary childhood have started to bemoan what the two German sociologists Helga and Hartmut Zeiher have called the "islanding" of childhood—the tendency to insulate children's spaces from one another, as well as from spaces used by adults.

Domestic Space

Throughout history, the home has been the institution most closely associated with children and childhood. In general, most housing types developed in the West assigned women and children to the most private and protected areas of the home. These layers of protection generally increased with the wealth of the family. In the large Roman *domus*, for example, the peristyle area furthest from the street was reserved for family life, while the atrium near the front of the house was for more public functions. Many Roman families, however, lived together in one-room homes, illustrated by the remarkable walk-up, multi-family dwellings, called *insulae*, at Ostia, the port of Rome.

The Important Visitors (17th century), Jan Brueghel the Elder. Special places were not set aside for children in western European houses before the modern period. Children and adults lived and worked together in communal areas within the home. © Francis G. Mayer/ CORBIS.

This is in sharp contrast to the relatively fixed patterns developed in Chinese courtyard houses. In the Chinese *siheyuan*, a walled enclosure of four buildings around a quadrangle with a north-south axis, the hierarchy of the family is clearly reflected in the rigid plan regardless of social class: the south building was for servants, the two side buildings were for unmarried children and married sons with families, while the main building facing south was occupied by the parents.

The Islamic urban house, on the other hand, was divided into two sections strictly according to gender: the *salamlik* and the *haramlik*. The *salamlik* was the public part of the house where male visitors and friends were received. The *haramlik*, on the other hand, was a secluded precinct for women and children. In larger homes each part of the house included a courtyard, while in smaller houses, the division was vertical, with women and children sequestered upstairs. Even the windows of the *haramlik* were carefully designed to prevent neighbors from seeing inside.

The urban medieval house in western Europe could boast no such clear divisions. Special spaces for women and children did not exist; children, including young apprentices, occupied every room in these remarkably sophisticated multipurpose dwellings that accommodated both work and domestic life. Youngsters occupied particular spaces according to the time of day (e.g., children might play during the day in a room reserved for sleeping adults at night), rather than through a predetermined division of space by age.

Since the Industrial Revolution, the development of special rooms for children has followed the larger pattern of increasingly specific spaces with regard to function. Special rooms for children appeared in the middle-class house about 1830, designed to protect children from the world, as well as to protect the rest of the Victorian house from children. Advice books generally forbade children to enter the main rooms of the house, especially the parlor, except when accompanied by their parents. Accounts in fiction and prescriptive literature suggest that Victorian-era children often

The nursery, often filled with toys and special child-sized furniture, was a fixture in the middle-class Victorian home. Children played, ate their meals, and sometimes slept in these rooms under the supervision of servants or a nanny, far from the adult areas of the house. © CORBIS.

ate separately from parents, perhaps in the kitchen or in servants' quarters. The high chair, which was purpose-built dining furniture, restricted a child's movements and protected the other furnishings from his or her touch.

The nursery was certainly a significant feature of grand eighteenth-century houses and an essential characteristic of the Victorian house. As the setting for PLAY, education, and sometimes sleeping, the nursery was frequently on the uppermost floor of a house, with direct connections to the family bedrooms or kitchen through a special corridor. This spatial separation of children in the middle-class home paralleled the rise of a specialist servant, the nanny, to care for them. The removal of children from the best rooms in the house may have served to alleviate maternal anxiety, but it was also evidence that children were seen as unique beings, rather than simply as tiny versions of adults. Specialty FURNITURE, china, and of course TOYS also support this notion, as do small purpose-built play houses by famous architects,

such as the one designed for the Breakers in Newport, Rhode Island, by Peabody and Stearns.

Most twentieth-century houses, especially those built after World War I, were smaller and servantless. With the disappearance of servant quarters and the "back stair" and with the identification of the kitchen with mother (rather than a servant) came an increasing integration of children's spaces into the heart of the house. Bedrooms for children were next to parents' bedrooms; bathrooms were shared. In general, the early twentieth century saw a relaxation of social regulations. The "living room" in the bungalow, for example, was much more likely to have accommodated children than was the Victorian parlor.

The most revolutionary change to the middle-class house came in the period immediately following World War II, both in terms of setting and room arrangement. The BABY BOOM inspired a mass exodus of middle-class families to suburbia, mostly picturesque neighborhoods with detached houses framed by front and back yards. Children occupied (and controlled) several key rooms in these ranch-style and split-level houses, especially the so-called multipurpose or family room. This room was typically at the rear of the house, visible from the kitchen, and featured the family television (after 1960 or so). Other important children's spaces in the post–World War II house were the basement and the back yard. Postwar basements were significant spaces of escape from parents, especially for TEENAGERS, and were the ideal setting for listening to rock music and playing games such as ping pong or pool which required too much space to fit the rooms on the main floor of the house. Backyards provided space and domestic equipment for play.

In the period since 1975, children typically occupy nearly every room in the middle-class home, with the exception of the living room. The family room remains the heart of family life, with the television at its center. Kitchens have become even larger, a sort of "super center" intended to facilitate cooking (by more than just mom), homework, and sometimes computer facilities. Bedrooms remain gender- and age-specific and continue to function as important places of solitude and self-expression for children of all ages.

Also significant in this era is the rise of the purpose-built daycare facility. Daycare is sometimes accommodated in non-purpose-built, "inherited" spaces, such as churches, schools, and community centers, or sometimes it is integrated into large workplaces, such as office buildings and hospitals. But the daycare has also become an important custom building type. In most cases, purpose-built daycare facilities draw directly on the language of domestic architecture, employing regional building materials, pitched roofs, bright colors, and easily legible room shapes. Daycare facilities typically comprise a series of small classrooms arranged along both sides of a corridor, as well as administrative offices and kitchens. Exterior play spaces, like the postwar private backyard, commonly feature equipment to encourage safe group play. Increasingly, security has become a concern in daycare centers (due to perceived increases in urban violence and child ABDUCTIONS) and as a result, daycare centers are frequently surrounded by fences and entered only by workers, parents, and guardians.

Spaces for Education

Schools were undoubtedly the first spaces outside the private home built specifically for the use of children. Indeed, a schoolroom was incorporated into Winchester College in England as early as 1394, while a number of purpose-built GRAMMAR SCHOOL buildings date from the fifteenth century. Typically financed by private benefactors, such schools were often part of extensive charitable foundations that could also include a church, almshouses, and a schoolmaster's house, as was the case for the two-story brick school building constructed in 1437 in Ewelme (Oxon.), England. In this Gothic building, a large schoolroom was located on the ground floor, while the room above it presumably served as a dormitory for the boys. By the sixteenth century, many English grammar schools used a similar schoolroom/dormitory core flanked on either side by living quarters for the master and usher. This arrangement was still in use in the late seventeenth century; Sir Christopher Wren used it in the initial designs for the grammar school at Appleby Magna (in Leicestershire) between 1693 and 1697. In these early schoolrooms, students sat on benches that lined the long walls at right angles to the master's seat at the end of the room. Lessons stressed oral performance; writing was not emphasized in early schools, and well into the seventeenth century, students were expected to use their knees for a table.

In the late eighteenth century, the specter of large numbers of poor children roaming the streets of London prompted educational reformer Joseph Lancaster to advocate a radical reorganization of the schoolroom in order to educate the largest number of children at the least expense. Lancastrian schools accommodated hundreds of students in each room, with students seated in long rows in the center of the classroom, facing the teacher's desk. Wide aisles on either side of the room provided space for students to stand in semicircles for small group lessons supervised by student monitors. Lancastrian schools were built in England, as well as in Philadelphia and New York, where they were constructed of brick and largely unornamented, in keeping with the movement's concern for economy. An emphasis on extending education to the children of the poor remained a primary concern throughout the nineteenth century, especially in England and other parts of the British Empire, where so-called Ragged Schools (tuition-free schools for poor children) were established at midcentury. The Ragged Schools Union was formed in Britain in 1844, while the first Ragged School was opened in Sydney, AUSTRALIA, in 1860. Initially housed in rented quarters in a grim, two-story, stone former warehouse with barred windows, in 1872 the school moved into a purpose-built school room paid for by funds raised by public appeal.

By the middle of the nineteenth century, there was a growing conviction that purpose-built schools were essential to good education, and school boards in many countries began devoting a great deal of attention to the design and construction of school buildings, often producing model building plans and specifications. In the United States, the spokesman for school reform was Rhode Island Commissioner of Public Schools Henry Barnard, who first published *School Architecture, or Contributions to the Improvement of School-Houses in the United States* in 1842. In England, London School Board architect E. R. Robson published his *School Architecture* in 1874, while in France La Commission d'hygiène des écoles was established in 1882. Although the architectural style of these buildings varied greatly—Barnard favored the Greek Revival, while Robson's schools were

Queen Anne—they all retained rectangular schoolrooms, with chairs bolted into place facing the teacher's (often elevated) desk and emphasized fenced in school grounds, separate entrances for boys and girls, and enhanced provision of natural light, heating, ventilation, and toilet facilities.

The nineteenth century also saw the establishment of KINDERGARTENS. These child-centered institutions sought to counteract the impact of the industrialized city by reconnecting young children to a coherent socializing system and by reestablishing their bond with the natural world. Although the founding kindergarten theorists—JOHANN HEINRICH PESTALOZZI and FRIEDRICH FROEBEL—worked in the early nineteenth century, purpose-built kindergarten buildings were few until the twentieth century. A notable exception is the New Institution for the Formation of Character, built in 1816 for Robert Owen as part of the model factory settlement at New Lanark, Scotland. Inspired by Pestalozzi's child-centered institution in Yverdon, Owen established an infant school in a room that he had furnished with maps and representations of zoological and mineralogical specimens. Even in the second half of the nineteenth century, kindergartens in England, the United States, and Germany were defined more by their pedagogical approach—particularly the use of Froebel's "gifts" (educational toys)—than by any architectural form. Many of these privately funded kindergartens were housed in buildings designed for other purposes.

In the early twentieth century, purpose-built kindergartens became more common. In the United States and England they tended to take the form of a specially shaped classroom attached to a primary school, while in Europe the kindergarten tended to be a distinct building type. Those associated with the Waldorf School Movement (which began in 1919 when RUDOLF STEINER started Die Freie Waldorfschule, for the children of the workers at the Waldorf-Astoria cigarette factory in Stuttgart) tended to favor organic forms that seemed to support Steiner's emphasis on cultivating higher mental faculties through the total harmony of the senses. More common in the 1920s and 1930s were kindergartens designed in a modern idiom, like the 1934 nursery school on the outskirts of Zurich where architect Hans Leuzinger provided direct access to the out-of-doors, ample daylighting, and light moveable furniture scaled to young children.

In the early twentieth century, Progressive pedagogical theorists (notably Karl Popper in Germany and JOHN DEWEY in the United States) began to apply the basic philosophy of the kindergarten movement—attention to the development of the whole child—to primary and secondary school students. In its modern manifestation, however, this educational reform movement was understood to depend absolutely on the transformation of the school's architectural form. Not only were school rooms fitted out with light, por-table furniture that could be rearranged to facilitate different classroom activities, but Progressive schools also included a wide range of other facilities: fully equipped playgrounds, baths, gymnasia, art studios, scientific laboratories, shops for woodworking and handicrafts, and home economics classrooms. Auditoria and libraries were often included as well, to serve both students and the wider community. In order to make these amenities more affordable, the Gary, Indiana, school system introduced the platoon system (also called the Gary plan) in 1909. Aimed at using all school facilities at once, this system divided the student body into two platoons, each of which used conventional classrooms for academic subjects while the other was involved in special activities. Schools planned for this system typically included a large auditorium at the center of the building, with special classrooms grouped together on lower floors.

In Europe, Progressive educational reform often went hand in hand with attempts to bring students into closer communion with the natural landscape. Early in the twentieth century, open air schools—with neither heating nor glazing—were built primarily for tubercular children; the first of these was the Waldschule (Forest School) established in Charlottenburg, Germany in 1904. By the 1920s, however, OPEN AIR SCHOOLS were recommended for nontubercular children as well. In Frankfurt, Germany, architects working under the leadership of Ernst May in the 1920s designed decentralized schools called *Pavilionschule* (pavilion schools) or *Freiflachenschule* (open air schools) with one-story wings disposed over large open sites to increase light and air circulation; the Niederursel School designed by Franz Schuster in 1928 may be the first of this type. Although there were some French pavilion schools (notably the open air school in Suresnes designed by Eugène Beaudouin and Marcel Lods), France retained a tradition of density, building multistory blocks with outdoor space provided on rooftop terraces.

In the post–World War II period, architects embraced prefabrication and modular planning as the best way to lower school construction costs in order to meet the acute demand for schools fueled by the baby boom. Educators, however, were equally drawn to the potential for providing spaces that could be quickly reconfigured for individualized or group instruction. The trend towards open planning developed rapidly in the 1960s and early 1970s. Half of all the schools built between 1967 and 1969 in the United States were open design, as were ten percent of all elementary schools in use in the United Kingdom in 1985. The Mt. Hope (New Jersey) Elementary School designed by Perkins and Will in 1971 displayed several characteristics of the type: a large floor plate, heavy reliance on fluorescent lighting, open classrooms on an upper level, moveable furnishing used as classroom partitions, and spatial continuity between classrooms and circulation space. Although such schools avoided the rigidity of conventional classrooms, they also sacrificed daylight and direct access to the out-of-doors, while creating new noise and discipline problems.

The last two decades of the twentieth century were a reaction against the open plan school. The self-contained classroom returned, albeit with greater attention to providing a variety of seating arrangements. Irregular planning also reemerged in order to enhance natural lighting, improve access to the out-of-doors, and decrease noise levels. Finally, the child's reaction to the qualities of place reappeared as an issue of concern to architects.

Libraries

The provision of children's space in public libraries was an American innovation that became widespread in the first two decades of the twentieth century, thanks in large part to the library-building campaign financed by industrialist Andrew Carnegie. Especially in the case of urban branches and small-town libraries, Carnegie-financed buildings devoted half their space to the use of children. The earliest children's rooms mimicked the arrangements of reading rooms for adults, with rectangular tables aligned in neat rows, a form intended to encourage orderly behavior in all parts of the library. By the 1910s, however, children's librarians (many of them women who had recently entered the profession) embraced progressive educational theories that emphasized fundamental differences between children and adults and between children of different ages. Thus, later children's rooms did not seek to create order, but used informal arrangements of circular tables, often sized specifically for children. A story-hour alcove, sometimes graced with a fireplace, was designed to allow the children's librarian to adopt a maternal role toward the children who sat at her feet.

This American innovation gradually spread to various parts of Europe. In Norway, children's reading rooms were opened at Oslo's Deichman Library in 1911 and at the public library in Bergen in 1918. CHILDREN'S LIBRARIES were established in Paris and Brussels just after World War I by an American organization called the Book Committee on Children's Libraries. Both libraries were called L'Heure Joyeuse, and the Paris library was housed in a sunny room on the first floor of an existing stone building, where it remained until the 1970s. Although the practice of including separate reading rooms for children continued throughout the twentieth century, children's reading rooms lost much of their distinctive character in libraries designed after World War II, when open, flexible plans predominated. Postmodernism, however, reinstated the practice, as is evident in the San Juan Capistrano (California) Public Library designed by Michael Graves in the 1980s to include a separate story-hour room, which is round in plan, with built-in benches, walls painted with clouds, and bean-bag chairs in the shapes of animals.

Spaces for Health and Welfare

Facilities for parentless children—either orphaned or abandoned—are a product of the early modern period in Europe.

The Ospedale degli Innocenti in Florence, a FOUNDLING hospital designed by Filippo Brunelleschi begun in 1419, is perhaps the best known of these early ORPHANAGES; on the building's facade, a series of rondels of infants in SWADDLING clothes announce the building's function to passersby. While some of these early orphanages were established by religious orders (like the refuge for young girls set up in sixteenth-century Rome by the Confraternity of St. Catherine of the Ropemakers), others were state-financed institutions that housed a wider range of inmates and adopted an ambivalent attitude towards the children in their care. In Leipzig, between 1700 and 1704, the city council built a combination poorhouse, orphanage, insane asylum, and penitentiary dedicated to St. George. Although the council recognized a difference between the undeserving and the deserving poor (the latter being orphans, widows, and others who were unable to fend for themselves), this eighteenth-century building housed both. Thus, it had a steeple ("to honor God, and the best of this house") and a strongly fortified appearance (to convey the harsh treatment meted out to the undeserving).

A unique architectural feature of foundling hospitals is the *tour* (or wheel), an ingenious revolving door that allowed the anonymous delivery of babies to the warmth and protection of those who ran the institutions. Many babies and children were actually only temporary residents of orphanages. In large industrial centers like Montreal, Quebec, children were stationed there during hard times or sickness, and later retrieved by their parents and guardians when things improved. The orphanage thus had a fluid relationship with the working-class urban home.

In the nineteenth century, the orphanage was joined by the asylum or House of Refuge, a new institutional type that aimed at removing orphaned or neglected slum children from the chaos and immorality of urban life. Initially constructed with private funds, the earliest American examples were built in the early 1820s in New York and Philadelphia. The type continued to be popular through the 1850s. The buildings themselves sought to reinforce DISCIPLINE and routine that were the hallmarks of these institutions. Although ostensibly built to protect children from the city, they often took in children whom reformers deemed as likely to become social problems.

Specialty hospitals for sick children were also first built in the nineteenth century. Before this time young patients were accommodated in general hospitals, or sometimes in hospitals designed for particular diseases, such as tuberculosis. The first hospital for children was the Hôpital des Enfants Malades in Paris in 1802. London's celebrated Hospital for Sick Children in Great Ormond Street opened in 1852. The first CHILDREN'S HOSPITAL in the United States opened in New York two years later. These Victorian hospitals relied heavily on domestic ideology to express their dual mission of medical science and moral amelioration, marked by pitched roofs, picturesque massing (or forms), the use of brick, and domestically scaled windows and doors. The idea behind the design of the buildings was to protect young patients from the harsh realities of the hospital environment by association with the comforts of the middle-class home.

After World War I, children's hospitals resembled other modern institutions, featuring up-to-date surgical facilities, outpatients' facilities, isolation wards, and facilities for the pasteurization of milk. In North America wealthy, paying patients were accommodated in luxurious private patients' pavilions that resembled hotels. Although the planning of most interwar health-care institutions showcased efficiency and modern business methods, the exteriors often drew on historical references. Pediatric health-care facilities after World War II, on the other hand, looked more like office buildings than traditional hospitals.

Finally, postmodern children's hospitals since about 1975 draw on imagery outside of medicine. Bright colors, ornamentation, human scale, and overt references to other building types—particularly the home, hotel, and shopping mall—are again deployed to comfort young patients.

Recreational Spaces

For centuries, the street was the primary play space for European and American children. Children spent a great deal of unsupervised time away from both home and school, often establishing their own social structure. Boys' gangs had their own territory and often engaged in fierce battles with trespassers. This tendency for children to create their own rules for the use of public space continued among working-class children into the twentieth century; in New York's working-class neighborhoods, for instance, in the early years of the century, stoops and sidewalks were reserved for girls, who looked after babies and toddlers, while the center of the street "belonged" to older boys, who patrolled their turf and guarded against incursions by boys from other neighborhoods.

By about 1800, however, the upper middle class began to devote greater attention to child rearing, and so began to supervise the activities of their children more closely. Kept inside the house to play with toys (rather than with cohorts from a different class), upper middle-class children only ventured out onto the street on "walks" in the company of adults. Indeed, throughout the nineteenth century, middle-class observers became increasingly alarmed by the idea of children roaming the streets and ever more critical of working-class play, which was dominated by games of chance that might reinforce "the taste for unearned pleasures." While such concerns prompted the establishment of ragged schools and other institutions aimed at removing poor children from the street, they also gave impetus for the establishment of parks and playgrounds. Although largely ornamental in nature, the great urban parks of the nineteenth century often included play spaces for children. Queen's Park in Manchester, England (designed in 1849), included circular swings, a ball and shuttle-cock ground, skipping rope and swing grounds, another shuttle-cock ground, a quoit alley, a skittle alley, an archery ground, and a cricket ground (some of these activities may have been intended for adults as well).

Playgrounds designed specifically for the use of children were introduced gradually in the second half of the nineteenth century, with the first English example—the Burberry Street Recreation Ground in Birmingham—established in 1877. Most nineteenth-century English playgrounds were sponsored by private organizations, such as the Metropolitan Public Gardens Association (which opened four playgrounds in London between 1882 and 1886) or the Children's Happy Evenings Association (which opened six play centers in London by 1888 and a total of ninety-six centers by World War I). By the turn of the century, however, there was an international movement to establish playgrounds in small parks in working-class neighborhoods, often with municipal support. The London County Council, for instance, opened over one hundred acres of London School Board playgrounds for Saturday use in 1890. In the United States, settlement house workers played an important role in establishing neighborhood parks (like Pulaski Park in Chicago), and also inspired the activities of playground associations abroad (including the Playground Association of Queensland, which opened three supervised playgrounds in Brisbane, Australia, between 1913 and 1927). Established at least in part to guide working-class recreational practices, these parks emphasized formal designs, containing well-defined spaces that allowed the sorting of park users by gender and age, as well as their supervision by professional, middle-class play leaders. In the 1940s, as playground supervision dropped off, municipalities depended more heavily on manufactured play equipment that was both low maintenance and safe. Stripped of dangerous equipment (such as the teeter-totter), the standard playground was comprised of a paved surface, fence, sandpit, swings and jungle gym, although by the 1960s, free-form play sculptures in bright colors began to supplement standardized equipment.

Perhaps the most significant "public" spaces designed for young visitors in the twentieth century are the Disney parks: Disneyland (Anaheim, California, 1955), Walt Disney World (Orlando, Florida, 1971), Tokyo Disneyland (1983), and EuroDisney (now Disneyland Paris, 1992). Inspired by cartoon characters first developed by the Walt Disney Company, the parks are comprised of a series of fantasy landscapes with rides. A sophisticated system of pedestrian-only circulation, based on subtly miniaturized buildings, grants children a greater feeling of control than they might experience in real urban environments.

By the late nineteenth century, the idea that the city was inherently detrimental to a child's well-being led to the establishment of SUMMER CAMPS where children could escape the city altogether. While many early camps—*colonies de vacances* in France, health camps of New Zealand, Fresh Air camps in the United States—were philanthropic endeavors aimed at safeguarding the physical health of poor children, others catered to the sons (and later daughters) of middle-class or well-to-do families, focusing on religious instruction or more generic character-building. In the United States, many of these early camps were instituted in response to turn-of-the-century anxieties about the impact of the feminized home on the social and physical development of boys, and often imitated the physical trappings of the military encampment—tents, mess hall, parade ground—in order to reconnect boys with the world of men. Although permanent buildings became more popular at American camps by the late 1930s, they retained a rustic flavor, while picturesque planning principles were introduced to disguise the extent of human intervention in the shaping of the camp landscape. In the post–World War II period, camps for children with special needs became increasingly common, as did skill-based camps teaching foreign languages, music, and computer programming. At the end of the twentieth century, however, the traditional, rustic, character-building summer camp enjoyed renewed popularity.

In studying the spaces and material culture of children from any culture or time period it is important to balance prescriptive and descriptive sources, because much of what we know about children of the past is solely from an adult point of view. Like toys and books, the spaces associated with childhood rarely record children's voices or perspectives. Diaries, letters, photographs, drawings, and other documents may provide important supplemental information on children's real spatial experiences.

See also: **Education, Europe; Education, United States; Montessori, Maria; Playground Movement; Progressive Education; Sandbox; School Buildings and Architecture; Street Games; Theme Parks; Zoos.**

BIBLIOGRAPHY

Adams, Annmarie. 1995. "The Eichler Home: Intention and Experience in Postwar Suburbia." *Perspectives in Vernacular Architecture* 5: 164–178.

Adams, Annmarie. 1996. *Architecture in the Family Way: Doctors, Houses, and Women, 1870–1900.* Montreal: McGill–Queen's University Press.

Adams, Annmarie, and David Theodore. 2002. "Designing for 'the Little Convalescents': Children's Hospitals in Toronto and Montreal, 1875–2006." *Canadian Bulletin of Medical History* 19: 201–243.

Boyer, Paul. 1978. *Urban Masses and Moral Order in America, 1820–1920.* Cambridge, MA: Harvard University Press.

Bradbury, Bettina. 1993. *Working Families: Age, Gender, and Daily Survival in Industrializing Montreal.* Toronto: McClelland and Stewart.

Cranz, Galen. 1982. *The Politics of Park Design: A History of Urban Parks in America.* Cambridge, MA: MIT Press.

Cromley, Elizabeth C. 1996. "Transforming the Food Axis: Houses, Tools, Modes of Analysis." *Material History Review* 44 (fall): 8–22.

Davin, Anna. 1996. *Growing Up Poor: Home, School, and Street in London, 1870–1914.* London: Rivers Oram Press.

de Martino, Stefano, and Alex Wall. 1988. *Cities of Childhood: Italian Colonies of the 1930s.* London: Architectural Association.

Downs, Laura Lee. 2002. *Childhood in the Promised Land: Working Class Movements and the Colonies des Vacances in France, 1880–1960.* Durham, NC: Duke University Press.

Dudek, Mark. 1996. *Kindergarten Architecture: Space for the Imagination.* London: E and FN Spon.

Dunlop, Beth. 1996. *Building a Dream: The Art of Disney Architecture.* New York: Harry N. Abrams.

Foy, Jessica, and Thomas J. Schlereth, eds. 1992. *American Home Life, 1880–1930: A Social History of Spaces and Services.* Knoxville: University of Tennessee Press.

Frawley, Jodi. 2000. "'Haunts of the Street Bully': Social Reform and the Queensland Children's Playground Movement, 1910–1930." *History of Education Review* 29, no. 1: 32–45.

Maack, Mary Niles. 1993. "L'Heure Joyeuse, The First Children's Library in France: Its Contribution to a New Paradigm for Public Libraries." *Library Quarterly* 63, no. 3 (July): 257–281.

Malchow, H. L. 1985. "Public Garden and Social Action in Late Victorian London." *Victorian Studies* 29, no. 1 (fall): 97–124.

Marling, Karal Ann, ed. 1997. *Designing Disney's Theme Parks: The Architecture of Reassurance.* Montreal: Canadian Centre for Architecture; Paris: Flammarion.

Maynard, W. Barksdale. 1999. "'An Ideal Life in the Woods for Boys': Architecture and Culture in the Earliest Summer Camps." *Winterthur Portfolio* 34 (spring): 3–29.

McClintock, Jean, and Robert McClintock, eds. 1970. *Henry Barnard's School Architecture.* New York: Teachers College Press.

Nasaw, David. 1985. *Children of the City: At Work and at Play.* Garden City, NY: Anchor Press/Doubleday.

Rothman, David J. 1971. *The Discovery of the Asylum: Social Order and Disorder in the New Republic.* Boston: Little, Brown.

Schoenauer, Norbert. 2000. *6000 Years of Housing.* New York: Norton.

Seaborne, Malcome. 1971. *The English School: Its Architecture and Organization, 1370–1870.* Toronto: University of Toronto Press.

Upton, Dell. 1996. "Lancasterian Schools, Republican Citizenship, and the Spatial Imagination in Early Nineteenth-Century America." *Journal of the Society of Architectural Historians* 55, no. 3 (September): 238–253.

Van Slyck, Abigail A. 1995. *Free to All: Carnegie Libraries and American Culture, 1890–1920.* Chicago: University of Chicago Press.

Van Slyck, Abigail A. 2002. "Housing the Happy Camper." *Minnesota History* (summer): 68–83.

Van Slyck, Abigail A. 2002. "Kitchen Technologies and Mealtime Rituals: Interpreting the Food Axis at American Summer Camps, 1890–1950." *Technology and Culture* 43 (October): 668–692.

Verderber, Stephen, and David J. Fine. 2000. *Healthcare Architecture in an Era of Radical Transformation.* New Haven: Yale University Press.

Weiner, Deborah E. B. 1994. *Architecture and Social Reform in Late-Victorian London.* Manchester, UK: Manchester University Press.

Zeiher, Helga, and Helmut Zeiher. 1994. *Orte und Zeiten der Kinder: soziales Leben im Alltag von Grossstadtkindern.* Weinheim, Germany: Juventa.

ANNMARIE ADAMS
ABIGAIL A. VAN SLYCK

Child Saving

The child-saving movement had its roots in privately funded mid-nineteenth-century charitable organizations for the protection and benefit of children, such as the NEW YORK CHILDREN'S AID SOCIETY. At the movement's height, between 1890 and 1920, child savers worked in such diverse reform efforts as fighting CHILD ABUSE, regulating CHILD LABOR, founding KINDERGARTENS, building playgrounds, establishing the JUVENILE COURT, campaigning for mothers' pensions, and reducing INFANT MORTALITY rates. The child-saving movement began in the latter half of the nineteenth century as a large, active coalition of women's club members, philanthropists, and urban professionals. In England in the 1860s and in the United States in the 1870s, the "charity organization" movement sought to make the doling out of charity more scientific and efficient, trying to keep the "undeserving" from receiving aid. Beginning around 1890, the Progressives increasingly professionalized and secularized child-welfare work. By 1920, the field of social work was filled largely with college-educated professional women rather than with volunteers.

In the United States, the child-saving movement grew in the Progressive period as reformers responded to the problems associated with rapid industrialization and massive immigration. Child savers believed that by alleviating the perils of poverty for the young and working to Americanize the children of immigrants, they could secure a better future for their nation. A large percentage of the new immigrants were Catholic and early child savers had a strong Protestant bias. The extent to which these reformers were influenced by a benevolent urge to help poor children, versus their desire to control the new masses of immigrants flooding the cities, is the subject of much historical debate.

Child Abuse and Neglect

The progression of child saving is in many ways exemplified by efforts to combat child abuse and neglect. Starting in 1853, the NEW YORK CHILDREN'S AID SOCIETY (CAS), headed by CHARLES LORING BRACE, sought to save children of the urban poor by sending those who were orphaned, neglected, abused, or delinquent to live on farms with surrogate families in the West. Brace and his followers believed that the country was inherently more wholesome and healthful than the city. Child savers believed in the environmental causes of children's misbehavior and felt that life with a farming family could redeem troubled youth. The CAS attracted the support of many philanthropists and reformers but was criticized by some westerners who complained that the ORPHAN TRAINS were overloading their small towns with unruly boys. Some reformers accused the program of providing free labor to farmers without sufficiently overseeing the treatment of the children.

In 1874, when a child named Mary Ellen was beaten by her guardian, the president of the Society for the Prevention of Cruelty to Animals, Eldbridge Gerry, found that the only way to prosecute the abuser was under laws protecting the rights of animals. The sensational case led to the foundation of the New York SOCIETY FOR THE PREVENTION OF CRUELTY TO CHILDREN. Early child-saving organizations such as the CAS and SPCCs were privately funded. According to historian Linda Gordon, child-saving organizations that focused on child abuse before 1910 were part of a feminist-influenced moral reform movement and emphasized illegitimate male power and the role of alcohol use in family violence. The period between 1910 and 1930 was marked by increased professionalization of social work, state regulation of child welfare, and a greater emphasis on child neglect, both physical and "moral," rather than abuse. The Cruelty, as the Massachusetts SPCC was known, worked as both a charity and a private law-enforcement agency, arbitrating custody and support arrangements and intervening in poor families. American SPCCs operated under a conservative feminist vision, trying to impose an middle-class ideal of domesticity on the immigrant poor at the same time that they offered some assistance to abandoned, battered, and overworked children.

Organizations to combat child abuse and neglect had an ambiguous attitude toward the family—they were at times child-centered, ready to intervene in private families in order to protect children, or to impose their notions of proper child rearing on immigrant and working-class families, and at times family-centered, anxious to keep families together even when the family patriarch was abusive. In general, the Progressives were less willing to remove children from their families than their predecessors (such as Charles Loring Brace). For instance, at the first WHITE HOUSE CONFERENCE ON THE CARE OF DEPENDENT CHILDREN in 1909, attendees easily agreed that poverty alone did not provide sufficient reason to remove a child from his family, but debated strenuously whether private aid alone or state aid was necessary to help bolster worthy impoverished families. Although most conference attendees argued against the benefits of state aid, by 1919, funds for dependents living at home were provided by thirty-nine states through mothers' pensions.

Child savers in Britain followed the American example, founding the Liverpool SPCC in 1883. Soon after, branches opened in London and other cities. Reluctant to prosecute parents, British SPCCs mainly relied on formal warnings and official visits to correct wayward parents. In 1889, the SPCC-supported Act for the Prevention of Cruelty to Children gave British authorities increased power to oversee the treatment of children. The National SPCC brought child abuse to the fore of British consciousness and remained a powerful organization under the leadership of Benjamin Waugh until its unsuccessful and unpopular campaign against child life insurance in the 1890s.

Child Labor

Child savers in the early twentieth century America argued that children under sixteen were not ready to face adult work responsibilities. From 1908 to 1916, at the behest of the NATIONAL CHILD LABOR COMMITTEE, LEWIS HINE photographed children working in textile mills, coal mines, and canneries throughout the South, providing powerful visual support for child savers who sought to end child labor in these industries. Although there were no federal statutes governing child labor before 1910, there were numerous state laws banning or regulating child labor passed between 1880 and 1910. Child labor laws were passed in twenty-eight states before 1900, but they were aimed at mining and manufacturing, rather than domestic service, street trade, or farm labor. Compulsory school attendance laws were also used to curb child labor. Although reformers took the credit for the decrease in child labor after 1900, changes in industry that made child laborers less useful, such as increased automation and the presence of more immigrant laborers to fill the positions previously held by children had much to do with decreasing use of child labor.

In Britain, child labor was regulated earlier. In 1833, the first effective Factory Act limited work-force participation of children aged nine to twelve in textile mills to forty-eight hours per week and required children to attend school for two hours a day. Silk factories, a major employer of children, were exempted from these restrictions. In 1844, the minimum age was lowered to eight, but child mill-workers were only permitted to work half-time and were required to attend school half-time as well. It was not until the 1860s and 1870s that laws limited child labor in other British industries, with the exception of the Mines Act of 1842, which was only minimally restrictive. Clark Nardinelli argues that these legal restrictions merely enforced the existing trend of decreasing child labor. Thus, in Britain, unlike in the United States, anti–child labor movements preceded other child-saving activities.

Education

Laws for COMPULSORY SCHOOL ATTENDANCE did exist in the United States before 1890, but they were poorly written and not widely enforced. In Great Britain, it was not until the late nineteenth century that truly effective compulsory-education laws were enacted. Child savers on both sides of the Atlantic worked to promote both privately and publicly funded kindergartens. In the United States at the turn of the century, followers of the CHILD-STUDY movement called for education reforms, criticizing overcrowded schools and stale teaching methods. Some child savers called for new VOCATIONAL EDUCATION programs that would give working-class children practical skills to help turn them into good industrial workers.

Youth Organizations and Child Leisure

Many child savers worked to organize the leisure time of children. In 1906, Henry S. Curtis and LUTHER GULICK founded the Playground Association of America, which gained municipal support and focused on providing outdoor play spaces and play leaders for children. The success of the PLAYGROUND MOVEMENT was based in the acceptance of the idea that PLAY was fundamentally important to the development of children and that the middle class should be involved in organizing the leisure time of the working class. Under the leadership of Gulick, between 1886 and 1896, the YMCA transformed itself into an athletic organization. It remained an explicitly evangelical Christian organization, but sought to gain young converts through organized sports.

In 1908, ROBERT BADEN-POWELL, who had gained acclaim in the Boer War, established the BOY SCOUTS in Britain, basing scouting on a system he used to train young soldiers. In 1910, the Boy Scouts of America was founded. Baden-Powell hoped that scouting would help boys to be physically fit and mentally prepared to protect their nation and that scouting would help boys safely negotiate the dangerous years of ADOLESCENCE. Scouting in both countries was mainly directed toward middle-class youth.

Juvenile Delinquency

Innovation in the treatment of juvenile delinquents eventually led child savers to establish a separate judicial system for juveniles in both the United States and Great Britain. In 1899, the first juvenile court was established in Chicago. One of the most famous spokesmen of the juvenile court was Denver judge Ben Lindsey. Lindsey argued that the court needed to be flexible in its approach to juvenile offenders and should focus on the best interest of the child. Juvenile courts tended to favor probation, either at home or with a foster family, over institutionalization. By 1915, nearly all states had established a juvenile court system. In the 1920s, a greater focus on psychiatry entered the juvenile courts and CHILD GUIDANCE clinics changed the way the courts looked at young offenders. In 1908, Britain established its own juvenile court system, which relied on probation and industrial schools in its efforts to rehabilitate troublesome youth.

Age of Consent

In 1885, the issue of the sexual abuse of girls exploded into British consciousness with W. T. Stead's "Maiden Tribute of Modern Babylon," an investigation of the world of vice published in the *Pall Mall Gazette*. One of the stories in this series described the "purchase" of a thirteen-year-old virgin by a brothel. The sensational coverage resulted in the AGE OF CONSENT for girls being raised from thirteen to sixteen. Police were also granted increased power to prosecute those involved in prostitution. In the United States as well, reformers fought successfully to raise the age of consent at the turn of the century in an effort to protect girls from sexual abuse.

Public Health

British and American child savers worried about public-health concerns that threatened children's well-being. Poor sanitation, tuberculosis outbreaks, and tainted food and milk supplies were all targeted by reformers. In 1874, British law required the registration of infant births and deaths and targeted foster parents for inspections, part of an effort to curb the abuses of BABY FARMING. A 1906 law made these policies stricter. Between 1906 and 1908, British schools began programs to provide meals to elementary students and provided for the medical inspection of school children.

In 1909, the White House held its first Conference on the Care of Dependent Children which drew attention to the child savers' concerns and helped lead to the establishment of the U.S. CHILDREN'S BUREAU in 1912. With Julia Lathrop at its head, the Children's Bureau first turned to the alarming infant mortality rate among impoverished city dwellers. The Bureau wrote popular instructional pamphlets on prenatal and infant care and encouraged "baby saving" campaigns. The Bureau also fought to expand birth registration campaigns and studies of infant mortality, though its focus was almost exclusively the high death rate among immigrants' infants—the equally high infant mortality rate among African Americans went largely unresearched. Between 1914 and 1920, the Bureau expanded, allowing it to explore the issue of child labor, to research maternal and child health, to fight for mothers' pensions, and to deal with the problems of illegitimacy and of children with disabilities.

Child saving did not end in 1920; however, the focus of child-saving efforts and the philosophy behind it changed. According to Hamilton Cravens, beginning in the 1910s, the emphasis of child savers shifted from reform to social-science research on "normal" children. The study of the child became paramount, numerous child-research institutes were founded, and legislative reform efforts took a secondary role. Furthermore, rather than focusing on environmental causes for children's developmental problems, the new professional child savers focused on internal emotional conflicts to explain problems with adjustment. The Progressives were most concerned with helping the so-called subnormal child, whereas the child savers of the later period focused their attention on understanding the so-called normal child.

See also: **Law, Children and the; Social Welfare; Street Arabs and Street Urchins.**

BIBLIOGRAPHY

Ashby, Leroy. 1997. *Endangered Children: Dependency, Neglect, and Abuse in American History.* New York: Twayne Publishers.

Behlmer, George K. 1982. *Child Abuse and Moral Reform in England, 1870–1908.* Stanford, CA: Stanford University Press.

Cavallo, Dominick. 1981. *Muscles and Morals: Organized Playgrounds and Urban Reform, 1880–1920.* Philadelphia: University of Pennsylvania Press.

Cohen, Ronald D. 1985. "Child Saving and Progressivism, 1885–1915." In *American Childhood: A Research Guide and Historical Handbook,* ed. Joseph M. Hawes and N. Ray Hiner. Westport, CT: Greenwood Press.

Cravens, Hamilton. 1985. "Child-Saving in the Age of Professionalism, 1915–1930." In *American Childhood: A Research Guide and Historical Handbook,* ed. Joseph M. Hawes and N. Ray Hiner. Westport, CT: Greenwood Press.

Cremin, Lawrence A. 1961. *The Transformation of the School: Progressivism in American Education, 1876–1957.* New York: Alfred A. Knopf.

Cunningham, Hugh. 1991. *The Children of the Poor: Representations of Childhood Since the Seventeenth Century.* Oxford, UK: Blackwell.

Dwork, Deborah. 1987. *War Is Good for Babies and Other Young Children: A History of the Infant and Child Welfare Movement in England, 1898–1918.* London: Tavistock Publications.

Fass, Paula S. 1989. *Outside In: Minorities and the Transformation of American Education.* New York: Oxford University Press.

Gillis, John R. 1975. "The Evolution of Juvenile Delinquency in England, 1890–1914." *Past and Present* 67: 96–126.

Gordon, Linda. 1988. *Heroes of their Own Lives: The Politics and History of Family Violence, Boston 1880–1960.* New York: Viking Penguin.

Hawes, Joseph M. 1971. *Children in Urban Society: Juvenile Delinquency in Nineteenth-Century America.* New York: Oxford University Press.

Lindenmeyer, Kriste. 1997. *"A Right to Childhood": The U.S. Children's Bureau and Child Welfare, 1912–46.* Urbana: University of Illinois Press.

Macleod, David I. 1983. *Building Character in the American Boy: The Boy Scouts, YMCA, and Their Forerunners, 1870–1920.* Madison: University of Wisconsin Press.

Mason, Mary Ann. 1994. *From Father's Property to Children's Rights: The History of Child Custody in the United States.* New York: Columbia University Press.

Mennel, Robert M. 1973. *Thorns and Thistles: Juvenile Delinquents in the United States, 1825–1940.* Hanover, NH: University Press of New England.

Nardinelli, Clark. 1980. "Child Labor and the Factory Acts." *Journal of Economic History* 40: 739–753.

Nasaw, David. 1985. *Children of the City: At Work and at Play.* Garden City, NY: Anchor Press/Doubleday.

Odem, Mary E. 1995. *Delinquent Daughters: Protecting and Policing Adolescent Female Sexuality in the United States, 1885–1920.* Chapel Hill: University of North Carolina Press.

Tiffin, Susan. 1982. *In Whose Best Interest? Child Welfare Reform in the Progressive Era.* Westport, CT: Greenwood Press.

Walkowitz, Judith R. 1992. *City of Dreadful Delight: Narratives of Sexual Danger in Late-Victorian London.* Chicago: University of Chicago Press.

CAROLINE HINKLE MCCAMANT

Child Stars

Ever since the popularization of the motion picture around 1900, child actors have achieved extraordinary success on the screen. From "America's Sweetheart," Mary Pickford, the nation's most popular actress in the 1910s to the *Our Gang* series of the 1920s to SHIRLEY TEMPLE and Judy Garland in the 1930s and 1940s, young actors have risen to levels of wealth and popularity rivaling those of their adult counterparts. As many a child star has discovered, however, success is often short-lived. Many young actors have fallen out of public favor upon reaching adolescence. Their fleeting fame is a testament to not only the fragility of stardom but America's ongoing obsession with youth.

Shirley Temple was the most popular child star in the world in the 1930s. President Franklin Delano Roosevelt credited her films with raising the nation's morale during the Great Depression, pointing to the tremendous influence of film on American culture. © Bettman/CORBIS.

Although the motion picture was the medium most responsible for the child star phenomenon, the first child stars appeared on the stage. In the mid-nineteenth-century United States, a girl named Lotta Crabtree, who had been pushed by her mother to become an actress as a means of supporting the family, became a national sensation and sparked a craze for young theatrical performers. The vogue launched the careers of two sisters, Elsie and Jenny Janis, who became the highest paid vaudeville headliners in the world, and also a child named Mary Pickford, who earned public acclaim when she appeared in the play *The Warrens of Virginia* in New York in 1906. In 1908, due to a slack season on Broadway, Pickford sought work in the fledgling film industry and became the first of many child stage performers to appear on the screen. After starring in several short films produced by director D.W. Griffith, by 1915 she had become not only the world's most popular actress but the highest-paid female in America. By 1927, Pickford, known for her trademark ringlet curls, had starred in over two hundred films in which she portrayed children or teens.

Pickford's phenomenal success sent a message to the film industry: young characters on the screen, whether portrayed by juveniles or adult actors, had genuine box office appeal. During the 1920s American filmmakers began producing a series of films with all-child casts; the most popular was the *Our Gang* comedy series, created by director Hal Roach. Between 1922 and 1929, Roach produced eighty-eight *Our Gang* films, which featured a troupe of rambunctious boys who became known throughout the country by their screen nicknames: "Wheezer," "Stymie," "Farina," and "Alfalfa," a character who sported a famous middle-part haircut with a long strand of hair sticking up at the back. Child performers also began starring alongside well-established actors, and in 1921 a six year old named Jackie Coogan earned worldwide fame when he appeared with Charlie Chaplin in Chaplin's silent melodrama *The Kid.* Coogan dolls, statuettes, and memorabilia were immediately produced by enterprising manufacturers, and they flew from store shelves. As Hollywood learned, children on the screen not only lured audiences but helped the film industry gain legitimacy. The aura of innocence conveyed by young stars helped the industry combat criticism from religious and social reform groups, which accused Hollywood of glorifying sex and violence and pressured the government to enact federal film censorship.

During the 1930s, the Great Depression years, America's obsession with young actors reached unprecedented heights. The craze began in 1934 with the appearance of a six-year-old singer, dancer, and actress named Shirley Temple in the musical *Stand Up and Cheer.* Charmed by Temple's angelic demeanor, perky on-screen antics, and remarkable talents, audiences catapulted her to stardom. Throughout the decade, Temple was celebrated by a legion of fans that included President Franklin Roosevelt, who credited "Little Miss Miracle" with raising the nation's spirits during the economic crisis. Between 1935 and 1938, Temple, who appeared in over a dozen films for the Fox studio, including *Poor Little Rich Girl* (1935), *Rebecca of Sunnybrook Farm* (1938), and *The Little Princess* (1939), was voted America's most popular star.

Not surprisingly, Temple's success spawned a host of imitators, who descended on Hollywood "like a flock of hungry locusts," in the words of movie gossip columnist Hedda Hopper. Across America, "Beautiful Baby" contests, with a screen test as the prize, were run in major cities by photographers and theater owners, and during the 1930s approximately one hundred child actors arrived in Hollywood each day. Hal Roach recalled that he tested over 140,000 children when casting for the *Our Gang* series. Though most dreams ended in failure—according to one estimate, less than one in fifteen thousand earned enough from one year of movie work to pay for a week's expenses—from the army of hopefuls a few genuine stars were born. Elizabeth Taylor, Freddie Bartholomew, Deanna Durbin, Mickey Rooney, and Judy Garland, who starred in the *Wizard of Oz* (1939), became *bona fide* celebrities during the 1930s and 1940s; in 1939,

Rooney and Durbin were given special Academy Awards for their "significant contribution in bringing to the screen the spirit and personification of youth."

The popularization of TELEVISION in the immediate postwar period created a further demand for child actors, who became a staple of the domestic drama/sitcom genre. During the 1950s several young television actors, including Jerry Mathers, star of *Leave it To Beaver*, and Ricky Nelson, on *The Adventures of Ozzie and Harriet*, rose to prominence. In the late 1950s, when Nelson began recording rock music, he initiated the phenomenon of the "crossover" youth celebrity, who starred simultaneously in two entertainment media. Like Elvis Presley, another young pop icon, Nelson sold thousands of records to his teenaged fans, capitalizing on the increased purchasing power of American youth in the affluent 1950s.

Like adult entertainment celebrities, child actors spurred an entire fan culture. Admirers of all ages organized fan clubs in honor of their favorite child actors, sent gifts and fan letters by the thousands, and purchased products bearing their idols' names and images. During the 1920s, actors in the *Our Gang* series initiated the phenomenon of child celebrity endorsement when they appeared in ads for Kellogg's Cereal; Temple, Garland, Rooney and Durbin similarly sold clothing, toys, and cosmetics for major corporations. Fans also read the many magazines and tabloids that reported the details of child stars' private lives and by the early 1930s could choose from over a dozen different fan magazine titles. Indeed, by World War II, the story of young stars' off-screen exploits had become as captivating to many Americans as their on-screen accomplishments. In a society obsessed with "rags to riches" stories, the phenomenal rise of stars like Rooney and Garland from impoverished backgrounds to celebrity status became an object of national fascination.

Almost as intriguing as the rise of child stars were the stories of their seemingly inevitable declines. During the 1940s the public was riveted by the story of Shirley Temple's fall from public favor—her career ended when she reached adolescence—and read about the troubles of Jackie Coogan, who as an adult became embroiled in a bitter lawsuit against his parents over control of his childhood earnings. Coogan's trials eventually led to the passage of the Coogan Act, a bill which required the parents of child actors to put aside at least half of their earnings. Jackie Cooper, star of *The Champ* (1931), battled alcoholism in his adulthood; Garland died from a drug overdose, and Rooney declared bankruptcy after seven failed marriages. It seemed that stardom, for many young actors, was more a curse than a blessing.

By the 1970s, child stars had become almost as famous for their misdeeds as their accomplishments. A series of well-publicized scandals and tragedies involving juvenile actors proved to an increasingly cynical public that young stardom was not as glamorous as it seemed. The three young stars of

A child star of the 1930s and 1940s, Judy Garland's most celebrated role was as Dorothy in the enormously popular 1939 screen adaptation of L. Frank Baum's *Wizard of Oz*. UPI/Bettman-CORBIS.

the popular 1980s sitcom *Diff'rent Strokes* made national news when, following the termination of the show, they fell into crime and drug addiction. The alcoholism of Drew Barrymore, star of the 1982 film *E.T.*, and the custody battles of Macaulay Culkin, star of the film *Home Alone* (1990) whose popularity sparked comparisons with Shirley Temple, also made headlines. Young celebrities had become an object lesson in the dangers of growing up on the screen—too famous, too rich, too soon.

The 1996 murder of six-year-old JonBenét Ramsey brought the potential perils of child stardom most poignantly to light. When images of Ramsey were shown in the national media—the winner of several child beauty contests, she was frequently photographed wearing lipstick and rouge—Americans were stunned. The issue of the sexualization of child performers was also raised around the adolescent singer BRITNEY SPEARS, who rose to fame in the late 1990s with her sexy costumes and dance routines. At the beginning of the twenty-first century, Spears and young actresses Jennifer Love Hewitt and Sarah Michelle Gellar, who played sexually charged roles in films, were frequently imitated by teenage girls, sparking concern from parents. As the media and advertising industries became more aggressive in their marketing of child performers, as more and more children found role models in young entertainers, and as American youth continued to pursue their own dreams of stardom, the child star phenomenon seemed destined to become an enduring part of American popular culture.

See also: **Images of Childhood; Media, Childhood and the; Movies.**

BIBLIOGRAPHY

Aylesworth, Thomas G. 1987. *Hollywood Kids : Child Stars of the Silver Screen from 1903 to the Present.* New York: Dutton.

Black, Shirley Temple. 1988. *Child Star: An Autobiography.* New York: McGraw-Hill.

Darvi, Andrea. 1983. *Pretty Babies: An Insider's Look at the World of the Hollywood Child Star.* New York: McGraw Hill.

Dye, David. 1988. *Child and Youth Actors: Filmographies of Their Entire Careers, 1914–1985.* Jefferson, NC: McFarland.

Serra, Diana Cary. 1978. *Hollywood's Children: An Inside Account of the Child Star Era.* Boston: Houghton Mifflin.

Whitfield, Eileen. 1997. *Pickford: The Woman Who Made Hollywood.* Lexington: University Press of Kentucky.

Zierold, Norman. 1965. *The Child Stars.* New York, Coward-McCann.

SAMANTHA BARBAS

Child Study

Child study, also called *paidology* or *experimental pedagogy*, was the attempt to apply the methods of modern science to the investigation of children in order to discover the laws of normal child development. The child-study movement arose in the last decade of the nineteenth century in several Western countries and was inspired by a number of social reform movements that aimed to improve the health and welfare of children. The connection between child study, schools, teachers, and movements for educational reform was particularly strong, because many reformers viewed the educational system as the most promising avenue to improve the conditions of children and to create the conditions for a better and more just society. They became convinced that scientific insights into the nature of children would aid their efforts. Initially, the child-study movement was inclusive: teachers, parents, ministers, psychologists, educational administrators, physicians, psychiatrists, and others concerned with the welfare of children participated in its research. After the turn of the twentieth century, psychologists and physicians aimed to make child study scientifically respectable by excluding lay researchers. In their hands, child study became the science of child development and developmental psychology. Consequently, research into child development became a field of academic inquiry and lost its ties to social and educational reform.

Educational reformers viewed the school as providing the means for improving social conditions and fostering the moral progress of society. They were inspired by a variety of ideologies, such as the social Darwinism of the English philosopher Herbert Spencer (1820–1903), which emphasized free competition as the prime condition for social betterment. In this view, a proper education equipped children with the tools for self-improvement and success in modern society, and would thereby help them lift themselves out of poverty. Other educational reformers were guided by the ideas of the French philosopher JEAN-JACQUES ROUSSEAU (1712–1778) and the educationalists JOHANN HEINRICH PESTALOZZI (1746–1827), a Swiss, and FRIEDRICH WILHELM AUGUST FROEBEL (1782–1852), a German. These thinkers embraced romantic idealizations of childhood as an innocent and untainted period of life and wanted to re-create the educational system to provide a stimulating environment for free PLAY and exploration.

Despite the variety in their philosophies and political orientations, educational reformers agreed in their attempts to reform old educational practices that relied on rote learning, character education, the training of mental discipline, and an academically oriented curriculum. Educational reformers argued that this curriculum was irrelevant for most children. According to them, education should become more practical and help children take their place in society. They proposed the introduction of project learning and practical and vocational training, and advocated the establishment of KINDERGARTENS.

The Beginnings of Child Study

The psychologist G. STANLEY HALL (1844–1924) initiated the child-study movement in the United States in the 1880s. Hall was influenced by the evolutionary theory of the nineteenth-century English naturalist Charles Darwin and adhered to the recapitulation theory, which states that children repeat in their development the physiological and cultural development of the species. Hall was also inspired by developments in psychology and education in Germany, where he had spent several years studying philosophy and psychology. His organizational efforts in the child-study movement stimulated and consolidated existing interests and activities in several countries. In 1882 Hall introduced a course in child study at Clark University, advocating child study as the core of the new profession of pedagogy. He became a prominent member of the National Education Association, where he found an enthusiastic response for his plans. Hall invited parents and teachers to participate in child-study research and sent out hundreds of questionnaires to collect observations of children. Hall used the results of this research to provide arguments for educational reform. In 1904 he published *Adolescence*, which he described as a period of life bestowed with special challenges and in need of special consideration. This book became very influential with parents, teachers, and individuals involved with child welfare agencies.

In 1891 Hall founded the *Pedagogical Seminary*, which became the most prominent outlet for research in child study worldwide. (The journal was renamed in 1931 the *Pedagogical Seminary and Journal of Genetic Psychology* and in 1954, the *Journal of Genetic Psychology*.)

Participants in the child-study movement investigated a wide range of topics, including the physical, cognitive, and moral development of children, health and HYGIENE, fatigue, educational practices and their effect on learning, the interests and imagination of children and the nature of their religious experiences, and children's attitudes toward various matters. A wide variety of methods were used: undirected observations of children at home and at school; personal letters or journals by children; quantitative and qualitative answers to a variety of questionnaires; observations of concrete behavior; measurements of weight, physical growth, and mental growth; results of a variety of special tests; diaries by mothers and teachers recording children's behavior; and autobiographical statements by adults reflecting upon their childhood.

During the first decade of the twentieth century, a number of psychologists and physicians argued that research in child study had resulted in vast amounts of incoherent data based on free observation under unspecified conditions, unguided by theories and hypotheses, and collected by untrained observers. They urgently advocated lifting the scientific standards of child study through more rigorous, laboratory-based research by qualified scientists. There were two approaches to doing so. The first one was advocated by education psychologists, who stated that pedagogy was the application of psychological knowledge that was based upon laboratory research or extensive psychometric testing. According to them, teachers and educational administrators needed to inform themselves about psychological research and apply its results. A number of educators and pedagogists advocated a second approach: they proposed the establishment of experimental schools and pedagogical laboratories to conduct educational research. They were convinced that pedagogy or the science of education could not be reduced to psychological research.

Psychologists made two contributions to educational research: they developed mental testing and investigated the fundamental laws of learning. The first INTELLIGENCE TEST was developed in 1905 by ALFRED BINET (1857–1911), who had been associated with the French Society for the Psychological Study of the Child (Société libre pour l'étude psychologique de l'enfant) and the educational system in Paris. For Binet, the intelligence test was an individualized diagnostic tool to diagnose pupils with mental RETARDATION or learning disabilities in order to place them in appropriate classes. The test was graded in terms of the age at which normal children would be able to solve a number of tasks. Psychologists in the United States and the United Kingdom found new uses for mental tests and developed the psychology of individual differences. In addition to developing men-

tal tests, behaviorist psychologists investigated the laws basic to all learning and claimed that educational practices needed to conform to these laws in order to optimize learning in schools.

Germany

Research in child development in Germany started with the publication of *Die Seele des Kindes* (The mind of a child; 1882) by the physiologist William T. Preyer (1841–1897), which was based on extensive physiological and psychological observations collected during the first three years of the life of his son. Preyer was influenced by Darwin's theory of evolution and proposed a developmental scheme in which instinct and reflex were gradually replaced by language and purposeful action. According to Preyer, scientific insights could be gained only through the continuous observation of a great number of healthy, normally developing children. He therefore encouraged mothers to observe their newborn babies by keeping diaries, starting at birth, making observations for several hours a day. Preyer's work suggested ways in which child development could be investigated scientifically, and it stimulated wide interest in the possibilities for such research.

The General German Society for Child Study (Allgemeiner Deutscher Verein für Kinderforschung) and the Society for Child Psychology (Verein für Kinderpsychologie) were founded in 1889. The latter society published the *Zeitschrift für Pädagogische Psychologie* (Journal for pedagogical psychology) in 1905, and the journal *Die Experimentelle Pädagogik* (Experimental pedagogy) commenced publication that year as well. Initially, German child study was dominated by the activities of teachers, who were active in a variety of associations and institutes. The methods of research were as eclectic and varied as those adopted by the American child-study movement, although German teachers were more interested in research conducted according to hermeneutic methods, which aimed at acquiring an intuitive understanding of how children think and learn, instead of quantitative research, which provided indications of the abilities and achievements of groups of children.

The different approaches of Wilhelm August Lay (1862–1926) and Ernst Neumann (1862–1937), two pioneers in pedagogical research in Germany, illustrate the development of experimental pedagogy or paidology in Germany. Both Lay and Neumann attempted to make child study more rigorous and scientifically respectable. Lay started out his career as an educator and conducted his research from the perspective of teachers. He advocated the establishment of experimental schools and viewed them as the ideal places for pedagogical research. Neumann was a psychologist who viewed education as a field in which psychological insights could be applied. The difference between these perspectives indicated the increasing tension between teachers and psychologists in their attempts to control the development of experimental pedagogy. Eventually, psychologists came to dominate the field. In Germany, however, pedagogy as a field remained influential within the educational system.

After World War I (1914–1918), German research on child development succeeded in acquiring a permanent place in the universities. The psychologist William Stern (1871–1938) had kept, with his wife Clara, detailed diaries of the psychological development of their three children. Stern later published his work on language acquisition and development of memory in young children based on this material. Other influential psychologists were the Austrian couple Karl (1879–1963) and CHARLOTTE BÜHLER (1893–1974), whose maturational and life-course psychology became very influential. Charlotte Bühler's research was based on guided observations of children, intelligence tests, the interpretation of diaries, and experiments with free play. She aimed to develop a unified scheme of psychological development from birth to early adulthood and focused on cognitive and personality characteristics of developmental stages.

United Kingdom

Child study in the United Kingdom followed developments in the United States and Germany, although it never reached the same level of activity. Interest in children and education grew when, during the 1890s, several medical surveys of schoolchildren, particularly those from poor working-class districts, revealed that many pupils were in poor health and suffered from malnutrition and a range of medical problems, including what was then called mental deficiency. In 1913 the Mental Deficiency Act was passed, mandating the proper treatment and care of individuals with this condition. Furthermore, philosophical psychologists in England had written several books on educational reform, educational philosophy, and the importance of modernizing the curriculum. And there were widespread calls for educational reform in order to increase national productivity through a better-educated labor force and calls to make education child-centered.

In 1898 the British Child Study Association was established by a number of individuals who had become acquainted with Hall's work in the United States and who wished to organize child study in England. The association started publishing the journal *The Paidologist* one year later (in 1908 the name was changed to *Child Study*; it ceased publication in 1921). In 1911 the rival *Journal of Experimental Pedagogy* commenced publication as well (it was renamed the *British Journal of Educational Psychology* in 1931).

Initially, educational psychology in England focused on the construction and administration of mental tests. Research into the nature of intelligence had been the lifework of Charles Spearman (1863–1945), who had analyzed a wide range of test results with a statistical technique called factor analysis and concluded that all intelligence tests measured a stable and inherited quality of general intelligence. In 1912

the psychologist CYRIL BURT (1883–1971) was appointed as psychologist at the London County Council, which was the central educational authority in London. In this position, Burt tested children recommended for special or remedial schools and classes. He also developed mental and diagnostic tests. In *The Backward Child* (1937), Burt argued that pupils who could not do the work of the grade they were supposed to be in on the basis of their age often suffered from environmental handicaps such as poverty, poor health, and inadequate housing. Despite that, he also believed that the majority of these cases were irremediably backward as a result of the general inferiority of their intellectual capacity, which, according to him, was inborn, hereditary, and therefore unalterable. According to Burt, the existing class structure was justified because it was based on innate differences in intelligence. Because he was convinced that intelligence did not improve because of education, he advocated the establishment of special educational tracks for children to match their innate general cognitive ability.

United States of America

At the turn of the twentieth century, psychologists criticized the child-study movement for the lack of scientific rigor and inconclusive nature of its research and the lack of clarity in its basic objectives. Consequently, the movement lost its momentum. In particular, educational psychologists attempted to make research into child development scientifically respectable. They aimed to provide teachers and educational administrators with the scientific tools to rationalize and improve educational practice. The *Journal of Educational Psychology*, which published their research, commenced publication in 1910.

According to the psychologist Edward Lee Thorndike (1874–1947), educational psychology could provide normative standards for the rational organization of educational practice. Thorndike promoted the widespread application of intelligence and achievement tests to make the work of schools visible in a numerical way: the statistics generated by these tests made classes, grades, and schools comparable, which made it possible to evaluate performance. In particular, educational administrators found this type of numerical information useful. Apart from developing psychometric tests, Thorndike presented the laws of learning as a rational foundation for educational practice, as behaviorist psychologists had formulated them. His most influential and controversial contribution was his opinion that there was little or no transfer of training between learning in different areas. This statement was used as an argument against the classical curriculum, in particular the teaching of Latin in HIGH SCHOOLS. After all, if the mental discipline acquired through learning Latin had no ramifications for learning in other areas, it became very difficult to defend teaching the subject.

The use of mental tests in education was promoted by Lewis M. Terman (1877–1956), a member of the faculty at

Stanford University who had translated Binet's intelligence test into English and published it as the Stanford-Binet test in 1916. Terman's version of the intelligence test could be administered to groups. According to Terman, intelligence, often expressed in the form of the intelligence quotient, or IQ, was a relatively stable and inherited quality. To accommodate students with a wide variety of intellectual ability, he proposed that schools organize different educational tracks suitable for different levels of mental ability. Similarly, Terman was convinced that modern society was essentially meritocratic in nature: intelligent individuals would naturally enter into the more desirable occupations. In his view, differences in income and socioeconomic status are based on intelligence rather than on differences in educational opportunity or the effects of discrimination, exclusion, and deprivation. Terman's views were very influential among psychologists and educators throughout the twentieth century.

Child Development Research in the 1920s

In the early 1920s, research into child development was a modest endeavor. It occurred on a small scale at a number of universities and received small amounts of funding. Researchers were engaged in research on different aspects of child health, child welfare, and educational research. The decisive impulse to make child study an area of scientific research came from the LAURA SPELMAN ROCKEFELLER MEMORIAL (LSRM), which, starting in 1924, funded interdisciplinary research at a number of research centers devoted to child development in the United States and Canada. As a result, CHILD PSYCHOLOGY or developmental psychology was transformed into a respectable profession with professional societies, journals, and university-based research and training centers. In 1925 the Committee on Child Development was founded by the National Research Council to coordinate research activities.

According to Lawrence K. Frank (1890–1974), who initiated this program within the LSRM, most research involving children had focused on DELINQUENCY, abnormality, and pathology. Relatively little was known about normal children and normal child development, knowledge of which he considered essential for guiding educational and child-rearing practices. Because the first years of life were essential for the formation of personality, Frank thought it essential that these would become the object of scientific research. The centers for research on child development funded by the LSRM generally opened a laboratory NURSERY SCHOOL where children from the age of about twelve months could be observed for longer periods. Researchers often had associations with elementary schools and high schools to investigate child development in its later stages. At several research centers, longitudinal research projects, in which individual children were followed for several decades to study their development, were undertaken. Other studies involved observational studies of children and the measurement of individual differences in intelligence and ability. According to

Frank, research in child development needed to be closely associated with the popularization of its results. He insisted that every center for child research institutionalize programs for public education. He also initiated the establishment of PARENTS MAGAZINE in 1926, a popular magazine with child-rearing advice for parents.

One of the first institutions to receive funding was the Iowa Child Welfare Research Station, which had opened in 1917. Researchers there developed measurements of physical development and investigated the importance of nutrition. Several observational studies were undertaken in a laboratory nursery school and at an adoption agency. Researchers at Iowa concluded that the IQ of young children could be highly variable: the IQ of children attending nursery school and adopted children generally rose several points. These conclusions were repeated by Helen Thompson Woolley (1874–1947) of the Merrill-Palmer school in Detroit but were contested by other researchers, in particular Lewis Terman and Florence Goodenough (1886–1959), who worked at the Institute for Child Welfare at the University of Minnesota. At his Yale University laboratory, ARNOLD GESELL (1880–1961) investigated the physical growth of children. According to Gesell, maturation and growth entailed the unfolding of inborn traits, which could be delayed by environmental deprivation. Gesell designed a number of normative scales measuring levels of mental and motor development in children. At the University of Toronto, several longitudinal research projects investigating the social behavior of children were undertaken. At the Institute of Child Welfare at the University of California at Berkeley, a similar research project was initiated. Researchers there also doubted the invariable nature of IQ scores in individuals. At the Child Development Institute at Teachers College, Columbia University, family relations and the personality development of children in nursery schools were studied. The research centers on child development provided career opportunities for women, who were excluded from most other fields of scientific research.

As a consequence of the funding provided by the LSRM, research in child development became scientifically respectable. Over time, researchers became less interested in public education activities, which were often discontinued. The association of research in child development with educational reform became increasingly tenuous over time as well. The research had developed a momentum of its own and lost its association with movements for social change.

See also: **Child Development, History of the Concept of; Scientific Child-Rearing.**

BIBLIOGRAPHY

Cahan, Emily D. 1991. "Science, Practice, and Gender Roles in Early American Child Psychology." In *Contemporary Constructions of the Child: Essays in Honor of William Kessen*, ed. Frank S. Kessel, Marc H. Bonstein, and Arnold J. Sameroff. Hillsdale, NJ: Erlbaum.

Chapman, Paul Davis. 1988. *Schools as Sorters: Lewis M. Terman, Applied Psychology, and the Intelligence Testing Movement, 1890–1930.* New York: New York University Press.

Clifford, Geraldine Jonçich. 1968. *The Sane Positivist: A Biography of Edward L. Thorndike.* Middletown, CT: Wesleyan University Press.

Cravens, Hamilton. 1993. *Before Head Start: The Iowa Station and America's Children.* Chapel Hill: University of North Carolina Press.

Depaepe, Marc. 1987. "Social and Personal Factors in the Inception of Experimental Research in Education (1890–1914): An Exploratory Study." *History of Education* 16, no. 4: 275–298.

Dickinson, Edward Ross. 1996. *The Politics of German Child Welfare from the Empire to the Federal Republic.* Cambridge, MA: Harvard University Press.

Gould, Stephen Jay. 1996. *The Mismeasure of Man,* rev. and expanded ed. New York: Norton.

Hall, G. Stanley. 1904. *Adolescence: Its Psychology, and Its Relations to Physiology, Anthropology, Sociology, Sex, Crime, Religion, and Education.* New York: Appleton.

Hearnshaw, Leslie S. 1964. *A Short History of British Psychology, 1840–1940.* London: Methuen.

Hearnshaw, Leslie S. 1979. *Cyril Burt, Psychologist.* Ithaca, NY: Cornell University Press.

Kett, Joseph F. 1977. *Rites of Passage: Adolescence in America, 1790 to the Present.* New York: Basic.

Minton, Henry L. 1989. *Lewis M. Terman: Pioneer in Psychological Testing.* New York: New York University Press.

Pols, Hans. 2002. "Between the Laboratory and Life: Child Development Research in Toronto, 1919–1956." *History of Psychology* 5, no. 2: 135–162.

Richardson, Theresa. 1989. *The Century of the Child: The Mental Hygiene Movement and Social Policy in the United States and Canada.* Albany: State University of New York Press.

Rose, Nicholas. 1985. *The Psychological Complex: Social Regulation and the Psychology of the Individual.* London: Routledge and Kegan Paul.

Ross, Dorothy. 1972. *G. Stanley Hall: The Psychologist as Prophet.* Chicago: University of Chicago Press.

Schlossman, Steven L. 1981. "Philanthropy and the Gospel of Child Development." *History of Education Quarterly* 21, no. 3: 275–299.

Siegel, Alexander W., and Sheldon H. White. 1982. "The Child Study Movement: Early Growth and Development of the Symbolized Child." In *Advances in Child Development and Behavior,* Vol. 17, ed. Hayne W. Reese. New York: Academic Press.

Stargardt, Nicholas. 1998. "German Childhoods: The Making of a Historiography." *German History* 16, no. 1: 1–15.

HANS POLS

Child Witch

Throughout history children have been involved in witchcraft accusations. They have appeared as witnesses in court, and they have had to defend themselves against accusations of using harmful magic. Although both boys and girls have been involved in witchcraft accusations, girls between five and eleven years old seem to have dominated the witness

stand in most of the afflicted areas. However, there were regional varieties. In some areas, such as North America, young adolescents (from twelve to eighteen years old), rather than children, were the most active in spreading rumors of witchcraft, and in the northern parts of Europe boys were as likely (if not more so) to fantasize about the witches' sabbath as girls.

In northern Spain in the fifteenth and sixteenth centuries, during the Inquisition, hundreds of children claimed to have been abducted by night to the witches' sabbath, where they had participated in large festivities mocking the Christian rites. They told horrifying stories about learning witchcraft and entering into pacts with the devil. Similar stories played a crucial role during the large Swedish witch trials in the late seventeenth century, and as late as the 1850s more than a hundred children created sensational headlines because of their fantasies about magical nocturnal flights to the witches' sabbath. In Germany in the 1720s a group of child witches were first imprisoned and then taken to a medical clinic for treatment, and the Salem, Massachusetts, witch trials in 1692 were initiated by a group of adolescent girls trying to divine their future by magical means.

Although the importance of child witnesses in witch trials differed both in time and location, it is evident that concern about children and child safety have been crucial. Children were supposed to be more vulnerable to magical attacks, and witchcraft beliefs have been connected to ideas about mothering, with the witch thus portrayed as the bad mother. Most accused child witches started out as witnesses claiming to be victims of magical attacks. However, it was not unusual that their testimonies were turned against them. If they showed too much knowledge about the magical flights, they could end up being charged with witchcraft.

It has been argued that children were more prone to becoming suspects in witch trials after the PROTESTANT REFORMATION, which brought about a growing concern about children's original sin and their ability to commit sins. According to Lutheran moralists, children had a natural tendency towards evil. Instead of seeing children as innocent victims, authorities showed a growing tendency to place blame on those who fantasized about the witches' sabbath regardless of age. This changed after the eighteenth century introduced a new concept of childhood. Children were seen as pure and innocent and in need of adult protection from corruption and evil. Their horrifying stories about the witches' sabbath proved to be incompatible with the new notion of childhood innocence.

Some historians have argued that children's stories about witchcraft forced parents to acknowledge their children's dark emotions and fantasies. Unable to relate to their needs or explain their behavior from contemporary ideals, some parents ended up accusing their children of witchcraft. But the children who were involved in witchcraft accusations not only challenged the concept of childhood innocence, they also broke the norms regulating the relationship between children and adults. Their accusations called adult authority into question, threatening fundamental hierarchical structures.

In the 1800s children's accounts of witchcraft continued to evoke controversy. By then, the ideals of childhood innocence were so cemented that children rarely were held responsible for their fantasies. Rather, the ungodly stories about the witches' sabbath were seen as symptoms of disease or parental neglect, thus freeing the children from responsibility and ultimately defending the idea of childhood innocence.

See also: **Early Modern Europe; Enlightenment, The; Theories of Childhood.**

BIBLIOGRAPHY

Boyer, Paul, and Stephen Nissenbaum. 1974. *Salem Possessed: The Social Origins of Witchcraft.* Cambridge, MA: Harvard University Press.

Roper, Lyndal. 2000. "Evil Imaginings and Fantasies: Child-Witches and the End of the Witch Craze." *Past and Present* 167: 107–139.

Walinski-Kiehl, Robert. 1996. "The Devil's Children: Child Witch-Trials in Early Modern Germany." *Continuity and Change: A Journal of Social Structure, Law, and Demography in Past Societies* 11, vol. 2: 171–190.

Willis, Deborah. 1995. *Malevolent Nurture: Witch-Hunting and Maternal Power in Early Modern England.* Ithaca, NY: Cornell University Press.

KRISTINA TEGLER JERSELIUS

China

In 1991, for a handbook on the history of childhood and children, historian John Dardess made a brief and masterful excursion into the history of childhood in premodern China, a subject he said had been "wholly untouched until recently" (p. 71). Some of the themes he struck are still with us ten years later, and provide a framework to assess changes in the field: the vast richness of potentially useful source material, both native and foreign; the intrinsic interest of childhood in China precisely because it is so different from Western traditions and practice; the problematic linkage between childhood in today's China, studied by social scientists and practitioners, and the deeper traditions and patterns studied by China scholars; the need continually to specify time, place, actors, and circumstances within a civilization so vast and complex that it continually surprises those who would claim to generalize about it.

Sources and Lenses

Some of that richness of source material has been mined in new books, particularly in *Chinese Views of Childhood* (1995) and *Children in Chinese Art* (2002). *Chinese Views of Childhood,* edited by Anne Behnke Kinney, brings together eleven scholars and the lenses of six academic disciplines: literature (fiction, necrology, biography, autobiography), institutional history (education, welfare, legal systems), the history of art, medicine, sociology, and cultural history. The authors scrutinize different types of written texts and visual representations for clues about children and childhood; the lines of inference are often long and tenuous, requiring qualifications and disclaimers and conditional language.

In this field, direct evidence about children's lives, especially nonelite children, is sparse before the twentieth century, and almost nonexistent before the Han dynasty (206 B.C.E.–220 C.E.). To put this in perspective, however, we must remember that overall the surviving body of visual and written materials in China is immense; the Chinese material focused on the lives of children available from the tenth, eleventh, and twelfth centuries, for example, is "substantially larger . . . than can be found anywhere else in the world." (Barnhart, p. 56). Surviving texts on elite family rituals and family instructions, explored by Patricia Ebrey, have yielded rich insights into the institutional context of children's lives.

Children in Chinese Art, edited by Ann Barrott Wicks, is the first book-length effort to draw out meanings about children and childhood from the vast treasury of Chinese visual imagery. Pre–Song dynasty (960–1279) visual depictions of children have been found on jade plaques, Han dynasty tomb decorations and furnishings, illustrations in pictorial biographies of cultural heroes, lacquer ware, woodblock scriptures, marble steles, and Buddhist murals and scrolls. In the Song period children became a recognized category within Chinese figure painting, and some court painters were individually known for their skills in this genre. The painter Su Hanchen (twelfth century) set a standard that later painters imitated.

Most of the essays in this book concern visual depictions of children from the Ming (1368–1644) and Qing (1644–1911) dynasties, around the themes of children at play, mothers and sons, fertility symbolism, family portraits, and child protectors from the folk religion. The focus of these depictions of children, says editor Wicks, was almost never on the child itself but on "the future role of the child as provider for aged parents and preserver of the patriline [line of male descent]." The representations were past-oriented and meant to encourage obedience to tradition (Wicks, p. 27).

The China Difference

China continues to offer some different angles on the study of childhood. Starting twenty years after their European counterparts, China scholars have not fixated upon the European debate over the quality of child rearing (nurturance versus abuse) and its improvement or deterioration over time. Instead the work has concentrated on more modest questions, such as those posed by Joseph M. Hawes and N. Ray Hiner, editors of the 1991 handbook *Children in Historical and Comparative Perspective*: What have been the attitudes of adults towards children and childhood, what conditions have shaped the development of children, and what have been the social, cultural, and psychological functions of children? Ongoing research keeps circling back to the prominence of filial piety, the influence of ancestral cults, and the domination of the patrilineage with its philosophically-grounded social hierarchies. Gender differentiation was also strongly marked. The depictions of children in art from the Song dynasty to the Qing dynasty revealed a persistent concern for the production of multiple sons, conveying the "accepted propaganda for a hundred generations" (Wicks, p. 30). A final element in Chinese traditions concerning childhood was the early introduction of state-sponsored Confucian education for a small elite, with occasional openings for a talented peasant child.

If China as an ancient historical civilization demonstrates the tenacity and power of traditions as well as the intricate interweaving of culture, society, and state, its twentieth-century story offers related insights. How does such a state, society, and culture remake itself? How do some young people break the hold of the group and of tradition? In his 1982 and 1990 studies, Jon L. Saari postulates that the supposedly monolithic family system had enough vulnerabilities and the cultural tradition sufficient variation to permit mischievous children to survive the intense pressures for filial behavior. New supports outside the family in coastal cities and in new-style schools after 1905 allowed some to become cultural innovators and political reformers.

The most controversial insights along these lines have come from the subfield of "political culture." Political scientist Richard H. Solomon argued that the twentieth-century Communist revolution has been in large part an unsuccessful Maoist effort to break out of the pattern of authoritarian leaders and deferential followers. A substantial part of his 1971 study, based on interviews and surveys, was a portrayal of traditional socialization within the family.

A sharp break between the two halves of childhood—indulgent care up to age six and strict and uncompromising DISCIPLINE and training thereafter—created ambivalence about authority and undermined the sense of individual autonomy. This view of the negative effects of traditional socialization, also promoted by a group of psychologists in Taiwan, led to counterarguments, particularly by Thomas A. Metzger in a 1977 study. Linking traditional socialization within the family to twentieth-century political movements has stirred up the most controversy in the field of the history of childhood; a related study by Mark Lupher focuses on activist youth in the Cultural Revolution (1966–1976), which pitted "revolutionary little red devils" against the Communist establishment (Lupher, p. 321).

Continuities, Changes, Breaks

The issue of continuity and change addresses not only contemporary China (1949–present) and its Republican (1912–1949) antecedents, but also the long centuries of what is simply classified as "premodern" China. Kinney points out that the history of childhood gives us a chance to see how a society perceives errors of the past, and might seek to shape a different future through its children. Republican China presents a strong example. Cultural critics and reformers like Lu Xun (1881–1936) raised the cry of "Save the children" (from the last line of his famous short story "The Diary of a Madman"), for they felt that only young people could forge new pathways for a society and polity mired in conservatism and reaction. The twentieth century has indeed seen the greatest structural and attitudinal changes affecting children: the breakup of the political monarchy and the attack on its counterpart the patriarchal family system, the coming of near universal schooling and literacy, the creation of ADOLESCENCE as a separate stage of the life cycle (at times in sharp tension with adult authority), and the spreading of ideals of considerate parenthood and of the legal rights of children.

Yet sensitivity to children also marked other periods as times of significant change: Richard and Catherine Barnhart (2002) and Pei-yi Wu (1989) depict Song China as a humane and enlightened era when reformers emphasized elementary learning and children were sometimes represented apart from adult preoccupations in art and poetry, the late Ming dynasty when the ideas of philosopher Wang Yang-ming (1472–1529) had spread sufficiently to help create a "cult of the child" (Pei-yu Wu 1995, p. 146), or the Six Dynasties (386–589) when, as Richard B. Mather argues, unconventional Taoist ideas facilitated positive portraits of "immoral" child behavior (such as impertinent but witty remarks to elders). How children are addressed, characterized, and understood can be a barometer, as Kinney puts it, of "the governing expectations and goals of particular eras in China's history" (Kinney, p. 1).

Signs of a Maturing Field of Study

The study of the history of childhood in China in 2002 resembles the development of the field elsewhere as described by Hawes and Hiner in 1991: a confusing and fruitful proliferation of multidisciplinary scholars, carefully extracting nuggets of insight out of more-or-less illuminating texts and visual images. The field may develop in diverse directions: the search for common ground (within China or worldwide) and/or the elaboration of complex syntheses within cultural regions and histories that are fundamentally incomparable. Both efforts are proceeding. Kinney and Wicks as editors both search for generalizations that can incorporate the separate insights of their contributors, just as Hawes and Hiner attempted the same for the entire field of the history of childhood in 1991. By themselves, the larger generalizations are abstract and incomplete, like shorthand compared to full text. What makes for understanding is not just the conclusions, but the full context of time and place and the shared process of minds working on evidence.

C. John Sommerville, who wrote a foreword to *Chinese Views of Childhood*, characterized the book, and by implication, the field, as relying heavily on literature and art for source material, and hence as documenting adult perceptions of children more than the actual lives of children. Documenting adult perceptions he regarded as the first stage, which would eventually lead to the next stage: a wider social history of children. These stages reflect the useful and common distinction between the history of childhood as a social and ideological construction and the history of children as a larger and more inclusive category. The latter is what scholars eventually want to achieve. Given the great reaches of time and geography in Chinese history, however, and the sparseness and indirectness of source material, it appears an almost Sisyphean task, with much scholarly effort supporting very tentative conclusions.

The twentieth century is more promising for complex syntheses, as the source materials are more abundant (both native and foreign) and theoretical models of humanization have given scholars ways to connect the pieces. A 1990 work by Jon L. Saari, *Legacies of Childhood: Growing Up Chinese in a Time of Crisis, 1890–1920*, seized these advantages by interviewing adult Chinese about their childhoods and youth, and by using the stage theories of ERIK H. ERIKSON as an orientation for understanding the early years of their lives. It is a collective biography of a generation of educated youth, who as children were heirs to the neo-Confucian tradition as well as to a specific historical juncture that permitted, even demanded, new behaviors from parents and children. Some children thrived on the opportunities and as youth and young adults created new pathways for their ancient culture. Mainstreaming the history of children by adding it to larger stories that address the transmission of culture is a promising long-range goal.

Signs indicate that the history of childhood in China is still an immature field. Warnings against simplifications are obligatory. No facile East versus West comparisons will do it justice. "China" as a self-evident reference point has dissolved into specific times, places, ethnic groups, classes, genders, families. At the same time scholars attempt China-centered understandings, seeking to minimize outsider perspectives, projections, and assumed Western impacts or standards. For the history of childhood these China-centered exhortations have been positive, for they have encouraged scholars to dig out Chinese understandings first and foremost. For example, Charlotte Furth has written nuanced accounts of the various cosmological, ritual, biological, and cultural perspectives that intersect with the Chinese medical understanding of human conception, infancy, and sexual maturation in the late Imperial period (1368–1911).

Similarly, much valuable research, particularly that of William de Bary and John Chaffee, has broadened and deepened our understanding of neo-Confucianism and education. The China-centered principle has also led some to criticize the work of modern social scientists like Solomon as insufficiently informed about Chinese traditions, as "decorative Sinology" (Mote, p. 116). No doubt a reverse charge could be leveled against theory-shy traditionalists. Such controversies indicate the high demands placed upon scholars in Chinese studies generally, for both language and disciplinary skills, not to mention the diplomatic and cross-cultural skills helpful in navigating Chinese bureaucracies. The subfield of the history of childhood in China is embedded in Chinese history generally, and not likely to mature any faster than the field of Chinese studies as a whole.

See also: **Images of Childhood; India and South Asia; Japan.**

BIBLIOGRAPHY

Barnhart, Richard, and Catherine Barnhart. 2002. "Images of Children in Song, Painting, and Poetry." In *Children in Chinese Art*, ed. Ann Barrott Wicks. Honolulu: University of Hawai'i Press.

Dardess, John. 1991. "Children in Premodern China." In *Children in Historical and Comparative Perspective: An International Handbook and Research Guide*, ed. Joseph M. Hawes and N. Ray Hiner. New York: Greenwood Press.

de Bary, Wm. Theodore, and John W. Chaffee, eds. 1989. *Neo-Confucian Education: The Formative Stage*. Berkeley: University of California Press.

Ebrey, Patricia Buckley. 1991. *Confucianism and Family Rituals in Imperial China: A Social History of Writing about Rites*. Princeton, NJ: Princeton University Press.

Furth, Charlotte. 1995. "From Birth to Birth: The Growing Body in Chinese Medicine." In *Chinese Views of Childhood*, ed. Anne Behnke Kinney. Honolulu: University of Hawai'i Press.

Hawes, Joseph M., and N. Ray Hiner, eds. 1991. *Children in Historical and Comparative Perspective: An International Handbook and Research Guide*. New York: Greenwood Press.

Kinney, Anne Behnke, ed. 1995. *Chinese Views of Childhood*. Honolulu: University of Hawai'i Press.

Lupher, Mark. 1995. "Revolutionary Little Red Devils: The Social Psychology of Rebel Youth, 1966–1967." In *Chinese Views of Childhood*, ed. Anne Behnke Kinney. Honolulu: University of Hawai'i Press.

Mather, Richard B. 1995. "Filial Paragons and Spoiled Brats: A Glimpse of Medieval Chinese Children in the *Shishuo xinyu*." In *Chinese Views of Childhood*, ed. Anne Behnke Kinney. Honolulu: University of Hawai'i Press.

Metzger, Thomas A. 1977. *Escape from Predicament: Neo-Confucianism and China's Evolving Political Culture*. New York: Columbia University Press.

Mote, Frederick W. 1972. "China's Past in the Study of China Today—Some Comments on the Recent Work of Richard Solomon." *Journal of Asian Studies* 32, no. 1 (November): 107–120.

Saari, Jon. 1967. "China's Special Modernity." In *China and Ourselves: Explorations and Revisions by a New Generation*, ed. Bruce Douglass and Ross Terrill. Boston: Beacon Press.

Saari, Jon L. 1982. "Breaking the Hold of Tradition: The Self-Group Interface in Transitional China." In *Social Interaction in Chinese Society*, ed. Sidney L. Greenblatt, Richard W. Wilson, and Amy Auerbacher Wilson. New York: Praeger.

Saari, Jon L. 1983. "The Human Factor: Some Inherent Ambiguities and Limitations in Scholarly Choices." In *Methodological Issues in Chinese Studies*, ed. Amy Auerbacher Wilson, Sidney L. Greenblatt, and Richard W. Wilson. New York: Praeger.

Saari, Jon L. 1990. *Legacies of Childhood: Growing Up Chinese in a Time of Crisis, 1890–1920*. Cambridge, MA: Council on East Asian Studies.

Solomon, Richard H. 1971. *Mao's Revolution and the Chinese Political Culture*. Berkeley: University of California Press.

Wicks, Ann Barrott, ed. 2002. *Children in Chinese Art*. Honolulu: University of Hawai'i Press.

Wu, Pei-yu. 1989. "Education of Children in the Sung." In *Neo-Confucian Education: The Formative Stage*, ed. Wm. Theodore de Bary and John W. Chaffee. Berkeley: University of California Press.

Wu, Pei-yu. 1995. "Childhood Remembered: Parents and Children in China, 800–1700." In *Chinese Views of Childhood*, ed. Ann Behnke Kinney. Honolulu: University of Hawai'i Press.

JON L. SAARI

Cholera. *See* Contagious Diseases.

Christian Thought, Early

Christianity offers a mixed legacy to the history of childhood. On one hand, the teachings of Jesus present childhood as the model for discipleship. Accordingly, newly baptized Christians regardless of their age were called *infants* (*infantes*), and stories of conversion often depict a physical return to childhood. Letters from the earliest Christian communities follow the Hebrew scriptures in urging children to honor their parents (Exod. 20:12), but in addition advise parents to love their children and not to provoke them to anger (Titus 2:4; Eph. 6:4). Early Christian writers protested customary practices of abortion, ABANDONMENT, and exposure of children, and their sale into slavery or prostitution. Evidence from texts and practices point to a positive evaluation of childhood and children from the early Christian communities.

On the other hand, Jesus commends those who leave behind parents and children to become his disciples (Matt. 19:29; Luke 14:26). Christianity offered an alternative community of brothers and sisters in Christ, and membership in this new family often disrupted ties of biology and blood. A young North African noblewoman, Vibia Perpetua, took Jesus' teachings literally, abandoning motherhood to choose martyrdom instead. During a period of intense persecution (c. 202), PERPETUA refused to offer sacrifice to the Roman gods, a move that landed her in prison and separated her from an infant son still nursing. Perpetua was martyred for her resistance; the fate of her son is not known. The story of Perpetua, recounted in Herbert Musurillo's *Acts of the Christian Martyrs*, remains one of the most vivid among early

Christian martyrologies, but the impact on her child is not recorded. Two centuries later, however, North African theologian Augustine of Hippo (354–430) tried to persuade another woman not to abandon her husband and children to live in an ascetic community of women.

From the first centuries of Christianity, material on childhood and children falls into three categories: descriptions of spiritual childhood, material on the care and education of children, and theological discussion of problems that childhood and children presented, specifically the issues of sin and suffering.

Spiritual Childhood

"Whoever does not receive the kingdom of God as a little child will never enter it" (Mark 10:15). The teachings of Jesus himself presented childhood as a model for the spiritual life. Initiation into the faith returned one to childhood, and the rites of Christian initiation were replete with the symbolism of birth and infancy, motherhood and childbearing. In the first four centuries after the death of Jesus, most converts to Christianity were adults, who were literally "born again" into the faith. From the fourth century onward, infant BAPTISM became more prominent. Newly baptized Christians were "infants" in name and in fact.

Christian faith reconfigured the family. Christ served as the true guardian of Christians, as Clement of Alexandria (c. 150–215) argued in a treatise entitled "The Teacher." Christ teaches Christians, but the child models the spiritual life. Clement urged believers to emulate the simplicity, freshness, and purity of the child in their spiritual lives. A later theologian, Isidore of Seville (c. 560–636), underscored the child's spiritual superiority to adults. On thin etymological grounds that *puer* ("boy" in Latin) derived from *puritas* ("purity" in Latin), he argued that a boy possessed virtues utterly lacking in adult males: he bore neither rancor nor grudges; he was immune to the charms of a beautiful woman; he did not think one thing and say another. Spiritual childhood existed as an ideal for the life of discipleship.

Not surprisingly, accounts of conversion borrowed imagery from birth. Recounting the story of his own conversion at the age of thirty-two, Augustine described himself weeping and flailing like a newborn. In a state of physical and spiritual vulnerability, Augustine saw a vision of Continence as "a fruitful mother of children" (p. 151). She urged him to take a few steps towards her, a scene that deliberately echoed the process of learning to walk. Childhood framed the narrative of conversion.

Care and Education of Children

Childhood functioned as a model for Christian spirituality, but the actual life of children was more problematic. In the Roman world children were routinely abandoned in rural places, in designated sections of the marketplace (*lactaria*), or later, on the steps of churches. Early Christian writers like

Justin Martyr, Athenagoras, and Tertullian in the second century and Lactantius in the third denounced the practice as infanticide, even as they acknowledged that not all exposed children fell prey to hunger or wild animals. More likely, children escaped death only to be raised as slaves or prostitutes. Tertullian and Lactantius admitted that extreme poverty might force parents into such a lamentable situation. Nonetheless, poverty in no way legitimated abandonment, as Lactantius made plain: parents who could not support their children should practice abstinence. Clement of Alexandria excoriated wealthy parents who abandoned children they could have afforded to raise. Christian writers urged restricting sexual intercourse to procreation, a move that has been popularly interpreted as fear of SEXUALITY and the body. It is more likely that these early Christian theologians were troubled by the fate of children in a world that regarded them as disposable.

The Edict of Milan in 313 made Christianity a legitimate religious option within the Roman Empire, no longer threatened by persecution. Christians were granted the right to assemble, build churches, and retain property. Children placed on the doorsteps of churches found care in church-supported ORPHANAGES. Monasteries regularly received young children, and Christian families kept them supplied. The reasons for this practice of oblation were various. Given the dangers of childbirth and limited life expectancies, some children had no parents. In other cases, poor parents felt oblation would enhance their children's chances of survival, while parents of more modest means could not always afford a dowry or patrimony for all of their sons and daughters. Still other reasons count as religious: some parents sought some spiritual benefits in this world or the next; others offered their children out of a sense of gratitude, following the example of Hannah in the Hebrew scriptures (1 Sam. 1:27–28).

Monastic rules attest to the practice of oblation and acknowledge its attendant problems. The monastic rules of Basil the Great (c. 330–379) required witnesses be present when parents offered a child to a community. Basil also insisted that at the age of sixteen or seventeen oblates make their own decision whether or not they wished to remain in religious life. The sixth-century Rule of St. Benedict, which gradually came to regulate monastic life in the West, assumed there would be children in monasteries. While imposing stiff punishments for childish pranks, the Rule nonetheless counseled mutual regard: children were to honor the older members of the community; the elders in turn were to love them.

Theological Issues of Children and Childhood

Children of poverty faced a spectrum of dangers ranging from hunger to abandonment, but disease and death cut across class lines. Indeed, the perils of childhood deeply impressed the early Christian writers, and with the end of persecution they turned their theological attention to children.

The plight of the Holy Innocents (i.e., Herod's slaughter of "all the male children in Bethlehem and in all the region who were two years old or under" [Matt. 2:16]) loomed large in the imagination of Christian men and women in late antiquity. Sermons considering Herod's cruel slaughter of the newly born (Matt. 2) proliferated in the late fourth and fifth centuries in the West. These infants had died without the rite of Christian baptism, and theologians speculated that they were baptized by the tears of their mothers and their own blood. They were the first Christian martyrs.

Nor were biblical children the only ones under scrutiny. Augustine, himself the father of one son, Adeodatus, observed children closely and put their world without language into words. In his autobiography he lamented the many beatings he received as a child at the hands of schoolmasters who were "behaving no better than I" (*Confessions*, 1:9, p. 12). With similar compassion Bishop of Antioch John Chrysostom (347–407) noted the simple trust of a child: no matter how badly its mother treated it, the child always longed for her. As bishops Chrysostom and Augustine spent a great deal of time caring for the physical and spiritual needs of children. Behind their observations one glimpses the hard life of children in the ancient world.

Eastern and Western views. As theologians from Eastern and Western Christianity reflected on the plight of children, however, a striking difference emerges. Western church fathers focused on a legacy of inherited sin; too often children died without the redeeming effect of baptism. Eastern church fathers worried about untimely infant death; too often children died before they could be educated or inducted into the life of faith that baptism inaugurated.

In the West Augustine focused debate on the legacy of Adam's sin, passed on by parents to their children. Original sin infected even the infant, and Augustine cited as evidence a newborn's jealous rage when, even after it had been fed, it saw another infant at the nurse's breast. Yet Augustine acknowledged stages in the life cycle, and these marked an increasing moral responsibility. An infant could neither speak nor reason; in addition, it was too weak to harm anyone. Infants were not innocent, but they were also not wholly sinful. Without speech and the capacity to reason, they were literally non-innocent, *non-nocens*. With the acquisition of speech, the child gained the capacity to understand commands and to obey or disobey them, and thus had a degree of moral accountability. With ADOLESCENCE the ability to reason and comprehend basic laws of human equity conferred greater accountability. Augustine illustrated this stage of the life cycle with an adolescent prank. As a youth he joined a group of young boys in stealing pears from a neighbor's tree. The boys were not hungry; they knew without being told that what they did was wrong. Their culpability as adolescents was therefore greater than if they had been infants or children. Augustine's theology featured a graduated accountability for sinning, beginning with infancy. For this reason Augustine urged infant baptism, as salvific redress of their inherited sin.

Eastern church fathers focused on the untimely death of infants, which cut short a life of ongoing formation in the Christian faith. In a treatise entitled "On Infants' Early Deaths," the great Cappadocian theologian Gregory of Nyssa (c. 335–394) tried to reconcile divine justice with the suffering and death of infants. Infants had had the opportunity neither to err nor to do good: what could they expect from eternal life? Without wishing to grant these tiny souls the rewards of the good, who had struggled successfully against temptation, Gregory settled for an afterlife of increasing participation in God and knowledge of divine goodness. He found in infancy an innocence born of ignorance, not Augustine's "non-innocence" begotten in sin.

Eastern church fathers remedied this ignorance with education, and from their pens emerged a whole literature on child rearing. Chrysostom charged parents with the Christian nurture of their children. In the treatise "On Vainglory and the Right Way for Parents to Bring Up Their Children," he offered a taxonomy of biblical stories appropriate to the child's place in the life cycle. Parents ought to teach infants and young children biblical stories, being certain to abstract the appropriate teaching from each. Older children eight to ten years of age were ready for more fearsome stories of divine punishment: the flood, the destruction of Sodom, and so on. Chrysostom advised waiting until a child was fifteen before relating stories of hell and grace.

Contrasting Chrysostom's graduated program of religious education with Augustine's graduated accountability for sin, one glimpses the difference between the Eastern and Western church fathers' approach to childhood. A comprehensive assessment of the impact of Christianity on childhood remains incomplete because the voices of the children themselves remain silent. The evidence available comes solely from the hands of adults, who view childhood through the distortions of time and theological interest.

See also: **Catholicism; Islam; Judaism; Protestant Reformation.**

BIBLIOGRAPHY

Athenagoras. 1953. *Early Christian Fathers*, ed. and trans. Cyril C. Richardson. London: SCM Press.

Augustine, Saint. 1991. *Confessions*, trans. Henry Chadwick. Oxford: Oxford University Press.

Basil of Caesarea. 1925. *The Ascetical Works of Saint Basil*, trans. W. K. L. Clarke. New York: Macmillan.

Boswell, John. 1988. *The Kindness of Strangers: The Abandonment of Children in Western Europe from Late Antiquity to the Renaissance*. New York: Pantheon Books.

Bunge, Marcia J., ed. 2001. *The Child in Christian Thought*. Grand Rapids, MI: W. B. Eerdmans.

Chrysostom, John. 1978 [1951]. "Address on Vainglory and the Right Way for Parents to Bring Up Their Children." In *Chris-*

tianity and Pagan Culture in the Later Roman Empire, trans. M. L. W. Laistner. Ithaca, NY: Cornell University Press.

Clement of Alexandria. 1954. *Christ the Educator*, trans. Simon P. Wood. New York: Fathers of the Church.

deMause, Lloyd, ed. 1974. *The History of Childhood*. New York: Psychohistory Press.

Goody, Jack. 1983. *The Development of the Family and Marriage in Europe*. New York: Cambridge University Press.

Gould, Graham. 1994. "Childhood in Eastern Patristic Thought: Some Problems of Theology and Theological Anthropology." In *The Church and Childhood*, ed. Diana Wood. Oxford, UK: Ecclesiastical History Society/Blackwell Publishers.

Gregory of Nyssa. 1972. *Gregory of Nyssa: Dogmatic Treatises*, ed. Philip Schaff and Henry Wace. Grand Rapids, MI: W. B. Eerdmans.

Guroian, Vigen. 2001. "The Ecclesial Family: John Chrysostom on Parenthood and Children." In *The Child in Christian Thought*, ed. Marcia J. Bunge. Grand Rapids, MI: W. B. Eerdmans.

Hayward, Paul A. 1994. "Suffering and Innocence in Latin Sermons for the Feast of the Holy Innocents, c. 400–800." In *The Church and Childhood*, ed. Diana Wood. Oxford, UK: Ecclesiastical History Society/Blackwell Publishers.

Holmes, Augustine. 2000. *A Life Pleasing to God: The Spirituality of the Rules of St. Basil*. Kalamazoo, MI: Cistercian Publications.

Justin Martyr. 1953. *Early Christian Fathers*. In *The Library of Christian Classics*, vol. 1, ed. and trans. Cyril C. Richardson. London: SCM Press.

Musurillo, Herbert, ed. and trans. 1972. *The Acts of the Christian Martyrs*. Oxford, UK: Clarendon Press.

Nelson, Janet. 1994. "Parents, Children, and the Church in the Earlier Middle Ages." In *The Church and Childhood*, ed. Diana Wood. Oxford, UK: Ecclesiastical History Society/Blackwell Publishers.

Rousselle, Aline. 1988. *Porneia: On Desire and the Body in Antiquity*. Trans. Felicia Pheasant. Oxford, UK: Basil Blackwell.

Stortz, Martha Ellen. 2001. "'Where or When Was Your Servant Innocent?' Augustine on Childhood." In *The Child in Christian Thought*, ed. Marcia J. Bunge. Grand Rapids, MI: W. B. Eerdmans.

Van Der Meer, Frederik. 1961. *Augustine the Bishop: The Life and Work of a Father of the Church*. Trans. Brian Battershaw and G. R. Lamb. London: Sheed and Ward.

Wood, Diana, ed. 1994. *The Church and Childhood: Papers Read at the 1993 Summer Meeting and the 1994 Winter Meeting of the Ecclesiastical History Society*. Oxford, UK: Blackwell.

MARTHA ELLEN STORTZ

Church, Charlotte (b. 1986)

Having released a solo album every year between the ages of twelve and sixteen, Charlotte Church has become the young face of classical music in the early twenty-first century. A self-initiated appearance on a popular local television show featuring talented children thrust Church into the international spotlight from her tiny hometown of Cardiff, Wales, where she was born in 1986. She attended school when home, but had a tutor when on tour performing for such distinguished audiences as Pope John Paul II, President and Mrs. Clinton, and Prince Charles. While she listened to popular singers such as P. Diddy and Gloria Estefan, her own albums included renditions of the Celtic folksongs "Men of Harlech" and "Carrickfergus," Andrew Lloyd Weber's "Pie Jesu," and "Ave Maria." Her personal and professional tastes evolved on each successive album as classical pieces made way for Broadway hits and popular classics.

Charlotte Church's image was defined by the title of her first recording, 1998's *Voice of an Angel*. Inspired in part by the success of the Three Tenors, or their marketing, record industry executives sought to broaden the audience for classical music. By packaging it in the form of a young performer, they hoped to further refute the genre's image as an inaccessible respite of the elite. While her cherubic image promised salvation through music, it also rescued classical music from poor record sales.

Church's music was nonthreatening to audiences, but critics argued that it was harmful to her still-developing voice. A soprano voice, such as Church's, only achieves full maturity in early adulthood. Some critics claimed that her voice was not technically suitable for the material she performed; others questioned how faithfully and passionately a young girl could sing such works as Stephen Adams's "Holy City."

While the description of Charlotte Church as a CHILD PRODIGY referred to her talent, her status as a CHILD STAR was a reflection of the image spun from it. Wolfgang Amadeus Mozart was commissioned to compose his first serious opera, *Mithridates, King of Pontus*, at the age of fourteen. However, Mozart's father was promoting only his son, while Church's record company began marketing an entire genre of music via one performer, one child. To many, Charlotte Church became the personification of opera.

Many hoped that Church's angelic image would herald a new age for classical music by bringing other musicians to the mainstream in her wake. This long-term goal was complemented by the immediate one of attracting an audience from among the largest CD-buying demographic groups—adults over forty-five and children between ten and nineteen. The fact that at the age of fourteen Charlotte Church was one of the sixty wealthiest people under the age of thirty in the United Kingdom was at least proof of her image's, if not her own, success.

INTERNET RESOURCE

Official Charlotte Church Website. 2003. Available from <www.charlottechurch.com>.

NIKA ELDER

Cinema. *See* Movies.

Circumcision

Male circumcision is evidently both the oldest and the most widespread surgical operation. It was practiced among several ancient Near Eastern cultures, but scholars have differed as to which of these first introduced the practice and how it spread. According to the Bible (Genesis 27:24–25), the first individuals to be circumcised at God's command were Abraham, who performed the procedure upon himself at the age of ninety-nine, and his son Ishmael, who was thirteen when he entered the "covenant." Voltaire, however, in his 1764 *Philosophical Dictionary* famously asserted that the Israelites had adopted circumcision from the Egyptians ("who revered the instrument of generation") rather than vice versa. "Would a master," he asked, "adopt the principle badge of his thieving and fugitive slave?" Whatever the direction of influence (if any), Israelite circumcision was performed on infants at the age of eight days, whereas among the Egyptians the rite seems to have been reserved for initiation into manhood, or possibly for prenuptial ceremonies.

Religious Circumcision

Since Biblical times, Jews have continued to circumcise male infants on the eighth day, but Muslims, among whom the rite (though not mentioned in the Qur'an) also became standard, have no set date for its performance, often waiting until several years after birth but rarely beyond the onset of PUBERTY. Whereas Jewish circumcision involves not only the excision of the outer part of the foreskin, but also a slitting of its inner lining (to facilitate the total uncovering of the glans), the Islamic rite calls only for the first procedure.

Female circumcision, which is also widely practiced in the Muslim world (especially in Egypt and other parts of Africa), always involves some cutting of, but not necessarily removal of, the clitoris, and sometimes cutting of labial tissue as well. Most proponents of female circumcision have seen it as a way of minimizing female sexual desire, thus ensuring the protection of a girl's virginity and her family's honor. Similar arguments have been made in favor of male circumcision, notably by the medieval Jewish philosopher Maimonides.

In Hellenistic times, many Jews who were influenced by Greek physical culture and wished to participate in nude athletic events underwent the operation of epispasm in order to conceal the shameful signs of their circumcision. It was under the Seleucid monarch Antiochus Ephiphanes (175–164 B.C.E.), a champion of intense Hellenization, that Jews were first prohibited from practicing circumcision. During the period of Roman rule in Palestine, circumcision was again prohibited by the emperor Hadrian, although scholars differ as to whether this was a cause or result of the Bar-Kokhba rebellion in the early second century. Although, following the teachings of Paul, most Christian sects abolished the practice of circumcision, it continued to be observed by Christian Ethiopians and by Egyptian Copts.

Circumcision is described in the Bible as a mark of the covenant between God and the Israelites, but later Jewish interpreters provided additional explanations for the practice. Philo of Alexandria, in the first century, saw the excision of the foreskin as a symbol for the excision of sensual desires, and Maimonides, in his *Guide of the Perplexed*, saw in circumcision a moral purpose, for "it weakens the faculty of sexual excitement and sometimes diminishes the pleasure." Some medieval Jewish exegetes stressed that Isaac was conceived only after Abraham purified his phallus through the act of circumcision. In Jewish mystical thought, circumcision was seen as having removed the barrier between Abraham and God, allowing him (and his descendants) a vision of the divine.

The seventeenth-century philosopher Baruch Spinoza argued that the sign of circumcision was so integral to Jewish identity that "it alone" could preserve the Jews as a nation forever. A number of early modern travellers, such as Michel de Montaigne and Thomas Coryate, witnessed Jewish circumcisions during their sojourns abroad, sometimes describing the ceremonies and their accompanying festivities in considerable ethnographic detail. Among artistic renditions of the rite, perhaps the best known is Romeyn de Hooghe's *Circumcision in a Sephardic Family*, executed in 1668.

Medical Circumcision

Some German-Jewish advocates of religious reform sought to nullify the rite of circumcision—a proposal first advanced in 1843 but ultimately rejected by the Reform movement. During the second half of the nineteenth century, some medical researchers in England and the United Sates advanced claims concerning the curative or prophylactic merits of circumcision, beginning with Nathaniel Heckford's 1865 *Circumcision as a Remedial Measure in Certain Cases of Epilepsy, Chorea, etc.* The most ardent advocate of circumcision on medical grounds was the prominent New York physician Lewis Sayre, who came to be known as the "Columbus of the prepuce" and who for three decades, beginning with his 1870 article in *Transactions of the American Medical Association* (of which he became president in 1880), argued persistently that serious orthopedic diseases could be prevented by early surgery on the foreskin.

During the latter half of the nineteenth century, some physicians who crusaded against MASTURBATION, such as the American pediatrician M. J. Moses, saw it as "one of the effects of a long prepuce." Similarly, in his 1891 *History of Circumcision from the Earliest Times to the Present* (more a polemic than a history) the California physician Peter Charles Remondino wrote that "the practice [of masturbation] can be asserted as being very rare among the children of circumcised races." It was his view that a wide variety of ailments, including asthma, penile cancer, and syphilis, could be avoided through early circumcision, and that consequently "life-insurance companies should class the wearer of the pre-

puce under the head of hazardous risks." By the end of the nineteenth century, male circumcision at birth became standard procedure in the United States.

During the 1970s, however, first the American Academy of Pediatrics and then the American College of Obstetricians and Gynecologists issued reports concluding that routine circumcision was not warranted. Moreover, by 1976 the influential pediatrician BENJAMIN SPOCK, who had originally endorsed circumcision, changed his mind, asserting that it was "unnecessary and at least mildly dangerous." In 1988, appearing on ABC's *Nightline*, he went even further: "I'm against circumcision. . . . If I had a baby now . . . I certainly would not want him circumcised. And if parents ask me, I would lean in the direction of saying, 'Leave his poor little penis alone.'"

See also: **Female Genital Mutilation; Islam; Judaism; Sexuality.**

BIBLIOGRAPHY

Gollaher, D. L. 2000. *Circumcision: A History of the World's Most Controversial Surgery.* New York: Basic Books.

ELLIOTT HOROWITZ

Coeducation and Same-Sex Schooling

The question of how to educate men and women together has had a long and rather turbulent history. It has been linked to questions of morality in the socialization of children, equality between the sexes, and higher academic achievement for both boys and girls. By and large, conservatives have advocated separate schooling for males and females, while liberal educational reformers typically have been champions of coeducation. In recent years this pattern has shifted somewhat in the United States, as feminists have endorsed separate schools as a means of supporting women's success, and reformers have explored the effect of all-male schools on African-American students' achievement. While coeducation has grown in popularity elsewhere, gender-segregated schooling continues to predominate in many other areas of the world. As a consequence, the question of gender and education continues to cause controversy.

Throughout much of history, separate education of boys and girls was the norm. This reflected the different roles society assigned to each gender and the unequal status of men and women in most premodern societies. By and large, male LITERACY rates were much higher than female literacy rates. Boys were trained for the worlds of work, politics, and war; while girls were prepared for the domestic spheres of home, hearth, and nursery. The very idea of coeducation posed a threat to this traditional division of labor, and it therefore held the potential to undermine the existing hierarchy.

Early Coeducation Efforts

During the eighteenth century, coeducation began to appear on a widespread basis in English-speaking regions of North America. Ideologically, the movement can be linked to Reformation-inspired religious dissent and to conditions of life in a frontier society. Coeducation was first practiced in New England, the region with the best-developed schools; most of these were intended to provide literacy instruction for religious education. The practice of enrolling both boys and girls in school together probably stemmed from the growing incidence of female church membership, as well as from the practical requirements of finding enough children to support the schools in a thinly inhabited countryside.

The years immediately following the American Revolution witnessed a surge of interest in female education and a growing perception that women had a critical role to play in the socialization of children of the new republic. This view—combined with a widely dispersed, largely agrarian population—helped to make coeducation a highly popular practice by the early nineteenth century, at least in the northern and western regions. Although coeducation was somewhat less commonplace in the larger U.S. cities, where traditional European norms prevailed, reformers vigorously urged its adoption, arguing that combining the sexes in school was a reflection of their "natural" mingling in two other important institutions: church and family. Pioneering experiments in coeducational higher education at Antioch and Oberlin Colleges in the antebellum period helped pave the way for more widespread acceptance of the practice. By the 1890s, the vast majority of American school children were enrolled in coeducational schools, a far higher percentage than in any other nation. Most children were enrolled in common or primary schools, but coeducation also had become widespread in secondary schools and colleges. By 1900 about 70 percent of American institutions of higher education admitted both men and women. Coeducation had become a standard American practice—one that clearly distinguished schools in the United States from educational institutions elsewhere.

The Case Against Coeducation

This did not mean that coeducation was adopted without controversy. It became a source of contention with regard to high schools and colleges, especially during the late nineteenth century. Certain male doctors argued that extended education was dangerous for women, who could be harmed by overexertion caused by competition with male students. Other opponents of coeducation protested on religious and moral grounds, maintaining that the hazards of impropriety were higher when young men and women were placed in such close proximity for long periods. But these arguments were countered by a host of voices defending coeducation as a practical success and a virtue of the American system of education. School authorities refuted claims that schooling made girls sickly, and parents willingly sent their daughters to coeducational high schools and colleges. School leaders also argued that coeducation was necessary for the success of secondary institutions, because restricting them to males would make the support of such schools impractical in all but the largest communities. Some educators even suggested that the girls represented a calming or "civilizing" influence on the boys, and that the presence of young men in the classroom may have helped to spur their female classmates to greater success. Taken together, these arguments represented a powerful affirmation of coeducation in the United States. Single-sex institutions persisted in larger cities, however, as well as in the American South, where conservative European traditions persisted.

Other Countries Consider Coeducation

The adoption of coeducation in other countries proceeded more gradually. Scandinavia was one of the earliest regions to adopt mixed-gender schools; coeducational institutions date from the eighteenth century in Denmark and the nineteenth century in Norway. Despite some isolated experiments in Great Britain, Italy, and Germany, however, the weight of tradition posed a powerful obstacle to its advancement elsewhere. Coeducation was closely associated with women's rights in the public mind, and the limited appeal of the early feminists constrained its acceptance. Europe's relatively high population density made sex-segregated primary schooling logistically practical, and secondary education was largely limited to elites and was dominated by male students. Women were admitted to institutions of higher education in the late nineteenth century, but except for a small number of intrepid pioneers, their absence from secondary schools made matriculation of women impractical at most universities. The first major challenge to this pattern occurred in Russia following the Bolshevik Revolution; there, women were afforded greater access to education, often on terms that were equivalent to those of men. Coeducation was consistent with radical conceptions of equality, and it was an efficient means of rapidly boosting student enrollments, helping the newly formed Soviet Union to meet its growing requirements for trained workers in a variety of fields. By and large, however, the Soviet model of coeducation was not followed by the rest of Europe.

A Backlash Develops in America

Coeducation became a matter of debate again in the United States in the opening decades of the twentieth century, as the number of high school students rose dramatically. New curricula were devised for female students, including courses in home economics, commercial (secretarial), and trades (especially garment-making). Boys, on the other hand, enrolled in such classes as industrial arts, bookkeeping, and commercial geography. These different courses reflected a growing recognition of the importance of schooling to the labor market, and of the sharp division of labor that continued to distinguish the work of men and women. Even if young men and women attended the same schools, the dictates of the larger society's conception of sex roles and gender-appropriate forms of work exerted considerable influence on educational institutions

At about the same time, certain groups resisted coeducation. Catholics objected to the practice on moral and religious grounds, arguing that it raised the specter of promiscuity and invited an unhealthy competition between the sexes. Echoing the arguments of curriculum experts who advocated separate vocational courses for young men and women, these critics claimed that the principle of differentiation was rooted in religion, and that males and females had profoundly different purposes to fulfill. For this reason, the vast preponderance of Catholic secondary schools remained single-sex institutions, even though many parochial grade schools observed the American practice of coeducational classes. Other private schools also resisted coeducation, largely in deference to traditions upheld within the upper echelons of society, which often followed European norms. Thus, while coeducation remained widely popular in the United States, its reach was hardly universal. The sexual division of labor and traditional concerns about propriety and the protection of young women continued to exert an influence on school policies. It would not be until after World War II that these limitations would change dramatically.

Coeducation Continues To Spread

Several developments accounted for the worldwide advancement of coeducation during the twentieth century, accelerating after 1945. One was the global spread of American influence after World War II. The conflict had devastated Europe and thus softened resistance to new modes of education for both sexes. Perhaps even more important was a gradual shift in gender roles, providing women with greater opportunity for involvement in life outside of the domestic sphere. This was especially manifested in rising rates of female participation in the labor force, perhaps most evident in America and Europe but also apparent in other countries. These developments bolstered arguments that educational opportunities open to women ought to be equivalent to those available to men, and coeducation came to be seen as the most direct and practical road to achieving such equity. Finally, a revolution in sexual mores came to characterize the decades during the second half of the century, becoming widely influential in the 1960s; this cultural change reduced popular resistance to coeducation on moral and religious grounds. Together, all of these influences helped to usher in a new period of swift progression in coeducational practices in the United States and elsewhere.

Coeducation spread slowly throughout America. Single-sex schools began to consider becoming coeducational in the 1950s and 1960s. These developments were abetted by the civil rights movement, which not only raised public awareness of racial inequities in education, but also helped to foster feminism. Calls for gender equity in education put pressure on institutions to respond to perceptions that single-sex

education was inherently unequal. Perhaps the greatest changes occurred at Catholic schools and colleges. Many of these institutions adjusted their admissions policies as a result of public pressure, partly due to the desires expressed by potential students. As demand increased for a coeducational experience in high school and colleges, many other private schools and colleges also altered their policies. Survey data suggested that fewer and fewer students were interested in the single-sex experience. While coeducation had long been popular in the United States, it reached unprecedented levels of public acceptance. At the same time, gender-segregated education remained most common in those curricula closest to the labor force. While the number of women increased sharply in such formerly male-dominated domains as law and medical schools, fields such as nursing, clerical work, carpentry, and auto repair remained segregated by sex.

Similar changes occurred throughout Europe. The spread of coeducation was even more pronounced, however, largely because the practice had been so rare. In many European cities, primary education became largely coeducational, although elite secondary schools in Germany and elsewhere continued to resist the practice. In France and Great Britain, coeducation became the norm more quickly; furthermore, the development of American-style "comprehensive" institutions eventually ushered in greater gender equity. Perhaps the biggest change, however, occurred at the universities; the preparation of larger numbers of women at the secondary level led to rising postsecondary enrollments.

Elsewhere in the world, the adoption of coeducation was less certain. In JAPAN women's matriculation consistently lagged behind other developed societies, and gender segregation persisted in higher education. Other countries witnessed dramatic improvements in women's education, however, and they widely practiced coeducation as educational opportunities expanded. This was true, for instance, in Cuba and CHINA. In some other developing countries, on the other hand, traditional and religious influences inhibited the growth of female education, especially at the secondary level and in universities. In much of AFRICA and in the Arab nations, coeducation continues to be frowned upon or strictly forbidden.

Same-Sex Schooling Regains Momentum

The drive for gender equity in American education continued during the 1970s and 1980s, pushing coeducation forward. Title IX legislation, passed by Congress in 1972, heightened public awareness of equity issues related to gender and contributed to institutional change in the 1980s and 1990s. At the same time, however, competing forces existed. An influential conservative political movement, represented by the presidency of Ronald Reagan; public concerns about sexual freedom; a rise in unmarried—particularly teenage—pregnancy; and the growth of sexually transmitted diseases led to a reexamination of coeducational policies. Simultaneously, feminists who were concerned about the slow advance of women into fields such as mathematics began to question the logic of coeducation as the principal means to educational equity. In the late 1970s, researchers began to note higher levels of female academic achievement at single-sex colleges compared to coeducational institutions. In a 1992 published report, the American Association of University Women questioned whether coeducation was the best way to achieve higher levels of accomplishment for young women. They postulated that females were likely to be ignored in class discussions and subjected to threats of sexual harassment. These findings contributed to a resurgence of interest in women's colleges. Educational reformers were similarly concerned about the low academic performance of young urban African-American males. They began to explore the feasibility of all-male academies, to provide an environment free of distractions in which these students could focus on achievement. These ideas and experiments posed a serious challenge to the principle of coeducation, and they marked the first major setback in its ascendancy during the postwar period.

Historically, coeducation has been associated with the idea of equality between the sexes in education and greater opportunities for women. Its advancement has marked the growth of women's rights and the expansion of the modern educational system to serve all segments of the population. The rise of coeducation has followed the movement of women into education, especially at the secondary and postsecondary levels. First widely observed in the United States, the practice of coeducation has spread significantly, although its advance has been uneven in many parts of the developed world, and slow to nonexistent in the developing world. As a rule, resistance has been greatest in societies where women's rights have been most rigidly constrained. Even in morally liberal societies such as the United States, recent developments suggest that there is a natural limit to the extent of coeducation's appeal. Renewed interest in single-sex schools indicates that the controversy over coeducation is not likely to subside soon.

See also: **Education, Europe; Education, United States; Girls' Schools; High School; Junior High School; Women's Colleges in the United States.**

BIBLIOGRAPHY

Albisetti, James. 1988. *Schooling German Girls and Women: Secondary and Higher Education in the Nineteenth Century.* Princeton, NJ: Princeton University Press.

King, Elizabeth, and M. Anne Hill, eds. 1993. *Women's Education in Developing Countries: Barriers, Benefits, Policies.* Baltimore, MD: Johns Hopkins University Press.

Komarrovsky, Mirra. 1985. *Women in College.* New York: Basic Books.

Riordan, Cornelius. 1990. *Boys and Girls in School: Together or Separate?* New York: Teachers College Press.

Solomon, Barbara Miller. 1985. *In the Company of Educated Women.* New Haven, CT: Yale University Press.

Tyack, David, and Elisabeth Hansot. 1990. *Learning Together: A History of Coeducation in American Schools.* New Haven, CT: Yale University Press.

Wilson, Maggie, ed. 1991. *Girls and Women in Education: A European Perspective.* New York: Pergamon.

JOHN L. RURY

Collections and Hobbies

In almost all cultures and societies, children have collected a broad spectrum of items. Although the activity seems to be universal, very little has been written on this subject. And even though collecting has played an important part in many individuals' lives, it is seldom described in memoirs or AUTOBIOGRAPHIES. This may be because many collections are suddenly abandoned when the collector grows up. Many of these collections are split up and disappear unless parents understand the fascinating world of the small collector and pay special attention to saving them. Some collections, however, continue into adult life, becoming lifelong passionate occupations; this is especially likely with collections that have some kind of economic value or present the adult with challenges or opportunities for further study.

The pleasure of founding and creating collections may lead children, as they grow, to collect a new category of items that are more acceptable to their age. The spirit of the collector once established never leaves the individual but is turned in new directions. Grand collections may end up in professional institutions, such as museums, which seems to be the dream of collectors, who do not want their passionate investments to disappear with them. But most collections are scattered by the years and do not survive their owners.

The Functions of Collections

Collecting serves a wide range of purposes and functions. Collecting trains the eye, creates a sense of order, and develops aesthetic appreciation. But collectors can primarily be characterized by their joyful dedication to their project. The world of collectors may be lonely, but can also be social when collectors share their pleasure with each other. The collector often participates in a community, whose connections may range from informal gatherings to organized networks. These give collectors the pride of showing and the pleasure of seeing others' collections, as well as an opportunity to exchange experience, advice, and actual items. Many collectors know that individuals outside the collectors' world consider them members of a special subculture that pays too much attention to an eccentric and limited sphere of interest.

Children's collections tend to be looked at with more tolerance, however strange or fantastical they may seem to the adult world. They form a space where childhood fantasy and imagination can be indulged. Contemporary tendencies reveal a change in the differences between the collections of children and adults. Many children start collections of valuable items that are marketed directly to them by the mass media and commercial powers. At the same time, adults show an increasing interest in collecting items that once belonged only to childhood or that possess a significance that may be regarded as infantile. Male and female toy collectors all over the Western world collect valuable antique matchbox CARS, TIN SOLDIERS, DOLLS, and dollhouses, as well as more recent miscellaneous objects that were once strictly children's TOYS. They seem to represent a dream of never-ending childhood, which never requires giving up the fascination with toys but supplies it with the new, playful ambition of the economically independent adult collector.

Sheer entertainment may be the purpose of one of the contemporary world's greatest collectors, Michael Jackson. His collections consist of amusement park attractions, a ZOO, and numerous kinds of toys, although he has a special devotion to toy animals. To some people he may represent the disappearance of well-defined borders between the ages in postmodern life: the boy who never grew up and the grown-up who never adapted to his new role and responsibility. Jackson may exemplify the collector's true identity, which confuses work with play, leisure with learning, childhood with adulthood, and creating new openings for possible and impossible identities.

Subsistence Economies

In subsistence economies, nature is a never-ending source of objects for infant collectors. Stones, shells, bones, twigs, leaves, flowers, feathers, teeth, and hair have been collected and appreciated by adults and children in most tribal cultures, although anthropologists have seldom described this activity within the specific context of childhood studies. They tend to study it in the context of the magical, religious, or festive. The basic instinct to behave like the parental group or other care givers may have been the origin of these childhood collections, whose durability and existence depended on the mobility and social stratification of the population.

Gender and division of labor may have been decisive factors shaping and structuring children's collections. Depending on the integration of children's work in subsistence economies, time for play and leisure varied. Hunter, nomad, and pre-agricultural societies generally offered less domestic space and thus less place for objects and collections that were not mobile.

Peasant Societies

Children in peasant societies worked, but they lived a much more settled, domestic life than did children in subsistence economies. This allowed for the possibility of more consistent collecting. Even though toys were seldom bought, they could be made, and depending on how much time was available for play, collections could be started. Sticks could be made into bows or used as throwing instruments. They could be carved in patterns or exchanged for other objects. In American immigrant milieus, it was easy to turn corn husks into dolls, and many girls had lots of them. No clear line exists between the possession of homemade toys and collecting.

In peasant cultures, children often reused objects from the adult world. It was common to collect pieces of glass or colored pieces of broken pottery. Yarn from worn-out knitwear could be sewn into balls in many patterns. The loose winter hair from cattle could be shaped and rolled with spit to make balls that bounced well. Braiding straw and flowers was often popular among girls. Paper could be folded or cut into more or less spontaneous patterns. Paper pierced with needles could provide children a great deal of joy. Children often collected beach stones with holes so they could put a string through the holes and pull them like cows. Exchanging such objects or using them for a lottery was common. Turnips, beets, and pumpkins could be hollowed and turned into lanterns, as is still done for HALLOWEEN. Clay could be shaped into small figurines or made into beads and then into bracelets or necklaces. Leaves, straw, shells, and many other objects could be fixed on the surface of any kind of box to create a home for one's treasures. Collecting in peasant cultures was generally a moneyless, outdoor activity, which appealed to both fantasy and social play. In the 1800s and 1900s, these collections were far more ephemeral than collections in the bourgeois culture and industrial society that developed alongside peasant culture.

Industrial Society

The bourgeois culture that began to develop at the end of the 1700s stressed consumption and domestic life. Even family life changed radically. Bourgeois children were given more physical space; training and education became more focused; and new intellectual borders between ages were established. More and more, the ideal domestic life excluded production and favored intimacy, reproductive activities, and leisure. Children began to have their own rooms in the home and were looked after by a differentiated staff, made up mostly of female servants. Education and schools played a still more important part in the child's life. Care and control developed side by side. Children's collections changed and were directed toward new aims.

The economic subordination of women and children in the reproductive and consumer spheres created new conditions for the small collector. Items became far more prearranged, dependent on money and the booming practice of giving gifts. During the 1800s, Christmas changed, becoming less of a social, religious feast and embracing the private, emotional, cocooning elements typical of the modern celebration. Parental love was increasingly connected with giving children gifts at Christmas and BIRTHDAYS and in other specific situations. The new collections often started and developed via such gifts. Children began making lists of items they wanted, which could be bought in shops and markets. However, homemade gifts were still usual and were often regarded as more personal. In the 1800s, Germany took a leading position in the production of toys. But the German paper industry developed innovations for children, including printed games, paper dolls, cards, sheets, and colored paper scraps.

Fascinating collections, however, could still be started without special expense. The birth of a consumer society meant large-scale production of luxury paper for packaging. Products were marketed in attractive paper wrappings, which children often saved. Food, sweets, cosmetics, tobacco, and many other goods were presented in new ways to the customers and their children. Mail-service companies started the printing of stamps, which initiated many young philatelists. Railway tickets and other items from the expanding world of transport and communication represented new collectors' items, enlarging the world of childhood.

Twentieth-Century Collections

The growth and democratization of consumption may be the outstanding feature of the recent period, and it changed children's collections decisively. After World War I, it became common to celebrate children's birthdays. Invitation cards became a new collector's item in the 1920s, functioning as social souvenirs. Girls started collections of exquisitely printed paper napkins, often brought home from birthday parties. Marketers introduced a new strategy, adding collector's items for children to products for adults. Cigarettes, soap, coffee substitute, chewing gum, and many other products contained collectibles for children. The expanding film industry, sports, and mass media sent children hunting for autographs, photos, or other memorabilia from the stars. Beautiful packaging was still popular, including matchboxes, tin boxes, fancy bottles, and shopping bags from fashion shops. Before World War II the Walt DISNEY Company launched a strategy of integrated consumption of trademarked goods, which appealed to young consumers and collectors. Film, magazines, cards, posters, soap figurines, bubble gum, printed napkins, and toys built up a total universe of desirable objects and experiences. This strategy was so successful that it turned into the contemporary business of merchandising, which puts trademarked characters on wallpaper, videos, computer games, towels, schoolbags, pencils, erasers, and clothes, and in fast food. Even though such collecting may worry some adults because of its prearranged character and the way it commercializes childhood, it mirrors the conditions of modern culture that also affect the adult world.

BIBLIOGRAPHY

Merrick, J., ed. 1988. *Merete Staack: Børns samlinger. Fra vaettelys til coca-cola-kultur.* Copenhagen, Denmark: Barndom.

BJARNE KILDEGAARD

Colonialism. *See* British Colonialism in India; Latin America: Colonialism.

Comenius, Johann Amos (1592–1670)

Johann Comenius was born Jan Amos Komenský on March 28, 1592, in Nivnice in Moravian Slovakia (now part of the Czech Republic). After completing GRAMMAR SCHOOL in Prerov, he studied at the universities of Herborn and Heidelberg from 1611 until 1614. He returned to the grammar school in Prerov and taught there from 1614 until 1618. From 1618 until 1621 he had a position as a minister at the Bohemian Protestant Church in Fulnek.

During the Counter-Reformation the Bohemian Protestant Church was crushed and those who refused to convert to Catholicism were forced to leave the country. This forced Comenius to live in various, sometimes secret, locations from 1621 until 1628. In 1628, Comenius, together with a number of other families, went into exile in Lissa, Poland, where he taught at the local grammar school until 1641. From 1641 to 1642 he lived in England. From 1642 until 1648 he lived in Elbing, Sweden, where he worked on the improvement of the Swedish school system and wrote school books in line with his pedagogical changes. The years 1648 through 1650 saw him in Lissa again. From 1650 to 1654 he devoted himself to the task of reforming the school system in Hungary, returning to Lissa in 1654. When Lissa burned down in 1656, Comenius moved to Amsterdam, where he died on November 15, 1670.

Comenius's Thinking

Comenius's thinking can be described as belonging to the pansophic-theological school of thought, according to which all things are connected with each other within the framework of a fixed order, which ultimately is the result of God's Creation. The presence of God manifests itself in nature, in the rationality of the law of nature, and in the beauty and harmony of the world. The order of nature itself is based on a principle of reason that ensures that all things are interrelated and nothing gets mixed up. Part of this sense of order is given to humans by God in the form of what Comenius called *ration*, so that humans could actively contribute their share in the divine creation of order. Ration is the link between God and human. It is the divine in each person; it justifies human supremacy in preference to all other creatures and also calls people to account for their actions. Anyone seeking cognition of God's wisdom must, however, be familiar with all three of the "books" in which God has laid down His wisdom: nature, spirit, and the Bible.

Comenius repeatedly endeavoured to establish a fundamental connection between pansophic-theological thinking and his own theoretical and practical pedagogy. Since humans could comprehend the harmony between nature and

A page from the 1780 edition of Comenius's illustrated textbook *Orbis sensualium pictus*. Comenius's work, first published in 1658, was translated into a number of languages and served as a model for textbooks throughout the eighteenth and nineteenth centuries. The Catholic University of America.

God only through reason, he argued, the proper use of reason must be taught to man; therefore a "universal education" (*Pampaedia*) is necessary and will eventually result in a "universal reform of things human" (1991, p. 67). Education would ensure that people could fulfil their duties on earth, and this must be true for all children since all human beings can be educated and are basically capable of being taught and of learning. The process of teaching should itself be guided by the principle of contemplation. In keeping with the ideas of universal harmony, Comenius believed that all knowledge can be acquired only through use of sensual perception. He further recommended that only those things should be taught at school that may be of use in later life. For Comenius, all of these considerations meant that new teaching disciplines had to be developed, in which students would be treated and taught individually, according to methods that make studying less burdensome and more pleasant.

In his *Didactica magna* (The great didactics), which was printed in 1657, Comenius laid down and substantiated the objectives and methods for pedagogical undertakings committed to pansophic-theological thinking. "Didactics," he wrote, meant the "art of teaching," and he ventured to provide a "Great Didactic," that is to say "the whole art of teaching all things to all men, and indeed of teaching them with certainty, so that the result cannot fail to follow; further, of teaching them pleasantly, that is to say, without annoyance or aversion on the part of the teacher or the pupil, but rather with the greatest enjoyment for both; further of teaching them thoroughly, not superficially and showily, but in such a manner as to lead to true knowledge, purity in morals and innermost devotion" (1985, p. 11).

Comenius believed in the possibility of lifelong learning. Humans, he believed, from the moment of their birth, are equipped with the ability to acquire knowledge of things. In the teaching process he did not recommend trying to infuse things from the outside into the human mind; instead he believed one should "single out, unfold and reveal what lies hidden within. . . . Consequently there is nothing in this world that a human being, endowed with senses and reason, does not wish to comprehend. Man is filled with the thirst for knowledge" (1985, p. 38).

Lifelong Learning

The idea that education is necessary is underlined by Comenius in the following words: "So do not think that anybody who has not learnt to act in the manner of man can really be a man" (1985, p. 86) and again, "Everything that man wants to know he must learn first" (p. 47). All creatures born human are born solely for the purpose of "being individuals, namely creatures endowed with reason, master over other creatures, and the identical image of the Creator. Therefore each individual should be promoted in a manner that they can pass their current life usefully and prepare suitably for the life to come" (p. 34). He emphasized the idea of rational creatures guided by reason again by writing that "all those born as human beings require education . . . exactly for the reason that they are intended to be human beings rather than wild animals, simple beasts or unhewn blocks" (p. 49). Those teachings must begin early in life, however, "because life should not be spent learning, but acting" (p. 50).

All human beings should be taught alike, he believed, "Boys and girls, both noble and ignoble, rich and poor, in all cities and towns, villages and hamlets, should be sent to school" (p. 55). Each child, irrespective of origin and sex, should be educated, the only decisive factor being ability.

Comenius was also convinced of the importance of giving an education even to those "who may seem stupid or dull by nature. Especially those who are stupid are in particular need of cultivation of the mind. The more children are weak-minded and stupid, the more they actually need help to free themselves of their stupidity. It is not possible to find a mind so inept that its cultivation cannot progressively improve it. . . . The dull and weak-minded may never boast of great achievements in science, nevertheless learning will at least improve the morality of their behaviour" (p. 56). The objective of universal education would be achieved by founding "schools as joint educational institutions for children in all the parishes, towns, and villages where people live together" (p. 55). Existing schools should be reorganized into "places of thorough and comprehensive education of the mind" (p. 59), which would ensure that "the entire youth is educated there and everybody is taught everything." "All human beings should be led equally to the goals of wisdom, morality and saintliness," he wrote, because "all human beings . . . have the same nature after all" (pp. 60, 73). Additionally, schools should be organized so "that the slow would be mixed with the fast, the ponderous with the agile, the stubborn with the compliant" (p. 74).

Johann Amos Comenius lived in a time marked by disruption and crises as well as wars. At a time at which the public education system was open only to a small group of children, his major concern was that "all men are taught all things." Unfortunately his ideas on education were not generally accepted by society, and his suggestions on school systems have not yet been implemented, even in part. However, the author of the *Didactica magna* lives on in our memory as a forerunner of modern pedagogy, a great reformer and crusader.

See also: **Basedow, Johann Bernard; Education, Europe; Locke, John.**

BIBLIOGRAPHY

Comenius, Johann Amos. 1985. *Grosse Didaktik.* Stuttgart, Germany: Klett-Cotta.

Comenius, Johann Amos. 1991. *Pampaedia—Allerziehung.* St. Augustin, Germany: Academia-Verlag.

NORBERT STÖRMER

Comic Books

While the comic book genre has traditionally been considered a form of children's entertainment, that distinction has almost never been entirely true. In fact, at the turn of the twenty-first century, the bulk of comic books produced in North America were aimed at an adolescent or adult audience.

Related forms include the comic strip, panel narratives (which date from the late nineteenth century in American newspapers), and the graphic novel, a long-form pictorial narrative, generally published as a book instead of the more ephemeral pamphlet form; the best-known graphic novels are Art Spiegelman's Pulitzer Prize–winning *Maus* (1986) and *Maus II* (1991). The term *comics* mistakenly connotes

humor, which is not an integral part of the form. This difficulty is mitigated in other linguistic traditions, such as French, which uses the term *bande dessinée* ("drawn strip"); Italian, which uses *fumetti* ("puffs of smoke," referring to speech balloons); and Spanish, which uses *historieta* ("little stories"). The Japanese term, *manga*, originally meant "humorous sketches," although that connotation no longer holds, and today the term is seen as a neutral way to indicate *comics*.

Background and History

There is much debate over the definition of the term *comic book*. Some critics such as Scott McCloud would argue that any narrative told with words and pictures could be considered a comic book. Others might place into this category any book that contains comic strip–like stories, such as those of the nineteenth-century Swiss humorist Rodolphe Töpffer or the adventures found in *Max und Moritz* (1865) by the nineteenth-century German illustrator and poet Wilhelm Busch.

The most common use of the term, however, denotes periodical publications in which the narrative is told through a combination of words and pictures, generally arranged in the form of comic strip panels on the page. Early periodicals like *Comic Monthly* (1922) and, later, the tabloid-sized *Famous Funnies* (1934–1955) contained reprints of newspaper comic strips. The intended audience for such publications was both children and adults, as both groups would be drawn to characters familiar from newspaper reading. Historian Ron Goulart notes in his *Comic Book Culture: An Illustrated History* (2000) that the first periodical to feature all-new content was Dell Publishing's short-lived weekly publication *The Funnies* (1929–1930). In 1935 Dell again published a tabloid with all-new material, *New Fun*, which quickly dropped in size from tabloid to magazine, making it the first genuine comic book of new material produced in America.

Burgeoning Popularity

While initially popular, the new form took a few years to become a cultural force. Originally created by teenagers Jerry Siegel and Joe Shuster for possible newspaper strip publication, the adventures of Superman first appeared in *Action Comics* (June 1938). Public reception of the character was immediate and overwhelming; *Superman*, a separate comic book established a year after the character's first appearance, sold in excess of one million copies an issue by 1940. Other costumed heroes followed, including Batman (in 1939), created by cartoonist Bob Kane and writer Bill Finger; the patriotic Captain America (in 1941), created by Joe Simon and Jack Kirby; and Wonder Woman (in 1942), created by psychologist William Moulton Marston. Superheroes engaged in the war effort in their pages during World War II; covers to the Captain America series, for example, urged readers to buy war bonds.

Superheroes were not the only popular comics at this time, however. Animal comic books, epitomized by the Disney line published by Dell Comics, were also successful. The Donald Duck and Uncle Scrooge stories by Carl Barks (whose work remained uncredited for years, as did the works of all Disney cartoonists) continue to be highly regarded for their adventure, humor, and visual accomplishment. Westerns were especially popular in the 1940s and 1950s, with television and film stars like Roy Rogers and Dale Evans, as well as characters like The Lone Ranger, starring in titles of their own, usually with photo covers.

So-called teen comics, particularly the Archie series, found popularity with pre-teen audiences, especially girls. Romance comics (a genre created in the 1950s by Joe Simon and Jack Kirby, who had created the Captain America series in the 1940s) also attracted predominantly female readers, although the stories in such comic books generally were created by men and upheld traditional gender roles.

The 1940s and 1950s: Crusade against Comic Books

Crime and horror comics, two genres that became popular after World War II, ignited a great deal of controversy. Featuring the sensational exploits of larger-than-life criminals (who enjoyed popularity in film and other media, as well) or gruesome revenge tales with monstrous protagonists, these comic books, with titles like *Vault of Horror*—published by E.C. (Entertaining Comics)—were admired by both children and adults. While the stories usually featured morality tales in which crime or evil is duly punished in the end, along the way there was plenty of opportunity for graphic gore.

These comics soon fell under the eye of educators and librarians. Like the comics that preceded them in the 1920s and 1930s, these comic books were seen to have a detrimental effect on children's reading habits. Some educators felt that the use of words and pictures together threatened the LITERACY of young readers. A more cogent argument was that most of these comics were not always well-written.

The most persuasive arguments of all had to do with story content. The campaign against "crime comics," as they were called, was led by the radical psychiatrist Fredric Wertham, whose *Seduction of the Innocent* (1954) was excerpted before publication in *Ladies Home Journal*. Based on Wertham's clinical research, it argued that violent and sexual imagery in comic books contributed to juvenile DELINQUENCY. Wertham was among the many witnesses who testified at the 1954 U.S. Senate Subcommittee on Juvenile Delinquency. As a result of these inquiries, and to protect themselves from further intervention and possible governmental control, many of the largest comic book publishers of the day banded together to create the Comics Code Authority (CCA), a self-governing censorship board. The goal of the CCA was to ensure that all published comic books would be perceived as wholesome family entertainment. The CCA required that depictions of parents, police, and other authority figures could not be portrayed as corrupt; crime could never succeed; the female body had to be drawn realistically, not las-

civiously; drug use could not be shown or described; and that monsters such as vampires or zombies could not be portrayed at all. Amy Kiste Nyberg discusses the history of the CCA in great detail in her *Seal of Approval: The History of the Comics Code* (1998).

These standards effectively limited the scope of comic book stories to those which could best be described as entertaining but blandly inoffensive. Comic book publishing thus became, for a decade, a practice aimed solely at entertaining children. While horror and crime and romance comics were still published, they were done so in far tamer, more conservative forms. E.C.'s popular satire *MAD* could not survive under the CCA; therefore, its format was changed to a black-and-white magazine, thus exempting it from the code governing traditional comic books. Of the major comics publishers, only Dell and Classics Illustrated did not join the CCA; their wholesome content assured that their books would be distributed widely even without the CCA seal.

Rebirth for Readers of All Ages

In the 1960s two different forces acted to broaden comics readership outside of young children. Beginning in 1961, Stan Lee, the publisher of Marvel Comics, in concert with artists such as Jack Kirby and Steve Ditko, re-invigorated the superhero genre with characters like the Fantastic Four, Spider-Man, and Doctor Strange, whose exploits combined cosmic adventure with soap opera–style narratives. Marvel Comics became popular with both children and older readers, with comic book clubs forming on college campuses across the country.

Near the end of the 1960s, underground comics (or *comix*) gained countercultural relevance. Cartoonists like R. Crumb, Trina Robbins, and Art Spiegelman, among many others, began publishing and distributing their own comic books through drug paraphernalia shops (or "head shops," bypassing traditional newsstand distribution (and thereby the CCA, as well). Influenced by youth movements of the day, these comic books tackled a wide variety of topics, breaking taboos with gusto and offering social and political commentary to their adult readers. Many of these comics outwardly resembled funny animal and other comics from the 1950s, which the cartoonists had grown up reading. The books also often featured parodies of the CCA symbol, a sarcastic reminder that two decades before, comic books did not have to rely on underground distribution if they wanted to address an adult audience.

While mainstream comics did not change drastically after the emergence of the underground comics, they did challenge CCA restrictions. When the U.S. Department of Health, Education, and Welfare asked Marvel Comics to promote drug awareness in its *Amazing Spider-Man* comic book, the CCA refused to approve the resultant three issues (numbers 96–98). Marvel published the books anyway in early 1971, and the publicity helped lead to a revision in the code, in part due to changed attitudes regarding the suitability of certain types of material for younger readers.

The Code was revised again in 1989, and while it is still in existence, it does not hold sway as it once did. The rise of comic book shops in the 1980s—along with the direct market distribution system, bypassing newsstand distribution altogether—resulted in fewer comic books being sold by newsstands. At the same time, this system enabled many new and smaller companies to print fewer copies of titles than their competitors and still make a profit. These so-called alternative comics made it possible for titles to be directed at smaller markets and produced comics on subjects that had not been profitable in decades, including nonfiction, fantasy, and humor.

While most of the alternative comics are intended for adult readers, others are designed with children in mind. Comics like Jeff Smith's Bone series, a nine-volume fantasy epic that began in 1991, is for young and old alike; portions were re-serialized in *Disney Adventures* magazine. Linda Medley's Castle Waiting series, which began in 1996, investigates what happens to peripheral fairy tale characters once the fairy tale ends. Her female-centered fantasies are as thought provoking for adults as they are enchanting for younger readers. Medley includes in her comic books and in their collected version guides for teachers, activities for children, and guides to further reading in comic books as well as traditional literary forms. Editors Art Spiegelman and Françoise Mouly, responsible for the avant-garde comics anthology RAW in the 1980s and 1990s, began in 2000 to produce Little Lit, a hardcover, annual anthology specifically designed for child readers. The first volume, subtitled *Folklore and Fairy Tale Funnies* (2000), and the second, *Strange Stories for Strange Kids* (2001), combine reprints of classic children's comics with newly produced stories by cartoonists and children's book illustrators.

Works influenced by Japanese *manga*, in addition to translations of *manga*, are another group of contemporary comic books deserving special attention. Both the visual style and the storytelling techniques of *manga*—such as open page designs and stories that continue over multiple volumes—are appearing with greater frequency in the works of newer American superhero and fantasy artists, who look increasingly to Japan for artistic inspiration.

Comics and Other Media

Early newspaper cartoonists, eager to expand their audience (and their profits), often licensed their characters to the burgeoning film industry. Winsor McCay, creator of the Little Nemo in Slumberland (1905–1911; 1911–1913; 1924–1926) and Dream of the Rarebit Fiend (1904–1913) comic strips, early on created his own animated cartoons by hand. Often based upon his comic-strip characters, his films, such as *Gertie, the Dinosaur* (1914), are regarded as hallmarks of early animation.

Comic book characters were soon licensed as well, with the most popular example being Superman. Within only a few years of the character's debut in 1938, Superman could be seen in the daily newspapers, heard on RADIO, and seen in motion-picture serials on Saturday afternoons. In the 1950s the Superman television series attracted new readers; shortly thereafter, it became one of the early color series. A decade later, the Batman television series brought a more faithful adaptation of a comic book character to the small screen; whereas the Superman series kept the comics' science fiction and super-villain elements to a minimum, Batman reveled in the exploits of classic villains like Catwoman and the Joker. Its high-camp, pop-art approach, however, reinforced for the general public that comic books were inherently trivial, childish material.

Hollywood has looked increasingly to comic books and strips for source material, producing films like *Superman* (1978), *Batman* (1989), *Dick Tracy* (1990), *The X-Men* (2000), *Spider-Man* (2002), and *The Hulk* (2003). Adaptations of lesser-known comic books, such as *Men in Black* (1997) and *The Road to Perdition* (2002) have proved successful as well, even though they were directed at an older (adolescent or adult) audience.

Most publishers of comics feature company- and character-related web sites, and newer cartoonists have found the Internet to be an effective way to get their work seen by a larger audience, often leading to eventual print publication. While there were some attempts in the 1990s at creating CD-rom comic books, the format never caught on with the public. Electronic comics remain more promotional tools and experiments, rather than an obvious new frontier in publishing.

See also: **Children's Literature; Series Books; Tintin and Hergé.**

BIBLIOGRAPHY

Barker, Martin. 1984. *A Haunt of Fears: The Strange History of the British Horror Comics Campaign.* London: Pluto.

Daniels, Les. 1971. *Comix: A History of Comic Books in America.* New York: Bonanza Books.

Foster, David William. 1989. *From Mafalda to Los Supermachos: Latin American Graphic Humor as Popular Culture.* Boulder, CO: L. Rienner.

Goulart, Ron. 2000. *Comic Book Culture: An Illustrated History.* Portland, OR: Collectors Press.

Groensteen, Thierry. 1999. *Système de la bande dessinée.* Paris: Presses universitaires de France.

Harvey, Robert C. 1996. *The Art of the Comic Book: An Aesthetic History.* Jackson: University Press of Mississippi.

Jones, William B., Jr. 2002. *Classics Illustrated: A Cultural History, with Illustrations.* Jefferson, NC: Macfarland and Co.

Kurtzman, Harvey. 1991. *From Aargh! to Zap!: Harvey Kurtzman's Visual History of the Comics.* New York: Arts.

Lent, John A., ed. 1999. *Pulp Demons: International Dimensions of the Postwar Anti-Comics Campaign.* Madison, NJ: Fairleigh Dickinson University Press.

McCloud, Scott. 1993. *Understanding Comics: The Invisible Art.* Northampton, MA: Kitchen Sink Press.

Nyberg, Amy Kiste. 1998. *Seal of Approval: The History of the Comics Code.* Jackson: University Press of Mississippi.

Pustz, Matthew J. 1999. *Comic Book Culture: Fanboys and True Believers.* Jackson: University Press of Mississippi.

Robbins, Trina. 1999. *From Girls to Grrrlz: A History of Women's Comics from Teens to Zines.* San Francisco: Chronicle Books.

Rubenstein, Ann. 1998. *Bad Language, Naked Ladies, and Other Threats to the Nation: A Political History of Comic Books in Mexico.* Durham, NC: Duke University Press.

Sabin, Roger. 1996. *Comics, Comix and Graphic Novels: A History of Comic Art.* London: Phaidon.

Savage, William W., Jr. 1998. *Commies, Cowboys, and Jungle Queens: Comic Books and America, 1945–1954.* Hanover, NH: Wesleyan University Press.

Schodt, Frederik L. 1996. *Dreamland Japan: Writings on Modern Manga.* Berkeley, CA: Stone Bridge Press.

Wertham, Fredric. 1954. *Seduction of the Innocent.* New York: Reinhart.

GENE KANNENBERG JR.

Commercial Curriculum

The teaching of commercial (business) subjects has a long history in American secondary education. Early in the nineteenth century, when such training prepared bookkeepers and merchants, most students were male, and these subjects were often taught in proprietary schools that prepared students for business careers. Prior to the Civil War, however, such instruction was not commonplace in HIGH SCHOOLS and ACADEMIES, and private business schools were concentrated in eastern cities, where there was a demand for clerks, bookkeepers, and other office workers.

As high schools grew in number following the Civil War, interest in commercial education increased. This was partly a response to demands to make the curriculum more practical, but it also reflected the changing urban economy. The growth of large-scale business enterprises, from railroads to manufacturing concerns to mail-order houses, created a need for clerical workers to manage records, handle correspondence, and keep accounts. This did not occur overnight, but had become quite evident by the 1890s.

At the same time, technological developments changed the nature of office work. The invention of the typewriter in the 1870s, along with adding machines and stenographic devices in later years, made clerical employment more routine and hierarchical. It was possible to hire large numbers of moderately skilled workers with little prospect for advancement. Under these conditions, employers began to hire more women, and by 1910 clerical work had become largely a female domain—at the time of the Great Depression this was one of the largest categories of women's work.

The growth of clerical work helped to make commercial education a major component of secondary education in the twentieth century. In the 1880s and 1890s, proprietary business schools trained about 80 percent of all commercial students. By 1920, however, public high schools dominated the field, enrolling almost half of these students, eventually eclipsing private schools in size and influence. Students enrolled in public-school commercial courses increased from fifteen thousand to more than three hundred thousand in this thirty-year span.

The commercial course was defined by the technical requirements of the largest employers; typing and stenography were the most popular classes (and the most highly feminized). Bookkeeping, accounting, commercial geography, and other courses enrolled larger numbers of boys. In this regard the rise of the commercial course reflected the emerging division of labor within the business world. The secretarial curriculum, which focused on the rote skills of typing, stenography, and record filing, was considered appropriate for women, while the higher-order tasks of keeping accounts, managing personnel, and planning change went to the men. Students mainly represented the lower middle classes (the children of skilled workers and white-collar employees), but gender was especially salient. As surveys from the period noted, boys in commerical positions were often promoted to the administrative ranks, while the girls remained clerks until they left to be married.

See also: **Coeducation and Same-Sex Schooling; Urban School Systems, The Rise of; Vocational Education, Industrial Education, and Trade Schools.**

BIBLIOGRAPHY

DeVault, Ileen A. 1990. *Sons and Daughters of Labor: Class and Clerical Work in Turn-of-the-Century Pittsburgh.* Ithaca, NY: Cornell University Press.

Krug, Edward A. 1964. *The Shaping of the American High School, 1880–1920.* New York: Harper and Row.

Powers, Jane B. 1992. *The "Girl Question" in Education: Vocational Training for Young Women in the Progressive Era.* London: Falmer.

Rury, John L. 1991. *Education and Women's Work: Female Schooling and the Division of Labor in Urban America, 1870–1930.* Albany: State University of New York Press.

JOHN L. RURY

Common Schools

The term *common school* refers to the predecessors of the public schools and systems of the United States. Common schools were quasi-public, originally mandated by colonial, and subsequently state, governments, though they were run locally. They offered an elementary level of schooling, were increasingly coeducational, and frequently were haphazard in instruction, curriculum, and duration.

The importance of schooling in a republic was a persistent theme among writers in the early national period. Citizens needed to be literate, moral, and industrious, reflecting the dominant Protestant ideology of the elite, and it was, ideally, the responsibility of the state, under the control of that same elite, to provide the means. Free schools, as Pennsylvania reformer Walter Johnson put it, were essential in order "to give every member of American society a portion of knowledge adequate to the discharge of his duties as a man and a citizen of the republic" (p. 2). But with few exceptions (New York and Connecticut especially), support and control of schools were mainly left to the localities, and, as communities grew in size, the number of school societies also grew adding to the fragmentation.

Considerable variation was the norm, with rural schools generally doing a better job than urban schools. Duration of the school year was uncertain, frequently not lasting more than a few months, and attendance was even more episodic. Common schools provided elementary instruction, the methodology was characterized by rote learning, harsh DISCIPLINE was common, and patriotic and Protestant messages were delivered insistently. All schools were crowded and ill-equipped, teachers served for brief periods and were ill-prepared, and the duration of the school term depended on the level of support from the community. Teachers were mostly men, who served brief terms, although women often taught in the summer terms. By the 1830s, however, women began to dominate the classroom. Some support was provided by the states, more by rates paid by local communities, but parents were expected to share in the cost of educating their young.

The so-called Common School Revival began during the third decade of the nineteenth century and flourished during the post–Civil War period. This movement emphasized the social and political role of publicly supported schools. During a period of incipient capitalism, increasing urbanization, and rapidly rising rates of immigration, political leaders turned to the schools to buttress the social order. The movement was strongest in the northern and midwestern states and was led by men such as James Carter and HORACE MANN in Massachusetts, Henry Barnard in Connecticut, John Pierce in Michigan, and Calvin Stowe in Ohio. The reformers had some allies in the southern states, but the movement never succeeded in that region prior to the Civil War.

The overriding goal of the reformers (who were mostly of the Whig persuasion) was the provision of schooling for all, or as Henry Barnard, the first U.S. commissioner of education, was wont to put it, schools which were good enough for the rich and cheap enough for the poor. Tax support for public schooling was crucial, and well-built and suitably furnished school houses, graded classes, common textbooks, and clearly defined procedures for attendance and reporting were constantly recommended. Most important was the emphasis on teacher training, either in short-term institutes or in state-provided normal schools. Supervision was to be a

state responsibility. Hence, the movement provided the basis for the systemization of schooling. Underlying the entire reform platform was the dominant Protestant, middle-class, capitalistic ethos, which the reformers saw as truly American.

Opposition to these reforms came not from those opposed to schooling, for there was consensus on that matter, but from advocates of local government and opponents of increased taxation. Members of ethnic, national, and religious minorities also objected to the exclusionary aspect of the movement. Thus, the seeds of controversy still prevalent today were sown in this period. Nonetheless, the Common School movement laid the foundation for the system of public education and for the myth of commonality that remains an American belief.

See also: **Compulsory School Attendance; Grammar School; Literacy; Parochial Schools.**

BIBLIOGRAPHY

Cremin, Lawrence A. 1980. *American Education: The National Experience, 1783–1876.* New York: Harper and Row.

Glenn, Charles Leslie. 1988. *The Myth of the Common School.* Amherst: University of Massachusetts Press.

Johnson, Walter R. 1830. *Remarks on the Duty of the Several States in Regard to the Public Education.* Philadelphia: W. Sharpness.

Kaestle, Carl F. 1973. *The Evolution of An Urban School System: New York City, 1750–1850.* Cambridge, MA: Harvard University Press.

Kaestle, Carl F. 1983. *Pillars of the Republic: Common Schools and American Society, 1780–1860.* New York: Hill and Wang.

Katz, Michael B. 1968. *The Irony of Early School Reform.* Cambridge, MA: Harvard University Press. Reprint, 2001, New York: Teachers College Press.

EDITH NYE MACMULLEN

Communion, First

For many Christians, the Eucharist (or Communion) is one of the three rites of initiation which incorporate an individual into the body of Christ—that is, membership in the Christian church (Matthew 26:26–28). The others are BAPTISM and CONFIRMATION. The Eucharist, which means "thanksgiving," is the recalling of the passion, death, and resurrection of Jesus (paschal mysteries) that guarantees eternal life for faithful disciples. Eucharist was considered to be the culmination of the initiation rite—the most important sacrament after baptism. For Roman Catholics, it is the source and summit of the faith. A few Christian denominations maintain a belief in the "real presence" of Christ in the Eucharist, including Roman Catholics, Eastern Orthodox Christians, and Lutherans. Most Protestants, however, reject the doctrine of real presence and maintain a belief in a spiritual or symbolic presence or simply a memorial. Roman Catholics regard the First Holy Communion of children as a RITE OF PASSAGE that marks the attainment of reason or discretion.

The Council of Trent's 1563 conception of the Eucharist evolved from the decrees of the Fourth Lateran Council in 1215, by which both boys and girls who had reached the age of discretion (seven) were required to confess their sins and to receive the Eucharist annually. It is assumed that before Trent both baptism and confirmation preceded the reception of the Eucharist. Children who had not attained the age of discretion could not receive the sacrament of the Eucharist validly because they did not understand its purpose and could not give assent to it. Thus the Western church in the High Middle Ages viewed young children under the age of discretion as catechumens, individuals who were intermediate between infants and adults. They were free from original sin but stained by concupiscence. Though infants were soldiers of Christ, they were not permitted to receive the Eucharist. The Council of Trent reinforced the Lateran decree and rejected the efficacy of infant communion. Since baptism protected the child from accountability, there was no reason to administer communion to infants.

Due to the ambiguity of language in the decrees of Trent, the Catholic Church has offered latitude in the age at which children should receive the sacrament of the Eucharist. In theory children could receive communion as early as the age of seven, but in the nineteenth century it was delayed frequently until a child was ten or twelve. The point to be made here, however, is that the Catholic Church, unlike most Protestant churches, has promoted the reception of the Eucharist before a child reaches PUBERTY. The Eucharist introduced the child to public life within the Church and the assumption of adult responsibilities, but it had nothing to do with the child's physical maturity.

Martin Luther developed a concept of the sacrament which was peculiar to himself and distinct from the mainstream of later Protestant theology. In addition to retaining the sacramental nature of the Eucharist, he taught that the purpose of the sacrament was to nourish the faith of the recipient and that its validity did not depend on the character of either the recipient or the minister. Moreover, Luther restricted the reception of the sacrament of the Eucharist to adolescents who had been instructed in the truths of Christianity. He required that all children should study the meaning and obligations of the Ten Commandments, the Creed, and the Lord's Prayer, and that they assume a catechumen status until they understood exactly what was expected of them. Admission into the Christian community depended on physical maturity as well as intellectual readiness.

For most Protestant churches, spiritual maturity is equated with physical maturity. Their rites of confirmation and the Eucharist are in effect twin rites of puberty—a public acknowledgement that the physically mature Christian is also spiritually mature and morally responsible.

See also: **Catholicism; Protestant Reformation.**

BIBLIOGRAPHY

DeMolen, Richard L. 1975. "Childhood and the Sacraments in the Sixteenth Century." *Archiv fuer Reformationsgeschichte* 66: 49–71.

Patterson, Lloyd G. 1990. "Eucharist." In *The New Dictionary of Sacramental Worship*, ed. Peter E. Fink. Collegeville, MN: Liturgical Press.

Power, David N. 1980. *Gifts That Differ: Lay Ministries Established and Unestablished.* New York: Pueblo Publishing.

Wainwright, Geoffrey. 2001. "Eucharist." In *The Encyclopedia of Christianity* vol. 2, ed. Erwin Fahlbusch, et al. Grand Rapids, MI: W. B. Eerdmans.

White, James F. 1989. *Protestant Worship: Traditions in Transition.* Louisville, KY: Westminster/John Knox Press.

RICHARD L. DeMOLEN

Communist Youth

Communism was one of the most important political movements of the twentieth century and communist leaders across the globe made young people central to their plans to create communist parties, states, and societies.

Communism as a Political Movement

The history of twentieth-century communism began in Russia. In November 1917, the Bolshevik Party overthrew the Provisional Government, which had been established after the collapse of the Russian autocracy in March 1917. The Bolsheviks, who emerged out of the Russian social democratic movement and based their revolutionary strategy on the writings of Karl Marx and their leader Vladimir I. Lenin, soon renamed themselves the Communist Party of the Soviet Union (CPSU) and set out to create a new communist state, the Union of Soviet Socialist Republics, or USSR.

As it developed, the Bolshevik approach to communism was based on state ownership of property and authoritarian political rule exercised by the party in the name of the proletariat, or working class. The Bolsheviks also worked to create an international communist movement. After the revolution, they sought to split socialist parties elsewhere in Europe to form communist parties in these countries, as well as in North America and Asia. Through membership in the Communist, or Third, International (Comintern), these parties were brought under Soviet leadership and were often compelled to follow Soviet instructions in the planning of their own revolutionary activities. After World War II, communist influence increased considerably. Communist regimes were installed in the Soviet sphere of influence in EASTERN EUROPE between 1945 and 1948, while communists took power in CHINA in 1949. Communist parties also played key roles in liberation and revolutionary struggles in many parts of AFRICA, Asia, and LATIN AMERICA during the postwar period. The importance of communism as an international political movement declined markedly after the collapse of communist regimes in Eastern Europe in 1989 and the disintegration of the Soviet Union in 1991.

Communism and Youth

Youth support was crucial to both the preparation of revolution and the establishment of lasting communist regimes and societies. In Russia, young urban male workers provided key support for the Bolsheviks and their armed forces during the summer and fall of 1917. When civil war broke out in 1918, members of the newly established Communist Youth League (or Komsomol) defended the revolution in various capacities within the Red Army, and they were lauded by Bolshevik leaders for their courage, bravery, and self-sacrifice. Elsewhere in Europe, young people—especially young working men—promoted revolution within both Communist Youth organizations (which belonged to a Soviet-controlled Communist Youth International) and the new communist parties. These young men's enthusiastic embrace of the Bolshevik model of revolution was sometimes used by Russian Bolsheviks as they attempted to marginalize older and less pliant prewar revolutionary activists and shape European communist parties in the image of the Russian Bolshevik Party. For example, in 1920s France, Comintern leaders promoted Young Communist militants to leading positions within the party, especially at moments of adult resistance to the implementation of Soviet strategies. Young people later played important roles in communist resistance movements during World War II.

Once in power, communist leaders made the transformation of the younger generation central to the attempt to create new communist societies. Because young people lacked prior political experience and were considered more malleable than adults, communist leaders believed they could be transformed into ardent supporters of communism and builders of new socialist societies. As Lenin declared in 1920, it was the youth of the world that were faced with the actual task of creating communist societies. To prepare the younger generation, communist regimes dismantled or undermined existing youth organizations and established party-controlled Communist Youth Leagues for young men and women and Young Pioneer sections for children. These organizations worked to educate young people in communist values and to aid the party as it worked to build communism. Thus, they provided political education for young people, sponsored communist cultural events and LITERACY campaigns, oversaw a range of activities in the schools, and served as a training ground for future membership in adult parties. Members of these youth groups, who often received privileged access to educational, professional, or political opportunities, were expected to devote themselves to the communist cause and participate actively in special campaigns.

During the first Five-Year Plan in the Soviet Union (1928–1932), young people were at the forefront; they were sent into the countryside to confiscate grain and force peasants onto collective farms, and they were deployed in factories and on construction sites as members of shock brigades who led the struggle to transform the Soviet Union into an industrial power. Many young people embraced these revolutionary tasks with great enthusiasm and spoke of the excitement they felt being on the front lines of the struggle to build socialism. In China, Mao used the revolutionary enthusiasm of Chinese youth to reinvigorate communism during the Cultural Revolution of the late 1960s. Communists also restructured education as they sought to mold successive generations of young supporters. Schools at all levels included political education in communist theory and values, and their curricula combined manual labor on behalf of socialism with more strictly intellectual labor.

Recent Trends in Scholarship

Scholars have recently begun to approach the relationship between youth and communism in new ways. For a long time, scholars focused largely on communist efforts vis-à-vis youth. They emphasized the ways communists abolished independent youth organizations, created party-controlled youth organizations that were firmly subordinate to adult parties, and used these organizations to shape and control young people. Recently, however, scholars have altered this picture, arguing that communist youth organizations were less monolithic than earlier scholarship described and, more importantly, that youth responses to communism were more complicated than they first appeared. Scholars now argue that even at moments of great revolutionary enthusiasm, young people responded in a variety of ways to communist messages: some were ardent believers, some learned what they needed to know to survive or advance within the system, while some believed very little (or not at all).

In fact, if young people were often builders of socialism, they were also among those willing to dissent from communist ideology. Critiques could come either through the adoption of new cultural styles and practices—indeed Eastern European and Soviet communists became concerned about the impact that Western cultural imports like jazz and ROCK AND ROLL had on youth during the 1950s and 1960s—or through outright political protest, as was the case in Czechoslovakia in 1967–1968 and 1989, and in China in 1989. Finally, scholarship has begun to explore how young men and women often had quite different experiences within communist youth organizations that professed gender equality, as well as the ways masculine ideals often predominated within these organizations.

See also: **Fascist Youth; Hitler Youth; Youth Activism.**

BIBLIOGRAPHY

Chan, Anita. 1985. *Children of Mao: Personality Development and Political Activism in the Red Guard Generation.* Seattle: University of Washington Press.

Fisher, Ralph Talcott, Jr. 1959. *Pattern for Soviet Youth: A Study of the Congresses of the Komsomol, 1918–1954.* New York: Columbia University Press.

Gorsuch, Anne E. 2000. *Youth in Revolutionary Russia: Enthusiasts, Bohemians, Delinquents.* Bloomington: Indiana University Press.

Konecny, Peter. 1999. *Builders and Deserters: Students, State, and Community in Leningrad, 1917–1941.* Montreal and Kingston: McGill-Queen's University Press.

Pilkington, Hilary. 1994. *Russia's Youth and its Culture: A Nation's Constructors and Constructed.* London: Routledge.

Tirado, Isabel A. 1988. *Young Guard! The Communist Youth League, Petrograd 1917–1920.* New York: Greenwood Press.

Whitney, Susan B. 1996. "Embracing the Status Quo: French Communists, Young Women and the Popular Front." *Journal of Social History* 30, no. 1: 29–53.

SUSAN B. WHITNEY

Comparative History of Childhood

Comparative work on the history of childhood can be extremely revealing. It highlights areas in which otherwise different societies have shared experiences, partly of course because of the standard biological and psychological aspects of being or having a child. But it also shows the considerable possibilities for variation, based on different cultures, family structures, or economic contexts. The comparative study of childhood has taken on new importance in the contemporary world because of huge debates over the applicability of Western (or industrial) standards of childhood to societies with very different kinds of traditions and very different economic settings.

At the same time, comparative work on childhood's history is not abundant. The relative newness of the field adds to the challenge of comparison across cultural lines. There is great opportunity for further work. It is revealing that some of the most significant comparative insights have come from anthropologists or other social scientists looking at historical materials, rather than from historians themselves.

Quite apart from the challenge of novelty, there are some key complexities in dealing with the comparative history of childhood. Generalizations are always complicated by gender. Most societies make significant distinctions between boys and girls, and these distinctions can be compared. But the distinctions also inevitably limit statements that try to talk about childhood in general. Social position is another issue. In contemporary Turkey, for example, lower-class mothers, when asked about good children, emphasize obedience and courtesy; very few place any premium on independence or autonomy. But upper-class Turks list these traits first, spending much less time on obedience or even niceness to parents. Their approach is closer to Western styles than to those of the Turkish lower class.

Distinctions of this sort are common in contemporary society, where individual communities are changing at different paces; but they crop up earlier in history as well, as different social groups shaped different cultures and influenced their treatment of children. Rural–urban differences are an-

other important variable, even in such prosaic matters as the nature and extent of CHILD LABOR. In modern history, for example, the rural–urban gap between children's experiences in Russia is noticeably wider than in the United States. Poverty is another factor. Children who are malnourished, or whose parents are so poor that they have no energy to devote to children or even resent them as competitors for resources, will obviously differ from children whose families face fewer problems in normal subsistence. Studies in twentieth-century LATIN AMERICA have documented the results of differential economic conditions within the same society.

Finally, there is the question of regional scale, a key issue in comparative work in general. Because of the importance of cultural factors in shaping childhood, many comparative studies use broad frameworks, talking about Chinese or Confucian versus Indian or Hindu versus Western. In Western history, however, there is also a tradition of making national comparisons, for example in commenting on distinctive aspects of childhood in the United States as commonly noted by European travelers. More rarely, still smaller regional units are used. In ancient Greece, for example, there was a vivid contrast between boyhood in Sparta, where upper-class boys were fiercely disciplined in preparation for lives of military service, and the more relaxed childhood and varied education available to upper-class boys in Athens.

Comparative distinctions in childhood often highlight significant aspects of the societies in which they are embedded. Sometimes they reflect differences in larger social purpose, as in the contrast between Athens and Sparta. Sometimes the distinctions themselves are the cause of wider structural differences. Some comparativists today, for example, grapple with the implications of the individualistic childhood in the Western world contrasted with the stronger family authority emphasized in many traditional societies: is the Western model essential as a basis for successful economic and political development?

Premodern History

Comparisons in the study of childhood until the eighteenth century usually emphasize the impact of cultural variables, that is, deeply held beliefs and values about children and their functions, using legal frameworks and family forms as secondary factors. Again, there are important commonalities. All the great agricultural civilizations extensively utilized child labor, for example, usually to supplement adult work in farming or craft manufacture. All enforced patriarchal distinctions between boys and girls, with girls carefully taught to be subservient to fathers and brothers as a prelude to their later role in marriage.

Cultural distinctions, however, loom large. Polynesian traditions encouraged widespread ADOPTIONS and shared parenting, for identifying a single-family derivation did not greatly matter. ISLAM, in contrast, with tremendous emphasis on family identity, prohibited formal adoption, favoring charitable care for children without family. Several cultural traditions, including the classical Greek and Chinese, tolerated widespread infanticide, particularly of female infants, as a means of reducing the burden of unwanted children on the family. But Islam expressly forbade infanticide and offered an unusual number of legal protections, including INHERITANCE rights, to female children.

Comparisons between the Confucian and Hindu cultural traditions as they emerged in CHINA and INDIA after about 100 B.C.E. have important implications for the study of childhood. Confucius (551–478 B.C.E.) viewed family relationships as a microcosm of broader political arrangements, and in both he sought order and hierarchy. Child rearing emphasized obedience and emotional control, and in the upper classes children were taught elaborate rules of courtesy. As was common in cultures that practiced primogeniture, first sons gained a special sense of privilege. Girls were instructed in humility and subordination, along with training in domestic tasks. Ban Zhao, the female author of a first-century manual on women (reprinted often into the nineteenth century), explained how girls should be placed in cots at the foot of their brothers' beds, to instill a proper sense of inferiority.

Later, beginning in the sixth century C.E., the practice of foot binding began to spread in China, first among the upper classes, then more widely. Young girls had their feet so tightly wrapped that small bones would break, creating a shuffling walk that was regarded as a mark of beauty—and an obvious incapacity that was seen as appropriate for women. Confucian culture did not cause this practice, but it proved consistent with it. Foot binding would begin to recede only as a result of reform movements beginning in the 1890s.

Hindu culture, though not wanting in insistence on obedience and female subordination, placed a much greater premium on children's imagination. Indian culture emphasized dramatic, adventure-filled stories. Some of them, like "Jack the Giant Killer" or "The Seven League Boots," would later make their way into world literature; they were formally written up during the Gupta period, in the fifth century C.E.. Some adventure stories, taken from the great Hindu epics, featured heroic actions by women (albeit on behalf of fathers or husbands) as well as by men. The Hindu moral code urged duties appropriate to particular castes rather than a single set of obligations. Again, popular stories illustrated different behaviors expected from warriors or merchants. Some analysts have suggested that this also encouraged a subjective approach to reality and an active life in the imagination, both in childhood and later adulthood. Indian culture placed more vigorous emphasis on love than Confucian culture did, and stories highlighted the loving and playful interaction between parents and children. Girls received greater encouragement for their beauty and lively personalities than they did in Confucian culture.

Hindu tradition, however, placed less emphasis on education than Confucianism did. In China, education was the key to success in the competitive examinations that opened the door to the government bureaucracy, the most prestigious source of employment in China for many centuries. Upper-class boys were widely educated first by tutors, then by state-sponsored schools, from the first century B.C.E. onward. Some lower-class youth might be identified as talented enough to be educated, under the patronage of an upper-class mentor; there was a limited opportunity for mobility here. And some girls were educated as well, like Ban Zhao herself, trained in domestic skills but also, under an indulgent father, granted LITERACY and other accomplishments.

Judging the impact of overarching cultural traditions on individual children and families is frankly difficult. Upper-class families followed better-defined or at least better disseminated traditions than did those in the lower class, particularly in systems like Confucianism: lower-class Chinese families might seek obedience and courtesy but they also needed work from their children. Personalities also played a role: individual parents might form intensely loving bonds with their children simply because of mutual personalities, even in seemingly restrained systems like Confucianism. On the other hand, some culturally induced differences were real and widely applied. The spread of foot binding demonstrates a distinctive system with measurable impact on the lives of many girls.

When Confucianism spread outside China, particularly to Korea, JAPAN, and Vietnam, it underwent some modifications. No society outside China copied foot binding for girls, for example. In Japan, from the sixteenth century onward, Confucianism encouraged a wider interest in education than ever developed in traditional China. By the eighteenth century a large minority of Japanese boys were sent to school for at least a few years and were gaining literacy.

Two other large cultural systems, Islam and Christianity, had a significant impact on the experience of childhood. Like Islam (but unlike Confucianism), Christianity discouraged the practice of infanticide that had been current in the Greco-Roman world. Christianity provided the first spur for schools in medieval Europe, though they were not widely accessible. Islam, spreading in a more prosperous part of the world and with stronger emphasis on the desirability of reading its holy text, the Qur'an, had wider educational impact, particularly in the cities, for several centuries.

Two later developments in Christian Europe invite comparative assessment. A strict disciplinary style developed there that involved the frequent use of physical punishments and also the instilling of FEAR. Children were often threatened with bogeymen or other monsters as an inducement to stay in line. Exactly when this approach arose is not clear. Some of it relates to Christian beliefs in original sin: children were born in sin because of Adam and Eve's fall, thus it was vital that they redeem themselves by behaving properly lest, in death, they be condemned to hell. Images and invocations of death were common in Christian culture into the nineteenth century, both in Europe and later the United States. Protestantism, on the whole, encouraged a strict disciplinary culture, in part because it emphasized original sin more starkly than CATHOLICISM did.

Martin Luther, the first leader of the PROTESTANT REFORMATION, was himself strictly raised by a coal-miner father in Germany, and he translated some of his own upbringing into his recommendations to parents. Protestant householders, particularly fathers, were responsible for the moral guidance and religious education of their children. This involved family Bible reading and also strict physical DISCIPLINE. Indians in North America were amazed at the frequency of spankings European immigrants administered to their children. Native American practice involved warmer interactions between children and parents.

The second development was not directly related to Christianity, though it also had disciplinary implications. By the fifteenth century, Western European families (except in the upper classes) began to emphasize a relatively late age in marriage (26 or so for women, a bit older for men). This was apparently intended to control the birth rate and reduce the burden of inheritance caused by undue numbers of children. But with later marriage, the importance of extended family relationships diminished greatly. Western Europeans married and had children when their own parents were either quite elderly or already dead. Nuclear families were on their own. American FAMILY PATTERNS, particularly in New England, departed from European precedents to some degree: marriage age was a bit earlier and longevity greater, which meant more GRANDPARENTS and grandparental influence on children. Even so, the Western European family style affected the colonial American experience.

The pattern had two results. In the first place, it helps explain the use of physical discipline. Mothers as well as fathers had to work hard; there was no wider group of relatives to help keep the family afloat. Young children were often isolated—swaddled and hung on a peg—so that mothers could work freely. Strict discipline helped keep older children in line. The second result was what many comparative analysts have seen as a slowly growing emphasis on children's individuality. Because they interacted with parents directly, with few intermediaries other than their SIBLINGS, children in Western Europe were encouraged to develop greater individual identity and self-reliance than was common in many other agricultural societies.

Other practices both reflected and encouraged this individuation. European families often sent teenage children to live in other households for several years. The motivation was economic: families with too many children could reduce their burden while providing another family with additional labor. Many parents argued that this helped with discipline, since other families could more easily insist that TEENAGERS toe the line than soft-hearted parents could. The practice stood in sharp contrast to other societies where extended families more commonly worked in groups, and was another factor that encouraged a child to develop an individual identity.

Modern Comparisons

Comparative histories of childhood emphasize two combinations when they approach the history of the past two to three centuries. First, they explore differences, usually national differences, within Western society. And second, they deal with differences between the West and other societies, here focusing particularly on twentieth-century comparisons. The two approaches involve interesting mutual tensions, since the latter assumes a roughly common and novel Western experience that can be juxtaposed with other areas, in contrast to the former's emphasis on distinctions within the West.

One of the most sustained comparisons, launched in the late eighteenth century by contemporary observers—European travelers to the United States—rather than historians, involves the juxtaposition of the United States and Western Europe. The two societies have displayed similar dynamics in many respects. The modern pattern of birthrate reduction began in roughly comparable ways in the late eighteenth to early nineteenth centuries, followed by a sweeping attack on INFANT MORTALITY after 1880. U.S. birth rates have tended to be higher than those of Europe, probably because of more abundant land and resources (for example, the mid-twentieth-century baby boom was more pronounced in the United States). But basic features are widely shared. In both societies nineteenth century industrialization generated new uses for child and youth labor (though few societies on either side of the Atlantic matched the British extreme, with its widespread conscription of ORPHANS). These were followed by child labor reforms—in the United States, initially mainly at the state level—that gradually curtailed the practice. The United States (except the South, which lagged behind) developed mass compulsory education a bit earlier than Europe—in the 1830s as opposed to the 1860s to 1870s—but again the process responded to similar forces and had similar results.

The big differences, however, involved children's position in the family and the looser patterns of authority on the American side. European visitors consistently commented, sometimes in praise, sometimes blame, on how openly children in American families were allowed to express themselves, even to dispute parental views and actions. The observation may seem surprising, given the emphasis on obedience and good manners in nineteenth-century child rearing. The comparison suggests how American childhood may informally have softened, despite the prescriptive literature. Even in the literature, the American enthusiasm for childish innocence and maternal affection surpassed most of Europe. The distinction has carried into the twenty-first century. New American efforts to protect children from emotional stress have continued to surpass those in Western Europe, despite some European (particularly British) imitations of American practice. Thus American attempts to promote SELF-ESTEEM and inhibit teachers from using ANGER or shaming in the classroom have not been matched in Western Europe. The measures constitute changes in American practice, compared to nineteenth-century standards, but they build on an earlier national sensitivity to and indulgence of children.

It is possible that labor conditions help explain the transatlantic difference. With labor in shorter supply in the United States, and with the frontier available as a recourse for older children seeking to leave family unpleasantness behind, American parents were more cautious in dealing with their children than were their European counterparts. Some analysis has suggested an undercurrent of parental fear in the United States—because of the importance of hanging on to children who might have other options—that was not present in Europe.

Whatever the causes, differences persisted, both outside of and within the schoolroom. The new generation of child-rearing literature that began to emerge in the United States in the 1920s, which recommended greater informality and, ultimately, greater permissiveness where children were concerned, was not matched in Western Europe until the late 1950s. Instead, in Europe, a more authoritarian parental approach persisted. American children may also have been introduced earlier and more widely to modern consumerism than their European counterparts: the practice of giving children ALLOWANCES and the possibility of obtaining driver's licenses both occurred earlier in the United States.

Some analysts have suggested that, by the late 1950s, the two societies began to converge, with more informal, less parentally controlled, more peer- and consumer-oriented childhoods in both groups. Even here, however, some comparative studies note a few ongoing distinctions. American fathers were more open to a best-friends approach to their children, emphasizing shared entertainment, than were otherwise permissive fathers in Sweden. American parents were much more reluctant than French parents to regulate and discipline children's eating, which was one reason child obesity increased more rapidly in the United States.

Other comparisons are also revealing. American patterns of schooling in the late nineteenth and twentieth centuries differed from those in Europe in their widespread use of co-education and in their emphasis on SPORTS and extracurricular activities, with less emphasis on achievement examinations and formal tracking. Where European (including Russian) and also Japanese systems featured decisive exami-

nations, often around age twelve, to determine what kind of secondary school a child would attend, the United States continued to emphasize a more comprehensive HIGH SCHOOL (an American invention), though with periodic bows to tracking distinctions, mainly on the basis of aptitude tests. American secondary education, as a result, was in some senses more democratic but also, by most comparative accounts, considerably less intensive, particularly for the college-bound. A higher percentage of American youth went to college, though the gap here narrowed by the early twenty-first century, with about 40 percent of Europeans, compared to almost 60 percent of Americans, going on to postsecondary study.

American moralism and religious commitment also differed from European attitudes. After the changes in adolescent sexual habits in the 1960s (similar in both societies) Europeans moved to greater advocacy of BIRTH-CONTROL devices, while Americans hesitated, preferring abstinence campaigns. By the 1990s this resulted in noticeably higher rates of TEEN PREGNANCY in the United States. By the 1980s, the greater American commitment to free market forces and the scaling back of welfare generated a higher percentage of children in poverty, particularly among racial minorities.

Several key comparisons suggest a somewhat more conservative approach to children in the United States than in Western Europe by the late twentieth century. Though the percentages of women working were similar, Americans were less confident about using CHILD-CARE facilities than were Europeans. American leisure, including VACATIONS, was somewhat more child-centered. Greater attachment to more traditional family values in the United States also helps explain the higher American birth rate. American parents were also still more likely to spank, particularly in contrast to Scandinavia, where laws banned the practice. American children were more likely to fight than French village children, who were schooled to restrain themselves physically while becoming adept at verbal insults. American YOUTH CULTURE made less reference to adult standards than in Western Europe, where the sense of range and spontaneity was smaller. The comparative differences remain intriguing, and they do not fit tidily together. Early childhood in the United States may, for example, have changed less rapidly than in Europe in recent decades, while youth culture, in contrast, seems more innovative on the American side of the Atlantic, despite many shared consumer and media interests.

Some comparative efforts have focused on national differences within Europe. By the 1930s a number of analysts sought to explain the rise of Nazism in Germany by focusing on particularly authoritarian patterns of child rearing and father–son relations, but results were inconclusive. Some specific comparative efforts stress common historical patterns despite big differences in other aspects of society. A study of ADOLESCENCE in late-nineteenth-century Britain and Germany—two countries very different politically at that point—stressed how both societies moved toward a very similar, and novel, identification of adolescence, including the creation of separate JUVENILE COURTS.

Studies that compare Western Europe and the United States with Russia deserve special attention. Though much work remains to be done, it is clear that the history of childhood mirrors the complex comparisons possible in other aspects of Russian history, with its mixture of distinctiveness and eagerness to import Western models. In the nineteenth century, Western-minded aristocrats absorbed the writings of Western thinkers like JEAN-JACQUES ROUSSEAU, who emphasized childhood as a period of innocence and learning. Writers like TOLSTOY described idyllic childhoods based on these concepts. Ordinary Russians were far removed from these flights. The SWADDLING of children lasted longer in Russia than in the West, and this set a strong disciplinary tone in combination with widespread use of CHILD LABOR in Russian agriculture.

With the Russian revolution of 1917, interest in children and youth crested. The state hoped to mold children to create the new Soviet citizen, though officials also reflected the older aristocratic interest in childhood as a time of learning. Education spread widely. As the birth rate dropped, many parents devoted great attention to their individual children, providing tutoring or private lessons in dance or acrobatics. Some of this mirrored what was happening in the West. Highly competitive schools and opportunities for advancement within the Communist Party beckoned successful children, and many parents tried hard to protect their offspring and encourage them to excel.

There were two clear differences between the Soviet Union and the West. First, the wars and dislocations of the Soviet era created an unusually large number of "lost" children, including refugees and ORPHANS. The Soviet system tried to provide for these children, but their numbers outstripped the available resources. Second, the collective emphasis for children—in terms of emphasis on group identity over individual achievement—was unusually strong. At least in the cities, schools worked children harder than in the West, with six days of classes. Soviet programs provided camps for many children in the summer, where they would do agricultural work and also learn to develop common bonds with one another amid extensive Communist propaganda. The state singled many children out for special service, as in the case of promising athletes. At an extreme, Soviet authorities hoped that children would learn loyalties to the socialist system that would supersede those due to their parents. (In a famous case in the 1930s, young Pavel Morozov turned his father in to the authorities for suspected dissident behavior. Morozov was held up by the state as a role model for other children.) Other Communist countries followed the Soviet model, as in the hothouse athletic-development program in East Germany.

Even after the Soviet system fell, distinctive Eastern European attributes remained, despite growing interest in Western-style media and consumerism. In Russia, many children reported a level of group loyalty unusual by Western standards, including a willingness to share work, even during examinations, on grounds that being a good comrade took precedence over official rules on cheating and over individual success. Several observers rate the intensity of FRIENDSHIP among Russian children, particularly boys, as higher than in the West. They also noted a longer childhood in Russia, especially in contrast to the United States. While Russian children were expected to perform more home chores, they were allowed to delay full emotional responsibility longer.

More general comparisons between Western (European and U.S.) patterns of childhood and those in other parts of the world highlight the several changes that began to take shape in the West from the nineteenth century onward. The growing Western hostility to child labor, the insistence on mandatory schooling, and the emphasis on warm emotional responses to childhood innocence added up to a demanding package by the early to mid-twentieth century. It was not always, of course, implemented in Western societies themselves. But Western observers, and international agencies that largely adopted Western ideas about the purpose of childhood and the rights of children, used the standards vigorously in judging other societies and urging reform. Ongoing differences reflected agonizing income inequalities, but also different conceptions of childhood itself.

Japan posed a fascinating case of a non-Western society that followed the Western lead very successfully in cutting child labor (after a period of intensive exploitation around 1900) and imposing schooling. The Japanese educational system, after the primary grades, was actually closer to that of Western Europe than the American system was. Japanese childhood continued to differ from Western patterns, however, in the greater emphasis placed on conformity. Early childhood education in Japan stressed good group relations and obedience to teacher authority, in contrast to Western efforts to stress individualism. Japan also routinely used shame in child rearing, while Western adults tried to minimize exposure to peer sanctions for the sake of individual self-esteem.

Contrasts between industrial societies and those that were slower to industrialize were of course more vivid. Many analysts compared villages in Kenya, for example, where the traditional emphasis on teaching children household and child-care tasks left little room to identify higher cognitive goals, to their modern Western equivalents. In one Kenyan village, six-year old girls were adept at housecleaning and sibling care, but could not repeat a story to an adult. Continued expectations that children should take care of older parents also marked great differences from Western patterns, again promoting a lower degree of individuation and more subordination to family and group goals.

Child labor persisted in many societies outside the West, and indeed often intensified with the pressure to increase production in the demanding global economy. Industrial observers, ignoring the fact that many of the responsible corporations originated in their own societies, expressed dismay at the work pressures, poverty, and lack of schooling that a majority of children still faced in countries like India. In contrast, even Western-oriented elites in India continued to find child labor—in the poorer classes—both natural and acceptable, a key reason that the practice persisted more strongly there than in some poorer countries. Even where school opportunities were better developed, as in Turkey, the lack of preschool preparation (only 7 percent of Turkish children were in preschools by the 1990s) explained significant differences in the childhood experience and in school performance, compared to the industrial societies.

Western ambivalence about children's SEXUALITY was another useful comparative marker. Few societies conformed to the Western idea that sexual innocence should extend through adolescence, particularly when Western films, widely marketed internationally, presented a highly sexual teenaged persona. Early marriage continued in many societies (early by Western standards of course), because teenagers were not seen as children, while sexual exploitation of teenage girls drawn from rural societies increased in the global economy.

Important comparative work has dealt with youth groups in contemporary history. Since the 1970s, student associations in places like India have been more strongly political than their counterparts in Western universities, and more critical of existing regimes. One explanation offered is that university education outside the West creates greater generational gaps with parents (often not university educated), which in turn promotes radicalization. With colleges and universities now drawing 40 to 60 percent of the relevant age groups in the West, political interests are inevitably more diffuse, particularly since the decline of student activism in the 1960s to early 1970s.

On the other hand, GLOBALIZATION did begin to reduce some differences, even between advanced industrial and less-developed societies. China's twentieth-century experience cut into Confucian traditions and patriarchy. A new concept of adolescence emerged, and at least in urban areas an interest in romance as part of the youth experience developed as well. Shared YOUTH CULTURE had a wide impact in many otherwise different societies after 1950, thanks to the spread of rock music and common sports and media idols. By the 1990s, village children in eastern Russia, ignorant of computers and knowing little about the United States, could nevertheless identify stars like BRITNEY SPEARS as epitomes of beauty. Common interests in the Internet, with which chil-

dren were more adept than most adults, aligned the interests of young people in places like Iran, in principle dominated by conservative Muslim clerics, with those in the industrial regions.

Other global trends from the 1970s onward included the continuing spread of education, despite persistent differences that depended on available resources, as well as some lingering hesitations about pulling children away from work and family. Birth rates declined, though again this general trend was combined with significant variations depending on when the decline began, and from what base. All societies were at least beginning to deal with the implications of smaller families for the experience of childhood and treatment of children.

Questions often asked in comparative contemporary history about the tension between traditional identities and homogenizing forces obviously apply to the study of childhood as well. Some societies used children as active agents in preserving distinctive ways of life, sometimes drawing children into violence as part of the process. People in key regions like the MIDDLE EAST have often divided between considerable attraction to Western-style education and a consumer-oriented childhood on the one hand and a commitment to religious schooling on the other that, in some cases, inflamed hatreds. Here, comparisons within societies might be more revealing than drawing contrasts between traditional civilizations and those more open to the changes of modernity.

The comparative history of Western society, or of Japan and the West, also reminds us that not all childhoods are alike even in places committed to advanced industrialization. Distinctions are less pronounced than those between a childhood of work and one of schooling, but they are significant nonetheless. Definitions of emotional goals, degrees of individualism, and other key issues can vary significantly in societies that seem equally adept in industrial economics and modern statecraft. Correspondingly, comparison remains an essential tool in identifying contrasts and commonalities.

See also: **Africa; Australia; Canada; Early Modern Europe; Eastern Europe; Education, Europe; Education, United States; Israel; Medieval and Renaissance Europe; New Zealand.**

BIBLIOGRAPHY

Bornstein, Marc H., ed. 1991. *Cultural Approaches to Parenting.* Hillsdale, NJ: Erlbaum.

Cunningham, Hugh. 1995. *Children and Childhood in Western Society since 1500.* London: Longman.

Delumeau, Jean. 1990. *Sin and Fear: The Emergence of a Western Guilt Culture, 13th–18th Centuries.* New York: St. Martin's Press.

Gillis, John R. 1974. *Youth and History: Tradition and Change in European Age Relations, 1700–Present.* New York: Academic Press.

Kagitcibasi, Cigdem. 1996. *Family and Human Development Across Cultures: A View from the Other Side.* Mahwah, NJ: Erlbaum.

Kahane, Reuven. 1997. *The Origins of Postmodern Youth: Informal Youth Movements in a Comparative Perspective.* Berlin: de Gruyter.

Lamb, Michael E. 1987. *The Father's Role: Cross-Cultural Perspectives.* Hillsdale, NJ: Erlbaum.

Lamb, Michael E., and Abraham Sagi, eds. 1987. *Fatherhood and Family Policy.* Hillsdale, NJ: Erlbaum.

McLoloyd, Vonnie C., and Constance A. Flanagan, eds. 1990. *Economic Stress: Effects on Family Life and Child Development.* San Francisco: Jossey-Bass.

Minturn, Leigh, and William W. Lambert. 1964. *Mothers of Six Cultures: Antecedents of Child Rearing.* New York: Wiley.

Stearns, Peter N. 1998. *Schools and Students in Industrial Society: Japan and the West.* Boston: Bedford Books.

Weiner, Myron. 1991. *Child and the State in India: Child Labor and Education Policy in Comparative Perspective.* Princeton, NJ: Princeton University Press.

Wylie, Laurence. 1964. *Village in the Vaucluse.* Cambridge, MA: Harvard University Press.

PETER N. STEARNS

Compulsory School Attendance

Between 1852 and 1918 all states and territories in the United States enacted compulsory school attendance laws. That children should be educated was a compulsory mandate in all state and territorial constitutions, but such proclamations said nothing about attendance at schools. Compulsory school attendance laws passed during the latter half of the nineteenth century represented more than the cessation of voluntary schooling; they formalized a significant broadening of state authority and its assumption of responsibility for the education of children.

The passage of compulsory school attendance legislation in the United States must be viewed as both a philosophical issue and a historical event. As a philosophical issue, the enactment of these laws reflected the demographic, economic, and cultural forces that were transforming nineteenth-century America. Opposition to compulsory attendance was defended by claims that such legislation would begin a decline in those values that distinguished the United States from the historical legacy of Europe. Such legislation would invite political intrusion into local communities and undermine traditional parental authority. Yet opposition could be quickly reversed on similar philosophical grounds. Passing compulsory school attendance would signify the benign role of the state, aligning it against sectarian and class divisions. In this view, compulsory school attendance was a means to a moral goal, for universal schooling best fit the emerging image of the nation as an organic unity that superceded particular groups or localities.

When viewed as a historical event, the timing of the enactment of compulsory schooling helps to explain much of the philosophical debate itself. A comparison of Western societies demonstrates that state enactment of compulsory schooling is not explained by economic factors, such as level of industrialization or urbanization. Some countries implemented compulsory schooling well before industrializing. The earliest state to do so, Prussia, illustrates the noneconomic motive behind enacting compulsory schooling. Enacting compulsory schooling was a means to reinvigorate national solidarity in a context where traditional, external modes of authority were weakening. Compulsory schooling was a form of nation-building, foreshadowing the larger historical movement to broaden the rights of individuals as citizens and linking this to an expanded moral jurisdiction of state authority. In contrast, England, a comparative latecomer to compulsory schooling, enacted its Elementary Education Act of 1870, well after taking the lead in inaugurating industrialization. Yet, like Prussia, a weak showing at the Paris Exhibition of 1867 signaled a threat to its international stature, in turn challenging traditional means of authority and technical training. The prompt to reinvigorate national solidarity fueled a sense of urgency and thereby gave legitimacy to an extension of state authority over universal primary education.

The comparison of Prussia and England is instructive for the American states. State variation in the timing of enactment was likewise weakly connected to economic factors. Rather, the timing of enactment must be viewed within the broader context of national formation. Most northern and western states and territories enacted compulsory schooling as part of a sequence of institutional formation, passing the law only after they had established the state reform school, the state lunatic asylum, and the state hospital for the deaf and blind. For these states, compulsory school attendance legislation was concrete evidence of their institutional strength; for young territories it was a symbol of their wish to obtain statehood. For both, the enactment of compulsory schooling laws had little to do with compelling attendance. Southern states, by contrast, enacted compulsory school attendance laws after 1900, and did so reluctantly. A planter class fearful of elevating the educational aspirations of ex-slaves and poor whites, whose labor was critical to an agrarian, plantation economy, effectively resisted the extension of universal public education. For these states, compulsory schooling symbolized the reverse of what it meant to their northern and western counterparts: it signaled a threat to the traditional means of social control, which the planter class sought to maintain in a racially divided form.

The passage of compulsory attendance laws in the American states had little to do with compelling school attendance, for school attendance was already high. To seek the reasons for their enactment in the requirements of an industrial economy is as misplaced as to seek their effects in expanding enrollment. Under such scrutiny, the laws may be seen as failures. Yet by legally positing universal schooling as a common goal, the laws helped to structure the social and legal categories of childhood and ADOLESCENCE that have become integral to American culture generally and to the organization of American education in particular.

See also: **Common Schools; Education, Europe; Education, United States; European Industrialization; Mann, Horace.**

BIBLIOGRAPHY

Anderson, James D. 1988. *The Education of Blacks in the South, 1860–1935.* Chapel Hill: University of North Carolina Press.

Fuller, Bruce, and Richard Rubinson, eds. 1992. *The Political Construction of Education, The State, School Expansion, and Economic Change.* New York: Praeger.

Melton, James Van Horn. 1988. *Absolutism and the Eighteenth-Century Origins of Compulsory Schooling in Prussia and Austria.* Cambridge, UK: Cambridge University Press.

Ramirez, Francisco O., and John Boli. 1987. "The Political Construction of Mass Schooling: European Origins and Worldwide Institutionalization." *Sociology of Education* 60: 2–17.

Richardson, John G. 1994. "Common, Delinquent, and Special: On the Formalization of Common Schooling in the American States." *American Educational Research Journal* 31: 695–723.

JOHN G. RICHARDSON

Computers. *See* Media, Childhood and the.

Conception and Birth

Human reproduction, from conception to birth, would seem to be one of the few historical constants across cultures and the centuries. While the basic biological features of reproduction have changed little over the last two millennia, the cultural understanding and social management of this fundamental human experience have varied enormously.

From the earliest records in the ancient world onward, birth attendants and parents sought to control fertility and to improve the experience and outcome of childbirth itself. While male philosophers and physicians starting with the Greek philosopher ARISTOTLE (384–322 B.C.E.) theorized about the nature of conception and embryological development, it was women as mothers and midwives who were ultimately believed to have authority over the practical aspects of conception and birth. But beginning in the seventeenth century, European male "natural philosophers" and doctors began taking a more active interest in the world of reproduction by exploring the microscopic world of conception and by beginning to practice routine midwifery in the British Isles, France, and North America.

By the late eighteenth century, men's incursions into these arenas led to the professional marginalizing of female midwives and the denigration of popular beliefs about reproduction. Physicians, biologists, and other researchers laid claim to knowledge of reproductive anatomy, fertilization, and embryological development in the nineteenth century and to heredity and hormones in the twentieth. As male scientists and doctors asserted their authority over conception and birth in the nineteenth and twentieth centuries, they influenced public and political opinion, which ultimately led to the state regulation of abortion, BIRTH CONTROL, out-of-wedlock births, midwifery, obstetrics, and prenatal and infant welfare.

The twentieth century witnessed phenomenal technological and social developments, from the invention of hormonal contraception in the 1950s and the legal right of Western women to terminate their pregnancies in the 1970s to the practice of surrogate motherhood and the surgical ability to repair fetal defects in utero in the 1980s. The spiritual and moral dimensions of conception and birth, such as when a fetus acquires a soul and whether the life of a mother or a fetus holds greater value, have been the subjects of debate for centuries. Yet twentieth-century scientific knowledge about reproduction, deep as it was, hardly resolved any of these issues. The extraordinary technological advances of the twentieth century only complicated the ethical, medical, and political questions regarding individual rights; the roles of the medical profession, the state, and the marketplace; and the question of when human life begins.

The Biology of Reproduction

Although it has been known in the West for centuries that both males and females contribute formative biological materials to a future child in the act of sexual intercourse, much beyond that remained mysterious. Exactly when and how peak fertility occurred in females, for instance, was not known until 1827 when the Estonian embryologist Karl Ernst von Baer discovered an ovum in a female dog and charted female ovulation. His work, combined with the late-eighteenth-century experiments of the Italian physiologist Lazzaro Spallanzani proving that sperm was necessary for fertilization, led to the insight that conception occurs when sperm from a male successfully fertilizes an ovum or ova released by the ovary of a female when she is ovulating.

The determination of the sex of the future child remained one of the great mysteries of human conception until the early twentieth century. While some classical authorities maintained that the male's left testicle held female seed and the right held male seed, the second-century Greek physician Galen argued that a not-yet-gendered fetus resting on the right side of the uterus would become male and one on the left would become female. For centuries, both popular and learned authors claimed that astrological forces, certain foods, and a woman's feelings during sexual intercourse could influence the future child's sex. According to the medical researchers Patrick Geddes and J. A. Thomson in 1889, there were at least five hundred distinct theories explaining sex determination by the nineteenth century. Though many of these theories argued that women somehow determined sex, it is in fact the father's sperm cells that carry the X and Y chromosomes that control sex, a discovery made in 1916 by the American biologist Calvin Bridges.

Sex ratios, however, are not perfectly even and can have significant geographic and historical differences. In late-twentieth-century Europe and North America about 105 boys were born for every 100 girls, but in Korea and Gambia that ratio was 116 to 100. At the turn of the twenty-first century it remains disputed why more boys are naturally born after wars, and why more firstborns are male.

In the vast majority of pregnancies, women have singletons. Twins and other multiples occur naturally either when more than one ovum is released and separately fertilized or when the fertilized ovum splits into genetically identical zygotes. Rates of multiples vary across ethnic and age groups, although on average in the 1990s in Europe and North America about one of every eighty-five pregnancies resulted in twins, with about a third of those identical. Multiples became more common in the West from the 1980s onward as more women delayed childbearing until their later thirties and forties (when their ovaries function less efficiently and more frequently release more than one egg per cycle) and as more women underwent assisted reproduction, a process that usually involves the implantation of more than one embryo.

The reproductive cycle in human beings, from the first day of the last menstrual cycle to the delivery, lasts approximately forty weeks. Conception occurs shortly after ovulation, usually about two weeks after the beginning of that month's menstrual cycle. The developing, multiplying cells are medically termed first as a *zygote* from conception to two weeks, then as an *embryo* from two to eight weeks, and from then until birth as a *fetus*. As soon as the zygote is implanted about ten days after fertilization—and the woman is now considered pregnant—whatever nutrients and other substances she intakes can affect the viability and health of the fetus. In 1959 the first medical reports appeared demonstrating that the sedative thalidomide caused severe fetal deformities, and by 1972 several researchers reported a high correlation between smoking in pregnancy and low birthweight. Especially during the first trimester, the pregnant woman can experience nausea, exhaustion, and tenderness throughout her body. At the same time, the fetal organ systems begin developing and maturing from two weeks to birth, with the basic structure of all the organ systems forming in the first six weeks.

In the late 1960s, animal researchers discovered that labor is launched by hormonal changes, first in the fetus and then the mother. When a normal fetus is nearly ready for birth, its pituitary gland is stimulated by the hypothalamus to begin secreting elevated levels of adrenocorticotropin (ACTH) and cortisol. These hormones help both to prepare the fetal lung tissue for breathing outside the uterus and to create enzymes that convert the mother's uterine progesterone into estrogen. This in turn triggers a cascade of maternal hormones that lead to labor: estrogen helps to increase oxytocin, secreted by the mother's pituitary glands and by the mother's mammary glands. Estrogen, oxytocin, and prostaglandins in the uterus ultimately trigger uterine contractions. The first stage of labor is this active phase when the uterine muscles powerfully contract to force open the cervix to ten centimeters. This can take several hours or even days. The second stage occurs as the baby exits the birth canal, a much shorter process of a few hours or less.

In about 97 percent of singleton pregnancies, the fetus presents itself upside down, often with its head facing toward the back of the mother, a position from which it is easiest to deliver. As the cervix thins and dilates and the uterine muscles contract, the head of the child drops into the birth canal; in the second stage of labor, the head turns through the pelvis—a mechanical process discovered independently by an Irish and a Scottish obstetrician in the 1740s. In about 3 percent of pregnancies, the fetus is positioned in difficult-to-deliver positions including a *breech*, in which the fetus's bottom is tucked into the pelvic basin. Before the twentieth century, attendants intervened in complicated births by performing internal or external *version*—the manual turning of the full-term fetus in utero; by introducing the attendant's hands or obstetrical forceps into the mother's birth canal to apply mechanical leverage during the delivery; or by changing the mother's position in labor to aid in delivery. In the late twentieth century, especially in the United States, obstetricians tended to resolve breeches and other obstructed deliveries with cesarean sections.

After the child is born, the umbilical cord is cut and the placenta, which has provided nourishment during the entire pregnancy, is delivered during a third stage of labor. In the twenty-first century, as in the past, attendants immediately examine and clean the newborn. In 1953 the American obstetrician Virginia Apgar developed a scoring system based on the infant's physiological signs to assess its condition; if the child appears to be in distress, neonatal specialists intervene. After delivery, the mother is cared for and allowed to rest. Before the twentieth century, the postpartum ideal in western Europe and North America was for a mother to rest and recuperate during at least an entire month of "lying-in" while her relatives and friends managed the household and cared for the newborn and the rest of the family.

Delivery Practices

Before the twentieth century, most mothers in the Western world were attended by female midwives in their own homes. The professional transition among birth attendants from female midwives to male obstetricians occurred first and most dramatically in the British Isles, the United States, and France during the eighteenth century, mostly among elite and middle-class families. Male doctors were far less successful in taking over pregnancy and childbirth in Catholic countries such as Italy and Spain. But despite their early success among an elite female clientele, male obstetricians have never delivered the majority of newborns in Europe, and in the United States they began to deliver the majority only after 1900. While obstetricians have firmly established themselves in modern America—managing from 95 to 99 percent of pregnancies in the 1990s—and while they handle complicated and high-risk pregnancies in all Western nations, it is only in the United States that midwives are no longer considered routine practitioners.

Before the late seventeenth century, medical men were usually called to births only in cases of severe complications requiring surgical intervention. But from the seventeenth century onward, male doctors developed techniques that improved the likelihood of survival among mothers and babies in some protracted labors. The most important and lifesaving included the obstetrical forceps, developed by the seventeenth-century Chamberlen family of physicians in England, and cesarean sections. Though cesarean sections had been attempted for centuries, until the 1880s few medical men had performed ones that resulted in the survival of both mother and child.

Obstetric medicine became increasingly associated with pain relief during labor. Beginning in the 1840s, British and American obstetricians began administering ether and chloroform as anesthesia during childbirth, and by the early 1900s, a full panoply of pain-reducing interventions had been deployed. By 1950, many techniques, such as spinal and epidural nerve blocks, were greatly improved, and some American obstetricians were commonly using continuous caudal anesthesia for use during vaginal labor and delivery. It became common practice by midcentury for women to be completely unconscious during labor and the birth of their children.

By the late 1950s, a handful of doctors in the Soviet Union and Europe and many women began arguing against this extreme "medicalization" of childbirth, including especially the administration of amnesiacs and anesthesia. Grantley Dick-Read's *Childbirth without Fear* (1944) and Ferdinand Lamaze's *Painless Childbirth* (1956) were instrumental in educating mothers about their bodies and the possibility of reducing pain during delivery without the use of drugs. By the 1990s, U.S. hospitals began incorporating "natural childbirth" education in prenatal courses, allowing women more control over the birth experience, and permitting partners to attend the birth. Yet a majority of American mothers in the late twentieth century continued to ask for pain relief; as of 2003, 60 percent of U.S. mothers requested epidural anesthesia during labor. This is not surprising given that research in the physiology of pain in the 1970s and 1980s showed that though Lamaze's methods can reduce discomfort by 30 percent on average, most mothers will still experience significant pain.

Obstetricians most successfully established nearly complete control over reproduction in the United States, especially as professional American medical groups helped to limit and even outlaw the work of midwives in the twentieth century. In Europe, however, midwives remain professionally powerful, fully trained and incorporated in hospital and clinical medicine. At the turn of the twenty-first century, about 75 percent of European births are attended by midwives, who are allowed to intervene medically in ways that only obstetricians are permitted in the United States. For instance, midwives are permitted to perform episiotomies and administer anesthesia in such countries as Great Britain and the Netherlands.

In the eighteenth century, medical men helped transform the experience of birth by establishing specialized "lying-in" hospitals in the British Isles and North America. These hospitals were initially reasonably safe places to give birth because female midwives handled most of the births, and, unlike doctors, they did not perform autopsies or attend other patients with contagious diseases. In the nineteenth century, however, as doctors increasingly attended hospital births, hospital mortality rates rose precipitously. La Maternité, a Paris hospital, for instance, saw the death of more than 180 mothers out of every 1,000 in the early 1860s. The American gynecologist Oliver Wendell Holmes (1809–1894) in 1842 and the Hungarian obstetrician Ignaz Semmelweis in 1847 observed how the disinfecting of birth attendants' hands reduced the spread of puerperal or childbed fever, but unfortunately their recommendations were little heeded until after the 1870s with the advent of modern germ theory.

Until the 1920s and 1930s, the American and European women who gave birth in hospitals were usually poor or objects of charity. Middle-class and elite mothers turned to hospital births beginning in the 1920s, first because of the growing reputation of medicine as an effective scientific discipline, and, second, because rapid urbanization and migration eroded traditional female networks that enabled mothers adequate social support to give birth at home. Paradoxically, however, maternal mortality rates were higher in hospitals than in home births throughout the 1920s and 1930s. Hospital mortality rates dropped only after 1935 with the introduction of sulfonamides and other antibiotics.

From the 1950s onward in the United States, the development of private, for-profit insurance and hospitals, plus the rise in plaintiff lawsuits, all influenced medical and hospital practices with controversial results. For instance, rates of cesarean sections increased dramatically starting in the 1970s, in part because surgical childbirths are more efficient, convenient, and even profitable for practitioners and hospitals than natural childbirths. The raised expectations of parents, combined with large jury settlements in some malpractice cases, have also led obstetricians to intervene in slow or difficult labors earlier and more aggressively. Less than 5 percent of U.S. births were cesareans before the 1970s, but by the 1990s, about 25 percent were. This contrasts with a rate of 15 percent in England and Wales and 40 percent of hospital births in Brazil and Chile in the same period.

At the turn of the twenty-first century, medical debate continues over whether an elective cesarean or vaginal delivery is safer for mother and child. In either case, maternal mortality rates are historically very low, running from 1 to 4 American mothers out of 10,000 dying in the 1990s depending on whether the delivery was vaginal, cesarean, routine, or emergency. Compared with mortality rates of nearly 70 mothers out of 10,000 dying as late as 1920 in the United States, the modern expectation that almost no women will die in childbirth is one of the most profound alterations in all of human history.

Popular Reproductive Beliefs

All cultures have sought to explain the mysteries of reproduction and to control the outcome of pregnancy. There have been thousands of various and contradictory cultural beliefs regarding sex determination, the explanation for fetal abnormalities, and every other imaginable aspect of conception and birth. Many Western beliefs rely on cosmological theories connecting macrocosmic forces such as astrological patterns with the microcosmic and invisible development of the fetus inside the mother's uterus. Other customs were based on the logic of resemblances; for instance in early modern Europe midwives and doctors recommended mothers wear an "eagle's stone"—a little rock that contained loose bits of mineral in the interior that were audible when shaken. This was said to prevent accidents that would lead to miscarriage, to prevent pain, and to help draw the child out during labor.

Most midwifery texts before the nineteenth century argued that a woman had to experience sexual pleasure during intercourse because if ejaculation after an orgasm was required for a man to impregnate a woman, so must a woman reach climax in order to release an egg or other material vital to conception. While such a theory endorsed female sexual pleasure, the idea also made it impossible for a woman to persuade most jurists that she had been raped if she became pregnant, because it was believed conception resulted from her enjoying the sexual encounter.

Both laypeople and the learned tried to explain negative outcomes. One of the most prevalent explanations for birth defects was *maternal imagination*, the belief that a mother's desires or fears could imprint themselves on her unborn fetus. Being startled by a rabbit could result in a baby having a harelip, for example, or strongly craving strawberries could mark the baby with red birthmarks. The most phenomenal case demonstrating the widespread belief in maternal imagination occurred in 1726 when a poor peasant woman persuaded much of the English nation that she had given birth to seventeen rabbits after being startled by a hare during pregnancy.

Reproductive Research

Aristotle, the Hippocratic Corpus, Galen, and other classical authorities offered a rich but contradictory range of theories about gender difference, conception, fetal development, and birth. Many of their ideas, such as the importance of bodily humors, survived among the learned well into the eighteenth-century ENLIGHTENMENT. But beginning with the sixteenth-century Italian Renaissance, artists and anatomists, such as the Belgian anatomist Andreas Vesalius, producer of *De humani corporis fabrica* (1543), focused on revealing the secrets of the human body. Several physiological aspects of conception and birth were discovered, including the discoveries of the fallopian tubes by Gabriele Falloppio in 1561 and of the foramen ovale, a hole between the chambers in the fetal heart that almost always fuses shut by birth, by Giulio Cesara Aranzi in 1557. Yet despite their focus on laying bare human physiology, anatomists were still heavily influenced by ancient theories and popular assumptions, such as the complementarity of the sexes. In Vesalius's 1555 dissections of the female body, he identified what are now called the ovaries as the "female testicles," basing his terminology on the assumption that the sexes were physiologically inside-out versions of each other.

The seventeenth century witnessed a flourishing of research into the beginnings of life and the nature of embryological development. Thanks to technical advances in microscopy, the Dutch naturalist Antoni von Leeuwenhoek and others discovered that male semen was filled with countless tiny, swimming sperm. Leeuwenhoek and his acolytes argued that each sperm cell carried if not a fully formed human, then all of the necessary rudiments of a future human. Although human ova were not actually seen until the nineteenth century, *ovists* contrarily maintained that female eggs housed miniature, fully formed humans. Others argued that both mothers and fathers contributed fundamental reproductive materials that allowed a future child to emerge *epigenetically*. These theorists proposed that living creatures were not preformed in either ova or sperm, but that once an egg was fertilized, unknown processes allowed unformed material to develop incrementally and gradually into different organ systems.

One important area of nineteenth-century research focused on embryological development. Von Baer, who had discovered the ovum in 1827, also observed how different layers developed sequentially in the zygote and embryo, showing how these different "germ layers" gave rise to different organ systems. The most significant developments in reproductive knowledge occurred from the 1890s onward in the burgeoning field of endocrinology, which charted the function of hormones as chemical messengers. Mid-nineteenth-century experiments showed that testes contained a material capable of preventing atrophy of the comb in castrated roosters, and in the 1890s Viennese researchers established the existence of female hormones when they triggered ovulation in spayed rabbits that had been implanted with ovarian tissue. By the 1910s, several researchers uncovered the hormonal changes involved in the female menstrual cycle and reproduction. Between 1923 and 1936 scientists isolated, synthesized, and determined the structure of the various female and male hormones. The discovery of the hormone human chorionic gonadotropin (HCG), which is present in the urine of pregnant females, led to the development of the first reliable pregnancy test (the Ascheim-Zondek test) in 1928.

At the same time that endocrinologists made these foundational discoveries, biologists began penetrating the nucleus of the cell, showing the genetic material and cellular processes of reproduction. Belgian Edouard van Beneden, for instance, demonstrated in 1883 that the fused gametes reduced their chromosome count by half so that the zygote contained the proper amount of genetic material. The most important contribution in this area was that of the Austrian monk Gregor Johann Mendel, whose 1866 work establishing the laws of heredity was rediscovered in 1900.

The Reign of Technology

Midwives and doctors offered advice for centuries to mothers telling them what signs to look for that showed the fetus was developing normally, such as feeling active movement of the fetus from about twenty weeks forward, when it was said to "quicken." Midwives and doctors could also usually determine by feeling a mother's belly the position of a full-term fetus. But the first advance that allowed an attendant to learn more about the fetus in utero was with the application of the French physician René Laënnec's invention of the stethoscope in the 1810s, which the French midwife Marie Anne Victoire Boiven Gillian and the Swiss surgeon François Mayor both independently used to detect the fetal heartbeat at about five months.

Other diagnostic developments included the application of X rays, discovered by the German physicist Wilhelm Conrad Röntgen in 1895, to diagnose the fetal position and detect such abnormalities as spina bifida and anencephaly. In the 1930s, American researchers used X rays to classify a woman's pelvic type and used such information to recommend whether she have a vaginal delivery or a cesarean section. Only in the 1950s did the medical profession recognize the dangers of excessive radiation, especially to the developing fetus, and obstetricians turned toward other diagnostic tools.

In 1958 Ian Donald of Glasgow University introduced ultrasound, a noninvasive and harmless technique used to visualize the fetus. Ultrasound has been routinely used since the 1960s to estimate the size of the fetus, gauge its position, determine whether it has certain abnormalities, and monitor its

heart rate, oxygen intake, and sleep and gasp patterns. In the 1950s, European researchers developed amniocentesis, in which a needle is inserted through the abdominal wall to withdraw amniotic fluid, which can then be examined for its cellular and biochemical content. Among other uses, this technique was used to determine the sex of the fetus beginning in 1953 and to diagnose Down syndrome by 1968. Because of the sharply elevated rates of Down syndrome and other chromosomal defects in pregnancies of mothers thirty-five and older, amniocentesis became routine for this group of women starting in the 1970s. Other prenatal diagnostics include fetoscopy, which involves inserting fiber optical technology in utero to examine the fetus, and chorionic villus sampling, in which tissue from the chorion, which develops into the placenta, is removed and examined for chromosomal abnormalities and sex.

During the second half of the twentieth century, many once-fatal complications began to be routinely treated. For example, mothers whose blood is negative for the rhesus (Rh) factor, but who carry a Rh-positive fetus, produce antigens that threaten the life of any subsequent Rh-positive fetuses; since the 1970s, such women have been treated with anti-D globulin to halt the production of antibodies. Since 1963, surgeons have also been able to perform intrauterine blood transfusions on the fetus, and in the 1980s, several specialists pioneered in utero surgery to repair spina bifida, hydrocephalus, diaphragmatic hernias, urinary tract obstructions, and other complications.

Hospitals have likewise dramatically helped to reduce newborn mortality rates through neonatal intensive care units, the first of which was established in 1960 at Yale-New Haven Hospital in Connecticut. These units have helped save the lives not only of many critically ill full-term newborns but also of extremely premature infants. In 1984 the Baby Doe amendment to the Child Abuse Prevention and Treatment Act was passed by the U.S. Congress and signed into law by President Ronald Reagan, making it illegal for doctors to do less than the maximum to save all neonates, no matter how premature. In 1990, only 40 percent of babies born at twenty-six weeks survived, but by 2000, 80 to 90 percent did, with the majority developing into normal children. Many of these babies have life-threatening respiratory problems, including respiratory distress syndrome (RDS), in which the lungs are too immature to function on their own. Synthetic hormones given to the baby after birth can treat RDS, but researchers also discovered in 1972 that glucocorticoid treatments given to mothers in preterm labor or having elective cesareans could prevent RDS. Thanks to ongoing new medical discoveries, "the edge of viability" has dropped substantially. At the turn of the twenty-first century, even "super-preemies" born before twenty-four weeks are in some cases able to survive, but most can expect enormous and expensive developmental and permanent complications.

Assisted Reproduction

In the 1990s, one-sixth of American couples were estimated to be infertile, that is, unable to conceive successfully without medical or technological intervention. Viable solutions to assist reproduction reach back at least to 1790 when the Scottish anatomist John Hunter performed the first successful case of ARTIFICIAL INSEMINATION. The first use of donated sperm occurred in the nineteenth century, and the concept of a sperm bank was developed in 1866, although the technology to preserve human semen was introduced only in 1953. By 1995, approximately five hundred thousand children had been born through artificial insemination in the United States, and the majority of these were conceived via donor insemination.

Women's fertility problems, such as blocked fallopian tubes, are far more difficult to remedy than male impotence or low sperm count, both of which can often be resolved through artificial insemination. The key breakthrough for women's infertility occurred in 1978 when Patrick Steptoe and Robert Edwards of Britain announced the birth of the first "test-tube baby," Louise Brown, conceived through IN VITRO FERTILIZATION (IVF). IVF involves retrieving mature ova from a woman who has often been given hormones to induce the production of several ova. In IVF the retrieved eggs are fertilized and kept in a laboratory for two to five days and then implanted in the uterus. By 1991 the pregnancy rate per retrieval was less than 20 percent in IVF, compared to an 80 percent success rate with artificial insemination. In the United States, for each attempt at IVF, medical, laboratory, and travel expenses typically ranged in the 1990s from $4,000 to tens of thousands of dollars, and in a significant proportion of cases in which implantation succeeds, the procedure results in multiples. Sometimes, especially in cases of triplets and more, parents choose "selective reduction"—that is, the termination of some of the pregnancies, an obviously highly controversial aspect of assisted reproduction.

As semen can be donated, so can ova, at least since 1983. The uterus also can be donated through surrogate motherhood. In biological SURROGACY, a woman agrees to use her ova, which are fertilized through IVF, to carry the resulting fetus to term, and to surrender the child to another individual or couple. In gestational surrogacy, a woman carries a fetus that is conceived from another woman's ovum through IVF. By 1993, approximately four thousand babies had been born through surrogacy in the United States since the late 1970s.

Birth Control and Abortion

While many couples have sought medical and technological means to reproduce successfully, so too have women and men sought for millennia to limit their fertility. For example, the ancient Egyptians used various herbal concoctions placed on vaginal pessaries during intercourse to block sperm from reaching the uterus. But the most dramatic leaps in manufacturing widely available, effective birth control did not occur until the nineteenth century with the vulcanization of rubber, used to make condoms and vaginal barriers including cervical diaphragms. Research in endocrinology in the twentieth century led to the contraceptive pill, made commercially available in 1960. Other contraceptive methods include injected and implanted hormones, introduced in the 1980s, and intrauterine devices (IUDs), in use since the 1960s. Permanent forms of contraception, including vasectomies in males and tubal ligations in females, were developed in the nineteenth century but did not become widely and electively chosen until the 1960s.

In scholarship published in the late twentieth century, Janet Farrell Brodie and Angus McLaren both argued that birth control existed on a continuum with early term abortion until the nineteenth century in the United States and Europe. Evidence suggests that herbal abortifacients, violent exercise, and even mechanical means were used for many centuries, in many societies, and among all classes and religions to terminate pregnancies, especially in the first trimester of pregnancy. Abortifacients were widely discussed (often in condemning detail that would enable their use) and also advertised as medications to release "obstructions" from the seventeenth century onward.

Demographic data of the dramatically declining size of nineteenth-century middle-class families in the United States, the British Isles, and France strongly suggests that married couples were turning to abortion when contraception failed. Popular belief until the nineteenth century maintained that though a woman might apprehend that she was pregnant in the first month or so, the fetus was not really "alive" until the moment of "quickening," which occurred at approximately four months into the pregnancy. Medical, legal, and even some religious texts well into the eighteenth century also endorsed this position that fetal life really began only once the mother herself experienced quickening, implying that the termination of an early pregnancy was not morally equivalent to a later term abortion.

Though abortion was never officially condoned, legislatures began criminalizing abortion for the first time in the nineteenth century, beginning with the British government's making abortion a statutory felony in 1803. In the United States, laws against abortion were passed piecemeal through state legislatures, and by 1900 all states had come to prohibit the practice. Historians of the subject have widely argued that the male medical profession drove antiabortion legislation as they sought to gain control over family's reproductive health and marginalize "irregular" practitioners—"quacks" and midwives. In so doing, they saw themselves as moral arbiters for society. The most stringent laws against abortion were enforced in Nazi Germany and Vichy France in the early 1940s, when providing abortions became a capital offense.

In the twentieth century, some advocates pushed for women's expanded access to abortion, first for reasons of physical and mental health. For instance, in 1927 German women could have abortions for therapeutic reasons (although this law was repealed under the Nazis), and some other European nations also passed similar legislation from the 1930s onward. In the 1960s several feminist groups, Protestant churches, and medical practitioners lobbied to repeal antiabortion laws in the United States, and by 1973, four states and the District of Columbia permitted elective abortions.

In 1973 the U.S. Supreme Court decided the landmark case of *Roe v. Wade*, with the majority stating that the right of privacy included a woman's right to abortion in the first trimester. From 1973 forward, states passed a wide range of laws that generally further expanded most adult women's access to abortion, for instance in later trimesters. Yet both Congress and certain states passed laws that limited many women's practical access to abortion, including mandatory waiting periods and parental consent for women younger than eighteen. The Hyde Amendment, first passed by Congress in 1976, annually prohibited federal funding of abortion, except in cases of rape or INCEST. In Europe, access to abortion was liberalized in most countries from the 1970s forward, but by the turn of the twenty-first century, most of these countries limited abortion by request to the first trimester or sixteen weeks of pregnancy.

In the United States, *Roe v. Wade* was deeply controversial, immediately leading to, on the one hand, advocates of abortion pushing states and the federal government to expand abortion rights, and, on the other, opponents lobbying for a repeal of abortion rights. In western Europe, a "prolife" movement has had little cultural or legal impact. But in the United States, both sides of the abortion debate have affected access to abortion, as in the case of RU-486, or mifepristone, a hormonal antiprogestin that halts gestation and is designed to be taken within nine weeks of the first day of the last menstrual period. Invented in France in 1980, RU-486 became available in France, Britain, and Sweden in 1989. RU-486 was not approved by the U.S. Food and Drug Administration until September 2000 after twelve years of strong lobbying by both sides.

A historical analysis of reproductive topics does not necessarily resolve these modern debates, but the varieties of accepted practices across time ultimately undermine any claim that there is a transcendent truth about the reproductive body or the ethics of reproduction. For instance, the high frequency of abortion for centuries challenges claims among late-twentieth-century opponents that the practice results from the rise of modern feminism and the secularized state. On the other hand, that abortion was widely condemned not only by the church and the state, but also by early modern midwives and nineteenth-century feminists, challenges some

assumptions among present-day pro-choice advocates that pro-life attitudes have been bred exclusively by the modern, male-dominated medical professions or by twentieth- and twenty-first-century conservative, special-interest groups.

See also: **Fertility Drugs; Obstetrics and Midwifery; Sonography.**

BIBLIOGRAPHY

Blank, Robert, and Janna C. Merrick. 1995. *Human Reproduction, Emerging Technologies, and Conflicting Rights.* Washington, DC: CQ Press.

Brodie, Janet Farrell. 1994. *Contraception and Abortion in Nineteenth-Century America.* Ithaca, NY: Cornell University Press.

Cadden, Joan. 1993. *Meanings of Sex Difference in the Middle Ages.* Cambridge, UK: Cambridge University Press.

Childbirth by Choice Trust. 1995. *Abortion in Law, History, and Religion,* rev. ed. Toronto: Childbirth by Choice Trust. Also available from <www.cbctrust.com/abortion.html>.

Clarke, Adele E. 1998. *Disciplining Reproduction: Modernity, American Life Sciences, and "the Problems of Sex."* Berkeley: University of California Press.

Cody, Lisa. 1992. "The Doctors in Labour; Or a New Whim Wham from Guildford." *Gender and History* 4, no. 2 (summer): 175–196.

DeLacy, Margaret. 1989. "Puerperal Fever in Eighteenth-Century Britain." *Bulletin of the History of Medicine* 63, no. 4 (winter): 521–556.

Gélis, Jacques. 1991. *History of Childbirth: Fertility, Pregnancy, and Birth in Early Modern Europe.* Trans. Rosemary Morris. Boston: Northeastern University Press.

Gould, Stephen Jay. 1996. *The Mismeasure of Man,* rev. and expanded ed. New York: Norton.

Jacob, François. 1976. *The Logic of Life: A History of Heredity.* Trans. Betty E. Spillmann. New York: Vintage.

James, William H. 1987. "The Human Sex Ratio." *Human Biology* 59, no. 5 (October): 721–752.

Laqueur, Thomas. 1990. *Making Sex: Body and Gender from the Greeks to Freud.* Cambridge, MA: Harvard University Press.

Leavitt, Judith Walzer. 1986. *Brought to Bed: Childbearing in America, 1750–1950.* New York: Oxford University Press.

Lee, H. S. J., ed. 2000. *Dates in Obstetrics and Gynecology.* New York: Parthenon Group.

Maienschein, Jane. 1984. "What Determines Sex? A Study of Converging Approaches, 1880–1916." *Isis* 75: 457–480.

McLaren, Angus. 1983. *Sexuality and Social Order: The Debate over the Fertility of Workers and Women in France, 1770–1920.* New York: Holmes and Meier.

McLaren, Angus. 1984. *Reproductive Rituals: The Perception of Fertility in England from the Sixteenth to the Nineteenth Century.* London: Methuen.

Melzack, Ronald. 1984. "The Myth of Painless Childbirth." *Pain* 19: 321–337. Reprinted in *Childbirth: Vol. 3. Methods and Folklore,* ed. Philip K. Wilson. New York: Garland Publishing, 1996.

Mitford, Jessica. 1992. *The American Way of Birth.* New York: Dutton.

Morton, Leslie T., and Robert J. Moore. 1997. *A Chronology of Medicine and Related Sciences.* Aldershot, UK: Ashgate.

Moscucci, Ornella. 1990. *The Science of Woman: Gynaecology and Gender in England, 1800–1929.* Cambridge, UK: Cambridge University Press.

Nathanielsz, Peter W. 1995. "The Role of Basic Science in Preventing Low Birth Weight." *Future of Children* 5, no. 1: 57–70. Also available from <www.futureofchildren.org/>.

Pinto-Correia, Clara. 1997. *The Ovary of Eve: Egg and Sperm and Preformation.* Chicago: University of Chicago Press.

Porter, Roy. 1997. *The Greatest Benefit to Mankind: A Medical History of Humanity.* New York: Norton.

Rhodes, Philip. 1995. *A Short History of Clinical Midwifery: The Development of Ideas in the Professional Management of Childbirth.* Cheshire, UK: Books for Midwives Press.

Walton, John, Paul B. Beeson, and Ronald Bodley Scott, eds. 1986. *The Oxford Companion to Medicine.* 2 vols. Oxford, UK: Oxford University Press.

Wilson, Adrian. 1995. *The Making of Man-Midwifery: Childbirth in England, 1660–1770.* Cambridge, MA: Harvard University Press.

Wilson, Philip K., ed. 1996. *Childbirth: Changing Ideas and Practices in Britain and America, 1600 to the Present.* 5 vols. New York: Garland Publishing.

LISA FORMAN CODY

Confirmation

For many Christians, confirmation is one of the three rites of initiation which incorporate an individual into the Body of Christ—that is, membership in the Christian Church (Acts 8:15–16). The other two are BAPTISM and Eucharist. The purpose of confirmation is to confer the presence of the Holy Spirit into the life of the child or adult. The practice of administering confirmation immediately after infant baptism was of ancient origin. Throughout the early church, and still today in the Eastern churches, infants received the three sacrament of baptism, confirmation, and the Eucharist within a few minutes of each other, and in that order. This tradition emphasized the innocence and equality of children with adults, in the eyes of the Church, by granting them full participation in the liturgy. Children did not have to prove their worthiness to receive the sacraments by mastering the catechism or by testifying to their belief in Christian dogma when they attained the age of discretion (i.e., seven). The early Church identified full participation with the spiritual maturity conferred by baptismal regeneration. Membership in the Church was spiritual. It had nothing to do with age or intellectual and physical maturity. Confirmation as an episcopal rite was characterized by the laying on of hands and chrismation, which involved the application of chrism, a consecrated oil. The bishop anointed the forehead with chrism and recited these words: "Be sealed with the gift of the Holy Spirit."

Throughout its early history, the Catholic Church did not assign any definite age for the reception of confirmation. Beginning in 1563, however, the Council of Trent determined that twelve was the ideal age for conferring confirmation, and that no child under the age of seven should be ad-mitted to that sacrament. The year 1563 was thus a watershed in the history of sacramental theology. With a simple decree, confirmation became one part of a trilogy of sacraments (confirmation, penance, and Eucharist) that was henceforth identified with the age of discretion. It is reasonable, therefore, to expect that many practicing Catholics starting in the late sixteenth century received penance and the Eucharist before they received confirmation at the age of twelve. In effect, the Council of Trent admitted that the order of the sacraments could be altered and that the change reflected its changing attitude toward children. Instead of associating confirmation with infancy, Trent saw it as the sacrament of discretion. Candidates for confirmation were now expected to display a measure of spiritual maturity. They were asked to profess publicly their own commitment to Christ and to his Church, fortified by the seven gifts of the Holy Spirit: wisdom, understanding, knowledge, counsel, fortitude, purity, and fear of the Lord. Trent's decision to postpone confirmation until prepuberty may have been influenced partly by the views of sixteenth-century reformers. For most Protestant reformers, spiritual readiness was equated with physical maturity. Their rites of confirmation and the Eucharist became in effect twin rites of PUBERTY—a public acknowledgment that the physically mature Christian was also spiritually mature and morally responsible.

Martin Luther rejected the idea that confirmation was a true sacrament and referred to it as a "sacramental ceremony." He saw it as a preparation for the reception of the Eucharist and as a sign of the remission of sins. For Protestants and the Orthodox, confirmation always precedes the conferral of the Eucharist, but for most Roman Catholics, it does not. The age at which confirmation is conferred on children varies among Christian denominations today, but it is most often conferred during ADOLESCENCE.

See also: **Catholicism; Christian Thought, Early; Communion, First; Protestant Reformation.**

BIBLIOGRAPHY

DeMolen, Richard L. 1975. "Childhood and the Sacraments in the Sixteenth Century." *Archiv fuer Reformationsgeschichte* 66: 49–71.

Marsh, Thomas A. 1984. *Gift of Community: Baptism and Confirmation.* Wilmington, DE: M. Glazier.

Marsh, Thomas A. 1990. "Confirmation." In *The New Dictionary of Sacramental Worship,* ed. Peter E. Fink. Collegeville, MN: The Liturgical Press.

Whitaker, Edward C. 1970. *Documents of the Baptismal Liturgy,* rev. ed. London: S.P.C.K.

RICHARD L. DEMOLEN

Construction Toys

Construction toys have been popular with generations of children. The underlying principle is that construction is basically a matter of assembly: a series of basic components are provided, designed to allow children to create objects of their own design that can later be taken apart again and rebuilt as something different. Construction thus becomes creative, and the child is in control.

Toys have become an essential asset in the pedagogical repertoire. Among the first were FRIEDRICH FROEBEL's "gifts," which were widely distributed in Europe and North America in the second half of the nineteenth century. Froebel was inspired by JEAN-JACQUES ROUSSEAU and the Romantic notion that children have an innate learning instinct which drives them to play and explore. Froebel's gifts were simple, unpainted geometric shapes, and the play sessions were conducted under adult instruction. In the early 1900s another pioneer, MARIA MONTESSORI, developed play material—blocks of various kinds and sheets or plates of wood, stone, iron, wool, or silk—that cultivated children's senses. The materials were as different as possible, in order to train all five of the human senses.

Construction toys gradually became commercialized, and enjoyed widespread popularity during the twentieth century, assisted by a market-oriented toy industry. Various types of material have been used for creating construction toys and models. Anchor Building Blocks were stone blocks popular in the early twentieth century. Structures were built of real stone according to the drawings of architects. The child became an apprentice and—as the toy became more difficult—journeyman, master, and grand master. The stone building blocks reflected long-standing craft traditions.

Great buildings also inspired toys. A construction such as the Eiffel Tower could be beautifully copied with Frank Hornby's iron construction kits. Initially, his invention was called Mechanics Made Easy, but in 1907 the name was changed to Meccano. The manuals were written in correct technical language. The basic system was made up of flat metal strips of different lengths, perforated with holes. Nuts and bolts were used to join them. Meccano developed children's imagination, dexterity, and sense of beauty, offering both functionality and pure, cool engineering beauty, a reviewer wrote in 1934.

Meccano attracted competitors. In the United States, Erector, a master builder set, was launched in 1913 by Dr. A. C. Gilbert, who wanted to teach boys the principles of construction and engineering. Numerous other metal construction sets reached the market. To a greater or lesser degree they were copies of Meccano (whose phenomenal success can be compared only with that of the LEGO Company and its little plastic brick, introduced in 1958). These construction kits were designed for older boys, and there was a clear segregation of the sexes: girls were not expected to play with them. It took precision, systematic thinking, and manual dexterity to put the many small parts together, and tiny,

LEGO's simple, colorful plastic modular building system, first introduced in 1955 and originally sold with no set rules or instructions, inspired children's imagination and gave them the freedom to build whatever they wanted. The Advertising Archive Ltd.

controlled movements. The toys disciplined and marshalled boisterous boys.

Lincoln Logs—a robust log cabin set—was marketed in the United States in 1920 by John Lloyd Wright, son of the famous architect. Sets could be used for building log cabins and forts. In the 1920s and 1930s the toy market was flooded with wooden building kits. Carpenters and joiners began making toys, and the market was filled with simple, well-made wooden playthings. Neutral components came in a wide variety of timbers, and advanced sets were available with special parts for recreating well-known buildings, houses, or skyscrapers. They were complete architectural models that allowed children to create a scaled-down version of the modern world. Contemporary architectural ideas and principles set the pace.

After World War II there was a decisive shift of perspective from the adult's viewpoint to the child's. The child was no longer expected to adapt to the adult world: Reforming educators took the child as their point of reference. Their aim was to liberate children's creative and natural abilities. In Denmark in the 1950s, highlighting children's own creative expression was emphasized, and developmental psychologists focused on play. The toy manufacturer Godtfred Kirk Christiansen evolved a system of play materials aimed at developing the imagination and creativity of boys and girls. The Danish wooden-toy manufacturer LEGO, influenced by the desire for attractive, colorful, simple, and hygienic playthings, had begun experimenting with plastics. The LEGO System of Play, based on the forerunner of the LEGO brick, was launched in 1955. The construction bricks quickly became recognized as an excellent toy to spark creativity and imagination. The simple, colorful modular building system with its open-ended potential brought to generations of children all over the world the freedom to build what they wanted with the bricks with the knowledge that whatever they made was right.

It can be said that children are getting older faster in the twenty-first century, and traditional toys are slipping from their hands earlier. The construction toy has its roots in a tangible world, the world of the craftsman and factory worker, the world of manual values. But ideas are the material of the visual world in a computer age. Still, the idea that children are designing their own virtual world in 3-D that they can build and then tear down does not exclude the theory that when children construct things out in the world, they construct knowledge inside their heads.

See also: **Theories of Play; Toys.**

BIBLIOGRAPHY

Ariès, Philippe. 1962. *Centuries of Childhood: A Social History of Family Life.* Trans. Robert Baldick. New York: Knopf.

Cunningham, Hugh. 1995. *Children and Childhood in Western Society since 1500.* New York: Longman.

INGE AAEN

Consumer Culture

In the West, childhood and child rearing are closely linked to the rise of consumer culture. Increased household wealth often freed children from work and harsh discipline, leaving time for PLAY and increasing adult toleration. Beginning in the eighteenth century, consumer goods redefined relationships between adults and children, especially when parents used playthings and books to indirectly guide children's behavior and expectations. Gifts to children were a key to the privatization and growth of symbolic and fantasy goods that displaced public, often religious, celebrations and rituals. By the sixteenth century in Europe, festival goods (like Christmas crèches) were miniaturized, introduced to domestic displays, and eventually transformed into play sets for children. By the eighteenth century in western Europe, children were treasured for how they expressed wonder and evoked emotional renewal when adults gave them TOYS and other pleasures. New children's goods (special clothing, FURNITURE, books, and playthings) in nurseries enveloped middle-class childhood in a cocoon of protected learning and imagination.

Modern Consumer Culture

In the nineteenth century, children's consumer culture shifted from training goods (like blocks and moralizing books) to playful and fantasy toys and stories. By the mid-nineteenth century, candy, toys, and books had become part of a new regimen of positive reinforcement for parent-pleasing behavior. A new indulgence reflected parents' attempts to relieve their offspring from their own austere upbringings and to display their new wealth. Fantasy entered into children's consumer culture with the emergence of stories like LEWIS CARROLL's *Alice in Wonderland* (1865) and J. M. BARRIE's *Peter Pan* (1904) with no or little didactic purpose, which celebrated children's special imagination. Although parents continued to supply most of children's consumer goods, working-class boys especially were able to purchase sweets and cheap magazines and books as well as attend plays with earnings from running errands, selling newspapers, and other petty jobs. In the 1870s middle-class children found the opportunity to own toys and gadgets offered as premiums for young readers who sold magazine subscriptions.

By the 1920s, adults bought playrooms, SANDBOXES, and swing sets to give their offspring autonomy and protected play. Pianos were purchased to raise children's cultural skills and Kodak snapshot and movie cameras were sold with the promise of capturing memory of the "delightful" early stage of childhood. Children, as representatives of change and the future, were often given commercial fads. The TEDDY BEAR craze of 1906 was perhaps the best early example of a pattern that would be repeated over and over again in the twentieth century—the celebration of the new through a consumer craze.

The emerging children's commercial culture was restricted to the comfortable classes. Working-class or African-American children even in 1900 were frequently finished with childhood by age ten. And many American children, especially in rural areas, had few manufactured toys, books, or other goods. These children used cans for "footballs" and played games like hopscotch, preserving traditional games and songs for generations. Still, the long-term trend was clear: when children were removed from the labor market, they became an essential part of a new market—the market of consumers—as parents spent their money to express the "pricelessness" of their children. By the 1910s, child experts began to advocate the weekly allowance to teach money management, but also to grant the child the right to "little pleasures" of personally selected trinkets, toys, or candy. Ads in children's magazines that invoked boys' longings for air rifles, bicycles, and TOY TRAINS insisted that children knew best in choosing the right purchases. While girls' access to ad-driven consumer culture lagged behind boys', they too connected to the emerging consumer culture when they made "paper dolls" from their mothers' fashion magazine ads. Parents also gave daughters DOLLS that featured store-bought and fashionable clothing sets. This was in contrast to nineteenth-century "sewing dolls" that required the girl to learn how to make her doll's own clothes. In any case, dolls, like many other aspects of children's play culture, were increasingly marketed directly to children rather than sold to parents via adult-oriented magazine ads and catalogs, as in the past.

While the GREAT DEPRESSION and war years slowed this process, the post-1945 BABY BOOM created instant markets for toys and layettes. Newfound affluence allowed parents to make their children the focal point for their spending. Despite moralists' complaints, parents gave to children as much to isolate and teach as to indulge them. This seeming contradiction is explained by the fact that many children's products were designed for indoor home use (such as games, books, records) and thus provided adults with the means to monitor their young and to give them enjoyable alternatives to wandering the streets.

Commercialization of Holidays

Throughout the nineteenth and twentieth centuries, children's consumer culture remained closely linked to traditional seasonal rituals, even as they were commercialized. Holidays, once associated with community identity and the reversal of authority roles, gradually became times of celebrating childhood and "gifting" children. In the United States, Christmas, long either ignored for reasons of religious purity or enjoyed in boisterous communal exchanges of food and drink, was identified with childhood and consumer goods by the mid-nineteenth century. The young symbolized the intimacy and innocence of family against the increasingly impersonal society that surrounded it. The child became a visible reminder of the adult's own youth and the hope of the future. In effect, money earned in the market was transformed through the child's presents into a sentiment of family life. Gradually, Santa Claus became the symbol of unrestricted giving to children. The story of his home at the North Pole, where elves, not sweatshop workers, made the toys, disguised the market origins of these gifts.

Other holidays, especially HALLOWEEN, long associated with rough communal practices like vandalism and intimidating demands for food and drink, were tamed when they were "given" to children in trick-or-treating in the late 1930s, a late tradition that stimulated the candy industry in the United States. VACATIONS too became an occasion for spending around and for children. Seasonal gifts of ice cream cones in the 1900s broadened to family vacations by the 1950s. Disneyland (opened in 1955) transformed the plebeian amusement park, which had been mostly patronized by young singles, into a middle-class family RITE OF PASSAGE, a setting for parent–child bonding through spending on rides and souvenirs.

Children's Control of Spending

Spending for children gradually became spending by children. In the nineteenth century, candy and small playthings and cheap novelties were available on the street to older children, and the introduction of manufactured candy bars and soda in the 1890s further increased the range of children's expressive spending. Children's demands, fueled by exposure to ads and store displays, helped shape consumer decisions, and merchandisers had learned by the 1910s that it was relatively easy to sell to the child who was not constrained by experience. Few children were able to purchase toys with their own money. But toy and candy companies recognized that children could influence parents' spending, and from the 1910s ads in children's magazines often brazenly encouraged this. Moreover, merchandisers relied upon children to teach their old-fashioned parents about new household products.

Media played a major role in shaping children's consumer culture, beginning with illustrated stories and comic strips which introduced characters whose images appeared in dolls, games, and toys from the 1890s. This process accelerated with sound MOVIES. In the 1930s, DISNEY characters from the cartoons were pictured or embodied in thousands of dolls, toys, lamps, watches, and toothbrushes. By 1937, Disney had mastered the art of tie-in marketing by selling Snow White and the Seven Dwarfs merchandise even before the movie appeared. By the early 1930s, RADIO advertisers in children's programs used premiums of toys and other novelties to increase sales of food and household products. Still, merchandisers were very careful not to offend parents by advertising for toys or sweets directly to children. Repeatedly moralists tried to ban children from the new commercial media. Beginning in 1909, city and state governments prohibited movies deemed dangerous to children and even banned children from exhibition halls. In reaction to violence and sexuality in COMIC BOOKS, moralists attempted to censor or even ban certain types of these books in the early 1950s.

Children increasingly were targeted after World War II when children's marketing specialists like Eugene Gilbert realized their potential spending power. Cereal makers found profit in sugared cereals designed for the childish sweet tooth and package designers learned to make shampoo and other containers in the shape of cartoon characters to attract the child's eye. Most important, television became a pipeline into the child's imagination when advertisers found that children responded to ads by the age of three, thus separating the parent's consumer culture from the child's. With the debut of the *Mickey Mouse Club* in 1955, cereal and toy ads began to be designed especially for children, leading to a continuous marketing barrage. By the second half of the 1960s, it is estimated that as a group children were annually spending two billion dollars on their own and influencing billions more in parental spending.

Childhood became linked with a vast interconnected industry built on licensed characters that encompassed movies, TV shows, video games, toys, and clothing. Moviemakers often joined forces with toy and fast food companies to offer novelty toys in fast food meals, making the commercial fad a nearly continuous part of childhood. Video games, in the mid-1970s directed toward teens and young adults, were marketed to children in the late 1970s with Atari, and by Nintendo and others by the late 1980s. Media-generated marketing to children created "additive" consumption, where the young were encouraged to accumulate whole "sets" of dolls, toys, books, and videos. This marketing became ever more sophisticated with the *Star Wars* trilogy (1977–1983). TV cartoon series based on toy and doll lines proliferated in the 1980s.

Children's goods became part of a new era of fast capitalism—the increasingly rapid shift from one product line to another on a virtually global scale. Toys and other children's products functioned less as vehicles connecting generations or linking past and future in the way that parental gifts to children once had done. Parents and other adults complained about an ephemeral consumer culture that took time from developmental activities, isolated children from reality in a fantasy world of fun, and seemed to expose the young prematurely to sex and violence. But increasingly, children's consumer culture was part of a separate fantasy world, which children and the merchandisers alone understood and which was designed to stimulate unending desire for more goods—even as it provided children with a measure of autonomy.

See also: **Advertising; Child Stars; Economics and Children in Western Societies: The Consumer Economy; Indoor Games; Media, Childhood and the; Television; Theories of Childhood.**

BIBLIOGRAPHY

Buckingham, David. 2000. *After the Death of Childhood: Growing Up in the Age of Electronic Media.* Cambridge, UK: Polity Press.

Cross, Gary. 1997. *Kids' Stuff: Toys and the Changing World of American Childhood.* Cambridge, MA: Harvard University Press.

Gilbert, James. 1996. *A Cycle of Outrage: America's Reaction to the Juvenile Delinquent in the 1950s.* New York: Oxford University Press.

Gillis, John. 1996. *A World of Their Own Making: Myth, Ritual, and the Quest for Family Values.* New York: Basic Books.

Jenkins, Henry. 1998. *Children's Culture Reader.* New York: New York University Press.

Nasaw, David. 1986. *Children of the City: At Work and at Play.* New York: Oxford University Press.

Seiter, Ellen. 1993. *Sold Separately: Children and Parents in Consumer Culture.* New Brunswick, NJ: Rutgers University Press.

Zelizer, Viviana. 1985. *Pricing the Priceless Child.* New York: Basic Books.

GARY CROSS

Contagious Diseases

Death in early childhood was a heartbreaking fact of life everywhere until the early twentieth century. Gravestones from the nineteenth century and earlier commemorate the death before the end of their first decade of life of between a quarter and half of all the children born into most families. Nearly all died of contagious diseases.

Definition of Contagious Disease

Contagious means infectious by direct contact, but in common usage the word usually applies to diseases that are highly infectious and dangerous, implying something more serious than a common cold (although colds are among the most contagious of all diseases). In his 1548 *De Contagione* the Italian monk Girolamo Fracastorius identified three modes of contagion: by direct intimate contact (as with sexually transmitted diseases); by "droplets" (as in coughing, sneezing, and talking); and by contaminated articles (such as clothing and kitchen utensils). Other modes of contagion that Fracastorius did not recognize include transmission by polluted water or contaminated milk or food and transmission by insect vectors such as mosquitoes.

The Nature, Origin, Ecology, and Evolution of Contagious Diseases

The agents, called pathogens, that cause contagious diseases vary in size and complexity from ultramicroscopic viruses, microscopic bacteria, and single-celled protozoa like the malaria parasite, to parasitic worms up to several meters long. The survival of pathogens depends on their ability to invade humans or other hosts, in which they are nourished and reproduce, and from which they can spread to new hosts. This capability is determined by biological, ecological, and behavioral factors, all of which render children especially vulnerable, as discussed below. Pathogens flourish at the expense of the health, and perhaps the life, of the human host. The most successful pathogens do not kill their hosts but merely make them ill while producing symptoms conducive to the pathogens' spread to fresh hosts. The viruses that cause the common cold are particularly successful in this respect.

When the world warmed up after the last Ice Age (i.e., about 10,000 years ago), human ancestors discovered how to domesticate animals for food, milk, and clothing, and how to plant and harvest crops. These discoveries made possible the transition from nomadic hunter-gatherers to settled agriculturalists, and transformed human communities forever. Brief generation times and prodigious reproductive rates enabled some microorganisms that had previously affected only animals to evolve into human pathogens, aided by the increasingly close and frequent contacts between humans and their domesticated animals. In this way some bacteria and viruses became human pathogens for the first time. This probably was how measles, smallpox, influenza, and tuberculosis originated as contagious human diseases. Some important pathogens developed survival mechanisms involving humans and other creatures—dogs, sheep, cattle, pigs, mosquitoes, ticks, freshwater snails, etc. The relationship of humans and mosquitoes to water set the stage for the evolutionary origin of malaria, which has caused enormous misery and innumerable deaths, mostly of children, since before the dawn of history. Similar ecological connections between humans, water, and various other living creatures led to the evolution of schistosomiasis and parasitic infestations with several kinds of worms. Archeological discoveries have revealed evidence that some of the great scourges of humankind—including smallpox, tuberculosis, malaria, and schistosomiasis—date from neolithic times, 10,000 to 15,000 years ago. Other diseases, including measles, influenza, typhus, and yellow fever, arose more recently, and the process continues. In the final quarter of the twentieth century, more than thirty new contagious diseases emerged and the pathogens that cause them were identified. Many of the newly emergent diseases are deadly—including HIV/AIDS, Lassa fever, Ebola, and Marburg disease and several other viral hemorrhagic fevers—and a few are not usually deadly but are unpleasant, like legionnaires disease and Lyme disease. Children are the main victims of many of these new diseases.

The development of agriculture ensured reliable food supplies, and this led to a population surge. Little clusters of families and clans grew into towns and cities that were the essential prerequisite for the rise of civilization—religions, laws, arts and culture, science, and literature. But increasing population density and a closer relationship of humans to domesticated animals such as pigs, sheep, cattle, and goats, transformed ecosystems, shaped the evolution of microorganisms, and increased the risk of transmission of pathogens.

In medieval times, cities and towns consisted mainly of ramshackle dwellings resembling the shanty towns surrounding modern cities in low-income countries. Domestic refuse, kitchen waste, and human and animal excreta were often scattered indiscriminately in places where children played. These conditions provided a favorable habitat for innumerable pests—flies, cockroaches, rats—which contribute to the transmission of several contagious diseases. Most people seldom bathed and changed their clothes infrequently, so they and their clothes were usually filthy and infested with vermin, a haven for lice and fleas—the vectors for two deadly diseases, typhus and plague. Pollution of water with human and animal excreta led to incessant outbreaks of contagious gastrointestinal diseases. Infectious diarrhea, spread by fecal contamination of drinking water or food, became even more prevalent as human settlements grew ever larger in the absence of adequate sanitary measures, reaching a peak at the time of the great cholera EPIDEMICS in the rapidly expanding industrial cities of nineteenth-century Europe and America. Pools of stagnant water as well as the rivers and lakes that attract human settlements provide breeding sites for mosquitoes, which are an intermediate host for malaria parasites. Malaria was endemic, with occasional epidemic flare-ups

The Sick Child (c. 1660), Gabriel Metsu. Prior to the era of antibiotics and reliable vaccines, even seemingly minor illnesses could result in death. The parents of a sick child would have been keenly aware of the transience and fragility of life. © Rijksmuseum Amsterdam.

throughout much of Europe and America, especially in the Mississippi River valley, until early in the twentieth century. Different species of mosquitoes transmitted other deadly contagious diseases—yellow fever, dengue, viral hemorrhagic fevers, viral encephalitis. Children were the principal victims of all these diseases.

As human settlements expanded and spread throughout the world, people came together in ever greater numbers. Increasing population density, trade, commerce, wars, and conquest led to frequent contacts among strangers. Many who survived the initial attack of contagious diseases acquired immunity, which protected them on subsequent exposure. But rising population density did not necessarily help to enhance immunity. On the contrary, it facilitated epidemic and pandemic spread of diseases, notably of those associated with lice and fleas, typhus and plague. Commerce and European exploration from the fifteenth to the nineteenth centuries led to increasingly frequent contact among people whose habitats were far apart and whose resistance to contagious diseases, because of prior exposures that conferred some inherited immunity, were very different. The consequences for those with no prior exposure were often disastrous. European conquests and colonization of the Americas were assisted by lethal epidemics of measles, smallpox,

МАТЕРИ, НЕ ЦЕЛУЙТЕ РЕБЕНКА В ГУБЫ и НЕ ДАВАЙТЕ НИКОМУ ЦЕЛОВАТЬ ВАШИХ ДЕТЕЙ!

Болезни, передающиеся через поцелуи:- ДИФТЕРИТ, СИФИЛИС, ИНФЛЮЭНЦА, ТУБЕРКУЛЕЗ И ДР.

"Mothers, don't kiss children on the lips and don't let anyone kiss your children!" reads the text of a Soviet postcard from the 1920s. State authorities commissioned posters and prints in their campaign to stop the transmission of contagious diseases, such as influenza, syphilis, and diphtheria, which were prevalent among the peasant population. © Rykoff Collection/CORBIS.

and tuberculosis, all of which had far higher death rates among the indigenous peoples of the Americas than among their European colonizers. Smallpox decimated the Aztecs, facilitating the Spanish conquest. Measles killed an estimated 90 percent of the people of Fiji in a single epidemic.

The Heightened Vulnerability of Children

Children have always been more vulnerable than adults to infection with most contagious diseases, for several reasons. Children are innately affectionate and undiscriminating in hugging and kissing playmates, PETS, and others. Young children, and toddlers in particular, explore their environment in part by tasting it—this is an inherent behavioral characteristic of all small children. Inevitably these behaviors expose children to frequent and repeated invasion by infectious pathogens of every kind. Most children are born with a partial immunity to common infections acquired from maternal antibodies and reinforced by additional antibodies in

breast milk. But this acquired immunity wanes when children are weaned, so by the time children are two to three years old, resistance to common contagious diseases is often low or nonexistent. This explains why young children have always been more prone to contagious diseases than adults, since adults are those who survive infections in childhood and acquire some immunity.

Malnutrition, which has always been common, impairs children's immune responses, making it more likely that infection can overwhelm their bodily defenses more rapidly than those of adults. Children's respiratory systems are smaller than adults'; their respiratory passages are narrower and more readily blocked by inflammatory swelling and exudates of mucus. All these factors contributed to the high risk of a fatal outcome when children were attacked by contagious diseases in the centuries before development of protective vaccines and modern treatment methods.

Varieties of Contagious Diseases

The contagious diseases that have afflicted children and infants throughout history can be classified according to their mode of spread and means and route of invading the human body.

1. Diseases spread by the fecal-oral route are transmitted by polluted water or contaminated food, milk, and so forth. They include several varieties of acute gastroenteritis that are characterized by diarrhea and vomiting. One of these diseases, cholera, has occurred in a series of worldwide pandemics; but over the centuries since medieval times, acute infantile gastroenteritis has had a higher toll of infant and early child deaths than cholera, because it was constantly present whereas cholera occurred only in occasional albeit devastating epidemics. Diarrheal diseases still kill 3 to 4 million infants and children every year, mainly in low-income countries in AFRICA and Asia. Other diseases spread by the fecal-oral route include poliomyelitis, which does not cause gastrointestinal symptoms but invades the nervous system after its entry into the body, and viral hepatitis, an inflammatory disease of the liver. Both polio and hepatitis were almost universal and mostly either symptomless or mild infections of infants and young children until improved sanitation in the twentieth century reduced the risk of acquiring them early in life; older children and adults often are vulnerable to severe attacks of these diseases, and this explains why POLIO and hepatitis became such prominent and dangerous contagious diseases of older children and young adults in and after the second or third decade of the twentieth century.

2. Diseases that invade or attack the respiratory sys-

tem (throat, windpipe, lungs) are primarily spread by droplets, such as the spray or mist suspended in the air after an infected person coughs or sneezes. Diseases spread by droplet include tuberculosis, bronchitis and croup, diphtheria, measles, scarlet fever, and whooping cough. The most common dangerous forms of acute respiratory disease, acute bronchitis and bronchopneumonia, still kill about 3 million infants and children every year in low-income countries. Diphtheria attacks the windpipe, causing its little victims to choke to death; the diphtheria bacillus also produces a toxin that damages the heart. Measles causes acute inflammation of the lungs—bronchitis and bronchopneumonia. It is often lethal when the affected children are malnourished. Until early in the twentieth century it was common for several children to share the same bed. Older children with measles or other contagious diseases often infected their younger siblings, with deadly consequences. Improved living conditions did more than anything else to reduce the role of measles, croup, and whooping cough as major child killers. By the time the measles vaccine was developed, death rates from measles had fallen to insignificant levels in the rich industrial nations. Tuberculosis is further discussed below.

3. Diseases transmitted to humans by insect vectors include several that have been terrible scourges of humanity—malaria, plague, typhus, and yellow fever. Nowadays these diseases mainly afflict people in low-income tropical countries, but until late in the nineteenth century all occurred in temperate regions of Europe and North America. Environmental and social conditions are important determinants of all of these vector-borne diseases, as discussed below.

4. Diseases spread by direct person-to-person contact are mainly sexually transmitted or mother-to-infant transmitted. They include several varieties of hepatitis and the current worldwide pandemic of HIV/AIDS, which so far has affected over 40 million people and killed more than 10 million. About two thirds of the affected live—and die—in sub-Saharan Africa. HIV/AIDS is having a catastrophic impact on child health in Africa, both directly, when it kills infants and children born to HIV-positive mothers, and perhaps even more so indirectly, when children orphaned after both parents have died of AIDS are left to fend for themselves.

5. Diseases caused by pathogens that reside in the environment include tetanus. Until anti-tetanus vaccine was developed in the 1930s and then widely used in vaccination campaigns after World War II, tetanus was among the great killing diseases of newborn infants. When tetanus spores lodge in the cut end of the umbilical cord, they produce a toxin that causes death within a couple of weeks of birth. Neonatal tetanus has always been associated with dirty midwifery and with unhygienic traditional childbirth practices. As recently as the 1960s it killed over half a million newborn infants every year. Even now, with vaccination of pregnant women to protect their unborn children, preserving antiseptic precautions during obstetric procedures is the best way to prevent infant deaths from neonatal tetanus.

The Great Killers

Throughout history, epidemic and pandemic contagious diseases have struck down prodigious numbers of people, sometimes damaging the fabric of society so gravely as to disrupt commerce and industry. Early in the twenty-first century this is happening in sub-Saharan Africa, where HIV/AIDS is devastating whole nations. The progress of European civilization was disrupted by the pandemic black death (almost certainly bubonic and pneumonic plague) that struck from 1347 through 1349. The nineteenth-century cholera epidemics, while less disruptive, had a comparable short-term impact, as have several epidemics of typhus and the worldwide influenza pandemic of 1918 through 1920, which caused an estimated 20 million deaths. Other diseases that have exerted a longer-term and ultimately more damaging effect on human affairs are smallpox, malaria, and tuberculosis. Several classes of contagious diseases, and the measures taken to control them, require further discussion.

Plague, caused by bacteria that are carried by fleas, is primarily a disease of rats, but when it kills the rats, their fleas seek other mammalian hosts, carrying the plague bacillus with them. Bubonic plague is so called because the infection causes large swellings, or buboes, in the armpits and groin. In humans, plague often infects the lungs, causing fatal pneumonia, or it invades the blood stream and causes generalized septicemia. It is among the most deadly of all pandemic diseases. The pandemic known as the black death killed about a third of the population of Europe between 1347 and 1349; it arrested the advance of European civilization for several generations. Most of the victims were children. Plague gave rise to the legend of the Pied Piper of Hamelin, and to the nursery rhyme "Ring-a-ring o' roses," both commemorating the terrible mortality among children. Epidemics of plague were associated with squalid living conditions that encouraged infestation with rats.

Epidemic typhus, like plague, relies on insects to assist its transmission. In this case it is the body louse, which flourishes in unwashed clothing on unwashed bodies. Typhus was typically a disease of campaigning armies, but it attacked townspeople too, so it was a child killer in epidemics from the Thirty Years War to the early twentieth century and it reappeared in the ghettoized populations of European Jews during World War II. Like the plague, its control depended mainly on eliminating the insect vectors—the lice that transmitted it. Cleanliness and frequent washing and changes of fresh clothing are the best way to prevent typhus. In 1944, an impending epidemic in Naples was prevented by widespread use of the insecticide DDT to kill the lice with which many of the people were infested.

Malaria remains extremely common in humid tropical regions where the mosquito vectors flourish. Formerly it was common in southern and central Europe, in England as far north as the Midlands, and in South, Central, and North America as far north as southern Canada. It killed innumerable children. It has been treated for centuries with quinine and more recently with modern quinine derivatives. But as with all the great killers, a population-based strategy of prevention is more effective than treatment of individual cases. The strategy relies on eradication of mosquito breeding sites, use of insecticides to kill mosquitoes, and window screens and netting surrounding beds to protect people from mosquito bites indoors and while they are asleep. This strategy was widely applied throughout many malarial regions of the world, including the southern United States from the early twentieth century onward, and has successfully eliminated malaria from most places except sub-Saharan Africa and parts of southern and Southeast Asia. At the beginning of the twenty-first century malaria kills about a million children annually, most of them in Africa.

Cholera has always been the archetype of fecal-oral infections. It existed in southern and Southeast Asia from ancient times. It was imported to Europe and North America when trade expanded in the eighteenth century and reached a peak in great lethal epidemics in the nineteenth century. Transmission was by polluted water, consequent on lack of sanitation and inadequate personal and kitchen hygiene. Control came with the introduction of sanitary disposal of human excreta and provision of safe water supplies. Cholera continues to flourish in southern and Southeast Asia. An epidemic occurred in the Pacific coastal regions of South America in 1990, caused by import of the cholera vibrio in ballast water on ships from the Bay of Bengal, combined with complex ecological factors associated with climate change, but the high death rates of former generations have been controlled by oral rehydration therapy.

Smallpox, a viral disease, has scourged humans since before the dawn of history. Great epidemics often cut a swath through the population, killing up to a third of all attacked, scarring many who survived and causing blindness when it affected the eyes. As with all epidemic contagious diseases, children were the main victims. In the late eighteenth century, the English family doctor and naturalist Edward Jenner

experimented on twenty-three child patients. He inoculated them with cowpox lymph and reported that this protected them against smallpox in an epidemic then raging in England. Jenner's 1798 book, *An inquiry into the causes and effects of the variolae vaccinae* may be the most important treatise on public health ever written; it stimulated VACCINATION programs against smallpox and led directly to the eradication of smallpox (which was officially proclaimed by the World Health Assembly in 1980). Samples of smallpox virus survive in secure laboratories in several countries and are a potential weapon in biological warfare.

Tuberculosis, also called the white plague or consumption, ravaged the people of Europe and North America in the eighteenth and nineteenth centuries. Typically it struck when its victims were young, often teenaged, but it usually did not kill them until they were in their third or fourth decade, or older. Its direct cause is the tubercle bacillus, but it hits hardest in the presence of poverty, poor nutrition, overcrowding, ignorance, unemployment, and alcohol abuse— a common combination among poor populations in the squalid industrial cities of nineteenth-century Europe and America.

Control of Contagious Diseases

Treatment of individual cases of contagious diseases was largely ineffectual until the discovery and development of antibiotics and other modern antibacterial remedies, which did not occur on a wide scale until midway through the twentieth century. Treatment of individual cases, however, remains a poor substitute for public health measures aimed at preventing contagious diseases from attacking the population. In only one group—sexually transmitted diseases—is treatment of individual cases an effective means of control.

Effective control requires an understanding of the epidemiological features of contagious diseases, which in turn requires an understanding of their ecology. VACCINATION and immunization programs have successfully controlled many contagious diseases, including smallpox, measles, whooping cough, diphtheria, and tetanus, but sometimes control of contagious diseases has occurred as a byproduct of societal changes, and the epidemiological insights and preventive measures have come later, after the waning of the great epidemics.

Ecological Approaches to Control

Although the necessary cause of each of the contagious diseases is a specific pathogen, other determining factors are required before a lethal epidemic occurs. The phrase *filth diseases* captures the sense of values that developed in the late nineteenth century as understanding about contagious diseases increased. Public health scientists and administrators recognized that effective control required an attack on what came to be regarded as filthy living conditions and behavior. Dirty, vermin-infested housing; squalid, overcrowded living conditions; fleas, lice, flies, and rats; lack of sanitation; and poor personal and domestic HYGIENE were all recognized as important environmental, social, and behavioral determinants. Effective control required attention to social and economic conditions, education about improving personal and domestic hygiene, as well as vaccination and immunization against vaccine-preventable diseases, sanitary engineering, and the provision of safe water supplies.

The Future of Contagious Diseases

The insights of history enable us to make educated guesses about possible futures. About halfway through the twentieth century, the optimistic view prevailed that soon all contagious diseases would be controlled and eliminated by the use of vaccines and antibiotics. The optimism was short-lived. It soon became apparent that antibiotic-resistant strains of dangerous pathogens would present an ongoing problem. Then deadly new contagious diseases emerged. This process of emergence continues. It is an inevitable consequence of evolutionary biology—pathogens will always continue to evolve, and because their reproduction rates are so prodigious and generation times so short, microorganisms evolve very rapidly. This explains the rapid development of antibiotic-resistant strains of many pathogens. The role of public health sciences is to anticipate the process and have public health practices ready to cope with each new contagious disease as it emerges.

See also: **Infant Mortality; Pediatrics.**

BIBLIOGRAPHY

Chadwick, Edwin 1965 [1843]. *Report on the Sanitary Condition of the Labouring Population of Great Britain.* Reprint, annotated by M. W. Flinn. Edinburgh, UK: Edinburgh University Press.

Chin, James, ed. 2000. *Control of Communicable Diseases Manual,* 17th ed. Washington DC: American Public Health Association.

Ewald, Paul. 1994. *Evolution of Infectious Disease.* New York: Oxford University Press.

Kunitz, Steven J. 1994. *Disease and Social Diversity: The European Impact on the Health of Non-Europeans.* New York: Oxford University Press.

McMichael, Tony. 2001. *Human Frontiers, Environments and Disease: Past Patterns, Uncertain Futures.* New York: Cambridge University Press.

McNeill, William H. 1976. *Plagues and Peoples.* New York: Doubleday.

Porter, Roy. 1997. *The Greatest Benefit to Mankind: A Medical History of Humanity from Antiquity to the Present.* London: HarperCollins.

JOHN M. LAST

Convent Schools (Cathedral Schools)

Convent schools (also called monastic schools) emerged in Europe during the Early Middle Ages (c. 500–1000). With the disappearance of classical Roman culture in western Europe, monasteries became sites for education. Oblates, boys of six or seven handed over to the care of the monastery by their parents and intended to become monks, were trained in reading and writing. According to the *Rule of Saint Benedict,* teenage novices, who were candidates for the monastic profession, had to receive instruction for at least a year before committing to monastic life. The novitiate, a separate part of the monastery with its own master and program of schooling, combined education in the liturgy and spiritual texts with acculturation in a monastic community.

The Early Middle Ages

One of the great early medieval figures in the attempt to heighten educational standards in monasteries was Hilda (614–680), the abbess of Whitby, a double monastery with separate wings for men and women in Yorkshire. She gathered books for an outstanding library and saw to it that both male clerics and nuns had an excellent knowledge of Latin language and literature. Centuries later, one of the first women's colleges at Oxford University was called Saint Hilda's.

Carolingian figures such as Alcuin of York (c. 732–804) tried to build on Hilda's efforts. Alcuin became the unofficial schoolmaster of the court of Charlemagne at Aachen, and he sponsored efforts to found cathedral schools all over the empire. Viking invasions quickly ended such dreams, however.

With the rebirth of European culture in the eleventh and twelfth centuries, new reform efforts again encouraged learning. Church councils attempted to ensure the presence of cathedral schools, primarily for teaching candidates for the priesthood. Monastic and cathedral schools thus became the first GRAMMAR SCHOOLS, teaching the rudiments of reading and writing. All instruction was in Latin, the international language of learning at the time. Meanwhile, wandering scholars were tramping across Europe in search of good teachers who were well-connected and could place them in lucrative jobs.

The High Middle Ages

Throughout this period, monastic institutions were being reformed and regularized, especially after the beginnings of a new monastic order that arose from the monastery at Cîteaux, founded in Burgundy in 1098. The Cistercians refused to accept oblates and imposed a minimum age of eighteen for novices. At the same time they placed more emphasis on what was to be learned in the novitiate. They expected their recruits to monastic life to have a background in Latin, often gained from parish priests or cathedral schools.

Grammar, rhetoric, and logic were the foundations of medieval education (the *trivium,* as they were called). Many a schoolboy had to spend painful hours in learning vocabulary and grammatical constructions by heart. Those who failed their lessons could be beaten, for the classical ideal of education left no mercy for the slow pupil. Eleventh-century monastic reform, however, gave rise to a debate about whether corporal punishment was a good idea. One great monastic philosopher and educator, Anselm (1033–1109), insisted on treating his novices with care and circumspection. He thought that they would learn more if they were motivated by love of the subject and of their teacher.

The end of the twelfth century saw the rise of a specialization of higher education in the new universities at Paris and Oxford. Boys of fourteen would enter these institutions after their trivium educations in parish, monastic, or cathedral schools. Religious orders such as the Cistercians at first stayed away from the universities, but around 1240 the order founded its own college at Paris and sent its intellectually brightest monks there. The new orders of friars, the Dominicans and the Franciscans, also produced members who became professors in the Paris schools.

Women did not have the same educational opportunities in the High Middle Ages (1000–1300) as they had been given in the double monasteries of the Early Middle Ages. But monasteries for women did provide instruction in reading and writing. In the twelfth-century in France, Heloïse (1098–1164), perhaps the most learned woman of her time, founded a convent for women and imposed high intellectual standards.

At the same time there was continuing pressure on cathedral schools to improve standards and educate people other than potential priests. In the growing towns of Europe, rich citizens began to found their own schools for boys, but these almost always had clerical teachers. At the end of the fourteenth century a secular priest and theologian named Jean de Gerson (1363–1429) headed the cathedral school of Notre-Dame in Paris. In a treatise entitled *On Bringing Children to Christ*, Gerson recommended a combination of strict discipline and humane treatment. He also worried that some teachers might sexually abuse their pupils, so he tried to make certain that boys would never be alone with their teachers—or with each other.

The Reformation
In the sixteenth century enormous changes were made following the Protestant and Catholic reformations. A new religious order in Catholic Europe, the Jesuits, placed great emphasis on education (especially of the nobility) in order to gain political influence and win over to the Roman Church areas of Protestant Europe. The Jesuits were firm disciplinarians and educational innovators in applying the classical humanist learning of the Renaissance to their schools.

The desire of women to form religious communities and obtain an education was also affected by the Catholic Reformation. The Ursulines began in northern Italy as a lay religious movement. The group did social work and opened schools, but the regimentation of reform at the Council of Trent in the mid–sixteenth century required the Ursulines to seclude themselves from the world and live a semicontemplative life. Some nuns, however, were allowed to teach girls, and the Ursulines became an educational success in Italy and France, with up to 12,000 sisters in 320 institutions in the seventeenth century.

Another French educational reform movement, the Brothers of the Christian Schools (known as the Christian Brothers) was founded by John-Baptist de La Salle (1651–1719). As canon at Rheims, La Salle had begun to found schools for poor boys, and he soon headed a religious community that specialized in teaching. He also avoided clericalization by forbidding priests to join. The order spread throughout France and opened many teacher training colleges.

La Salle left a monument to his educational ideas in his *Conduct of Christian Schools*. Like his medieval predecessors he saw education as an integral part of a Christian upbringing. Schools existed to fashion devout Christians, but teenage boys were also given an opportunity to understand the intellectual and historical foundations of their faith.

Convent Schools in the United States
The ideals and practices of the Ursulines and the Christian Brothers were exported to America in the convent and PAROCHIAL SCHOOLS of the nineteenth and twentieth centuries. Some of the finest achievements of medieval civilization thus became available to new generations of young people. Catholic educational culture, with its emphasis on celibacy and a chronic suspicion of women and SEXUALITY, has had to face many problems and conflicts in modern education. At its best, however, this orientation has emphasized humanistic learning, an international outlook, and a dialogue between teacher and pupil.

See also: **Early Modern Europe; Education, Europe; Latin School; Medieval and Renaissance Europe.**

BIBLIOGRAPHY

Leclercq, Jean. 1979. *Monks and Love in Twelfth-Century France.* Oxford, UK: Clarendon Press.

McGuire, Brian Patrick. 1996. "Education, Confession, and Pious Fraud: Jean Gerson and a Late Medieval Change." *American Benedictine Review* 47: 310–338.

Mullett, Michael A. 1999. *The Catholic Reformation.* New York: Routledge.

Nicholas, David. 1992. *The Evolution of the Medieval World, 312–1500.* London and New York: Longman.

BRIAN PATRICK MCGUIRE

Cosmetics

Cosmetics are generally defined as products applied externally to improve appearance. The purpose—enhancing beauty—defines cosmetic use, as opposed to painting the body for religious, ritual, or medicinal purposes. With the exception of "permanent cosmetics," a late twentieth-century innovation, cosmetics' temporary nature separates them from permanent body alterations such as TATTOOS, PIERCINGS, or scarification.

Virtually all cultures have used cosmetics. Nail lacquer (gum arabic, egg whites, gelatin, and beeswax) originated in China at least 3000 years B.C.E. Ancient Egyptian women lined and shadowed their eyes with green (malachite) and black (kohl). Henna was used on fingernails in the Middle East. In Britain, Gilbertus Angelicus's *Compendium Medicinae* (1240) contains recipes for beauty aids; by the 1400s women were using ceruse, a mixture of vinegar and powdered lead, to whiten their faces and bosoms.

In Western culture makeup originated as theatrical paint. While late-nineteenth- and early-twentieth-century actresses like Lillie Langtrey, Sarah Bernhardt, and Theda Bara pioneered the use of cosmetics off-stage and -screen, most American women did not consider makeup an "everyday" ritual until the early twentieth century, when entrepreneurs such as Max Factor, Elizabeth Arden, and Helena Rubenstein introduced products that looked more natural and were easier to use. And for children—aside from the ritual of face-painting at county fairs, dressing up for HALLOWEEN, and the occasional opportunity to play "dress up" with mom's makeup kit—cosmetics were largely off-limits.

Because cosmetics are designed to enhance beauty and increase sexual appeal, cosmetic use has always been a RITE OF PASSAGE. In the 1920s FLAPPERS battled their parents not only for the right to smoke and dance in public but for the right to wear makeup. In the film *Rebel Without a Cause* (1955), Judy's (Natalie Wood) father forces her to wipe off her red lipstick, which he considers too "grown up." In the 1950s, however, cosmetic manufacturers saw gold in the burgeoning baby-boom youth market, and the race was on.

Throughout the 1950s, 1960s, and 1970s, cosmetic manufacturers targeted the seemingly endless teenage market. In the United States, Bonne Bell targeted TEENAGERS, while in Britain Mary Quant launched her own "Youthquake." Until the end of the twentieth century, however, children largely remained off limits. Tinkerbell, for example, launched the children's market in the 1950s, but it steadfastly refused to sell eyeshadow and rouge, which it considered improper for girls so young, and targeted its ADVERTISING to parents, rather than directly to children. In the 1980s and 1990s, however, in America and in Europe, cosmetics were designed for and marketed to "tweens" (girls between childhood and teen years) and then to children as young as three. Japan, which saw its first "toy" makeup introduced in 1993, was not far behind.

The practice of encouraging young children to learn to apply makeup is not without controversy. Some critics are concerned about product safety (cosmetic ingredients other than color were unregulated in the United States in the 2000s) while others question whether such products encourage children to grow up too fast, or undermine their SELF-ESTEEM. But at $10 billion a year in the United States alone by the beginning of the twenty-first century, the market for children's cosmetics wasn't going away anytime soon.

See also: **Fashion; Girlhood; Youth Culture.**

BIBLIOGRAPHY

Brumberg, Joan Jacobs. 1998. *The Body Project: An Intimate History of American Girls.* New York: Vintage Press.

Fass, Paula. 1977. *The Damned and the Beautiful: American Youth in the 1920s.* New York: Oxford University Press.

Palladino, Grace. 1996. *Teenagers: An American History.* New York: Basic Books.

Peiss, Kathy. 1999. *Hope in a Jar: The Making of America's Beauty Culture.* New York: Owl Press.

ELIZABETH HAIKEN

Custody. *See* Divorce and Custody.

D

Dating

Dating is a ritualized courting process that developed in the twentieth century as a means for adolescents to engage in approved heterosexual activities. It emerged first in the United States in response to significant social and gender changes in schooling and work, family life, and recreational activities. During the twentieth century, dating spread to other Westernized societies, although it has become increasingly attenuated in the context of the revolution in premarital sexual behavior after the 1960s.

In the early modern world most courtship was supervised by family or other adult community institutions. Formally arranged marriage was never the dominant practice among most Americans, as it was among the European aristocracy and upper middle class, but informal arrangements existed which directed young people's desires toward suitable partners who remained within racial, class, and other boundaries. Most young people did not have either the time or the privacy to engage widely in experimental activities, and the importance of chastity for women among respectable people meant that girls and young women did not venture very far on their own without adult chaperones. These informal controls were able to adapt initially to the emergence in the nineteenth century of the ideal of romantic LOVE and to companionship as a replacement for patriarchy in marital values. More challenging were the dramatic dislocations that accompanied the urban and industrial transformations of the second half of the nineteenth century.

Among the wealthy elite, well-orchestrated rituals surrounding elaborate debutante balls and coming-out ceremonies largely assured that family choices would continue to define the horizons of adolescents and young adults as they moved toward a season of courtship. Thus eighteen- and nineteen-year-old girls were introduced to the proper society from among whom they could choose and be chosen. But among others, especially the large and growing middle class

and the respectable working class, the fact that young men and women spent more time away from the watchful guidance of parents became a source of considerable cultural concern and anxiety in the late nineteenth and early twentieth century, a concern most effectively articulated by social reformer JANE ADDAMS in *The Spirit of Youth in the City Streets*. Especially problematic was the new freedom of young women. Both boys and girls were now more often found mixing promiscuously in unsupervised work and play environments as adolescent girls went out to work in factories, shops, and offices. These young people often spent their money and free time in unsupervised commercial recreations such as MOVIES, dance halls, and amusement parks. Both male and female adolescents were also staying in school longer as new school attendance laws began to include more older children. The schools, pressed to engage their charges, provided more opportunities for socializing as they searched for ways to keep older and recalcitrant student populations at school. As schools became the arenas for extracurricular clubs, SPORTS, PROMS, and other events, they also became the site for spontaneous heterosexual socializing. Young people developed dating in these new work and educational contexts as a means to order mate selection and to contain the erotic possibilities that the new freedom from adult supervision made possible.

The apparent freedom of dating and its association with out-of-home and paired activities made the new practice seem risqué and daring in the early twentieth century. By the 1920s, however, it had become generally regarded as a legitimate means of interaction between young men and women during later adolescence and young adulthood. Some immigrant and religious groups still resisted and were appalled by the freedom that dating permitted between strangers, but most native white young people understood that while dating was not supervised by adults it nevertheless had clearly established boundaries enforced by peers that regulated respectability, eligibility, and the routines of sexual access. Moreover, the young not only defined what was attractive, permissible, and popular, but continued to maintain clear class, racial, and ethnic boundaries.

The vast extension of schooling between the world wars to the majority of adolescents (including immigrants) in public HIGH SCHOOLS, and to a substantial minority in colleges and universities, made these new peer definitions possible. The long hours at school and the shift of authority from home and work to youth-based institutions, along with the coeducational nature of the great majority of these institutions, made peer standards in dating dominant. At schools, a complex social system that included extracurricular activities, sports competitions, fraternities and sororities, literary activities, beauty contests, and other means to define identity and popularity regulated dating behavior. But the system was not closed since the young drew on nonschool institutions for inspiration in setting new nonfamily-based fads and fashions. These relied on both the heterogeneity of populations at school and the enormous expansion of popular culture, especially via movies, popular music, and sports, that provided sources and models for approved behavior, appearance, style, language, dress, and beliefs around which standards of popularity and datability revolved. In expanding the vocabulary of acceptable and proper behavior, popular culture idols helped the young redefine eligibility and expand the limits on sexual propriety in their dating behavior toward more liberated forms.

Starting in the 1920s, a date usually involved one or two couples going out together to a movie, a dance, a soda shop, or a roadside restaurant. In places outside of large cities, this increasingly relied on access to an automobile and became dependent on the outlay of significant amounts of cash to ensure that the treat for the afternoon or evening was acceptable to the dating partner. Commercial considerations were thus embedded into the very structure of the dating relationship, which required that the male treat the female to a good time. Women too were required to expend money on their appearance, wearing fashionable clothes and stylish hairdos, and relying on beauty treatments and up-to-date cosmetics. These consumer-based standards became crucial to the evaluations that each side made of the prospective date and the subsequent decisions about whether dating would continue. They were the basis for at least initial conclusions before other, more subtle, considerations could intervene.

In the 1920s and 1930s, exclusivity was not considered either essential to dating or its only necessary result. Instead, a dating-and-rating syndrome sometimes overwhelmed the long-term courtship objectives of dating, as young men and women of the middle class engaged in a whirl of heterosexual social activities which defined their status in a complex hierarchy of popularity and desirability. Class differences also surfaced, particularly in high school, with working-class youth more likely to see dating as part of marriage-partner selection, while middle-class youth engaged in dating more

in terms of entertainment. At the same time, both dating which led to exclusive attachments and dating which was part of a busy social life included a variety of erotic practices that became a standard part of the expected sexual initiation of twentieth-century youth before the premarital sexual revolution of the late 1960s and 1970s.

Some historians have argued that in return for the expenses incurred by the male dating partner some sexual compensation was expected from the female. Whether the exchange was quite so direct and calculated or evolved from a set of expanded possibilities for intimacy and graduated expectations, dating certainly resulted in mutual sexual experimentation. In most cases, these activities fell short of intercourse, involving instead an elaborate pattern of sexual play that included hand-holding, kissing, petting, and fondling. It was well understood that within this evolving pattern women would define the limits of acceptable behavior, while men would try to push those boundaries as far as possible. Most studies of the 1920s and 1930s show that among those whose dating had become exclusive, especially those who were engaged to marry, intercourse would become an occasional or regular part of the dating relationship for about half of these couples. This was usually rationalized as a legitimate expression of the commitment to a long-lasting loving relationship oriented to marriage.

These newly established dating rituals were disrupted by America's entry into World War II, when dating was largely suspended for older couples in the context of a national emergency which emptied schools, colleges, factories, and offices of eligible young men. The war also encouraged more rapid sexual involvement and a rush to marriage. In a related way, war often led to short-term casual sex that some young women saw as their contribution to the war effort, but that seemed to liberate others from the artificial standards that had previously been in place. Among these were thousands of VICTORY GIRLS, urban camp followers who catered to men on short-term leave, and whom the army targeted as potential carriers of VENEREAL DISEASE.

Adolescents, though not so clearly affected by the war, were not entirely shielded from its effects, especially since older adolescents might be inducted as the war accelerated draft call-ups. More significantly, the war changed the pattern of delayed marriage that had become common for all classes and groups during the Depression of the 1930s and the postponement of first conception that had a longer twentieth-century history. After the war, the trend toward early marriage continued and in the 1950s a dramatic baby boom altered American family life in significant ways. While peacetime conditions allowed a return to earlier dating behavior, that behavior had now become more than in the past a matter of adult concern and intervention. It was also shorter since women now married younger than at any time in American history and began to contemplate the road to marriage throughout adolescence. Dating as a route to marriage became both more serious and more hurried. Younger adolescents and even preteens began to appropriate some of their older brothers' and sisters' behaviors, while serious relations became more common earlier in the dating process. Pinning (wearing the fraternity or club pin of a boyfriend), wearing a love anklet, and going steady became regular rituals of 1950s and 1960s dating behavior.

At the same time, adults became more clearly involved in these behaviors. The most obvious form this took was in the elaboration of advice in newspapers, TEEN MAGAZINES, and manuals for adolescents. Adult family and relationship experts, who drew on the increasing American infatuation with the science of psychology as a guide to daily life, intervened in this as in many other arenas of child rearing and self-development. But popular culture too began to reflect new concerns about dating, and a whole genre of movies, including films such as the teen classics *Where the Boys Are*, and *Splendor in the Grass*, were based on the erotic charge that resulted from breaking dating taboos.

This whole structure was fundamentally weakened in the late 1960s and 1970s when the rapid legitimization of premarital sexuality removed some of the need for dating etiquette, at least among young adults. For adolescents, too, the more open sexuality that developed during this period made dating rules far less stringent and enforceable. While dating certainly continued and continues to define many heterosexual relationships, the rules became much more flexible (and included the possibility of same-sex dating). The effective use of BIRTH CONTROL and the availability of abortion, even for adolescents, after the 1970s meant that rules which had been in place for most of the century and whose objective was always to maintain social standing during a life-cycle phase marked by sexual desire, were hardly as necessary anymore.

While dating has by no means disappeared even in the twenty-first century as adolescents and young adults seek to define just what is permissible and what is not in their mating behavior as they move toward adult life, it now coexists with a range of other activities. Some of these are less dependent on isolated pairing and include group activities associated with alcohol, DRUGS, and music. Matchmaking and dating services—many newly dependent on computers and the Internet—have also become much more common and acceptable. Dating has in the meantime shifted to older people, many of whom seek companionship and remarriage after divorce. Dating has become less obviously part of adolescence as age of marriage has once again shifted upward and taboos against premarital sexuality have become less harsh and judgmental.

See also: **Adolescence and Youth; Life Course and Transitions to Adulthood; Sexuality; Youth Culture.**

BIBLIOGRAPHY

Addams, Jane. 1972 [1909]. *The Spirit of Youth in the City Streets.* Urbana: University of Illinois Press.

Bailey, Beth L. 1988. *From Front Porch to Back Seat: Courtship in Twentieth-Century America.* Baltimore, MD: Johns Hopkins University Press.

Bailey, Beth L. 1999. *Sex in the Heartland.* Cambridge, MA: Harvard University Press.

Fass, Paula S. 1977. *The Damned and the Beautiful: American Youth in the 1920s.* New York: Oxford University Press.

Glenn, Susan A. 1990. *Daughters of the Shtetl: Life and Labor in the Immigrant Generation.* Ithaca, NY: Cornell University Press.

Hine, Thomas. 1999. *The Rise and Fall of the American Teenager: A New History of the American Adolescent Experience.* New York: Bard.

Modell, John. 1989. *Into One's Own: From Youth to Adulthood in the United States, 1920–1975.* Berkeley and Los Angeles: University of California Press.

Peiss, Kathy. 1987. *Cheap Amusements: Working Women and Leisure in Turn of the Century New York.* Philadelphia: Temple University Press.

Rothman, Ellen K. 1984. *Hands and Hearts: A History of Courtship in America.* New York: Basic Books.

Tentler, Leslie Woodcock. 1979. *Wage-Earning Women: Industrial Work and Family Life in the United States, 1900–1930.* New York: Oxford University Press.

PAULA S. FASS

Death. *See* Grief, Death, Funerals; Infant Mortality.

Delinquency

Delinquency occurs in every country in the world. In many countries, delinquency first arose as a distinct problem in the late nineteenth century. In Germany, juvenile crime was first distinguished from adult crime in 1871 and in Britain in 1908. The United States' first JUVENILE COURT was established in 1899.

Delinquency and Society

As a social problem, delinquency came into being with ADOLESCENCE itself. As Western societies prolonged childhood dependency and postponed the age of expected independence through the second half of the nineteenth century and the early twentieth century, problems specific to the period of prolonged childhood emerged. In a rural, peasant society, for example, a fifteen-year-old boy missing school was not greeted with official opprobrium; a sixteen-year-old girl who was becoming sexually active might be rushed into marriage, not into court.

No matter the time period, delinquency is often closely tied to poverty and to the degree of difference between the rich and the poor in a society. In addition, delinquency is a

A still from the movie *Boys Town* (1938). Methods of dealing with delinquent children have become more punitive in the late twentieth and early twenty-first centuries, making a change from the paternalistic approach represented by Spencer Tracy's (admittedly idealized) Father Flanagan. THE KOBAL COLLECTION/MGM.

symptom of larger disruptions to tradition. Public concern for, and even panic over, delinquency peaks when major social patterns are changing. The first real attention to delinquency in the United States occurred in the 1880s and 1890s, for example, a time of rapid urbanization, massive immigration, and major shifts in labor patterns and the workplace. More recently, scholars focused on ethnic and racial difference as indicated by youth crime during the turbulent 1960s and 1970s.

Scholars in eastern Europe have understood youth crime as an indicator of the breakdown of traditional authority resulting from the disruptions associated with the fall of the Soviet Union and the instability of succeeding political and economic regimes. In western Europe, two trends have emerged. Some countries, including Great Britain, Germany, and Finland, have witnessed a constantly increasing amount of juvenile crime from 1950 to 2000. Others, including Austria, Switzerland, and the Scandinavian countries, saw a sharp rise in juvenile crime from 1950 to about 1970, with a leveling-off occurring after 1970. On the other hand,

all European countries have seen an increase in juvenile violent crime since 1950, with marked upward trends during the 1980s and 1990s. While adult crime rates stayed steady, rising juvenile violent crime rates mirrored rising unemployment and poverty rates. The most recent statistics, for 1995 through 2000, show a slight increase in juvenile violent crime in Germany, a slight decrease in Great Britain, and a significant increase in France, especially in sexual assaults by juveniles.

In South Africa, juvenile crime in the period from 1948 to 1994 was associated with apartheid, resistance to apartheid, and with the divide between blacks and whites in income, housing, and education. Since the new government came to power there in 1994, it has tried to address youth crime by instituting socioeconomic change and by revising the criminal justice system. Unfortunately, reliable information on the results of these efforts is difficult to find.

Definitions of Delinquency

The *Oxford English Dictionary* defines delinquency as the condition or quality of being a delinquent; delinquent means "failing in duty or obligation; one guilty of an offence against the law." Juvenile delinquency is the term used to denote any offense against the law performed by a youth under a certain age. In many countries, that age is eighteen, but it varies across the globe.

In the United States, police may charge a youth with delinquency when he or she is alleged to have committed a crime. In addition, juveniles may be charged when they have committed a "status offense," a violation of a specific restriction that applies to people under a certain age, such as breaking a curfew.

Delinquency and its definitions have changed over time. Scholars have found that girls and boys are apprehended for different offenses. In addition, what constitutes delinquency has changed over time.

In the late nineteenth and early twentieth century United States, boys and girls were most often charged with crimes far different from those they are charged with early in the twenty-first century. Delinquent boys were primarily charged with property offenses, such as stealing copper pipes to sell to junkmen. In the same period, girls were mainly charged with status offenses, such as incorrigibility or running away—terms that often masked sexual activity. Boys were rarely charged with such crimes. In the early twenty-first century, both girls and boys have been charged more often with violent crime than they were in 1900, although property theft is still the largest category for boys charged with delinquency. What was once considered an offense—frequenting dance halls, for example—is often not considered a crime at all today. On the other hand, crimes related to the drug trade and the easy availability of weapons are much more prevalent than at the turn of the last century.

A surge of violent youth crime in the United States took place in the 1980s and was closely tied to a new wave of DRUGS on the streets. During the 1980s and 1990s, more children under age twelve were committing violent acts than before. Between 1980 and 1995, arrests for violent crime doubled for youths aged twelve or younger. From 1980 to 1995, the number of arrests for forcible rape were up 190 percent for juveniles under twelve and arrests for carrying or possessing weapons were up 206 percent. African-American juveniles were arrested disproportionately compared to their numbers in the population. In 1995, African-American children represented about 15 percent of the U.S. youth population but accounted for nearly 50 percent of all arrests for violent crime. The government responded to the dramatic increase in juvenile crime with a host of punitive measures: reducing the age at which an adolescent can be considered an adult and tried in adult court; creating new military-style "boot camp" programs; sentencing juveniles to longer periods of incarceration and stricter oversight. The number of adolescents incarcerated skyrocketed. After 1994, violent youth crime decreased, but property crime did not decrease proportionately. Female violent crime, moreover, did not decrease at the same rate as that for males. It is unclear whether the decrease in violent juvenile crime was a result of new policies, a decline in crack cocaine use, federal efforts to control the distribution of guns, community and school prevention programs, or some combination of these factors.

Responses to Delinquency

At bottom, the governmental response to delinquency is inherently repressive, relying on the coercive power of the state and the threat of incarceration. During the 1960s and 1970s, both the United States and Great Britain saw a more anti-institutional approach hold sway, with a greater focus on welfare, probation, and supervision, but now both countries have returned to a more punitive method of dealing with delinquent youth.

Researchers have spent decades examining juvenile delinquents and their offenses. Time and again, they come up against the difficult question posed by any study of crime: why did this particular person and not another commit a crime? Was the cause of his of her delinquency physical, medical, psychological, social, or something else entirely? Cross-cultural comparisons of delinquents have pointed to useful facts: that where family power breaks down and when traditions lose their grip, one is most likely to find delinquent behavior. In-depth studies of certain delinquent groups have also pointed to the growth of an alternative family structure in gangs and to a growing tradition of rootlessness and violence. For many youth, there is no tradition but violence and aimlessness. Some investigators have found that delinquency increases during wartime because of this rootlessness; others find that wartime employment means lower rates of delinquency.

Conclusion

It is impossible to discuss delinquency as though it is the same the world over, but important patterns can be distinguished. Delinquency is often seen as a social problem, a symptom of a deeper social malaise. When societies undergo long periods of upheaval, official attention is focused on delinquency and youth behavior. Even though delinquency goes through periods of increase and decrease, it never disappears altogether. Governments and social agencies also go through periods of increased or decreased effort in dealing with delinquency, swinging back and forth between repressive and less restrictive measures.

See also: **Children's Rights; Homeless Children and Runaways in the United States; Juvenile Justice; Youth Gangs.**

BIBLIOGRAPHY

Addams, Jane. 1909. *The Spirit of Youth and the City Streets.* New York: Macmillan.

Boehnke, Klaus, and Dagmar Bergs-Winkels. 2002. "Juvenile Delinquency under Conditions of Rapid Social Change." *Sociological Forum* 17, no. 1 (March): 57–79.

Butts, Jeffrey A., and Howard N. Snyder. 1997. "The Youngest Delinquents: Offenders Under Age 15." *Juvenile Justice Bulletin* (September): 1–2.

Cross, William E., Jr. 2003. "Tracing the Historical Origins of Youth Delinquency and Violence: Myths and Realities about Black Culture." *Journal of Social Issues* 59, no. 1: 67–82.

Estrada, Felipe. 1999. "Juvenile Crime Trends in Post-War Europe." *European Journal on Criminal Policy and Research* 7: 23–42.

Hoffman, Allan M., and Randal W. Summers, eds. 2001. *Teen Violence: A Global View*. Westport, CT: Greenwood Press.

Humes, Edward. 1996. *No Matter How Loud I Shout: A Year in the Life of Juvenile Court*. New York: Simon and Schuster.

Jenson, Jeffrey M., Cathryn C. Potter, and Matthew O. Howard. 2001. "American Juvenile Justice: Recent Trends and Issues in Youth Offending." *Social Policy and Administration* 35, no. 1 (March): 48–68.

Mennel, Robert M. 1973. *Thorns and Thistles: Juvenile Delinquents in the United States, 1825–1940*. Hanover: University of New Hampshire Press.

Office of Juvenile Justice and Delinquency Prevention. 2001. *Research 2000*. Washington, DC: U.S. Department of Justice, Office of Justice Programs.

Rothman, David. 1980. *Conscience and Convenience: The Asylum and Its Alternatives in Progressive America*. Boston: Little, Brown.

INTERNET RESOURCES

Interpol. "International Crime Statistics." Available from <www.interpol.int/>.

Pfeiffer, Christian. "Trends in Juvenile Violence in European Countries." Available from <www.ncjrs.org/txtfiles/fs000202.txt>.

VICTORIA L. GETIS

Dentistry

Dentistry began to emerge as a recognized specialty within medical surgery in seventeenth-century Europe, although scattered examples of basic dental practice (especially extractions) and attention to oral hygiene can be traced to earlier centuries. The French surgeon Pierre Fauchard, author of *Le Chirurgien Dentiste* (1728), is generally recognized as the "father" of modern dentistry. Among his select clientele was an occasional child, usually a daughter of one of his (mainly female) patients, who would present with a badly carious, visible tooth that she was reluctant to extract because an empty space or replacement tooth might threaten her physical appearance and social position. Fauchard's creative solution, which apparently met with some success, was to withdraw the diseased tooth and then replace it immediately in its socket. Beyond providing pain relief, Fauchard and his contemporaries also experimented with new procedures to straighten misaligned teeth; children ages twelve to fourteen were the principal clientele.

These early examples notwithstanding, it was rare for a child of any social class to visit a dentist in the eighteenth and nineteenth centuries. Even among leading professional spokesmen, the traditional view still held that children's primary (deciduous) teeth were expendable, unworthy of financial investment, and unrelated to future oral health. The reparative treatment of carious teeth improved in quality and gained in popularity during the late nineteenth century, but its primary reliance on expensive gold fillings militated against its general extension to children. Extraction remained the primary response to children's dental diseases. Trained dentists—few in number, located mainly in cities, and expensive—were largely peripheral to the extraction trade, which was dominated by barbers, nostrum salesmen, and itinerant "tooth-pullers" who promised instant, pain-free relief. Not surprisingly, business boomed for replacement teeth and prosthetic devices in the nineteenth century, not just for the elderly but also for young adults who emerged from childhood with few usable teeth and constant mouth pain. Dentists and craftsmen worked singly and collaboratively to meet public demand and to improve the quality and fit of prosthetic devices (famous portraits of George Washington's clenched mouth exemplified why technical improvements were considered necessary). Dentists in the United States established clear superiority in "mechanical dentistry" and in the production, quality, variety, and economy of prosthetic devices.

Education, Child Welfare, and the Rise of Children's Dentistry

Children's dentistry emerged as a distinct subspecialty in Canada, Great Britain, and the United States in the first half of the twentieth century. Oddly, the field took shape mainly outside rather than inside dentists' offices, and under public rather than private sponsorship. Most dentists remained ambivalent, if not hostile, to integrating children into their private practices. The challenges and rewards of technically sophisticated, adult-oriented mechanical dentistry, not child-oriented, poorly compensated, preventive dentistry, drove the bulk of the profession. Nonetheless, a major shift in scientific direction, professional orientation, and public discourse about dental disease was evident by the early 1900s. For the first time, dentists seriously questioned the panacea of extraction and the presumed inevitability of toothlessness. A new gospel of "prevention" became a clarion call for dentistry to transform its customary assumptions about children's dental needs, and to make "mouth hygiene" a vital concern in medicine, public health, and education.

Several scientific advances in the 1880s and 1890s underlay the new viewpoint. Most important were Dr. William Miller's "chemico-parasitic" theory, which described the bacteriological process by which caries emerged under gelatinous plaques, and his "focal infection" theory, in which an unclean oral cavity was seen as the prime avenue of penetration for infectious disease in children. Also important in building professional confidence were Dr. Edward Angle's creative inventions for straightening teeth, which raised hopes for addressing the entire range of difficult problems surrounding malocclusion. New techniques and equipment for saving carious teeth with better, longer lasting, and cheaper filling materials also promised a bright future for reparative dentistry.

Children's dentistry was integral to the Progressive Era's (1890–1920) wide-ranging child welfare and Americanization campaigns, and, in particular, to the school health movement. Educational programs made prevention the central theme of children's dentistry. While educators emphasized the importance of nutrition and regular prophylaxis, they urged above all that children maintain lengthy, stringent, technically perfect standards of brushing their teeth: three, four, and ideally five times per day. Mothers as much as children were the audience for the new conventional wisdom. As with other elements of the Progressive child welfare agenda, mothers were assigned major responsibility for sparing their children needless pain and suffering, and thereby ensuring their success in school and assimilation into American life.

The provision of operative treatment via schools and clinics was the boldest innovation of early-twentieth-century children's dentistry. In the 1910s, several dozen dental clinics were established exclusively or primarily to serve children in public schools and in local health departments; a few clinics with private support, most notably in Boston and Rochester, were also founded. These clinics brought prevention-and-treatment oriented dentistry to the masses for the first time. In many clinics, dentists not only inspected children's teeth but also performed reparative treatments and extractions. Equally innovative was the introduction of regular prophylaxis, usually performed by members of the new, entirely female, school-centered specialty of dental hygienists. Despite its acknowledged importance in caries prevention, prophylaxis was time-consuming, laborious, and generated low fees. Dentists rarely performed prophylaxes in their private offices until hygienists or comparably trained assistants became more widely available. Although male dentists provided most school- and clinic-based operative service, it was lower-level women professionals—teachers, nurses, and hygienists—who mainly carried the banner of children's dentistry, much as in other areas of Progressive child-welfare reform.

A small corps of women dentists also emerged in the early twentieth century that began to focus primarily on children. M. Evangeline Jordon was arguably the first specialist in children's dentistry, beginning in 1909. Jordon authored the field's first expert textbook, *Operative Dentistry for Children*, in 1925. In his preface to Jordon's text, the prominent dental scholar Rodrigues Ottolengui observed that prior to 1915 he "had never heard of a dentist specializing exclusively in dentistry for children," and that "Dr. Jordon, so far as we have been able to learn, was the first dentist to practice exclusively for children, and thus she is the pioneer pedodontist of the United States, and perhaps of the world" (p. vii). In 1927, around the time of her retirement as a practitioner, a small group of dentists formed the American Society for the Promotion of Dentistry for Children, based on a common understanding that "if children are to be served, general dentists would have to provide most of the treatment." In 1933, the *Journal of Dentistry for Children* was founded.

General dentists did begin to serve children in larger numbers during the Great Depression, but mainly as paid employees in schools and clinics that expanded under government auspices. The Depression brought considerable hardship for dentists, and publicly funded programs in school and clinic settings were essential for their professional survival. Now numbering in the hundreds, these clinics provided around half of the total amount of dental treatment that children received from *any* source during the 1930s. (As the draft examinations in World War II would reveal, however, the oral health of American children and youth was still abominable, especially in rural communities and in the South, where publicly financed school and dental clinics never took hold.) Thus, out of necessity more than design or desire, children and dentists were no longer strangers to one another. A base of professional experience and client expectation for integrating children into general dentistry had been laid. Signifying the subspecialty's gradual arrival at professional legitimacy, the American Society for the Promotion of Dentistry for Children was renamed the American Society of Dentistry for Children in 1940.

Toward the Cavity Free Child: New Advances and New Horizons in Children's Dentistry

The provision of free reparative and restorative dentistry to several million servicemen during World War II also did much to create a new consumer base for children's dentistry in the postwar era. With the return of prosperity, this potential was soon realized—but now in the private rather than in the public sector. In the decade following the war, the private practice of American dentistry boomed as never before, and the share of children receiving private dental care expanded dramatically. By the late 1950s, nearly half of the school-age population was visiting a dentist about once per year. Organized dentistry—which, unlike organized medicine, had largely supported free school and clinic dental programs for children during the previous half-century—adopted a condescending stance toward such programs in the 1950s, claiming that they provided inferior treatment, used outdated equipment, misled parents about their children's true dental needs, and were no longer necessary. School clinics and other public agencies that had grown accustomed to calling upon unemployed or underemployed dentists on an hourly per capita or fee basis to treat children now found that dentists no longer had the time or financial inclination to participate in such arrangements. The long-sought ideal of the "family dentist" was finally becoming a reality.

An equally major change emerged in the postwar years that would profoundly transform children's oral health by the 1980s. This was the discovery of the preventive possibilities of fluorides for dental caries. Schools returned briefly in the 1970s to a central role in children's dentistry as the National Institute of Dental Research launched a major publicity campaign to convince educators and dentists alike that school-based fluoride rinse programs represented the most cost-effective, school-based means available to prevent tooth decay. By 1980, nearly one-quarter of the nation's school districts were participating in fluoride rinse programs, which may have reached as many as 8 million children. Although bitter fights over water fluoridation occurred in numerous communities, with some opponents casting fluoridation as a Communist plot, the fluoridation of water supplies grew rapidly in the postwar era. By the end of the 1950s, nearly two thousand communities serving over 33 million people had fluoridated their water supplies. By 1980, over eight thousand communities and more than half of the U.S. population was drinking from artificially or naturally fluoridated water supplies.

In addition, the advent of fluoride-based toothpastes beginning in the 1960s and the growing availability of fluoride mouth rinses in the 1970s further increased the likelihood that children, whether their community had fluoridated its water supply or not, had ready access to fluorides' preventive possibilities. The impact of pervasive exposure to fluorides on children's dental health was spectacular. By the late 1970s, a precipitous nationwide decline in the incidence of dental caries was evident, in non-fluoridated as well as in fluoridated communities. Dentists began to report substantial growth in the numbers of cavity free children, who were virtually unknown just two decades earlier. While the precise causes were uncertain, the omnipresence of fluorides in the food chain, as well as their widespread ingestion via community water supplies, tablets, mouth rinses, and toothpastes, contributed substantially to the decline.

By the beginning of the twenty-first century, the perceived crisis in "mouth hygiene" that had given rise to the specialty of children's dentistry was clearly over. To be sure, dental caries still compromise children's health, and some subgroups of children, particularly among the disadvantaged, continue to suffer disproportionately from caries. But leaders in the field have understandably turned their attention to a variety of new issues and unmet needs. These include paying more attention to periodontal diseases in children; intervening earlier to treat malocclusions; grounding dentist–child relations more consistently on scientific principles of child development; extending dental care to disabled children; expanding the dentist's responsibility in recognizing CHILD ABUSE and neglect; managing medically compromised patients, such as those with AIDS; and inventing a caries vaccine. Concerns about aesthetic issues as well as health issues led to growing rates of treatment with braces and other straightening devices from the mid-twentieth century onward.

Perhaps bolder still, some leaders in "preschool dentistry" insist that the relatively recently established ideal age for children to see a dentist for the first time—age three—is in fact far too late to preserve optimal dental health. Instead, they recommend that parents schedule their child's first dental appointment between six months and one year of age. The entire field of preschool dentistry was inconceivable a century ago. But its basic premise remains consistent with that of Jordon and other pioneers in early-twentieth-century children's dentistry: "The prevention of disease can never be started too early" (Pinkham, p. 4).

See also: **Hygiene; Pediatrics.**

BIBLIOGRAPHY

Adams, Tracey I. 2000. *A Dentist and a Gentleman: Gender and the Rise of Dentistry in Ontario.* Toronto: University of Toronto Press.

Campbell, J. M. 1963. *Dentistry, Then and Now.* Glasgow, UK: Pickering and Inglis.

Dunning, James Morse. 1970. *Principles of Public Health,* 3rd ed. Cambridge, MA: Harvard University Press.

Gies, William J. 1926. *Dental Education in the United States and Canada.* New York: The Carnegie Foundation for the Advancement of Teaching.

Jordon, M. Evangeline. 1925. *Operative Dentistry for Children.* Brooklyn, NY: Dental Items of Interest Publishing.

King, Roger. 1998. *The Making of the Dentiste, c. 1650–1760.* Brookfield, VT: Ashgate.

Lambert, Camille, Jr., and Howard E. Freeman. 1967. *The Clinic Habit.* New Haven, CT: College and University Press.

Loevy, Hannelore T. 1984. "M. Evangeline Jordon, Pioneer in Pedodontics." *Bulletin of the History of Dentistry* 32, no. 1 (April).

McBride, Walter C. 1945. *Juvenile Dentistry.* Philadelphia: Lea and Febiger.

McCluggage, Robert W. 1959. *A History of the American Dental Association: A Century of Health Service.* Chicago: American Dental Association.

McDonald, Ralph E. 1963. *Dentistry for the Child and Adolescent.* Saint Louis, MO: C. V. Mosby.

Nettleton, Sarah. 1992. *Power, Pain, and Dentistry.* Buckingham, UK: Open University Press.

Pelton, Walter J., and Jacob M. Wisan. 1955. *Dentistry in Public Health.* Philadelphia: W. B. Saunders.

Pinkham, J. R. 1988. *Pediatric Dentistry: Infancy through Adolescence.* Philadelphia: W. B. Saunder.

Schlossman, Steven L., Joanne Brown, and Michael Sedlak. 1986. *The Public School in American Dentistry.* Santa Monica, CA: Rand.

Welbury, Richard R. 2001. *Paediatric Dentistry.* Oxford, UK: Oxford University Press.

STEVEN SCHLOSSMAN

Dependent Children

The contemporary idea of childhood in the United States is distinctly domestic: it regards the home and its appendages, such as schools and churches, as the child's proper places. Although U.S. attitudes toward childhood and children have European roots, approaches to child welfare in parts of Europe and non-Western societies often differ from American attitudes, since they have included the separation of children from their homes for purposes of maturation, APPRENTICE-SHIP, and early employment. From the American view, such practices are aberrant, harmful, and tantamount to ABAN-DONMENT in so far as they fall short of providing children with nurturing, parental home environments. Contemporary Western notions of abandonment sprang from this particular representation of domestic childhood and from normative judgments about a child's actual and ideal life course.

The Years Prior to the Civil War

Dependent children are those who, through various circumstances, become dependent on private charity or public assistance. In the United States, ideas about children's welfare were inherited from the English Poor Laws under the principle of *parens patriae*, whereby the state is the ultimate parent of all children. In the colonial era, this resulted in two forms of relief for dependent children: indoor relief (assistance to parents in the home) and outdoor relief (alternate homes, such as ORPHANAGES and poor houses). For most of the seventeenth and eighteenth centuries, public administration was local and the household was the immediate source of authority, with the result that dependents had little direct contact with the state. Many thousands of children were brought to the colonies as indentures and the death rate in the Chesapeake was high for children as well as adults. Consequently, the indenture system tried to maintain household governance and the family system by placing children in homes while training them for future employment. It made little difference whether the child was poor, illegitimate, or orphaned and, regardless of cause, children who were left on their own were regularly indentured or apprenticed. Indenture afforded a reasonable solution to uncared-for children while reducing public responsibility for colonial dependents, including those who were orphaned, whose parents were unfit, or who misbehaved. In 1648 Virginia, for example, following the British model, the state could remove a child from a home with parents who were overly fond or if the child was "perversely obstinate."

The first private orphan asylum in North America appeared in 1738 in Georgia, and the first public orphanage did not open until a half century later, in 1790, in South Carolina, with 115 orphans. Others followed in New York City, Philadelphia, and Baltimore. The founding of orphanages demonstrates that by the late eighteenth century, congregate alternatives for dependent children were being tried. Whereas binding out and indenture favored the family setting and foreshadowed the subsequent shift to FOSTER CARE and ADOPTION, almshouses and orphanages foreshadowed a preference for congregate institutions.

The years prior to the Civil War witnessed a movement away from indenture and apprenticeship toward the rise of congregate institutions, based in rising objections to indenture for children, and an increase in the real numbers of dependent children. Moreover, as industrialization changed the size and nature of the family, the value of children shifted from their productive contribution to the family to parental bonds of affection for the child. The nineteenth-century cult of motherhood eroded the traditional patriarchal control over child custody, forging instead a romanticized ideology in which children were innocent and vulnerable and mothers had a special responsibility for protecting them. In 1838, a new judicial policy marked the shift from father's rights to mother's love in the adjudication of child custody. EX PARTE CROUSE declared that children have needs, not rights; that they need custody, not liberty; and the place for a child was school, not prison. While the case is noted for shifting the parental responsibility of child custody from the father to the mother, it was also pivotal for legitimizing and elevating the practice of institutional custody.

Between 1820 and 1860, 150 private orphanages were founded across the United States, some in response to EPI-DEMICS that orphaned many children. Orphanages were largely religious and largely for white children under ten years of age. Most orphanages indentured the older children, and few received public funds. It was not long before congregate institutions became overcrowded, underfunded, and less and less rehabilitative. By mid-century, congregate institutions that only a few years earlier had been models of care were losing their luster. An 1855 report to the New York State Legislature chastised almshouses for the outrageous conditions in which they sheltered some 3,000 children under sixteen. The problems were intensified with the children orphaned in the Civil War and as numbers of immigrants multiplied. Nevertheless, despite criticism, congregate institutions grew through the end of the nineteenth century.

Placing Out

The idea of PLACING OUT marked a departure from apprenticeship, indenture, and congregate homes. Whereas removing children from the home under those circumstances did not necessarily sever ties with the children's families, placing out included permanent transfer to foster or adoptive homes, illustrated by the NEW YORK CHILDREN'S AID SOCIETY (NYCAS) and CHARLES LORING BRACE's famous ORPHAN TRAINS in the mid-nineteenth century. Brace was a critic of congregate institutions, and the NYCAS placed thousands of dependent youth in private homes. (NYCAS, however, overwhelmingly favored white western European children, who represented 95 percent of its placements; it could not or would not place black or eastern European children.) Brace romanticized the image of children being "rescued" from urban streets and placed in families in the midwestern countryside and the plains states. He spoke passionately about the practice that eventually affected some 200,000 youngsters over seventy-five years. As rapid urbanization, immigration, and industrialization widened social class divisions, reformers like Brace looked to protect society by removing children from those "dangerous" classes.

Brace's objective was to place children in caring, moral, and stable family environments, and this program signaled the triumph of the ideology of domesticity, with its emphasis on affection, romantic marriage, and innocent children. He preferred foster care to adoption, as most of his children's parents were destitute but not absent or dead, and ties of affection and Christian charity to legal bonds. Brace found a middle ground between involuntary apprenticeship or indenture on the one hand and adoption on the other. With the support of New York's upper-class reformers, he shared their concern for the waif as well as disdain for the poor and immigrant parents.

In the colonial era children outside the bloodline could not share legal status with natural-born children. However, by the mid-nineteenth century the courts, under the best interests of the child doctrine, were more willing to consider the place of affection, choice, and nurture in the family structure. In 1851, two path-breaking court cases terminated the natural rights of birth parents. More and more, judges moved the parent-child relationship from patriarchal kinship lines to a contractual relationship that reflected sentimental ties and emphasized child nurture. That year, Massachusetts passed an act to provide for the adoption of children, substituting artificial ties for those of birth. By the end of the century, the Massachusetts model existed in almost every state, and adoption became routine.

While Brace's system of fostering challenged institutional care for dependent children, asylums continued to grow in size and number but increasingly were on the defensive. In 1864 the Boston Children's Aid Society (BCAS), for example, rejected long-term care in favor of keeping the families intact to the greatest extent possible. Where Brace wanted homes for children who were homeless or in jeopardy, the BCAS developed strategies for placing dependent children, paying other families to board them, and finding places where single mothers could both work and keep their children, carefully selecting and monitoring the foster homes. Taken together, these projects encouraged the formation of foster care and the passage of adoption laws intended to place children in family environments where the relocated children would be treated like natural sons and daughters. Brace wanted to place children permanently, separated from their birth families, which, especially regarding poor or immigrant families, he considered to be incapable of raising good "American" children. The BCAS, on the other hand, wanted to place children in ways that their parents could see them, and perhaps reclaim them when their situations improved. Moreover, Brace and his peers succeeded in articulating new language that included the rights of the child, not for independence or personal liberty, but for safety from risk and corruption. Welfare policies were profoundly influenced by the idea of the child as a special category of citizen, and state-sponsored children's institutions supported this view. By the end of the nineteenth century, the best interest of the child doctrine facilitated the creation of age-segregated state laws restricting child labor and prohibiting children from buying tobacco or alcohol. It also shaped adoption and custody laws. The new laws rested on an assessment of the child's needs and the public good rather than the parents' interests. Poor and black families after the Civil War were particularly vulnerable to having their children bound out for apprenticeships without parental approval, and the best interest of the child idea sometimes resulted in injustices as the authority to control the child shifted from the parent to the state.

Mothers' Pensions

The first White House Conference on the Care of Dependent Children, which assembled 200 leading child welfare advocates to discuss the problem of the dependent child, was convened by Theodore Roosevelt in 1909. The White House Conference marked a turning point in state responsibility for the care of dependent children where advocates sanctioned the idea that poverty alone should not justify disrupting the home became official policy. It introduced ideas upon which the modern welfare state would be based and signaled a new relationship between women, the family, and the state, while retaining familiar patronizing judgments about women in poverty, the working class, and race. Consensus among reformers reified the ideal of the nuclear family as the best environment in which to raise children. They encouraged placing out and making congregate institutions more homelike with family-style cottages and self-governing formats. In principle, however, the conferees agreed to keep children with their natural families whenever possible, an objective that set the groundwork for the most important innovation regarding child dependency: widows' pensions, intended to enable needy and morally "fit" widows to care for their children in their home.

In 1910, the report of the New York State Commission on Relief for Widowed Mothers claimed that, "No woman, save in exceptional circumstances can be both homemaker and the breadwinner of her family." By and large, interest in working mothers reflected the reformers' preoccupation with children as a national resource rather than with the needs of mothers themselves. According to this view, a mother's employment negatively influenced her child's development. The commission found that the work available to poor women outside the home inevitably broke down the physical, mental, and moral strength of the family. It disrupted the home life through an inadequate standard of living and parental neglect due to the enforced absence of the mother at the time the children most needed her care.

Through this reasoning, working mothers were blamed for juvenile DELINQUENCY and other problems children faced.

Such was the first modern public welfare program in the United States focused on keeping children with their families of origin. In 1911 Illinois enacted the first statewide law, and within eight years thirty-nine states had their own versions. States, one by one, adopted laws that concurred with the White House Conference report that said, in part, "Children of . . . deserving mothers who are without the support of a normal breadwinner, should as a rule be kept with their parents, such aid being given as may be necessary to maintain suitable homes for the rearing of children" (Abramovitz, p. 194). The nineteenth-century desire to save the child was transformed into a twentieth-century desire to save the family. Mothers' pensions continued the nineteenth-century pattern in which the state interposed itself between parents and children; however instead of breaking up poor families by removing children from homes viewed as unfit, the twentieth-century strategy was to help families stay together on the grounds that no child should be removed from home for reasons of poverty alone.

From the beginning, however, pension rules emphasized that subsidies should go to only the "fit and worthy poor," elevating the image of the blameless widow while at the same time creating a category of those who were deemed unworthy. Inefficiency or immorality were justifications for withholding support. The pensions no longer stigmatized pauperism or blamed its victims for idleness, but they did establish a new moral litmus test. "Suitable home" provisions allowed for surveillance and investigation, and "unfitness" devolved into a set of moral judgments, especially regarding immigrants and minorities. For example, in Los Angeles, prior to the Social Security Act of 1935, no Mexicans were eligible and nationally few African Americans received pensions. While mothers' pensions worked for some, for others the program excluded whole categories of poor women with children.

The shift from institutional care and placing out to mothers' pensions as a means for the care, support, and socialization of poor children reflected not only the desire to keep families united, but also the existing SOCIAL WELFARE system's declining ability to protect children. Private charities could not provide adequately for destitute children, and family management ideas generated by social workers were gaining confidence. Indeed, mothers' pensions reflected both a critique of institutional care and the placing out system and also the belief that money going to institutions could be redirected to mothers in their homes at less cost. The acceptance of mothers' pensions constituted public recognition by the states that the contribution of the unskilled or semiskilled mothers in their own homes exceeded their earnings outside the home and that it was in the public interest to support the child-rearing function of mothers. Nevertheless, inadequate

pensions, prohibitions against supplemental work, and traditional moral surveillance over women limited the effectiveness of the program from the beginning.

The Century of the Child

The Progressive Era ushered in the CENTURY OF THE CHILD. States took on enlarged public responsibility for needy children, and JUVENILE COURTS collected information about dependent and neglected children, which was used in deciding matters of placement. Emerging groups of social science professionals focused their expertise on the special needs of children. Among educators, a crusade against corporal punishment in the public schools was added to concerns about child labor and parental neglect. Over the next decade, however, despite the best intentions of reformers, the limitations on who could receive support meant that too few children would be beneficiaries of the new thinking. By the end of the 1920s, less than one percent of all children under the age of fourteen benefited from aid to mothers.

In 1934, in the depths of the GREAT DEPRESSION, President Franklin Delano Roosevelt created the Committee on Economic Security to draft a social security plan that went beyond emergency relief programs and established permanent federal governmental strategies to deal with recurrent problems such as unemployment. The U.S. CHILDREN'S BUREAU, author of the mothers' pensions, was called upon to draft the provision for aid to children, and in 1935 AID TO DEPENDENT CHILDREN (ADC) was established by Title IV of the Social Security Act.

Harry Hopkins, director of the Federal Emergency Relief Act programs and a trained social worker, favored a comprehensive welfare system that included an income maintenance program. In his view, direct assistance to the poor was more important than rehabilitating families. Hopkins defined a dependent child as anyone under sixteen for whom no adult person, other than one needed to care for the child, could work and provide a reasonable subsistence compatible with decency and health. This definition broadened the concept of dependent children to include those who lived in two-parent families in which unemployment or underemployment prevailed, or in foster homes, or with relatives. Congress, however, rejected this expansive plan.

Aid to Dependent Children, was a more comprehensive version of the mothers' pension program. From the beginning, it was "designed to release women to their natural role as mothers, and to save children from social misfortune, but more affirmatively to make them citizens capable of contributing to society" ("The Report on the Committee on Economic Security," pp. 35–36). The program provided funds to the states rather than cities or counties to establish financial assistance programs for needy children. The Social Security Administration (SSA) required ADC programs to be implemented statewide, unlike mothers' pensions which were not always distributed by the local units authorized to do so. This system increased women's access to relief funds. Moreover, the program expanded the reasons children could receive support and the range of possible caretakers. However, most states delayed putting the program into place. By 1939 ten states still had not implemented a program for dependent children.

From the beginning, a pattern of lower payment rates was set for ADC participants than for the blind and the aged. The lower wage, it was reasoned, would guarantee that public aid would not become more attractive than the lowest paying job, or more attractive than conventional marriage and family life. ADC remained limited to single parents, despite efforts to extend it to two-parent households if both were unemployed. Roosevelt's Committee on Economic Security rejected the Social Security Advisory Council's 1935 efforts to include two-parent families, fearing that if it asked too much for ADC it might undercut the whole Social Security Act. The effort failed again in 1949 on the grounds that it undercut the work ethic.

The Social Security Act established a two track welfare system. One track was oriented toward social insurance whereby government would make up for wages lost by injury, unemployment, or retirement; the other focused on public assistance. Social insurance flowed automatically from one's age or condition. However, public assistance in the form of ADC was discretionary and had the taint of public charity. Congress rejected the Federal Emergency Relief Administration's broad definition of dependence and funded ADC at $18 per month for the first child and $12 for any others, a sum that was "utterly inadequate and completely out of line with pensions of $30 per month to individual old people" (quoted in Gordon, p. 278). Congress further weakened ADC by enlarging state control; many states refused to pay anything, or paid well below any standard of subsistence. States demanded "suitable" homes as an eligibility requirement and, although the Social Security Act did not require it, they were allowed to do so. From the beginning, the dilemma was whether to meet the economic needs of children or judge the morals and behavior of adults. The suitable home requirement immediately became discriminatory.

In the years following World War II, the number of ADC recipients more than doubled, growing from 372,000 families in 1940 to 803,000 in 1960. ADC costs rose from $133 million to $994 million, and the profile of the ADC recipient changed. By 1961, widowed families were no longer the face of ADC, comprising only 7.7 percent of the ADC caseload, down from 43 percent in 1937; the majority of ADC mothers were separated, divorced, or unwed. Absolute numbers of white women were higher, but the percent of black women receiving ADC benefits was higher than in the general population. Nonwhite Hispanics and blacks produced a nonwhite majority, and whites were 42 percent nationwide. Discrimination against black men in the workplace led to low-wage and vulnerable employment situations. In 1940, black unemployment exceeded white by 20 percent, and in 1955 was twice that of whites. Black women were equally vulnerable to workplace discrimination; in 1950, sixty percent of employed black women worked in domestic service, compared with sixteen percent of white women. Between World War II and the 1960s, ADC's policies also became more punitive and moralistic, focusing on the personal characteristics of the ADC mother.

Changing ADC From Needs to Rights

The civil rights and social protest movements of the 1950s and 1960s, however, created a context for new ideas about the rights of mothers, the rights of children, and the very definition of the family. Social attitudes shifted from the idea that mothers should stay home to the idea that mothers should work, and shifted from the idea that the best interest of the child meant the child should be protected to the idea that children have rights. In the early 1960s, moreover, the nation rediscovered poverty. Although the percentage of poor persons dropped from 22.4 percent in 1959 to 21 percent in 1961, the real numbers remained very high. Inside the White House, it was thought that providing services rather than giving direct assistance would both rehabilitate families and move them off welfare rolls. In 1962 President John F. Kennedy added amendments to the Social Security Amendments to strengthen family and self-support for ADC families. One amendment authorized ADC funds for foster care when children were removed from an "unsuitable" home; another provided funds to assist two-parent homes in which the wage earner was unemployed and no longer entitled to unemployment insurance. For the first time, unemployed men could remain present in an ADC household. With this change, the government symbolically changed Aid to Dependent Children to Aid to Families with Dependent Children.

Aid to Families with Dependent Children (AFDC) had two fundamental and warring goals: to provide a decent standard of living for children and to encourage the self-sufficiency of parents. It was held that cash transfers to families with children could eliminate child poverty, but not without discouraging parents from working. The inherent conflict led to insufficient funding and provisions that made work an unattractive option. Mothers who worked lost benefits for every earned dollar and faced the loss of Medicaid, food stamps and other AFDC benefits. Moreover, AFDC was administered at the state level, allowing states to choose the standards that determine eligibility, set income and asset limits, and chose benefit levels. As a result programs varied considerably from state to state. Despite its flaws, however, the program grew. By the end of 1964, AFDC rolls numbered 975,000, and during the next four years AFDC expanded by 58 percent, to more than 1.5 million families. This and other factors provoked a backlash against AFDC mothers. Detractors thought recipients were lazy and undeserving. In the face of a developing National Welfare Rights Organization, some states began to channel AFDC mothers into the labor market. A punishing 1967 amendment (the Work Incentive Program), imposed a freeze on all federal aid to states for AFDC cases arising from desertion or births outside of marriage and continued unlimited matching funds for cases where the father had died or was unemployed. Outrage over this policy caused two presidents not to enforce it, and it was finally repealed in 1969. A dramatic reversal in congressional attitudes toward working mothers was almost complete: in 1935, the best interest of the mother, the child, and the nation was to keep the mother at home. In 1969, to receive AFDC, mothers had to register to work.

Meanwhile, between 1950 and 1970, the system of foster care became an integral part of the child protection network. In 1958, the number of children in foster care was 38 per 10,000—lower than it had been in 1933, when 59 per 10,000 were in the system. In 1969, however, 75 per 10,000 of all dependent children were in foster care. A heightened awareness of CHILD ABUSE accounted for some increase; the 1962 increase in payments to AFDC foster families and the decline of children's institutions may account for more of it, as may other factors. While orphanages were in decline (an unexpected consequence of ADC) in favor of foster care, even foster care came under criticism for its intrusions into the homes of the poor and minorities. In the climate of returning to "family values," foster care was criticized for being class biased in its removal policies, and too emotionally destabilizing for children. The Adoption Assistance and Child Welfare Act passed by Congress in 1980 privileged adoption over long-term foster placements and redefined fostering as a temporary situation until the child could be returned home or adopted. No child was to enter the foster care system without a long-term plan in place. In contrast to the 1974 Child Abuse Prevention and Treatment Act, the 1980 law was to be noninterventionist and sought to protect children from extended foster care itself.

Adoption proved to be an alternative to foster care and unsafe familial homes, but adoption, too, was subject to the race and class divisions existing in the larger society. In 1972 the National Association of Black Social Workers declared that black children should only be adopted by families of their own race, and over the next twenty years 77 percent of state and almost half of private agencies had unwritten understandings which enforced that policy. Similar questions arose regarding NATIVE AMERICAN CHILDREN. In 1978, some 90 percent of adopted Native American children were in the custody of non-Indian families. Between 1969 and 1974, states had placed 35 percent of Native children in adoptive or foster care, often in forced separations from parents. The Indian Child Welfare Act of 1978 discouraged the removal of children from Indian settings, preferring, where possible, that the child should remain in the Indian commu-

nity. Consequently, by 1986 some 62 percent of Indian children were placed with Indian families.

Changing AFDC

Under the Reagan administration (1981–1989) criticism of welfare programs intensified. The failed 1979 Family Protection Bill attempted to end federal spending for child abuse prevention; however, conservatives continued to criticize AFDC, which for them symbolized the welfare state, collapse of the family, and a decline of morality. Cutbacks under Reagan reduced AFDC income to 47 percent of what was necessary for basic needs. With food stamps, AFDC income was at 70 percent of the poverty threshold. By 1989, one in four children lived in poverty. As the federal government shifted responsibility to the states between 1980 and 1992, real state spending on AFDC per poor family declined by 31 percent. The 1990s saw a developing consensus in favor of reduced federal budgets, family restoration, and a reinvigorated national debate about adoption. Issues arising from open records and new reproductive technologies emerged, exposing tensions between birth and adoptive parents, and between surrogate and adoptive parents. States tested the acceptance of homosexual adoption, and how open the adoption process should be. With the foster care system overwhelmed with a new class of drug-addicted parents and babies, the courts, legislatures, and welfare professionals believed that the goal of family reunification was not always in the best interest of the child.

In the 1990s, various new ideas were proposed for dependent children, while some old ones, such as a return to congregate institutions (orphanages) were also discussed, although it was clear that this proposal was unlikely to prosper. Dissatisfaction with welfare did, however, bear fruit. On August 22, 1996, President Bill Clinton signed a bill to abolish the sixty-year-old AFDC program. The WELFARE REFORM ACT set a five-year lifetime cap on welfare benefits and required most recipients to enter the workforce within two years. It provided federal block grants to states to establish their own programs. The law was opposed by the Children's Defense Fund, the Urban Institute, and other groups, which estimated that it would increase the number of children living in poverty by a million. Others argued that AFDC, by supporting children in their own homes, was less expensive than the alternatives, which would have to include expenses for day care. Nonetheless, by 1993, according to the Children's Defense Fund, 15.7 million children, including 27 percent of all American children under the age of three, already lived in poverty. Poverty remains unevenly distributed. According to statistics issued in the spring of 2003, almost a million African-American children live in extreme poverty and the number of all African-American children who are poor has increased by almost 50 percent since 1999. Clearly, the problem of poverty and social dependency has not disappeared, but the solution has become much less clear.

Historically, society's obligation to assist dependent children has been undisputed and has produced a range of alternatives, from reproducing the home through indenture, apprenticeship, fostering, and adoption, to replacing the home with orphanages and group homes. Each solution involved children's separation from their families of origin. In the twentieth century, both reformers and mothers preferred to keep children at home wherever possible, agreeing that poverty alone should not separate children from their parents. By the end of the twentieth century, however, the question of assistance to dependent children was inextricably linked to the country's deep ambivalence about what children need, which mothers deserved help, the size of the welfare state, and the degree to which government should intervene in private family matters. Welfare rights supporters asserted that the programs were insufficient and created family disruption, while opponents countered that the family was being undermined by interference from the state. Laws geared to protecting children from abuse and neglect both protected children and undermined parental authority. At the heart of the matter was conflict over the rights and needs of the child, set against equally powerful beliefs about the proper responsibility of the poor single mother: whether she should work or to be home with her children. Attitudes toward mothers reflected larger national attitudes toward race, class, sex roles, ethnicity, and values surrounding work and welfare. Public assistance to children was thus linked not only to the social construction of CHILDREN'S RIGHTS and needs, but also to the social construction of mothers in poverty.

See also: **White House Conferences on Children; Work and Poverty.**

BIBLIOGRAPHY

Abramovitz, Mimi. 1988. *Regulating the Lives of Women: Social Welfare Policy from Colonial Times to the Present.* Boston: South End Press.

Ashby, LeRoy. 1984. *Saving the Waifs: Reformers and Dependent Children, 1890–1917.* Philadelphia: Temple University Press.

Ashby, LeRoy. 1997. *Endangered Children: Dependency, Neglect, and Abuse in American History.* New York: Twayne.

Brace, Charles Loring. 1894. *The Life of Charles Loring Brace: Chiefly Told in His Own Letters / Edited by His Daughter.* New York: Charles Scribner's Sons.

Currie, Janet M. 1995. *Welfare and the Well-Being of Children.* Chur, Switzerland: Harwood Academic.

Gordon, Linda. 1994. *Pitied but Not Entitled. Single Mothers and the History of Welfare, 1890–1935.* New York: Free Press.

Grubb, W. Norton, and Marvin Lazerson. 1982. *Broken Promises.* New York: Basic Books.

Hawes, Joseph. 1991. *The Children's Rights Movement: A History of Advocacy and Protection.* New York: Twayne.

Ladd Taylor, Molly. 1994. *Mother-Work: Women, Child Welfare, and the State, 1890–1930.* Urbana: University of Illinois Press.

Ladd Taylor, Molly, and Lauri Umansky, eds. 1997. *"Bad" Mothers: The Politics of Blame in Twentieth-Century America.* New York: New York University Press.

Platt, Anthony. 1969. *The Child Savers.* Chicago: University of Chicago Press.

"The Report on the Committee on Economic Security," 1985. Reprinted in *50th Anniversary Issue, The Report of the Committee on Economic Security of 1935 and Other Basic Documents Relating to the Social Security Act.* Washington, DC: National Conference on Social Welfare.

Swift, Karen J. 1995. *Manufacturing "Bad Mothers": A Critical Perspective on Child Neglect.* Toronto: University of Toronto Press.

Tiffin, Susan. 1982. *In Whose Best Interest? Child Welfare Reform in the Progressive Era.* Westport, CT: Greenwood Press.

ROBERTA WOLLONS

Desiderius Erasmus of Rotterdam (c. 1469–1536)

Erasmus is often described as one of the first "modern" persons, closer to our time than to the medieval world. In looking at his writings on childhood, however, it is apparent that his teaching was based on classical and medieval debates about upbringing and schooling. Here the basic question had been: how do children learn best, by the stick or the carrot? Erasmus's answer was: spare the rod and stimulate the child.

Early Life

Erasmus never knew his father, and his illegitimate status haunted him through his life, with the result that his own autobiographical account cannot be trusted for what it tells about his parents. At an early age he was handed over to a school in Deventer run by the Brethren of the Common Life. Here there were some good teachers who taught Erasmus the classical Latin that would become one of his lifelong passions. But here he also experienced the beatings and humiliations that he later condemned as a disciplinary method for children.

In 1487 Erasmus was convinced by his guardians to enter a monastery, thus ending their obligations toward him. The Canons Regular of Saint Augustine gave him good opportunities for study and also for writing, but Erasmus disliked most of the brethren, many of whom were probably country boys with shallow vocations and limited interest in learning. In 1493 he received permission to leave the monastery, but not the order, in order to be secretary for the bishop of Cambrai. In the bishop's company Erasmus began to make contacts with other aspiring young intellectuals and their powerful patrons.

Thanks to a leave of absence from this position, Erasmus later attended the University of Paris. If he had been critical of his monastery, he soon became equally dissatisfied with the dry theological discussions of late scholasticism. After four years and many new friendships, especially with English students, Erasmus made his first journey to England. He met central intellectual and political figures such as John Colet and Thomas More. Because of them, he revised his opinion about sterile theology and decided to concentrate his life not on the classics but on the Bible and the church fathers.

Erasmus became a leading light of what has been called Christian humanism and had passionate intellectual contacts and heated controversies with many of his humanist colleagues. He learned Greek and fathered an important edition of the New Testament; he journeyed to Italy and received new inspiration for his studies; he returned several times to England. In 1517 the Pope dispensed him from his religious vows. Soon after he was forced to realize that another Augustinian canon, Martin Luther, was threatening the unity of the Western Christian Church. Erasmus recognized the importance of Luther's criticisms of abuses but eventually distanced himself out of a desire to preserve the unity of the Church.

Early Liberal Education for Children

During these years the political and religious situation forced Erasmus to move from Louvain to Basel and finally to Freiburg im Breisgau, where he arrived in 1529. Here he published a "Declamation on the Subject of Early Liberal Education for Children" (*De pueris statim ac liberaliter instituendis declamatio*), which he had first composed in Italy in around 1509. This is Erasmus's central work on education and had immediate success. It is addressed not only to professional educators but also to parents, and the central argument is that they are to invest time, effort, and money in seeing to it that their children, especially their sons, get access to humane and humanistic schooling from the earliest possible age.

Erasmus accepted the teaching of Saint Augustine (d. 430) that children are not born into innocence but are marked by original sin and so have a proclivity toward evil. But as a Christian humanist, he was convinced that generous love and careful instruction by both parents and teachers would bring out the best in children. Education's first task was to teach children to speak clearly and accurately, and so parents were obliged to spend time with children and make sure that they heard good speech. Erasmus claimed, on the basis of his vast knowledge of classical culture, that civilization went into decline when parents began to hand over the upbringing and education of their children to slaves.

Classical writers such as Plutarch, as well as medieval monastic teachers such as Anselm of Canterbury (d. 1109), had already discussed how educators should treat children. Erasmus, like Anselm, insisted on gentleness. The teacher must be liked, for through his own personality he makes learning attractive. Schools, he complained, had become "torture chambers," recalling his own experience and warning against sadistic and cruel practices, including those among students in initiation rituals.

Erasmus related his recommendations to statements by Saint Paul and also to the teachings of Jesus. The teacher was to become a father to his students, and Erasmus was confident that love would be able to overcome almost any challenge. Such a regime did not allow laziness or indifference:

children were to begin to learn languages as early as possible. He remarked on the openness of small children to rote learning and how they excelled in memory and imitation.

The best teacher, he wrote, is the one who makes learning letters into a game, who uses pictures and illustrative stories, who knows how to make school into something attractive. Children should not be kept at home until PUBERTY and then sent off to school. Erasmus implied that sending children away to boarding school was not good for them, but his main point was that formal and informal schooling should take advantage of the early years.

On Good Manners for Boys

Also in 1530 Erasmus wrote his "On Good Manners for Boys" (*De civilitate morum puerorum*), which has been noticed for its lively descriptions of vulgarity and uncouth manners. Cultural historians such as Norbert Elias have seen the treatise as an indication of a new emphasis on civility after medieval barbarism, but again it must be emphasized that Erasmus drew on a discussion beginning in the classical world and continuing in medieval monasteries and court life. Erasmus here again pleaded for a gentle approach to the young, but now he addressed the young themselves and described how they were responsible for their outward behavior as an indication of inner life. Physical gestures should show respect for other people. Bodily functions should be kept under control. Erasmus emphasized modesty and propriety. The treatise, like its companion, reflects Erasmus's search for loving, caring authority figures and humanistic educational models.

See also: **Education, Europe; Medieval and Renaissance Europe.**

BIBLIOGRAPHY

Desiderius Erasmus. 1965. *Christian Humanism and the Reformation.* Ed. and trans. John C. Olin. New York: Harper and Row.

Desiderius Erasmus. 1985. "A Declamation on the Subject of Early Liberal Education for Children." Trans. Beert C. Verstraete. In *Collected Works of Erasmus,* vol. 26, ed. J. K. Sowards, pp. 291–346. Toronto: University of Toronto Press.

Desiderius Erasmus. 1985. "On Good Manners for Boys." Trans. Brian McGregor. In *Collected Works of Erasmus,* vol. 25, ed. J. K. Sowards, pp. 269–289. Toronto: University of Toronto Press.

Huizinga, Johan. 1984 [1924]. *Erasmus and the Age of Reformation.* Princeton, NJ: Princeton University Press.

BRIAN PATRICK MCGUIRE

Dewey, John (1859–1952)

America's foremost philosopher of education, John Dewey grew up in rural Vermont, earned his doctorate at The Johns Hopkins University, and taught at Michigan, Chicago, and Columbia universities. Dewey was one of the founders and the leading philosopher of PROGRESSIVE EDUCATION, an important late-nineteenth-century and twentieth-century movement for school reform that emphasized meeting the needs of the whole child—physical, social, emotional, and intellectual. In addition to his work in developing a new philosophy of education, Dewey, along with Charles Sanders Peirce and William James, created a uniquely American approach to philosophy—Pragmatism.

Dewey developed his educational philosophy when he joined the faculty of the University of Chicago in 1894 and added a department of pedagogy to his responsibilities. Aided by his wife, Alice, he founded the university's Laboratory School to test scientifically his ideas for improving schooling.

As a philosopher who was profoundly affected by the English naturalist Charles Darwin's thinking, Dewey believed that in a post-Darwinian world it was no longer possible to envision life as a progress toward fixed ends. His reading of Darwin's *On the Origin of Species* (1859) convinced him that the only constant in life was change or *growth* (the term Dewey preferred). Therefore, Dewey held that the purpose of formal education was not to prepare children for any fixed goal, but rather that schools should be devoted to encouraging children to grow and to prepare them to continue to grow and develop as adults in the uncertain future that they would face. Childhood was not merely a prelude to adulthood; it was a stage of development that was important and valuable in its own right. Accordingly, schooling should be based on meeting the needs of children, as children, rather than only striving to prepare them for adulthood.

Dewey faulted contemporary schools for regarding children as empty vessels to be filled with intellectual content. Schools treated pupils as passive learners. Dewey argued that children were naturally curious and that outside of school they learned through activities. They came to school with many interests, which he classified in his 1899 publication *The School and Society* as "the interest in conversation, or communication; in inquiry, or finding out things; in making things, or construction; and in artistic expression." These, he maintained were "the natural resources, the uninvested capital, upon which depends the active growth of the child" (1956, pp. 47–48). The role of the teacher, Dewey argued, was not merely to give pupils the freedom to express these impulses, but rather to guide them toward the learning they needed. As he noted in his 1902 work *The Child and the Curriculum*, this would not ignore traditional learning. "It must be restored to the experience from which it has been abstracted. It needs to be *psychologized*; . . . translated into the immediate and individual experiencing within which it has its origin and significance" (1956, p. 22). Progressive teachers, therefore, should construct a curriculum based on both the interests of the pupils and knowledge of the subject matter that children should master.

Influence

Dewey was the most significant educational thinker of his time and he influenced educational discussion for a century. His followers took his ideas in many directions. Dewey's disciples, most notably William Heard Kilpatrick, emphasized one part of Dewey's philosophy—the need to appeal to the natural interests of the child—at the expense of consideration of the importance of the traditional fields of study. For Kilpatrick, subject matter was not important. Moreover, some of Dewey's followers extended the idea of relying on the natural curiosity and interests of children to define the curriculum in the upper grades and in secondary schools. This conflicted with Dewey's philosophy: "The new education is in danger of taking the idea of development in altogether too formal and empty a way. . . . Development does not mean just getting something out of the mind. It is a development of experience . . . into experience that is really wanted. . . . What new experiences are needed, it is impossible to tell unless there is some comprehension of the development which is aimed at . . . adult knowledge" (1956a, p. 19). Dewey maintained that the study of traditional subjects was important because "they represent the keys which will unlock . . . the social capital which lies beyond the possible role of . . . limited personal experience" (1956b, p. 111).

Dewey did agree with Kilpatrick that one of the ultimate goals of education must be social reform. For Dewey the ideal society was thoroughly democratic and the school should be organized as an "embryonic community. . . . When the school introduces" children "into membership within such a little community, saturating . . . [them] with the spirit of service, and providing . . . [them] with the instruments of effective self-direction, we shall have the deepest and best guaranty of a larger society which is worthy, lovely, and harmonious" (1956b, p. 29).

During the GREAT DEPRESSION Progressivism's social reform impulse turned increasingly into a critique of the capitalist system that was blamed for the economic disaster. This, in turn, helped fuel a strong reaction against Progressive education during the anticommunism of the post–World War II period. In addition, in the 1950s Progressive education was increasingly blamed for the academic shortcomings of American students. In this setting, Dewey's reputation waned. The movement toward establishing rigid standards that began with the Reagan administration's 1983 report, *A Nation At Risk*, regarded Dewey's ideas as not only wrong but harmful. The states joined in a movement to establish knowledge standards and a schedule of rigid testing to see if the children met those standards. Teachers increasingly taught to the test—an educational program that neglected Dewey's ideas of relying on children's natural curiosity and interests.

While a distorted version of Dewey's educational philosophy had weakened the curriculum, especially in secondary schools, a proper understanding of the kinds of schools that Dewey wanted to establish is still regarded as relevant by a dissenting minority who believe that schools need to meet the broader needs and interests of children.

See also: **Child Development, History of the Concept of; Education, United States.**

BIBLIOGRAPHY

Cremin, Lawrence A. 1962. *The Transformation of the School: Progressivism in American Education, 1876–1957.* New York: Alfred A. Knopf.

Cremin, Lawrence A. 1988. *American Education: The Metropolitan Experience, 1876–1890.* New York: Harper and Row.

Dewey, John. 1938. *Experience and Education.* New York: Macmillan.

Dewey, John. 1954 [1910]. "The Influence of Darwinism on Philosophy." In *American Thought: Civil War to World War I,* ed. Perry Miller. New York: Rinehart.

Dewey, John. 1956a [1902]. *The Child and the Curriculum.* Chicago: The University of Chicago Press.

Dewey, John. 1956b [1899]. *The School and Society.* Chicago: The University of Chicago Press.

Dewey, John. 1966 [1916]. *Democracy and Education: An Introduction to the Philosophy of Education.* New York: The Free Press.

Dewey, John. 1967–1972. *The Early Works, 1882–1898,* 5 vols. Carbondale: Southern Illinois University Press.

Dewey, John. 1976–1983. *The Middle Works, 1899–1924,* 15 vols., ed. Jo Ann Boydston. Carbondale: Southern Illinois University Press.

Dewey, John. 1981–1990. *The Later Works, 1925–1953,* 17 vols., ed. Jo Ann Boydston. Carbondale: Southern Illinois University Press.

Ravitch, Diane. 2000. *Left Back: A Century of Failed School Reforms.* New York: Simon and Schuster.

Westbrook, Robert B. 1991. *John Dewey and American Democracy.* Ithaca, NY: Cornell University Press.

Zilversmit, Arthur. 1993. *Changing Schools: Progressive Education Theory and Practice, 1930–1960.* Chicago: The University of Chicago Press.

ARTHUR ZILVERSMIT

Diapers and Toileting

For as long as there have been babies, there has been mess; but how parents have contended with that mess has changed over time and varied from culture to culture. Some Native American tribes packed grass under rabbit skins to contain their infants' waste. Inuits placed moss under sealskin. In Japan during the Edo era (1603–1868), farmers used an *ejiko,* a wooden bassinet layered with absorbent materials topped by a mattress with a hole cut out for the baby's buttocks. Urine was collected by the lower layers of ash, rags, and straw, and the baby stayed dry while the parents worked. In many warm places, even today, toddlers simply go naked below the waist or, as in China, have pants with a hole cut out of the bottom.

In Europe in the Middle Ages, babies were swaddled in long, narrow bands of linen, hemp, or wool. The groin was sometimes left unwrapped so that absorbent "buttock clothes" of flannel or linen could be tucked underneath. Often in warm weather SWADDLING bands were removed and children were left unclothed or swaddled only on top. After about a year, babies wore small dresses or blouses that fell to the ground with nothing underneath. A handful of ashes was thrown over the infant's excrement which allowed it to be easily swept away.

In the seventeenth and eighteenth centuries in Europe, babies were infrequently bathed or changed. When swaddling clothes were removed to attend to babies' waste, the infants' bottoms were usually just wiped without soap or water and then powdered with absorbent worm-eaten wood dust. Urine-soaked swaddling clothes were dried in front of the fire without being washed and then used again. Urine was believed to have disinfecting properties and filth was often considered protective for infants. It was not until the end of the eighteenth century that doctors began to recommend that cloths used as diapers be changed promptly.

In the mid-eighteenth century, philosophers such as JEAN-JACQUES ROUSSEAU criticized swaddling as unhealthful. These criticisms altered the behavior of European urbanites and the wealthy but had little effect on the practices of the rural poor. English children were not commonly swaddled but dressed in diapers, underpants, and long woolen dresses with swaddling bands only around their abdomens. Swaddling cloth of oiled silk was developed in the eighteenth century in an attempt to prevent leaks.

A great advance in diapering was the invention of the safety pin, patented by Walter Hunt in 1849, but not widely used in place of the straight pin for securing diapers until the 1880s. By the late 1800s, infants in Europe and North America were wearing garments similar to the modern cloth diaper. A square of linen or cotton flannel was folded into a triangular or rectangular shape and held in place by safety pins. The diaper was covered with an absorbent pant called a "soaker" or "pilch," made of tightly knitted wool. In the late 1890s, rubberized pants were sometimes used to cover diapers. Diaper rash in the nineteenth century was commonly remedied with burnt flour or powdered vegetable sulfur.

One of the most common responses to the difficulties of diapering has been to toilet train early. At the end of the seventeenth century JOHN LOCKE recommended putting babies on a "pierced chair"—a chair with a hole in the bottom under which a chamber pot could be placed. Some of these chairs had a space for a hot brick to help keep infants warm for the time, sometimes considerable, in which they were strapped to the chair while their mothers waited for them to "produce." Throughout the nineteenth and early twentieth centuries, parenting manuals commonly recommended that TOILET TRAINING begin almost immediately after birth. Some manuals promised mothers that diapers could be dispensed with altogether within three or four months. After

Disposable diapers, first introduced in the 1960s, have become the most popular form of diaper in the early twenty-first century due to their convenience of use, despite the criticism they have received for the impact the discarded diapers have on the environment. Courtesy of Karen Wisinski.

the 1940s, the idea of insistent early toilet training began to give way to the notion that the child should be the guide in toilet training. The child-guided process recommended putting off toilet training until the child was considerably older, meaning at least an additional five thousand diaper changes per child, according to one scholar's estimate.

Changing and cleaning diapers could be very laborious. Beginning in the twentieth century, mothers were encouraged by doctors and other child-rearing experts to wash diapers with soap and water and, by the 1930s, diapers were washed and then sterilized with a hot iron or boiled. Commercial diaper laundering services appeared in the United States in the 1930s. Cloth diapers were overlaid with a highly absorbent muslin, oilcloth, or gauze, or, in Great Britain, underpants made of sterilized latex. The Maternity Center Association, a nonprofit organization devoted to improving maternity care, advised parents that they could use "stork pants" with tightly gathered legs when they went visiting,

but they were discouraged from using these regularly since they could irritate the baby's skin. In 1946 Marion Donovan invented a waterproof diaper cover made of a nylon parachute cloth that was reusable, leak-proof, and closed with snaps. She called it the "Boater" and when it debuted at Saks Fifth Avenue in 1949 it was an immediate success.

Some form of one-use diapers appeared as early as the 1890s, but they were not widely available (and affordable) until the 1960s. The modern disposable diaper was developed by Victor Mills and launched in 1961 under the brand name Pampers. Pampers were an immediate success, even though they initially came in only two sizes, had no tapes, and were quite bulky. Competition for the disposable diaper market soon took off and remedied these flaws. Some doctors worried that disposable diapers would adversely affect infants' development because of the bulk between the legs, but this fear was assuaged by hourglass-shaped diapers and then by the development of super-absorbent polymers, first patented in 1966, which allowed for the introduction of super-absorbent diapers in 1984. In 2001, disposable diapers were, on average, three times less bulky than they were in the early 1980s, significantly decreasing transportation, workforce, and storage costs. Since the early 1980s, disposable diapers have faced a great deal of criticism for their environmental impact, a subject which continues to ignite research and debate. Because of their efficiency, some have also accused disposable diapers of delaying toilet-training for young children.

See also: **Child-Rearing Advice Literature; Hygiene; Pediatrics.**

BIBLIOGRAPHY

Bel Geddes, Joan. 1964. *Small World: A History of Baby Care from the Stone Age to the Spock Age.* New York: Macmillan.

Fontanel, Béatrice, and Claire d'Harcourt. 1997. *Babies: History, Art, and Folklore.* Trans. Lory Frankel. New York: Harry N. Abrams.

Gladwell, Malcolm. 2001. "Smaller; The Disposable Diaper and the Meaning of Progress." *The New Yorker,* Nov. 26: 74.

Kohno, Goro. 1987. "History of Diapering in Japan." *Pediatrician* 14 (suppl. 1): 2–5.

Thurer, Shari L. 1994. *Myths of Motherhood: How Culture Reinvents the Good Mother.* Boston: Houghton Mifflin.

INTERNET RESOURCES

Krafchik, Bernice. 2000. "Diapers: History and Development." Available from <http://cp.pdr.net/hostedfiles/docs/papc_diapers_site/history.htm>.

Richer, Carlos. 2000. "History of the Diaper." Available from <www.gpoabs.com.mx/cricher/history.htm>.

CAROLINE HINKLE McCAMANT

Diaries. *See* Autobiographies.

Dickens, Charles. *See* Oliver Twist.

Disability. *See* Birth Defects; Retardation; Special Education.

Discipline

Throughout American history adults have sought to produce orderly behavior in children. Although many parents and educators expressed their own frustration with a boisterous, willful, or recalcitrant child, most sought to instill values and behaviors that would govern the individual as an adult. Their degree of reliance on corporal punishment, habit formation, control of the environment, or moral suasion has fluctuated through the centuries, reflecting change in concepts of desirable behavior and expectations of children in the family, workplace, and society.

Native American and Colonial Children

NATIVE AMERICAN CHILDREN prior to European contact seem to have enjoyed an indulged childhood followed by initiation rites, which occurred at the onset of PUBERTY. Born on an average at four-year intervals, they received protracted breast-feeding and the attention of their mothers, who carried them on their backs in cradleboards. Allowed to crawl when they were ready and to run about freely by the age of three, children were not disciplined with corporal punishment. Instead, instructed by their parents and members of the community in tasks designated by gender, they were chastised by shaming. At the onset of menstruation, girls were separated from the group and told to fast. Boys of the same age were isolated, confined, and given substances that induced visions as guides to life. Such practices marked a clear line between childhood and adulthood, as young men and women assumed the tasks designated by their cultures.

In seventeenth-century England, infants were shaped by midwives and then swaddled in the belief that the human body could not support itself. Children were breast-fed for about a year by their mothers or a wet nurse whose care could sometimes be negligent. Because crawling was thought to indicate animal behavior, children were encouraged to remain upright by the use of tight corsets under their long robes, leading strings attached to their shoulders, and standing or walking stools in which they could be left for long periods of time. Both boys and girls were corrected with corporal punishment as they grew. When the English settled the Chesapeake colonies, these practices were altered by the circumstances of the new environment. Some 70 to 85 percent of the immigrants arrived as indentured servants, one-third to two-thirds of whom were under the age of twenty. These youngsters and youths were disciplined by the routines of tobacco production and chastised with corporal punishment or shaming. They and the children born in Virginia and Maryland suffered the effects of the region's high mortality rate. Half of the children born would not live to the age of twenty, and over half of those who survived lost one or both parents. Although ORPHANS were placed under the care of guardians and sent to live with another family, they came under the direction of adults who may themselves have lacked the loving care of parents. These conditions, however, also mitigated discipline by limiting the power of a patriarchal father and throwing youngsters on their own at an early age.

Religious beliefs also mitigated practices of discipline. English Puritans, who settled New England, believed in the depravity of the newborn child, who inherited original sin. Infants may not have been swaddled and were breast-fed by their mothers, but when they showed signs of autonomy, their parents restrained them in order to create habitual tractability. As children grew, fathers as well as mothers participated in their governance, instructing them by example and exhortation, and correcting with corporal punishment when they considered it necessary. Yet Puritans were restrained by their belief in the reciprocity of relationships: children owed parents honor and obedience, but parents owed children protection and care. Quakers—the more radical Puritans who settled Pennsylvania—rejected belief in the depravity of the newborn child and encouraged spiritual development in a loving family atmosphere. In order to protect children, they sought to shelter them from sinful influences. The Quaker family became a controlled environment in which the child's will was subject to that of the parents. But Quaker authority was nurturing and sought to buttress autonomy; parents appealed to reason in their children and taught them subordination less to individuals than to a community of values.

Influence of John Locke

In his 1693 *Some Thoughts Concerning Education* JOHN LOCKE suggested that child-rearing practices be designed to develop the rational, autonomous adult. He had argued in his 1690 *Essay Concerning Human Understanding* that the child resembled a blank tablet (*tabula rasa*) at birth and received knowledge through sense impressions, which were ordered by the innate power of reason. The task of the parent was to build in the child the strong body and habits of mind that would allow the capacity of reason to develop. To build the strong constitution, Locke advocated loose clothing, fresh air, and exercise. To teach denial of appetite, he urged little behavioral lessons in the first year of life, in which the parent denied the child something he clearly wanted. Once habits of self-denial and obedience were established, parents could reward good behavior with their esteem and punish bad behavior with disgrace—the withdrawal of parental approval and affection. As the child developed the capacity to reason, he could be granted increasing independence while the parent assumed a new role of friend.

Locke's advice was directed to the education of a gentleman's son but was applied to the education of girls in the periodical the *Spectator* (1711–1714), copies of which inundated the colonies in the eighteenth century. Stories addressed to women and girls spurned fashion while advocating reason, virtue, and gentle wit, and popularized new conceptions of the affectionate, anti-patriarchal family. By the 1740s, British physicians elaborated on Locke's advice, and John Newbery began to print books designed to amuse as well as to instruct children. Avant-garde colonial parents purchased alphabet blocks to make learning pleasant and had children's portraits painted in slightly relaxed attitudes, celebrating the playful aspects of childhood. Popularizations of Locke's advice arrived in America with imports of an expanding consumer economy and widespread aspiration to genteel behavioral ideals. Parents attempted to mold their children to gentility, and some youngsters drew on these materials to

discipline themselves. For example, the printer's apprentice Benjamin Franklin taught himself to write in the 1720s by copying articles in the *Spectator*. In 1746 the fourteen-year-old George Washington consciously acquired self-restraint by copying "Rules of Civility & Decent Behavior" into his commonplace book.

Slavery and Revolution

In the eighteenth century, however, increased transport of African slaves brought large numbers of teenagers and many children to the colonies. These youngsters and youths, cut off from their families and original cultures, were put to work in agricultural labor and disciplined harshly with corporal punishment. Slave children were subject to the discipline of both their masters and their parents or kin. Children born in the colonies shared their mothers with the tasks required of slaves and often lived separately from their fathers. Although they were allowed to play when young, their parents may have curbed signs of autonomy in order to prepare them for survival in slavery. Growing up in a slave society also affected parental discipline of white children, who found themselves masters at an early age. Thomas Jefferson, who agreed with Locke that personality was formed by environmental influences, feared that children observing the harsh discipline of slaves would learn to imitate it and not attain mastery of their own behavior.

The American Revolution imparted political significance to the discipline of children, as cultural leaders sought to create a genuinely republican society. Personal independence and individual autonomy became desirable goals, but self-restraint was deemed essential in future citizens. The task of forming personality in early childhood was allocated to mothers and the creation of common social bonds was allocated to schools. Although Americans did not wholeheartedly approve JEAN-JACQUES ROUSSEAU's 1762 *Émile*, they did adopt his concept of the natural child, whose personality could be formed through manipulation of the environment. In his 1825 *Treatise on the Physical and Medical Treatment of Children*, Dr. William Potts Dewees recommended maternal breast-feeding and the loose clothing, fresh air, and exercise that had been advocated by eighteenth-century physicians. But he also urged parents to instill obedience through strict control of issues such as the child's diet. And he allocated to children special nursery space in the middle-class household, where they could play with a proliferation of new TOYS under the constant surveillance of the mother.

The Nineteenth Century

By the mid-nineteenth century a widespread movement of evangelical Protestantism reinforced the emphasis on affectionate maternal persuasion to help the child develop internalized restraint through guilt. As the middle class became more child-centered, a romantic concept of childhood emerged, in which the young seemed to possess a special spiritual sensibility. But the lives of children also became more regimented with the development of systems of age-graded public schools. With maturation of a capitalist economy, class differences in discipline became pronounced. Working-class parents expected children to contribute to family support inside and outside the home. Those who were immigrants demanded deference from their children and lacked the time and energy for moral suasion. Many resorted to corporal punishment and were frustrated when the freedom of urban streets lured children from their control. Some urban children found themselves committed by city magistrates or their parents to institutions such as the Houses of Refuge, where they were placed under strict regimens designed to instill orderly habits and reform character. Children who grew up on farms also were expected to work, continuing earlier patterns through which parents instructed the young in daily tasks designated by gender.

As the nineteenth century progressed, social critics became alarmed that mothers and female teachers had assumed the rearing of middle-class boys, while working-class and immigrant youth lacked adequate outlets for dangerous male instincts. The result was an emphasis on masculine aspects of Christianity and the founding of organizations such as the Young Men's Christian Association (YMCA), which championed the manly, character-building force of competitive SPORTS. By the turn of the century, after-school GYMNASTICS, BASKETBALL, and volleyball became a means to acquire physical discipline and practice teamwork. The scientific study of children produced works such as the 1904 ADOLESCENCE, by G. STANLEY HALL, which defined the teenage years as a period of emotional stress and which also prolonged the protected middle-class childhood. Progressive educators who followed the ideas of JOHN DEWEY advocated liberty in classrooms to achieve self-direction and creative expression for children, but the general trend was toward increasing adult direction of young people's leisure time.

The Twentieth Century

In the early twentieth century, child-rearing experts abandoned a romantic view of childhood and advocated formation of proper habits to discipline children. A 1914 U.S. CHILDREN'S BUREAU pamphlet, *Infant Care*, urged a strict schedule and admonished parents not to play with their babies. JOHN B. WATSON's 1924 *Behaviorism* argued that parents could train malleable children by rewarding good behavior and punishing bad, and by following precise schedules for food, sleep, and other bodily functions. Although such principles began to be rejected as early as the 1930s, they were firmly renounced in the 1946 *Baby and Child Care*, by pediatrician BENJAMIN SPOCK, which told parents to trust their own instincts and to view the child as a reasonable, friendly human being. Dr. Spock revised his first edition to urge more parent-centered discipline in 1957, but critics blamed his popular book for its permissive attitude during the youth rebellions of the 1960s and 1970s.

The affluent consumer society that followed World War II provided parents with the tactic of disciplining children by denying toys or the right to watch a favorite TELEVISION program. Contemporary experts favor reasonable discussion and nonpunitive techniques that will allow the child to maintain a positive attitude toward the parent. Adults demonstrate the consequences of actions, set firm boundaries and rules, and punish with time-outs and isolation. Yet national surveys show that many parents still resort to corporal punishment. And as mothers as well as fathers participate in the work force to survive or to achieve or maintain middle-class status, many children still are thrown on their own without parental guidance much of the time.

See also: **Child-Rearing Advice Literature.**

BIBLIOGRAPHY

Calvert, Karin. 1992. *Children in the House: The Material Culture of Early Childhood, 1600–1900*. Boston: Northeastern University Press.

Clement, Priscilla Ferguson. 1997. *Growing Pains: Children in the Industrial Age, 1850–1900*. New York: Twayne.

Demos, John. 1970. *A Little Commonwealth: Family Life in Plymouth Colony*. New York: Oxford University Press.

Illick, Joseph E. 2002. *American Childhoods*. Philadelphia: University of Pennsylvania Press.

Rawlins, Roblyn. 2001. "Discipline." In *Boyhood in America: An Encyclopedia* ed. Priscilla Ferguson Clement and Jacqueline S. Reinier. Santa Barbara, CA: ABC-CLIO.

Reinier, Jacqueline S. 1996. *From Virtue to Character: American Childhood, 1775–1850*. New York: Twayne.

JACQUELINE S. REINIER

Disney

Walt Disney's name has not always been synonymous with childhood. In the 1930s his work was seen as populist and avant-garde. It was considered populist because, three decades earlier, he had been born into poverty, and his cartoons had the simple outlines of folk art. (They were seen as "his" cartoons even though, as the story goes, one of his animators had to teach him to draw his signature Mickey Mouse.) Disney's cartoons were considered avant-garde because the cinema was a new art form, and at this time when photography still had only dubious claims to artistry and live-action motion pictures could be seen merely as moving photographs, animated cartoons could make a greater claim to artistry. The preeminent name in the art of animation—thanks to Mickey Mouse, the Silly Symphonies, and "The Three Little Pigs"—was Walt Disney.

Early in his career Disney was both a popular success and the darling of intellectuals. Between 1932 and 1941 his work won thirteen Academy Awards, and he was granted honorary degrees by Yale and Harvard. The philosopher Mortimer

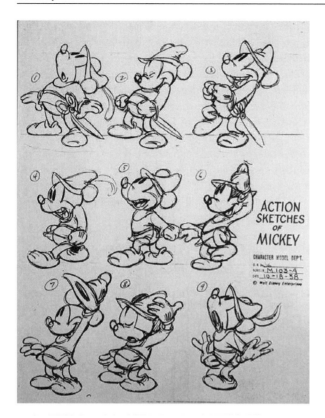

Original sketches of Mickey Mouse, by Walt Disney. Mickey Mouse, perhaps Walt Disney's most popular creation, was not considered solely a children's character in the early years of animation. Prior to the 1940s Disney's work was considered avant-garde and received wide critical acclaim. AP/Wide World Photos.

Adler rhapsodized about Disney's greatness, as did the Russian filmmaker Sergei Eisenstein; the French filmmaker René Clair called his artistry sublime; the artist David Low called him the most significant graphic artist since Leonardo. The film historian Lewis Jacobs referred to Disney as the most acclaimed of current directors: Disney's willingness to plow profits into new technology and to take financial risks to achieve desired effects was, for Jacobs, a sign of artistic integrity—not, as it would later be construed, entrepreneurial savvy.

Disney's audience included both young and old. Critics often praised his films for addressing the young, the old, indeed "artists, intellectuals, children, workers, and everyday people the world over," to quote the *Atlantic Monthly* in 1940. Consider the Disney merchandise of the 1930s, which included not just Mickey Mouse dolls but also ashtrays, beer trays, negligees, and Donald Duck Coffee. (Disney pioneered tie-ins and cross-merchandising, and the corporation is now the industry leader in cross-promotion.)

Changing Attitudes

In the 1940s Disney's productions continued to be popular with the general public, but his reputation among critics and intellectuals waned. In the 1950s it plummeted. This shift may have resulted from Disney's decision to include human figures in his feature-length cartoons, starting with *Snow White and the Seven Dwarfs* in 1938, and that these figures imitated real life only imperfectly. Perhaps disenchantment derived from the bitter strike at Disney Brothers Studios in 1941, or from the experimentalism of *The Three Caballeros* in 1945. Perhaps, too, critics resented the fact that Disney simply did not focus as much on his cartoons as he had in the past, producing live-action films, nature documentaries, TELEVISION programs, and THEME PARKS, launching what has been called the first multimedia empire.

Disney's reputation continued to suffer in the 1950s. The reason may have had something to do with the advent of television. Previously cartoon shorts had been an expected part of an evening's entertainment at the MOVIES, no matter how sophisticated the feature film. But in the decades following World War II, cartoons appeared less often in the theater and more often on Saturday morning television. Eventually, they were regarded as strictly for children.

In other words, once Disney's cartoons came to be seen as suitable only for children, and once he himself became Uncle Walt to millions of viewers, Disney's cartoons were no longer suitable for intellectuals. In a twentieth-century intellectual climate where anything considered juvenile was suspect (a very different climate from that of the nineteenth century) Disney's productions were devalued.

Some critics disapproved of Disney's works even in the 1930s. As a Mickey Mouse book was placed on the recommended reading list for New York City schools in 1938, Louise Seaman Bechtel, in the *Saturday Review of Literature*, regretted "the pressing semi-reality of all the hurrying scenes in color on the screen, the over-elaborated story and crowded canvas" of the film *Snow White*. In later decades one of the louder salvos was fired by the librarian Frances Clarke Sayers, who in a 1965 letter to the *Los Angeles Times* (later expanded into an article for the *Horn Book Magazine*) made an often-quoted statement bemoaning the obviousness of Disney's work, particularly its violence, mediocrity, vulgarity, and its "pretending that everything is so sweet, so saccharine, so without any conflict except the obvious conflict of violence." Other critics include Richard Schickel, who in his *The Disney Version: The Life, Times, Art and Commerce of Walt Disney* (1968) lamented, "In this most childlike of our mass communicators I see what is most childish and therefore most dangerous in all of us who were his fellow Americans."

I'm Going to Disney World!

In recent years Disney's popularity with the general public has soared. Disney products are seen as cute, safe, and cheerful. The company's CEO Michael Eisner claimed, in the 2001 annual report, that Disney's various studios had been number one at the U.S. box office for six of the previous seven years and number one internationally for five of them.

A still from *Snow White and the Seven Dwarfs* (1938), Walt Disney's first full-length animated film, a breakthrough in animation history. Cultural critics have questioned the patriarchal and ethnocentric biases sometimes apparent in Disney's retelling of classic tales (only in Disney's version does Snow White become a mother figure for seven dwarfs). AP/Wide World Photos.

He added that Disney was the largest publisher of children's books in the world and that more than a billion people worldwide had used a Disney product during the previous year. Giants slugger Barry Bonds exclaimed, upon hitting his record-breaking homerun in 2001, "I'm going to Disney World!," and in the wake of terrorist attacks on September 11, 2001, President George W. Bush advised the American public, "Go down to Disney World in Florida. Take your families and enjoy life the way we want it to be enjoyed."

Yet cultural critics and film historians continue to accuse the entertainment company of reinforcing corporate, patriarchal, ethnocentric, and imperialistic values by modifying, for instance, traditional tales such as "Snow White," "Cinderella," "Sleeping Beauty," and "Beauty and the Beast." Only in Disney's version is Snow White such a happy housewife for the dwarfs. While traditional tales with oral sources have been altered throughout their history to reflect the concerns and biases of individual tellers and transcribers, once Walt Disney Productions (as the company is now known) creates a version of a story—whether it is a traditional tale or a classic text such as *Pinocchio* or *Alice's Adventures in Wonderland* or *Winnie-the-Pooh*—Disney's version becomes the

standard one for millions of children. *The Little Mermaid*'s underwater witch is now visualized around the world as a drag queen named Ursula, and the American Indian Pocahontas is a brunette Barbie.

Other cultural critics and historians find points of contestation in Disney's films. In *From Mouse to Mermaid: The Politics of Film, Gender, and Culture* Elizabeth Bell found visual images of strength and discipline in the fairy-tale heroines, whose bodies were modeled on those of classical dancers. Lori Kenschaft, in her essay "Just a Spoonful of Sugar? Anxieties of Gender and Class in *Mary Poppins*," reminded us that not everyone experiences a film such as Disney's *Mary Poppins* in the same way, especially in this age of multimedia and fast-forwarding: whereas one individual might register the energy of the chimney sweeps in the film, another viewer might pick up on the film's intermittent critiques of class and gender.

The company struggled financially in the 1930s and 1940s, achieving stability only in the late 1950s, and since Walt Disney's death in 1966 the corporation has experienced a number of ups and downs. In 1999 and again in 2002

Fortune magazine called it the "world's most troubled entertainment giant." Nevertheless, it is one of the largest media corporations in the world, firmly ensconced in the Fortune 100, with annual revenues of more than twenty-five billion dollars. Its holdings include Touchstone Pictures, Miramax, the Disney Channel, Radio Disney, Hyperion Books, Hollywood Records, the various theme parks, and the television networks ABC and ESPN. It is arguably the most influential corporation in the world. For Disney gets us young and helps to shape our understanding of who we are, getting us to whistle while we work, to be unafraid of the big bad wolf, to wish upon a star that some day our prince will come, indeed to accept Disney products as the spoonful of sugar that helps any medicine go down, in this small world after all.

BIBLIOGRAPHY

Bell, Elizabeth, Lynda Haas, and Laura Sells, eds. 1995. *From Mouse to Mermaid: The Politics of Film, Gender, and Culture.* Bloomington: Indiana University Press.

Kenschaft, Lori. 1999. "Just a Spoonful of Sugar? Anxieties of Gender and Class in *Mary Poppins.*" In *Girls, Boys, Books, Toys: Gender in Children's Literature and Culture,* ed. Beverly Lyon Clark and Margaret R. Higonnet. Baltimore: Johns Hopkins University Press.

The Project on Disney. 1995. *Inside the Mouse: Work and Play at Disney World.* Durham, NC: Duke University Press.

Sayers, Frances Clarke, and Charles M. Weisenberg. 1965. "Walt Disney Accused." *Horn Book Magazine* 40: 602–611.

Schickel, Richard. 1968. *The Disney Version: The Life, Times, Art and Commerce of Walt Disney.* New York: Simon and Schuster.

Smoodin, Eric, ed. 1994. *Disney Discourse: Producing the Magic Kingdom.* New York: Routledge.

Watts, Steven. 1997. *The Magic Kingdom: Walt Disney and the American Way of Life.* Boston: Houghton Mifflin.

BEVERLY LYON CLARK

Disneyland, Disney World. *See* Theme Parks.

Divorce and Custody

The history of child custody following divorce reflects the changing view of children and the evolving relationship between husbands and wives. During the colonial period and the early Republic, children were viewed as economic assets whose labor was valuable to their parents and other adults. In this early era, the father as the head of the household had the complete right to the custody and control of his children both during the marriage and in the rare event of divorce. Over the course of the nineteenth century, the child's value as a laborer decreased and more emphasis was place on child nurture and education. The legal concept of *the best interest of the child* was initiated. Under this rule, mothers gained favor as the parent better able to handle the emotional and nurturing needs of children of tender years and mothers were likely to prevail over fathers in the custody battles following the increasingly common event of divorce. In the late twentieth and early twenty-first centuries, fathers regained ground in the now-common event of divorce as women and men struggled for equal standing before the law. There are no longer clear rules on what is in the best interest of the child and psychological experts have increasingly usurped much of the power from judges in custody determinations.

The Colonial Era and Early Republic: 1630–1830
In the modern era child custody is automatically thought of in the context of divorce, and, indeed, beginning in the last half of the twentieth century, divorce has been the setting for the vast majority of custodial disputes. Earlier in American history, however, custodial issues surfaced far more frequently on other occasions: the death of a father or both parents, the incompetence or financial inability of parents to care for their children, and the birth of illegitimate children. With these events the two major considerations in determining who should have custody and control of the child were the labor value of the child and the ability of the adults to properly maintain and supervise the child. Widows often lost custody of their children because they were no longer able to support them. In the era before ORPHANAGES and formal ADOPTIONS, such children were usually apprenticed or "placed out" to another family who would support them in exchange for their services. A child born out of wedlock was known as *filius nullius* ("child of no family") and the town's poor law official was authorized to place out the child with a family.

Within marriage, fathers had complete right to custody and control of their children. Married women were considered, under common law, *femmes couvertes* (literally "covered women") who were covered by their husband's identity and authority. A father could hire out a child for wages or apprentice a child to another family without the mother's consent. In the very rare event of divorce, the father normally maintained his legal right to custody and control. The right to divorce was not uniformly established in colonial America and therefore there are few examples of custody decisions following divorce. South Carolina, for example, did not grant its first divorce until 1868. Colonies like New York and Virginia followed the English tradition where full divorce was an ecclesiastical affair and only rarely granted. English law, until 1753, retained the principle of canon law that no marriage can be destroyed. In those states following English tradition, divorce could be obtained only by a private bill in the legislature. In New England, divorce laws were more liberal, as marriage fell under the jurisdiction of the civil courts and legislatures. Following what they believed to be the laws of God, states granted divorce (with the right to remarry) when either party to a marriage could prove that the other had neglected a fundamental duty. The usual grounds for divorce were adultery, desertion, and absence for a length of time determined by the government.

The two most divorce-prone states, Massachusetts and Connecticut, have been fairly well studied. The most important aspect of records of these divorces is that children were not considered at all. In no cases do the courts speak about the best interests of the children, or indeed, show any concern for the children's welfare.

The absence of dispute over the custody of children before the nineteenth century has at least two possible, not mutually exclusive explanations. The first is that mothers believed they had no chance to gain the custody of their children and therefore did not even advance this cause. Fathers alone were entitled to custody and control of their children, as they were to all forms of property. There is, in fact, anecdotal evidence that some women avoided divorce because they feared their husbands would take the children away from them. Nancy Shippen Livingston, a woman from a prominent Philadelphia family, endured a loveless marriage in which her husband forced her to turn the baby over to his family to be brought up. As she was living in New York, she could obtain a divorce only by a private bill in the legislature, which was a notoriously difficult feat. She considered hiring the dashing lawyer Aaron Burr to plead her case to the legislature, but lost courage when she realized that if she won the divorce her husband would gain complete custody and she could be prevented from ever seeing her child again.

Women's belief that they had no legal right to their children was reinforced by English precedent. In *Rex v. DeManneville* (1804), a mother ran away from an allegedly brutal husband, but Lord Ellenborough of the King's Bench, emphasizing a father's paramount right to custody of his children, returned the child to her father, even though "she was an infant at the breast of the mother."

A second explanation for the absence of custody disputes during the colonial period is that mothers often got custody of the children without a fight. Women were most often granted divorces in cases of adultery or desertion, and it is unlikely that the father deserted with children in tow. In fluid, expanding colonial America, the father most often "went west" in search of new opportunities and failed to send for his family. More than likely, many deserted wives never took the matter to court at all.

The Nineteenth Century

The legal and social status of the child was transformed during the first century of the new republic. The colonial view of children as helping hands in a labor-scarce economy gave way to a romantic, emotional view of children who were no longer legally akin to servants under the complete control of their fathers or masters but instead were deemed to have interests of their own. Increasingly, these interests became identified with the nurturing mother.

The reasons for this shift are complex, reflecting the rising middle-class culture where educational and emotional investment on the part of parents replaced the economic value to the parents which children earlier represented. The newly emerging women's movement at mid-century also took up the right to child custody as an important plank in their campaign for women's rights. This priority is illustrated in a passage from the 1848 Seneca Falls Convention Declaration of Rights and Sentiments, the founding document of the women's rights movement:

> He [the legislative and judicial patriarchy] has so framed the laws of divorce as to what shall be the proper causes, and in the case of separation, to whom the guardianship of the children shall be given as to be wholly regardless of the happiness of women—the law in all cases going upon the false supposition of the supremacy of man, and giving all power into his hands.

The growing number of custody disputes in the nineteenth century most likely reflected two trends: the rise in divorce and the uncertainty of the laws governing custody. Divorce became easier to obtain in most states, and by the second half of the nineteenth century many people were taking advantage of this new opportunity. A U.S. Census Bureau study reveals a rapidly escalating pattern of divorce. While there were 53,574 divorces granted in the years 1867 to 1871, the figure nearly tripled to 157,324 between 1887 and 1891. In about 40 percent of the divorces, children were involved; another 20 to 40 percent did not report either the presence or absence of children. These figures do not account for couples who separated but never divorced. In a culture where a strong stigma was attached to divorce, separated couples were probably far more numerous than those who sought legal termination.

Judges continued to be torn between applying common law rights of the father and the more modern rule of *the best interest of the child*. Eventually, however, the trend favored children. The best interests of the child, particularly for very young or female children, became increasingly associated with the child's mother. This tendency of courts to award infants and young children to their mothers later became known as the *tender years doctrine*. In awarding a four-year-old boy to his mother, the court in *People ex rel. Sinclair v. Sinclair* stated:

> Nature has devolved upon the mother the nurture and care of infants during their tender years, and in that period such care, for all practical purposes, in the absence of exceptional circumstances, is almost exclusively committed to her. At such periods of life courts do not hesitate to award the care and custody of young infants to the wife as against the paramount right of the husband where the wife has shown herself to be a proper person and is able to fully discharge her duty toward the child.

The almost universal exception to the growing rule of awarding children of tender years to their mother occurred when the mother was considered unfit. The very high moral standards attributed to mothers in the nineteenth century allowed judges to view them more positively in custody disputes, but it also meant that judges turned harshly against them when they strayed from conventional moral standards. The two transgressions that most frequently caused women to lose custody of their children were adultery and leaving their husbands without, in the opinion of the judge, just cause.

The Early Twentieth Century

In 1890, the date often used to mark the beginning of the reform-minded Progressive Era, there were 33,461 divorces in the United States. In the year 1920, at the end of the reform era, there were 167,105 divorces. While these numbers may not be precise, as local records are often incomplete or missing, they suggest that a remarkable increase occurred in the numbers of couples who experienced divorce. Not all of these couples had children; in fact, less than 50 percent of these divorces involved children. Still, for the first time, the number of children who lost a parent from divorce began to approach the number who lost a parent through death. Moreover, countless parents simply deserted, with no divorce sought, and many couples lived apart without divorce.

For the courts and the legislatures, the formerly unusual event of divorce was now commonplace; child custody was no longer an arcane and rarely exercised area of the law and the lives of thousands of children and their parents were affected by custody decisions. These realities accelerated trends that had begun in the nineteenth century, such as the father's obligation to support his children without the benefit of custody, for which there previously had been little precedent. The judiciary still took the lead in developing rules to resolve the private disputes between divorcing couples, but state legislatures increasingly codified these rules, often narrowing the margin of judicial discretion.

The case of Mr. and Mrs. Harmon (*Harmon v. Harmon* [1922]) provides a glimpse of the changing attitudes of the "Roaring Twenties" and reveals that a woman's sexual conduct was no longer a complete bar to custody. Two married couples in Kansas, Mr. and Mrs. Harmon and an unnamed husband and wife, associated in the same social circles and became good friends, going on late-night rides together and spending much of their free time together. One day Mr. Harmon found Mrs. Harmon engaged in an act of adultery with the other husband. He insisted that she must go to live with her parents and renounce the custody of their five-year-old daughter. Both men made her sign a written agreement admitting her guilt and agreeing to the custody arrangement.

Mr. Harmon then sued for divorce on the ground of adultery and sought custody of their daughter. The court agreed that adultery had been encouraged by the husband. "He must have known the absurd lengths to which extraordinary

intimacy, informality, and unconventionality [with the other couple] had grown, it was bound to culminate as it did." The court affirmed the denial of a divorce to the Harmons but granted temporary custody of the daughter to the mother, reasoning that "except for defendant's temporary infatuation for her paramour, she was a good mother."

Other courts concurred with this assessment, gradually turning away from the double standard of moral fitness which viewed a mother's sexual misconduct as damning and a father's as forgivable. The leading family law treatise of the 1920s, *Keezer on the Law of Marriage and Divorce*, states the "new" rule: "Where the children are of tender years, other things being equal, the mother is preferred as their custodian, and this more especially in the case of female children, and this though she may have been guilty of delinquencies in the past but there is no evidence that she was delinquent at the time of determining the matter by the court." In *Crabtree v. Crabtree* (1922) the court even overlooked the fact that Mrs. Crabtree had almost murdered Mr. Crabtree, cutting his throat with a razor blade, slicing through his fingers and stabbing him in the back. The court explained: "It does not follow that because the wife tried to kill him in a fit of anger, she did not have any parental affection for the children. On the contrary the record discloses that she loved them and was properly caring for them."

The Late Twentieth and Early Twenty-First Centuries

By the last third of the twentieth century, law relating to child custody had permeated the casual conversation of everyday life; indeed, few households were untouched by a custody matter. A child born in 1990 had about a 50 percent chance of falling under the jurisdiction of a court in a case involving where and with whom the child would live. The great majority of these child custody determinations were the products of an exploding divorce rate.

While the divorce rate soared, the rules governing child custody grew increasingly confused. "The simple fact of being a mother does not, by itself, indicate a capacity or willingness to render a quality of care different from that which the father can provide" a New York court stated in 1973, challenging nearly a century of a judicial presumption in favor of mothers. The court rejected the notion that mothers and their children shared a special bond, invoking the authority of social scientist MARGARET MEAD, who once wrote, "This is a mere and subtle form of anti-feminism which men—under the guise of exalting the importance of maternity—are tying women more tightly to their children than has been thought necessary since the invention of bottle feeding and baby carriages."

Not all courts were as outspoken in reducing the importance of mothers or in suggesting that maternal presumption is a male conspiracy. Nevertheless, the presumption that the interest of a child of tender years is best served in the custody of the mother was legally abolished or demoted to a "factor to be considered" in nearly all states between 1960 and 2000.

With the old rules gone, state legislators and judges have turned to social science to develop new guidelines to aid judges in making this most difficult decision. Two popular psychological theories are enlisted to support two opposing models of custody. The first model assumes that one parent should take primary responsibility of the child's care, but that parent need not be the mother. This model embraces sole custody (with visitation) and a primary caretaker preference. The second model stresses the importance of both parents in the child's development and promotes some form of joint or shared custody. Neither model gives any preference to mothers and neither model considers the age or developmental stage of the child, as was the case in the tender years doctrine.

Evidence to support this subjective criterion can be obtained only outside the courtroom by lay eyewitness testimony, or by the evaluation of the parties by mental health professionals. Thus, experts are increasingly utilized in child custody cases and are engaged in every step of the proceeding; parents can jointly seek the services of a mental health consultant to aid them with private mediation, or one party, often on the advice of his or her attorney, can employ the consultant with a view to settlement or potentially, trial testimony. Increasingly, the court itself, or the *guardian ad litem* (an attorney, or sometimes a layman or a psychiatrist, appointed by the court to represent the child), requests a psychological evaluation. These evaluations, usually performed by court social workers or by psychologists, provide a wide range of information about the parents and children, including social and economic data, but especially focus on psychodynamic factors.

While mental health experts are prominent in pretrial procedures, where most disputes are settled, their presence has also increased dramatically in those cases that find their way to trial. Between 1960 and 2000, the pattern of expert utilization at trial changed dramatically; the number of experts soared and these experts were more likely to be appointed by the court rather than by the parents. In addition, the nature of expert testimony shifted from an evaluation of the sanity of the parent (usually mother) to observations regarding the relationship between parent and child, and in a substantial number of cases these experts testified regarding alleged sexual or physical abuse.

Outside the courtroom, a battle rages among the social and behavioral scientists on what effect divorce has on children. This question has serious implications for a nation considering whether or not to actively promote marriage and discourage divorce. The scientists, however, have reached no consensus. Some studies indicate that divorce has lifelong negative consequences for most children. Others insist that most children fare well and that those negatively affected most often recover completely.

At the start of the twenty-first century, a few observations can be made with some certainty: the proper role of the social and behavioral sciences in custody matters is still a subject of controversy but their continuing influence is an established fact. Finally, it can also be said that what constitutes the "best interests of the child" is a matter of continuing dispute.

See also: **Beyond the Best Interests of the Child; Law, Children and the.**

BIBLIOGRAPHY

Anthony, Susan B., and Ida Hustead Harper, eds. 1902. "Seneca Falls Women's Rights Convention of 1848, Declaration of Rights and Sentiments." In *The History of Women's Suffrage*, vol. 1. Rochester, NY.

Grossberg, Michael. 1985. *Governing the Hearth: Law and Family in Nineteenth-Century America*. Chapel Hill: University of North Carolina Press.

Heatherington, E. Mavis, and John Kelly. 2002. *For Better or For Worse*. New York: W.W. Norton.

Mason, Mary Ann. 1994. *From Father's Property to Children's Rights: The History of Child Custody in the United States*. New York: Columbia University Press.

Mason, Mary Ann. 1999. *The Custody Wars: Why Children Are Losing the Legal Battles and What We Can Do About It*. New York: Basic Books.

Mead, Margaret. 1954. "Some Theoretical Considerations of the Problems of Mother-Child Separation." *American Journal of Orthopsychiatry* 24. In *State ex rel. Watts v. Watts*, 350 N.Y.S.2d. 285 (1973).

Morland, John W., ed. 1946. *Keezer on the Law of Marriage and Divorce*, 3rd edition. Indianapolis: Bobbs-Merrill.

O'Neill, William. 1967. *Divorce in the Progressive Era*. New Haven, CT: Yale University Press.

Wallerstein, Judith S. 1980. *Surviving the Breakup*. New York: Basic Books.

Wallerstein, Judith S. 1989. *Second Chances*. New York: Ticknor and Fields.

MARY ANN MASON

Dolls

Dolls are known in all cultures and are one of the oldest and most widespread forms of TOYS. A doll in its most basic form is a cone-shaped figure which can be made of clay, wood, stone, bone, cloth or different natural materials. It is believed that in prehistoric societies, dolls made in a human likeness had a magic or religious significance. At what point these figures became toys for children is not clear, but discarded doll-like figures were doubtless picked up and used for PLAY.

History

Small human figures made of wood and clay have been found in Egyptian graves from 2000 B.C.E.; dolls of clay, marble and alabaster have been found in children's graves of ancient

Girl with a Doll (Franzi) (1910), Erich Heckel. Like many works of art, Heckel's painting explores the boundary between childhood and adulthood. Courtesy of Serge Sabarsky Collection.

Greece and Rome; dolls are also referred to in some written sources from the early European Middle Ages. Doll-makers can be traced to Nuremberg in Germany from as early as 1413. Several depictions of German doll-makers exist from the fifteenth century. The earliest doll-makers carved dolls out of wood and some even attempted to provide the toys with moveable limbs. Germany and France were early centers of European doll manufacture. Since the fifteenth century, both toy dolls and fashion dolls—dolls attired in the latest costumes and coiffures and commissioned so that European courts could follow fashionable trends—were produced in Paris. Several oil paintings of the early seventeenth century depict noble children playing with wooden dolls dressed in finery. A colored drawing in the British Museum in London

of 1585 shows an Indian girl with a European doll, presumably taken to America by the early English settlers.

Materials

Wood is the oldest material used for making dolls for sale. Turned dolls were mass-produced in Sonneberg in Thüringen from the seventeenth century. Wooden dolls were very popular throughout the eighteenth century. The head and body were carved by professional doll-makers and the face and hair were painted directly onto the wood.

A mixture of paper, sawdust, plaster and glue, called composition, was developed around 1800 as a cheap alternative to wood. It could be formed under pressure, allowing for the mass production of dolls. At the toy center in Sonneberg heads were pressed in papier mâché after 1810, while bodies were made of a soft material and then stuffed. Papier mâché heads could also be overlaid with wax to give them a more lifelike appearance. For a time dolls with heads made entirely of wax were much in demand, but these were costly and were superseded by porcelain dolls. After about 1830 porcelain manufacturers, especially in Germany, France and later Denmark, started serious production of dolls, and dolls with cast heads became very popular.

The glazed china used in the 1860s was succeeded by unglazed biscuitware, which, especially in its pink coloring, acquired a very lifelike appearance and became enormously popular. Coiffures were ingeniously modeled and precisely followed contemporary fashions. After 1870 wigs and glass eyes became common. Beginning in 1880, some manufacturers began to sell dolls that could close their eyes. At the same time jointed dolls were introduced with bodies and limbs of papier mâché, the head and limbs being attached by strong inbuilt elastic. Commercially produced rag dolls were also introduced by English and American producers in the nineteenth century.

The synthetic material celluloid was discovered around 1870 and was used for doll manufacture after the end of the nineteenth century. This material became brittle with age and was extremely flammable. However, it was cheap and was used for the mass production of dolls until the mid-1950s at German, French, American, and Japanese factories. More durable materials such as vinyl and plastic overtook celluloid as the preferred materials for dolls in the second half of the twentieth century.

Doll Types

The oldest dolls were all adult "lady" dolls representing well-dressed women. The Great Exhibition in London in 1851 saw the first appearance of infant dolls with round heads and soft bowed limbs created by the London doll-maker Mme. Montanari. The "baby" doll was born. The golden age of doll manufacturers was 1860 to 1890, when demand for dolls rose and new and elegant types were constantly being produced. Many patents were taken out at this time as mechanical dolls which could walk, sing and dance were invented. The most desirable and expensive types were and are the French fashion *Parisienne* dolls, which are equipped with exclusive wardrobes.

Paper dolls were produced in Europe—especially in England, Germany and France—from the early nineteenth century. Paper dolls are cut-out dolls with matching clothes printed on card and models were often inspired by famous people of the time. Perhaps as a reaction to perfect, expressionless faces which did not appeal to the child's imagination, dolls' faces with individual characteristics reflecting natural child types were modeled around 1900. The first character doll was the so-called Kaiser baby, created by the German doll manufacturer Kämmer and Reinhardt. Another very popular doll was the Dream Baby, produced in 1913 by the German firm Armand Marseille. Dolls with an ethnic appearance—especially Asian and African—were also popular; as were celebrity dolls representing royals and actors.

At the end of the nineteenth century the majority of dolls represented children, both boys and girls, of about ten years old. By the beginning of the twentieth century, baby dolls had taken the upper hand and remained popular until the 1950s, when adult dolls returned with a new form of fashion doll: BARBIE. Later came Action Man, a series of military dolls for boys, which broke what had for generations been a female monopoly on doll use. Famous dolls of the twentieth century included the Kewpie Doll (1912), Bye-lo-baby, the Million Dollar Baby (1922), Barbie (1959), and the Cabbage Patch Kids (c. 1980).

Role Models

Products of their times, different dolls cannot be judged without reference to wider economic and social conditions. Dolls are created for play and recreation, but their purpose is also to prepare girls for their later roles as mothers and housewives.

Until the end of the eighteenth century, children were regarded as small, unfinished, adults who had to be trained for adult life. Miniature tools from the adult world were designed to familiarize them with that world and prepare them for the tasks that would later await them. In the nineteenth century a young woman's task was to marry and look after the home as mother and housewife. Marriage was the only conceivable career and dress was of the utmost importance. Luxurious dress was the only effective way for a woman to show her social standing. Lady dolls of the nineteenth century were pure extravaganzas, especially the Paris dolls with their sumptuous wardrobes, with clothes in the latest French fashion and a range of personal articles including a fan, dressing table set, parasol—and even a dance card for a doll's ball. Everything needed to make the home function was part of the doll's life—doll's furniture, dinner service, kitchen articles and similar items.

Children's play mirrors to some degree what they see in the home. Some evidence suggests that baby dolls have faded into the background as women enter the workplace and fewer look after children at home. In 2003 young girls are primarily interested in mannequin dolls. Barbie dolls reflect the new female role as the active, independent, career woman, but also the "dream girl next door" that every girl wishes to be. The Barbie doll is an expression of late-twentieth-century CONSUMER CULTURE, and apart from glamorous clothes its accessories include things like a mobile phone, laptop computer, and sports car.

Conclusion

A doll is not simply an impersonal play object. It becomes the child's natural and trustworthy guide in daily life. Children become attached to their dolls and share with them their deepest wishes, sorrows, and joys. A doll is given a name and an identity of its own. Dolls often cannot, therefore, simply be thrown out when the age of play has passed.

In the twentieth century, a market for dolls began to emerge among adult collectors. As a result, the price of antique and finely made dolls began to grow. The price of a doll depends on its type, make, age, and condition. It also matters whether the doll's clothing is original, whether it has other accessories and whether it has its original box. Collectors and museums are often interested in the doll's provenance. It is also important to ensure that the doll has not been restored, that wig and eyes have not been replaced and that arms, legs and fingers are original and intact. Historical dolls can be seen at the following museums of cultural history, special museums and private collections: Legoland, Billund, Denmark; Musée de la Poupée, Paris, France; Coburger Puppenmuseum, Coberg, Germany; Bethnal Green Museum of Childhood, London and Museum of Childhood, Edinburgh in the United Kingdom; Yokohama Doll Museum, Yokohama, Japan; and Rosalie Whyel Museum of Doll Art, Bellevue, Washington, DC and Wenham Historical Association and Museum, Wenham, Massachusetts, in the United States.

See also: **Construction Toys; Infant Toys; Teddy Bear; Toy Soldiers.**

BIBLIOGRAPHY

Bristol, Olivia. 1977. *Dolls: A Collector's Guide.* London: De Agostini Editions Ltd.

Coleman, Dorothy S., Elizabeth A. Coleman, and Evelyn J. Coleman. 1968. *The Collector's Encyclopedia of Dolls.* New York: Crown Publishers Inc.

Goodfellow, Caroline. 1993. *The Ultimate Doll Book.* New York: Dorling Kindersley.

King, Constance Eileen. 1977. *The Collector's History of Dolls.* New York: St. Martins Press.

KIRSTEN F. SCHMIDT

Dr. Seuss (1904–1991)

The children's-book author Dr. Seuss was born Theodor Seuss Geisel on March 2, 1904, in Springfield, Massachusetts. He drew constantly as a child and always had an ear for meter, as well as a penchant for the absurd. Geisel had little interest in academics or athletics. He contributed cartoons, often signed with creative pseudonyms, to his high school newspaper. At Dartmouth College he spent most of his time working on the *Jack-o-Lantern*, a campus humor magazine. He became editor during his senior year, signing his contributions "Seuss" after school authorities penalized him for drinking bootleg gin. He studied English briefly at Oxford University, where he met Helen Palmer, who admired the cartoon sketches in his lecture notes. In 1927 the couple married and moved to New York, where they immersed themselves in the nighttime pleasures of Jazz Age New York, drinking, smoking, and going to parties. Geisel loved to play practical jokes and to put people on (especially anyone pompous). He had a childlike imagination but also harbored insecurities and vulnerabilities that made him intensely private. Geisel and his wife were unable to have children, a loss they felt strongly, but that also freed Geisel to behave childishly himself. Helen mothered Geisel; she drove the car, balanced the checkbook, paid the bills, and ministered to his domestic needs. They traveled frequently to such far-off locales as Peru. Geisel and Helen remained married until her death in 1967; in 1968 he married Audrey Stone, who survived him.

Geisel began his career as a cartoonist in 1927, primarily contributing drawings and writings to the humor magazine *Judge*, in addition to *College Humor, Liberty,* and *Vanity Fair,* and signing his work "Dr. Seuss." During the 1930s Geisel also created cartoon ads for Standard Oil Company. His bug-spray catchphrase, "Quick, Henry, the Flit!" became a popular saying. In 1937 he sold his first children's book, *And to Think That I Saw It on Mulberry Street,* to Vanguard Books after twenty-seven publishers rejected the manuscript because it lacked a moral message. *Mulberry Street* established the Dr. Seuss template; it was written in verse and illustrated with comically exaggerated drawings—a marked contrast from the pretty pictures then typical to children's books. In the next few years Geisel published several more books, including the classic *Horton Hatches the Egg* (1940), before he joined Frank Capra's Signal Corps and devoted his artistry to the war effort.

After a brief postwar spell in Hollywood, Geisel and his wife moved to La Jolla, California, and he resumed writing children's books. A string of successes followed, including *The Sneetches and Other Stories* (1953), *Horton Hears a Who!* (1954), *On Beyond Zebra!* (1955), *How the Grinch Stole Christmas* (1957), and *Yertle the Turtle and Other Stories* (1958). None could compete however with the enormous popularity of Geisel's breakthrough book, *The Cat in the Hat* (1957). Inspired by a challenge from his wartime friend William Spaulding, an editor at Houghton Mifflin, Geisel wrote his classic as a reading primer, using just over 200 words.

Propelled by the baby boom, *The Cat in the Hat* sold nearly one million copies by 1960 and seven times that figure by 2000. Its success instigated the Random House division Beginner Books, which published *The Cat in the Hat Comes Back!* (1958) and *One Fish Two Fish Red Fish Blue Fish* (1960). *Green Eggs and Ham* (1960), which uses only fifty words—all of them one syllable except for the word "anywhere"—became his most popular work, selling over six million copies by 1996.

Over the following three decades, Geisel continued writing books for little children, big children, and adults. His bizarre humor, made-up words, and mellifluous rhymes attracted generations of readers, making him a celebrity. Some of his later books carried strong moral messages. *The Lorax* (1971) advocated conservation; *The Butter Battle Book* (1984) attacked the nuclear arms race. Even so, Geisel never departed from the basic formula for his success: amuse first, educate later. Geisel died in 1991 after a long battle with cancer.

See also: **Children's Literature.**

BIBLIOGRAPHY

Fensch, Thomas. 1997. *Of Sneetches and Whos and the Good Dr. Seuss: Essays on the Writings and Life of Theodor Geisel.* Jefferson, NC: McFarland.

Morgan, Judith, and Neil Morgan. 1995. *Dr. Seuss and Mr. Geisel: A Biography.* New York: Random House.

RACHEL HOPE CLEVES

Drugs

Drug use by children and adolescents periodically comes under state and social scrutiny, fueled both by actual incidence of increased drug use and popular and parental fears about it. Prior to the twentieth century "soothing syrups" consisting of paregoric and laudanum (both dilute opiates) were among the few effective medications available to treat cholera and childhood diseases by physicians, lay healers, and family members responsible for health care. Criticisms of their use in infants and children were present from the earliest days of the United States. Early campaigns against infant "doping" by mothers and nursemaids were led by nineteenth-century "regular" physicians who employed such warnings as part of their bid to consolidate professional control over pharmaceutical opiates.

Clinicians observed congenital addiction to opiates as early as the 1830s. Restlessness, moral and mental weakness, and "blue baby" (cyanosis) were attributed to maternal opiate use. An 1832 dissertation by William G. Smith criticized the "youthful, inconsiderate mother and the idle nurse" who quieted infants with opiate-laced proprietary medicines "rather than forego the pleasures of a crowded assembly, or the gaudy charms of a dramatic scene, a single evening." Nineteenth-century physicians practiced gradual withdrawal techniques. However, the *American Textbook of Applied Therapeutics* (1896) applauded the poor prognosis of "infants born of mothers who are morphinists" because "the moral and mental strength of these children is so far below par as to make them liable to much subsequent suffering." Under the influence of the Women's Christian Temperance Union (WCTU), all states required physiology and HYGIENE instruction in public schools that emphasized the dangerous effects of alcohol, tobacco, and other drugs by the turn of the

twentieth century. Mothers who "drugged" their children came under public scrutiny during the Progressive campaigns to regulate patent medicines. These campaigns took place in the context of broader concerns about widespread popular use of proprietary medicines, adulteration of them, and exaggerated advertising of them, which ultimately led to their regulation under the Pure Food and Drug Act (1906).

"Morphinist mothers" were depicted as direct threats to their babies when in 1913 a physician found that babies' blood was "as much saturated with the drug as the blood of the mother," thus confirming that narcotics crossed the placenta. "Morphinist fathers" were also thought to impair their offspring: "How could it be otherwise, since every influence within the body tells in the upbuilding of protoplasm, and since the composite protoplasm of the germ borrows its qualities from every form of protoplasm in the parental organism?" (Terry and Pellens, p. 416). The first congressional attention to narcotics use among schoolchildren occurred in 1910 in Philadelphia. States such as New York, which had the highest number of addicts, regulated opiates prior to the federal Harrison Act of 1914, which effectively ended the administration of narcotics by physicians once its constitutionality was ascertained through *United States v. Jin Fuey Moy* (1916) and *Webb v. United States* (1918). With Prohibition enacted, reformers turned to organizations such as the World Narcotic Defense Association (WNDA), headed by Spanish-American war hero and temperance reformer Richmond Pearson Hobson. The WNDA held a conference on narcotics education in 1925 at which a speaker maintained that addiction was spread through "intergenerational transmission": "Babies are born in drug addiction and, horrible as it may seem, they actually begin life under the influence of narcotics. . . . what can society expect of children whose father and mother, or both, are criminal addicts? What will be the children's attitude toward society?" Claims concerning high numbers of child addicts were also made by public officials who ran the New York City Clinic, operated by the City of New York Department of Health and administered by the state, which served over 7,000 addicted persons from 1919 to 1920.

Addiction among children was rarely mentioned until the mid-twentieth century and there were long periods when most physicians knew little about how to treat it. When Charles Terry and Mildred Pellens surveyed physicians in the 1920s for *The Opium Problem* they concluded that most lacked accurate and rational knowledge about congenital addiction. A 1924 questionnaire with a response rate over 50 percent that was administered to 687 schools in New York State failed to turn up any cases of drug addiction despite popular press reports. The same survey sent to JUVENILE COURT judges and chiefs of police only yielded a handful of cases throughout the state. During World War II few opiates were available as the U.S. government stockpiled them as strategic materials, thus keeping the numbers of addicted persons low until the postwar period.

Warnings that a "frightening wave" of narcotics addiction was about to engulf New York City youth fueled a state-wide popular panic that spurred officials to action after the war's end. The first televised congressional hearings before the Senate Crime Investigating Committee and the Subcommittee to Investigate Juvenile Delinquency, stimulated intense fervor among an estimated 20 to 30 million viewers. Chaired by Senator Estes Kefauver, the hearings lasted from May 1950 to August 1951. Mention of teenage drug addiction aided November 2, 1951 passage of the Boggs Act, which mandated the first minimum sentences for drug offenders. New York hearings on teenage narcotic addiction held by State Attorney Gen Nathaniel L. Goldstein in the summer of 1951 in Buffalo and Albany helped establish the first state institution dedicated to the treatment and rehabilitation of female drug addicts at Westfield State Farm in Bedford Hills, New York.

New York City and state became a locus for public discussion of teenage addiction. The prestigious New York Academy of Medicine held conferences titled "Drug Addiction among Adolescents" in 1951 and 1952. The Research Center for Human Relations at New York University conducted the classic addiction research of the 1950s. Their social-psychiatric study of heroin use among adolescents in three boroughs of New York City between 1949 and 1954 was published as *The Road to H* (1964). Considered the definitive study on the topic for decades, it criticized federal drug policy for confusing a minor symptom with a major epidemic—a view shared by many treatment professionals who worked directly with drug users.

The heightened attention to adolescent narcotics use in the 1950s focused on the increased availability of drugs to teenagers and the role of PARENTING, especially mothering, in producing it. Postwar addicts were depicted as racial and ethnic "others," and sometimes as sexual "deviants" in the steady trickle of films depicting narcotic use that began to appear in the late 1940s. The press played up the lurid and novel aspects of the 1950s epidemic, but professionals who remembered the aftermath of the Harrison Act referred to it as the "second peak of an old problem." Until this point, opiates, especially heroin, were the real concern and the basis for policy.

Drug control officials were taken aback by the explosion of widespread popular youthful experimentation with illicit drugs that took place in the 1960s. The emergence of ADOLESCENT MEDICINE and neonatology as clinical specialties; the expansion of the federal and state treatment and research apparatus; and the movement of community mental health into the substance abuse area paralleled the explosion of youth participation in the counterculture that developed in the second half of the twentieth century. As youthful users' "drug of choice" changed from LSD to marijuana to heroin to crack-cocaine to methamphetamines to Ecstasy specific drug-using subcultures emerged among younger users. The social context in which drugs are used continues to determine which subpopulations gravitate towards specific substances. Peer influence plays a role, as do high levels of undiagnosed depression among teenagers, suggesting that youthful drug use may represent a form of "self-medication." Due to the United States' commitment to incarceration for drug offenses, juveniles began to experience higher levels of involvement with the criminal justice system in the later twentieth century. Some states and municipalities began experimenting with alternative justice systems called "drug courts" to respond more appropriately to youth drug use by diverting some young offenders to treatment and rehabilitation programs.

The National Institute of Drug Abuse (NIDA), a component of the National Institutes of Health, has funded a nationwide survey of the extent of drug use among high school seniors called "Monitoring the Future" since 1975. In 1991 the survey was expanded to include eighth and tenth graders. A decade later, the 2002 survey showed not only an overall decline in illicit drug use but a significant decline in the proportion of children who had used any illicit drug for the sixth year in a row. Following cyclic trends similar to those seen in adults, drug use among children tends to follow the cycles of social learning demonstrated by historians Courtwright and Musto rather than the notions of "intergenerational transmission." For instance, children who observed adult crack-cocaine use tended not to become crack-cocaine users themselves. As the crack-cocaine epidemic subsided, the nation's concern about "intergenerational transmission" seemed to have been largely unwarranted. Longitudinal studies show that cognitive abilities and other "outcomes" measures differ little between children who were exposed to cocaine in utero, and those whose basic needs go unmet for reasons of economic deprivation.

See also: **Smoking; Teen Drinking; Youth Culture.**

BIBLIOGRAPHY

Campbell, Nancy D. 2000. *Using Women: Gender, Drug Policy, and Social Justice.* New York: Routledge.

Courtwright, David T. 2001. *Dark Paradise: A History of Opiate Addiction in America.* Enlarged edition. Cambridge, MA: Harvard University Press.

Goldstein, Nathaniel L. 1952. *Narcotics: A Growing Problem, A Public Challenge, A Plan for Action, Report to the Legislature Pursuant to Chapter 528 of the Laws of 1951, 175th Session.* No. 3. Albany, New York.

Kandall, Stephen R. 1996. *Substance and Shadow: Women and Addiction in the United States.* Cambridge, MA: Harvard University Press.

Musto, David F. 1999. *The American Disease: Origins of Narcotic Control Policy.* 3rd edition. New York: Oxford University Press.

Prescott, Heather Munro. 1998. *A Doctor of Their Own: The History of Adolescent Medicine.* Cambridge, MA: Harvard University Press.

Terry, Charles, and Mildred Pellens. 1970 [1928]. *The Opium Problem*. Montclair, NJ: Patterson Smith.

White, William L. 1998. *Slaying the Dragon: The History of Addiction Treatment and Recovery in America*. Bloomington, IL: Lighthouse Institute.

NANCY CAMPBELL

Dumas, Alexandre (1802–1870)

The French novelist and dramatist commonly known as Dumas *père*, to distinguish him from his writer son (also named Alexandre Dumas), was born in Villers-Cotterêts, a small town in northern France, in 1802. Dumas's own colorful life reads like a novel. His father, a general in Napoleon's army, was born in Santo Domingo to the Marquis de la Pailleterie and a black slave, whose family name he assumed when he enlisted. The death of the father he idolized before Dumas's fourth birthday left the family in dire financial straits. At fourteen, Dumas, who had little formal schooling, began working as a clerk for a local notary. Eventually, the theater lured him to Paris, where he obtained a position with the Duc d'Orléans in 1823. An ardent republican, he took part in France's revolutions of 1830 and 1848, and joined Italian republican Giuseppe Garibaldi in 1860. His renown as a dramatist and then as a historical novelist earned him immense wealth, but an extravagant lifestyle left him almost penniless at his death.

Dumas is one of the most prolific, popular, and perhaps underrated authors of all time, but interest in popular culture is attracting new critical attention to his work. His stories written intentionally for children generally first appeared in his own newspapers, *Le Mousquetaire* and *Le Monte-Cristo*; they include *La Bouillie de la Comtesse Berthe* (1845), *La Jeunesse de Pierrot* (1854), *Le lièvre de mon grand-père* (1857), and adaptations of well-known fairy tales. E. T. A. Hoffman's dark, morbid story *The Nutcracker and the Mouse King* was transformed into a children's tale, titled *Histoire d'un Casse-Noisette* (1845), which inspired Tchaikovsky's famous ballet.

The works that children know best, however, are the popular historical novels he wrote for adults. Like those of Walter Scott, Dumas's novels were immediately adopted by young readers who were enthralled by this master storyteller. His exciting plots, fast-moving action, lively dialogue, and memorable characters had universal appeal. Generations of readers worldwide owe their first, indelible impressions of French history to Dumas's novels, the most popular of which are *Les Trois Mousquetaires* (*The Three Musketeers*) (1844) and *Le Comte de Monte-Cristo* (*The Count of Monte Cristo*) (1844-45). *Les Trois Mousquetaires*, a swashbuckling adventure tale that has become a children's classic, is the first novel in a trilogy about Athos, Porthos, Aramis, and D'Artagnan, who are legendary characters the world over, as is Edmond Dantès, wrongfully imprisoned for years in the Château d'If before enacting his delayed revenge as the Count of Monte Cristo. Few young people today read the integral text of Dumas's prodigiously long novels, especially in the English-speaking world where they have often been heavily abridged. A prime example is *The Man in the Iron Mask*, excerpted from the third novel in the *Mousquetaire* trilogy, *Le Vicomte de Bragelonne*, and published separately in English.

Born in the popular press, where they were serialized, Dumas's novels live on in the mass media of cinema and television. *The Three Musketeers* is one of the most remade stories in motion picture history. Contemporary teen audiences were deliberately targeted in films like *The Musketeer* (2001), with its martial arts choreography, and *The Man in the Iron Mask* (1998), with its casting of Leonardo DiCaprio in the dual role of Louis XIV and his twin brother.

See also: **Children's Literature; Images of Childhood.**

BIBLIOGRAPHY

Hemmings, F. W. J. 1979. *The King of Romance: A Portrait of Alexandre Dumas*. London: Hamish Hamilton.

Stowe, Richard S. 1976. *Alexandre Dumas père*. Boston: Twayne.

SANDRA L. BECKETT

E

Early Modern Europe

Historians have reached no consensus over definitions of early modern Europe. Published work on the period roughly spans the years between 1400 and 1800 but chronological boundaries vary by region and discipline. The term itself is largely Anglo-American. Historians in continental Europe refer to the period between the Middle Ages and the contemporary world simply as "modern history," but again there is little consensus over its meaning. In contrast, the French *Annaliste* tradition, advanced by Fernand Braudel and his followers, largely refutes dating altogether in favor of the tripartite *longue durée* (long-term structures), *conjoncture* (short-term trends), and *histoire événémentielle* (individual events). In the United States and the United Kingdom early modern European studies gained ground in the 1970s. Historians began with the breakup of feudalism and the emergence of the western European state in the fifteenth century and ended with the eighteenth-century revolutions in politics and economic life. The literature spotlighted advances in science and secularism, the transition from feudalism to capitalism, and the rise of the modern state, developments that were linked to the concept of modernization.

The period did witness significant strides in state building in England, France, and Spain, where growing bureaucracies levied taxes to finance large-scale warfare and territorial expansion. But at the same time encroachment on the long-standing powers of the nobility invited feudal reaction, while the breach with tradition, particularly by creating new taxes in an era plagued by war, famine, and disease, triggered widespread peasant revolts. The road to modernization theme quickly led to a literature of adjustments that demonstrated failures to modernize as well as the demographic and technological limits hindering economic growth. Still, a number of historiographical trends emerged to give the period firm contours: the fragmentation of Christendom and growing secularism; pronounced demographic and economic fluctuation; the development of the European state system; and the emergence of a global, Europe-centered system of production and trade.

These grand narratives, however, did little to include women's roles in reproduction and production, or the travails of ordinary people; nor did they work well for comparativists in world history circles. Thus historical output in the last decade of the twentieth and the early years of the twenty-first centuries has attempted to redress these omissions as well as to reconceptualize how historians arrive at periodization. Like definitions of early modern Europe, discussions of childhood experience have also continued to evolve. Was there an awareness of childhood as a distinct stage in the life cycle? In the predominantly agrarian economy of early modern Europe, childhood and adolescence quickly progressed into adulthood for peasants and workers whose lives revolved primarily around reproduction and production. In contrast, improved material conditions among the middle class fostered more awareness of childhood as separate from adulthood. Commercialization and urbanization required more formal education for the young. As a result, civic groups, church, state, and parents made larger investments in child rearing and education with efforts that divided along gendered lines.

The Religious Reformations

In the second decade of the sixteenth century, the Christian church experienced the first in a series of religious divisions along geographic lines. The sequence of splits, beginning in the Holy Roman Empire and spreading to the whole of Europe by the end of the century, transformed the relationship of the reformed churches with state, society, and the individual. It also transported Christianity to the indigenous peoples of the Americas and Asia. There was a fervent desire for religious homogeneity, marked by compulsory conversions of Moors and Jews to Catholicism in Spain and missionary zeal both in Europe and abroad. At the same time in nearly every area of Europe religious conflict and calls for a redistribution of power became virtually indistinguishable, evoking crises in authority at state and local levels.

Unruly School (also known as *The Village School* and *A School for Boys and Girls,* c. 1670), Jan Steen. The Protestant Reformation, with its emphasis on reading the Scriptures, encouraged the expansion of education throughout early modern Europe, although the extent to which schools involved excessive discipline has been the subject of intense debate. (NG 2421. National Galleries of Scotland, Edinburgh).

The Protestant and Catholic Reformations affected family life, and by extension children's upbringing, in important ways. Protestants advanced new family models that overrode Catholic doctrine and canon law, models which presumably would affect the character formation of children. They refuted the celibate ideal, closing convents and monasteries and celebrating the status of husband and wife over that of monk and nun. Reformers like Martin Luther found marriage to be the appropriate place for sexuality and a prophylactic for fornication. Pastors and former nuns took marriage vows. Both lay and clerical Protestants were encouraged to form companionate marriages, where husbands still held authority over wives but where spouses were encouraged to divide family responsibilities. In contrast, the Catholic clergy continued to make strenuous efforts to restrict sexuality, particularly that of women. In order to defend family purity as well as maintain social order, women were either to marry or undergo religious enclosure.

While Protestant theologians created the legal possibility of divorce and remarriage, Catholic reformers made strenuous efforts to tighten the rules on marriage and family formation with the Council of Trent (1545–1563). The church sought to regularize and stabilize marriage and to protect women and children. Unlike Protestant theology, divorce was proscribed by canon law but legal separations of bed and table were permitted under extreme circumstances. After the Council of Trent Catholic theologians lay greater claim to the regulation of the marriage contract. The Tametsi decree ruled that banns be published and that a couple pronounce their vows in the presence of a parish priest and several witnesses. Although parental consent was not required or enforced, secret marriages were discouraged. Some children used the reform to have their arranged marriages annulled, arguing that their parents had forced them to take vows. Others married against the wishes of their parents.

Religion, Science, and Popular Beliefs

Religious evangelism advocated greater spiritual education of the young. At the same time the rise of scientific inquiry provided new, conflicting methods of learning, grounded in empirical observation and the material world. Thus children of the educated classes were brought up in a world of competing models of knowledge advanced by churchmen and scientists, while the offspring of ordinary people were exposed to some combination of evangelical claims, folk wisdom, and the repressive powers of the Reformation churches.

Among the goals of religious reformers was that of molding parent–child relationships. Beginning with DESIDERIUS ERASMUS (c. 1466–1536), Christian humanists and other intellectuals stressed the importance of childhood for character formation among the middle and upper classes. Religious thinkers debated whether children were born innocent or depraved, but in either case emphasized a parental duty to invest in the upbringing of the young, not only at home but also at school. Schooling was provided both by the churches and through a growing number of secular tutorials. Throughout Europe the number of new schools increased significantly with the advent of the religious reformations. As during the Renaissance, both girls and boys of the upper classes received primary education, but following the Reformation many reformers encouraged girls as well as boys to become more literate so as to be able to read the Scriptures and to instruct their children. Boys from wealthy families were prepared for prestigious professions. Girls, whose training revolved around home life, at best attended finishing schools. In some respects the school replaced the family as parent, particularly for wealthy boys who boarded out. Whether child rearing and schooling included excessive discipline has been the subject of intense debate. Catholic or Protestant, the middle and upper classes increasingly attempted to separate children from the spheres of adult living, removing them from the workplace, prolonging schooling, and repressing their SEXUALITY.

Both Protestant and Catholic teachers also strove to delineate the boundaries of official doctrine more rigorously. Their encounters with common folk produced serious tensions. Popular beliefs were quickly judged pagan and labeled heretical, and their exponents were repressed. Evangelists and inquisitors sought to impose religious uniformity and eliminate groups or individuals who could not be assimilated into mainstream orthodox Christianity. In particular, the office of the Holy Inquisition denied the laity's claims to spiritual powers in an effort to make them the exclusive purview of the clergy. It was an attempt to divest the laity, and also medicine and science, of a spiritual dimension. The religious campaign to denounce magic, feigned sainthood, and witchcraft thus helped prepare the ground for the late-seventeenth-century and eighteenth-century scientific claims that the cosmos was mechanized. In the modern age science would marginalize and undermine magical beliefs and reduce the spiritual influence of the clergy.

The religious Reformation, together with the critical and antiauthoritarian nature of Renaissance humanism, shattered the unity of intellectual thought, developments that were vital to the advancement of science. The discovery of new worlds and peoples and that the earth was round; the invention of movable type; the development of firearms and of a lens that improved the visibility of the stars and planets; improved mechanical clocks; and the development of ship-building and navigation opened up new intellectual perspectives and methods of discovery that relied increasingly on rationalism rather than religion. Scientists made new claims to authority and objectivity, tending toward explaining the world in mechanical terms. Scientific inquiry complemented secularism and the focus on how to improve material life. Separating the observable world from the spiritual sphere represented a fundamental shift in thought. To see the world operating on basic principles discoverable by reason fostered hope that humans could control their environment, a change in attitude that helped pave the way for nineteenth-century industrialization.

Scientific emphasis on reason also encouraged new views about children themselves. JOHN LOCKE, writing in the late seventeenth century, argued against the importance of innate concepts and implicitly, original sin, urging that children were blank slates (*tabulae rasae*) open to education as a source of rapid self-improvement. These views promoted increasing attention to education, at least in theory, during the eighteenth century, as a crucial part of the ENLIGHTENMENT. It may also have encouraged other developments in child care, such as a decline of SWADDLING, in the interest of permitting children more opportunities for development in early childhood. In this cultural context, emphasis on children as loving and lovable creatures also increased, as did (by the end of the early modern period) the creation of TOYS and books explicitly designed to promote children's abilities.

Demography

Demographic patterns in early modern Europe were critical determinants of life experience for the majority of people. The periodic expansion and contraction of the population helped define the limits of the possible, the balance between available resources and demand, and the standard of living. Economic and demographic trends affected changes in age at marriage for peasants and workers. In the sixteenth century, for example, when the population was swollen and there were land shortages, marriage was generally delayed, at least in areas like northwest Europe where the custom was to form nuclear households. Postponing marriage to the late twenties for men and early twenties for women limited fertility and helped to prevent an excess supply of children. Conversely, following great EPIDEMICS or long periods of war, smaller populations with sufficient landed resources generally married younger and had the potential to have more children. Their resources permitted their children to be raised at home. Such trends were critical to economic life since marriage and reproduction created the basic units of production. A significant number of men and women did not marry at all, becoming servants or auxiliary members of the households of married kin.

War, famine, and epidemic disease had catastrophic effects on mortality rates in early modern Europe. INFANT MORTALITY was high, particularly for babies farmed out to wet-nurses by the upper class and the destitute as well as for those born illegitimate. Infanticide also contributed to the mortality rate, despite the harsh laws designed to prevent it. As much as a quarter of all babies died in their first year, and another quarter never reached adult age. The high mortality rate of the young is a factor that sparked a lively historical debate, beginning with the work of PHILIPPE ARIÈS, on whether parents held much regard for their children or much awareness of the early stages of life. Perhaps parents and children who were fortunate to live out their lives together cared very much for one another. However, large numbers of children received little PARENTING at all. The excess children of the poor either died of malnutrition or left at an early age to live as servants or apprentices with another family. Moreover, one or both parents could be expected to die during a child's lifetime, making childhood brief.

Children represented a large percentage of the poor in early modern Europe. ORPHANS and the abandoned presented new challenges for both church and state who sought to reduce the numbers of beggars and vagrants and to provide children with sustenance, vocational training for boys, and small dowries for girls. England devised the Poor Law. In the rest of Europe, cities, civic organizations, and religious orders established foundling hospitals and encouraged the wealthy to bequeath resources to sustain charitable institutions. Efforts intensified after 1520 in correspondence with the spread of Christian humanism and the religious reformations. At the upper levels of society, wealth-conserving strategies helped determine children's life experiences. Fathers decided sons' careers and whether daughters would marry. Many unmarried Catholic daughters were forced to take the veil. Restricted marriage was common. In Venice, the *fraterna* (brothers in business together) limited marriage to one brother while other male siblings shared the family wealth and acted as an association. Some unmarried siblings entered ecclesiastical institutions. Few daughters were dowered to be married but instead were placed in convents, particularly as dowry levels steadily rose. Roman law on the Continent and common law in England, on the other hand, rested on the principle of primogeniture, whereby siblings did not inherit the land earmarked for the patrilineal lineage. The result was a large number of displaced children of the nobility whose destinies were determined in accord with gender expectations.

Economy

The early modern economy witnessed dramatic changes in the global spheres of transoceanic voyage and market exchange. State building and colonialism shifted the center of gravity from the Mediterranean to the wider Atlantic world, Africa, and the Americas. Spain and Portugal experienced temporary prosperity during this global expansion, while England and the Low Countries thrived well beyond the sixteenth century. Global markets and new goods linked people of different continents through sugar, tobacco, and coffee. Neither women nor most men, however, were highly visible at this economic level, where capitalism was at work and European states were in competition to control global trade networks, for most people did not have access to large resources, to companies and monopolies of control, or to the power of the state that would enable them to invest in capitalist enterprise.

Peasants and workers did, however, witness significant changes in production. The urban guilds that had prevailed in the Late Middle Ages waned in the sixteenth century, and production shifted to rural households where all family members took part in both productive and reproductive labor. Economic historian Carlo Cipolla states that the preponderance of demand centered around food, clothing, and housing, a phenomenon that determined the structure of production. Women, men, and children from the age of seven worked the land, cared for the livestock, and produced essentials for the family unit. They also tended and harvested crops that provided raw materials for manufactured products, such as flax, hemp, silk, and plants for dye. Capitalist investors found it in their interests to bypass the urban guilds and to hire women (and children), whose wages were more determined by custom than by the market. They bought from urban and rural households for export to Atlantic markets. Thus commercial capitalism and the globalization of the economy stepped up production based on hand technology in the family household.

The domestic industrial system changed the kinds of work opportunities available to women and children. It also transformed the functions of the family as men, women, and children began to receive individual wages for work. Nonetheless, Europeans had to work harder between 1500 and 1800 than during the previous centuries in order to maintain what were stagnant living standards, for their purchasing power did not increase much. It was not until the nineteenth century that capitalism transformed definitions of work. In the Middle Ages it included all tasks that contributed to a family's sustenance. With nineteenth-century industrialization and capitalism work became more exclusively participation in production outside the home and the market economy. When the household lost its central economic role to capitalist production and became more a center for reproduction, the status and importance of women's work and work in the household declined. Productive labor was seen as men's sphere, while women's labor, largely involving childbirth, infant care, and WET-NURSING, took place in the home and was of no monetary value. Women and children's roles in economic development were hardly recognized until gender analysis among late twentieth-century scholars reevaluated the importance of reproduction and domestic work as well as proto-industry in the home, connecting public and private spheres.

See also: **Education, Europe; Medieval and Renaissance Europe; Protestant Reformation.**

BIBLIOGRAPHY

Ariès, Philippe. 1962. *Centuries of Childhood: A Social History of Family Life.* Trans. Robert Baldick. New York: Knopf.

Berg, Maxine. 1985. *The Age of Manufactures: Industry, Innovation, and Work in Britain, 1700–1820.* London: Fontana.

Boxer, Marilyn J., and Joan Quaertert, eds. 1999. *Connecting Spheres: Women in a Globalizing World, 1500 to the Present.* New York: Oxford University Press.

Cipolla, Carlo Maria. 1980. *Before the Industrial Revolution: European Society and Economy, 1000–1700.* New York: Norton.

Cunningham, Hugh. 1995. *Children and Childhood in Western Society Since 1500.* London: Longman.

Davis, James C. 1962. *The Decline of the Venetian Nobility as a Ruling Class.* Baltimore, MD: Johns Hopkins University Press.

deMause, Lloyd, ed. 1974. *The History of Childhood.* New York: Psychohistory Press.

De Vries, Jan. 1994. "The Industrial Revolution and the Industrious Revolution." *Journal of Economic History* 54, no. 2: 249–270.

Ferraro, Joanne M. 2001. *Marriage Wars in Late Renaissance Venice.* New York: Oxford University Press.

Ferraro, Joanne M. 2003. "Families and Clans in the Renaissance World." In *The Blackwell Companion to the Worlds of the Renaissance,* ed. Guido Ruggiero. Oxford: Blackwell.

Goldstone, Jack A. 2002. "Efflorescences and Economic Growth in World History: Rethinking the 'Rise of the West' and the Industrial Revolution." *Journal of World History* 13: 323–389.

Heywood, Colin. 2001. "Child Rearing and Childhood." In *The Encyclopedia of European Social History, 1350–2000,* ed. Peter Sterns. New York: Scribners.

Heywood, Colin. 2001. *A History of Childhood.* Cambridge, UK: Polity Press.

Marshall, Sherrin. 1991. "Childhood in Early Modern Europe." In *Children in Historical and Comparative Perspective,* ed. Joseph M. Hawes and N. Ray Hiner. New York: Greenwood Press.

Ozment, Steven. 1983. *When Fathers Ruled: Family Life in Reformation Europe.* Cambridge, MA: Harvard University Press.

Perry, Mary Elizabeth. 1990. *Gender and Disorder in Early Modern Seville.* Princeton, NJ: Princeton University Press.

Pollock, Linda A. 1983. *Forgotten Children: Parent–Child Relations from 1500 to 1900.* Cambridge, UK: Cambridge University Press.

Pomeranz, Kenneth. 2000. *The Great Divergence.* Princeton, NJ: Princeton University Press.

Ruggiero, Guido. 1985. *The Boundaries of Eros: Sex Crime and Sexuality in Renaissance Venice.* New York: Oxford University Press.

Shorter, Edward. 1977. *The Making of the Modern Family.* New York: Basic Books.

Sperling, Jutta. 1999. *Convents and the Body Politic in Late Renaissance Venice.* Chicago: University of Chicago Press.

Starn, Randolph. 2002. "The Early Modern Muddle." *Journal of Early Modern History* 6, no. 3: 296–307.

Stone, Lawrence. 1977. *The Family, Sex, and Marriage in England, 1500–1800.* New York: Harper and Row.

Wiesner, Merry. 1993. *Women and Gender in Early Modern Europe.* Cambridge, UK: Cambridge University Press.

Wiesner-Hanks, Merry. 1999. "Women's Work in the Changing City Economy, 1500–1650." In *Connecting Spheres: Women in a Globalizing World, 1500 to the Present,* ed. Marilyn J. Boxer and Joan Quaertert. New York: Oxford University Press.

Wilson, Adrian. 1980. "The Infancy of the History of Childhood: An Appraisal of Philippe Ariès." *History and Theory* 19: 132–153.

JOANNE M. FERRARO

Eastern Europe

BALKANS
   Traian Stoianovich

POLAND
   Bogna Lorence-Kot

BALKANS

Because of common biological foundations, societies have tended to divide childhood into two main categories, children under seven and children from seven to fourteen or fifteen. The age group from fourteen to twenty-one comprises a third life category, which most societies did not, for a long time, associate with childhood.

In classical Greek antiquity, Hippocrates distinguished between three phases of early human life: that of the *paidion,* the child until age seven; that of the *pais,* the child of seven to fourteen; and that of the *mourakion,* the person between fourteen and twenty-one, when males usually were admitted into their father's *deme* and females were married. In western Europe, in response to urbanization, commercialization, the development of schools, and the rise of chivalry, this third stage was recognized between the eleventh and fourteenth centuries. With the diffusion of chivalry to the Serb lands between the thirteenth and fifteenth centuries, which required long training in knightly games, delayed marriage may have become almost as common among privileged Serbian males of the warrior class as it was in the West. For most social categories of the western and central Balkans, however, a long transitional stage between childhood and adulthood came into existence only after 1830.

The Domestic Family

From the fifteenth century until 1830, the Balkans divided on the basis of biosocial regimes into three areas: the western and west-central or Serb, Croat, western Bulgarian, and Albanian lands; the east-central Balkan or eastern Bulgarian

TABLE 1

Percentage of Children in Total Population

Place	Year	Ages 0–14/15	Ages 0–18	Uncertain Age
Adriatic Zara/Zadar city	1593		34.4	
Zara's islands	1593		44	
Zara's *terraferma*	1593		46.7	
Dubrovnik's rural communities	1673/74			35
Montenegro	1692	47.6		
Venetian Albania	1692	44.5		
Old Hercegovina districts: Grahovo, Hercegnovi, Nikšići	1692	52.5		
Savska Varoš, Belgrade suburb	1734	39.2		
Serbia	1846	48.9		

SOURCE: Courtesy of author.

lands; and the Adriatic, Aegean, and Black Sea coastlands. In the western and west-central lands, 60 to 80 percent of the population was included in extended households. In the east-central regions, the proportion fell to 40 percent; in the coastlands, to 20 percent.

Epistion was the ancient Greek term for household, meaning, literally, "(pertaining) to the hearth." The hearth was the place of assembly for the smallest socially defined unit for such common purposes as eating, celebrating, and grieving. The household could be small or large. Among the descendants of the Slavs who migrated into the Balkans in the sixth and seventh centuries, the term for household was the same as the word for house. In the early nineteenth century, however, south Slavic thinkers adopted the term *zadruga* to denote extended household, a term meaning "harmony" or "for the other." Anthropologist Claude Lévi-Strauss has suggested the use of another term, *domestic family*, for the extended household. We accept the suggestion but will define it in the sense of the extended household of the south Slavic or Balkan type. The latter was not just the product of a process of continuing lineal and lateral expansion and contraction but also of the aspiration to perdurability. It was a corporate body whose members identified land, work implements, and livestock as their common property.

Extension was a response to three circumstances. Pastoral transhumance, which needed the labor of male children from seven to fourteen years old, may have given an initial impetus to the formation of households of many adults and children. It was also a response to the need of agriculturalists and raisers of livestock alike for a household of more than two adults to assure the presence of someone to care for children in case of the death of one or two adults. Finally, large and strong families were a response to the need for protection against intruders during periods of insecurity.

By its very size, the vast Ottoman Empire created conditions under which long-distance transhumance was able to prosper and expand. It also engendered insecurity in the extensive marchlands formed with neighboring European states. Between the latter part of the fifteenth century and 1830, these marchlands remained an area of insecurity and of wide diffusion of a biosocial regime of domestic households, in which children up to fourteen years old made up well over 40 and even close to 50 percent of the population.

The Stages of Childhood

Records regarding the first phase of Balkan childhood are meager. Among the Balkan Turks, however, the sixteenth-century naturalist Pierre Belon du Mans, in a comparison of urban populations, says that children there were "never so stinky" or so difficult to bring up as the children of the "Latins," or Roman Catholics of western Europe. Turkish mothers breast-fed their infants until they were at least ten months old. They fed them no cereals or milk from a nonhuman source until that age, in contrast to the Latins, who gave them such foods much earlier. The infants were cradled until they were able to control their physiological needs. Through their cradles, which were made of taut leather, a hollow tube attached to the child's urinary member passed out through a small hole into a receptacle. In this way, mothers avoided the soiling of their rugs or carpets, diminished the need for linens, and kept their infants clean and comfortable.

Nineteenth-century and later observers note that infants were swaddled in almost all Balkan rural districts—lightly in Albania, round and round in Macedonia. In Macedonia, infants were allowed to have one hand free after their first smile; in Albanian districts, after they were forty days old. In southern Macedonia, mothers changed their children as soon as they wet themselves. Macedonian mothers fondled or tapped them playfully, tickled them around the lips, and told them stories. In Macedonia and Montenegro alike, infants normally were weaned in their third or fourth year. The functions of Balkan mothers later shifted to accustoming children to recognize male authorities and to teaching them the requirements of communal survival: to honor elders, observe age and sex differences, economize by not dropping crumbs, and respond to household needs.

In the second stage of childhood, the head of the household and the fathers and paternal uncles took over the task of teaching male children work tasks and instilling in them the need for collaboration. Mothers prepared female children for wifehood and motherhood.

ADOLESCENCE was virtually absent. Early marriage was common. In 146 of the villages enumerated in the county of Belgrade in 1530, only 13 percent of the male adults (males fourteen or fifteen years of age and over) were unmarried. In the Croatian Military Frontier during the Napoleonic era, females were married at age thirteen or fourteen, males at sixteen or seventeen. Table 1 shows certain other contrasts in the percentage of children in the total population.

Celibacy and late marriage suggest a low representation of children. Many Dubrovnik nobles married after age forty or fifty or remained celibate. Dubrovnik noblewomen did not marry until they were twenty-five or thirty. In the new city of Sarajevo in 1516, only 13.5 percent of the Orthodox males over fourteen or fifteen were unmarried compared to 39.6 percent of the Muslim males. In 1528, the proportion among Muslim males rose to 52.8 percent. In late nineteenth-century Istanbul, most males married after age thirty, and many remained bachelors. The city's females married after age twenty.

The practice of abortion, other means of BIRTH CONTROL, and venereal disease curtailed the number of children. A French consul versed in medical matters, F. C. H. L. Pouqueville, noted in the 1790s that Muslim Moreot (Peloponnesian) women practiced abortion and had fewer children than the Orthodox Greek women of the peninsula. Ottoman attempts to curb abortion were of no avail. Instead, Orthodox Christian women, rural and urban alike, also resorted to the practice. Long known to the western Asian and Mediterranean cultures, the practice of abortion and of other modes of birth control was less common in interior Balkan districts. Conducive to their diffusion were a growing acceptance between 1830 and 1880 of European ideas of fashion, an increasingly favorable attitude toward European conceptions of modernity and individuality, and the affirmation of European models of urban organization. Such influences emanated from two directions. They spread from the east (Istanbul) and south (Thessaloniki), moving northward and westward. They were also diffused—and ever more vigorously during the second half of the nineteenth century—southward from Vienna and Hungary. Finding acceptance among the Serbs of Hungary, they made their way to Serbia and Bosnia. In their wake and under the effect of compulsory male military service, urbanization, growing literacy, intensified contact with Europe, the relaxation of the authority of elders, and a growing propensity to delayed marriage, birth-control practices and abortion—which together were known as the "white plague"—spread southward.

The practice of delayed marriage acted to promote an upward creeping in the rate of illegitimacy in Serbia. From 1880 to 1884, however, the illegitimacy rate in that country still stood at less than 1 percent of all births. In 1877, it was 1.41 percent in Greece, 4.74 percent in Romania, 7.1 percent in France, and 7.4 percent in Hungary. In 1878, it stood at 7.15 percent in Italy, 7.44 percent in Germany, and 14.1 percent in Austria.

Revision of the Biosocial Regime
The revision of the biosocial regime of the Balkan interior, however, was a product not simply of diffusion but of earlier changes promoted by Balkan elites: demographic growth, urbanization, improved communication and transportation, commercialization, the obligation of military service for males, the diffusion of an ideology of freedom and individuality, and the voluntary adoption of western European political, social, economic, and cultural models. These innovations included the establishment of governments of law, with provisions for the security of life and property and a favorable disposition toward the formation of an informed, communicating society. These innovations were introduced in Wallachia and Moldavia after 1830, and in Greece, Serbia, and Croatia in the 1830s and especially 1840s. Aided by a growing cereal economy, they spread to the Ottoman Danube *vilayet* (northern Bulgaria). After the Crimean War and the Congress of Berlin, they found root in Bosnia and Herzegovina.

The best-informed person in a domestic household was likely to be the *pater familias* or *starešina*. The following incident suggests that he sometimes may also have been the member most responsive to the new institutions supportive of individual initiative and an informed society. The Serbian ethnographer Milan Đuro Milicevic (1831–1908), relates that when he was a child, his eighty-five-year-old grandfather gathered together his sons, grandsons, and older nephews to tell them that what hitherto had been known as "ours" henceforth would be "ours, yours, and theirs." The household would have to separate. Eager to favor their own children, the women of such households later would also favor separation.

By the mid-nineteenth century, the spread of elementary, intermediate, and higher schools, and of opportunities for the sons of the privileged to study in other European countries, aided the process of creating self-instituted generations, made up of persons in their late teens and twenties who, under the impetus of some great issue, interest, or idea, emerged as groups able to influence the rest of the population until another strong interest or idea gave rise to the formation of a new generation. In Croatia, Serbia, Vojvodina, and Greece, such a generation, informed by the ideology of liberalism, arose in the 1840s. Its elders, constitutionalist notables, regarded the demonstrations and polemics of this generation in 1848 as the "games of children." In fact, the extension of higher education to the sons of the privileged had resulted in the creation of a life cycle of delayed marriage. One demand of the students of the Licej (lyceum, the future university) of Belgrade in 1848 was that they be allowed to wear swords and marten-skin caps, parts of the uniform of the Serbian bureaucracy, in recognition of their right to fill future governmental positions. In 1868, Svetozar Markovic (1846–1875), the son of a Serbian prefect, urged the formation of a "radical party" to wage a "struggle against everything that has grown too old." The Bulgarian poet Hristo Botev emerged as a critic of Bulgarian mothers for striving to prevent their sons and daughters from becoming realists. A fellow Bulgarian, Ljuben Karavelov, discoursed on the conflict of generations.

Another consequence of the new societal model was that rural houses began to be built of more durable materials and with more rooms. The typical Balkan rural house in lowland districts grew from a dwelling of one or two rooms (without the kitchen) in 1830 to a dwelling of four rooms in 1900. In highland rural districts, it grew from nothing more than a kitchen and all-purpose room to a building of two or three rooms. Households became smaller. Houses became larger. The idea of a separate room for children or of the separation of the sexes could be conceptualized only around or after 1900.

The formation of a new biosocial regime of childhood and adulthood similar to that of Western Europe, which was simultaneously furthered and arrested by two world wars and by political and economic crises, continued after 1945, at first mostly under communist but ultimately again under capitalist direction. Its affirmation has been least complete among rural Albanian, Kosovo, and Bosnian Muslims. Specific conditions under communism, however, did generate some distinctive features. Housing shortages in countries like Hungary, for example, generated more multigenerational households after World War II, when these were virtually disappearing in western Europe. More recent developments point to a resumption of convergence in the experience of childhood between the Balkans and the rest of Europe.

See also: **Eastern Europe: Poland.**

BIBLIOGRAPHY

Golden, Mark. 1990. *Children and Childhood in Classical Athens.* Baltimore, MD: Johns Hopkins University Press.

Hajnal, John. 1965. "European Marriage Patterns in Perspective." In *Population in History: Essays in Historical Demography,* ed. D. V. Glass and D. E. C. Eversley. London: Edward Arnold.

Halpern, Joel Martin. 1967. *A Serbian Village.* New York: Harper and Row.

Hammel, Eugene A. 1968. *Alternative Social Structures and Ritual Relations in the Balkans.* Englewood Cliffs, NJ: Prentice-Hall.

Hammel, Eugene A. 1972. "The Zadruga as Process." In *Household and Family in Past Time: Comparative Studies in the Size and Structure of the Domestic Group over the Last Three Centuries in England, France, Serbia, Japan, and Colonial North America, with Further Materials from Western Europe,* ed. Laslett, Peter, with the assistance of Richard Wall. Cambridge, UK: University Press.

Lévi-Strauss, Claude. 1971. "The Family." In *Man, Culture, and Society,* ed. Harry L. Shapiro. New York: Oxford University Press.

Quataert, Donald. 1994. "The Age of Reforms, 1813–1914." In *An Economic History of the Ottoman Empire, 1300–1914,* ed. Halil Inalcik, with Donald Quataert. Cambridge, UK: University Press.

Stoianovich, Traian. 1992–1995. *Between East and West: The Balkan and Mediterranean Worlds.* 4 vols. New Rochelle, NY: Aristide D. Caratzas.

Stoianovich, Traian. 1994. *Balkan Worlds: The First and Last Europe.* Armonk, NY: Sharpe.

TRAIAN STOIANOVICH

POLAND

The values of the nobility shaped the rearing of Polish children until the mid- to late eighteenth century, when ENLIGHTENMENT influences and political developments led to major reforms. Enlightenment ideas about the nature and treatment of children had been seeping into Poland prior to the First Partition in 1772, when its territory was divided among Russia, Prussia, and Austria. The loss of territory, along with fear of further losses, also spurred reforms dedicated to national priorities instead of the goals of the nobility, because child-rearing practices and educational norms were perceived as being basic to national interests. Reforms included the secularization, nationalization, and Polonization of schooling. Girls were to be educated and mothers were encouraged to raise good citizens from infancy by taking physical and emotional care of their young. These measures contrast with the preceding distant and intimidating attitude of adults toward the young.

Public discussion about children waned following the Third Partition in 1795, because the occupiers had little interest in Polish issues and even less in progressive ideas. During the period of subjugation (1795–1918), Austrians did little to proscribe Polish identity, viewing Poland as the empire's hinterland. The other two occupiers, Prussia and Russia, sought absorption of Poles into their own cultures, but Polish resistance to integration became apparent with the failed Uprising of 1830 in Russian Poland. By the second half of the nineteenth century, the failed 1863 Uprising in Russian Poland provoked elimination of all Polish topics from public school curricula. Prussians pursued similar measures in the wake of German unification and Bismarck's *Kulturkampf.* But Poles, who made clear distinctions between nationality and state authority, felt no affinity for either Russians or Germans, and continued covert inculcation of Polish national identity in the young.

Historically, Polish cultural intransigence came as a surprise to those who knew that prior to the partitions, progressive Poles had shown little interest in Polish identity, preferring cosmopolitanism and everything French. In its serious version, that sentiment promoted the modernization of Polish culture for the purpose of preserving independence by aligning it with developments in Western Europe. Upon loss of independence Poles refocused on neglected national traditions, rediscovering some of what they had scorned in the eighteenth century. It may well be said that the partitions helped forge a modern Polish identity.

Identity apart, Poles always followed developing Western European trends. They were particularly interested in PROGRESSIVE EDUCATION, such as the educational ideals promoted by FRIEDRICH FROEBEL and MARIA MONTESSORI. To the extent that private school funding was available and the censors were satisfied, a minority of Polish children experienced the best that the educational world could offer. As for the rest, improvised home education augmented, if not negated, state schooling. Efforts to sustain the Polish ethos in the children of literate parents were expanded to illiterate peasant children. Progressives supported these efforts because they viewed peasant children as Polish nationals in the making; conservatives shared those goals because they were anxious to buttress class distinctions and inculcate the proper work ethic.

By the 1880s, when political activism turned to improving society instead of battling for independence, young Poles of both genders were proselytizing on behalf of Polish culture. The defeat of 1863 had turned Poles toward so-called organic work, which focused on social and economic improvement rather than armed struggle. Norman Davies points out that thirty years of such missionary activity yielded a bumper crop of private, informal, and covert Polish cultural enterprises, which swamped the Prussian and Russian educational system. Poles were culturally intact when they gained independence in 1918, but they faced enormous practical difficulties. The task of creating an organic infrastructure for three territories that had been apart for over a century was daunting. The problem of unification was compounded by the high rate of illiteracy and by the existence of several ethnic minorities who did not necessarily identify with Polish culture. The nation was still in the process of becoming when World War II began.

Loss is the operative word for the Polish experience of World War II. Estimates indicate that Poland lost over 2.6 million children under the Nazi and Soviet occupations. The children represent 38 percent of all Polish human losses during the war. Of the two hundred thousand children taken to Germany for the purpose of Germanization, only 20 percent returned. Both German and Soviet invaders destroyed school facilities and annihilated educators. Yet in the midst of terror, Poles managed to print books to teach their children Polish subjects, their teenagers finished high school, and graduates took university courses. It is as if wartime was just a variation on the period of partitions.

At the end of the war Poles expected to pick up where they had left off in 1939. That illusion lasted only three years. In 1948, having gained political control, the communists began organizing school reforms whose stated goal was raising the level and quality of education, but whose real purpose was indoctrination of the young. Polish texts were replaced with Soviet works. Contact with Western educational practice disappeared. Again, Polish families did their best to offset what children learned in school by exposing them to views that were not politically correct.

Following the dissolution of communist control in 1989, members of the Solidarity Party—with the support of the Catholic Church—embarked on new school reforms. In 1991, a law was passed authorizing the post-communist National School Reform Act. This act opened the door to the establishment of private schools by individuals, foundations, municipal governments, and religious institutions, none of which was possible earlier. According to observers, the reforms have had mixed success so far. Their stated goal has been to modernize Polish education and to meet the criteria of the European Union. But, according to some Polish critics, the constant search for new programs, new texts, and new pedagogical approaches has, at times, undermined the stability of the public school system. Ironically, democracy appears to present greater educational opportunity, but also greater challenges, than Poles faced under various occupiers.

See also: **Eastern Europe: Balkans; Education, Europe.**

BIBLIOGRAPHY

Davies, Norman. 1982. *God's Playground: A History of Poland.* New York: Columbia University Press.

Lorence-Kot, Bogna. 1985. *Child-Rearing and Reform: A Study of the Nobility in Eighteenth-Century Poland.* Westport, CT: Greenwood Press.

Lorence-Kot, Bogna, and Adam Winiarz. 2000. "Education in Poland." In *Kindergartens and Culture: The Global Diffusion of an Idea,* ed. Roberta Wollons. New Haven, CT: Yale University Press.

BOGNA LORENCE-KOT

Economics and Children in Western Societies

FROM AGRICULTURE TO INDUSTRY
David Levine

THE CONSUMER ECONOMY
Gary Cross

FROM AGRICULTURE TO INDUSTRY

Studying the family's organization of production and consumption can only be carried out if one also keeps its reproductive behavior in the same field of vision. For the vast majority of people, for most of the time, the act of balancing "hands" (i.e., production) with "mouths" (i.e., consumption and reproduction) was a precarious act; whether they were peasants, landless proletarians, or artisans, the slightest hint of adversity could destabilize the family unit enough to drive it down into poverty and destitution, from which escape was difficult, if not impossible.

Before 1750 most proletarianization was the result of downward mobility by the landholding peasantry into the ranks of the landless poor; such people became vagrants and migrant workers who frequently ended up as the *lumpenproletariat*, the lowest class of worker, which made up a majority of the urban population. After 1750 this trajectory of social decline was supplemented by a massive increase in a new kind of lateral mobility as industries in rural areas expe-

Cranberry Pickers (1910), Lewis Hine. Children began earning money in rural households at an early age. Five-year-old Jennie Capparomi is pictured here alongside adult workers harvesting cranberries in a New Jersey cranberry bog. © CORBIS.

rienced dramatic growth, sometimes in competition with—but more often as a complement of—factory industrialization. Marginal peasants having little or no land, sometimes called cottagers or dwarf-holders, who together made up a huge proportion of the rural population of northwestern Europe, found that their tenuous hold on the land was terminated when the products of the first phase of the Industrial Revolution destroyed the income supplements they derived from rural proto-industry. In North America, similar processes of downward (and outward) mobility were in evidence in the colonial and early federal towns, but the accessibility of the frontier meant that the day of reckoning could be postponed by starting life over again as pioneers.

The Demographic Revolution

The European population grew from about 65 million in 1500 to around 127.5 million in 1750, reaching almost 300 million in 1900. In North America, the population in 1750 was perhaps 2 million but grew almost exponentially—as a result of massive immigration from Europe as well as the natural increase of the native-born Americans—so that by 1900 there were about 81 million people living from sea to sea north of the Rio Grande. In this demographic revolution, population increased after 1750 in response to falling levels

of mortality and gently rising levels of fertility. The mix of factors was by no means homogeneous because in some places the whole population rise was accomplished by rising birth rates while elsewhere it was the result of falling death rates. Of course, in many places it was some combination of the two factors. The rise in FERTILITY RATES was itself remarkable because, all other things being equal, it would be expected that fertility rates would have declined in response to declining mortality. But all other things were not equal.

What is now known as the demographic revolution may have stemmed from declining mortality rates but, like the sorcerer's apprentice, this new state of affairs released uncontrollable forces when unexpected levels of survival of youths and married adults combined with earlier marriage and skyrocketing illegitimacy rates. Thus, more people married, they married at younger ages, and they stayed married longer. Around 1800, perhaps one English child in twelve was born out of wedlock (the comparable figure in 1700 was about one in fifty); in parts of Germany, the rates of illegitimacy were occasionally as high as one in five. This is especially significant to the birth rate, which is itself the product of length of marriage and fertility rates per year of marriage, for even small changes in mortality and birth rates when aggregated and allowed to multiply over several generations have profound implications.

It was within the changing tempo of daily life during the demographic revolution that family formation strategies were affected. The older world of family farming and family-workshop production was not lost for everyone, but the success of the few was predicated on the failure of the many. The majority of that population was forced to migrate—either socially or physically—and to establish wholly new routines. As a consequence, new ways of social life were simultaneously created and abandoned. Cottagers first became wage-earners and then lost their purchase on the land altogether. Furthermore, the value of women's and children's labor was initially enhanced and then radically depreciated. In handicraft cottage industry women and children supplied "hands," but they were subsequently marginalized by the emerging political economy of urban and industrial capitalism. In moving towards the patriarchal breadwinner economy, in which a male household head commanded both economic and moral authority over the family group, these urban wage-earning families were re-creating the social norms of the villages from which they came and in which the peasant patriarchs usually ruled the roost, controlling all women as well as unmarried males. The other side of this process is that the social standing of those who were neither patriarchs nor breadwinners was increasingly jeopardized. While individual families struggled desperately against these larger historical forces, it is only possible to understand their demographic and family formation behavior if we conceive of it as just one of a series of proactive coping maneuvers.

The explosive demographic implications of cottage industrialization were at least as much the result of more frequent marriages, by more people, as of earlier and more fertile ones. So too, the dynamic of rural industrialization permitted married couples to stay together whereas in the earlier social mode of production marriages were constantly being fragmented, and wives and children deserted. The economic base of the marginal peasant family was flimsy because it was subject to cyclical strains, resulting from the impact of war, climate, and the harvest. In this sense, the proletarianized cottagers who formed the backbone of many handicraft industries were able to move into new zones of economic and social freedom that translated into the formation of new families. The preindustrial cottagers, therefore, formed a large population reserve; the growth of rural industries allowed such people to be siphoned out of the rural economy connecting their individual movements with larger population processes. Furthermore, before 1750 delayed marriage and permanent celibacy had acted as a check on population growth but afterwards boom times meant more frequent and earlier marriage as well as a decline of celibacy.

In the preindustrial demographic-economic system of reproduction, about three-fifths of all families were likely to have had an inheriting son while another fifth would have had an inheriting daughter, which meant that about one-fifth of all niches in the landed economy became vacant in each generation. Urbanization, with its filthy environment breeding microorganisms so lethal to babies, partially counterbalanced the global improvements in life expectancy. Overall, however, mortality rates dropped and it is probable that improvements in infant, child, and adult health were especially significant in the rural environment. Married couples remained intact and continued to reproduce for longer periods of time while a higher proportion of children was likely to reach adulthood and themselves marry.

These trends raise some questions, however. Why, when rising life expectancy yielded more survivors, did people produce so many children over and above replacement? How were these additional children to find their way in a world that was already overcrowded? How were new economic niches created? Were such niches in agriculture, industry, or service sectors? The key point to bear in mind in answering these questions is that children were brought into the rural industrial family's productive activities at an early age. In cotton spinning or straw plaiting, girls as young as five or six were working long hours; in nail making, boys of seven or eight were apprenticed to older, stronger workers. Both girls and boys in such rural-industrial households were probably able to cover the cost of their upkeep by the time they reached twelve or thirteen; as older teenagers, they probably made a "profit" for the parents who kept them working in the family enterprise. The economics of child labor—and the early opportunity for independence that came with it—had two important implications: first, it meant that such

piece-workers could assemble the wherewithal to marry at a young age even though they had no expectation of inheriting anything of substance, unlike their peasant forebears; and second, it was peculiar insofar as more children were a good thing because a large family would not only change the ratio of "hands to mouths" but it would also extend the period of the family cycle when there would be surplus income from the ratio of producers to consumers.

There were other effects that resulted from shifts in the fertility schedule. The age-pyramid rapidly broadened at its base as enhanced child survival combined with the diminishing chance of marital break-up to swell the lower age groups at the end of the eighteenth century. Generations followed one another more quickly, contributing to the maintenance of high aggregate fertility rates. But something else was at work in maintaining high levels of age-specific fertility at later ages. Marginal groups—such as non-inheriting children—felt the full force of the nonlinear implications of population growth, as over the course of three generations the number of places remained the same but the population increased exponentially. Villagers who were over and above replacement, then, could either wait in the hopes of marrying into a niche or they could emigrate, that is, they could move *socially down* and *physically out* of their native land. This second alternative had been the reality presented to generations of their predecessors, for whom non-inheritance meant downward social mobility and demographic death. People who had been unable to inherit a niche in the rural economy were at the end of a family line, which stopped because they were unable to marry and reproduce themselves.

For a time, however, cottage industry was a godsend for these non-inheriting, marginal people; the luckiest ones could even find a way to subsidize the formation of a new household without having to leave their native hearth. The less lucky ones could move to the villages, towns, and cities where rural proto-industries were located; once there, they could set up on their own and support themselves with income derived from their labor, often with common rights to keep livestock and even a small garden. Children were enmeshed in the labor cycle: as young as four or five, they could watch their infant siblings; at six, seven, and eight they could gather dung and firewood, sweep the floor, clean pots and pans and dishes and cutlery, carry water from the well to the hearth, and prepare foodstuffs by chopping and peeling, as well as going out of the cottage on errands. Nine through twelve year olds could spin, knit, mend clothes in need of repair, attend the fire in the hearth, wash and dry clothing and bedding, herd and milk domestic animals, watch the poultry, and prepare food for the family meal. By the time these children were on the cusp of what we would call ADOLESCENCE, they were able to cover their costs through a mix of domestic labor and productive work. They were also very nearly "adult equivalents" in that they may have lacked some strength, endurance, and skill but otherwise were capable of a full day's work—and a full day's pay, too. Families engaged in rural industry were therefore less willing to see their teenaged children move away from home and into domestic service. Having paid for the cost of their child's upbringing, parents wanted to benefit from their labor.

During the classic Industrial Revolution (1760–1840) a large segment of the population experienced what have been called "lifetime moves" into the proletariat. And while their actions may have consisted of efforts to retain or recapture individual control over the means of production, they were swimming against a powerful historical current that ultimately pulled most of them down into the ranks of the proletariat. This occurred with astonishing frequency as the population in the countryside thickened. If boom times were like a siphon sucking population out of their rural cottages, then proto-industrial communities were like sponges in their ability to soak up these footloose extras.

But what about those who stayed behind? In what ways were their lives and the lives of their children altered by the outlet provided by rural industrialization? We have already had a glimpse of the rising reproductive levels in rural areas that provided some of the migrants, so it would seem obvious that the opportunity to export non-inheriting children relaxed the pressure on resources the exporting regions would have experienced. Parents with additional non-inheriting children would have had the knowledge that their offspring could relocate. Proto-industry acted not only as a magnet, then, by attracting migrants, but also as an insurance policy in perpetuating the reproduction of those who would become migrants. In addition to absorbing excess people rural industry also provided a source of ready cash for children who would eventually inherit but were in the meanwhile required to wait for an economic niche to open. If only one of the children was to inherit the family farm or household, that does not mean that he or she was unavailable as a source of income while waiting. Indeed, most had usually spent some time as live-in servants or in husbandry during the long wait between PUBERTY and marriage or INHERITANCE. In the preindustrial period, annual service for cash wages was of enormous importance in the rural economy of England and northwestern Europe. Children from poorer cottage households frequently moved away from home at twelve and worked for ten to fifteen years in the houses of the peasant patriarchs. But in the period of the classic Industrial Revolution this life-cycle system came into direct competition with more attractive, better-paid opportunities in proto-industrial households.

Cash earned in proto-industry was a kind of income transfer to the cottage economy: it gave some the opportunity to buy into an available, vacated economic niche; it gave others money to purchase the consumer products and the capital goods being produced more cheaply in an age of early industrialization; and it provided a valuable infusion of funds into a sector that was notoriously undercapitalized. Rural industrial communities therefore provided both an outlet for and a stimulus to this demographic dynamic in those villages that were the source of migrants. Consequently, the countryside filled up quickly. Dwarf-holdings multiplied, intensive cultivation and new crops, along with a more vigorous division of labor in the service sector, combined to make it possible for the land to fill up to the point of supersaturation. It couldn't continue, and it didn't.

The Change from Rural to Urban Industry

If rural industrialization and population increase were the most prominent features of the countryside in the period after 1750, then deindustrialization and depopulation typified the countryside in the middle half of the nineteenth century, from 1825 to 1875. For children, in particular, this switch from rural-industrial production in the cottage to urban workshops and factories had a profound impact. When the economic prop of child labor was knocked out from under the cottage economy, children were among the first victims of sectorial unemployment. Thus while individual couples desperately tried to protect themselves and their children from the self-defeating cycle of high rates of replacement, the respiration of the countryside inhaled the majority of marginally propertied peasants and exhaled its landless proletarians. Unemployed children were soaked up by the emerging school systems that developed across the North Atlantic world in the middle half of the nineteenth century.

By the mid-nineteenth century the forces holding villagers to their land in England and on the northwest European continent were in tatters. Many tried mightily to stay, but more left out of despair. The second half of the century also witnessed unprecedented levels of migration, both external—millions left Europe, most of them after mid-century—and internal—continental urbanization proceeded furiously to catch up with British levels, where 40 percent of the population lived in six large conurbations by 1881. Together, the demographic revolution and the Industrial Revolution wreaked disaster on an over-stretched peasantry clinging to proto-industry as a supplement to their subdivided holdings by undermining the continued viability of the family farm.

The family production unit's reliance on its own labor power merely served to expose it when the terms of trade swung violently against it in the mid-nineteenth century. The significant if simple and repetitive tasks by which women and children had contributed to the domestic economy of the peasant household—first and most notably in spinning—inexorably declined in the face of competition from specialized, factory-based production. The mechanization of spinning in the last decade of the eighteenth century effectively demolished this cottage industry at the moment when population growth was creating increasing stress on the income of these rural industrial households.

Compounding this decline, the mutuality of the cottage was displaced as women and children were further marginalized in the world of work by the increased emphasis on gender roles and age-stratified activities in the new domestic economy, which replaced the family-based system of cottage production. The ideology of domesticity provided the key entry-point for a new culture of breadwinning respectability as work was reclassified as a masculine endeavor and masculinity, in turn, was judged by the harmony of domestic discipline and its respectable independence. Accordingly, observers of the time worried that the supposed "natural" character of rural, proletarian women was threatened by "masculine" work. Such women would not only be "unsexed" but also socially deranged since they would be indisposed to "a woman's proper duties at home." Powerful as this prescription was, it was irrelevant to the lives of working women, who had never conformed to bourgeois expectations nor given "femininity" priority over family subsistence needs—always their primary focus.

Proletarians' high fertility during the early era of industrialization was incomprehensible to the bourgeoisie, who considered their additional children to be mouths to feed, while the working class considered them to be hands to work and insure the family against the ill-luck of any particular member. Sharing misfortune was a way of coping with the inevitable vicissitudes of daily life; this kind of mutuality found deep resonances in class-specific family formation practices. In England as well as in France, the mutuality of the proletarian family—which stood in contrast to the individuality so prized by social policy makers and reformers—was cited as evidence of its deficient moral education.

The organization of national social systems of education and welfare during the later nineteenth century provided the historical context in which the ongoing revolution in the family was keynoted by the decline in fertility. The average English woman marrying in the 1860s had 6.16 children; her daughters, marrying in the 1890s, had an average of 4.13 children; her granddaughters, marrying in the 1920s, had on average 2.31 children. The decline of marital fertility was both an innovation and an adjustment; it not only responded to macro-level changes in social organization but also represented one of the primary ways in which individual men and women acted to make their own history. Not only were the numbers of children dropping dramatically but the period of the family cycle devoted to child raising was likewise abridged. Some demographers have explained this phenomenon in terms of a shift from "quantity to quality" in relation to the time, energy, and resources devoted to each individual child; but something even greater was at work: the family had been deindustrialized and children had been unemployed. The modern family was built on a very different set of priorities from its predecessors and the experience of childhood was intimately affected by this transition to privacy, domesticity, and, above all, child-centeredness.

See also: **Child Labor in the West; European Industrialization; Family Patterns; Work and Poverty.**

BIBLIOGRAPHY

Anderson, Michael. 1971. *Family Structure in Nineteenth-Century Lancashire*. Cambridge, UK: Cambridge University Press.

Cobbett, William. *Cottage Economy*. 1979 [1822]. New York: Oxford University Press.

Collins, Brenda. 1982. "Proto-Industrialization and Pre-Famine Emigration." *Social History* 7: 127–146.

Durand, John J. 1977. "Historical Estimates of World Population: An Evaluation." *Population and Development Review* 3: 253–296.

Goldstone, Jack. 1991. *Revolution and Rebellion in the Early Modern World*. Berkeley and Los Angeles: University of California Press.

Hajnal, H. J. 1965. "European Marriage Patterns in Perspective." in *Population in History*, ed. David V. Glass and David E. C. Eversley. London: Edward Arnold.

Hajnal, H. J. 1983. "Two Kinds of Preindustrial Household Formation Systems." In *Family Forms in Historic Europe*, ed. Richard Wall. Cambridge, UK: Cambridge University Press.

Hobsbawm, Eric J. 1968. *Industry and Empire: An Economic History of Britain since 1750*. London: Weidenfield and Nicolson.

Hufton, Olwen H. 1974. *The Poor of Eighteenth-Century France, 1750-1789*. Oxford, UK: Clarendon Press.

Kussmaul, Ann. 1981. *Servants in Husbandry in Early Modern England*. Cambridge, UK: Cambridge University Press.

Levine, David. 1977. *Family Formation in an Age of Nascent Capitalism*. New York: Academic Press.

Levine, David. 1987. *Reproducing Families: The Political Economy of English Population History*. Cambridge, UK: Cambridge University Press.

Malthus, Thomas Robert. 1970 [1798]. *An Essay on the Principle of Population*. Ed. Anthony Flew. Harmondsworth, UK: Penguin.

Mendels, Franklin. 1972. "Proto-Industrialization: The First Phase of the Process of Industrialization." *Journal of Economic History* 32: 241–261.

Sharpe, Pamela. 1996. *Adapting to Capitalism: Working Women in the English Economy, 1700–1850*. Basingstoke, UK: Macmillan Press.

Smith, Ruth L., and Deborah M. Valenze. 1988. "Mutuality and Marginality: Liberal Moral Theory and Working-Class Women in Nineteenth-Century England." *Signs* 13: 277–298.

Tilly, Charles. 1984. "Demographic Origins of the European Proletariat." In *Proletarianization and Family History*, ed. David Levine. Orlando, FL: Academic Press.

Wrigley, E. A. 1978. "Fertility Strategy for the Individual and the Group." In *Historical Studies of Changing Fertility*, ed. Charles Tilly. Princeton, NJ: Princeton University Press.

DAVID LEVINE

THE CONSUMER ECONOMY

Throughout the twentieth century, children's roles in providing labor and income for families decreased while their functions as consumers increased, leading to dramatic changes in their relations with parents. This trend coincided with what scholars call the family consumer economy—the organization of the nuclear family around purchasing and using market commodities—which emerged in various forms in economically advanced regions of the world.

The Reduction of Children's Work Load

Several factors created this new family setting: the introduction of electrification, central heating, and indoor plumbing to the home, a process which began around 1890 but was not completed until after 1950, all reduced the traditional chores of children (hauling water, helping with hand laundry, and carrying wood, for example). The gradual replacement of home-preserved and kitchen-prepared foods with canned, packaged, and refrigerated goods similarly lessened the need for children's domestic labor. So did the process of family migration from rural farms to cities, which eliminated chores such as caring for poultry, horses, and cattle, and tending gardens. Thus, by one estimate, at the end of the twentieth century children did four to six hours of domestic work per week compared to the same number of hours per day in 1900. Paralleling these economic and technological trends was a substantial reduction of fertility and thus of the number of babies and toddlers requiring care from older children.

While the need for children's manual labor in support of the family declined to token amounts, technological and social changes outside the home reduced the demand for children's wage labor. Mechanization had reduced the need for child workers as early as the mid-nineteenth century in textile factories. Improved communications networks (telephones and home newspaper delivery, for example) diminished the demand for errand boys and newsboys by the 1920s. The decline in the demand for domestic servants in the early twentieth century equally reduced the need for child assistants to paid house cleaners and cooks. Increased wages, especially for fathers, contributed also to the decline in parents' expectation that their offspring contribute wage income to the household budget.

Children's school work roughly replaced the time they had formerly devoted to domestic chores and paid work. In 1900, children seldom attended school after twelve or fourteen years of age and, even before the teen years, parents frequently withdrew them from school to help out the family with wages or work. After World War I, school-leaving was gradually pushed into the teens, coming first to urban and then to rural children after World War II. Leading these trends were urban and middle-class families. Adults, especially in the working classes (as well as employers in child-dependent industries), resisted compulsory schooling and legal restrictions on the age at which children could enter the workforce. Fears of child idleness prevented successful legislation against child labor until 1938 in the United States. Still, the need for more skilled workers and, even more, long-term economic trends reducing the jobs available for children encouraged parental acceptance of extended schooling by mid-century.

The Changing Role of the Family

All this increased the time required to care for and nurture children and extended the years of childhood economic dependency into the teens and even beyond. Not only did children remain in the home until full maturity, but adults' daily interaction with them increased insofar as the family had become primarily an institution that socialized future workers and met their increasingly complex consumer needs. As a result, parents had a reduced incentive to bear large families, leading to the two- or three-child family of the twentieth century instead of the four- to six-child family of the nineteenth century. Because higher income and educational expectations over the century raised these time and money commitments, parents had increased incentives to bear fewer children. With the striking increase in the rate of married women in the workforce (around 60 percent by the end of the century in many economically advanced countries, compared to 10 percent to 30 percent in 1900), married women had to weigh the cost of bearing and raising children in terms of lost income when children required their leaving the workforce (and expenditures in raising them in a consumer economy) against any psychic benefits of children in the family. By the end of the century, it was estimated that the cost of raising an American child ranged from $410,000 to $1,500,000 (rising with family income). Even though all children's education contributes indirectly to the well-being of all adults, the shift of children's time toward education means that the young seldom pay back in labor and income the effort and money expended on them by their parents. Thus the traditional reciprocity between generations at the personal level has largely disappeared.

Another long-term effect was for mothers to enter the workforce in place of older children. This decision was motivated both by the shorter span of total years that young children were in the home and even more by the perceived need for mothers to contribute income to support the long-term costs of children (e.g., for further training, especially university) instead of children financially supporting their families of origin. This transformed older forms of reciprocity between parents and children, dramatically reducing the expectation that older children provide labor and income to parents in compensation for the parents' investment of time and money in children's early upbringing. Instead offspring gave back, not to their parents, but to the next generation of children, producing the contemporary pattern of one-way sacrifice, or staggered reciprocity.

This new economic relationship between parents and children, which placed such a large burden on parents, was in part sustained by a shift in the rationale for bearing and raising children. No longer could children be understood as economic assets or investments. Instead, they became emotionally priceless treasures, valued for their capacity to bring happiness into the home and for representing life beyond the market and work. Once parents widely accepted the doctrine of the priceless child (as it trickled down from the affluent), they could no longer expect their children to spend substantial time on domestic chores or earn money for family (as opposed to personal) use. The good parent could spend on the child but not expect the child to work for money beyond token amounts.

Family and Children as Consumers

Economically speaking, children became primarily recipients and agents of family consumer spending. Increasingly, most family goods and services were purchased rather than produced at home. As family incomes rose, the range of consumer goods, and especially symbolic or psychic goods, increased as well. By 1900, advertising appealed to parental concerns about protecting the health and enhancing the future opportunities and status of their offspring. New products, from appropriately sized furniture and clothing to baby cleaning and feeding products, were designed for parents eager to accommodate their children's perceived needs. Middle-class parents especially bought educational TOYS, backyard play sets, and uplifting magazines in the hope of giving their children the character and intellectual training necessary to prevail in competitive schools and later the business world. From the 1910s, child-care experts, who were especially influential in Britain and the United States, began advocating that children be given weekly money ALLOWANCES to train them in the arts of consuming. The allowance was intended to be educational, substituting training in well-considered consumption and money management for the older lessons in hard work and thrift.

While the allowance gave parents indirect influence and control over their children's decisions, the practice also affirmed CHILDREN'S RIGHTS to their own desires and to participate in the CONSUMER CULTURE. The child was increasingly expected neither to contribute money to the family nor to save for the future, but to use her or his earnings for personal gratification and self-expression. Moreover, from early in the twentieth century, children gained influence over family consumer decisions, especially in progressive, middle-class families. In the United States, ADVERTISING appealed to children's desires in the selection of foods, toiletries, and clothing, and in the 1930s merchandisers used premiums directed toward children to increase sales.

Deeper psychological motivations induced adults to bestow non-utilitarian goods on their offspring. In part, this was a form of vicarious consumption—adults enjoying spending, and the status that it brought, through purchases for their children. Starting with the mid-Victorian middle class, parents recognized that their wealth and domestic comfort allowed their children a less regimented growing up than they had experienced. As a result, childhood became more playful and involved more celebrations of fantasy. This trend culminated in the early twentieth century with a great upsurge of new toys, DOLLS, games, and fads designed for children or passed on to them. To a degree, spending on these goods was a substitute for older customs of transferring skills. Gifts of CONSTRUCTION TOYS and miniature TOY SOL-

DIERS "prepared" children by inviting them to imagine themselves as engineers or military leaders. Presents of baby dolls were substitutes for the real care of younger siblings (increasingly absent from smaller families) and preparation for later parenting. Yet the trend was gradually toward non-utilitarian spending on toys, sweets, and entertainment, which celebrated childhood as an emotional and expressive world apart from the care and competition of adult life. Beginning with the international TEDDY BEAR craze in 1907 and the play PETER PAN in 1904, toys and entertainment gave children permission to enjoy a playful, imaginative world. Although the hardships of the Depression and World War II reduced family discretionary spending on children's goods, merchandisers continued to appeal to parents' desire to please offspring with a widening range of toys, MOVIES, and other fantasy products. DISNEY, for example, not only distributed his cartoons globally from the early 1930s on, but also licensed products based on his characters.

Spending on children increased dramatically in the second half of the twentieth century, especially as Europe and JAPAN became affluent. In 1999, four- through twelve-year-olds spent $11 billion and teenagers spent $94 billion in the United States. And while a survey found shopping the favorite activity of 55 percent of American children from seven through twelve years of age, the percentage for children in other advanced consumer societies was also high: 47 percent in Japan and 37 percent in Germany. This consumption prompted oft-repeated fears that children were being spoiled by gifts that contributed little toward enhancing their life chances or developmental needs. Yet adults tolerated this form of fantasy consumption because it gave them permission to share it with their children, whatever their own guilt about excessive consumption might be, and it met other emotional needs.

Much of this type of spending on children took place during holidays, especially Christmas and BIRTHDAYS. The old potlatches of extravagance that had formerly taken place around community celebrations increasingly were focused on children. This trend was accelerated after World War II with the family vacation. The opening of Disneyland in 1955, Disney World in 1971, and sister sites in Tokyo in 1983 and Paris in 1992, was only a small part of this growing accommodation of children on VACATIONS.

At the same time, however, children's consumer desires were never controlled by parents. From the beginning of the century, makers of cheap fiction, films, candy, novelties, and playthings found ways to market directly to children, despite their lack of significant pocket money. With the development of peer groups on neighborhood streets and, with the lengthening of school years, in school and at extracurricular events, parental authority declined. In the United States, merchandisers of children's goods began advertising directly to children in the mid-1950s on television. In many other countries, however, restrictions on commercial TELEVI-SION—and in Scandinavia outright prohibitions—limited this trend. Everywhere, children used their "pester power," the income they accumulated from gifts during holiday pot-latches, their allowances, and increasingly their own wages from part-time work to gain access to the children's consumer market.

In the family consumer economy children have a reduced role in contributing to the material and social well-being of their families. Parents, however, have accepted this change in the hopes that schoolwork will provide their offspring with skills that will help them establish successful family consumer economies in the future. Gifts have become the means for parents to share and communicate with their children in a culture where older transfers of skill and even religious and ethnic values have declined. At the same time, consumer goods have become crucial in the formation of children's identity, giving them material expressions of their growing independence from parents and markers of their roles and participation in peer groups. As a result, modern children in affluent families may also become separate from parents and siblings through their pursuit of consumer goods. Because parents expect that bestowing gifts on their offspring will create bonds across the generations, children's consumer culture frequently frustrates adults insofar as it is alien to their memories of childhood and their expectations for their children's futures.

See also: **Child Labor in Developing Countries; Child Labor in the West; Globalization.**

BIBLIOGRAPHY

Burggraf, Shirley. 1997. *The Feminine Economy and Economic Man: Reviving the Role of Family in the Post-Industrial Age.* Reading, MA: Addison-Wesley.

Caldwell, John Charles. 1982. *Theory of Fertility Decline.* London: Academic Press.

Kline, Stephen. 1993. *Out of the Garden: Toys and Children's Culture in the Age of TV Marketing.* London: Verso.

Mizen, Philip, ed. 2001. *Hidden Hands: International Perspectives on Children's Work and Labour.* London: Routledge.

Sutherland, Anne, and Beth Thompson. 2001. *Kidfluence: Why Kids Today Mean Business.* Toronto: McGraw-Hill Ryerson.

Tilly, Louise, and Joan Scott. 1978. *Women, Work, and Family.* New York: Holt, Rinehart and Winston.

Zelizer, Viviana. 1985. *Pricing the Priceless Child: The Changing Social Value of Children.* New York: Basic Books.

GARY CROSS

Education, Europe

LITERACY in Europe has always been affected by conflict and competition among religious movements. The PRO-TESTANT REFORMATION and the Catholic Counter-Reformation are examples that confirm this fact. Religious doctrines encouraged education of a select few in the Middle Ages, but additional reasons developed to educate more people from the Renaissance onward. For example, the growth of the urban economy in northern Italy during the fifteenth century necessitated that large numbers of children be taught about secular life.

The Frame and the Drive

Since the sixteenth century, the education of every young person in Europe has been framed by the dialectical relationship between the spiritual and the secular, which in practice has differed from century to century and from country to country. And these differences—between Protestants and Catholics, country folk and townspeople, girls and boys, the Mediterranean and the Nordic countries, and Eastern Europe and the West—have created a tension that formed the conditions for challenge and response.

From the Renaissance to the Reformation

By the fifteenth century, urban residents of northern Italy had developed a self-assured attitude toward life. People began to feel less subject to the will of God and more responsible for their own decisions. Thus, it became appropriate to teach according to humanistic principles, based on reason, contrary to the traditional religious scholastic ideals of education. In the arts, objects were no longer depicted from God's perspective, but instead were viewed from a human's place in the landscape. At the same time, scientists learned that the Earth was not located at the center of the universe; instead, it was just one of several planets that revolved around the sun. Both these understandings were crucial to the European belief that it was necessary to educate the public at large—not just a small clerical elite.

The Reformation

In the Middle Ages the Roman Catholic Church dominated both religion and education, controlling nearly all the schools and universities. There was, however, some growing opposition to the church's monopoly. The Renaissance humanism that was concerned with individualism posed the greatest challenge to the ruling scholastic thinking. In the beginning of the sixteenth century, a German monk named Martin Luther, who was a child of the Renaissance, declared himself opposed to the Roman Catholic Church. He wanted every person to read the Bible; thus, it became necessary to promote universal literacy. Subsequently, the Protestant movement began to develop its own school system.

After one of his visitations to a village in 1529, Luther compared many of its local priests unfavorably to cattle and pigs. Luther then began to write textbooks, one of which, *The Small Catechism*, still is used throughout Protestant Europe. This booklet was widely circulated, made possible by cheap distribution. According to Luther, the school was to be the daughter of the church. Most of the education of the

Marie Bashkirtseff's *The Meeting* (1884) was painted in the period immediately following the passage of the Ferry Law of 1883, which instituted free compulsory education in France. No longer a threatening political force, the young working-class boys shown here are on their way to school. Musée d'Orsay, Paris.

rural peasant children took place in the church after the Sunday service; in the towns, separate schools, including GRAMMAR SCHOOLS, were established.

The Society of Jesus

The Protestant movement had set the pace of change in the field of education. A Spanish nobleman named Ignatius Loyola, however, took up the challenge to defend education on behalf of the Roman Catholic Church. In 1553 he established the Collegium Romanum, a secondary school in Rome, which became a laboratory for the development of an effective school system in the Catholic world.

After a few years, similar schools were established in Italy, Spain, Portugal, India, and Germany. Each of these new institutions employed at least a dozen priests as teachers, contained a suitable house for the priests in connection with a church, and also included a garden. This educational establishment, which required a sound economic foundation, aimed to produce competent theologians, skilled professors of Latin and Greek, but most of all, excellent teachers who would be able to create a pious atmosphere. Of course, the overall aim of the new schools was to educate young people to be faithful Roman Catholics and thereby form a buffer against the expanding Protestant movement. By the seventeenth century, Jesuit educational institutions had been established in all the predominantly Catholic countries in Europe, as well as among the unlettered residents of the Spanish and Portuguese colonies outside of Europe. During the eighteenth century, secular authorities accused the Jesuits of using the end to justify the means. Some also questioned whether it was appropriate to allow an ecclesiastical group to educate children.

Enlightenment

In 1783 the German philosopher Immanuel Kant asked the question "What is enlightenment?" He answered "*Sapere Aude!*" meaning "have the courage to leave behind your ignorance." Not all children could do this, but the eighteenth-century ENLIGHTENMENT movement helped to modernize and secularize education throughout the developed countries in Europe.

Despite the efforts of such reformers as Czech theologian JOHANN AMOS COMENIUS and British philosopher JOHN LOCKE, most eighteenth-century European parents paid a fee to send their children to dame schools, which provided nursery care rather than formal education. In a typical British parish of Islington between 1767 and 1814, for example, about 75 percent of poor boys and girls were illiterate. In the eighteenth century it was commonly believed that the poorer classes should not receive any education. In 1803 the bishop of London expressed it in this way: "It is safest for both the Government and the religion of the country to let the lower classes remain in the state of ignorance in which nature has originally placed them" (Hibbert, p. 450). The French philosopher JEAN-JACQUES ROUSSEAU developed a theory of education based on the assumption that children were naturally good. He offered a different perspective; namely, that all teachers should give their students the liberty to learn from their own experience. In *Émile*, Rousseau's model boy had to be taught by a professional teacher, not by his parents. Rousseau wrote that Émile should avoid the conventions of

civilization and learn from nature. He should be educated to be a good citizen and taught to work with his hands. Although many philosophers argued that the elementary education curriculum should be the same for boys and girls, in Rousseau's work, Émile's sister, Héloïse, was educated in preparation for life as a housewife.

Industrialization and Modernization

The growing urban economy, along with the new philosophies of the Enlightenment, made it possible for more people to think of themselves not just as workers, but as members of the larger society. Contrary to Martin Luther's statement that a shoemaker should stick to his last, more and more people in the nineteenth century could move to new jobs or new social classes. Industrialization demanded a new middle class, which in turn required an education system that could produce a literate and broadly educated section of the population. To this end, the eighteenth-century grammar school curriculum was broadened from Greek and Latin to include history, science, chemistry, modern languages, and the national language. Educators needed to find out what parts of the different scientific subjects should be included in the curriculum, however, and this led to interesting discussions among teachers, university professors, and politicians. The measure or standard was to be *Allgemeinbildung*, that is, liberal education.

During the nineteenth century, all European states assumed responsibility for education at all levels. Private institutions were permitted, and often received public aid, but they had to conform to the laws of the state. The aims of universal elementary education were no longer considered to be simply religious and economic, for in an age of increasing democracy, the school also had to prepare the pupils for participation in political and civic life. The elementary school and compulsory military service, which became common in Europe in the nineteenth century, prepared males for trade and citizenship. This process of national unification had a high priority in the so-called new countries—namely, Greece and Belgium—in 1830, followed by Germany and Italy in the 1860s. In most European countries people were bilingual, and a condition for effective nation-building was a uniform national language. In Brittany, a region of France, for example, in order to prevent pupils from speaking the local language teachers forced children who spoke Breton to wear an ox bone or a wooden choker around their necks.

To develop an effective primary school system which could support the new nation-state, teachers had to be educated in training colleges, and this process stimulated the pedagogical debate. How should classroom discipline be maintained? Which were the best ways of teaching calculation? How should schools be constructed and classrooms organized?

Better economic conditions in the 1830s encouraged the development of new and more effective forms of education.

These changes were barely noticeable in university education or at the secondary level, but major advances occurred in the primary schools. As long as the gross domestic product relied more heavily on agrarian production than on trade and industry, however, access to higher education had to be limited (because few professionals would be needed in such a society). From 1840 to 1880 the population in Europe rose by 33 percent, but the number of children attending school jumped by 145 percent. In Italy the number of children attending primary school doubled in the fifteen years after the country was unified in 1840. France, after being defeated by the Germans in 1870 in the Franco-Prussian War, gave a high priority to education under the Law of 1873. The minister of education, Jules Ferry, had great visions for the educational system, which at the primary level was to be free, compulsory, and secular. In 1883 he wrote an open letter to all teachers in France concerning the main principles for the public school. Ferry said the new schools should stress morals and civics instead of religious instruction, which was to be the obligation of the family and the church.

Literacy rates varied widely throughout Europe in the last quarter of the nineteenth century. In Germany, Scotland, Switzerland, and the Scandinavian countries, over 90 percent of the population could read; in France, England, and Belgium, approximately 80 percent of the citizens were literate, while in Austria-Hungary, Spain, Portugal, Italy, and Greece the percentage dropped to around 50 percent. Allowing for difficulty in collecting the data, these differences were nonetheless remarkable. The main cause was likely to have been the varying degrees of industrialization, but this factor is not sufficient to explain all the differences. For instance, in 1870 Germany was no less industrialized than England and France, but nevertheless the educational systems in each country were very unlike one another. Universal elementary education, financed by the state, was established in Scandinavia and Germany by the beginning of the nineteenth century, whereas it was not made compulsory in Britain and France until the 1870s. The nation's governments varied in their ideological commitments to private education.

The Democratization of the Schools

The growth and the increasing sophistication of industrial production in the first half of the twentieth century made society far more complex; this complexity posed a challenge to all kinds of education.

If the solution in the nineteenth century had been primary education for all, the answer in the twentieth century was to be secondary education for all. This aim was the title of a pamphlet written by R. H. Tawney for the British Labour Party in 1922, recommending a break at age eleven, when pupils were to be allocated to different categories of schools. Under the 1944 Educational Act, secondary education was made universal and free. Reformers hoped that the system would develop along tripartite lines: grammar schools, technical schools, and secondary modern schools. Placing the children in different types of schools would allow educators to provide a curriculum that suited their needs. Many European countries practiced the break at eleven. In 1896 Norway created a so-called middle school, and Denmark and Sweden followed suit. In France the urban academic pupils could choose a more advanced line of education which would prepare them to either take jobs such as bank clerk or railway company servant, or to continue their education at an upper secondary school.

Girls were allowed to participate in elementary education, but they were normally excluded from secondary schools, except those run privately or by the church. By the end of the nineteenth century, however, girls were legally allowed to enter the universities; this development compelled European governments to make equal secondary school provisions for female students. As the family evolved during the twentieth century from a traditional extended family to a nuclear structure, new jobs were created in the public sphere, where educated women were in demand.

The educational pedagogy in the first half of the twentieth century was dominated by traditional classroom teaching. This practice had its virtues; namely, the teacher could take personal conditions into consideration to meet the needs of most students. But in many cases, teaching conditions did not favor respect for the individual pupil. Big classes, insufficient teaching material, choleric teachers, and the necessity in some rural areas to teach children of different ages in one room complicated the traditional approach. In most European countries, reform-minded educators became inspired by pioneer educators such as the United States' JOHN DEWEY, Italy's MARIA MONTESSORI, and the German anthroposophist RUDOLF STEINER. But nonetheless, the overall tendency was an education rooted in a centralized curriculum, controlled by examinations, and taught by teachers who were at best authoritative or at worst authoritarian. In most European countries, if the parents were not satisfied with the public school, they had three other options: they could send their child to a private school, to a so-called free school with a milder discipline and democratic ethos, or they could teach their children themselves.

The Posttraditional Society

After World War II, the Cold War infiltrated European classrooms. In France and Italy the communists were supported by more than a fifth of the population; moreover, regions of Eastern Europe from Lübeck to Trieste had been transformed into Communist states which promoted a utilitarian, politically dogmatic educational pedagogy. Although the United States wanted to establish comprehensive education in its German occupation zone, West German politicians wanted to return to the pre-Nazi tripartite system. Spain and Portugal, however, remained as they were before the war—fascist dictatorships where no reforms were expected.

As industrial production became more technological, demand grew for white-collar workers to supplement the traditional blue-collar labor force. In the 1970s, conventional wisdom referred to the service society; in the 1980s, economists described the information society; and in the 1990s, experts coined the term the knowledge society. These developments had a great impact on education. Furthermore, new scientific discoveries entered the classrooms, which necessitated new forms of teaching. For example, knowledge of computers and the Internet had to be integrated in all subjects.

In a rapidly changing society, it is not sufficient to maintain one's competence; rather, it is necessary to engage in lifelong education. Given the extent of GLOBALIZATION it is not possible for nation-states to maintain their own individual standards. For example, international organizations such as the United Nations Educational, Scientific and Cultural Organization (UNESCO) have created channels to further global communication in the educational field. British sociologist Anthony Giddens described what he called the *post-traditional period.* He suggested that tradition should no longer be the guideline for education and for life; in the modern world, risks dominate and individuals must continually assess the pros and cons of their decisions. In such a complex world, education must also be more complex, and the solutions to teaching problems could be to create new subjects or to combine existing subjects in new ways. Thus, interdisciplinary work has become common in all types of secondary schools and the universities.

There are at least two paths to choose when planning an educational approach. One is the Anglo-Saxon curriculum, popular in Great Britain and the Scandinavian comprehensive schools. All pupils follow the same core curriculum and progressively they are given more choices in order to follow their individual talents. The comprehensive system responds to the challenge of globalization by teaching a variety of school subjects. Each student's proficiency is tested periodically to ensure that the teaching objectives are being satisfied. Another approach is the German or continental didactical method. Instead of choosing elective courses, students decide to attend one of three types of secondary schools: Hauptschule (26 percent), Realschule (27 percent) or Gymnasium (32 percent). Only a few students choose to go to private schools; the remaining 9 percent attend a comprehensive school. The pupils do not have a free choice between different institutions, however; their teachers at the lower level decides for them. The pupils in the Hauptschule can continue their studies at the vocational training schools, those who attend the Realschule can go to technical schools, and the pupils in the Gymnasium can go to the sixth form and continue their studies at the university and academy. In

fact, although there are relatively few choices between subjects in the German system, it ensures coherence and progression. Moreover, the teachers are free to develop a personal didactic approach to teaching, often with student participation, in order to prepare their pupils for the final state-controlled examinations.

In the 1990s, to prepare their citizens to contribute to the knowledge society, several European countries formulated an education plan. This approach expected 95 percent of young people to graduate from secondary school, with 50 percent of those students going on to university. In order to fulfill this plan, it was appropriate to stress the learning rather than teaching; educators discussed terms such as the Process for Enhancing Effective Learning (PEEL, a method developed in Australia) in order to focus on the responsibility of the pupils. Because the individualization of education made it difficult to know whether all students had reached an acceptable proficiency level, it was therefore necessary to evaluate the educational process and its results. Swiss psychologist JEAN PIAGET's theory of children's maturation influenced these educators. They also incorporated the ideas of German philosopher Wolfgang Klafki, who promoted categorical learning as a synthesis of material and formal education.

The development of globalization presented a challenge to the European nation-state; one of the responses has been the development of the European Union (EU), a trading bloc with a common currency. Another was the collaboration between the industrialized countries of the world in the Organisation for Economic Cooperation and Development (OECD). This organization developed a program called PISA (Programme for International Student Assessment) which in 1998 published a review called *Knowledge and Skills for Life.* This comprehensive account showed "evidence on the performance in reading, mathematical and scientific literacy of students, schools and countries, provides insight into the factors that influence the development of these skills at home and at school, and examines how these factors interact and what implications are for the policy development." More than a quarter of a million students, representing almost seventeen million fifteen-year-olds enrolled in the schools of the thirty-two participating countries, were assessed in 2000. The literacy level among students in the European countries differed very much from one nation to the next. Finland was at the top, followed by Ireland, the United Kingdom, Sweden, Belgium, Austria, Iceland, Norway, France, Denmark, Switzerland, Spain, the Czech Republic, Italy, Germany, Poland, Hungary, Greece, Portugal, and Luxembourg. All sorts of explanations for the differences can be brought forward, and there probably is no single underlying factor. Economic variation is likely to be a contributing factor, but it is not sufficient. The report concludes that the socioeconomic background of the students, although important, does not solely determine performance. Religious affiliations are no longer a decisive factor, but combined with the fact that countries like Germany and Luxembourg have a comparatively large number of immigrants with a different cultural background, religion may have had some influence on reading proficiency. Other factors could be the regional differences in teacher training, the structure of the native language, or the reading traditions in the home.

The Trend

The Reformation in the early sixteenth century gave illiterate children in Europe an opportunity to learn basic reading skills in order to understand the holy texts. The Enlightenment of the eighteenth century questioned the power of the church and gave the new nation-states more control over the education of ordinary girls and boys. During the nineteenth century, European states increasingly wanted to provide a universal, free, and compulsory secular education, practiced by trained teachers in suitable buildings. The sophistication of the industrial production was a new challenge to schools in the twentieth century, and educators began to provide a secondary education for all. Globalization presented a challenge to the pedagogical thinking through the implementation of new teaching material and the Internet. In the knowledge society, the schools began to compete not only at a national or regional but also at an international level. The European school of the third millennium needs to prepare its students to participate in lifelong learning.

See also: **Education, United States; Gymnasium Schooling; Lycée; Public Schools: Britain.**

BIBLIOGRAPHY

Center for Educational Research and Innovation, ed. 1992–2002. *Education at a Glance: OECD Indicators.* Paris: Organisation for Economic Cooperation and Development.

Hahn, Carole S. 1998. *Becoming Political: Comparative Perspectives on Citizenship Education.* Albany: State University of New York Press.

Hibbert, Christopher. 1987. *The English: A Social History 1066–1945.* London: Grafton.

Martin, J. P., and E. Owen, eds. 2001. *Knowledge and Skills for Life: First Results from PISA 2000.* Paris: Organisation for Economic Cooperation and Development.

HARRY HAUE

Education, United States

From the colonial period to the present, the question of how to properly educate and socialize children and youth has preoccupied parents, teachers, and other adults. With the establishment of more fully inclusive, free public schools in the nineteenth century, Americans increasingly made formal instruction outside of the home or workplace a significant aspect of most children's experience. Prolonged school attendance, rare before the Civil War, became increasingly

common by the early twentieth century. HIGH SCHOOLS, which enrolled a small fraction of adolescents even in the late nineteenth century, soon became mass institutions. By the 1920s, there were already more students attending secondary schools in some American cities than in some European nations. Over the course of the century, attending school became an integral part of growing up in America.

Schools in Colonial America

The modern emphasis on attending school contrasts sharply with the experiences of most children and adolescents in colonial America. A wide variety of schools existed, especially in the northern colonies, but they were not compulsory or necessarily linked together in any kind of system. Most famously, the early Puritan settlers required the establishment of schools in local towns and villages; communities sometimes evaded the laws, but many established elementary schools and even a local Latin GRAMMAR SCHOOL, the latter usually restricted to a few bookish boys preparing for college. Schools paled in significance, however, compared with the authority of parents and churches. Parents, particularly fathers, were expected to teach children to read, in order to ensure their capacity to read the Bible, before they attended the elementary school, which emphasized the importance of reading, Christian morality, and to a lesser extent numeracy.

Before the American Revolution, generations of children would recite their ABCs from successive editions of the *New England Primer*. Every school child, whether Puritan or not, was explicitly reminded by these primers of the sacred quality of language, which Christians had long regarded as a divine gift, as well as of their own sinful nature: "A: After Adam's Fall, We Sinn'd All." School children in reading classes also recited the Lord's Prayer and memorized scripture; older boys in Latin grammar schools memorized Latin and advanced math as they prepared for their college entrance exams.

Children growing up in places with heterogeneous populations—for example, New York City or rural communities in Pennsylvania—also attended schools, and adults there similarly assumed that pupils should learn basic LITERACY, numeracy, and religious faith. Anglicans, Presbyterians, and other Protestants often built denominational schools, sometimes with a mix of public and private funds. By the middle of the eighteenth century, Quakers in greater Philadelphia established schools for their own children as well as for free black adults and children. The slave South, in contrast, with its rural, dispersed population, had fewer schools, especially outside of the cities, leading to lower literacy rates among poor whites and especially among black slaves, 90 percent to 95 percent of whom may have been illiterate at the time of emancipation.

As in Europe, colonial Americans debated the nature of children and the best ways to educate them. There was never any clear consensus on the nature of children or on how they should be educated or reared. Evangelicals often proclaimed that children were evil by nature, thanks to the misdeeds of Adam and Eve; their wills needed to be broken, which reinforced the familiar use of the switch. More moderate voices among Protestants held a more balanced view of the young, emphasizing Christian nurture, parental understanding, and the human potential made possible by free will. To most parents and educators, however, learning was widely seen as a form of moral discipline. Nearly every child who attended any school faced a regimen of study, memorization, and recitation, which was essential in learning religious truths as well as the alphabet or the rules of grammar and multiplication.

For the great majority of children and adolescents, school remained a minor aspect of life. Benjamin Franklin, while not a typical American as an adult, was perhaps typical in terms of his childhood. Reared in a large, poor family in Boston, he had some private tuition and attended the Boston Latin School, which he disliked, preferring to read on his own outside the constraints of educational institutions. Self-help long remained an attractive ideal to many citizens.

Some colonials certainly had access to schools. Modest one-room district schools dotted the New England countryside after the mid-eighteenth century, and many northern villages and towns (as well as southern communities) had private pay schools that taught such specialized subjects as French, drawing, or navigation. Other children had access to various elementary and grammar schools. But school attendance even in the North was not universal and was usually brief or irregular. The majority of children everywhere mostly learned what they needed in life at home, where girls worked with their mothers to learn the art of gardening and housewifery and boys tended animals and helped work the fields. To learn a trade or special skill, boys in particular, at around the age of twelve, were sometimes apprenticed to a master outside of the home, though such arrangements dramatically declined in the early 1800s. The modern world—with its age-graded, compulsory school systems, CONSUMER CULTURE, and linkage of jobs with educational credentials—was largely unknown during the colonial period. A tiny percentage of the male population attended colleges, nine of which existed by 1776, providing the nation with ministers, professionals, and members of its political elite.

The Creation of Public Schools

In the nineteenth century, the most important developments in the history of childhood and adolescence included the creation of public schools, first in the North in the antebellum period and in the South after the Civil War. This was an age of rising expectations for schooling, born in an age of intense evangelical Protestantism and dramatic social change, including the rise of cities, expanding commerce, and intensified industrialization. Late in the century, however, most children, even in the best financed school districts in the North, left school by the age of ten to twelve due to the pri-

macy of work and other family obligations. The creation of free high schools, an integral part of the public school movement, also led to the decline of private academies, particularly in the North, where they had provided most secondary education before the 1870s. In the South, the public schools created during Reconstruction were soon segregated by race, and they were poorly funded compared to the North, with African-American schools routinely starved for money. As in the colonial past, regional differences remained very visible.

The evangelical as well as secular reformers who built free, tax-supported public schools in the decades before the Civil War imposed an expansive mission upon them. Reformers claimed at different times that schools could end social conflict, create American citizens, save the republic, and reduce public immorality as well as poverty. This was a tall order, and impossible to fill, but it reflected the millennial hopes of the era. Ideas about education as well as school practices remained heavily shaped by religious values, particularly nondenominational Protestantism. Many schools began the school day with the Lord's Prayer and a reading without comment by the teacher from the King James version of the Bible; this offended enough Catholics that a fledgling PAROCHIAL SCHOOL system began to emerge in some northern cities by mid-century.

Shaping children's character—by having them attend school punctually, obey authority, honor rules and regulations, and attend to their lessons—was central to the thinking behind all of these schools. By the 1820s and 1830s, young scholars typically studied the proverbial three Rs plus English grammar and some geography and history. The Mc-Guffey Readers, which became more secular and less religious in later editions, taught the values of piety and virtue, and Webster's ubiquitous spellers, as well as their rivals, emphasized the English language, uniform spelling and punctuation, and proper diction. Children studying geography learned of the grandeur of America and its material riches, and those studying history of its greatness among nations.

Boston established the first free high school as an alternative to the Latin grammar school and classical education in 1821. Other big cities in the North followed suit and similarly restricted admission to boys, a trend that was soon reversed in most communities. Separate male and female high schools remained common in the urban South and the larger northern cities, but the trend, as in the lower grades, was toward coeducation. At mid-century, whether in the ubiquitous, ungraded rural schools of the North or in the age-graded classrooms in the cities, boys and girls increasingly attended school together, even if they entered the building through separate entrances or sat in different rows within the classroom. This was seen as an alternative to Catholic and European practices, which often practiced strict gender separation.

Public high schools enrolled only a minority of adolescents in the nineteenth century. As late as 1890, only about 5 percent of all adolescents were enrolled. In most places the majority of pupils were girls, many of whom, whether or not they graduated, became elementary school teachers. Boys became clerks or white-collar professionals, and only a minority of high school pupils of either gender enrolled in college. Drawn mostly from a broad range of middle-class families, high school pupils usually maintained their family status and position through secondary education. Like children in the lower grades, students of the higher branches memorized reams of material, which they learned from textbooks and recited to their teachers. High schools also largely remained urban institutions, though northern villages after the 1850s often built larger central schools, which offered secondary classes for the more mature and advanced pupils.

Public School Expansion

Children in the cities were widely regarded as having the best educational opportunities in the nineteenth century. At least that was the point of view of most professional educators, who saw the cities, with their greater and more concentrated wealth and student populations, as model sites for educational experimentation and improvement. Cities over the course of the century increasingly hired women to teach, especially in the lower grades; had a more standardized and uniform curriculum; and added additional subjects late in the century, such as sewing for girls and drawing and manual training for everyone. Reformers who were inspired by romantic notions of the child called for more social cooperation and less competition in the classroom and demanded the elimination of corporal punishment and rote teaching methods. Most schools, however, embraced tradition and rejected these ideas as unsound and impractical. In contrast, schools everywhere seemed to catch the spirit of nationalism and patriotism sweeping over the nation in the 1890s. The nation's flag increasingly appeared atop school houses, and an early version of the pledge of allegiance became a common opening school exercise.

In the South, public school expansion after the Civil War progressed slowly. Despite some initial success at building racially integrated schools in such places as New Orleans in the early 1870s, schools throughout the South became formally segregated, reflecting a policy of racial apartheid enshrined in 1896 by the U.S. Supreme Court in *Plessy v. Ferguson*. Northern schools were also frequently racially segregated, sometimes by conscious intent, sometimes by custom; below the Mason-Dixon Line, separation was complete and legally mandated. Under this Jim Crow system, African-American schools suffered the most, and the South overall remained economically backward compared to the more urban, industrial North. In 1900, the much poorer South had twice as many children to educate as the North. Having a dual system of public education, one for whites and one for blacks, spread scarce resources even thinner.

In all regions, the twentieth century witnessed the continual expansion of the power and authority of public schools in the lives of children and adolescents. New ideas about childhood—that the young should be sheltered from the workplace; that compulsory school laws should be extended and strengthened; that the schools should offer a more diverse curriculum; and that the schools should provide more social services and welfare—also gained support. High schools, which for many decades had served relatively few adolescents, expanded dramatically and by the middle of the century had become mass institutions. In the second half of the twentieth century, schools became even more intensively linked with the job market and took on greater credentialing roles. Similarly, for different reasons, federal interest in the schools, which had historically been low, intensified in the liberal 1960s and even in the more conservative decades that followed. On the eve of the twenty-first century, few citizens downplayed the importance of a quality education for everyone, even if the rhetoric outpaced the reality and precise definitions of such an education remained unclear and contested.

School attendance in the elementary and grammar level grades became increasingly universal in the early decades of the twentieth century. The assimilation of immigrants had long been a goal of the public schools, and this only accelerated with the massive foreign migrations from central and southern Europe between the 1890s and World War I, which swelled enrollments in many parts of the urban and industrial North. In addition, a range of reformers during this period pressed for an expanded social role for the schools, including the addition of broadened social welfare services. Responsibilities traditionally regarded as the purview of the home, charitable institutions, or the workplace were increasingly assumed by the school. Locally funded school lunches, especially for the poor, were common in many cities decades before passage of the National School Lunch Act after World War II. In many cities, schools built playgrounds, gyms, and even swimming pools, as physical education grew in importance. Medical and dental inspection of children became common. The three Rs and academic subjects remained central to most schools, but the social functions of public education continued to expand by World War I. With the intense consolidation of rural schools into larger units over the course of the century, reforms that began in the cities increasingly became commonplace in most school systems.

In elementary schools, new forms of classroom organization, such as ability grouping, first found in urban graded classrooms in the early 1900s, forever changed the experience of going to school. Scientific testing, reflecting the larger fascination with scientific management in the business world, produced an array of "objective" measures to determine the academic potential and achievement of every child. Newly developed intelligence tests became popular and were used in concert with achievement test scores and teachers' reports on children's reading ability. This helped in assigning children to a particular ability group. In some schools, teachers separated pupils within classrooms into slow, average, and accelerated reading groups; in others, pupils were placed in separate classes with academically similar children. Critics then and later warned that the use of scientific, "objective" measures discriminated against poor, immigrant, and minority children. Testing also promoted the expansion of special classes for "exceptional" children, later known as SPECIAL EDUCATION classes (whose enrollments in a diversity of programs would begin to skyrocket by the 1970s and 1980s).

Elementary and especially grammar and high school enrollments in the early 1900s were given a boost with the arrival of millions of adult immigrants, who displaced older children and especially adolescents from the work force. Technological innovations—the use of the pneumatic tube in department stores and office buildings, growing reliance upon the telephone, changes in the sale and distribution of newspapers—also displaced youthful workers such as messenger boys and the newsboys on the street corner. Adolescents were especially affected by these economic changes and by competition from adult laborers. As a result, high school enrollment grew dramatically in the northern states in the early decades of the twentieth century, followed by equally impressive growth in the Jim Crow South. Nationally, about half of all adolescents attended high school by 1930, leading to remarkable changes in the nature, purposes, and character of the institution.

The High School as a Mass Institution

By the 1920s and 1930s, as the high school became a less socially and academically selective institution, it increasingly became part of mass public education. Historically, elementary and secondary schools were fairly distinct institutions, poorly articulated with each other. Most children before the 1920s had never attended high school, but it was now a more common experience, whose social functions, like that of the lower grades, changed dramatically. As the GREAT DEPRESSION further eliminated many job opportunities for TEENAGERS (the term itself was coined in the early 1940s), the high school became a more custodial institution, one that tried to meet a rising demand to educate everyone. By the 1950s, expectations rose even higher, as more Americans increasingly thought that everyone, perhaps, should graduate.

In response to a larger and more diverse student population, the curriculum of the typical high school correspondingly became more diversified. Unlike their European counterparts, who differentiated pupils at an earlier age for separate academic or vocational secondary schools, American policymakers favored the comprehensive high school. Increasingly common by World War I, the comprehensive high school had separate curriculum tracks, or streams, under the same roof. This was seen as democratic in the sense that pupils attended the same school, even though they were enrolled in different programs, presumably to match their academic achievement and potential (as determined by previous grades, IQ test scores, etc.) and likely destination in life. Academic subjects were directed more toward the high-achieving students, especially those aspiring to college, whose enrollments were growing and would dramatically expand in the 1960s. The high school had always been academically oriented, but the academic curriculum increasingly became synonymous with college preparation. Vocational courses of study, which disproportionately served the lower classes, were typically less prestigious and academically weaker, but they contained a breadth of offerings. These included commercial subjects (such as typing or shorthand) and home economics for girls, and classes such as carpentry, leather craft, and automobile repair for boys. The college and non-college bound alike thus found a niche in the comprehensive high school.

The expanding array of courses, programs, and pupils in the high school blurred its academic mission, which was further clouded by a dramatic rise in nonacademic activities, collectively known as the extracurriculum. Just as the diversified curriculum presumably addressed the varying intellectual needs and potential of youth, so too did the appearance of an increased number of social activities that promised to appeal to the now less-than-selective student body. Competitive SPORTS, for example, became enormously popular. By the 1920s, complaints about the excesses of high school BASKETBALL in Utah and Indiana and football in Texas were already heard in the national press. School-based student clubs proliferated, from academic specialties like the French club or honor society, to the radio club, ukelele club, Future Teachers of America, and Future Farmers of America. Still other pupils worked on the school newspaper or yearbook staff or served in STUDENT GOVERNMENT. After studying community life in Muncie, Indiana, in the 1920s, sociologists Robert and Helen Lynd concluded that the local high school was a "social cosmos" unto itself. It was no longer simply an academic institution, but a social world whose parameters seemed to know no bounds. This troubled some taxpayers and parents, and complaints about the subdued attention to academics echo to this day.

In a nation as diverse as America, high schools, like elementary schools and JUNIOR HIGH SCHOOLS below them, remained very diverse, even though they were all shaped by the same general trends. In some major cities in the North, specialized high schools focused on the sciences or the arts, and they remained academically elite, with admission guarded by competitive admission exams. The American high school was a study in diversity. High schools within the same town or city could differ enormously, reflecting the makeup of particular neighborhoods or which children were assigned to particular institutions. Some high schools were a cross-section of their communities, while others overrepresented particular ethnic, racial, or social classes. In many small towns, high schools became an important way for people to identify with their community. Some citizens cared more about athletic success than academic programs; others counted the ever-expanding number of high school graduates as a sign of progress, while naysayers assumed that the academic quality of the high school had been unduly sacrificed along the way. Although adults frequently argued among themselves about whether academics counted for much in high school, alumni by the 1940s and 1950s probably remembered, for good or ill, its social side—dances, friendships, peer cultures, and athletic events—more than what they learned in algebra or shop.

Reform and the Role of the Schools

Traditional teaching methods were occasionally altered in some schools in the first half of the twentieth century, adding to the diversity of classroom experiences. A variety of Progressive educators called for a more experimental approach to teaching and learning, usually involving a more active role for the child in an assault on teacher- and subject-centered classrooms. Such ideas found expression more in the lower than the higher grades. This was accomplished through more group work on school projects, learning by doing, field trips, or other innovative approaches. Some of these ideas bore fruit, but mostly in affluent suburbs such as Winnetka, Illinois, in the 1930s; even there, however, flexibility did not come at the expense of mastering the basics. For most children in most elementary schools, the traditional emphasis on academic subjects, especially on reading and math in the early grades, remained common, and textbooks and their new allies, workbooks, were ubiquitous. Progressive educators despaired over the traditional ways of the high schools, where subject matter and teacher authority had long reigned supreme, and critics discovered that even shop teachers lectured or read to pupils out of textbooks. The curricula of high schools had undergone important changes with the rise of vocationalism, but teachers often ignored pleas for a more student-centered pedagogy.

In the second half of the twentieth century, about 90 percent of all children and teenagers were enrolled in the public schools. The exodus of teenagers from the workplace during the Depression was somewhat reversed with the rise of the service and fast food industry, but after-school jobs did not diminish the centrality of the public high school in the lives of most young people. As high school attendance increased, it provided a basis for the booming expansion of college enrollments of the 1960s, fueling fears from some parents and citizens that the schools were not academic enough. The launching of Sputnik by the Soviet Union in 1957 had convinced many citizens that the Soviets had superior schools; America's schools, they said, should raise standards and return to the basics in the interests of national defense. But the 1960s also inherited a quite different legacy from the Eisen-

hower era: the prospect of racial integration and the schools. In a landmark 1954 decision, BROWN V. BOARD OF EDUCATION, the U.S. Supreme Court unanimously ruled segregated schools to be unconstitutional, leading to rancorous debates that again focused attention on the place of schools in the lives of children and adolescents; these debates live with us still.

Thanks to the rise of the civil rights movement and the Great Society reforms of President Lyndon Baines Johnson in the 1960s, the importance of public schools in American society remained evident, as liberal activists attempted to make them part of a wider campaign for social justice. Federal monies poured into elementary schools to try to improve the academic success of underprivileged children, and numerous programs at the high school level reached for the same lofty goal. HEAD START grew out of this liberal moment but over time gained bipartisan support. Bicultural and BILINGUAL EDUCATION programs, less popular with conservatives, gained more ground and federal support. After the 1960s, as liberalism faded and conservative views gained popularity, the role of public schools in American culture would be the subject of heated public debates, but these schools continue to serve the vast majority of children and adolescents and continue to play an important role in their socialization and education.

In the 1960s, liberal policy makers emphasized the importance of federal programs to promote greater equality, opportunity, and racial and economic justice in the schools. Since the 1980s, more conservative policy makers in Washington, as well as many on the state and local levels, have emphasized the importance of setting high academic standards for the nation's schools. They have also reemphasized the traditional notion of civic education, character education, and the importance of training the young to become productive workers. The standards movement reflected revived support for free market, competitive values, the reorientation of the economy away from heavy industry and toward the service industry and technology, and the spread of an economically integrated global economy. Since the Reagan years, presidents and governors of both major parties have regularly endorsed proposals to strengthen the academic character of the public schools, with mixed results. At the same time, the experience of attending school continues to reflect their many and varied social purposes.

In many communities, despite various movements for reform, the local public school often continues to have a blurred academic purpose. Special education programs, with a diverse student population, have proliferated, making universal academic standards difficult to set or at least impossible for every child to meet. And the great diversity of schools—in inner city northern ghettos, southwestern barrios, rich suburbs, small towns, and everything in between—ensures that having common intellectual outcomes in such wildly different environments remains a utopian goal. Some schools continue to enroll many poor and minority pupils, many from families where English is a second language, and many who qualify for a free school meal. For very poor children, a free breakfast and lunch or a safe haven from violent streets may be as important as high standardized test scores are for upper-class parents living in gated suburbs.

The drive for more testing in academic subjects became irresistible in the early years of the twenty-first century, as exemplified by the requirements in President George W. Bush's No Child Left Behind legislation. After some success at building more racially integrated schools in the 1970s, a trend toward resegregation has become apparent. How schools are to construct a more uniform curriculum in a multicultural world, where assimilation is not unquestionably accepted, also remains a heated issue. The fairness of common, even high-stakes, tests for everyone when disparities in school funding from district to district remain so wide similarly leads many to wonder whether testing will have much impact on school improvement. And finally, despite all the joys and importance of learning academic subjects, for many children the schools still remain to an important degree part of a social experience. In addition to their intellectual functions, schools have evolved as key social institutions, a place where friendships are made and broken, where social skills are taught if not always learned, and where learning about academic subjects competes with other human needs. The intellectual aims and social purposes of schools will remain in tension in the lives of children and adults into the foreseeable future.

See also: **Coeducation and Same-Sex Schooling; Compulsory School Attendance; Education, Europe; Progressive Education; Urban School Systems, The Rise of; Vocational Education, Industrial Education, and Trade Schools.**

BIBLIOGRAPHY

Greven, Philip. 1977. *The Protestant Temperament: Patterns of Child-Rearing, Religious Experience, and the Self in Early America.* Chicago: University of Chicago Press.

Kaestle, Carl F. 1983. *Pillars of the Republic: Common Schools and American Society, 1780–1860.* New York: Hill and Wang.

Kliebard, Herbert M. 1986. *The Struggle for the American Curriculum 1893–1958.* Boston: Routledge and Kegan Paul.

Ravitch, Diane. 1983. *The Troubled Crusade: American Education, 1945–1980.* New York: Basic Books.

Ravitch, Diane, and Maris Vinovskis, eds. 1995. *Learning from the Past: What History Teaches Us about School Reform.* Baltimore, MD: Johns Hopkins University Press.

Reese, William J. 1986. *Power and the Promise of School Reform: Grassroots Movements during the Progressive Era.* Boston: Routledge and Kegan Paul.

Reese, William J. 1995. *The Origins of the American High School.* New Haven, CT: Yale University Press.

Rorabaugh, W. J. 1986. *The Craft Apprentice: From Franklin to the Machine Age.* New York: Oxford University Press.

Smith, Wilson, ed. 1973. *Theories of Education in Early America 1655–1819.* Indianapolis, IN: Bobbs-Merrill.

Tyack, David B. 1974. *The One Best System: A History of American Urban Education.* Cambridge, MA: Harvard University Press.

Tyack, David, and Larry Cuban. 1995. *Tinkering toward Utopia: A Century of Public School Reform.* Cambridge, MA: Harvard University Press.

Wishy, Bernard. 1968. *The Child and the Republic: The Dawn of Modern American Child Culture.* Philadelphia: University of Pennsylvania Press.

Zelizer, Viviana A. 1985. *Pricing the Priceless Child: The Changing Social Value of Children.* New York: Basic Books.

WILLIAM J. REESE

Egg Donation

Egg donation involves, first, the synchronizing of the egg donor and egg recipient's menstrual cycles, the stimulation of multiple egg production in the donor, and the stimulation of endometrial lining development in the recipient through hormone injections. Then, the donor's eggs are removed with a small needle, fertilized in vitro, and several days later successfully fertilized eggs are transferred to the recipient's uterus. A successful birth from a donated egg was first reported in Australia in 1984. By 1994, it was estimated that there had been at least 750 births from donated eggs in the United States. Egg donation has generally been used in cases in which the recipient is infertile but wants to experience pregnancy and give birth to a child who is genetically related to the recipient's (male) partner, or in cases in which the recipient is a surrogate, carrying the fetus of a donor who has fertile eggs but who cannot sustain a pregnancy.

Despite there being many fewer births from donated eggs than from donated sperm, egg donation has attracted more criticism and regulation in Europe and the United States than has sperm donation. While sperm donors are generally paid for their donations, in Great Britain, payment for egg donors beyond compensation for time and expense has been banned out of fear that women's reproductive capacities will be exploited, either by themselves or by others. In contrast, in some poorer countries, such as Brazil, women can receive access to reproductive technologies in return for egg donation. While it is not clear that refusing women compensation for their donated eggs constitutes a nonexploitative policy, it is true that health risks and discomfort are much greater for egg donors than for sperm donors. Complications from the procedure can cause infection and possible infertility, and hormone injections put women at greater risk for various cancers. Donors are also asked to undergo a battery of tests before donating, and the hormone injections and surgery can have extremely uncomfortable side effects.

Egg donation has also attracted particularly widespread controversy in cases where nonwhite recipients have chosen to receive eggs from white donors. While many are uncritical of the eugenic implications of white recipients examining elaborate donor dossiers and paying tens of thousands of dollars in order to choose the eggs of white, blond, blue-eyed, athletic donors with graduate degrees, the apparently eugenic choice by a nonwhite woman of a white donor raises popular ire to a much greater degree. Controversy has also erupted around the donation of eggs to postmenopausal women, and it has been made illegal in some countries. For example, in 2000, the donation of eggs to postmenopausal women was banned in Italy by the self-regulatory body of the medical profession, and in the Netherlands eggs could be donated only to women up to age 44, which is well under the average age of menopause. While egg donation provides opportunities to challenge some norms of motherhood and kinship, legal and popular censure often stem those opportunities, and the norm of women as mothers is inevitably promoted.

Typically, egg donors, unlike sperm donors, have not remained anonymous, and have often been recruited by egg recipients and their partners through personal connections with family and friends, as well as less personal methods such as newspaper ads and e-mails. Anthropologist Gay Becker points out the extensive work recipients and their partners do to define egg donors' relationships to, and within, the family, trying to include donors in some way as family members while refusing them any status as "mothers." Becker also describes recipients' efforts to "naturalize" egg donation, claiming kinship to their children though the biological link of pregnancy and birth rather than that of genetics. Like other new reproductive technologies, egg donation highlights, sometimes challenges, and in some ways reinforces cultural ideas about kinship, motherhood, and gender.

See also: **Adoption; Artificial Insemination; Conception and Birth; Fertility Drugs; Obstetrics and Midwifery; Surrogacy.**

BIBLIOGRAPHY

Becker, Gaylene. 2000. *The Elusive Embryo: How Women and Men Approach New Reproductive Technologies.* Berkeley: University of California Press.

Meyer, Cheryl L. 1997. *The Wandering Uterus: Politics and the Reproductive Rights of Women.* New York: New York University Press.

LARA FREIDENFELDS

Emotional Life

Scholars debate how much children's actual emotions have changed in the last five hundred years of Western history, yet all agree that the nature and extent of cultural interest in the emotional lives of children has shifted dramatically. From the sixteenth century to the twenty-first, from theologians to moralists, to novelists, to psychologists, to sociologists and anthropologists, adults interested in defining and regulating emotion have often trained their eyes and ears on the lips and tongues of children. Whether children's souls were viewed as stained with sinful passions waiting to be cleansed, their hearts regarded as empty vessels ready to be filled with finer feelings, or their psyches seen as the seat of complex emotions ripe for discovery and discussion, over time the emotional life of children has been the focus of ever-increasing levels of adult attention. Historians charting such changes have been able to make few authoritative pronouncements about the lived inner experiences of children's emotions for most of this period. There simply are no records to consult that can reliably reveal the subjective texture of children's emotional lives in past times. On the other hand, historians have employed an incredibly creative array of methods and sources to try to make sense of the outward tracks and traces of children's emotion that have been left behind.

Emotional History in Context: Scholarly Debates about Historical Change

The first contemporary historians of emotions found fewer differences between the emotional lives of early modern adults and their children than between early modern and modern adult emotional attitudes. In the mid-twentieth century, many historians of early modern Europe argued that, regardless of age, the people of past times were universally childlike in their emotions, at least compared to contemporary standards. They cast early modern people as given to frequent, unpredictable, and extravagant outbursts of emotion, especially of rage, grief, jealousy, lust, and avarice. In this model, LOVE was portrayed as a rare feeling which, when it existed at all, passed mutely between male fellows, or flamed briefly in romantic entanglements outside the realm of marriage.

There was, according to this argument, little love within the family, either between husbands and wives or between parents and children. The family was simply a cooperative economic unit in which children were regarded as little adults in training, to be set loose in the world the moment they were able to earn their livelihood. This situation supposedly held until the rise of the modern era, an era begun by Protestant reforms, shaped by the rise of market capitalism, and marked by the growth of individualism. Released from its earlier economic frame, the family was free to develop more elaborate moral and affective functions. The emergence of what some scholars have called "affective individualism" led to an increasing emphasis on loving relations within the family. In the early 1970s, many historians of colonial America applied this paradigm to their subjects and argued that, as late as the seventeenth century, emotional ties were at most a limited feature of family life.

Subsequent work has tempered these extreme views, however; many historians have since unearthed evidence of the importance of emotional bonds within early modern families, especially between parents and children. Most historians now reject extremist characterizations of early mod-

Child Bitten by a Crayfish (c. 1558), Sofonisba Anguissola. This sixteenth-century drawing is a tender image of an upsetting event in a young boy's life. © Pedicini Napoli, Archivio dell'Arte, Galleria Nazionale de Capodimonte.

ern people as childlike in their rages and stunted in their love. Considerable evidence, from religious writings to court cases, indicates that early modern people were extremely troubled by the dangers they perceived to be inherent in violent emotion; moreover, poetry, letters, and diaries from this period contain ample evidence of strong family feelings.

Yet, even as recent historians have largely come to agree that loving relations between parents and children were likely quite prevalent throughout the early modern period, they have also come to a renewed appreciation of the fact that—whatever the continuities of the currents of subjective emotional experience—there have been marked changes in the kinds of ideals espoused and the extent of emotions expressed by and about children in past times. In fact, current

scholarship recognizes that while historians in the mid-twentieth century may have overstated claims that early modern emotion was fundamentally and experientially different from modern emotion, they were quite right to remark that attitudes and ideas about children and the ideal role of emotion in family life have undergone significant changes from the early modern to the modern period.

Just as claims of radical disjuncture in the emotional lives of early modern and modern children now seem unlikely and exaggerated, models of undifferentiated continuity appear overly simplistic, not to mention ahistorical. Postmodern critical perspectives have brought home an awareness that experience itself is shaped at least in part by cultural ideas. The range of emotions identified and expressed by children inevitably would have been molded to a great extent by the prevailing culture's understanding of emotion. Thus, historians have recently become aware of the importance of making cross-cultural as well as chronological comparisons. Attention to the changing cast of observers who took upon themselves the responsibility of cataloging and critiquing children's emotions is an important starting point for sorting out the changing nature of interest in children's emotional life.

Children's Emotions in Early Modern Europe and Seventeenth-Century British America

In sixteenth- and seventeenth-century Europe, during the years following the Protestant Reformation, theologians and litigants left the most extensive records concerning attitudes towards children's emotions. In much of northern Europe (especially in England and Germany where a good deal of research has been focused) as well as in colonial English America, Calvinistic attitudes towards sin and salvation dominated concerns about children's emotions. Emotions in this period were most often referred to as passions, and they were regarded with suspicion as a primary manifestation of the sinful and selfish will.

A central belief of Calvinist Christianity was that each believer should submit his or her will to God's will, in order to experience his saving grace. Therefore, ministers preached that passions ought to be eliminated as much as possible, with every effort made to discipline the will. For parents and children, this meant that one of the primary obligations of family life was to teach children to conquer their passions. From infancy, parents began to discipline their children's emotions, meeting cries and tears with the switch and schooling their children to contain their emotions at all costs.

Some parents may have relished their religious duty to break their children's wills; others, however, may have found this process painful to inflict. Scholars have speculated that the common process of "putting children out," that is, sending them to live and work as servants or apprentices in the homes of neighboring families, resulted from parents' concerns that their natural affection for their own offspring would inhibit their ability to impose proper emotional discipline. In this view, excessive parental love could potentially imperil children's immortal souls.

One unintended consequence of this extreme cultural emphasis on the importance of emotional containment was that rebellious outbursts of emotion were extremely common. Early modern court records are rife not only with instances where anger overflowed into violence, but also with examples of cases where verbal violence alone was enough to send people to seek public redress against anger. Most plaintiffs in court cases were adult men suing for compensation on behalf of themselves or their female dependents. Occasionally, however, some fathers brought suit against their children for angry and disrespectful behavior. On the one hand, the prevalence of court cases involving outbursts of anger supports the notion that early modern people, parents and children alike, were, by modern standards, especially passionate. On the other hand, the fact that these emotional outbursts were litigated in a court of law, rather than simply negotiated as a private matter, indicates how seriously early modern Europeans and European Americans took religious injunctions against the passions.

Immoderate emotions were not only an instrument of spiritual sin, they also could cause physical sickness. In this period, the germ theory of disease was as yet undeveloped. Instead, early modern medical theory posited that bodily health depended on the proper balance of the four humors, or bodily fluids, including blood, phlegm, black bile, and yellow bile. If any of the four humors accumulated to excess, the body would become too hot, too cold, too dry, or too moist, and thus subject to disease. To be "out of humor" was not simply to be in a bad mood, but actually to be in bad health. When parents urged their children to master their wills and subject their passions, they did so out of fear for both their spiritual and physical well-being.

Indeed, death and disease were ever-present in the early modern world. At a time when many children would not live to see adulthood, and when those that did might well lose a parent along the way, it is possible that family affection had less room to flower than it would have in later periods. This fact has led some scholars to argue against the development of a great degree of familial love between early modern parents and children. Scholars favoring this view have noted the common practice of reusing the name of a deceased child at the births of subsequent children and have argued that this implied a lack of strong feeling for the lost child. Other scholars have viewed the same evidence from the opposite angle and made the point that a desire to preserve and pass on traditional family names, even in the face of grave loss, actually indicates the great importance of familial bonds.

Another important piece of indirect evidence indicates that, for all of Calvinism's emphasis on the discipline of the will, loving relations were still the family ideal. Ministers frequently described themselves in their sermons as nursing fathers and mothers, and a common metaphor for conversion (for men and women alike) was to take Christ as one's bridegroom. The church's reliance on loving and nurturing family metaphors to describe emotional connections between God and his believers or between preachers and their flocks indicates that early modern children probably did experience important degrees of familial love. That said, the emotional discipline and material challenges such children would have been subjected to daily, accompanied by frequent family separations due to death or servitude, would have made the cultural influences on their emotional lives distinct from those of later periods.

A final point remains to be made regarding the use of familial metaphors in this period. Church authorities and government officials across Europe drew on comparisons of parents (most often fathers) and children to describe relations of power and authority between rulers and their subjects. While noting the use of familial metaphors by ministers highlights the importance of familial love as a cultural ideal, it also reinforces the point that love and authority were explicitly intertwined in the lives of early modern children in ways which would be unfamiliar today.

Children's Emotions during the Enlightenment Era

In the eighteenth century, the number and variety of commentators interested in assessing and advising on emotion increased exponentially. From political theorists to moral philosophers, from theologians to novelists, writers and thinkers of the ENLIGHTENMENT became newly intent on explicating the importance of emotions. Where early modern writers had linked passions to sin and humors to bodily sickness, Enlightenment writers began to focus on feelings as a key to salvation and on sentiments as a source of social virtue. Unregulated by reason, passions could still be dangerous and undesirable. In such cases, physicians now believed they could be a potent source of debilitating nervous disorders. But, properly governed, emotion came to be viewed as a source of good. Children had to be taught a new, more balanced approach to emotions which continued to emphasize self-control and domination of the will, but which now also included a positive role for some kinds of feeling.

Historians who have focused their attention on religious writings have provided the most evidence of emotion's increasingly positive cultural valence. The 1700s saw the rise of pietistic religions in Germany, the growth of Methodism in England, and the emergence of evangelical awakenings in British America, all of which placed a new emphasis on the importance of emotion in the process of religious conversion. The path to salvation lay in the emotional conviction of sin, followed by the experience of the saving grace of God's love. Unlike biblically based Calvinism, which had stressed the need to be literate to know God's Word, these new religions placed feelings at the center of faith. The result was that even unlettered children could choose to give themselves to God. In fact, many contemporary depictions of religious revivals, including the widely read work of the colonial Massachusetts minister Jonathan Edwards, described the pious emotions of child converts in considerable detail. Children had once been taught that their own passions were the source of sin; now they were learning a new lesson—that the cultivation of religious affections could bring them closer to God.

Another important line of scholarly inquiry into the improving cultural status of emotion comes from research in intellectual history. One important philosophical strain of the Enlightenment, Scottish moral philosophy, developed around the idea that emotions were the seat of social virtue. The capacity to imaginatively identify with the emotions of others provided the inner guide that made possible moral human actions. Neither theologians nor philosophers recommended emotion as a means to self-knowledge or self-promotion. On the contrary, the ideal of submission of the self to the will of God, as well as to the greater social good, continued to be of fundamental importance. Children remained bound by requirements for emotional discipline. But the desire to eradicate the passions had begun to be replaced by a desire to channel them for virtuous ends.

Not all historians who have considered society's changing attitudes towards emotion would chart the time line in quite this way. Some have contended that the eighteenth century inaugurated a newly antagonistic attitude towards emotion. The best evidence for this stance comes from the growth of a particular kind of literary genre: the etiquette manual. Writers of advice books began to focus their observations on children more forcefully in the eighteenth century than they had previously. Where once admonitions concerning proper conduct had been directed at adults (who were expected to enforce observance of these standards by their children and other subordinates), instruction in MANNERS began to be aimed directly at children themselves. This new emphasis on self-regulation has led some historians to write as if emotion itself took on a new negative valence in this period.

The chief argument of these historians—that conduct books exhibited a new concern with providing instruction in the modulation of emotion—is key and remains valid. It is probably more accurate, however, to argue that the advice about the regulation of emotion became increasingly elaborate because emotion was now seen to have positive potential in certain controlled circumstances. In fact, of course, invariable antagonism to emotion was far easier to enforce and to understand than the more complicated position that some kinds of emotion could serve useful religious and social ends, while others remained dangerous and undesirable. Conduct books thus began to address themselves to the task of sorting out such nuances.

Another key insight from conduct literature is that changing ideas about emotional regulation led parents and their children to redefine their relationships with one another. Once parents had held primary responsibility for disciplining the unruly passions of their children; now, however, parents began to expect young people to learn to regulate themselves. This shift released parents from their punitive positions as enforcers and allowed new ideals of family affection to flourish. Research indicates that advice writers began to instruct parents to express love for their children rather than to physically correct their children's unruly displays of emotion. Under this new system, parents were expected to teach their children by example to control outbursts of undesirable emotions, such as anger. Similarly positive messages concerning emotions spilled from the pens of poets, playwrights, and novelists. The novel as a literary form was essentially invented in the eighteenth century, and its hallmark was the exploration of characters' inner emotions.

Of course, it is important to remember that evidence gleaned from prescriptive commentators—whether theologians or philosophers, writers of advice manuals or of novels—reveals ideals rather than practice. What some scholars have come to call emotionology—that is, the dominant constellation of cultural ideas about emotion—is not the same as emotion. The actual extent of loving feelings within families may not have changed markedly between 1500 and 1800; however, the importance attached to the idea of family feeling did.

As parents embraced these new ideas wholeheartedly, so did their children. By the mid-eighteenth century, many middling and elite young people began to keep commonplace books. They copied rules of conduct advice gleaned from etiquette manuals into these scrapbooks, along with various poems and literary snippets. Just as conduct literature was increasingly aimed at young people, so too were novels. Authors frequently wrote in epistolary style (a series of letters) and dealt with issues of courtship and seduction, of successful marriages and of suits gone awry. Meanwhile, ordinary eighteenth-century young people filled their own letters and diaries with a new, more emotional style of address. Many historians trace the beginnings of a distinctive youth culture to this period.

Some scholars argue that emotion began to be feminized in the late eighteenth century as well, but this is a point that has come under considerable dispute. It seems most likely that young men and women alike read and enjoyed novels, followed conduct advice, and shared concern for their souls and their societies in more or less equal measure. Indeed, as emotion became tied to civic virtue, and as the public sphere became masculinized, boys and young men maintained an especially marked interest in emotion. The one exception here probably had to do with anger, which may well have been more permissible in boys (in certain circumstances which required displays of masculine mastery), than in girls (where it continued to be regarded as necessarily sinful).

Because expressions of emotion came to be seen as desirable in certain circumstances, they gradually found their way into ideas about gentility and civility. The complex code of permissible versus reprehensible emotions was one ideally suited to the subtle signaling of social distinctions. Over the course of the eighteenth century, as people and goods circulated with increasing frequency, making social mobility possible, emotional agility emerged as an important badge of gentility, on par with dancing or other forms of polite behavior. Children and parents alike responded to these trends with a greater emphasis on emotion.

What of social and cultural diversity in eighteenth-century attitudes toward emotion? Surely not everyone espoused or experienced the version of emotion just described. Because the writing of political history usually precedes social and cultural history, and because Western European history has long predominated over that of other areas, it is clear that much remains to be discovered about the contours of the emotional lives of children outside those of the white elite. Still, certain arguments have emerged.

Some evidence exists to suggest that members of the lower orders (soon to become recognized as a distinct economic class) did not embrace the new ethos of emotional cultivation and control, but rather followed their own less-constrained inclinations. This appears particularly likely to have been the case with men and boys, who gave rein to everyday anger and participated in boisterous recreational fighting, such as wrestling. In any case, the same debates about gentility, assimilation, and imitation that accompany all studies of eighteenth-century manners and culture also apply to questions about class differences in the emotional lives of European and European-American children.

By contrast, the emotional lives of NATIVE AMERICAN CHILDREN and of AFRICAN-AMERICAN CHILDREN, whether free or enslaved, would have been markedly different from the European patterns just described. Differences in religious beliefs and forms of political and social organization would have led these groups towards a distinct set of emotional expectations and experiences. At the same time, exigencies imposed by interactions with Europeans would have further distinguished the emotional lives of these children in crucial ways.

According to colonial observers, surviving oral accounts, and contemporary scholarship, affection far outranked discipline as a concern of Native American parents. Native American children in North America (from the Northeastern woodlands to the desert Southwest) would most likely have been raised in matrilineal households where cooperative work habits would have ensured young children great amounts of time with their mothers and female kin. Later on, boys would have received greater attention and training from fathers and uncles. While both girls and boys would have had to undergo ritual trials before becoming recognized as adults— trials that would have tested their emotional as well as physical endurance—Native American children would not have had to submit to daily parental efforts to punish their passions. Love not only flowed freely between parents and children, but also between men and women. All but the most elite marriages were by mutual consent and divorce was easy and voluntary.

Still, this openness does not mean that Native American children faced no strictures concerning emotion. On the contrary, stoicism in the face of suffering was a highly valued trait amongst Native Americans, while mourning in response to death was culturally patterned and especially important among the northeastern Iroquois nations. So great was their grief when a family member died, that in many cases mourners would attempt to replace lost family members by adopting a captive from another tribe or, following the contact period, from a European settlement. It is a testament to the relatively pleasant emotional lives of Native American children that many European-American children so adopted were reluctant to return to the homes of their birth, even when offered the opportunity. The reverse was not true, however; Native American children forced into servitude in the households of colonial Europeans usually languished there unhappily. Furthermore, the arrival of European weapons and especially of European diseases dramatically increased deaths and family disruptions in the lives of Native American children, perhaps making the experience of grief a more dominant companion than love.

African-American children would also have grown up amidst great emotional and familial challenges. In the seventeenth century, when slavery was just being established as a labor system in British America, various factors combined to limit the numbers of African-American children. Plantation owners preferred male bondservants to female, and living conditions were severe enough to ensure high rates of INFANT MORTALITY. Perhaps because of this, very little research has been done on African-American children in this era. By the eighteenth century, however, as male-female ratios became more even and basic living conditions improved somewhat, the numbers of African-American children increased. In fact, recent research indicates that in the eighteenth century as many as a third of forced African migrants enslaved in North America may have been children at the time of their departure from Africa.

Children living under slavery faced an unprecedented degree of family disruption, whether snatched from Africa or born in North America. Not only were family bonds torn asunder by death and disease, but they were also liable to be severed at the whim of slave masters who were more sensitive to their own fluctuating labor needs than to their slaves' enduring human desires for family. Still, considerable indirect evidence, such as family naming patterns and the transmission of specialized job skills from parents to children, testifies to the strong bonds of love that tied enslaved families together. Meanwhile, rich traditions of spirituality, song, and storytelling, passed down from one generation to the next, show the resilience and dignity with which children living under slavery were taught to confront daily injuries and injustice.

Like Native American children, most African-American children lived with their mothers in matrilineal family groups. Less clear is whether this arrangement was simply created at the convenience of masters, or whether it reflected African traditions and preferences. On the one hand, it appears that free black families often chose to live in nuclear, father-headed households. Some historians believe that this indicates that the mother-centered households typically found in slave quarters reflect the difficulty of sustaining family life under bondage. On the other hand, the prevailing view among historians is that matrilineality was a revered African tradition. In fact, many scholars argue that, even in free black families that appear to have followed a European model, greater equality in work roles meant that loving partnerships departed from the more authoritarian patriarchal model of European families. In either case, some of the challenges of family life under slavery would have been mitigated by the development of far-flung kin networks. Extended family and fictive kin provided parents and children alike with an important measure of emotional as well as practical support.

Children's Emotions in the Emerging United States

From the creation of the United States to the present day, Americans have placed an ever-increasing emphasis on the importance of children and their emotions. Just as emotions themselves have undergone a shift, from an exclusive association with sin to a potential alliance with salvation, so views of children have changed. Once seen as naturally depraved and in need of emotional discipline, children came to be seen as naturally innocent, innately sensitive, and in need of tender care. In the history of the United States, the turn towards a decidedly positive view of children's emotions came after the American Revolution.

The American Revolution heralded an era dominated by a republican political philosophy accompanied by a new political and cultural interest in the family. Much as the new nation stirred optimistic visions of expanding democracy and economic progress, it also provoked anxious images of moral decline and decay. One way to banish shadows and burnish republican dreams was to turn to the family as a haven from the vices of the marketplace and the dangers of political divisiveness. In such a context, the emotional sensitivity of children came to be construed as an important aspect of republican virtue, something to be nourished and encouraged by republican wives and mothers from the safety of hearth and home. Aiding and augmenting this trend among Protestants was the arrival of the Second Great Awakening in the 1830s, which once again placed a premium on the importance of emotion for salvation and which introduced a new optimism about the perfectibility of the self.

By the early nineteenth century, the cult of sensibility reached full flower. Taking off from the premise of eighteenth-century moral philosophers that emotion was the basis of virtue, citizens of the new nation sought to cultivate their capacities for finer feeling, their ability to appreciate pathos in art and literature. Initially, this emotional quality was expected of all good republicans and seems to have been more a mark of virtue than a trope of gender. As time went on, however, and economic and political developments led to a widening conceptual gap between public and private life, the home came to be regarded as the feminine sphere. With this shift came an increasing feminization of emotion. At the turn of the nineteenth century, both little boys and little girls would have aspired to emotional sensibility. But, increasingly, girls learned to cry tears, while boys were taught to pat them dry. Such was the work of boys in training to be citizens and the girls who would grow up to be their republican wives.

For the children of those excluded from both actual citizenship and symbolic roles as republicans—namely, white men who did not own property and their working wives, Native Americans, and African Americans—emotional life appeared very different. Poor white children living in rural areas may have continued to experience emotional conditions akin to those of the eighteenth century. But for the poor living in cities, among them many immigrant Catholics, the long working hours of their parents and the squalid conditions of daily existence made for a very different set of emotional experiences. Court records and popular accounts make clear that verbal and physical violence were frequent features of daily life. Courage and a ready fist in defense of honor came to be seen as signal traits of the working-class man, whether immigrant or native, as well as among upper-class Southerners. Boys schooled their own emotions according to this ideal. Girls, meanwhile, learned from their mothers' examples the importance of sympathy as an emotional tool for survival. Often, female solidarity was the only thing that produced a fresh pail of water in times of sickness, or an extra bite of bread when a husband's wages went to drink.

As propertied white men came to define themselves as citizens of the new nation, they held fast to the idea that other Americans were their dependents. The parents of African-American and Native American children were not only excluded from the formal rights of citizenship, but actually denied recognition as adult members of society. Southern slave masters likened enslaved adults to children and referred to "my family black and white." President Andrew Jackson, architect of Indian removal, referred to Native Americans as "my red children." When these white male leaders spoke of their paternal affection for their "children," the centuries-old link between family feeling and public power continued to evolve.

African-American and Native American children faced particular emotional challenges growing up in a society increasingly intolerant of family forms that deviated from the republican norm, yet hostile to any attempt by non-elites to lay claim to the possibilities of republicanism. From Cherokee children forced west on the Trail of Tears, to African-American children sold south in the service of King Cotton, many children never experienced the cozy security of the re-

publican fireside. Their feelings of loss, of grief at separation from their mother, or shame at watching their father whipped, of rage against oppression never more than partially subdued, could not be fully assuaged even by ample amounts of love and affection shared among their friends and kin.

Surveying the distinctive contours of emotional life among elite white men, as opposed to white women and people of color, some scholars have argued that only American men were encouraged to embrace the individualism that supposedly characterized the nation as a whole by the turn of the twentieth century. Emotional distinctions loomed large in the socialization of middle-class children. Boys were urged to restrain certain emotions, such as fear. Not only parents and teachers, but also boys' own play patterns, emphasized the importance of this kind of emotional control. Boys who were too emotional were regarded as sissies. For girls, control of fear was seen as largely irrelevant; shyness and timidity were the desirable feminine traits. But control over anger was urged along with a positive emphasis on the importance of loving qualities. Children's toys, including dolls for girls, encouraged the same complex, gender-specific emotional release and control.

The Emotional Lives of Children in the Twentieth and Twenty-First Centuries

This split in emotional life finally began to change over the course of the twentieth century. By then, ever-increasing racial, ethnic, and religious pluralism (the result of large-scale immigration that included, among others, Jews and other Eastern Europeans, Asians, Latinos, and members of other groups only minimally represented in the United States at the time of the Revolution) made many old strictures untenable. Schooling, commercial popular culture, and psychological advice began to affect the large variety of groups now present in the society.

In the early modern period, Europeans believed the self and its passions posed so many dangers as to require total submersion. By contrast, in mid- to late-twentieth-century America, children learned of the importance of accessing and expressing their emotions in service of self-development or what came to be called self-actualization. YOUTH CULTURE, assumed to be more spontaneous, more sincere, and more open in its approach to emotion, gained a kind of social currency unimaginable in 1600. Black power movements in the 1960s allowed African Americans of all ages to express rage at last. In the postfeminist age, many Americans still assume that women are the more emotional sex; yet they often view this discrepancy as a masculine failing rather than a feminine sin. Children and their parents are both routinely encouraged to get in touch with their feelings. Emotional well-being has come to be sought for its own sake, not in service of bodily purity or in fear of spiritual sin.

While encouraging American children to identify their emotions was the most obvious change from the nineteenth to the twentieth century, it was not the only one. Concern about exposing children to unduly intense emotions was another key development; it promoted new efforts at control despite the apparent trend toward greater openness. Spurred by psychological advice, parents were urged to become more concerned about fear and anger in children, while a campaign against sibling jealousy brought new attention to this emotion as well. Twentieth-century advice manuals encouraged children to talk about these negative emotions, but discouraged them from acting on their feelings. Other ploys, including the use of toys to distract children from feelings of envy or fear, accomplished the same objective. It was widely believed that parents had a responsibility to prevent many emotions from festering in their children in order to prepare them for successful adulthood. While gender differences persisted, commitment to radically different patterns of emotional socialization for boys and girls declined; instead, all children were taught to moderate their emotional intensity. Keeping children away from experiences of deep grief was another aspect of this new approach. Finally, awareness of children's emotional vulnerability focused attention on other issues such as promoting self-esteem.

Furthermore, the emotional lives of children continue to change, as do attitudes towards children and emotion itself. For example, scientists have recently begun rediscovering the "mind-body" connection, that is, the links between emotional and physical health. Ironically, the freer and more developed the self has become, the more that emotional self-control has come to be valued. Where parents once monitored and corrected the passions of their children, and courts controlled the unruly emotions of adults as needed, modern Americans expect emotional control to be a wholly individual matter. Meanwhile, many postmodern theorists have begun to argue that the very idea of an autonomous self is itself a Western illusion, a relic of the Enlightenment, and by no means the only, or even the best, way of considering emotions, identity, and social relations. In short, the history of children's emotional lives is still being written and still being lived.

See also: **Anger and Aggression; Child Psychology; Child-Rearing Advice Literature; Fear; Friendship; Gendering; Guilt and Shame; Grief, Death, Funerals; Jealousy and Envy; Shyness.**

BIBLIOGRAPHY

Ariès, Philippe. 1962. *Centuries of Childhood: A Social History of Family Life.* Trans. Robert Baldick. New York: Vintage Books.

Barker-Benfield, G. J. 1992. *The Culture of Sensibility: Sex and Society in Eighteenth-Century Britain.* Chicago: University of Chicago Press.

Bloch, Ruth H. 1987. "The Gendered Meanings of Virtue in Early America." *Signs* 13: 37–58.

Bumstead, J. M. 1976. "Emotion in Colonial America: Some Relations of Conversion Experience in Freetown, Massachusetts, 1749–1770." *New England Quarterly* 49: 97–107.

Burke, Peter and Roy Porter, eds. 1991. *Language, Self and Society: The Social History of Language.* Cambridge, UK: Polity Press.

Bushman, Richard L. 1992. *The Refinement of America: Persons, Houses, Cities.* New York: Knopf.

Corrigan, John, Eric Crump, and John Kloos, eds. 2000. *Emotion and Religion: A Critical Assessment and Annotated Bibliography.* Westport, CT: Greenwood Press.

Cushman, Philip. 1995. *Constructing the Self, Constructing America: A Cultural History of Psychotherapy.* Boston: Addison-Wesley.

Demos, John. 1994. *The Unredeemed Captive: A Family Story from Early America.* New York: Knopf.

Ekman, Paul and Richard J. Davidson, eds. 1994. *The Nature of Emotion: Fundamental Questions.* New York: Oxford University Press.

Fiering, Norman S. 1976. "Irresistible Compassion: An Aspect of Eighteenth-Century Sympathy and Humanitarianism." *Journal of the History of Ideas* 37 (April): 195–218.

Frost, J. William. 1973. *The Quaker Family in Colonial America: A Portrait of the Society of Friends.* New York: St. Martin's Press.

Hemphill, Christine Dallett. 1999. *Bowing to Necessities: A History of Manners in America, 1620–1860.* New York: Oxford University Press.

Hendrix, Scott. 1995. "Masculinity and Patriarchy in Reformation Germany." *Journal of the History of Ideas* 56 (April): 177–193.

Hirschman, Albert O. 1982. *The Passions and the Interests: Political Arguments for Capitalism before its Triumph.* Princeton, NJ: Princeton University Press.

Howe, Daniel. 1997. *Making the American Self, Jonathan Edwards to Abraham Lincoln.* Cambridge, MA: Harvard University Press.

Huizinga, Johan 1996. *The Autumn of the Middle Ages.* Trans. Rodney J. Payton and Ulrich Mammizsch. Chicago: University of Chicago Press.

Kamensky, Jane. 1997. *Governing the Tongue: The Politics of Speech in Early New England.* New York: Oxford University Press.

Kasson, John F. 1990. *Rudeness and Civility: Manners in Nineteenth-Century Urban America.* New York: Hill and Wang.

Kerber, Linda. 1976. "The Republican Mother: Women and the Enlightenment—An American Perspective." *American Quarterly* 28: 187–205.

Levy, Barry. 1988. *Quakers and the American Family.* New York: Oxford University Press.

Lewis, Jan. 1983. *The Pursuit of Happiness: Family and Values in Jefferson's Virginia.* New York: Cambridge University Press.

Lockridge, Kenneth. 1992. *On the Sources of Patriarchal Rage: The Commonplacebooks of William Byrd and Thomas Jefferson and the Gendering of Power in the Eighteenth Century.* New York: New York University Press.

Lutz, Catherine A., and Lila Abu-Lughod, eds. 1990. *Language and the Politics of Emotion.* New York: Cambridge University Press.

MacFarlane, Alan. 1986. *Marriage and Love in England: Modes of Reproduction, 1300–1840.* New York: B. Blackwell.

Miller, Jacquelyn C. 1996. "An 'Uncommon Tranquility of Mind': Emotional Self-Control and the Construction of a Middle-Class Identity in Eighteenth-Century Philadelphia." *Journal of Social History* 30: 129–148.

Morgan, Edmund S. 1966. *The Puritan Family: Religion and Domestic Relations in Seventeenth-Century New England.* New York: Harper and Row.

Radcliff, Evan. 1993. "Revolutionary Writing, Moral Philosophy, and Universal Benevolence in the Eighteenth Century." *Journal of the History of Ideas* 54: 221–240.

Reddy, William. 1997. "Against Constructionism: The Historical Ethnography of Emotions." *Current Anthropology* 38: 327–352.

Rotundo, Anthony. 1993. *American Manhood: Transformations in Masculinity from the Revolution to the Modern Era.* New York: Basic Books.

Scott, James C. 1990. *Domination and the Arts of Resistance: Hidden Transcripts.* New Haven: Yale University Press.

Smith, Daniel Blake. 1980. *Inside the Great House: Planter Family Life in Eighteenth-Century Chesapeake Society.* Ithaca, NY: Cornell University Press.

Sobel, Mechal. 2000. *Teach Me Dreams: The Search for Self in the Revolutionary Era.* Princeton, NJ: Princeton University Press.

St. George, Robert. 1984. "'Heated' Speech and Literacy in Seventeenth-Century New England." In *Seventeenth Century New England,* ed. David D. Hall and David G. Allen. Boston: The Colonial Society of Massachusetts.

Stansell, Christine. 1986. *City of Women: Sex and Class in New York, 1789–1860.* Urbana: University of Illinois Press.

Stearns, Carol Z., and Peter N. Stearns. 1986. *Anger: The Struggle for Emotional Control in America's History.* Chicago: The University of Chicago Press.

Stearns, Peter N., and Jan Lewis, eds. 1998. *An Emotional History of the United States.* New York: New York University Press.

Stone, Lawrence. 1977. *The Family, Sex, and Marriage in England, 1500-1800.* New York: Harper and Row.

Wallace, Anthony F.C. 1972. *The Death and Rebirth of the Seneca.* New York: Vintage Books.

White, Deborah Gray. 1985. *Ar'n't I a Woman?: Female Slaves in the Plantation South.* New York: Norton.

Zagarri, Rosemarie. 1992. "Morals, Manners, and the Republican Mother." *American Quarterly* 44: 192–215.

NICOLE EUSTACE

Enlightenment, The

In 1784 the German philosopher Immanuel Kant gave a simple answer to the difficult question "What is enlightenment?" He defined this intellectual movement as man's emergence from his self-imposed tutelage. This emancipatory view of the Enlightenment was widely shared, as was his interest in education as shown in his lectures on the subject, *Ueber Paedagogik* (Lectures on pedagogy). Writers as divergent as JOHN LOCKE, Montesquieu, Voltaire, JEAN-JACQUES ROUSSEAU, David Hume, Denis Diderot, and Benjamin Franklin all saw themselves as educators of mankind. Their common goal was greater freedom: freedom from arbitrary power, freedom of speech, freedom of trade, and freedom to realize one's talents. However, enlightenment also had a different meaning to every author. The Enlightenment was more a loosely organized family of progressive thinkers than a phalanx of modernity. Recent studies have shown that each country had its own variety of Enlightenment, and that Christian forms of Enlightenment were much more widespread and influential than the better known deist and the even more exceptional atheist variants. Another new insight is that the Enlightenment focused not only on rationality, but also on emotionality. Many writers stressed the importance of passions and sentiments and were convinced of the necessity of studying them.

Enlightenment Pedagogy

To a large extent, the Enlightenment and pedagogy were synonymous. In his introduction to the *Encyclopédie ou dictionnaire raisonné, des sciences et des métiers,* a cornerstone of the movement, published between 1751 and 1772, Diderot wrote that the project was undertaken to make future generations more enlightened, more virtuous, and happier. Diderot and his colleagues saw themselves as pedagogues, and their task was the emancipation of mankind. To educate the people, they believed, one had to start by educating its youth. Beginning with Erasmus, scholars and theologians had published advice books for parents and teachers, but in the eighteenth century pedagogy developed as a science in its own right. Modern pedagogy was an invention of the Enlightenment; as an anonymous author wrote in 1788, "Today we live in an age in which book after book is written or translated about education." This stream of publications sprang from two sources, John Locke and Jean-Jacques Rousseau.

John Locke's *Some Thoughts Concerning Education* was published in 1693, and is now seen as a starting point of the Enlightenment. Locke introduced a new approach to children. He compared the child with a *tabula rasa,* a blank slate, in contrast to earlier writers, who regarded children as born with innate ideas and marked by original sin. A child developed by experience, argued the empiricist Locke, and parents should mainly stimulate and steer those experiences. In that way children would channel their passions and learn skills. Locke's treatise originated with a series of letters to a friend during the 1680s, while he was in exile in the Dutch Republic. He was influenced by Dutch child-rearing practices, which were relatively mild and involved little distance between parents and children. He stressed the need for an individual approach to each child. He also gave many pieces of practical advice about food, clothing, exercise, and reading. Not everything he wrote was new (much was obviously taken from an earlier Dutch treatise), but his pedagogical message fitted well into his other philosophical writings. In the article on *enfance* (childhood) in Diderot's *Encyclopedia,* the reader is explicitly advised to read Locke's book on education.

While Locke's contribution to pedagogy was influential, that of Jean-Jacques Rousseau was no less than explosive. Although his *Émile ou de l'éducation* was immediately forbidden after its publication in 1762, within a few years the pedagogical ideas he had formulated were discussed all over Europe. *Émile* is a pedagogical treatise in the form of a utopian novel mixed with many bits of practical advice. *Émile* made all earlier ideas about education obsolete, Rousseau claimed. Only his predecessor Locke received some friendly words, but he ridiculed Locke's idea that parents should argue in a rational way with their children. The fundamental mistake of earlier writers was, in Rousseau's view, to base their pedagogy on the goal they aimed at, the adult person a child had to become. "Everything is good coming from the Creator, every-

Girl Mourning over Her Dead Bird (1765), Jean-Baptiste Greuze. Typical of eighteenth-century art, Greuze's painting plays off sexual innuendo (the dead bird symbolizes lost virginity) against a new Enlightenment belief in the natural purity of children. (NG 435. National Galleries of Scotland, Edinburgh).

thing degenerates in the hands of men." This is the first sentence of *Émile*, and it states the basic principle of the book. A child is good because she or he is part of nature, and educa-

tion and culture can only spoil the natural child, he warned. The exemplary education of the little orphan Émile by his tutor—named Jean-Jacques—took place in the countryside, and nature was his teacher. Books were forbidden—with the exception of Defoe's *Robinson Crusoe*—because a child had to learn from empirical encounters. Freedom was the highest good in life, and therefore a child should, for instance, learn to walk without leading strings or reins, since "the joy of freedom compensates for many injuries."

Émile was seen by contemporaries as both compelling and chaotic, as a paradoxical mix of reason and incongruity, religion and godlessness, meddlesomeness and love for freedom. Despite all criticism, though, *Émile* became the foundation and touchstone of Enlightenment pedagogy. Although Rousseau afterwards explicitly stated that his book was not meant as a guide—he preferred to call it an utopian text— some parents tried it out in practice. Some of these experiments are well documented, such as that of Richard Edgeworth, born two years after *Émile* came out. His father wanted to make of his son "a fair trial of Rousseau's system." The first results were encouraging, because as a boy Dick turned out to be "bold, free, fearless, generous" and "ready and keen to use all his senses." At the age of seven, his father took him to Paris to visit Rousseau, who thought that the boy was intelligent, but also stubborn and conceited. These traits soon got the upper hand, and Dick was removed from school and sent to the navy, where he soon deserted and finally went to America, to the great relief of his father.

Émile led to discussions all over Europe, but even its greatest adherents realized that Rousseau's ideas were unworkable and should be transformed into practical guidelines.

The Philanthropinists

Nowhere was the new science of pedagogy more enthusiastically developed than in Germany. This was no coincidence. The Enlightenment there occurred when the country was emerging from a period of retarded political and intellectual development. The German word *paedagogik* was introduced in 1771, and the period 1770 to 1830 is now called the *paedagogisches Zeitalter*, the age of pedagogics. A congenial group of writers, clergymen, and teachers developed a dense network. They were called the *philanthropen* ("friends of men"). J. B. BASEDOW (1723–1790), J. H. Campe (1746–1818) and C. G. SALZMANN (1744–1811) were the most famous among them. They were all enlightened and progressive, but on essential points they differed with Rousseau. For instance, they developed systems of punishments and rewards on which Rousseau would have frowned. They made a German translation of *Émile* with elaborate comments and criticisms in footnotes, which overshadowed the original text. In this revised version, Émile is tamed into a well-behaved bourgeois boy. The first footnote is a comment on Rousseau's famous opening sentence, cited above, and it reads: "It could be argued as well that many things degenerate when they are left to Nature only, without being helped by human diligence." The philanthropinist version of *Émile* was translated into other languages, as were many of the books and journals produced in abundance by German pedagogues.

An important difference with Rousseau was their rejection of the possibility of education outside of society. These pedagogues strove to improve education within the family and at school. They wanted to educate not only the children of the elite, as early enlightened writers such as Locke and Rousseau had, but also children of the lower classes. Basedow was invited by the enlightened prince of Dessau to establish a school according to these new principles. This school, the Philanthropinum, became a model for many other schools. The small garden, in which each pupil had to work, and the little lathe which stood in each pupil's room were distant echoes from Rousseau's *Émile*.

The new generation of pedagogues concentrated on educating the common people. They observed that schools, both in cities and in the countryside, were old fashioned and that most teachers were incompetent. In the middle of the eighteenth century there still was a broad gap between the cultural elite and the majority of people, who were illiterate. Newly established societies aimed at bringing the message of the Enlightenment to the common people. In the Dutch Republic, for instance, the Society for Public Welfare established schools for the poor and published cheap schoolbooks according to modern principles.

The German philanthropinists and kindred spirits elsewhere in Europe produced new teaching methods on a large scale. Basedow tried to present children with all existing human knowledge in his 1774 *Elementarwerk*, and this became a model for later authors. They also invented a new literary genre, children's books. Rousseau's idea that children should not read at all was partly a choice based on principle but was also based on the lack of suitable books. That changed rapidly after around 1770. The Dutch novelist and pedagogue Betje Wolff wrote, "This is the century in which we have started to write for children" (quoted in Dekker, p. 46). Although in many of these books the ideals of the Enlightenment were presented in a rather crude way, they were a great step forward.

Enlightenment and Revolution

In the age of the democratic revolution, from the American War of Independence to the French Revolution, new ideas about children also took on a political dimension. However, while the rights of men were formulated, no separate rights of children were even discussed (nor were the rights of women). Children nevertheless were very visible in revolutionary ceremonies and festivities, such as the planting of liberty trees. Revolutionary catechisms were published to explain to children the ideals of freedom, equality, and brotherhood. Revolutionaries developed plans for school reform. In the French constitution of 1791, education was made a task of the state, and the writer and politician the Marquis de Condorcet, and later on the politician Michel

Lepeletier, were asked to create blueprints for a new system of public schools.

Politics no longer was the domain of old men. Many French revolutionaries who came to power in 1789 were remarkably young. One example of the political youth was Marc-Antoine Jullien Jr., who had just finished an education of the sort inspired by Rousseau. Only sixteen years old, he was a regular visitor at the Jacobin Club in Paris, the meeting place of the radicals. One year later he was sent to England to establish contacts with the opposition there. In 1793, he was made a deputy in the provinces by the radical leader Robespierre and became responsible for the Terror in the northwest of France. Louis-Antoine-Léon de Saint-Just, another young revolutionary and one of the forces behind the French Terror, claimed that his moral authority was based on his youth: "Because I am young I am closer to Nature," he said. Not much later, at twenty-eight, Saint-Just died on the guillotine. Jullien escaped that punishment and after the revolution became a writer in the field of pedagogy. In 1817 he published *Esquisse et vue préliminaire d'un ouvrage sur l'education comparée*, the first study in comparative pedagogy.

The legal status of children changed in many countries. In France, the voting age was lowered in 1792 from twenty-five to eighteen. In the Netherlands after the Batavian Revolution of 1795, the voting age was set at twenty. Other rights of children were extended at the expense of parental power in many countries. Children gained greater freedom to choose a marriage partner despite parental protest. Children could also no longer be completely disinherited by their parents. During the Restoration in 1814, these rights were to some extent restricted again in many countries. The voting age in France, for instance, became thirty. The discussion about rights and the age of majority was often implicitly about boys, not about girls. However, girls were not completely forgotten, and many pedagogues paid attention to their education, often in separate chapters or books, in the way Rousseau added the education of Sophie to the upbringing of Émile.

The Influence of the Enlightenment

In the end, the Enlightenment had its greatest impact in and through pedagogy and education. The last of the Enlightenment pedagogues was JOHANN FRIEDRICH HERBART, author of *Allgemeine Paedagogik* (1806), who held the Kant's chair at the university of Koenigsberg (Kaliningrad) after Kant's death. While most philanthropinists were forgotten in the nineteenth century, the Swiss schoolmaster J. H. PESTALOZZI and his collaborator FRIEDRICH FROEBEL, who, although often regarded as belonging to the Romantic period, were closely connected to their predecessors. Another link between the Enlightenment pedagogues and those of later times is found in the methods invented by the director of the Paris School for Deaf Children, Jean Itard, in his effort to educate the Wild Boy of Aveyron. His work exercised a last-

ing influence, despite the failure of what may have been the most daring experiment of Enlightenment pedagogy. The world of children today was to a large extent created in the age of Enlightenment, and several elements of today's standard school curriculum, including PHYSICAL EDUCATION, manual training, and school gardens, can be traced to the advice given by Rousseau in his *Émile*.

See also: **Desiderius Erasmus of Rotterdam; Education, Europe; Theories of Childhood.**

BIBLIOGRAPHY

Dekker, Rudolf. 1999. *Childhood, Memory and Autobiography in Holland from the Golden Age to Romanticism*. London: Macmillan.

Douthwaite, Julia V. 2002. *The Wild Girl, Natural Man, and the Monster: Dangerous Experiments in the Age of Enlightenment*. Chicago: University of Chicago Press.

Lempa, Heikki. 1993. *Bildung der Triebe Der deutsche Philanthropismus (1768–1788)*. Turku, Finland: Turun Yliopisto.

Lévy, Marie-Françoise, ed. 1990. *L'enfant, la famille et la Révolution française*. Paris: Olivier Orban.

Rothschild, Emma. 1998. "Condorcet and Adam Smith on education and instruction." In *Philosophers on Education: New Historical Perspectives*, ed. Amelie Oksenberg Rorty. London: Routledge.

Todd, Janet, ed. 1996. *Female Education in the Age of Enlightenment*. London: Pickering.

ARIANNE BAGGERMAN
RUDOLF M. DEKKER

Epidemics

From the onset of the statistical era (which began around 1840 in Britain and the United States) until the present time, roughly half the world's population were (and are) infants and children under the age of fifteen. This must also have been the situation among all humankind before 1840. In the eighteenth century in the West, in those regions for which some crude figures exist, such as Massachusetts, Britain, the core lands of modern France, Sweden, and the German lands, it can be said with some confidence that life expectancy at birth occasionally touched forty years but even there it was generally less. Given that measles and several other epidemic diseases tended to target people under fifteen—half of the population—it follows that they had a very large clientele to work on.

An endemic disease is one that is continuously present in any given population in nascent form. Its rate of occurrence as an illness—which is to say, its prevalence—may differ according to the season of the year and other variables, but its causal agent is almost always found within the locality. Heading the list of today's endemic, or always present, child killers are the water-borne ailments collectively known as dysentery and the diarrheal diseases. In contrast, an epidemic disease, such as smallpox in its most virulent forms (extinct since 1977 in its free-ranging state) or measles (which still exists), only occasionally attacked any given human population. The disease agents, or pathogens, which had the potential to periodically set this sort of epidemic in motion almost always came in from outside the place in which victims lived.

Smallpox

Unlike a dread disease such as bubonic plague (essentially a disease of rats and other rodents), smallpox had no nonhuman host. Thus, over time it was vital to the perpetuation of the smallpox variola that it not kill off all its child hosts. If it did, the children would not be there in a few years, in their capacity as sexually mature adults, producing children of their own, who in turn could host the variola. Without hosts, the variola would become extinct.

It is essential to understand that the causal agents of infectious disease are living things that have the potential to change their forms over time. These mutations make their presence felt in the altered way the disease makes its presence felt among humankind.

In the case of smallpox as it affected populations in western Europe and the Middle East before around 1650, it was most commonly a benign endemic disease that did not kill its victims. Aside from sickly infants, who in any case could not be expected to live, pre-1650s smallpox neither killed nor scarred nor blinded nor neutered its victims. It was in this benign form that smallpox first entered the medical record.

Writing in Baghdad before 925 C.E., the Persian physician-philosopher Abu-Bakr al-Razi reported that smallpox was a common disease which most Middle Eastern children underwent with no ill effects. Al-Razi noticed that the illness never struck the same person twice. Nearly 700 years later, this was apparently still the situation in the British Isles. William Shakespeare, who died in 1616, in his many sonnets in praise of beautiful young men and women nowhere mentioned the threat of disfigurement or death from the disease. Thus, before 1616, it would appear that rampaging lethal smallpox was still unknown in England.

Opinions are divided about when and where the variola virus of smallpox first changed into its violently nasty forms. On the one hand, many historians argue that the Spanish, Genoese, and other European adventurers who went to the Caribbean Islands in the New World in and after 1518 were responsible. Having acquired smallpox immunity by hosting a benign case of the disease in their infancy at home, they brought forms of smallpox with them that, when let loose, quickly changed into lethal forms that killed millions of nonimmune Native Americans who had never before been exposed to smallpox. If these events—so catastrophic from the First Nation point of view—actually happened, it can be suggested that disease mutation may have first occurred in the New World.

Or it may have already happened in parts of sub-Saharan Africa, or in Bengal, in northeastern India. In both regions, sometime before medically aware European observers came on the scene in the late seventeenth century, village curers recognized that some cases of smallpox were now lethal. They also observed that little children who survived a bout of the disease in any of its forms were immune to further attacks. Putting two and two together, they devised the control technique known as inoculation.

In this process, a curer took a bit of a smallpox scab from a moderately sick child, diluted it, and then scratched it into the skin of the child being inoculated. The curer and the parents realized that this process was not risk free, yet they continued to use it. In the 1870s it was found that more than eighty percent of the Bengali men who were imprisoned in government jails in that province had already been inoculated.

The processes of inoculation first described by Western observers in Bengal in the late seventeenth century were also being commonly used at that time in parts of West Africa, from whence they were brought to the New World. In 1706, the slave Onesimus taught his master, the Reverend Cotton Mather of Old North Church, Boston, the mysteries of smallpox prevention through inoculation. In earlier years, between 1620 and 1700, Massachusetts had been blessed by an exceptionally benign disease environment and a low infant mortality rate that had allowed far more babies to survive to adulthood than was the case in the middle colonies and in Europe. However, in the years just before 1706, Old World diseases, including smallpox, had begun to strike youthful New Englanders. For this reason, Mather was atypically willing to listen to what his African dependent said and to put it into practice. He had the children in his immediate circle inoculated and encouraged his friends to follow suit.

Massachusetts-style inoculation against smallpox caught on in the New England colonies and in some of the more smallpox-prone parts of Europe. Thus in authoritarian Sweden, the central government gradually realized that if smallpox were allowed to rage among its infants unchecked the country would be in danger of being depopulated. During bad periods, such as the years between 1779 and 1782, nearly a fifth of all deaths were from smallpox; most of the victims were children under the age of nine. Aware of this, the Swedish government strongly encouraged parents to have their offspring inoculated.

Among western Europeans and European-Americans, inoculation processes may have turned the tide against smallpox, even before the immunization process known as VACCINATION was devised by Edward Jenner in the late 1790s and put into common use early in the next century.

Measles

At the opening of the twenty-first century, twenty-five years after smallpox was abolished in its free-ranging state worldwide, measles—an air-borne virus—continues to kill one million children each year and to make an additional 42 million seriously ill. First tentatively identified as a separate disease by the Persian philosopher-physician al-Razi in the tenth century, measles today is most common among the third of the world's children who are chronically malnourished and who live in the non-West.

In addition to children with an unfavorable nutritional status, young children living in large families are also much more prone to being infected with measles than are children living in families with one or two siblings. Nowadays, when the total population of most western European countries is rapidly shrinking due to the limitation of family size, and at a time when most European and European-American parents have their children immunized against all common infectious diseases, measles has become rare in the West. This means that it has become one of the many infectious diseases most commonly found in the non-West. Its non-Western survivors, their immune systems weakened through a bout with the disease, often fall prey to pneumonia.

Bubonic Plague

From 1348 through 1351, western Europe and Egypt were ravaged by a terrible disease, which killed between a quarter and a third of the population. The first great onslaught was called the Black Death. In Europe visitations of what used to be regarded as the same disease (at the time there were no means for identifying disease agents) recurred until the late seventeenth century. In western Europe, the last major outbreak was imported into Marseilles, France, in 1721 by a rogue ship coming from the Orient.

Conventional scholarship once held that humans who survived one attack of the bubonic plague did not develop immunity against a subsequent attack. Conventional scholarship also held that bubonic plague did not necessarily target children. Given that roughly half of the population in any place was under the age of fifte, one could expect that roughly half the victims of the disease would be non-adults. However, according to Samuel K. Cohn Jr. (2002), the late medieval plagues that repeatedly hit western Europe after 1351 directed their attention primarily against children; children who survived acquired life-time immunity.

Given that these events happened before the advent of modern laboratory medical science and before the statistical age, we have no sure way of knowing just what disease agents were actually at work in Europe between 1347 and 1721. In time, new scholarship may permit the writing of comparative studies based on findings from the non-West. It is already clear, however, that the Bubonic plague that continued to kill people in Egypt until 1844 was the same as, or closely related to, modern laboratory-certified Bubonic plague.

Poliomyelitis

Much more certain is our knowledge of the so-called summer plague, more usually known as poliomyelitis or infantile paralysis. In the summer of 1916, several thousand middle-class children in New York City and the surrounding region were struck with a strange new disease. Although outright death was rare—because hospital care was available—many survivors were left severely crippled in their legs and unable to walk. Other less fortunate survivors suffered impairment of their breathing apparatus and had to be placed in an iron lung.

Caused by viruses (there are three main viral strains), POLIO spreads from one person to another by a fecal-oral route and in the East Coast of the United States was very often contracted by middle-class young people who had access to public swimming pools. Polio was a high-profile disease—its victims included President Franklin Delano Roosevelt. Accordingly, it attracted the attention of highly qualified American scientists. In the development of a preventive vaccine suitable for mass distribution, the first great breakthrough was by Dr. Jonas Salk in the 1950s. In most areas of the world, Salk's techniques, which were based on the use of an injection, have now been replaced by an orally administered vaccine by Dr. Albert Sabin that was released in 1961.

Thanks to preventive immunization, polio has all but disappeared in the United States and elsewhere in the West. Yet in India, Nigeria, and some other parts of the non-West, young children and infants over the age of six months are still at risk from the disease. As of 1998, more than 18,000 fatalities were reported. Given that the quality of hospital care found in most non-Western countries is far below the standard found even half a century ago in the United States, cases that in the United States might have been successfully treated are left all but unattended and commonly result in death.

AIDS

Human Immunodeficiency Virus (HIV) and Acquired Immuno-Deficiency Syndrome (AIDS) was first reported in 1981 and has become the world's fourth most common cause of death. As of 2002, 40 million people bore the lethal virus, 70 percent of them in sub-Saharan Africa.

According to the conventional wisdom of leading funding agencies as expressed by the World Health Organization (WHO), "99 percent of the HIV infections found in Africa in 2001 are attributable to unsafe sex." (WHO 2002, p. xv). However, four years earlier, the same organization admitted that half a million victims were under the age of fifteen (WHO 1998, p. 93).

An alternative assessment of the situation was found in the *International Journal of STDs and AIDS* in October 2002. Here, David Gisselquist and his colleagues found that a sizeable percentage of Africans suffering from HIV had not yet reached the age of puberty. Though none of these children had engaged in sexual activity involving a partner, all of them had been the recipients of clinically administered injections which were intended to prevent communicable diseases, fevers, or other childhood illnesses. On-site study showed that the cash-strapped clinics often reused syringes simply because no other instruments were available; more than half of all HIV and AIDS victims in Africa may have been infected in this way. In many cases, newborn infants may have been infected in utero by infected mothers who had made use of the disease-prevention services of clinics.

The current AIDS epidemic affects infants and young children under the age of fifteen in financially hard-pressed sub-Saharan regions in two ways. First, many of them will die of pneumonia and the other killers that strike down people whose immune systems have been rendered useless. Very often their deaths will be recorded as having been caused by something other than AIDS.

Second, and more difficult to capture statistically, millions of young Africans are becoming ORPHANS through the AIDS deaths of their parents, aunts and uncles, and other potential care-givers. In several countries in southern Africa, where nearly half the adult population is HIV-positive, orphans have little chance of survival. For this reason, many of these who do survive do not acquire the veneer of civilization and instead become teenaged mercenary soldiers, drug-dealers, extortionists, or all-purpose terrorists.

As of 2003, the AIDS epidemic continues, and in the next two or three years is expected to make its presence heavily felt in China and in India, nations which between them are the home of half the world's population. Because many non-Western countries are burdened with debt repayment to financial institutions based in the West and are thus unable to fully fund proper health services, the AIDS epidemic may well become the non-Western world's principal childhood killer. The prognosis is not good.

See also: **AIDS; Contagious Diseases; Infant Mortality.**

BIBLIOGRAPHY

Cohn, Samuel K., Jr. 2002. "The Black Death: End of a Paradigm." *American Historical Review* 107, no. 2: 703–38.

De Waal, Alex. 2003. "How Will HIV/AIDS Transform African Governance?" *African Affairs* 102: 1–23.

Gisselquist, David, Richard Rothenberg, John Potterat, et al. 2002. "HIV Infections in Sub-Saharan Africa Not Explained by Sexual or Vertical Transmission." *International Journal of STDS and AIDS* 13, no. 10: 657–666.

Gisselquist, David, John Potterat, Paul Epstein, et al. 2002. "AIDS in Africa." *The Lancet* 360, no. 9343L: 1422–1423.

Gould, Tony. 1995. *A Summer Plague: Polio and Its Survivors.* New Haven: Yale University Press.

Joralemon, Donald. 1982. "New World Depopulation and the Case of Disease." *Journal of Anthropological Research* 38, no. 1: 108–127.

Lovell, W. George. 1992. "'Heavy Shadow and Black Night': Disease and Depopulation in Colonial Spanish America." *Annals of the Association of American Geographers* 82, no. 3: 426–446.

Mercer, Alex. 1990. *Disease, Mortality, and Population in Transition: Epidemiological-Demographic Change in England since the Eighteenth Century as Part of a Global Phenomenon.* Leicester, UK: Leicester University Press.

Watts, Sheldon. 1997. *Epidemics and History: Disease, Power, and Imperialism.* London: Yale University Press.

World Health Organization. 1998. *World Health Report 1998.* Geneva: World Health Organization.

World Health Organization. 2002. *World Health Report 2002.* Geneva: World Health Organization.

SHELDON WATTS

Erasmus. *See* Desiderius Erasmus of Rotterdam.

Erikson, Erik H. (1902–1994)

Erik Erikson was born of Danish parents in 1902 and brought up in Germany as the stepson of a pediatrician. His first love was art, which he studied in Munich and Florence. He came into contact with the psychoanalyst ANNA FREUD when he took up a post as a teacher in a Viennese school. He was analyzed by her and, following her example, worked with both children and adolescents as well as with adults. Erikson spent six years in Vienna, becoming a member of the Freudian community there and studying the methods of Montessori education. In response to the threat posed by the rise of the Nazi movement, Erikson moved to the United States with his wife and sons, setting up as one of the first child analysts in Boston. He carried out research on children with the Harvard Psychological Clinic and made contacts with both psychologists such as Henry Murray and Kurt Lewin and anthropologists such as Ruth Benedict and MARGARET MEAD. Although he had no academic qualifications, Yale University offered him a teaching and research appointment.

In 1939 the Eriksons moved to California, where Erikson did longitudinal studies on children at the University of California, Berkeley, worked as a child and training analyst, and carried out anthropological studies. Eventually he returned to the East Coast to teach at Harvard, particularly on his theory of the cycle of psychological development throughout life. He subsequently retired to the San Francisco area, where he died in 1994.

A major focus for Erikson, as both analyst and researcher, was the study of children, and he drew together his ideas about childhood in his first major and seminal work, *Childhood and Society*. Here he elaborated his approach of "triple bookkeeping": that understanding a person or behavior involves taking into account somatic factors, social context, and ego development, each in relation to the other. To unpack the somatic aspect, Erikson developed and clarified SIGMUND FREUD's theory of psychosexual development. He explored the power of social context in relation to child-rearing practices and their effects on later personality through some fascinating anthropological-psychoanalytical analyses of Sioux and Yurok Indian cultures. He looked at ego development in particular through an analysis of the significance and role of PLAY. In this book, as in all his work, Erikson emphasized the need for integration: that these three processes (somatic, social, ego developmental) are interdependent, and that each is both relevant and relative to the other two.

Childhood and Society also contains an early statement of his theory of the life cycle (which he subsequently elaborated in 1959, 1964, and 1977). This extends the notion of developmental stages, each with its own character, dynamics, and conflicts, beyond childhood into ADOLESCENCE, young adulthood, maturity, and old age. For example, he placed considerable emphasis on the significance of school experience for the developing ego. Erikson took a particular interest in adolescence (e.g., in *Identity, Youth, and Crisis*). He was fascinated by this transitional stage where identity is being forged, and by the conflicts and turbulence that this can provoke. He became best known in the 1960s for his articulation of the adolescent "identity crisis."

In summary, then, Erikson's primary contributions to the understanding of childhood rest on his:

elaboration and modification of the theory of psychosexual development,

theorizing and case studies on the development of ego in childhood, and

anthropological and other explorations of the significance of social context, child-rearing, and cultural processes for personality development

He made a further contribution in unraveling the processes involved in the development of identity, particularly during adolescence.

See also: **Child Development, History of the Concept of; Child Psychology.**

BIBLIOGRAPHY

Erikson, Erik H. 1950. *Childhood and Society*. New York: Norton.

Erikson, Erik H. 1959. *Identity and the Life Cycle*. New York: International Universities Press.

Erikson, Erik H. 1964. *Insight and Responsibility: Lectures on the Ethical Implications of Psychoanalytic Insight*. London: Faber.

Erikson, Erik H. 1968. *Identity, Youth, and Crisis*. London: Faber.

Erikson, Erik H. 1977. *Toys and Reasons: Stages in the Ritualization of Experience*. London: Marion Boyars.

Stevens, Richard. 1983. *Erik Erikson: An Introduction*. New York: St. Martin's Press.

RICHARD STEVENS

Eugenics

During the first half of the twentieth century, the movement known as eugenics profoundly influenced children and reproduction in most Western societies. The term *eugenics* was first popularized by Charles Darwin's cousin, Sir Francis Galton, who defined it as the use of science to improve human heredity. But that definition left many key questions unresolved: What is an improvement? What is heredity? How can science improve heredity? Who has the authority to answer these questions?

Self-proclaimed eugenics experts, drawn largely from middle-class professional and managerial backgrounds, formed a network of formal institutions, such as the American Eugenics Society and the British Eugenics Education Society, which promulgated a set of orthodox answers to these questions. These groups enjoyed political success disproportionate to their relatively small numbers, but they did not monopolize the meaning of eugenics. Public discourse included a variety of conflicting alternative answers to each of these questions, with differing implications for children.

What Is an Improvement?

Eugenicists' diagnoses of good and bad human traits were molded by their particular cultures' values, including their racial, religious, gender, and class prejudices. Eugenicists in the United States focused on racial and ethnic distinctions more than did British eugenicists, who tended to see class as more important than race, while French eugenicists instead emphasized nationality. Eugenic leaders from elite or managerial backgrounds depicted poverty as an inherited disease, while socialist eugenicists portrayed greed and capitalism as the pathologies. Eugenic intellectual leaders emphasized what they called the "menace of the feebleminded," but in mass culture eugenic popularizers often ranked an attractive body ahead of a brilliant mind. Although the subjective, culturally derived nature of these diagnoses is obvious in retrospect, at the time each was presented as the objectively proven verdict of science.

What Is Heredity?

Early-twentieth-century scientific understanding of heredity was transformed by rediscovery of Gregor Mendel's research on the patterns of inheritance of specific traits, and by August Weismann's demonstrations that heredity is unaffected by environment. However, many eugenicists campaigned against conditions from infectious diseases to malnutrition whose causes science now attributed to environment, not genetics. This expansive version of eugenics did not result from ignorance of science, but from a different set of concerns. In this view, calling something hereditary meant that you got it from your parents, regardless of whether you got it via genes or germs, precepts or probate. The 1922 U.S. Public Health Service film *The Science of Life* defined a man's heredity as "what he receives from his ancestors." What made a trait hereditary was the parents' moral responsibility for causing it, rather than the technical mechanism of its transmission. On this view, eugenics meant not simply having good genes, but being a good parent.

How Can Science Improve Heredity?

Eugenicists often categorized their methods as either positive—increasing the reproduction of those judged fit—or negative—decreasing the fertility of those judged unfit. Positive measures ranged from proposed government stipends for parents of large healthy families, to Better Baby and Fitter Family contests modeled on rural livestock shows. Negative measures included forced sterilization, ethnic restrictions on immigration, and euthanasia. In France and Latin America eugenicists generally emphasized positive measures, while the United States and Germany led in negative measures.

However, positive and negative were meant as simply arithmetic not evaluative distinctions. Negative measures often relied on coercion, but so did some pronatalist methods. In addition, negative techniques from BIRTH CONTROL to euthanasia often were not imposed by the government, but chosen by families, sometimes even when they violated the law. Furthermore, most eugenicists employed a mix of positive and negative methods. Both positive and negative methods shared the same goals, based on shared definitions of good and bad heredity.

Eugenics and Children

Different versions of eugenics affected children in different ways. Eugenic efforts to control who had children did not explicitly prescribe how to raise them. But the eugenic assumption that heredity determined a person's essential characteristics could undercut support for efforts to improve children's environment through such means as education or health care. Furthermore, many eugenicists such as Charles Davenport endorsed Social Darwinist and neo-Malthusian assertions that disease in general, and INFANT MORTALITY in particular, were valuable means of natural selection. On this view, death was nature's method for eliminating children with inheritable defects. For example, from 1915 to 1918, a prominent Chicago surgeon, Dr. Harry Haiselden, refused to treat and sometimes actively hastened the deaths of infants he diagnosed as eugenically unfit. His practice won widespread public support.

On the other hand, eugenics was also frequently invoked to support improved medical treatment, education, and welfare programs for children. The American Association for the Study and Prevention of Infant Mortality had a formal section on eugenics, while America's first major eugenic organization, the Race Betterment Foundation, promoted a broad range of preventive health measures for children, from exercise to clean milk. Eugenicists who supported social services for children argued that infant mortality was insufficiently selective—too random, or too likely to kill children

with valued traits (such as intelligence). They also tended to define eugenics as good parenting, not limited to good genes. Such views were especially appealing to maternalist social reformers, who believed that power for women would make society more nurturing, and to advocates of scientific motherhood, who sought to professionalize homemaking. These versions of eugenics attempted to help all children, but they still depended on distinguishing between good and bad parents.

Support for programs labeled as eugenic declined in the 1930s and 1940s in the United States, in reaction to the Nazi use of eugenics to promote genocide, and in response to growing scientific understanding of the complexity of genetics. To protect genetic medicine from the prejudiced values of past eugenics, many post–World War II scholars insisted that doctors should treat only objectively defined diseases. However, medicine has always required some evaluative judgments to distinguish good health from disease. Well-intentioned efforts to keep medicine value-free actually replicated past eugenicists' faith in the objectivity of their own diagnoses. Such efforts could not succeed in eliminating the need for value judgments in medicine, but they could obscure and delegitimate the political and ethical analyses necessary if a culture is to make such value judgments wisely.

See also: **Family Patterns; Fertility Rates; Pediatrics.**

BIBLIOGRAPHY

Adams, Mark B., ed. 1989. *The Wellborn Science: Eugenics in Germany, France, Brazil and Russia.* Oxford, UK: Oxford University Press.

Briggs, Laura. 2002. *Reproducing Empire: Race, Sex, Science, and U.S. Imperialism in Puerto Rico.* Berkeley: University of California Press.

Dikotter, Frank. 1998. "Race Culture: Recent Perspectives on the History of Eugenics." *American Historical Review* 103: 467–478.

Kevles, Daniel. 1985. *In the Name of Eugenics: Genetics and the Uses of Human Heredity.* Berkeley: University of California Press.

Kline, Wendy. 2001. *Building a Better Race: Gender, Sexuality, and Eugenics from the Turn of the Century to the Baby Boom.* Berkeley: University of California Press.

Larson, Edward J. 1995. *Sex, Race, and Science: Eugenics in the Deep South.* Baltimore: Johns Hopkins University Press.

Meckel, Richard. 1990. *Save the Babies: American Public Health Reform and the Prevention of Infant Mortality.* Baltimore: Johns Hopkins University Press.

Paul, Diane. 1996. *Controlling Human Heredity 1865 to the Present.* Atlantic Highlands, NJ: Humanities Press.

Pernick, Martin S. 1996. *The Black Stork: Eugenics and the Death of "Defective" Babies in American Medicine and Motion Pictures since 1915.* New York: Oxford University Press.

Pernick, Martin S. 1997. "Eugenics and Public Health in American History." *American Journal of Public Health* 87: 1767–1772.

Pernick, Martin S. 2002. "Taking Better Baby Contests Seriously." *American Journal of Public Health* 92: 707–708.

Proctor, Robert N. 1988. *Racial Hygiene: Medicine Under the Nazis.* Cambridge, MA: Harvard University Press.

MARTIN S. PERNICK

In eighteenth-century Britain, as the Industrial Revolution created new wealth, children from affluent families are sometimes depicted in portraits as symbols of parental status, as are these elegantly dressed children in William Hogarth's *The Graham Children* (1742). © Art Resource, NY. National Gallery, London, Great Britain.

European Industrialization

It is tempting to assume that the Industrial Revolution of the nineteenth century was a disaster for children. There are the familiar images of child workers struggling in the mills, of wretched street urchins in the slums, and of poor OLIVER TWIST half starving on gruel in the workhouse. Yet even in the British case this was a very partial reflection of reality. The young factory operative or the slum child was the exception rather than the rule during the nineteenth century. In the first place, industrialization was a slow and protracted process that affected different regions of Europe in a number of ways. During the first half of the nineteenth century, a core of western European nations began to industrialize, with Britain leading the way, followed by Switzerland, Bel-

gium, France and Germany. This left a huge periphery of backward regions which had barely begun the process. Similarly, the massive urbanization characteristic of modern society only began in earnest around the middle of the nineteenth century in most of Europe, the exceptionally precocious British case apart. Even within the more developed western "core," important regional differences were much in evidence. The most spectacular forms of industrial development were confined to a handful of well-known localities around Manchester, Birmingham (both in England), Liège (Belgium), Mulhouse (France), Elberfeld (Germany), Brno (Austria-Hungary), and so on. This meant that in Britain, and more so in continental Europe, small islands of modern industry were surrounded by a large sea of "pre-industrial" forms.

Second, industrialization brought benefits as well as misery to the people of Europe, though how this panned out for individuals depended on such influences as class, gender, and region. If the factories and sweatshops blighted the existence of some young people, the wealth they created would eventually release many others from the need to work at all. Mass immigration to the towns may have swamped basic facilities such as housing and schools for a while, but in the long term urban civilization proved favorable to medical, educational, and cultural advances. In short, any account of the impact of industrialization on children in Europe must take account of continuity as well as change, of material and cultural advance as well as poverty, and, bearing in mind the massive social inequalities persisting through the period, of winners as well as losers.

Work, Play, and Education

People in the West now take it for granted that the children should be free from adult responsibilities—notably the need to earn a living—so that they can develop a healthy body, complete their education, and have time for PLAY. However, this type of "long" childhood, quarantined from much of what goes on in the world, is a comparatively recent phenomenon. Until mass schooling began to make an impact during the late nineteenth and early twentieth centuries, most young people in Europe gradually moved into the world of adults at an early stage in their lives. They helped with little tasks around the farm, the workshop, or the home, and learned their trade, and the values that went with it, on the job, by means of a formal or informal APPRENTICESHIP. This latter approach was not without its advantages, avoiding the more modern tendency to infantilize the young. It certainly involved a very different balance in everyday life between time spent at work and time passed on the school benches.

Children in preindustrial Europe gradually drifted into work from around the age of seven or eight. Much of their labor was casual and undemanding, for they were not strong enough to take on most of the tasks required on a farm or in a workshop. It was only when they reached their teens that they began the more serious business of an apprenticeship in a trade or work beside adults. In the meantime, they often occupied themselves with simple but time-consuming jobs, such as caring for younger siblings or running errands, which released adults for more productive labor. Girls in particular looked after younger children for their mothers or earned a few pence minding a baby for another family. On the farms children helped by picking stones from fields, scaring birds from crops, minding pigs and sheep, and similar work appropriate to their size and experience. In the towns they might start work in some of the lighter trades, such as making clothes, manufacturing nails, or doing deliveries. Many also tried their luck on the streets, sweeping crossings for pedestrians, performing tricks, or cleaning shoes. Some of this work required long, lonely hours out in the fields or

TABLE 1

Occupations of children under sixteen in French industry, 1839–1845

Industry	Number	Percentage
Textiles		
Cotton	44,828	31.2
Wool	26,800	18.7
Linen and hemp	7,232	5.0
Silk	9,326	6.5
Mixed fibers	15,803	11.0
Mines, quarries	6,256	4.4
Basic metallurgy	6,340	4.4
Metalworking	6,315	4.4
Leather	751	0.5
Wood	262	0.2
Ceramics	4,089	2.8
Chemicals	606	0.4
Construction	2,930	2.0
Lighting	71	0.0
Furnishings	0	0.0
Clothing	410	0.3
Food	6,889	4.8
Transport	223	0.2
Paper, publishing	2,841	2.0
Luxuries	95	0.1
Miscellaneous	1,598	1.1
Total	143,665	100.0

SOURCE: Statistique de la France, *Industrie* (4 vols, Paris, 1847–1852).

on the streets, not to mention facing rain, mist, and cold winds during the winter. Tiennon, hero of the peasant novel *The Life of a Simple Man* (1904), recalled time hanging heavily as he watched his flock in the Bourbonnais region of France during the early nineteenth century:

> Sometimes fear and sadness overtook me, and I started to cry, to cry without reason, for hours on end. A sudden rustling in the woods, the scampering of a mouse in the grass, the unfamiliar shriek of a bird, that was enough during these hours of anxiety to make me burst into tears.

At the same time, it was often possible to lighten the load by combining work with play. The young shepherds, for example, could amuse themselves carving wood or joining with others to play games.

Authorities in EARLY MODERN EUROPE were generally worried more by the lack of work for poor women and children than by any abuses of their labor. They therefore welcomed the first signs of industrialization: the spread of industry in the countryside, notably in the northwestern parts of the continent. These new "protoindustrial" forms brought a grueling round of agricultural and industrial work unknown in earlier centuries that bore down on children as on the rest of the family. During the early nineteenth century, for example, among the handloom weaving families of the Saxon Oberlausitz, young children wound bobbins and prepared spools, while adolescents of both sexes learned to weave. Besides handloom weaving, village children were employed in large numbers by protoindustries in hand spinning, hosiery, embroidery, lace making, braiding straw, and metalworking. The early textile mills of the late eighteenth century were a further boon for governments saddled with large numbers of ORPHANS by war and revolution. Robert Owen employed around 500 parish apprentices in his famous cotton mill at New Lanark in Scotland. Although the early spinning machinery was specifically designed for use by young people, most factory children continued with the traditional role of helping adults. Best known are the little piecers working beside the mule-spinners in the textile mills, the trappers operating ventilation shafts in the mines, and the carriers of bottles for glass blowers. The French example shows CHILD LABOR concentrated in a small number of industries during the 1840s, above all in textiles, mining, metalworking, and food production (see Table 1).

Overall, industrialization may have drawn more children into the labor force, though historians argue whether in the British case the maximum level of participation occurred during the late eighteenth and early nineteenth centuries, with protoindustrialization, or during the 1830s and 1840s, with the spread of the factory system. It may also have required a more intensive work regime in terms of working hours and effort, at least for that minority employed in the mills and "sweatshops." Children like those in the cotton mills of Ghent, in Belgium, who worked from dawn until 10:00 P.M. in winter, and from 5:00 A.M. until 8:00 P.M. in summer, would have had little time for leisure. As one young Londoner lamented, there was "never no time to play."

Yet it is easy to exaggerate the misery involved. Historians frequently note that children might start work in the mills "as young as seven or eight"—but the majority probably waited until they were closer to ten or twelve, and even later in a heavy industry like iron- and steel-making. To take the best-documented case, the British census of 1851 recorded that only 3.5 percent of children aged 5 to 9 had an occupation. Even in the next age group, 10 to 14 years, no more than 30 percent was gainfully employed (37 percent of boys and 22 percent of girls). If the new industrial system sucked in child labor during the early stages, it also spewed it out later. The reasons for the decline in child labor in Western Europe during the second half of the nineteenth century remain controversial, but it was not necessarily due entirely to intervention by the state. Historian Clark Nardinelli has pointed out that the proportion of children among workers in the British silk industry fell during the 1840s and 1850s, even though they were not covered by factory legislation at this period. New technologies were one influence, such as the self-acting mule in the spinning industry, which largely made it possible to dispense with the piecers (though not all employers chose to do so, notably in Lancashire). At

the same time, rising wages may have allowed working-class parents more leeway for keeping their offspring in school.

The favoring of work at the expense of leisure during the opening phase of industrialization is unlikely to have created a vacuum in popular leisure activities. Some of the old holidays and festivals persisted; children had the run of the fields or streets around their homes; and even on the factory floor child workers had some scope for "larking about." Witness the two French girls revealed to have been dancing together in a mill at Saint-Pierre-les-Calais during the 1850s, until they suffered broken arms when their skirts became caught up in the machinery. Doubtless it was children from well-off backgrounds who principally benefited from innovations such as board games and jigsaw puzzles, not to mention visits to ZOOS, circuses, and puppet shows. Even so, the capacity of industrial centers such as Nuremberg in Germany and the Black Country in England to churn out cheap wooden and metal TOYS ensured a certain democratization in this sphere. There was, in addition, a section of the market catering for popular tastes by the late nineteenth century, with "penny dreadfuls" and *romans à quatre sous* to read, and "penny gaffs" and music halls to visit. By this time young people in the towns would scorn their country cousins for their unfashionable clothing and traditional dances, preferring the varied delights of a consumer-oriented urban culture.

In terms of drawing children into the schools, industrialization emerged as an ambiguous influence. On the one hand, during its early stages the rapid movement of population into the new industrial areas played havoc with the school system, depressing levels of literacy in areas such as Lancashire or Flanders. Certain trades were particularly associated with illiteracy, notably coal mining and construction. In northern Europe Protestant churches took the lead in encouraging education during the early modern period; they were joined in this aim in the late eighteenth century by reformers promoting a national system of education. Prussia, hardly a leading industrial power during the early nineteenth century, led the way: by the late 1830s, an estimated 80 percent of children aged six to fourteen were attending the elementary schools. On the other hand, the more progressive industrial employers tended to insist on some schooling for their employees, even if it was more to instill religious and moral values than to promote learning. Skilled craftsmen, retailers, and at the very least a new elite of foremen, technicians, and clerks in the factories depended more on literacy than did peasants and farm laborers. The atmosphere in the towns was more favorable to education than that of the villages, given the more vigorous political and intellectual life. By the time education was made compulsory in Britain and France during the 1880s, most children were probably receiving some elementary education. Yet the pressures of poverty and parental indifference meant that, even during the late nineteenth and early twentieth centuries, many children in Western Europe still had to combine work with school. Aurelia Roth, for example, complained from Bohemia that with her long hours spent grinding glass, "I didn't get much time to learn, and still less to play, but it hurt me the most if I had to skip school." Nonetheless, at this time children in Western Europe were a dwindling force on the shop floor; the only problem was the need to enforce more regular attendance at school among the poor.

The "Middle-Class" Family and a New Ideal of Childhood

Industrialization made an impact on the family, as surely as on the workshop. During the early modern period, particularly in northwest Europe, many families had routinely sent off their sons and daughters to a boarding school or to another family. A spell as a farm servant or an apprentice was a common experience for young people between leaving home and getting married. An unfortunate minority was separated from their parents from a very tender age, as young as seven, but most could afford to wait until some point in their teens before going off into service. With the coming of protoindustrialization to the countryside, families in the affected areas chose to keep their young people at home, given the wide variety of tasks that needed to be performed on the farm and in the workshop. Similarly, working-class families in nineteenth-century mill towns had their sons and daughters living with them well past childhood, as the pioneering study of Preston (Lancashire, England) by Michael Anderson has revealed. The exceptions, until the early twentieth century, were the young women living away from home as domestic servants in the big cities. Even so, the general drift was for young people to live at home until they married.

There was in addition a long-term change in the function of the family during the period of industrialization. With the rise of specialized institutions, such as factories, schools, and hospitals, the family began to lose some its earlier roles. Rather than a unit of production, education, and so on, it became above all a source of emotional support for its members. Nowhere was this more the case than among the new "middling strata" which flourished during the nineteenth century, from the wealthy bankers and industrialists at the top to the shopkeepers and master artisans at the bottom. Aristocratic parents had a tendency to distance themselves from their children: Talleyrand, born into a noble family in France in 1754, noted that neither of his parents ever showed him any affection, for "paternal care had not yet come into fashion." Peasant and working-class parents were often too hard-pressed by work and insecurity to be able to pay much attention to their offspring. Hence it was among the affluent professional and business groups that domesticity flourished, and, as Philippe Ariès has put it, the family organized itself around the child. It was above all mothers who were supposed to devote themselves to their families: breastfeeding their infants, teaching them sound religious and moral values, and cosseting them in a nursery far removed from the harsh realities of adult life. This was the milieu which proved most receptive to new ideas on the nature of childhood emerging from leading figures in the ENLIGHTENMENT and the Romantic Movement.

JEAN-JACQUES ROUSSEAU is the thinker usually credited with challenging the Christian tradition of original sin with the contrary notion of original innocence in the child. His *Émile* (1762) was not entirely original in its ideas, but its witty and engaging style of writing ensured a ready reception in educated circles. Rousseau asserted that the child was born innocent, but became stifled by all the prejudices and authority of society. His advice was to respect childhood, and "leave nature to act for a long time before you get involved with acting in its place." The Romantics went even further in idealizing childhood. The German Jean Paul Richter, for example, suggested in his *Levana* (1807) that children were "messengers from paradise." Most influential of all on nineteenth-century conceptions of childhood was the poet William Wordsworth, and his *Ode. Intimations of Immortality from Recollections of Childhood* (1807). Lines such as "Heaven lies about us in our infancy!" echoed down the years, as later writers quoted, plagiarized, or adapted them for their own purposes. As Peter Coveney observed, in the Machine Age the child could symbolize Imagination and Sensibility. Yet it required a wealthy, urbanized society to accept the view that children were essentially innocent, vulnerable, and asexual. The way was open for a range of philanthropic and legislative initiatives to protect children from the dangers they were perceived to face.

Philanthropy, the State, and Child Welfare

The nineteenth century brought a series of private charitable initiatives and government regulations to improve child welfare. Most directly linked to industrialization were the campaigns to eliminate the abuse of child labor. The motives of the reformers were a combination of humanitarianism and more mercenary considerations. Thus the textile magnates of the Société Industrielle de Mulhouse, in Alsace, who campaigned for a law on child labor from the 1830s onwards by petitioning the government, had their eyes firmly set on their own profits as well as on the health and morality of their employees. The British pioneered such legislation in 1802 with an act protecting apprentices in the new cotton mills. Subsequently they and their continental neighbors proceeded by a process of trial and error, gradually extending the scope of factory legislation and tightening the systems of enforcement. In Britain Althorp's Act of 1833 replaced an earlier one of 1819 by introducing the first viable inspection system, while the 1867 Factory Extension Act finally reached out beyond the factory system. Both Prussia and France experimented with child labor laws around 1840, but neither had an effective means of enforcement. The former produced a more comprehensive system in 1853, the latter in 1874. All such legislation aimed to regulate child labor rather than abolish it, setting minimum ages for working, grading hours according to age, banning night work, and insisting on some schooling. It doubtless curbed some of the worst abuses, though it also had the perverse effect of driving some children into small, unregulated workshops.

The nineteenth century also transformed the relationship between the state and the family. In the French case, a group dominated by doctors and administrators launched the challenge to the traditional authority of the head of the household. Appalled by the waste of infant life around them, and the high cost of supporting single mothers, they founded societies for the protection of children during the 1860s and a series of laws that shifted control from cases of "morally deficient" parents to philanthropists and magistrates. The 1889 Roussel law on the divestiture of paternal authority, for example, allowed courts to deprive parents of their rights on the grounds of drunkenness, scandalous behavior, or physical abuse. In Germany zealous Protestants took charge of the reform process, placing what were known as "wayward" children in a *Rettunghaus*, or House of Salvation. As in France, because private initiatives were all too easily thwarted, the reformers turned to the state for support. A Prussian law of 1878 made possible the placing of juvenile delinquents in a *Rettunghaus*. Similarly, in Britain, reformers like Mary Carpenter blamed parents for crime and vagrancy among children, and in the 1850s responded with industrial and reformatory schools. Later in the century, the Cruelty to Children Act of 1889 permitted the courts to take into care children who had been abused or neglected by their parents. The good intentions of these reformers need not be doubted, though in retrospect one can discern a desire to refashion poor, working-class families in their own middle-class image.

Finally, the spread of industrialization coincided with that of mass schooling, at the expense of informal methods of education in the family or the local community. Various German states attempted to make elementary schooling compulsory during the seventeenth and eighteenth centuries, but there were simply too few teachers and school buildings available for such measures to have any chance of success. They did at least enjoy a considerable lead over surrounding parts of the continent where schools were few and far between, notably in Scandinavia, Ireland, Southern Italy, and Eastern Europe. Other nations gradually took the path pioneered by the Germans, taking over responsibility for education from the churches, and making schooling both free and compulsory. In Britain and France, for example, this latter shift occurred during the 1880s. The social inequalities that had always marked access to education were far from eliminated by the early twentieth century, but at least the widespread illiteracy of the past disappeared. Compulsory education had long-term significance for children. More than any factory legislation, which was always difficult to enforce, it ended most forms of child labor (part-time work excepted). It also made everyone familiar with the notion of an age-graded society, with children starting school at the same age, and working their way up the system year by year. A "long" childhood had come to replace the gradual transition into adulthood by the early twentieth century.

See also: **Compulsory School Attendance; Education, Europe; Social Welfare; Street Games; Theories of Childhood; Work and Poverty.**

BIBLIOGRAPHY

Anderson, Michael. 1971. *Family Structure in Nineteenth Century Lancashire.* Cambridge, UK: Cambridge University Press.

Ariès, Philippe. 1962. *Centuries of Childhood.* Trans. Robert Baldick. New York: Knopf.

Bolin-Hort, Per. 1989. *Work, Family and the State: Child Labour and the Organization of Production in the British Cotton Industry.* Lund, Sweden: Lund University Press.

Bowen, James. 1972–81. *A History of Western Education.* Vols. 1–3. London: Methuen.

Coveney, Peter. 1967. *The Image of Childhood,* revised edition. Harmondsworth: Penguin.

Cunningham, Hugh, and Pier Paolo Viazzo, eds. 1996. *Child Labour in Historical Perspective.* Florence: UNICEF.

Davin, Anna. 1996. *Growing Up Poor: Home, School and Street in London, 1870–1914.* London: Rivers Oram Press.

Dickinson, Edward Ross. 1996. *The Politics of German Child Welfare from the Empire to the Federal Republic.* Cambridge, MA: Harvard University Press.

Furet, François, and Jacques Ozouf. 1982. *Reading and Writing: Literacy in France from Calvin to Jules Ferry.* Cambridge, UK: Cambridge University Press.

Gomersall, Meg. 1997. *Working-Class Girls in Nineteenth-Century England.* London: Macmillan.

Hair, P. E. H. 1982. "Children in Society, 1850–1980." In *Population and Society in Britain, 1850–1980,* ed. Theo Barker and Michael Drake. London: Batsford.

Hendrick, Harry. 1994. *Child Welfare: England, 1872–1989.* London: Routledge.

Heywood, Colin. 1988. *Childhood in Nineteenth-Century France: Work, Health and Education among the "Classes Populaires."* Cambridge, UK: Cambridge University Press.

Heywood, Colin. 2001. *A History of Childhood: Children and Childhood in the West from Medieval to Modern Times.* Cambridge, UK: Polity.

Hopkins, Eric. 1994. *Childhood Transformed: Working-Class Children in Nineteenth-Century England.* Manchester, UK: Manchester University Press.

Horrell, Sara, and Jane Humphries. 1995. "'The Exploitation of Little Children': Child Labor and the Family Economy in the Industrial Revolution." *Explorations in Economic History* 32: 485–516.

Jordan, Thomas E. 1987. *Victorian Childhood.* Albany: State University of New York Press.

Laqueur, T. W. 1976. "Working-Class Demand and the Growth of Demand of English Elementary Education, 1750–1850." In *Schooling and Society: Studies in the History of Education,* ed. Lawrence Stone. Baltimore: Johns Hopkins University Press.

Lavalette, Michael. 1994. *Child Employment in the Capitalist Labour Market.* Aldershot, UK: Avebury.

Nardinelli, Clark. 1990. *Child Labor and the Industrial Revolution.* Bloomington: Indiana University Press.

Quataert, Jean H. 1985. "Combining Agrarian and Industrial Livelihood: Rural Households in the Saxon Oberlausitz in the Nineteenth Century." *Journal of Family History* 10: 145–162.

Schleunes, Karl A. 1979. "Enlightenment, Reform, Reaction: The Schooling Revolution in Prussia." *Central European History* 12: 315–342.

Sieder, Reinhard. 1986. "'Vata, derf I aufstehn?': Childhood Experiences in Viennese Working-Class Families around 1900." *Continuity and Change* 1: 53–88.

Weissbach, Lee Shai. 1989. *Child Labor Reform in Nineteenth-Century France: Assuring the Future Harvest.* Baton Rouge: Louisiana State University Press.

COLIN HEYWOOD

Ewald, Wendy (b. 1951)

Wendy Ewald was born into a large family in Detroit, Michigan, in 1951. She studied photography at Massachusetts Institute of Technology under the photographer Minor White and graduated from Antioch College in 1974. Ewald's work has earned her numerous prizes and fellowships, including Fulbright and MacArthur fellowships.

Ewald creates photographs through subtle collaborations with children. Giving children cameras while also photographing them demands that Ewald acquire the visual vocabulary the children themselves use in this process of self-representation. This complex work confronts the lopsided relationship introduced as the subject is framed and contextually defined by the camera's gaze. While imparting to the photographer the spectacular power to extract from the world a controlled visual story, the camera also inserts an almost incontrovertible, hierarchical distance between subject and photographer. Ewald, recognizing the limited dialogue available to an artist within traditional photography, first began photographing alongside children on a First Nations reservation in Canada in 1969. Viewing the photographs the children made against her own, she saw the differences between the children's perceptions of their community and her own view as an outsider.

Ewald sought new processes to make images that would be drawn out of a shared interaction between herself and the children. The resulting collaborative approach resists placing a frame around another's world; instead she engages with the children, allowing their vision to shift her own sense of seeing and guide the artistic process. Though the photographs possess their own narrative power, which is similar to the work of other documentary photographers like Dorothea Lange and W. Eugene Smith, it is the creative process rather than the artifact that Ewald emphasizes. The intricate negotiations among her child collaborators, herself, and the worlds they are seeing challenge notions of photographic objectivity and sole authorship. The subsequent layered images operate from a documentary vantage point established

by Walker Evans in the 1930s, which contests the privileged narrative of photographs composed by an outsider. Ewald's collaborative photography is also strongly connected to conceptual art like that of Alfredo Jaar, which requires not only observation but reflection on the logic of ideas present throughout his politically confrontational work.

Ewald worked with students in the Appalachian Mountains of eastern Kentucky from 1975 to 1982. Four central themes emerged from this work: self, family, community, and dreams. Giving the children simple point-and-shoot cameras, she asked them to make photographs. Together they developed and printed the film in school darkrooms, demystifying the photographic process and offering the children complete ownership of their image, from conceptualization to production of the final print. The children then wrote from these photographs, sharing their stories and elaborating their images into powerful narratives, rich with the embedded detail of their lives. This established the framework for Ewald's later projects in such places as India, apartheid-era South Africa, Colombia, Saudi Arabia, and Durham, North Carolina.

Ewald's work with children disrupts the notion that only adults can use artistic tools for personal expression or documentary intent. By revealing children's interior worlds, Ewald's approach complicates and questions the view of children usually attributed to adult society. These conventional conceptions perpetuate a homogenous portrayal of children's experiences that is ruptured as the children with Ewald both interrogate and construct the world using the extraordinarily populist medium of photography.

See also: **Images of Childhood; Photographs of Children.**

BIBLIOGRAPHY

Ewald, Wendy. 2000. *Secret Games: Collaborative Works with Children, 1969–1999.* Zurich: Scalo.

Ewald, Wendy, and Alexandra Lightfoot. 2001. *I Wanna Take Me a Picture: Teaching Photography and Writing to Children.* Boston: Beacon Press.

DWAYNE EMIL DIXON

Ex Parte Crouse

The 1838 Pennsylvania Supreme Court decision *Ex parte Crouse* elaborated the doctrine of *parens patriae* by establishing that the state has a right and an obligation to remove children from improperly supervised households. The common law doctrine *parens patriae*, or "the state is the father," provides that the state has the responsibility to care for those who are legally incapable of caring for themselves. During the nineteenth century, JUVENILE JUSTICE advocates frequently relied on this doctrine to justify their efforts to protect children, both from the harsh adult criminal justice system and from parental neglect and abuse.

Ex parte Crouse was heard by the court as an appeal brought by a father whose daughter was committed to the Pennsylvania House of Refuge. The House of Refuge was established in 1826 to house and rehabilitate children who were charged with or convicted of committing criminal offenses. In 1835, the law governing the House of Refuge was amended to provide that girls under age eighteen and boys under age twenty-one could also be committed to the care and supervision of the House of Refuge for incorrigible or vicious conduct. The local magistrate committed Mary Ann Crouse to the House of Refuge under this provision after her mother filed a petition alleging that she was no longer capable of controlling Mary Ann's "vicious conduct." Following the commitment, Mary Ann's father filed a petition with the court in which he argued that the commitment was a violation of Mary Ann's constitutional rights because the magistrate did not conduct a trial before placing her in the House of Refuge.

The Pennsylvania Supreme Court disagreed with the argument that Mary Ann's commitment was a violation of her constitutional rights. Instead, the court held that Mary Ann's proper place was in the House of Refuge because, according to the doctrine of *parens patriae*, the state had an obligation and a right to assure her well-being. According to the court, if Mary Ann's parents were unable to control her, to educate her, or to protect her virtue, it became the state's responsibility to protect her. The court stated that although parents have a right to parental control, the right is not absolute, and if parents fail to exercise their rights in the appropriate manner, the rights and responsibilities of caring for the child are transferred to the state. Furthermore, Mary Ann's commitment was not a violation of her constitutional rights because the House of Refuge was a place of rehabilitation, not of punishment. The court reasoned that Mary Ann's placement in the institution would save her from a course of certain harm and that to release her from the House of Refuge would itself be an act of cruelty.

According to historian Michael Grossberg, *Ex parte Crouse* can be considered "the most influential antebellum judicial analysis of newly created children's asylums." In addition to providing an explanation of the rehabilitative goal of houses of refuge, the case was also important because it expanded the application of the doctrine of *parens patriae*. The expansion of this important legal doctrine was later relied upon by legal reformers to support the expansion of the legal powers of JUVENILE COURTS.

See also: **Children's Rights; Law, Children and the.**

BIBLIOGRAPHY

Grossberg, Michael. 1985. *Governing the Hearth: Law and Family in Nineteenth-Century America.* Chapel Hill: University of North Carolina Press.

Krisberg, Barry, and James F. Austin. 1993. *Reinventing Juvenile Justice.* Newbury Park, CA: Sage.

Ramsey, Sarah H., and Douglas E. Abrams. 2001. *Children and the Law in a Nutshell.* St. Paul, MN: West Group.

Vito, Gennaro F., and Deborah G. Wilson. 1985. *The American Juvenile Justice System.* Newbury Park, CA: Sage.

AMY L. ELSON